The Genesis of Flight

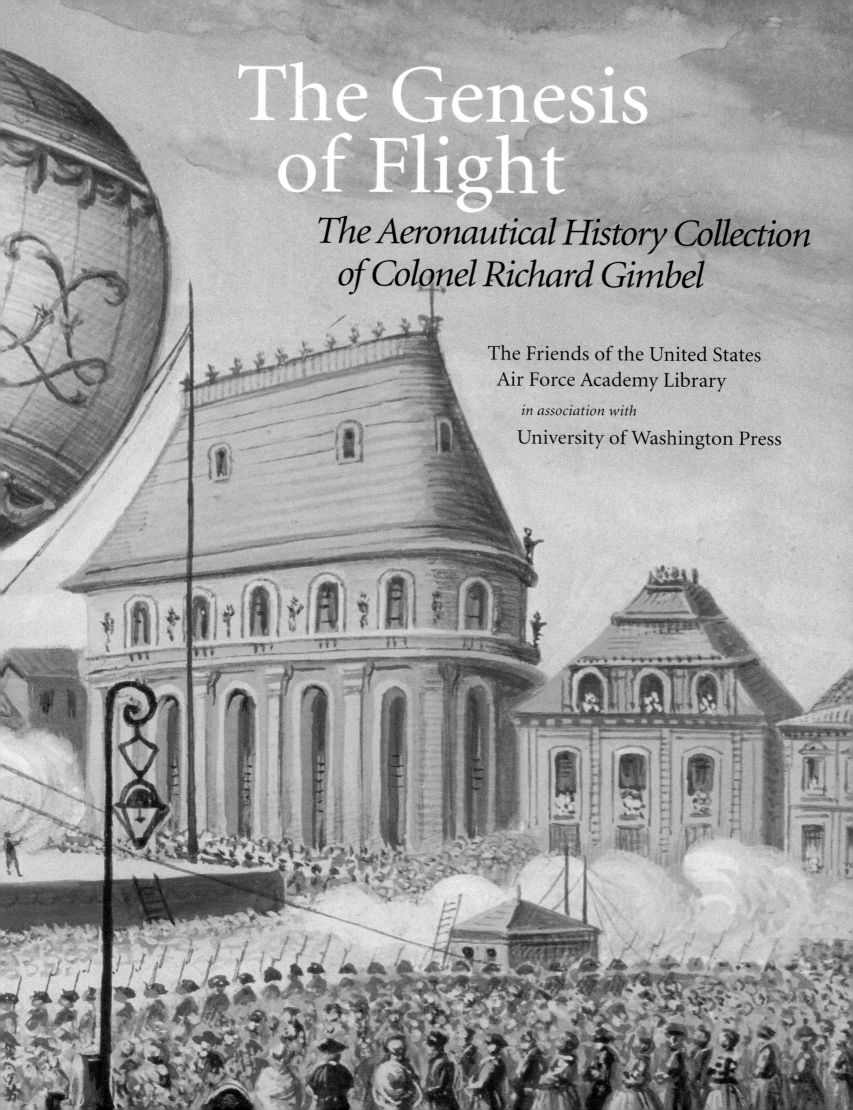

The Genesis of Flight

The Aeronautical History Collection of Colonel Richard Gimbel

The Friends of the United States
Air Force Academy Library
in association with
University of Washington Press

The Genesis of Flight was produced
for the University of Washington Press
and The Friends of the United States Air Force Academy Library
by Perpetua Press, Los Angeles
Design by Dana Levy
Production administration by Letitia Burns O'Connor

Copyright © 2000 by The Friends of the United States Air Force Academy Library

Printed in Japan

Library of Congress Cataloging-in-Publication Data
Gimbel, Richard.
     The genesis of flight : the aeronautical history collection of
  Colonel Richard Gimbel.
       p. cm.
     Includes bibliographical references and index.
     ISBN 0-295-97811-2 (alk. paper)
     1. Aeronautics—Bibliography—Catalogs. 2. United States Air
Force Academy. Library—Catalogs. 3. Gimbel, Richard—Library—
Catalogs. I. Untited States Air Force Academy. Library. Friends.
   II. Title.
   Z5063.G53 1999
   [TL506.A1]
   016.62913—dc21   99-10107
                              CIP

FRONT COVER: Detail of a print illustrating the first human flight—the Montgolfier
balloon ascent from Paris on November 21, 1783

BACK COVER: Photograph of Wilbur Wright piloting the Wright Model A aircraft

PAGES ii-iii: Detail of a print illustrating the launch of an unmanned Montgolfier
balloon from Versailles in September 1783 before an audience that included
King Louis XVI (page 173)

(Unless otherwise noted, the illustrations in the catalogue are from the Gimbel collection.)

This volume is dedicated to
Lt. Gen. A. P. Clark, USAF (Ret.),
sixth superintendent of the
United States Air Force Academy,
without whose dedication,
inspiration, sacrifice, and example
it would never have been published.

Contents

viii
Acknowledgments

ix
Sponsors

x
The Friends of the United States Air Force Academy Library

xi
Contributors

1
Introduction: A Gift of Tradition
Tom D. Crouch

37
Printed Books, 1489–1850
Clive Hart

91
Printed Books, 1851–1914
Tom D. Crouch

147
Manuscripts
Clive Hart

165
Prints
Paul Maravelas

261
Other Holdings
Dominick A. Pisano

313
Seals
Ellen Morris and *Holly Pittman*

327
Numismatics
Edward Rochette

346
Chronology of Flight

348
Appendix

361
Bibliography

363
Editors

364
Index

Acknowledgments

THIS BOOK IS A TRIBUTE TO RICHARD GIMBEL. In his correspondence and during his visits with Air Force Academy officials, Colonel Gimbel always said that if he were to donate his aeronautical history collection, he would like the Academy to someday publish an illustrated, annotated catalogue.

The development of this catalogue was a very complex undertaking and was accomplished over a period covering almost a decade. The project was spearheaded by the dynamic leadership of Lt. Gen. A.P. Clark and by the skillful professionalism of the Academy archivist, Duane J. Reed. It was also labor intensive and required the skills, talents, and support of many people. Foremost among them were the volume's sponsors, listed on the following page.

The members of The Friends of the Air Force Academy Library Executive Committee were involved in every phase. They included the late Lt. Gen. Thomas S. Moorman, Lt. Gen. A. P. Clark, Brig. Gen. George V. Fagan, Brig. Gen. Philip D. Caine, Col. Henry A. Kortemeyer, Willis I. Ketterson, Lt. Col. Dona R. Hildebrand, and the late Lt. Col. John J. Ward.

Former directors of the Academy libraries, Lt. Col. Reiner H. Schaeffer and Lt. Col. James W. Hopkins, and the present director, Dr. Edward A. Scott, all vigorously supported the project. Dr. Elliott V. Converse III, Dr. Richard W. Lemp, Alice Levine, and Shena Redmond served as co-editors. Generous advice and counsel was offered by John T. Schwartz, former editor, Knopf publications. The high-quality photography was provided by Stewarts Photographers and Custom Lab of Colorado Springs.

Others who participated in the development of the manuscript include: Donald J. Barrett, John S. Beardsley, Sgt. Maj. Julius L. Denning, Michele Greeder, Rae Hellen, the late Lt. Col. David Hollenbaugh, Thelma Hostetter, Gwen Krasikov, Peggy Litwhiler, Maria D. Mobley, Gertrude Pollok, and Dr. Neville Prentice.

The Friends particularly want to acknowledge the encouragement and efforts of Donald R. Ellegood and Pat Soden of the University of Washington Press, as well as Dana Levy and Letitia O'Connor of Perpetua Press.

Note: All of the military listed in the acknowledgments are retired from active service.

Sponsors

Mr. & Mrs. Donald J. Barrett

Lieutenant General & Mrs. A.P. Clark, USAF (Ret.)

Major John H. Craigie, USAF (Ret.)

Lieutenant General & Mrs. Laurence C. Craigie, USAF (Ret.)

Brigadier General & Mrs. Philip J. Erdle, USAF (Ret.)

Brigadier General & Mrs. George V. Fagan, USAF (Ret.)

Mrs. B. Christine Fessler

The members of the Gimbel family:

    Mr. & Mrs. Daniel Gimbel

    Mr. Roger Gimbel

    Mrs. Ann Goff

    Mrs. Pamela G. Lehman

    Mr. & Mrs. R. J. Lewis

    Mrs. Joyce Gimbel Trifield

Lieutenant Colonel & Mrs. Jean C. Hempstead, USAF (Ret.)

Colonel & Mrs. Floyd G. Hildebrand, USAF (Ret.)

Lieutenant General & Mrs. Bradley C. Hosmer, USAF (Ret.)

Brigadier General & Mrs. Marcos E. Kinevan, USAF (Ret.)

Rear Admiral John E. Kirkpatrick, USN (Ret.)

General & Mrs. Robert M. Lee, USAF (Ret.)

Mr. Harold U. Littrell

Colonel & Mrs. William J. Mahon, USAF (Ret.)

Lieutenant Colonel Naomi M. McCracken, USAF (Ret.)

Brigadier General Robert F. McDermott, USAF (Ret.)

General & Mrs. T. Ross Milton, USAF (Ret.)

Lieutenant General Thomas S. Moorman, USAF (Ret.)

The Lieutenant General Thomas S. Moorman Memorial Fund

Mr. & Mrs. David Pollak

Major General Ramsay D. Potts, USAF (Ret.)

Mr. & Mrs. Frank A. Saunders

Lieutenant General & Mrs. Winfield W. Scott, Jr., USAF (Ret.)

Mr. & Mrs. Robert S. Shaffer

Silver Falcon Association of the Air Force Academy

The Stalag Luft III Former Prisoners of War

General Jacob E. Smart, USAF (Ret.)

Mrs. Jean S. Snodgrass

General Horace M. Wade, USAF (Ret.)

Major General Richard A. Yudkin, USAF (Ret.)

The Friends of the
United States Air Force
Academy Library

THE FRIENDS OF THE UNITED STATES AIR FORCE ACADEMY LIBRARY is a tax-exempt charitable foundation established in 1987 to enhance the quality of the Academy as an educational, research, scientific, and cultural institution. The Friends enable the library to acquire materials, to pursue projects, to create publications, and to implement services beyond those made possible through funds allocated by the United States Air Force.

This catalogue has been put together in response to a need expressed to The Friends by the director of Academy libraries. It was clear that a collection of such historical significance with its richly documented and illustrated account of the slow, evolutionary fulfillment of humankind's dream and aspiration to fly in the air should be better known and more available to scholars and researchers around the world. The Friends also envisioned a catalogue as an appropriate way to assist cadet studies at the Air Force Academy.

At the outset, The Friends realized that the opportunity to produce a catalogue of this marvelous collection would not likely occur again and that the resulting work should be of unsurpassed quality. Because it would be impossible to include all of the Gimbel collection's 20,000 items, 300 of the most representative were selected, each to be described briefly and illustrated in full color. An additional number were also selected for listing in an appendix. Recognized experts in each of the collection's main categories were engaged to make the selections and to write brief descriptions of their history and significance. Thus an authentic and rich collection of narratives and illustrations fills this volume.

Contributors

TOM D. CROUCH
Dr. Crouch wrote the introductory essay and selected and annotated books printed from 1851 through 1914. He is Senior Curator of Aeronautics, National Air and Space Museum, Smithsonian Institution, Washington, D.C., and is the author of nine books and numerous articles on the history of flight technology, including the award-winning: *A Dream of Wings: Americans and the Airplane, 1875-1905* (1981); *The Eagle Aloft: Two Centuries of the Balloon in America* (1983); and *The Bishop's Boys: A Life of Wilbur and Orville Wright* (1989).

CLIVE HART
Professor Hart selected and annotated books printed through 1850, and in a separate section selected and annotated a number of significant letters and manuscripts for inclusion in the catalogue. Clive Hart is a professor at the University of Essex, England. In addition to numerous publications in the field of literature, he has written extensively about the early history of aeronautics. His books include: *Kites: An Historical Survey* (1967), *The Dream of Flight* (1972), and *The Prehistory of Flight* (1988). Professor Hart is a member of the Royal Aeronautical Society, and president of the Suffolk Aero Club, Ipswich, England.

PAUL MARAVELAS
Paul Maravelas selected and annotated the prints from the Gimbel collection. As curator of the Aeronautical Book Collection of the University of Minnesota libraries, he served as consultant for the University of Minnesota Art Museum in planning an extensive exhibit that commemorated the bicentennial of ballooning. The exhibit included the publication of an illustrated, annotated catalogue entitled *The Balloon: A Bicentennial Exhibition.* He is also the editor of the "Balloon Historian's Friend," a newsletter published by the University of Minnesota.

ELLEN MORRIS
Ellen Morris co-authored the descriptions of the ancient seals included in the catalogue. She is a Kolb Fellow at the University of Pennsylvania, studying Egyptian and Near Eastern Archaeology in the Department of Asian and Middle Eastern Studies. She is writing her dissertation on "The Architecture of Imperialism: An Investigation into Frontier Strategies in New Kingdom Egypt."

DOMINICK A. PISANO
Dr. Pisano selected and annotated "Other Holdings," a variety of ephemeral items including, among other things, advertisements, news clippings, dime novels, and sheet music. Dr. Pisano is Chairman of the Division of Aeronautics, National Air and Space Museum, Smithsonian Institution, Washington, D.C. He is the author of *To Fill the Skies with Pilots: The Civilian Pilot Training Program, 1939-1946* (1993), and the co-author of *Legend, Memory, and the Great War in the Air* (1992). Currently he is editing a book of essays entitled *The Airplane in American Culture*, to be published by the University of Michigan Press.

HOLLY PITTMAN
Dr. Pittman selected the ancient seals to be included in the catalogue and co-authored their descriptions. She is a professor of the history of art at the University of Pennsylvania where, since 1989, she has taught the art and archaeology of the pre-Islamic Ancient Near East and Egypt. Before beginning an academic career, she was a curator in the Department of Ancient Near Eastern Art in the Metropolitan Museum of Art in New York City for fourteen years. She received her M.A. and Ph.D. from Columbia University under the direction of Edith Porada. Professor Pittman wrote her dissertation on cylinder seal types in the Fertile Crescent in the third millennium B.C.E. She has excavated sites in Cyprus, Turkey, Syria, and Iraq.

EDWARD ROCHETTE
Edward Rochette selected and described the history and significance of the numismatics included in the catalogue. He is the chief executive officer of the American Numismatic Association and has assisted in selecting the design of several U.S. Mint commemorative coins. Edward Rochette serves on the staff of the U.S. Olympic Committee and has prepared exhibits for the new International Olympic Museum in Lausanne, Switzerland. He maintains a widely syndicated column on coins and is the author of *The Other Side of The Coin* (1987).

Introduction: A Gift of Tradition

The Aeronautical History Collection
of Colonel Richard Gimbel
at the United States Air Force Academy

Tom D. Crouch

A Prophecy Fulfilled: London, 1942

For I dipt into the future, far as human eye could see
Saw the Vision of the world, and all the wonders that would be; . . .
Heard the heavens fill with shouting, and there rain'd a ghastly dew
From the nations' airy navies grappling in the central blue;

—Alfred, Lord Tennyson
"Locksley Hall" (1851)

B Y 1942, Tennyson's prophetic vision of war and peace in an air age had long since come to pass. The Blitz, the "ghastly dew" of German bombs that had rained down on London in the high summer and fall of 1940, was over. The Luftwaffe struck Bath, Norwich, Exeter, and other provincial cities in a series of "Baedeker raids," while the capital enjoyed several months without a night alert. That June, officials reduced the number of West End tube stations outfitted as air raid shelters from ten to four as a cost-saving measure. The "little Blitz" of 1944, and the terror of the flying bomb campaign, lay in the future. For the moment, however, beleaguered Londoners could breathe a little easier and grow accustomed to sleeping through the night.

The tables were turning. Night after night, the men of Royal Air Force's Bomber Command set out from airfields all along the North Sea coast of Britain, determined to carry the war to the cities of the Reich and Fortress Europa. Moreover, Londoners were becoming thoroughly familiar with American accents and uniforms. The 8th Air Force struck its first blow against the Axis in August 1942, when a dozen B-17s attacked the railway yards at Rouen, France. The first U.S. strike against a target in Germany was still six months away.

If life in London seemed a bit more cheerful and less threatening in the spring of 1942, it was still impossible to escape the war. On the evening of June 13, nineteen residents of Gurney Street, Southwark, died in the explosion of a UXB (unexploded bomb) that had remained hidden in the rubble for thirteen months. Authorities speculated that the vibration of trains moving through nearby Elephant and Castle station had detonated the bomb. Relatively small raids followed that summer and fall. Civil defense authorities were particularly concerned about the appearance of a new and more powerful incendiary bomb.[1]

Colonel Richard Gimbel, 1898–1970

Lt. Col. Richard Gimbel, an administrative officer with the 8th United States Army Air Force (USAAF), arrived in England on July 1, 1942. Like other Americans, he had watched London burning in the newsreels and had listened to Edward R. Murrow's broadcasts from the city during the height of the Blitz. Now he could witness the devastation for himself.

Gimbel, one of America's leading rare book collectors, must have been particularly saddened by the destruction of the Paternoster Row neighborhood, the traditional center of British publishing and the book trade. An estimated 6 million volumes, ranging from new books waiting distribution to rare surviving examples of the earliest printed volumes, had gone up in flames on the night of December 29, 1941, when bombs rained down on the quarter square mile of crowded streets in the shadow of St. Paul's Cathedral.

"There was nothing left to recognize," one observer noted as he walked through the area the next morning. "Such a scene of destruction I have never seen or imagined."

In publishers' basements...glowed and shuddered the remnants of a million books. Gusts of hot air and acrid smoke blew across the streets.... From Warwick Square on the west to Ivy on the east, from Paternoster Row to Newgate Street, there lies now an undulating sea of broken yellow bricks. As I picked my way gingerly across from brick to brick, hot gusts of sulphurous fumes from buried fires seeped up between my feet; desultory flames played on the remains of a rafter here, or a floor joist there; and on either side the smoking causeway fell sharply away into cavernous glowing holes, once basements full of stock, now the crematories of the City's book world.[2]

The smoke had cleared by the time Richard Gimbel arrived in England six months later, but one of the most historic neighborhoods in the City of London remained an urban wasteland of broken glass and brick. Soon thereafter, Gimbel noticed an advertisement for a London bookshop that, in spite of the best German efforts to the contrary, would be "Open for Business as Usual." Impressed by the spirit of the bookseller, Gimbel called at the shop and looked around for something to purchase. Noticing that his customer was a USAAF officer, the shopkeeper produced a box filled with an assortment of books on aviation. Richard Gimbel, a veteran bibliophile who had already built three world-class book collections of American and English authors, had found a new world to conquer.[3]

The Merchant Prince

Richard Gimbel was born in Atlantic City, New Jersey, on July 26, 1898, the son of Ellis A. and Minnie Mastbaum Gimbel, and the grandson of Adam, who had journeyed from Bremerhaven to New Orleans in 1835 as an impoverished teenager. This first American Gimbel earned his living as an itinerant peddler, traveling up and down the Mississippi Valley until 1842, when he established his first dry goods store, The Palace of Trade, in the small town of Vincennes, Indiana.

Adam met and married Fridolyn Kahnweiler, the 17-year-old daughter of a German-Jewish family, during a buying trip to Philadelphia in 1847. The couple would produce fourteen children over the next twenty-four years. The Gimbel empire was to be a family enterprise. Within a few years of his marriage, Adam was operating four stores in Vincennes and a fifth in Danville, Illinois. One after another, each of the seven surviving Gimbel brothers would learn the ropes working in one of the growing chain of family stores. "Others may have had their paid helpers and assistants," Adam Gimbel explained, "I have had my seven sons."[4]

The Gimbels began their period of serious expansion in 1887, when Jacob and Isaac, the eldest of Adam's merchant princes, established a department store in Milwaukee. Five years later, father and sons purchased the Granville B. Hayes store in Philadelphia, where they installed the first escalators in the city, created a much publicized merchandise testing bureau,

Library After Air Raid, London, 1940 (Archives of The Royal Commission on the Historical Monuments of England)

and established a reputation for "truth in advertising." Ellis, the youngest son, and Richard Gimbel's father, established the New York store, the flagship of the family fleet, in 1910.[5]

"I was fortunate in being born with a sort of silver spoon in my mouth," Richard Gimbel once explained.[6] He grew up in a family already famous for its bargain basement; a feud with Macy's that had been manufactured for its public relations value; an annual holiday parade in Philadelphia; and lavishly decorated store windows at Christmastime. Education was taken very seriously in this family. Young Richard attended Philadelphia's prestigious School of Pedagogy and graduated from Central High School, an institution famed for its high standards and classical curriculum. He entered Yale in 1916.

Richard Gimbel was a brilliant student and something of a character. "From the time he was a child," his cousin Rose recalled many years later, "he loved to give the impression he was crazy." He was, in any case, always eager to make a buck. As an undergraduate, he established a tutoring service, complete with a money-back guarantee of the sort people had come to expect from Gimbel's. Even with four months off in 1918 for service as a lieutenant with the 310th Field Artillery, 79th Division, he was still able to qualify for Phi Beta Kappa and graduate with the class of 1920.[7]

Richard Gimbel's first important assignment in the family business was to plan and supervise construction of a new $18-million Philadelphia store that opened in 1927. He rose to the position of vice president of the Gimbel Corporation and succeeded his father as president of the Philadelphia store. During these years the company's Philadelphia operations averaged annual sales of $100 million. This phase of Gimbel's career came to an abrupt end in 1935, when he lost a management dispute with his older cousin Bernard, who insisted on placing Arthur C. Kaufmann, scion of a Pittsburgh retail family, in effective command of Gimbel's Philadelphia operation. "I'm very fond of Bernard," Gimbel explained years later:

> There was a heated proxy fight and the whole thing blew up in smoke. We just had a basic disagreement; he and his group wanted outsiders in the management, and I didn't. I wanted the business run by the family; there were fifteen Gimbels in it at one time. That way, you could take longer vacations and sort of rotate. I know that some Gimbels are better at business than others, but I believe that owner management makes up for lack of brilliance, and anyway my motto is "Let the strong carry the weak."[8]

Clearly, Richard Gimbel, speaking many years later to a reporter from the *New Yorker*, was putting the best possible face on the matter. Having lost the fight, he was not only forced out of company management; for a time he was barred from entering the Philadelphia store.[9]

Retaining a large block of Gimbel's stock, but unable to use the company name, Gimbel moved to Miami, Florida, in 1937, where he took over Richard's Department Stores. He diversified his business interests as well, investing heavily in both the broadcasting industry and the IBM Corporation. Although Richard Gimbel took business very seriously, it was clear that he reserved his deepest enthusiasm for his collection of rare books and manuscripts. Beginning not long after his graduation from Yale, the young businessman had begun to build the first of his four great collections, three of which were loosely connected to his interest in the history of Philadelphia.

Gimbel took special pride in having gathered the world's finest collection of the writings of Thomas Paine, the radical thinker who had provided a rationale for American independence. Fascinated by Edgar Allan Poe, who had lived and worked in Philadelphia between 1838 and 1842, Gimbel built an enormous collection of U.S. and foreign editions of his work. Poe met Charles Dickens when the English author visited Philadelphia in March 1842. Perhaps as a result of this encounter between two literary giants, Gimbel began a world-class collection of Dickens' books and magazine serials, with an emphasis on materials autographed by the author.

Asked to provide a list of his three leading credit references during the years after World War II, Gimbel named Philadelphia's two leading banks—and a Walnut Street bookstore. Brig. Gen. George V. Fagan, a former director of the Air Force Academy Library, explains that Gimbel was a sophisticated bookman with a deep understanding of the inner workings of the rare book trade:

> For many years, Col. Gimbel had been a client and admirer of another Philadelphian, Dr. A.S.W. Rosenbach, the unexcelled doyen of American rare book dealers and collectors. From Dr. Rosenbach, Richard Gimbel had acquired a sense of the pure joy and excitement of collecting as well as an understanding of the significance of rare materials in the realm of scholarship. Gimbel was a life-long member of the American Bookman's Association and regularly attended national and international meetings. At these gatherings, rare materials were displayed, sold and traded among dealers throughout the world. Richard was also a very active member of the Grolier Club which is made up of wealthy collectors and bibliographers as well as dealers.[10]

Prior to World War II, Gimbel also turned his attention to the other great interest of his life—flying. His love of aviation began in 1910, when as a boy of twelve he witnessed two great events that he would never forget. On April 23, while visiting London with his parents, young Richard watched English aviator Claude Grahame-White roar away from the Park Royal, steering his Farman biplane through the early morning fog and darkness in an unsuccessful attempt to win the £10,000 *Daily Mail* prize for the first flight from London to Manchester. Gimbel's father was one of those who established a $10,000 prize for the first flight from New York to Philadelphia and back. On June 13, 1910, Richard shook the hand of the man who won that prize, Curtiss aviator Charles K. Hamilton, and proudly announced that he planned to become a pilot himself.

He made good on that promise three decades later. The senior members of the Gimbel family did not approve of flying lessons for young associates with positions of responsibility in the firm. Once he was on his own, however, Gimbel lost no time in earning his license (#39293) and purchasing a Stinson Reliant (N14187). He flew on business and to savor the sheer joy of spending a few hours in the sky. Eventually he acquired two smaller Fairchild aircraft and became active in aviation affairs, serving as chairman of the aviation committee of the Miami Chamber of Commerce; director of the Miami Air Pilots Association; and chairman of the contest committee of the Cuban National Air Races.[11]

Richard Gimbel launched his third and final career in 1940, when he transferred from his position as a lieutenant colonel in the field artillery reserve to the U.S. Army Air Corps. Called to active duty on June 15, 1941, he commanded various administrative and service units prior to being ordered to England with the 8th Air Force Service Command. Initially, Gimbel was assigned to duties as an officer in charge of reception centers and rest homes. He also attended aerial gunnery school at the 11th Combat Crew School in Bovington, England.

Gimbel had been promoted to full colonel, earned his wings as a USAAF service pilot qualified to fly single- and twin-engine aircraft, and had almost completed his twelve-month tour of duty in England before he tasted combat. Early on the morning of June 15, 1943, he flew as a nose gunner and observer with the 510th Bomb Squadron, 351st Bomb Group, on a mission against Le Mans, France, that was aborted because of poor visibility over the target.

Things were a good deal more exciting one week later when Colonel Gimbel flew aboard one of the six aircraft that the 510th contributed to the first 8th Air Force raid on targets in the Ruhr Valley. The Luftwaffe was waiting for them. The group lost one aircraft. Another

Colonel Richard Gimbel [back row center] of Philadelphia, Pa., of the 8th Air Force Service Command, with the officers of *The Duchess,* the Flying Fortress in which he flew his first combat mission over enemy territory. (National Air and Space Museum, Smithsonian Institution)

limped home with heavy damage. The group's gunners were credited with destroying seventeen enemy aircraft that day. Richard Gimbel claimed responsibility for one of those fighters—an FW190. Four days later, Capt. Clark Gable took Gimbel's place as an observer-gunner flying off to war with the 510th Bomb Squadron.[12]

When Gimbel returned from England in July 1943, USAAF officials assigned him to administrative and personnel duties where he could put his extraordinary business skills to work solving the procurement and logistical problems of the first global air war. Having qualified as a service pilot while still in Europe, Gimbel was assigned to flying duties with the 13th, 20th, and 10th Air Forces following World War II, then returned to his alma mater as Professor of Air Science in 1951. Retiring from the U. S. Air Force two years later, he remained at Yale as curator of Aeronautical Literature until his death in 1970.[13]

During the last three decades of his life, Richard Gimbel focused increasing time, energy, and enthusiasm on the acquisition of rare items of aeronautica. Fascinated by the contents of the first box of aeronautical items purchased from the bomb-damaged bookstore, he decided to begin building a new collection that would link his deep interest in rare books with his love of aviation. He scoured the bookshops and auction houses of wartime London, taking great delight in shipping coffin-shaped crates filled with aeronautical books home to his wife. In addition, he commissioned Maggs Brothers and Bernard Quaritch, English rare book dealers with a long interest in aeronautica, to seek out fresh treasures for his new collection.

Gimbel cast a wide net, creating the world's finest collection of materials illuminating five millennia of persistent human dreams and efforts to achieve flight. "I've never catalogued it," Gimbel admitted to a *New Yorker* reporter who inquired about his collection,

> but I must have over one hundred thousand items now, including books, manuscripts, pictures, Babylonian seals, coins, stamps, postcards, fans, cigarette cards, Siege of Paris balloon mail, carrier-pigeon mail, aeronautical dinner plates, watches, snuff boxes—everything reflecting man's endeavor to fly and his interest in flight. Everything up to the Wright brothers, that is to keep from being swamped, I end the collection there. As it is, people send me doorknobs and shower curtains with balloons on them, and I'm in constant communication with about four hundred dealers, all over the world.[14]

His timing was impeccable. Economic conditions in postwar Europe increased the amount of rare aeronautical material on the market. As a knowledgeable and seasoned bibliophile who had established a deep and long-standing relationship with the leading rare book dealers of the United States and England, Gimbel was willing to pay top dollar.

He took a great interest in references to flight in the earliest printed books, which are perhaps better represented in his library than in any other private collection of aeronautica. He also learned from the experience of earlier collectors like Bella Landauer, a New York matron who pioneered new collecting areas, including advertising ephemera, song sheets, and juvenile books with aeronautical themes. Recognizing the importance of rocketry and space travel in the postwar world, Gimbel would include in his library volumes related to that subject from the earliest volumes on black powder rocketry and pyrotechnics to volumes of science fiction that had inspired the birth of the space age. By 1955 Gimbel's growing collection of aeronautica was already recognized as the finest in the world.

Gimbel spent the last two decades of his life in New Haven. "I was retired, as a full colonel, in 1953," he explained to an interviewer from the *New Yorker,* "and stayed on here, with the Library, of which I am a trustee."

> The university offered me space, a curatorship, and two bursary students to work on my collection. I have a house near the [Yale] Bowl, where my wife and I live with our two youngest children—thirteen year old girls, identical twins. We have two grown-up sons and three married daughters. I'm a Fellow of Pierson College; I attend some classes that interest me; I gave a dinner for forty professors last night; and all I can say is that my cup runneth over.[15]

Letter from Charles Lindbergh to Lt. Gen. Hubert R. Harmon, Feb. 18, 1956

He enjoyed the prestige that accompanied a formal relationship with a great university. Moreover, Yale officials provided safe and secure storage for his books and enabled him to publicize the treasures of his collection through the medium of two major exhibitions staged in university library gallery space. "Five Thousand Years of Going Up: An Exhibition of Aeronautical Books and Prints Ending with the Discovery of the Secret of Flying by the Wright Brothers," opened in December 1953 in honor of the 50th anniversary of the invention of the airplane and ran through January 1954. Four years later, at the height of excitement over the launch of Sputnik I, Gimbel produced a second exhibition on the prehistory of the space age, including such rare materials as his original 1493 first published edition of *Vera Historia*, the story of a voyage to the moon by the Greek satirist Lucian.

Richard Gimbel died of a heart attack near Munich, Germany, on May 27, 1970. He was among friends, visiting Europe on a trip sponsored by the Grolier Club of New York, the nation's most prestigious society of rare book collectors. He died engaged in what had always been his favorite pursuit.

J. Pierpont Morgan, Harry Elkins Widener, Henry E. Huntington, Henry Clay Folger, and other leading American philanthropist-collectors had achieved a sort of immortality by establishing great public or private research libraries named for themselves. Gimbel preferred to will his treasures to a series of carefully selected research libraries with strong supplementary collections that would extend the scholarly value of his materials. The Thomas Paine Collection, for example, went to the American Philosophical Society, a Philadelphia institution with extraordinarily strong holdings in the area of early American history. Gimbel, who decorated his Yale office with a stuffed raven, willed his Poe materials to the Edgar Allan Poe Museum and Library, a Philadelphia institution that he had established some years before. He boasted to friends that he had succeeded in getting Poe's name into the Philadelphia telephone book.

He rewarded Yale University, where he served on the library board of trustees and held an appointment as curator of aeronautical literature for almost twenty years, with the gift of his Charles Dickens collection. Yale had lost the real prize, however. The treasures of the Colonel Richard Gimbel Aeronautical History Collection were destined for the Air Force Academy.

* * *

ON THE MORNING OF APRIL 11, 1955, Charles Augustus Lindbergh telephoned Lt.Gen. H. R. Harmon with news that "the finest and most valuable collection of aeronautical documents in the world, covering a period of 5,000 years—up to the Wright brothers' first flight," might be available to the Air Force Academy. Lindbergh, a resident of Darien, Connecticut, who was in the process of donating his own papers to Yale, had made the acquaintance of Richard Gimbel.

Just a year before, Lindbergh and General Harmon had served on the five-man committee created to advise Secretary of the Air Force Harold Talbott on a site for the Academy. Now Harmon was serving as the first superintendent of the academy-in-the-making, with headquarters at Lowry Air Force Base, near Denver, Colorado, while work was underway on the new facility at the foot of the majestic Rampart Range of the Rockies, just outside Colorado Springs.

As a retired officer who had commanded the Air Force ROTC detachment at Yale, Gimbel was enthusiastic about the notion of an Air Force Academy. Moreover, he was certain that his collection of aeronautica could be of extraordinary value in connecting Academy cadets to a

TOM D. CROUCH

dream of flight as old as humanity and a rich tradition of airmanship and innovation almost as old as their nation. Familiarity with the cultural and historic roots of aviation, he felt, should be an important element in the professional education of the cadets.

Searching for a suitable repository to house his personal papers, Lindbergh had visited Yale's Sterling Library at the suggestion of his friend Harry Guggenheim, a Yale alumnus. It was only natural that the library staff introduce their guest, the world's most famous pilot, to the local aviation celebrity and honorary curator of aeronautical literature. Surviving correspondence indicates that Gimbel immediately asked Lindbergh to assist him in opening discussions with Air Force leaders. Gimbel pursued serious negotiations regarding the donation of his collection to the Academy through the early 1960s and remained in touch with Academy officials until the time of his death.

Gimbel's correspondence files reveal that he was careful to keep Yale library officials fully informed of his discussions with the Air Force. As the negotiations dragged on for years with no resolution, Yale officials who sought to hold on to the collection must have begun to relax. Gimbel had always indicated that the location of his collection during his lifetime and its ultimate disposition were two distinct matters, however. He remarked on several occasions that he intended to donate his aeronautical collection "to the institution best qualified to house it, preserve it, exhibit it, and make the best use of it for scholars."[16] In willing his collection to the Air Force Academy, Gimbel accomplished a great deal more. The Gimbel collection was destined to become part of the intellectual life of the Academy.

Ancient Wings

When Yale's curator of aeronautical literature was giving a tour of his collection or planning an exhibition of the materials, he liked to move chronologically. "Well, I thought at first that I'd...start with the Bible—angels, you know—but I found that angels in the Bible didn't get wings until quite late; the cherubim guarding the tree of life, in the third chapter of Genesis, don't have any in the early illustrations," he explained.

> So I started with the Babylonian legend of Etana. Etana, a prince who could not have children and was worried about high taxes, was advised by holy men to consult an eagle. He found a beat-up eagle on a mountaintop, nursed it back to health, and talked it into flying to Heaven with him on its back. I haven't been able to get an Etana seal myself, but the Morgan Library has one and was kind enough to give me a wax impression of it.[17]

In fact, Gimbel did manage to acquire a handful of the seals and stamps produced by the peoples of southern Mesopotamia. The Academy archivist once allowed me to hold the oldest of these tiny dark stone cylinders in my white-gloved hand. It is as old as civilization, dating to 2700 B.C.E., and one of the earliest representations of the symbolic power of wings.

When the seal is rolled onto a strip of moist clay, repeated images of an eagle with outspread wings appear, separating a series of naked men, wearing what specialists recognize as the belt of a hero, holding two goats aloft by their heels. The precise meaning of this image is unclear. Representations of Etana and his magical eagle would not appear for another two centuries. This might be Anzu, the lion-headed eagle who obtained the tablets of life from the air-god Enlil, or the Imdugud-bird, who decreed the fates and befriended the hero Lugalbanda.[18]

It is enough to know that from the very dawn of civilization winged creatures were thought to link the mortal world with the power of the gods. "The natural function of the wing is to soar upwards and carry that which is heavy up to the place where dwells the race of gods," Plato explained in *Phaedrus*. "More than any other thing that pertains to the body it partakes of the nature of the divine."[19]

From the beginning, we placed our gods in the heavens and regarded flight as a symbol of supernatural power. It is scarcely surprising that the mythologies of the ancient world are filled with stories of heroes who traveled into the sky to commune with the gods.

The oldest printed book in the Gimbel collection, *Historia Alexāndri Magni* [The romance

Peter Brueghel, *Interumque vola, medio tutissimus ibis,* 1553

of Alexander] (1489), tells of the legendary flight of Alexander the Great, who is said to have been carried aloft by winged griffins harnessed to a basket. This is the first published version of a tale that had inspired ancient poetry and medieval illuminated manuscripts. Alexander was by no means the only hero who ventured aloft by hitching a ride with birds or mythical flying creatures. The Gimbel shelves contain rare accounts of Etana, the Babylonian eagle tamer; K'ai Ka'us, the Persian monarch who harnessed himself to eagles; and Sinbad, the hero of *A Thousand and One Nights,* who tied himself to the leg of a giant Roc.

There can be no doubt as to the identity of the classic myth of the air, however. The story of Icarus and Daedalus is very different, and much more powerful, than what had come before. Appropriately, the oldest printed illustration in the Gimbel collection is a woodcut entitled "The Fall of Icarus." Prepared by the German master Albrecht Dürer for Friedrich Riedrer's *Spiegel der waren Rhetoric* (1493), it is also the very first image of human beings in flight to appear in a printed book.

The Roman poet Ovid offered the best account of the legend of Daedalus, the ingenious artificer commissioned by Minos, king of Crete, to design and build a great labyrinth, or maze, in which to imprison the monstrous bull, the Minotaur. Falling from the king's favor, he was imprisoned in a tower with his young son, Icarus. Unable to escape in any other way, Daedalus collected feathers and worked them into wings with great care. The larger feathers were sewn to the frame with twine, the smaller attached with wax. When the work was complete, "he bent them with a gentle curve, so that they looked like real birds' wings."[20]

Daedalus cautioned Icarus not to fly too low, where "the damp will clog your wings," or too high, where the sun would melt the wax. Thomas Bulfinch, the Harvard graduate and Boston bank clerk who published a popular retelling of the classic myths in 1855, imagined what an impact the sight of these first two men in the sky must have had on those who saw them. "As they flew the ploughman stopped his work to gaze, and the shepherd leaned on his staff, and watched them, astonished at the sight and thinking they were gods who could thus cleave the air."[21]

They had flown past the islands of Samos and Lesbos, when Icarus climbed too close to the sun and fell to his death. Daedalus retrieved the body and buried it on an island west of Samos. He named the island Icaria and the body of water surrounding it the Icarian Sea. Daedalus continued his aerial journey to Sicily, where he dedicated a temple to Apollo in which he hung up his wings as a divine offering.

The story is memorialized on modern maps—Icaria and the Icarian Sea—testimony to the antiquity and popularity, if not the reality, of the legend. It is by no means difficult to understand the depth and power of this myth. This is not some tall tale about a fellow who believes that he can be drawn through the air by a team of birds. Daedalus relies on his ingenious brain and clever hands to design artificial wings with which to trespass on the domain of the gods. But this is far from being a story of unalloyed triumph. The ancients understood that those who would imitate the gods must be prepared to suffer their wrath. Later generations would understand the extent to which the legend underscores the risks involved in the technological enterprise.

TOM D. CROUCH

Dürer's historic illustration is a forceful portrayal of the very moment of disaster. A bearded Daedalus, flying in formation with two ducks, glances down to see Icarus plummeting into a sea that is dotted with islands, each capped by a castle. The young man's left hand has just broken the surface, preceded by two loose feathers and a duck with folded wings whose head has already disappeared beneath the water. Clearly, the dive that will prove fatal to Icarus is quite natural for the duck. It seems to be Dürer's artistic restatement of the widespread assumption: "If God had meant humans to fly, He would have given them wings."

Like other myths that touch a fundamental cord in the human psyche, the story of Icarus and Daedalus has inspired generations of artists. In addition to the Dürer woodcut, the Gimbel collection contains illustrations of the story in a wide variety of media. "The Flight of Icarus," for example, is a deeply sculpted bronze medal produced by artist Joseph Sheppard in 1992 for the American Society of Medalists. The obverse illustrates the moment of wonder as father and son rise into the air. The reverse shows a terrified Icarus, shorn of his wings, falling toward the sea.

Gimbel's wonderful collection of sheet music on aeronautical themes includes the sonnet *Icare* (1840) by French composer Victor Masse. The cover shows the body of Icarus lying on the rocks, his wings smashed and broken. Gimbel also acquired a large stippled engraving titled "Daedalus & Icarus," published by Johann and George Facius in November 1779. Based on a painting by Le Brun, who had been charged by Louis XIV with the decoration of Versailles, the print shows Daedalus, the loving father, carefully fitting a set of wings to his son.

Here we have four very different works of art, produced over a period of almost five hundred years, each illuminating and extending our understanding of the classic myth of the air. The availability of so many artistic interpretations of Daedalus and Icarus in one place demonstrates the extraordinary value of a collection of this scope and scale. Far more important, it underscores the longevity of the legend and its continuing power to inspire us with the dream of flight.

Tower Jumpers and Kite Flyers

The volumes lining the shelves of the Gimbel collection demonstrate both the role of flight symbolism in medieval and early modern times and the history of the earliest attempts to realize the ancient dream of wings. The symbolic importance of flight in religion is represented in Pietro Terameno's popular tract of 1495 recounting the angelic transportation of the Blessed Virgin's home from Nazareth, where it was threatened by infidels, through the air to Loreto.

If some citizens of the medieval world regarded flight as a symbol of supernatural intervention in human affairs, others, including the learned English monk Roger Bacon (*ca.* 1220–1292), assumed that mechanical flight was not only possible but had been achieved in ancient times, then forgotten.[22] In addition to his early printed edition of Bacon's work, Richard Gimbel obtained a copy of Athanasius Kircher's 1641 account of a mechanical flying dove said to have been created in the fourth century B.C.E. by an acquaintance of Plato's, Archytas of Tarentum. One of the most widely circulated and influential stories of mechanical flight in the early modern world, the tale of Archytas' dove gave confidence to those who believed that the classical world had achieved many technical wonders, including powered flight, the secrets of which were waiting to be rediscovered.

Robert Hooke (1635–1703), the seventeenth-century English philosopher who served as secretary of the Royal Society, was also inspired by the story of Archytas' dove. In his *Philosophical Collections* (1682), a copy of which survives in the Gimbel collection, Hooke describes his own spring-powered ornithopter, "which rais'd and sustain'd itself in the Air."[23] The opinion of Girolamo Cardano (1501–1576), an earlier scholar whose work is also preserved here, was much more prescient. A successful mechanical ornithopter, he believed, was highly unlikely. A very light, fixed-wing model might be quite a different matter:

> that it should rise of its own accord is hardly possible...[but a mechanical] dove may certainly fly properly if the lightness of the body, the size of the wings, the strength of the wheels, and assistance provided by the wind (which geese and other heavy birds do not ignore), are sufficient.[24]

Octave Chanute, 1832–1910
(National Air and Space
Museum, Smithsonian
Institution)

Richard Gimbel collected a wide range of volumes describing the experience of individuals who attempted to follow in the footsteps of Icarus and Daedalus, testing their homemade wings in what can best be described as semi-suicidal leaps from high places. *Mirrour for Magistrates* (1620), for example, tells the story of King Bladud, the legendary father of King Lear and founder of the city of Bath, who is said to have died *ca.* 850 B.C.E. as the result of an unsuccessful attempt to fly from the roof of the Temple of Apollo. Christian and Islamic literature records over fifty such tales of would-be aviators during the millennium following the death of Bladud. In a fine edition of *Pinacotheca imaginvm* (1645), author Gian Vittorio Rossi describes how the artist Paolo Guidotti broke his thigh in an attempt to fly with whalebone wings covered with feathers. Such tales seldom contain extravagant claims for long flights, are often filled with intriguing details, and usually end in the death or serious injury of the hero. In short, they have the ring of truth to them.

The accounts of "tower jumpers" may well be distant, fragmentary, and exaggerated echoes of the earliest flight-test reports, but they contributed little to the solution of the problems of flight. Other volumes record the work of those individuals, less venturesome but no less curious, who made some of the earliest discoveries in practical aerodynamics. Fausto Veranzio did not invent the parachute, but he did provide the earliest printed illustration of such a device in his *Machinæ novæ Favsti Verantii siceni* (*ca.* 1595).

Giovanni Battista della Porta (*ca.* 1535–1615) provided something far more important for the future in his *Magiæ naturalis libri viginti*, one of the earliest descriptions of the diamond-shaped paper kite. The book is represented in the Gimbel collection by an edition of 1591. Della Porta described a new kite design introduced by seamen returning from voyages to the Far East. The essentially plane-surface Asian kite was so successful that it quickly replaced the traditional European sleeve, windsock, or tailed pennon designs. The Eastern origins of the kite are also celebrated in two Gimbel collection kite prints by the great Japanese artists Hiroshige and Hokusai.

The wide variety of uses to which kites have been put are reflected in the wealth of books on the subject preserved in the Gimbel collection. They range from the early descriptions of the fully developed European version of the diamond kite offered in John Bate's *The Mysteries of Nature and Art* (1635); through nineteenth-century handicraft guides, such as E. Landells' *Boy's Own Toymaker* (1859), which introduced youngsters to the fine art of kite-building and bridling; to enormously detailed treatises on kite history and technology like Joseph Lecornu's 1902 classic, *Les Cerfs-Volants*.[25]

At one end of the spectrum, kites have delighted and inspired children and playful adults for centuries. That is no small matter. It does not take much browsing through the Gimbel shelves to make a case for the importance of the play impulse as a factor encouraging technological change.

Octave Chanute (1832–1910) provides a case in point in the description of helicopter toys offered in his classic survey of pre-Wright flight technology, *Progress in Flying Machines* (1894). "The most popular of such toys," he noted, "have been the various single spinning screws, either of cardboard or metal, which are attached to a spindle around which a string is wound, and which are set in rapid motion by briskly pulling and unwinding the cord."[26]

Helicopter toys of the sort Chanute describes date at least to 1325, when the first illustration of such a device appears in a Flemish manuscript. Over the next two centuries the toy appears in several portraits of children. It remained essentially unchanged until 1784, when, as Chanute explains, the French experimenters Launoy and Bienvenu produced a self-propelled model powered by twisting a bowstring around the shaft. Sir George Cayley, the first genuinely significant figure in the history of aeronautical engineering, was inspired by this version of the old toy,

TOM D. CROUCH

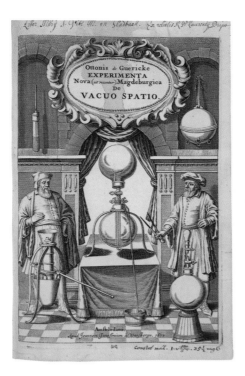

Frontispiece of *Experimenta nova...magdeburgica de vacuo spatio,* 1672

which he described in the pages of his three-part paper, "On Aerial Navigation," a milestone publication of engineering preserved in the Gimbel collection.[27]

Three-quarters of a century later, Bishop Milton Wright returned from a church trip with a present for his two youngest sons, a variant of the now centuries-old helicopter toy, this one developed by the French engineer Alphonse Pénaud. Orville Wright dated his earliest interest in flight to the toy and described subsequent events in a court deposition available to researchers in the Gimbel collection in *The Papers of Wilbur and Orville Wright:*

> We built a number of copies of this toy, which flew successfully. By "we" I refer to my brother Wilbur and myself. But when we undertook to build the toy on a much larger scale it failed to work so well. The reason for this was not understood by us at the time, so we finally abandoned the experiments.[28]

The "experiments" were only temporarily "abandoned." "They made helicopters out of bamboo, paper, corks and rubber bands and allowed us to run after them when they flew them," their nephew recalled of his famous uncles many years later.[29] After more than five hundred years, the little helicopter toy was alive and well and inspiring a new generation of children with an interest in flight. Its history can be traced on the shelves of the Gimbel collection.

So it was with the kite. The oldest aerodynamic device capable of sustained flight, it was manufactured in many variants by generations of youngsters anxious to feel the tug of the wind on a string. Ultimately, however, *no* device was of more importance to the invention of the airplane than the kite. It was an invaluable tool enabling a century of experimenters, from Sir George Cayley to the Wright brothers, to investigate wing design, structural forms, and aeronautical control systems without risking their lives in gliding flight.

Unfortunately, the suitability of the kite as a model for a heavier-than-air flying machine was not apparent prior to 1800. For the moment, those who dreamed of heavier-than-air flight continued to focus on the chimera of flapping wings.

Lighter-Than-Air Balloons

Human beings first took to the sky on the basis of a completely different and much simpler principle, one for which nature offered few clues and no obvious examples. Rather, as the shelves of the Gimbel collection demonstrate, the technology of buoyant flight was rooted in the growing interest of seventeenth- and eighteenth-century natural philosophers in the nature of the atmosphere.

Researchers can examine a very late edition (1672) of *Experimenta nova...magdeburgica de vacuo spatio* in which Otto von Guericke (1602–1686), a city official of Magdeburg, announced his discovery that air, like any other fluid, could be pumped out of a sealed vessel. Fascinated, the English experimenter Robert Boyle (1627–1691) asked his two laboratory assistants (one of whom was Robert Hooke) to design and build a new and improved air pump.

Using the new pump, Boyle (represented in the Gimbel collection by *Occasional reflections upon several subjects,* 1665) conducted a series of experiments that became the basis for his most important discoveries: a statement of the relationship between temperature, pressure, and volume that would be known as Boyle's law; confirmation of the fact that air pressure explained the operation of Torricelli's mercury barometer; and proof that air was required for the propagation of sound, and for combustion and respiration.

Francesco Lana de Terzi, 1631–1687 (National Air and Space Museum, Smithsonian Institution)

The work of the pneumatic physicists had immediate technological consequences, notably the introduction of the earliest steam pumps by Denis Papin and Thomas Savery during the years 1681 to 1698. The new discoveries also inspired the earliest useful speculations on buoyant flight. Gaspar Schott (1608–1666), whose *Magia universalis naturae et artis* (1657–1659) had introduced Robert Boyle to the work of Otto von Guericke, was the first thinker to suggest that copper globes filled with ether, a very light substance presumed to fill the empty space of the universe, might rise into the air.

Richard Gimbel was fortunate to obtain five copies of an even more influential volume, *Prodromo* (1670) by the Jesuit priest Francesco Lana de Terzi. One of those volumes is an especially impressive bibliographic prize, for it once belonged to Gaston Tissandier, the great French balloonist who was the most significant aeronautical collector of the nineteenth century. Published at Brescia in 1670, the thin volume, bound in vellum, contains a proposal for a lighter-than-air flying machine that, while clearly inspired by Schott, went a step further.

Lana de Terzi suggested that if the air were pumped from a large, thin-walled copper sphere, the device might then weigh less than the amount of air it displaced and rise into the sky. Four such globes, each 20 feet in diameter, might be light enough to carry a human being aloft. Theoretically, Lana was on the right track. A hot-air balloon functions because the heat expands the air inside the envelope, so that the balloon weighs less than the amount of fluid it displaces. Unfortunately for Father Lana, it is still not possible to construct globes of any material that are sufficiently large, light, and strong as to become buoyant when evacuated.

Historians of flight have exhibited an unfortunate tendency to dismiss Lana as an impractical dreamer who had little impact on the future. On the contrary, as the shelves of the Gimbel collection demonstrate, Lana's proposal was widely republished, much commented on, and enormously influential. Father Bernardo Zamagna (1735–1820) produced one of the most impressive of those volumes. Published a century after *Prodromo*, Zamagna's *Navis aeria et Elegiarum monobiblos*, an epic of the air in Latin hexameters, describes a voyage around the world in Lana's aerial ship.[30]

In addition to his own speculations on winged flight, Robert Hooke included a discussion of "P. Fran. Lana's way of making a Flying Chariot…," complete with an illustration, in his *Philosophical Collections* (1682). Antonio Vanossi offered an extended commentary on the plan in his *Placita physica…* (1724?), while a 1789 issue of *European Magazine* featured an illustration of the aircraft, identified as "an air-balloon invented in the last century." The print is a copy of an original first published in 1714. Tiberius Cavallo, a chemical experimenter and the author of *The History and Practice of Aerostation* (1785), was one of the pioneer historians of the balloon who described Lana's work with great respect.

If Gaspar Schott and Father Lana conceived the notion of a lighter-than-air flying machine, a Brazilian priest, Bartholomeu Lourenço de Gusmão (1685–1724) may have been the first to actually build and fly a small balloon. His story begins with a book in the Gimbel collection, *Nachricht von dem fliegenden Schiffe*, published in Vienna in 1709. The little volume provides what we can safely assume to be a somewhat exaggerated account of Gusmão's aerial voyage from Lisbon to Vienna in 1709 aboard a craft named the *Passarola* (great bird). The precise nature of *Passarola* is not clear in this marvelous fictional account, and accurate information as to what Gusmão actually did achieve is difficult to obtain.

We do know that in 1709 the king of Portugal granted Gusmão a patent for a flying machine called *Passarola*. There are stories to the effect that Gusmão flew a small fixed-wing glider model that year. Even more convincing, however, are the accounts suggesting that on August 8, 1709, Gusmão flew a small balloon in the presence of the king of Portugal at the Salla das Embaixadas in Lisbon. The burning spirits employed to heat the air inside the envelope, or "canopy," are said to have set fire to the wall hangings and carpets in the room.

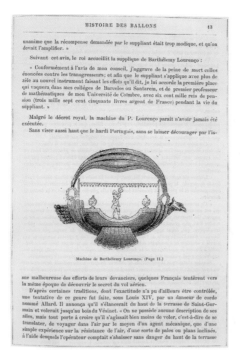

The *Passarola*, a flying machine conceived by Bartholomeu Lourenço de Gusmão

Whatever occurred in Lisbon in 1709, news of Gusmão's project spread quickly from one end of Europe to the other. In addition to the anonymous German account, Richard Gimbel acquired a second version of the story in Pierjacopo Martello's *Versi, e prose* (1710) and a rich assortment of the drawings of *Passarola* that began appearing across Europe after 1709, often in conjunction with illustrations of Lana's craft.

The illustrations of *Passarola* show a bird-shaped fuselage, complete with a beaked head and outstretched feathered wings and tail, and a huge, billowing canopy stretched overhead. The various versions of this print have usually been thought to be conjectural illustrations of a large ornithopter, or a fixed-wing glider. In view of the very strong evidence in favor of Gusmão's demonstration of a model hot-air balloon, however, it is possible that the print is a depiction of what a full-scale balloon might look like, prepared by an artist who had not actually seen the little craft flown at Lisbon. The canopy could be a misguided attempt to represent what in any case may have been an unconventional envelope.

If Gusmão did fly a small balloon in Lisbon, the world would have to wait three-quarters of a century for the second public flight of a hot-air balloon. The place was the public square of Annonay, a provincial market town and administrative center in the southern French district of the Vivarais. The date was June 4, 1783. Fortunately, the scene was recorded in a contemporary print that is preserved in the Gimbel collection. We see a handful of people, far fewer than were actually there that day. The flight had been timed to coincide with the meetings of the *États particuliers* of Vivarais, a local legislative and judicial assembly. The town was crowded with officials, visitors with business before the assembly, and local citizens.

Attention is focused on the balloon, trailing tendrils of smoke as it rises slowly into the air. It measured 10 feet in diameter and was constructed of a sandwich of paper and fabric. The material was cut into gores, appropriately shaped strips that could be combined to form a sphere. The print also shows some puzzling nubs running along the edge of the gores. They are the buttons—yes, buttons—that, along with the glue, hold the whole thing together.

This illustration of the first public flight of the brothers Joseph and Étienne Montgolfier has a value quite beyond the information that it communicates about the birth of the air age. It is the rarest aeronautical print in the Gimbel collection and may be the only original copy of this image in the United States.

If seventeenth-century studies of pneumatic physics inspired the notion of buoyant flight, the eighteenth-century effort to analyze the constituent gases of the atmosphere led directly to the invention of the balloon. It is a story told in several volumes contained in the Gimbel collection, notably Tiberius Cavallo's *The History and Practice of Aerostation* (1785). Cavallo, a Neapolitan experimenter living in England, knew the principal chemists involved in analyzing the atmosphere and helped to bridge the gap between the laboratories of the chemists and the workshops of the men who built and flew the first balloons.

The first step was taken in 1756 when the Scottish chemist Joseph Black identified the first truly elemental gas, "fixed air," or nitrogen. A decade later Henry Cavendish announced the discovery of "phlogisticated," or "inflammable," air, a gas (from the German *geist*—"spirit") that was much lighter than either nitrogen or atmospheric air. The balloon would be seven years old before Antoine-Laurent Lavoisier applied the name hydrogen to the gas discovered by Cavendish.

The discovery of a new gas six times lighter than air inspired several pioneering chemists to explore just how much weight "inflammable air" might lift. Joseph Black considered inflating the

Joseph Montgolfier,
1740–1810

Étienne Montgolfier,
1745–1790

bladder of a calf with the gas but did not do so. Tiberius Cavallo actually tried Black's experiment but could not find a bladder that offered sufficient volume for weight. He did, however, devise an apparatus for blowing hydrogen-filled soap bubbles that rose to the ceiling.

Joseph Montgolfier (1740–1810) was one of many curious Frenchmen who were fascinated by the work of the English pneumatic chemists. The twelfth of sixteen children born to a family that had been involved in the manufacture of paper since the fourteenth century, Joseph was an absent-minded eccentric, quite unlike his younger brother Étienne, the fifteenth child and the best businessman of his generation of Montgolfiers. Yet Joseph was the one who would immortalize the family name.

Following the invention of the balloon, some writers wondered if the Montgolfier brothers had been inspired by Joseph Galien's *L'art de naviger dans les airs* (1757), published in Avignon, where Joseph had lived for a time. In this fantasy, represented in the Gimbel collection by a copy once owned by Gaston Tissandier, the author follows the line of reasoning pioneered by Gaspar Schott, speculating that an airship filled with ether might be used to escape flood or pestilence.

If Joseph did read the book, he kept that fact to himself. In general terms, he was much more interested in science than in science fiction. Matthieu Duret, a younger physician and Joseph's cousin, remembered that as early as 1777 Joseph had repeatedly quizzed him on the content of the public lectures offered in Paris on the new discoveries in pneumatic chemistry. Matthieu objected when Cousin Joseph suggested that an understanding of pneumatic chemistry might lead to the design of a flying machine. "All that you have taught me of chemistry, only confirms me more fully in my ideas," he responded. "I must make some experiments."[31]

Joseph conducted the most critical of those experiments in November 1782. Convinced that "heat" was a fluid related to the other new "airs" and that the combustion of organic materials would produce a very lightweight "rarified air," he constructed a frame of very light wood covered with finely woven taffeta and filled it with very hot air. It flew. "Get in a supply of taffeta and cordage, quickly," he wrote to Jacques-Étienne, "and you will see one of the most astonishing sights in the world."[32]

News of the Montgolfier flight on June 4, 1783 was slow to reach Paris. The controller general of finance, who received the official report of the *États particuliers* late in June, was probably the first man in Paris to discover that the age of flight had begun. On July 10, a Paris newspaper published an extract of a very brief account of the flight by a witness. The first relatively full and accurate account did not appear in a Paris newspaper until July 27, 53 days after the flight.

TOM D. CROUCH

J.A. C. Charles, 1746-1823

Jean-François Pilâtre de Rozier, 1754-1785

By the time the first detailed article appeared, however, a subscription had already been filled to fund the construction of a balloon to be flown in Paris. The original report from Annonay had been communicated to the savants of the Academy of Science, who were willing to wait for the Montgolfiers to arrive in Paris. Barthélemy Faujas de Saint-Fond (1741–1819), a naturalist at the Musée d'Histoire Naturelle in Paris, was less patient.

As a young man Faujas had abandoned a promising legal career in order to pursue a deep interest in science, earning his reputation with a study of ancient vulcanism in the Vivarais. Sir Joseph Banks, president of the Royal Society, was fond of Faujas but described him as a bumptious fellow, possessed of "effrontery" to "an eminent degree."[33]

Certainly, Faujas showed little restraint in the spring of 1783. When he learned of the events in Annonay and realized that the members of the Academy were going to watch and wait, Faujas simply announced that he was selling tickets to a balloon launch and turned the money over to Jacques Alexandre César Charles, the man whom he had selected to construct a balloon.

Charles, one of the best known scientific lecturers in Paris, had given up a budding career as a government administrator after reading Benjamin Franklin's treatise on electricity. The notion of "inflammable air" was very much on his mind. In mid-June Antoine-Laurent Lavoisier had demonstrated for the first time that water was a compound of that very light gas and "dephlogisticated air," or oxygen, which Joseph Priestley had identified in 1774. It probably did not even occur to Charles that the Montgolfiers had filled their balloon with anything other than hydrogen.

With the assistance of the brothers A. J. and M. N. Robert, who had developed a process for coating fabric with natural rubber, Charles built a demonstration balloon and an apparatus for generating large quantities of hydrogen. An enormous crowd of Parisians gathered near the Champ de Mars, the great parade ground in front of the *École militaire* on the afternoon of August 27, 1783, to witness the first flight of a gas balloon, just as Faujas had promised. "It diminished in Apparent Magnitude as it rose," Benjamin Franklin reported, "till it entered the Clouds, when it seem'd to me scarce bigger than an Orange." At the conclusion of the demonstration, Franklin, the leader of the American diplomatic community in Paris, overheard a spectator remark that the balloon was nothing more than a useless toy. "Of what use," the American responded, "is a new born babe?"[34]

One balloon after another rose above the Paris skyline during the next three months. The royal family was in attendance on September 19, when Étienne Montgolfier sent a sheep, a duck,

Mr. BLANCHARD

Citoyen de Calais et de plusieurs autres Villes, par adoption Pensionaire de S.M.J.C et de plusieurs Academies

« Quelques amis le suivirent à cheval et arrivèrent près de Saint-Pierre-Woluw(

JOHN JEFFRIES.

Jean-Pierre François
Blanchard, 1753–1809

Dr. John Jeffries, 1745–1819

and a rooster aloft from the palace at Versailles. Pilâtre de Rozier, who lectured on science under the patronage of the Comte de Provence, and François Laurent, the Marquis d'Arlandes, the first two human beings to make a free flight, rose from the grounds of the Château de la Muette on November 21 aboard a Montgolfier hot-air balloon. Less than two weeks later, J.A.C. Charles and M. N. Robert became the first human beings to make a flight with a gas balloon. Less than a year after the first flight of a small balloon from Annonay, the air age was well under way.

The shelves of the Gimbel collection contain a wealth of materials that enables us to reach back more than two centuries and recapture some sense of the incredible excitement occasioned by the invention of the balloon. Here are manuscript letters from the Montgolfiers and their relatives, Pilâtre de Rozier, and other participants, commenting on everything from the cost of hats and difficulties of travel to the details of the first balloon ascents.

Pamphlets and articles by the Montgolfiers, J.A.C. Charles, the Robert brothers, Pilâtre de Rozier, and the Marquis d'Arlandes grace the Gimbel shelves. Other first-generation aeronauts represented in the Gimbel collection include Paolo Andreani, who made the first flight outside of France; Jean-Pierre François Blanchard, the first of the great professional aeronauts; Dr. John Jeffries, the first American to make a free flight, and the man who accompanied Blanchard on the first flight across the English Channel; and André Jacques Garnerin, who earned his early reputation by making parachute jumps from balloons.

It was the irrepressible Barthélemy Faujas de Saint-Fond, however, who quickly emerged as the most significant historian of the birth of flight. Angry at the false and misleading accounts that were rushed into print in the immediate aftermath of a flight, Faujas set out to produce an extended, detailed, and accurate account of the events that he had witnessed and helped to shape. His first book on the subject, the two-volume *Description des expériences de la machine aérostatique...*, was published so quickly that it was dated 1783–1784. The Gimbel collection holds Dutch, Belgian, German, English, and Italian editions of the work, all published before the end of 1784.

In addition to letters, newspapers, pamphlets, and books, the citizens of the late eighteenth century relied on inexpensive and widely distributed printed images to help them visualize the distant places, people, and events of their day. The creation, production, distribution, and sale of such single-sheet images was a minor industry prior to the rise of illustrated newspapers and magazines in the nineteenth century. The invention of the balloon inspired an outpouring of

TOM D. CROUCH

Melancholy Death
OF
MADAME BLANCHARD,
At Paris, through her Balloon taking Fire.

THE Fete at Tivoli, which had long been announced, took place on the 6th of July, and was marked by a dreadful catastrophe. Among the amusements which had been announced, was the ascension of Madame Blanchard in an illuminated Balloon, ornamented with fire-works. At half-past ten the intrepid aeronaut, dressed in white, with a white hat and feathers, entered the car. At the signal given, Madame Blanchard rose rapidly. Bengal fire-pots illuminated the ascension. The aeronaut waved her flag, and the air resounded with shouts. On a sudden the Balloon entered a light cloud, which completely extinguished the fire-pots.—Madame Blanchard then set light to the fire-works, which produced the intended effect; but it was observed, that some of the fiery matter took a direction towards the Balloon, and the fire communicated to its base. Immediately, the most dreadful fright seized all the spectators, there being no doubt of the deplorable fate of the aeronaut.

It is impossible to describe what passed at that moment at Tivoli; cries of grief were heard in all quarters; a great number of women became a prey to the most violent nervous attacks, and consternation was depicted in every countenance, and in a quarter of an hour afterwards the lifeless body of Madame Blanchard was brought back to Tivoli. She was in the car, enveloped in the cordage, which had attached it to the Balloon.

A subscription was immediately opened for the family of Madame Blanchard. The unfortunate lady was about 45 years of age. The proprietors of the garden offered the produce of the receipts for the benefit of her family. The height from which the Balloon fell was about 400 feet.

THE BALLOON:
A FICTITIOUS DREAM ABOUT FACTS.
Or Occurrences of every Day.

A SCENE which I beheld in my sleep some time ago, has occupied my waking thoughts ever since. As the circumstances which then seemed to happen, certainly take place every day, the recital may both please and edify, and stamp a solemnity upon Time which was not observed before. The remembrance of it has both moderated my joy and regulated my sorrow, upon various occasions. In my sleep I supposed myself seated in a Balloon, and they were all happy and cheerful. Some were losing, others gaining. A thoughtless young man lost his whole property at one throw of the dice!—He slipt away to another apartment, and seemed ready to tear out his very heart. He had several brothers and sisters entirely dependent upon him for support, who had all been brought up in the first style. How to reveal his ruin to his friends he knew not:—but do it he must. He called the gentle- living in the utmost profusion; their dishes at table are so numerous, they can hardly taste half of them, and yet they are not thankful; they say, "This fowl is too old; that one is not well cooked; this pudding is bad; and that pie is intolerable." The patience of Job could not bear with the constant ingratitude of such creatures, yet God has patience to bear with such persons for many years; but if his goodness does not lead them to repentance, his wrath

Newspaper account of the death of Madame Blanchard, "The Religious Tract Society," *ca.* 1819

prints unmatched by any other event in the late eighteenth century.

The Gimbel collection contains multiple prints illustrating each of the great Paris ascents of 1783. At least a dozen different views of the first flight of human beings on November 21, 1783, were on sale in the shops and stalls of Europe before the end of 1785. Richard Gimbel acquired two illustrations of that flight as seen from the terrace of Benjamin Franklin's home, the Hôtel de Valentinois, in the Paris suburb of Passy. In addition to the eighteenth-century prints, Richard Gimbel collected a number of more recent artistic interpretations of the moment when human beings first took to the sky, including a misty and evocative painting on wood and a print by Marcel JeanJean, a World War I aviator and official painter to the French minister of air.

The tradition of commemorating the great events in the history of flight with fine examples of numismatic art began in 1783, when the Paris Mint issued a lovely medal honoring the Montgolfier brothers, "POUR AVOIR RENDU L'AIR NAVIGABLE." The Mint issued another medal the following year commemorating the first flights of human beings aboard the Montgolfier and Charles balloons. Gimbel obtained examples of both medals restruck using the original dies, as well as a variety of additional numismatic items celebrating the achievements of the great aeronauts of the nineteenth century from the time of Vincent Lunardi, who made the first hydrogen balloon flight in England in 1784, to Charles Green, the most experienced and famous of the Victorian aeronauts, and his American contemporary Thaddeus Sobieski Constantine Lowe, who earned fame as the leader of the Union army balloon corps during the Civil War.

The Uses of a Newborn Babe

The Gimbel collection is a treasure trove of materials tracing the history of ballooning through the end of the nineteenth century. The sheer number of prints and published accounts documents the wave of interest in flight that swept across Europe following the annus mirabilis of 1783. The new invention had shattered the chains of gravity and offered the promise of conquering the old barriers of time and space. People expressed this sense of new possibility in very personal terms. "If it were possible to have one of the new aerial carriages," a French nun remarked to her brother in a letter surviving in the Gimbel collection, "I could travel through the air…to tell you what my heart would…say and would return from that content to savor the happiness of my solitude."[35]

As the large number of satirical prints in the collection demonstrates, however, the invention of the balloon also inspired considerable cynicism. Some prints, including "The Aerostatic

NADAR

Gaspard-Félix Tournachon (Nadar), 1820–1910 (National Air and Space Museum, Smithsonian Institution)

Man or My Poor Uncle" and "The Definitive Judgment in Favor of Srs. Miolan and Janinet," seem calculated to puncture the scientific pretensions and pomposity affected by aeronauts of the period. Others, like "The New Mode of Picking Pockets" and "Aerostation out at Elbows," raised questions as to the basic utility of the new technology. In spite of Franklin's *bon mot*, there remained a great deal of doubt as to the "use of a newborn babe."

During the nineteenth century, many aeronauts in Europe and America earned their living by performing feats of aerial derring-do high above a crowd of paying spectators and by capturing newspaper headlines with spectacular long-distance flights. The names of those who made aeronautical history are preserved on the posters, tickets, news clippings, letters, and books of the Gimbel collection: Jeanne-Geneviève Garnerin, the first woman pilot-in-command; Louis Charles Guillé, who introduced parachute jumping in the United States; Marie Madeleine Sophie Blanchard, the second wife of J.-P.F. Blanchard and the first woman to die in a ballooning accident; and George and Margaret Graham, the husband and wife aeronauts who thrilled crowds in Victoria's England.

Some aspects of nineteenth-century aerial showmanship apparent in the Gimbel collection may surprise modern readers. Consider, for example, a print showing a series of large inflated animals soaring over the Paris skyline. It is a reminder that the delightful helium-filled comic figures associated with American holiday parades are simply the latest versions of the hydrogen-filled fabric creations produced for public celebrations in Europe and America during the late eighteenth and early nineteenth centuries.

Those who delight in hangar flying tales of aerial adventure will enjoy discovering the stories of the great balloons, aeronauts, and long-distance flights of the nineteenth century preserved in the Gimbel collection. Take the case of Gaspard-Félix Tournachon's great balloon, *Le Géant.* Tournachon, a pioneering French photographer who worked under the professional name of Nadar, became fascinated by aeronautics in the 1850s. Along with the American Samuel Archer King, he was one of the first practitioners of aerial photography. He unveiled his huge balloon, *Le Géant,* in the fall of 1863. It stood 196 feet tall, could lift 4.5 tons of useful load, and featured a two-story, six-room, wicker-work gondola complete with four berths, a lavatory, a darkroom for developing aerial photographs, and a printing press.

Le Géant carried fifteen people, including the "young and personable" Princess de la Tour d'Auvergne, on its first flight. The great adventure ended only about 30 miles from the take-off point with the bungalow of the gondola being dragged for a mile across the landscape while the passengers hung on for dear life. Between 1863 and 1867, Nadar made a series of celebrated ascents, including one long-distance flight into Germany. The adventurous details of the various flights were published in illustrated newspapers on both sides of the Atlantic.

As the Gimbel collection attests, Nadar and his enormous balloon inspired everything from advertisements to children's board games. Many published accounts of the adventures of this real life Jules Verne hero are to be found on the Gimbel shelves. Nadar himself wrote the preface for one of the best: Alfred Sircos and Th. Pallier, *Histoire des ballons et des ascensions célèbres* (1876).

The dream of very long distance flights, however, was born and nurtured in America.

TOM D. CROUCH

Crash of Nadar's *Le Géant*

The notion of flying the Atlantic can be seen in a variety of materials preserved by Richard Gimbel, including accounts of transoceanic dreamers like John Wise and Washington Harrison Donaldson, both of whom disappeared during the course of long-distance flights over the Great Lakes. Wise published *A System of Aeronautics* (1850), his history and guide to ballooning, close to the outset of his career, and his fully developed autobiography, *Through the Air* (1873), more than a quarter of a century later. Both volumes remain as classics of the literature of flight. M. L. Amick's *History of Donaldson's Balloon Ascensions* (1875) offers a classic, and comical, account of the career of one of the most colorful aeronauts of the nineteenth century, complete with a series of lively and delightful primitive woodcut illustrations.

Materials related to the two most famous American newspaper hoaxes of the nineteenth century are also preserved on these shelves. Edgar Allan Poe perpetrated the "balloon hoax" with the best of motives. In order to feed himself and his invalid wife, he wrote the false account of Thomas Monck Mason's supposed aerial crossing of the Atlantic. The other hoax—the "moon hoax"—we will come to in due time.

The Gimbel collection includes a wealth of additional materials documenting the ultimate dream of an Atlantic crossing, including a letter describing Richard Clayton's 1835 record-setting 350-mile flight from Cincinnati to Monroe County, Virginia; a published account of the 1859 flight of the balloon *Atlantic*, piloted by John Wise, John LaMountain, and two companions, 809 miles from St. Louis to Henderson County, New York; and a rare medal struck in 1859 and sold to raise funds for T.S.C. Lowe's effort to fly the Atlantic in the *City of New York*.

Having failed to raise the funds to fly from New York, Lowe relocated the project to Philadelphia and renamed his giant balloon the *Great Western*, a comment on the huge steamship *Great Eastern*, designed and built by the English engineer I. K. Brunel. The project collapsed when the citizens of the City of Brotherly Love proved no more enthusiastic about the huge balloon than their New York cousins. In addition to the medal commemorating the *City of New York*, Richard Gimbel acquired a marvelous comic print comparing the balloon and Brunel's leviathan steamship, which was also the butt of a great many jokes.

Throughout the nineteenth century, however, there were those who believed that the balloon ought to be put to some more worthy purpose than that of a vehicle for adventurers or as a centerpiece around which to organize public spectacles. A recognition that the ability to fly would have revolutionary military applications dated at least to Francesco Lana de Terzi, who believed that for all of his own plans, God would never permit human beings to fly. The prospect of an attack from the sky on defenseless civilians was too terrible to contemplate.

The Gimbel print files contain several images of *L'Entreprenant*, the world's first military aircraft. Constructed by Charles Coutelle and N. J. Conte, who had organized a Corps d'Aérostiers for the Army of Revolutionary France, the observation balloon first saw service at Maubeuge and Fleurus in 1794. Additional popular prints illustrate the use of the observation balloon in the American Civil War and the Spanish-American War. Interested researchers will also find a copy of Thaddeus S.C. Lowe's written report of his service with the Army of the Potomac preserved in the Gimbel collection, along with photographs of his balloons and equipment.

One of the most interesting Gimbel items relating to military aeronautics is a long Chinese scroll illustrating the various stages in the deployment of an observation balloon. The scroll probably documents the scene at the Tientsin Military Academy in 1887, when French contractors, including the aeronaut Pillas-Panis, instructed students in the management of the equipment required to maintain and operate an observation balloon in the field. Gimbel, an experienced military airman, amassed personal accounts, official reports, illustrations, and historical studies detailing the full range of experiments undertaken in military aeronautics prior to 1914.

In bibliographic terms, however, there can be no doubt that the wealth of materials relating to aeronautics in the Franco-Prussian War constitutes a unique strength of the Gimbel collection. Seldom has a nation entered a conflict with more enthusiasm, or collapsed as quickly, as did the France of Louis Napoleon. Thousands of French troops had marched out of Paris in July 1870, clad in colorful uniforms beneath waving flags, the cry of "on to Berlin" ringing in their ears. By September 20, the Emperor had surrendered at Sedan and the first of General Moltke's 150,000 gray-clad troops were knocking on the gates of Paris.

Although both nations had given some thought to aerial warfare, observation ballooning did not play at important role in the early phases of the conflict. Henry Tracey Coxwell, the famous English balloonist, working as a contractor, had provided the Prussian army with two balloons and the equipment, except for gas generators, required to maintain them in the field. He had also trained two companies of twenty men each to move and operate the balloons. Without a means of inflation on the march, however, the single balloon that accompanied the invading army was worthless. The entire unit was ordered back to Germany. Coxwell's memoir of this effort, *My Life and Balloon Experiences, with a Supplementary Chapter on Military Ballooning* (1887), offers a rare account of aeronautics on the Prussian side of the lines.

Marshal Leboeuf, the French minister of war, had opposed the use of balloons, so that it was not until after the surrender at Sedan and the death of the Second Empire that Nadar, the colorful photographer and aeronaut, made a tethered ascent inside the city to observe the movement of besieging German troops. M. Rampont, the minister of posts, then announced the creation of a balloon post that would carry mail out of the city over the heads of the besieging Germans. There would be two classes of balloon mail: "*monté*" and "*non-monté*." Letters *monté*, prepared on small sheets of lightweight paper weighing less than 4 grams, would be carried aboard manned balloons. *Non-monté* communications would be written on special postcards and sent aloft aboard unmanned balloons in the hope that they would come down inside French lines and be forwarded to the addressee.

When the siege began, there were seven balloons in Paris. At the rate of a flight or two a week, the supply was soon exhausted. Nadar, Eugène Godard (a veteran of 800 ascents), and other experienced aeronauts organized 60 seamstresses and transformed the city's great railroad stations, where the trains no longer ran, into balloon factories. The supply of experienced aeronauts was also limited. Before the siege was over, 18 trained balloonists, 17 volunteers, and 30 sailors who were trapped in the city would pilot balloons out of Paris.

Some 58 of the more than 65 balloons launched from Paris during the siege (September 1870–January 1871) reached safety. They carried 2,500,000 pieces of mail and 102 pas-

TOM D. CROUCH

GASTON TISSANDIER.

Gaston Tissandier, 1843–1899
(National Air and Space
Museum, Smithsonian
Institution)

Copper medallion
commemorating a balloon
flight during the Siege of
Paris, September 1870–
January 1871

sengers, including Leon Gambetta, a government official who was wounded by a Prussian bullet and barely escaped capture. Fearful of coming down within German lines, one team of aeronauts flew about 520 miles to a landing in Longsburg, Norway, 14 hours, 40 minutes after takeoff. Another balloonist flew 285 miles in fewer than 3 hours, averaging 95 miles per hour!

Of course, getting mail and personnel out of the city was only half of the problem. Several methods of getting messages *into* Paris were considered and rejected—including the use of dogs and the notion of floating objects down the Seine. Ultimately, ingenious postal officials decided to combine carrier pigeons with advanced technology.

The first step was for M. Dagron, a specialist in microphotography, to leave the city aboard the balloon *Niepce*. Reaching the wartime capital of Tours, he established a photographic facility and began producing microfilm copies of government dispatches and letters intended for Paris. Eventually, as many as 40,000 pages could be carried by a single bird. The homing pigeons were flown out of Paris aboard the balloons, loaded with messages, and released to fly back to the city. Once retrieved, the film was processed and the messages projected onto a wall, copied by stenographers and distributed. The people of Paris were reduced to eating rats during the siege, but their mail arrived on time.

Memories of the disastrous war with Prussia would shape French policy for seven decades. Patriots could take pride in the role that the aeronauts of Paris had played during the siege, however. Autobiographical accounts of the leading aeronauts of the siege, like Gaston Tissandier's *En Ballon!* (1871), as well as the descriptive volumes and histories of the balloons and the pigeon post, sold well during the years following the conflict.

In addition to holding published accounts unmatched by any other American library, the Gimbel collection contains a treasure trove of other materials describing the role of aeronautics in the Franco-Prussian War. The collection includes a rich assortment of the newspapers published in the city during the siege based on information supplied by the pigeon post: *Lettre-Journal de Paris, Dépêche-Ballon, La Cloche Journal-Poste* and *L'Indépendant*. Researchers will also find thirty examples of letters delivered "*par ballon monté*" and a pair of microprints.

The Gimbel siege collection also contains printed images, notably "Au Bastion," a lithograph illustrating a lovely Parisienne standing atop a city bastion with a balloon passing overhead. One of Richard Gimbel's most interesting numismatic acquisitions is a small *jeton* or token, celebrating the pigeon post. During the course of the siege, Paris entrepreneurs produced for sale a total of 83 distinct copper or lead medallions of this sort commemorating the escape of one or another of the balloons from the city. Moreover, the provisional government of Paris authorized proof sets of coins featuring the balloons. The coins themselves were not issued after the siege.

The *jeton,* along with the wealth of other materials in the Gimbel collection relating to aeronautics in the Siege of Paris, represents a priceless scholarly resource enabling researchers to examine a critically important moment in the early history of military aviation from a number of points of view.

Navigating the Air

The balloon had opened the skies to human beings, but it remained a captive of the winds. Numerous materials documenting the evolution of designs for a dirigible balloon, a powered airship capable of navigating the air, are found in the Gimbel collection. Prints illustrate the early airship designs of Louis Charles Guillé, Muzio Muzzi, Carmien de Luze, Ernest Pétin, and Russell Thayer. A wonderfully optimistic handbill dated 1835 announces the imminent departure of the airship *Eagle* on a round-trip flight from Kensington, England to Paris with 17 passengers on board.

Rufus Porter, the founder of *Scientific American,* established the Aerial Navigation Company in 1852. Intended to develop a passenger carrying airship, the project is memorialized in a stock certificate, complete with an illustration of the cigar-shaped *Aeroport,* which is preserved in the Gimbel collection.

Solomon Andrews, the mayor of Perth Amboy, New Jersey, during the Civil War, went a step further than his predecessors, commissioning the Pennsylvania balloonist John Wise to construct a one-man version of the *Aereon* airship, some 60 feet long. Andrews' craft did fly and generated some public enthusiasm. Ultimately, however, he was pursuing a will-o'-the-wisp, seeking to employ the power of the air flowing around the descending airship to both propel and control the motion of the craft. It was an aeronautical version of perpetual motion. The details of the story are fully recorded in Richard Gimbel's copy of Solomon Andrews' 1865 publication *The Art of Flying.*

French engineer Henri Giffard took the first serious step toward the navigation of the air in 1852, when he guided his steam-powered airship through the first circle in the air. A contemporary print in the Gimbel collection shows the Giffard craft with an enclosed gondola rather than the open platform on which the intrepid aeronaut, clad in a frock coat and top hat, actually stood. The subsequent experiments of Gaston Tissandier, Paul Haenlein, Charles Renard and Arthur Krebs, and Karl Woelfert are detailed in a series of volumes found on the Gimbel shelves.

Alberto Santos-Dumont's autobiographical account, *My Air-Ships,* remains a particular favorite. The son of one of the wealthiest coffee planters in Brazil, Le Petit Santos had come to Paris to study engineering and became fascinated by the subject of flight. He burst onto the public scene in 1901, when he won the rich prize offered by Henri Deutsch de la Meurthe for the first flight from the Aéro-Club field at St. Cloud to the Eiffel Tower and back. Thousands of Parisians turned out to watch and to cheer their new hero on to victory. In one of those grand gestures so typical of him, the young Brazilian divided the prize money among the members of his ground crew.

The sight of Santos-Dumont cruising above the rooftops of the city in a one-man airship powered by an internal combustion engine delighted residents of the City of Light. All of Paris knew that Santos carried his obsession with flight to such an extraordinary degree that he dined at a table and chairs suspended from the ceiling of his apartment. The story of the day on which he landed on a boulevard, tethered his craft, and enjoyed an apéritif in a sidewalk cafe became a legend of the city.

But the efforts of Santos-Dumont and other early twentieth-century aeronauts who operated one-man airships were overshadowed by the achievements of Count Ferdinand von Zeppelin. The Count organized his first joint stock company in 1894; flew his first rigid airship in 1900; achieved practical success with the *LZ6* in 1906; and, by 1913, was regularly carrying pas-

sengers on excursion flights over German cities. A symbol of German national pride and technological achievement, the giant rigid airships were universally recognized as the first practical
strategic weapons system.

The Gimbel collection includes prints (like "Zeppelin über den Bodensee" and a child's
cut-out paper model of a "dirigible militaire") that speak volumes. The frail airplanes of the
period scarcely seemed to offer much of a threat, but the image of a German airship cruising
high over a defenseless city provided the people of London and Paris with food for thought.
Three centuries before, Francesco Lana de Terzi had predicted that this day would come. The
power to fly had carried the world to the doorstep of total war.

Wings

The age-old dream of winged flight was also realized during the first decade of the new century. The Gimbel collection traces the notion of flying like a bird from the legends represented
on the Mesopotamian seals, through the era of Leonardo da Vinci, to the development of the
earliest aerodynamic devices such as kites and helicopter toys. The fact remains that Sir George
Cayley (1773–1857), an English baronet with an estate at Brompton Hall in Yorkshire, took
the first serious steps toward the realization of the dream.

One of the genuine rarities preserved in the Gimbel collection is a thin, 56-page German pamphlet titled *Dresdener Chroniken, und Geschichts, Calender 1809*, containing an illustration of a
brave soul wearing a pair of trussed, ornithopter wings developed by a Swiss clock-maker named
Jacob Degen. Reports that Degen had actually gotten his machine off the ground circulated widely
between 1807 and 1817. What this illustration does not show, and what most other accounts of the
project failed to mention, was that Degen had tested his machine dangling beneath a large balloon,
without which it would not have risen an inch into the air.

The Degen hoax had one great consequence. It convinced George Cayley to publicize his own
aeronautical experiments. By 1809, when he first heard that Degen had flown, Cayley had already
conducted a series of experiments to gather data that could be used in designing a flying machine; developed the modern conception of an airplane as a craft with separate systems for lift,
propulsion, and control; and built and flown a full-scale but unmanned glider, the first in the
world of which we can be certain. At work for over a decade, he had decided not to publish the
results of his studies—until the article on Degen convinced him that if he did not publicize his
own thoughts and information he would be by-passed and forgotten.

Sir George Cayley, 1773–1857
(National Air and Space
Museum, Smithsonian
Institution)

Otto Lilienthal, 1848–1896

The Gimbel collection does not contain any more influential volumes than the November 1809 and February and March 1810 issues of Nicholson's *Journal of Natural Philosophy, Chemistry, and the Arts* in which Sir George Cayley published his three-part paper "On Aerial Navigation." Along with a handful of eighteenth-century studies of windmills, waterwheels, and ballistics, this paper is the foundation stone of aeronautical engineering.

Cayley launched a new era in which the enormous power of engineering research would be brought to bear on the flying machine problem. The most influential nineteenth-century aircraft designs also reflected Cayley's influence. And none was more influential than the Aerial Steam Carriage of John Stringfellow and William Samuel Henson, an illustration of which is preserved in the Gimbel collection.

Much of what is important with regard to the history of aerodynamic research in the nineteenth century is contained in the twenty-three volumes of *Reports* published by the Aeronautical Society of Great Britain, 1866–1893, and preserved in the Gimbel collection. The best of these papers represent milestones in the history of flight, marking the path of technological progress from the age of Cayley through the invention of the wind tunnel (which Francis Herbert Wenham reported in these pages), to the experiments with power plants, models, and gliders that prepared the way for the final steps toward the invention of a successful airplane.

The great aeronautical pioneers who dominated the second half of the nineteenth century —Hiram Maxim, Samuel Pierpont Langley, Clément Ader, Louis Mouillard, Lawrence Hargrave, and others—describe their own work in volumes found on the Gimbel shelves. Here researchers will find a copy of the single most important aeronautical book published between Sir George Cayley's triple paper of 1809–1810 and the turn of the century—Otto Lilienthal's classic *Der Vogelflug als Grundlage der Fliegekunst...* (1889). Having published the engineering data resulting from his meticulous research, Lilienthal turned his attention to the design and construction of gliders. Between 1890 and his death in 1896, as a result of injuries suffered in a glider crash, Lilienthal completed about 2,000 glides in at least 18 distinct glider types.

Octave Chanute (1832–1910), a leading American civil engineer and an international authority on aeronautics, was Otto Lilienthal's chief American correspondent and the link between the German pioneer and the brothers Wilbur and Orville Wright. Chanute's classic, *Progress in Flying Machines* (1894), summarized a century of research into flight science and technology. His correspondence with the Wright brothers, published in *The Papers of Wilbur and Orville*

TOM D. CROUCH

Wright Flyer
at Kitty Hawk, 1903

Wright (1953), helps us to understand the way in which the two men from Dayton, Ohio, solved the final problems barring the way to success and launched the world into the age of wings.[36]

One of Colonel Gimbel's rarest acquisitions relating to the Wrights is a copy of a monthly journal with the unlikely title *Gleanings in Bee Culture*. The editor, Amos Ives Root, the proprietor of a Medina, Ohio, apiary supply house, was fascinated by technology. In the fall of 1904, hearing rumors of strange goings-on in a cow pasture 8 miles east of Dayton, Root drove his automobile to the place, where he met Wilbur and Orville Wright and witnessed the first complete circle flown by an airplane. Returning home, he wrote an account that treated the beekeepers of America to the very first eyewitness account of a Wright airplane in the air. The great newspapers of the world had been scooped by an unlikely competitor.[37]

The Wrights were the first great heroes of the twentieth century and symbolic figures of enormous importance. Some notion of the enormous range of attitudes toward the brothers and the meaning of their achievement is to be found in two cartoon portraits of Wilbur Wright preserved in the Gimbel collection. In one, a hugely smiling Wilbur, pipe clenched in his teeth, takes a clinging, corpulent, and obviously adoring *Marianne*, the symbol of the French nation, for a ride in his airplane.

The other image, a caricature on the cover of the French comic journal *Le Rire*, is a caustic portrait of a mechanistic Wilbur, complete with bolted metal bars for arms and legs, a bellows for a body and bat wings. A scowling grimace spreads across his face, and vultures perch on his wings and cap. One can only wonder what solid, upright Wilbur Wright thought of these two images that were anything but flattering. The son of a bishop of the Church of the United Brethren in Christ—and a man who seems never to have touched tobacco, liquor, or women—Wilbur would have been appalled and offended by the two very different caricatures that indicate the failure of the world's press to understand the two brilliant Americans or their achievement.[38]

The excitement and energy of the early years of powered, heavier-than-air flight are clearly expressed in the wide range of paper ephemera in the Gimbel collection. Produced by showmen who never dreamed that these items would survive once they had performed the function for which they were intended, the advertisements, tickets, posters, and similar objects remain as colorful and evocative reminders of a bygone time when the sight of an airplane in the sky caused people to stop and stare. They bring the past to life.

A postcard shows a Wright Model A aircraft cruising high over lower Manhattan beneath a slogan suggesting, "High Flyers From Coast to Coast Use Lash's Bitters, The Great Tonic

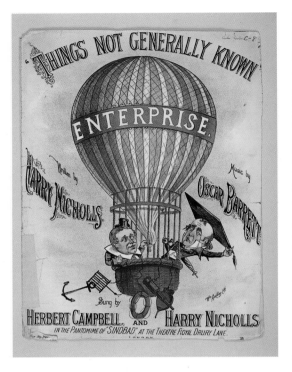

Sheet music, "Things Not Generally Known," with balloon motif

Laxative." Other items remind us of the great aeronautical events of the era: The tickets to the first and greatest of all the pre-war air meets, sponsored by the Champagne producers on the Plains of Betheny, near Reims, are shaped like champagne corks. The price of admission to the International Aviation Tournament at Belmont Park, New York, October 26–30, 1910, was $1, as indicated on each of the four tickets surviving in the Gimbel files. There is a lovely crimson and white program for the 1910 Harvard-Boston Meet, along with an invitation to attend a special educational demonstration by the English aviator Claude Grahame-White during the course of the event.

A handbill invites members of the Aero Club of Great Britain and Ireland to meet Louis Blériot, the hero of the first flight across the English Channel. More than any other aeronautical event between the emergence of the Wright brothers and the sound of guns in August 1914, Blériot's achievement shocked the English nation. "It has been raining warnings on us," H. G. Wells noted. "Never was a slacking, dull people so liberally served with warnings of what was in store for them....In spite of our fleet, this is no longer, from the military point of view, an inaccessible island."[39]

The number of songs published on aeronautical themes during the first decade of the new century is an indication of the public's fascination with the subject. The Gimbel collection of song sheets includes "Up in My Flying Machine," a tune dedicated to Dick Ferris, the impresario of the great Dominguez Field Air Meet in Los Angeles, January 10–20, 1910; "Aeroplane, or Flying Machine," a British song sheet illustrated with a photo of S. F. Cody's biplane; "A Hundred Years from Now," Tin Pan Alley's vision of a future in which the sky would be filled with airplanes. "Come Josephine in My Flying Machine" is one of the few aeronautical songs in the collection that most people can still hum.

Less than a decade after the first flight of the Wright brothers at Kitty Hawk, the airplane was already performing useful work. One of the treasures of the Gimbel collection is a small postcard that pilot Henri Pequet carried aboard a Sommer biplane at Allahabad, India, in February 1911 as part of the United Provinces Industrial and Agricultural Exhibition. The flight, which covered only 5 miles, nevertheless qualifies as the world's first official airmail flight by airplane. A second postcard in the collection was flown between London and Windsor, September 11, 1911, in celebration of the coronation of King George V.[40]

Junior Birdmen

The early twentieth-century fascination with flight was by no means limited to adults. Since the middle of the nineteenth century, the authors and publishers of children's books had drawn on aeronautical themes in order to capture the attention of young readers. Books of educational toys and games had long been popular in America. E. Landells' *The Boy's Own Toy-Maker* (1859), was typical, offering plans and instructions for a variety of kites and small fire balloons. It remained for the founder of mass market children's publishing in America, however, to take full and shrewd advantage of youthful enthusiasm for flight.

Samuel Griswold Goodrich is a name with which many researchers in the Gimbel collection would not be familiar. He is one of the genuinely forgotten men of American history. In

TOM D. CROUCH

spite of that, he was responsible for a series of important juvenile titles surviving in the Gimbel stacks. A Massachusetts legislator and U.S. consul to Paris, Goodrich may have sold more books than any other publisher in nineteenth-century America. Between the time of his entry into the business in 1816 and his death in 1860, the companies under his control had published as many as 7 million volumes. In addition, Goodrich operated several long-running children's magazines.

Goodrich set the pattern that would prevail in children's publishing for the next century. He issued books in series, bearing the names of fictitious "writers," notably Peter Parley and Robert Merry, who became wildly popular and attracted an enormous audience of young readers who would want to devour book after book bearing the familiar name. In fact, Goodrich hired a stable of writers, including Nathaniel Hawthorne, to churn out literary product.

Goodrich had given as much thought to the subject matter of his books as to every other aspect of his business. Balloons appear time after time in his series, and *The Balloon Travels of Robert Merry...* may have been the most popular of all the Goodrich titles. The appeal of the theme is not difficult to understand. A balloon voyage offered a sense of ultimate adventure to young readers, as Jules Verne and other writers would discover.

The popularity of flight themes with young readers was a lesson that later publishers were quick to learn. If S. G. Goodrich was the king of children's publishing during the first half of the nineteenth century, the brothers Erasmus and Irwin Beadle launched a whole new era in 1859 when they formed a partnership with Robert Adams. Beadle and Adams gave birth to what would become known as the "dime novel," a piece of cheap and thrilling fiction printed on even cheaper paper, just in time to meet the cultural needs of Civil War soldiers. The addition of a lurid cover, usually underscoring the moment of maximum danger to the hero, completed the pattern for a "literary" genre that would survive into the new century.[41]

Richard Gimbel was born a bit too late for the heyday of the dime novel, but he was clearly a connoisseur of those with aeronautical themes. Most of these books, from the era of Beadle and Adams to those issued by the firm of Street and Smith in the early years of the twentieth century, were western novels. Military combat, crime, exploration, and romance were also popular themes. It is astounding, however, how many aeronautical titles were issued. The Gimbel collection holdings range from reasonably realistic tales of aerial adventure aboard the observation balloons of the Civil War to wildly imaginative yarns in which heavier-than-air machines fly *Across the Continent in the Air* or *Over the Andes*. In one unforgettable issue of *Motor Stories*, "Motor Matt" made use of his airship to best "the rival inventors," while "Diamond Dick" used a balloon to thwart a robbery.

Edward Stratemeyer, the Samuel Goodrich of the twentieth century, was a graduate of the Street and Smith school of dime-novel literature. Like his nineteenth-century predecessor, Stratemeyer created a literary assembly line on which a stable of writers labored to produce books by the dozen. The Bobsey Twins, the Rover Boys, the Motor Boys, the Motor Girls, and Tom Swift became wildly popular with young readers. Stratemeyer sold 4 million Motor Boy books, 6 million of the Rover Boys series, and as many as 6.5 million Tom Swifts.[42]

Often focused on the wonderful products of a young inventor or mechanically inclined youths, publications for juveniles featured the theme of aeronautics. *The Airship Boys* and *The Boy Aviator* series were Stratemeyer productions entirely devoted to flight. Perhaps the most interesting of all the aviation juveniles on the Gimbel shelves, however, is the complete series of Bill Bruce books produced in the 1920s by Henry Harley "Hap" Arnold, future commander of the victorious U.S. Army Air Forces of World War II.

Parents and librarians alike hated both the dime novels and the products of Stratemeyer's juvenile fiction factory. The literary quality was poor and the story lines outrageous. For all of that, Richard Gimbel, an elite bookman, knew just how important a book could be in the life of a child. He could point to one area of his collection containing books that had inspired generations of youngsters to dream of the day when humanity would move beyond its home planet.

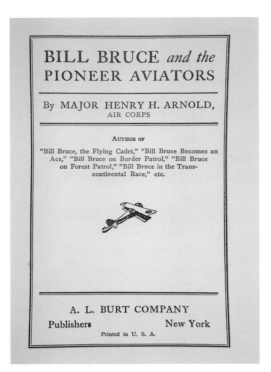

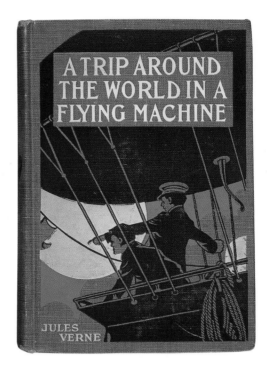

Frontispiece, *Bill Bruce and the Pioneer Aviators,* Henry H. Arnold

A Trip Around the World in a Flying Machine, Jules Verne

Across the Space Frontier

Few writers are better represented in the Gimbel collection than the French master of science fiction, Jules Verne. Earlier in his career Richard Gimbel had concentrated on building definitive collections of particular authors: Paine, Poe, and Dickens. He approached Verne in the same way, buying every edition, translation, and bibliographic variation of the novels relating to flight that he could lay his hands on.

There can be no doubt as to the impact of Jules Verne. "I owe my interest in flight to the well-known science fiction writer, Jules Verne," the great Russian space theorist and pioneer Konstantine Tsiolkovskii remarked in 1926. "He caused my mind to work...a desire was born."[43] Hermann Oberth, Tsiolkovskii's Romanian counterpart and the man whose own writing had sparked the wave of interest in space flight that swept across Weimar Germany, agreed. Having read *From the Earth to the Moon* as a young teenager in 1906, Oberth studied mathematics and physics and devised simple experiments as a means of checking the elements of Verne's story. It was the beginning of a lifelong commitment to the dream of space flight.

Of course, Verne was not the first science fiction writer. The Gimbel collection contains several editions of the work of Lucian of Samosata (*ca.* C.E. 135–190), the oldest of which is a volume published in Venice in 1551. In two of his satirical tales, *Icaromenippus* and *Vera Historia,* Lucian described voyages to the moon and planets. For Lucian, however, space was nothing more than an imaginary theater in which to stage biting commentaries on the political, social, and cultural events of the day.

Johannes Kepler (1571–1630) may have been the first human being to believe that it might actually be possible to travel into space. Moreover, it would be difficult to identify a more fascinating, or influential, book in the Gimbel collection than Kepler's masterpiece, *Somnium.* Johannes Kepler was a remarkable citizen of an extraordinary age. Slowly and painfully, a new Europe was emerging from an era of chaos, confusion, and change. During the century before Kepler's birth, a renaissance of art and literature had swept across Italy and France, the Protestant Reformation had shattered the unity of medieval Christendom, and mariners had planted their countries' flags on the shores of continents whose existence they had not even imagined.

It was a time of deep contradictions. Bigotry, intolerance, and persecution flourished at the very moment when geographic barriers were falling and intellectual horizons expanding exponentially. As Europeans struggled to deal with religious wars, unprecedented social and

TOM D. CROUCH

Johannes Kepler, 1571–1630

economic upheavals, and shifting international rivalries, they were also growing accustomed to the excitement of change and the thrill of discovery. Johannes Kepler personified the ironies of his age. He was, on the one hand, a major contributor to the most significant intellectual revolution in history, nothing less than a rearrangement of the cosmos. The philosopher Immanuel Kant, surely a creditable judge of such matters, regarded Kepler as "the most acute thinker ever born." For all of that, his life was deeply rooted in a traditional world of darkness, superstition, and violence.

His father, an alcoholic mercenary with a criminal record and a penchant for wife beating, deserted the family when Johannes was 17. His great aunt was burned as a witch, and his mother barely escaped the same fate. Giordano Bruno, a contemporary of Kepler's, was less fortunate. Having insisted that the stars in the night sky were suns warming "a plurality of worlds," some of which might shelter life, he was burned alive as a heretic in Rome on February 17, 1600.

Kepler, an aloof and unpopular neurotic who admitted to a "dog-like horror of baths," was not a particularly pleasant fellow. He may have laid the foundation for the science of celestial mechanics, but in his own time he was better known as a mystic, an astrologer, and a numerologist. While acknowledging that astrology was only "the foolish step-daughter of astronomy," he cast horoscopes for Duke Albrecht von Wallenstein, the preeminent military commander of the day, and predicted everything from the weather to the outcome of battles on his observations of the heavens.

Yet if Kepler lived his life with one foot firmly planted in the past, his mind ranged further than the ships of the great explorers of his day. Christopher Columbus and those who followed him crossed oceans and began the process of exploiting the wealth of newly discovered continents; Kepler dreamed of journeys into the cosmos. He was one of the first to honestly believe that men and women might one day set out on the ultimate voyage into space. "Let us create vessels and sails adjusted to the heavenly ether and there will be plenty of people unafraid of the empty wastes," he remarked. "In the meantime, we shall prepare, for the brave sky-travellers, maps of the celestial bodies—I shall do it for the moon, you Galileo, for Jupiter."[44]

Kepler, who had "established the astronomy" for such a voyage through his statement of the three laws of planetary motion, relished the notion of a trip to the moon. Other authors, including Greek satirist Lucian had written of journeys to the moon in the second century. Kepler's approach was very different. He used fiction as a means of presenting the best science of his day in the most appealing fashion.

Kepler's *Somnium* reflects the ironies and contradictions of the author's life. He conjures up demons to carry him to the moon, yet fills the books with the very best contemporary science and some startlingly accurate predictions of what future astronomers would discover. Anxious to excite his readers by encouraging them to imagine what a journey to the moon might be like, he based his inspired speculations on what little he knew, or thought he knew, and was the first author to describe the airlessness and weightlessness that might be encountered in space. And instead of telling his readers what the moon looked like through a telescope, he stood them on its surface, gave them a guided tour of lunar topography, and described what the earth would look like, suspended over the lunar surface.

In addition to Kepler's *Somnium*, the Gimbel collection contains a group of rare early volumes describing fictional journeys into space. Many, including those offered up by Cyrano de Bergerac, Francis Godwin, and John Wilkins, were firmly rooted in the scientific revolution of the seventeenth century, a revolution to which men like John Wilkins, an important figure in the Royal Society, had made substantial contributions. For these men, the moon was no longer a silver shield in the sky. It was an astronomical body whose motions could be calcu-

La terre me fut importune,
Ie pris mon essort vers les cieux,
Iy vis lesoleil, et la lune,
Et maintenant. Iy vois les Dieux.

Cyrano de Bergerac, Savinien, 1619–1655

lated and whose changing appearance could be understood. Its surface, seen for the first time through a telescope, was composed of peaks, valleys, and plains like those of the earth. The planets were far more than wandering points of light in the night sky. They were real bodies, geographic locations. One of them, Jupiter, had four moons of its own. Another, Saturn, had beautiful rings.

The notion of a plurality of worlds, the possibility that the moon or a planet might harbor sentient life, was a popular, if sometimes dangerous, topic for discussions among natural philosophers of the period. It would have been extraordinary indeed if those interested in the new science had not used fiction to more fully explore the implications of these discoveries. The moon that Kepler describes in *Somnium*, for example, is not the imaginary land of Lucian but the astronomical body he has seen through his telescope. Having been shaped by lunar conditions, the life forms that he discovers are quite unlike those on earth.

Domingo Gonsales, the hero of Francis Godwin's *The Man in the Moone* (1638), was also a man of science. His mode of transportation (he was carried to the moon by migrating birds) was as old as Alexander. That aside, Godwin filled his hero's notes with a description of conditions in the upper atmosphere and space, and the regions through which he was passing, as well as the motions of the earth, moon, and planets. His observations supported the Copernican heliocentric hypothesis, which Godwin described in considerable detail.

Most of the seventeenth-century authors wrote fictional accounts of travel to the moon and planets as a means of popularizing new scientific theories, including the Copernican hypothesis and Kepler's laws of planetary motion. Stories of space travel enabled them to communicate fresh information on the appearance of heavenly bodies resulting from telescopic observations. Moreover, by describing the details of an extraterrestrial journey, serious researchers could extrapolate from what little they knew to what they believed.

By the eighteenth century, writers of fiction were also exploring the implications of technological change. Richard Gimbel acquired a copy of *Le philosophe sans prétention...*, by Louis Guillaume de La Follie (1775), for example, a book describing a flight from Mercury to the earth in the *Scintilla*, a spacecraft powered by static electricity. Although *Gulliver's Travels* is clearly not science fiction, it is interesting to note that Jonathan Swift made use of magnetism to levitate an entire island.

Widely reported advances in telescope technology inspired a classic nineteenth-century hoax. From the late eighteenth to the mid-nineteenth century, popular enthusiasm for astronomy flourished. By the mid-nineteenth century, no astronomer was better known than Sir John Frederick Herschel, son of the legendary astronomer royal, Sir William Herschel. Like his father, John Herschel was famous for the design, construction, and use of very large telescopes. He had drawn the attention of newspapers around the world with his studies of the southern sky using a huge instrument that he had constructed at the Cape of Good Hope.

In August and September 1835, the *New York Sun* ran a series of articles announcing that the great Herschel had discovered a strange new world on the moon, complete with bat-winged men and women. Couched in pseudo-scientific jargon, the story was widely believed. Eventually, the editor of the *Sun* admitted that the story was a hoax intended to divert attention "from that bitter apple of discord, the abolition of slavery." The public, however, remained fascinated. In addition to a published set of the articles from the *Sun*, the Gimbel collection houses an American print illustrating the "Lunar Animals and Other Objects."

There can be little doubt, however, that Jules Verne launched a new era in the history of science fiction. Verne captured the spirit of the age on the pages of his books. The central figures of his books, misguided as they sometimes were, employed the enormous power of science and technology to overcome barriers and conquer new frontiers. They traveled beneath the sea, journeyed to the center of the earth, soared through space aboard both balloons

TOM D. CROUCH

Robert Hutchings Goddard, 1882–1945 (National Air and Space Museum, Smithsonian Institution)

and heavier-than-air machines, and even traversed the gulf of space between the earth and the moon and back. Small wonder that Verne's marvelous tales retain their power to inspire more than a century after they were written and long after the wonders they predict have come to pass. The notion that there is little that a human being armed with the power of science and technology cannot achieve remains compelling, if more than a bit tarnished by the experience of the twentieth century.

In January 1898 the *Boston Post* and a number of other American newspapers began publication of a serialized adaptation of a new novel by Herbert George Wells, who shared with Jules Verne the power to inspire. *War of the Worlds* had originally appeared in *Pearson's Magazine* between April and November 1897. In an effort to enhance local interest, the editors of the *Post* relocated the action of the story and provided a more riveting title: *Fighters from Mars, or, The War of the Worlds, In and Near Boston*. The series was such a success that Garrett Putnam Serviss was commissioned to write a sequel, *Edison's Conquest of Mars*, in which the great inventor invades the red planet to defeat the tentacled extraterrestrials introduced in Wells' classic tale.

The publication of the two serializations was a turning point in the life of one 16-year-old reader of the *Boston Post*. Two decades later, Robert Hutchings Goddard could still recall the way in which the two stories had gripped his imagination. "Wells' wonderfully true psychology made the thing very vivid," he remarked, "and possible ways and means of accomplishing the physical marvels set forth kept me busy thinking."[45]

Goddard was still thinking a few weeks later when, on October 19, 1898, he climbed a tall cherry tree behind Maple Hill, the family home in Worcester, Massachusetts. While trimming dead branches from the crown of the tree, he paused to enjoy the beauty of a fall afternoon in New England, and his thoughts returned to Wells' exciting story:

> I imagined how wonderful it would be to make some device which had even the *possibility* of ascending to Mars, and how it would look on a small scale, if sent up from the meadow at my feet....In any event, it was a different boy when I descended the tree from when I ascended, for existence at last seemed very purposeful.[46]

Young Robert Goddard's experience in the cherry tree can best be understood as something akin to a religious vision. For the rest of his life, he would remember October 19 as "Anniversary Day." He carefully preserved photos of the cherry tree and the wooden ladder he had used to climb it among his most cherished possessions. The destruction of the tree in a hurricane that swept across New England in 1938 was clearly an enormous emotional blow. "Cherry tree down," he wrote in his diary, "have to carry on alone."[47]

H. G. Wells remained tied to Robert Goddard's dreams of space flight, both literally and figuratively. On July 19, 1915, Goddard noted in his diary that he had read Wells' *The First Men in the Moon*. He glanced through the book once more on the afternoon of July 29, then, on August 8, he relived Wells' trip to the moon in a dream. Goddard dreamed that he made the voyage in a rocket with folding tripod legs and set off a "red fire" on the surface of the moon to prove that he had arrived. It was cold, he recalled, and when he opened his helmet to take pictures of the earth with his Kodak, there was not enough air to breathe.[48]

The following evening, Goddard was reduced to watching the moon through his telescope once again. But he did not forget the dream. By December 1915 he had devised an experiment that demonstrated how much flash powder would have to be exploded on the moon to produce a flash that would be seen from earth. The results were published in Goddard's classic paper of 1919, *A Method of Reaching Extreme Altitudes.*

Goddard continued as a faithful reader of Wells, Serviss, and Jules Verne until his death in 1945. At one point he even wrote an updated version of Verne's book, *From the Earth to the Moon*. Recognizing the role that science fiction had played in shaping his work, Robert Goddard expressed his appreciation in a letter to Wells written on April 20, 1932. Having described the impact of *War of the Worlds* and the subsequent cherry tree incident and quickly outlined his rocket research, Goddard closed the letter with a moving statement of his own commitment to the dream of space flight:

> How many more years I shall be able to work on the problem, I do not know; I hope, as long as I live. There can be no thought of finishing, for "aiming at the stars," both literally and figuratively, is a problem to occupy generations, so that no matter how much progress one makes, there is always the thrill of new beginning.[49]

The Collection

A quarter of a century after its arrival at the Air Force Academy the Colonel Richard Gimbel Aeronautical History Collection is very much a part of the intellectual life of the institution. The dedicated librarians and archivists who have exercised wise stewardship over Gimbel's treasures, working in cooperation with Air Force Academy officials and faculty members, have added new materials to the collection and have used it to introduce cadets to the history and traditions of flight and to encourage an appreciation for the extent to which the literature of aeronautics inspired and informed the generations of would-be airmen who came before them.

On any given day, a visitor to the Gimbel collection is likely to find a variety of activities under way. The lovely, wood-paneled, book-lined, and very secure reading room on the top floor of the Air Force Academy Library may be hosting a group of "doolie" (fourth classmen, or freshmen) English students taking turns reading aloud from an early edition of Alfred, Lord Tennyson's prophetic poem "Locksley Hall"; a history major preparing a report on the use of balloons in the Siege of Paris; a student of German translating an article from an aeronautical journal published in Berlin prior to 1914; a professor of art history from the University of Colorado at Boulder studying French engravings of the late eighteenth century; or an entire class receiving an orientation lecture on the history of aviation based on materials in the collection. Richard Gimbel would be pleased.[50]

The Gimbel Room in the Air Force Academy Library

NOTES

1. The account of continued German attacks on London is based on Philip Ziegler, *London at War* (New York: Alfred A. Knopf, 1995), p. 208; Niall Rothnie, *The Baedeker Blitz: Hitler's Attacks on Britain's Historic Cities* (Runnymeade, England: Ian Allan, 1992); Winston G. Ramsey, *The Blitz Then and Now* (London: Battle of Britain Prints International, 1990), vol. 3, pp. 142–143.

2. "Books Versus Bombs," *Journal of the Aeronautical Sciences Aeronautical Review Section,* March 1941 (vol. 8, no. 5), p. 3.

3. Richard Gimbel, military and civilian personnel records, Gimbel collection, Air Force Academy Library; "New Haven Gimbel," *New Yorker,* June 7, 1958 (vol. 34), pp. 25–27.

4. Nan Tillson Birmingham, *Store* (New York: G. P. Putnam and Sons, 1989), p. 231.

5. "Ellis A. Gimbel, 84, Merchant, Is Dead..." *New York Times,* March 8, 1950.

6. "New Haven Gimbel," *New Yorker,* p. 27.

7. Leon Harris, *Merchant Princes* (New York: Kodansha International, 1994), pp. 81–82.

8. "New Haven Gimbel," *New Yorker,* p. 25. For additional information on key members of the Gimbel family see "Bernard F. Gimbel Dies at 81; Led Chain of Stores 34 Years," *New York Times,* September 30, 1966; "Jacob Gimbel Dies of Heart Disease," *New York Times,* November 8, 1922; "Daniel Gimbel, 75, Merchant Is Dead," *New York Times,* September 9, 1939; "Charles Gimbel, Merchant, Is Dead," *New York Times,* September 10, 1932.

9. "New Haven Gimbel," *New Yorker,* pp. 25–27.

10. George V. Fagan, An unpublished biographical sketch of Richard Gimbel, in "The Colonel Richard Gimbel Aeronautical History Collection Catalogue; Second Draft in Three Volumes, August 1996, Vol. 1." Manuscript in possession of the author.

11. For additional biographical information on Richard Gimbel, see "Col. Richard Gimbel Dies at 71; Flier Was Yale Library Curator," *New York Times,* May 28, 1970; "Co-founder of Gimbel's Dies at 71," *Hartford Courant,* May 29, 1970, p. 4; "Col. Richard Gimbel Is Dead in Germany," *Philadelphia Inquirer,* May 29, 1970, p. 18; "Gimbel Aeronautic Collection Donated to Air Force Academy Library," News Release no. 91, February 10, 1971, Air Force Academy.

12. Edgar L. Mattock, "The Red Devils: A Journal of the 510th Bombardment Squadron (H)," vol. 1. Manuscript in the Gimbel collection, Air Force Academy Library.

13. For additional information on the military career of Richard Gimbel, see the variety of military records and personnel reports in the Gimbel collection, Air Force Academy Library.

14. "New Haven Gimbel," *New Yorker,* p. 26.

15. *Ibid.*

16. Richard Gimbel to Col. William Taylor, June 6, 1958, Gimbel collection, Air Force Academy Library .

17. "New Haven Gimbel," *New Yorker,* p. 26.

18. For a popular treatment of winged creatures in Mesopotamian mythology, see Samuel Noah Kramer, *History Begins at Sumer* (Garden City, N. Y.: Doubleday Anchor Books, 1969).

19. Thomas Cahill quotes the alternative Benjamin Jowett translation in *How the Irish Saved Civilization: The Untold Story of Ireland's Heroic Role from the Fall of Rome to the Rise of Medieval Europe* (New York: Doubleday, 1995), p. 52.

20. Ovid, *Metamorphoses* (Cambridge, Mass.: Harvard University Press, 1916), vol. 1, pp. 417–423.

21. Thomas Bulfinch, *Mythology* (New York: Dell, 1959), pp. 128–130.

22. See Clive Hart's commentary on Roger Bacon in the annotation for Claudius Cælestinus, *De mirabili potestate artis et natvrae...*(1542).

23. Robert Hooke, *Philosophical Collections...*(London: John Martyn, 1679–1682).

24. Girolamo Cardano, *De rerum libri* (Basileae, 1557), in Clive Hart, *The Dream of Flight: Aeronautics from Classical Times to the Renaissance* (New York: Winchester Press, 1972), p. 79.

25. Joseph Lecornu, *Les Cerfs-Volants...*(Paris: Librairie Nony et Cie, 1902).

26. Octave Chanute, *Progress in Flying Machines* (New York: American Engineer and Railroad Journal, 1894), p. 56.

27. George Cayley, "On Aerial Navigation," *A Journal of Natural Philosophy, Chemistry, and the Arts,* November 1809 (vol. 24), pp. 164–174; February 1810 (vol. 25), pp. 81–87; March 1810 (vol. 25), pp. 161–169.

28. Marvin W. McFarland, *The Papers of Wilbur and Orville Wright: Including the Chanute-Wright Letters and Other Papers of Octave Chanute,* vol. 1 (New York: McGraw-Hill, 1953), p. 3.

29. Milton Wright, "Press Release," December 17, 1948, in Ivonette Wright Miller, *Wright Reminiscences* (Dayton, Ohio: privately published, 1978), p. 68.

30. Bernardo Zamagna, *Bernardi Zamagnae S. J. Navis aeria et Elegiarum monobiblos* (Rome: Paullus Giunchius, 1768).

31. Charles Coulston Gillispie, *The Montgolfier Brothers and the Invention of Aviation* (Princeton, N. J.: Princeton University Press, 1983), p. 15.

32. *Ibid.,* p. 17.

33. Sir Joseph Banks, quoted in Patrick O'Brian, *Joseph Banks: A Life* (Boston: David Godine, 1993), p. 212.

34. B. Franklin to J. Banks, August 30, 1783, in A. L. Rotch, *Benjamin Franklin and the First Balloons* (Worcester, Mass., 1907), p. 5.

35. Soeur Michel, from the Convent of the Visitation of Saint Mary, to Père Michel, of the Oratory of Toulon, December 26, 1783 (Gimbel collection call no. XF-2-1 2394 1783/DEC. 26).

36. McFarland, *The Papers of Wilbur and Orville Wright*.

37. Amos Ives Root, "Our Homes," in *Gleanings in Bee Culture,* January 1, 1905 (vol. 33, no. 1), pp. 36–38.

38. Victor E. Ostoya, *Vole, Wright!* (Paris, 1908); "Les Gens du Mans," *Le Rire,* September 5, 1908.

39. Herbert George Wells, in C. H. Gibbs-Smith, *The Invention of the Airplane, 1799–1909* (London: Faber and Faber, 1965), p. 212.

40. Donald Dale Jackson, *Flying the Mail* (Alexandria, Va.: Time-Life, 1982), p. 19.

41. Russel Nye, *The Unembarrassed Muse: The Popular Arts in America* (New York: Dial Press, 1970), pp. 200–202.

42. Nye, *The Unembarrassed Muse,* pp. 76–85.

43. Konstantine E. Tsiolkovskii, *Investigation of Universal Space by Reactive Devices,* in *Works on Rocket Technology by K. E. Tsiolkovskii* (Washington, D. C.: NASA TT-243, 1965), p. 111.

44. Arthur Koestler, *The Sleepwalkers: A History of Man's Changing Vision of the Universe* (New York: Macmillan, 1959), pp. 372–373.

45. Robert H. Goddard, "Materials for an Autobiography," in Esther C. Goddard and G. Edward Pendray, eds., *The Papers of Robert H. Goddard,* vol. 1 (New York: McGraw-Hill, 1970), p. 7.

46. Goddard and Pendray, *The Papers of Robert H. Goddard,* vol. 1, p. 9.

47. R. H. Goddard Diary, November 1938, in Goddard and Pendray, *The Papers of Robert H. Goddard,* vol. 3, p. 1216.

48. R. H. Goddard Diary, July 19 to August 8, 1938, in Goddard and Pendray, *The Papers of Robert H. Goddard,* vol. 1, p. 163.

49. Robert H. Goddard to H. G. Wells, April 20, 1932, in Goddard and Pendray, *The Papers of Robert H. Goddard,* vol. 2, p. 821.

50. The original group of cadets, the Class of 1959, were called doolies, from the Greek *duolos,* or servant, when they were in basic training at Lowry Air Force Base in Denver, Colorado. Since that time the term has been used to describe fourth classmen, or freshmen.

ILLUSTRATED
HOLDINGS

Printed Books, 1489–1850

CLIVE HART

THE COLONEL RICHARD GIMBEL AERONAUTICAL HISTORY COLLECTION is especially valuable in containing items that bear on the very early history of aviation in a wide variety of ways. In addition to rare books and pamphlets from the time of the first balloon ascents and tracts offering designs for heavier-than-air machines, there are books of flying legends (many of them attractively illustrated), imaginative tales in both verse and prose of voyages to the moon and planets, books of scientific theory and quasi-scientific speculation, treatises on the flight of birds, and works of angelology that examine the human aspiration to flight from the point of view of religious belief.

The diversity of the collection greatly facilitates the wide-ranging interdisciplinary studies that are necessary if the technological achievements of the early modern period are to be properly understood. The development of winged aircraft was delayed not only by inadequate technology and the failure of all experimenters before the nineteenth century to understand the basis of bird flight but also by the deep-seated unease of many thinkers. The doubts of philosophers and theologians and the generally negative response of the early Christian church had a notable effect on the speculators. Although flying prophets and other men of virtue figure frequently in pagan myth and religion, early Christianity wished to reserve almost all virtuous flight for the seraphs. Ordinary angels were not represented as winged until some centuries after Christ. For Christians, flight through the atmosphere was most clearly associated with demons, sorcerers, and (later) witches. (Contrary to popular opinion, witches were an obsession of the Renaissance rather than of the Middle Ages.) Satan was "the prince of the power of the air" (Ephesians 2:2) and any man who aspired to fly might be thought potentially in league with him. At times more positive effects of Christian thought and iconography can nevertheless be perceived: the joyous story of the aerial journey of Mary's house in Terameno's little tract (see below, Terameno, *Translatio, ca.* 1495) caught the imagination of designers of large machines.

The collection includes many books of importance not described here. There are early editions of John Donne, John Milton, Ovid, Johannes Sambucus, and Alfred Tennyson, all of scholarly and bibliographical interest. Early and rare books on fireworks bear on the history of rocketry. There are works by the British astronomer Sir John Frederick Herschel and other important astronomers and scientists. The shelves also hold a large number of items from among the thousands of publications that appeared in the two or three years following the first ascent in a Montgolfier balloon in 1783. These include not only the best-known books and pamphlets in French and English but also an especially rich collection of publications in Italian. Together with these is a large and valuable collection of the many satirical plays, vaudevilles, squibs, and broadsides published, mainly in French, in the years immediately following the Montgolfiers' success. (Perhaps the only collection to rival the Gimbel in that

Detail of page from novel by Restif de la Bretonne (Page 73)

respect is the Bibliothèque de l'Arsenal, Paris.) The books described in this section and those in the Appendix inevitably represent no more than a sample. Although I have tried to identify items that reveal the special qualities of the Gimbel collection, other choices could readily have been made.

∗　∗　∗

Following the standard bibliographic data for each item in this and the next section (Printed Books, 1851-1914), the Gimbel collection call number is identified. Additionally, where appropriate, references are given to corresponding entries in such standard bibliographies as Hain, Brockett, Gamble, and Randers-Pehrson (the last coded R-P) listed in the "Printed Books, 1489-1850" section of the Bibliography at the end of the catalogue. For books published before 1701, numbers are given for the Pollard or Wing short-title catalogues coded STC and also listed in the Bibliography. If the entry in any of the bibliographies refers not to the holding in the Gimbel collection but to a closely related book or edition, the number is placed in brackets. Finally, and again where appropriate, other copies and editions in the Gimbel collection of the item described are noted. Thus for *Historia Alexāndri*, the first item described in this section, the Gimbel call number is AC10.A4 1489, and "Hain 780" refers to the number of the relevant entry in Ludwig Hain, *Reportorium bibliographicum*. 4 vols. Stuttgart and Paris, 1826-1838 (listed in the Bibliography at the end of the catalogue).

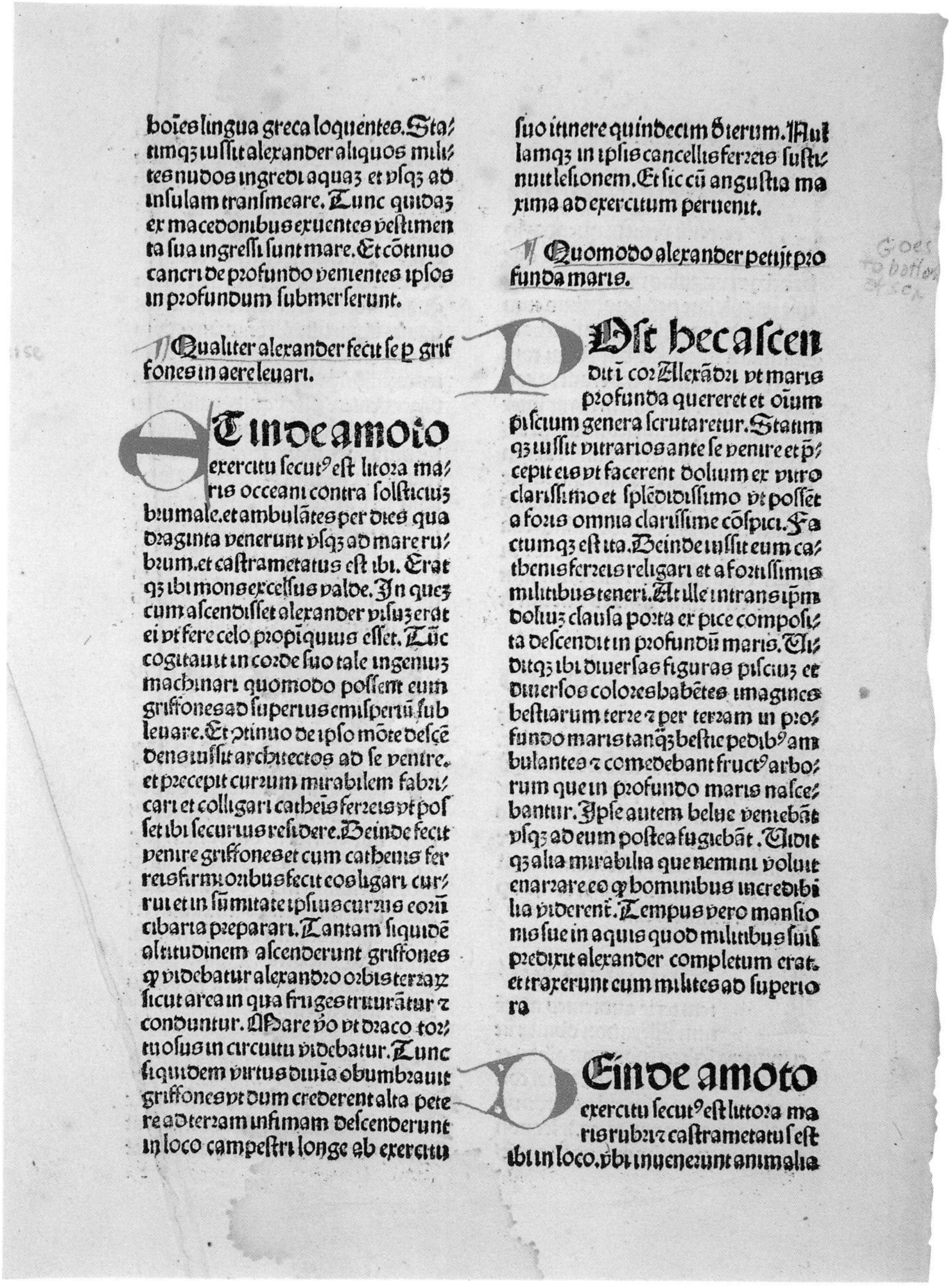

Alexander the Great (romances, etc.)

Historia Alexandri | magni regis | mace | donie de prelijs.
Colophon: Historia Alexandri magni finit feliciter
impressa Argentine anno domini M.CCCC.LXXXIX …

37 leaves. 28.5 cm.
Title-page with verso blank. Illus. of king on t.-p.
  Signatures: a4-f4, [g¹].
Printer: Johannes Gruninger.
AC10.A4 1489
Hain 780

The romance of Alexander, a fabulous account of the life of Alexander the Great (356–323 B.C.E), was immensely popular in the Middle Ages and the early Renaissance. Alexander not only conquered all known countries on land but also used a primitive submarine to explore the bottom of the sea and a flying machine to carry him through the regions of the air. His machine consisted of a basket to which two or sometimes four griffins were tethered. Alexander held a dead carcass on a pole. When he raised the carcass above the griffins' heads, they attempted to fly up to it and so carried the basket through the air. When Alexander wanted to descend, he lowered the pole to make the griffins fly down. The land and sea below Alexander are described as if on a large map. Offended by Alexander's presumption, divine power finally caused the griffins to think that they were rising when in fact they were descending. The machine, which was damaged when it landed, came down fifteen days' walk from Alexander's army, thus complicating Alexander's return. Along with the story of Icarus (see below, Riedrer, *Spiegel*, 1493), this is among the most frequently quoted cautionary tales about the consequences of excessive ambition. (The story is told on fol. f2ᵛ of this printing of the book.)

Riedrer, Friedrich

Spiegel der waren Rhetoric | vsz M. Tulio C. vnd andern | getütscht: Mit Irn glidern cluger reden | Sandbriefen, vnd formen. Menicher con | tract, seltzam. Regulierts Tütschs vnd | nutzbar exempliert, mit fügen vff | göttlich vnd keiserlich schrifft vnd rech | te gegründt: nuwlich (vnd vormaln | In gemein nÿe gesehen) ÿetz loblich vsz | gangen. [fol. 188ʳ:] friburg in Briszgaw, Durch fridrichen Riedrer versamelt, gedruckt, vnd volendet...An mittwoch vor sant Lucien tag [11 December] 1493.

[188] leaves, 2–180 so numbered. 31 cm.
With several woodcuts, incl. t-p.;
     fall of Icarus on fol. 61ᵛ.
AC10.R4 1493
Hain 13914

Although illustrations of flying men had long been common in manuscripts and other media, Albrecht Dürer's woodcut in Riedrer's *Spiegel* is the first such representation in a printed book. The story of the flight of Daedalus and his son Icarus was best known from a passage in Ovid:

> he lays feathers in order, beginning at the smallest, short next to long, so that you would think they had grown upon a slope. Just so the old fashioned rustic pan-pipes with their unequal reeds rise one above another. Then he fastened the feathers together with twine and wax at the middle and bottom; and, thus arranged, he bent them with a gentle curve, so that they looked like real birds' wings.

Using these wings, Daedalus and Icarus flew away from captivity but "led by a desire for the open sky," Icarus flew too high. "The wax melted; his arms were bare as he beat them up and down, but, lacking wings, they took no hold on the air" (*Metamorphoses*, VIII. 189–195, 224, 227–228).

Dürer makes an ironic parallel between Icarus' fall into an element to which he is physically unsuited and the entirely natural dive of the seabird to his left. Variants of the old adage "if God had meant us to fly, He'd have given us wings" were often invoked in response to early attempts to build flying machines.

This little tract, hugely popular during the Renaissance, was reprinted many times and translated into several languages. After the Reformation, its Marian theme made it wholly unacceptable to Protestants. Two different translations of modified versions of the original, both by R. Corbington and both printed in 1635, were nevertheless widely circulated among English recusants during the seventeenth century. Facsimiles of the translations were published as folded broadsheets at the back of D. M. Rogers, ed., *English Recusant Literature, 1558–1640* vols. 75 (1971) and 108 (1972). According to the legend, in 1291 angels transported the Virgin's house from Nazareth through the air and deposited it in Loreto to protect it from invading infidels. The story serves in part to counter pagan stories of mystical flight, such as an oracle that flies after being lifted by priests in Lucian's *De Syria dea* (sect. 37). Images of the flying house—including frescos, sketches, and paintings by Tiepolo (1692–1769)—are common. In Catholic countries the story strongly influenced later speculations about the relationship between the flight of angels and their power to move material objects. In this vignette they are carrying the house without effort through the upper air, above the clouds. This region was thought to be one of total serenity; if human beings could reach so high, they, too, would be able to move objects without muscular effort. Together with Saint Joseph of Copertino (1603–1663), Mary is one of the patron saints of aviators.

De his quę mundo mi-
RABILITER EVENIVNT: VBI
de sensuum erroribus, & potentijs animę,
ac de influentijs cælorum, F. Clau=
dij Cæleſtini opuſculum.

De mirabili poteſtate ar
TIS ET NATVRAE, VBI DE
philoſophorum lapide, F. Rogerij Ba=
chonis Anglici, libellus.

¶ Hæc duo gratiſſima, & non aſpernanda opu-
ſcula, Orontius F. Delph. Regius Mathe=
maticus, diligenter recognoſcebat,
& in ſuam redigebat har=
moniam, Lutetiæ
Pariſiorum.

Apud Simonem Colinæum
1 5 4 2.

Cælestinus, Claudius

De his quę mundo mirabiliter evenivnt: vbi de sensuum
erroribus, & potentijs animę, ac de influentijs cælorum,
F. Claudij Cælestini opusculum. De mirabili potestate
artis et natvrae, vbi de philosophorum lapide, F. Rogerij
Bachonis Anglici, libellus. Hæc duo gratissima, & non
aspernanda opuscula, Orontius F. Delph. Regius
Mathematicus, diligenter recognoscebat, & in suam
redigebat harmoniam. Lutetiæ Parisiorum. Apud
Simonem Colinæum, 1542.

[4], 52 p. 21 cm.

1. Science—Early works to 1800. I. Bacon, Roger,
1214?–1294. II. Fine, Oronce, 1494–1555. III. Title.
IV. Title: De mirabili potestate artis et natvrae.
Q155.C13
[Gamble 4678, 4679]

An important contributor to medieval science,
the Franciscan monk Roger Bacon was
somewhat irascible and prone to hyperbole. In
De mirabili potestate artis et natvrae, written
about 1260, he alleged that "it is possible to
make flying machines such that a man may sit
in the middle of the machine turning some
kind of device by means of which artificially
constructed wings strike the air in the manner
of a flying bird." Speaking of this and a number
of other mechanical devices, he goes on to say
that it is certain that they were made both in
ancient times and in modern, with the possible
exception of the flying machine, which he has
not seen, nor does he know anyone who has
seen such a thing. He does, however, claim to
know a man who has thought through the art
of building one. In medieval times it was
common to believe that the achievements of
the classical world—mechanical as well as
moral—surpassed those of the civilizations of
the day. The conviction that in those times
men had solved the problem of flight inspired
many experimenters.

Ariosto, Lodovico, 1474–1533

*Orlando Fvrioso di M. Lvdovico Ariosto ornato di uarie figure, con alcvne stanze del medesimo nuouamente aggiunte, et alcune altre del S. Aluigi Gonzaga in lode dell'istesso...*In Vinegia appresso Gabriel Giolito de Ferrari, 1547.

264, [30] numb. leaves, illus. 21 cm.
"Espositione di tvtti i vocaboli e lvoghi difficili...raccolte da M. Lodovico Dolce..." (leaves [1–25] has special t.-p.).
With bookplates of Thomas Isted and C.W.H. Sotheby.
Printer's device (phoenix on pyre staring at the sun with motto *semper eadem*) on t.-p.s and last p.
PQ4567.A2 1547

Other copies and editions in the Gimbel collection: PQ4567.A2 1572: *Orlando Fvrioso...tvtto ricorretto...* , illus. with woodcuts attrib. to Dosso Dossi (*d.* 1542), Venetia, 1572; PQ4582.E5 A35: *Orlando Furioso*, trans. from the Italian...with notes by John Hoole, 5 v., illus., London, 1799.

One of the greatest Italian writers of the Renaissance, Ariosto wrote plays that imitated those of Plautus and Terence and lyric poems in both Latin and Italian. His fame, however, rests almost entirely on *Orlando Furioso*, a long and complex romance in forty-six cantos, the first version of which was published between 1516 and 1532. Among its many episodes is the story of how Astolfo flies to the moon in aid of Orlando, whose "wit" (rational faculty) had been taken from him and deposited there three months earlier. To reach the moon, Astolfo first rides on his winged horse, the offspring of a griffin and a mare, and then in the chariot of Elijah (2 Kings 2:11) with Saint John the Evangelist as charioteer:

> ...to the *Moone* he guides the running wheel,
> The *Moone* was like a glasse all void of spot,

Or like a peece of purely burnisht steel,
And look'd, although to us it seem'd so small,
Welnigh as big as earth and sea and all.

(Canto 34.70.4–8, in Sir John Harrington's translation of 1591.)

Astolfo returns safely with the "wit" and restores Orlando to mental health. In 1784 Vincent Lunardi was to propose that Astolfo's flight was a hint that the principle of the balloon had long since been discovered. (See below, Lunardi, *An account*, 1784, p. 28n.) Ariosto's is one of the many stories of journeys to the moon that proliferated in the literature of the late Middle Ages and the Renaissance. As later holdings in the Gimbel collection reveal, these became still more numerous after the observations of the moon made with the telescopes of Galileo and others.

INCOMINCIA IL PRIMO LI
bro di Luciano delle uere narrationi.

Essendo una fiata uscito fuore delle collone di Herco
le, & condotto nel mare occidentale, nauigaua con
prospero uento & bonaccia la causa della peregrinatione
& del proposito mio era desiderio de cose nuoue, pero che
desideraua sapere qual fusse il fine del mare Ociano, &
che huomini oltra esso habitassino, per questa ragione
adonche fornite la naue de uettouaglie & cose necessarie,
conducendo con meco cinquanta compagni de mia etade,
liquali erano di quello medemo uolere che io, & arman
do la naue di buona copia d'arme, per gran precio uno ot
timo gubernatore condusse, Era la naue mediocre, robu
sta pero & forte contra l'imperio delle onde marine, di e
notte adoche co bonaccia nauigando, non molto longi da
terra, non con gran forza di uento procedeua il uiaggio
nostro, nel seguete giorno nel nascere del sole crebbe il ue
to & gusionsi l'onde, & una caligine tenebrosa per tutto

M iij

Lucianus Samosatensis, *ca.* C.E. 135–190

I dialoghi piacevoli, le vere narrationi, le facete epistole di Luciano philosopho. Di greco in volgare tradotte per M. Nicolo da Lonigo: & historiate, & di nuouo accuratamente reuiste, et emendate. In Venetia, per G. Padoano, 1551.

223 numb. 1. illus. 15 cm.
With 30 woodcuts. Bound in vellum.
Bookplate of George Charles Bright, M.D.
I. Lonigo, Nicolò da, tr.
PA4231.A2 1551
[Gamble 80]

Other copies and editions in the Gimbel collection: PA4232.F8 1613: in *Les oeuvres*, with 10 vignettes on t.-p., Paris, 1613; PA4236.G3P: *Lucians Werke, übersetzt von August Pauly,* Stuttgart, 1829 (v. 10 of set only); PA4230.A2F13: in *Lucian: with an English Translation,* 8 v., Loeb Classical Library, 1913–1967.

In classical literature voyages away from the surface of the earth, both to Hades and to Heaven, were relatively common, among the most celebrated and amusing being the dramatic visit to an aerial civilization in Aristophanes' play *The Birds* (414 B.C.E.). Better known among readers of the Renaissance, however, were two journeys described by the Greek poet Lucian. The more familiar of these is his satire *Icaromenippus,* the hero of which travels to the heavens in search of truth. The other is a story in this "true history," which is in fact a parody of travelers' tales. Lucian tells us,

tongue in cheek, that he made an involuntary journey to the moon when he was traveling beyond the Pillars of Hercules (the Straits of Gibraltar). In the translation by Francis Hicks (1634) Lucian describes how "upon a suddaine a whirlewinde caught us, which turned our shippe round about, and lifted us up some three thousand furlongs into the aire." After a week without sight of land, they "came in view of a great countrie in the aire, like to shining Island." He proceeds to describe the inhabitants and their surroundings in terms intended as a satirical commentary on life in Rome.

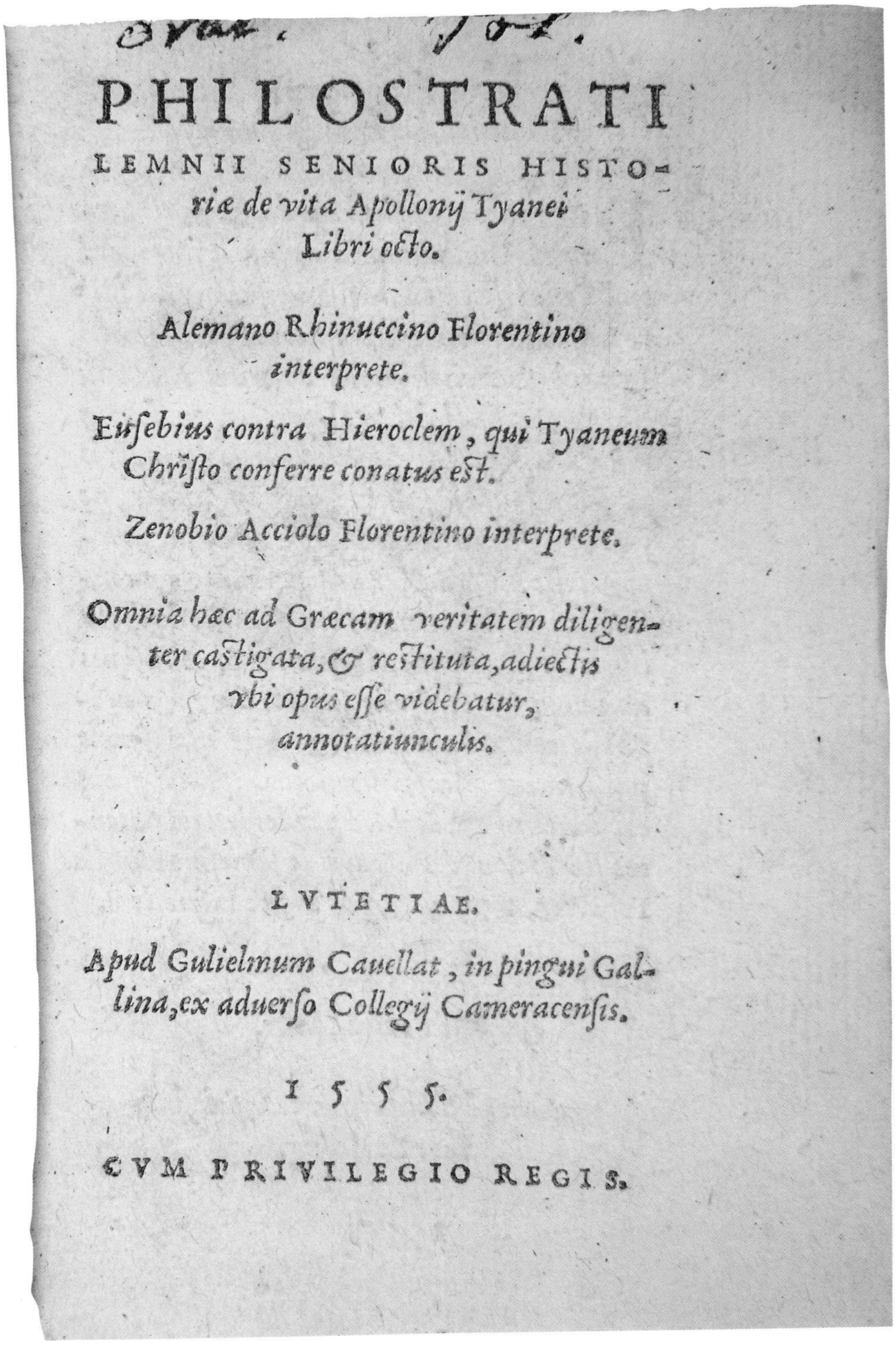

PHILOSTRATI

LEMNII SENIORIS HISTO-
riæ de vita Apollonij Tyanei
Libri octo.

Alemano Rhinuccino Florentino
interprete.

Eusebius contra Hieroclem, qui Tyaneum
Christo conferre conatus est.

Zenobio Acciolo Florentino interprete.

Omnia hæc ad Græcam veritatem diligenter castigata, & restituta, adiectis
vbi opus esse videbatur,
annotatiunculis.

LVTETIAE.

Apud Gulielmum Cauellat, in pingui Gal-
lina, ex aduerso Collegij Cameracensis.

1 5 5 5.

CVM PRIVILEGIO REGIS.

Philostratus, Flavius, *ca.* C.E. 170–245

Philostrati Lemnii senioris historiæ de vita Apollonij Tyanei libri octo...Lvtetiae, Apud Gulielmum Cauellat, 1555.

16 p. l., 571 p. 11.5 cm.

1. Apollonius, of Tyana. I. Title: De vita Apollonii Tyanei.

TLB154.P5 1555

Apollonius of Tyana (in Cappodocia, an ancient name for a district of what is now Turkey) was a peripatetic philosopher and mystic, born about the time of Christ. The accounts of his magical powers gained him such fame that he was treated by pagans, both in his own day and for some time thereafter, as a god to be revered in direct competition with the claims that were being made for Christ by the early church. The story of his life was written in Greek by Flavius Philostratus (second to third centuries C.E.). Like many mystics, of whom Simon Magus is perhaps the best known, Apollonius was credited with being able to fly (see Book VII, chap. x). Although the ability to fly was a standard attribute of virtuous pagan mystics, any flying human being was, in the apprehension of Christians, almost certainly in league with demonic powers. (See introduction to this section.)

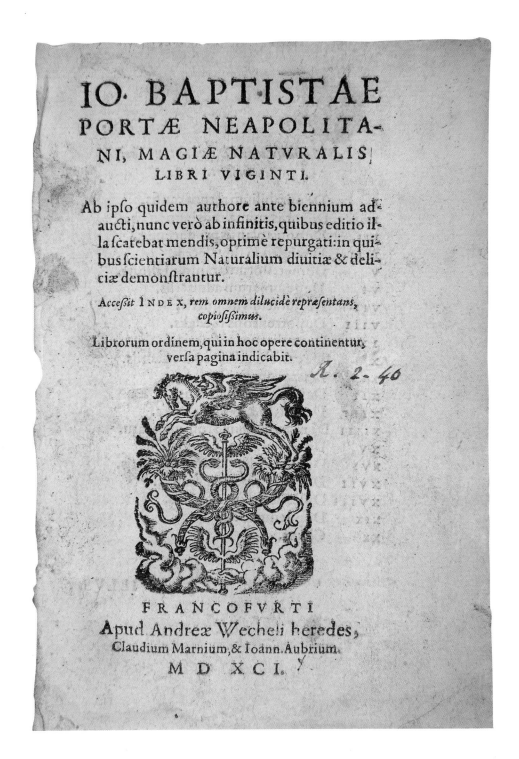

IO· BAPTISTAE
PORTÆ NEAPOLITA-
NI, MAGIÆ NATVRALIS,
LIBRI VIGINTI.

Ab ipſo quidem authore ante biennium ad-
auƈti, nunc verò ab infinitis, quibus editio il-
la ſcatebat mendis, optimè repurgati:in quibus ſcientiarum Naturalium diuitiæ & deliciæ demonſtrantur.

Acceſſit INDEX, rem omnem dilucidè repræſentans,
copioſiſſimus.

Librorum ordinem, qui in hoc opere continentur,
verſa pagina indicabit.

FRANCOFVRTI
Apud Andreæ Wecheli heredes,
Claudium Marnium, & Ioann. Aubrium.
MDXCI.

Porta, Giovanni Battista della, 1535?–1615

Io. Baptistæ Portæ neapolitani, Magiæ natvralis libri viginti...Francofvrti, Apud A. Wecheli heredes, C. Marnium, & I. Aubrium, 1591.

[36], 669 p. 17 cm.
Index on first [36] p. Publisher's device on t.-p.
1. Science—Early works to 1800. I. Title: Magiæ naturalis libri viginti.
Q155.P83 1591
[Gamble 4985]

First published in 1558 when Porta was in his early twenties, Porta's book was reissued in greatly expanded form in 1589 and reprinted several times thereafter. It became one of the best known and most frequently quoted collections of "natural wonders." On pp. 69–70 of the first edition (pp. 668–669 of this edition) he describes how to make a *draco volans* (flying dragon: the ordinary Latin term for a paper kite, which he believes to be the probable reality behind the wooden dove of Archytas; see below, Kircher, *Magnes*, 1641). The passage was influential in spreading knowledge of how to build and fly a dia-

mond-shaped kite of the kind that returning sailors had recently introduced into Europe from the East Indies. Among other writers to quote the description was Johann Jacob Wecker (1528–1586), a copy of whose *Les secrets et merveilles de natvre* is in the Gimbel collection (see Appendix; the quotation is found on pp. 1219–1221 of Wecker). This design quickly ousted the more complicated native European kite (which was indeed shaped like a dragon) and eventually played its part in the development of the airplane, especially with the aerodynamic experiments of Sir George Cayley in the early nineteenth century.

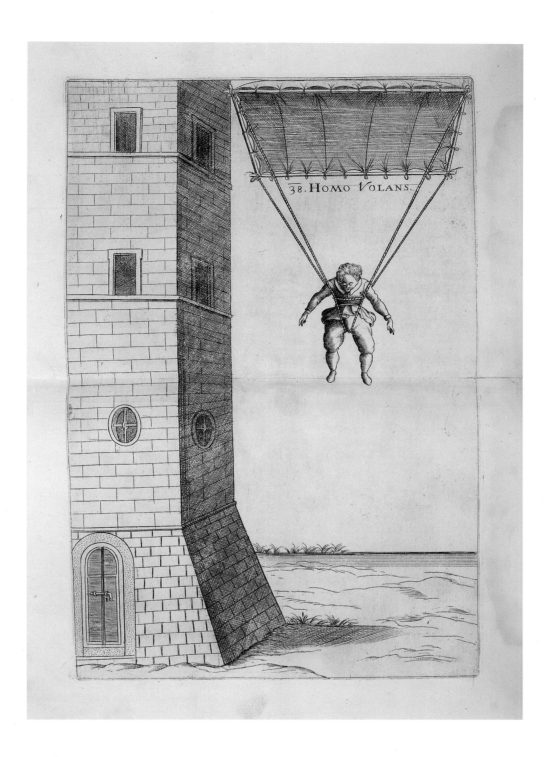

38. HOMO VOLANS.

Veranzio, Fausto, bp., 1551–1617

Machinæ novæ Favsti Verantii siceni. Cvm declaratione latina, italica, hispanica, gallica, et germanica. Venetiis [*ca.* 1595].

 1 p. l., 49 pl. (double pages) 19, 18 p. 38 cm.
  1. Mechanical engineering—Early works to 1800.
   2. Machinery—Early works to 1800.
    3. Parachutes. 4. Inventions. I. Title.
 TJ144.V47
 Gamble 2527

The earliest Western drawing of a parachute is probably that found in British Library Add. MS 34113, fol. 200ᵛ, dated about 1480 and very likely antedating Leonardo's famous design of about the same date. Whether Veranzio could have known of either of these manuscript sketches is uncertain. In any event, the parachute reproduced here is the first to have appeared in a printed book. Like Leonardo's, it uses a rigid rectangular frame, though unlike Leonardo's pyramidal design the canopy is very flat—so flat as to be unstable. The illustration is in any case rather schematic: the uncomfortably harnessed parachutist, whose tunic is quite unruffled, is dropping very slowly. This design appears to have had little if any effect on later inventors. The first recorded free fall by a human being using a parachute was not made until André Jacques Garnerin descended from a balloon on October 22, 1797.

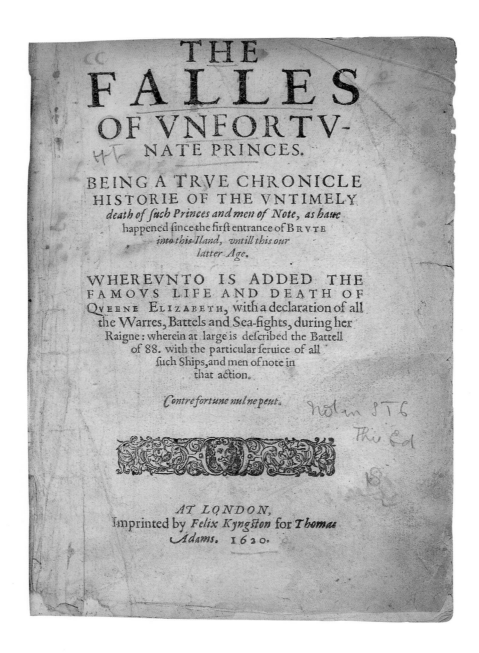

Mirrour for magistrates

The | falles | of vnfortv- | nate Princes. | Being a trve chronicle | historie of the vntimely | death of such Princes and men of Note, as haue | happened since the first entrance of Brvte | into this Iland, vntill this our | latter Age. | Wherevnto is added the | famovs life and death of | Qveene Elizabeth, with a declaration of all | the Warres, Battels and Sea-fights, during her | Raigne: wherein at large is described the Battell | of 88. with the particular seruice of all | such Ships, and men of note in | that action.… At London, | Imprinted by Felix Kyngston for Thomas | Adams, 1620.

Originally published *ca.* 1555, but suppressed; a first part covering the earliest period was added later; this edition adds *A winter nights vision* and *Englands Eliza*.

The three parts have separate title pages: *The Variable Fortvne and Vnhappie Falles Of Svch Princes As hath happened since the Conquest*, 1609; *A Winter Nights Vision*, 1610; *Englands Eliza*, 1610.

1. Gt. Brit.—Hist.—Poetry. I. Niccols, Richard, 1584–1616. II. Baldwin, William, fl. 1547.

III. Higgins, John, fl. 1570–1602. IV. Title.

PR2199.M67 1620

[Not in STC. This edition appears to be a reissue, with new t.-p., of the edition of 1610: STC 13446.]

A legendary king of England, Bladud was supposed to have lived in the middle of the ninth century B.C.E. The story of his death was repeatedly cited in Renaissance England as an example of punished hubris. Accounts of his life vary. The founder of the city of Bath, Bladud is said either to have given healing power to the waters by means of spells and mechanical arts or to have been banished as a leper and to have discovered their curative qualities when wandering as a swineherd in 863 B.C.E. The former version is more commonly found. *The Mirrour for Magistrates* (an anthology of historical narratives) represents him as a kind of British Daedalus, master-inventor. He is said to have died when hoping once too often to outwit nature. Having attached feathers to his body and

wings to his arms, he tried to fly from the top of the temple of Apollo but fell onto the building and broke his neck. The limp verse in the *Mirrour* implicitly Christianizes the story by saying that he flew from the top of the "temple" but fell onto the "church." This is one of many medieval and Renaissance moral tales of men who died or were maimed as a result of their arrogant attempts to fly with wings. Because of Bladud's association with Apollo, he was sometimes identified with the flying prophet Abaris.

The Mirrour for Magistrates was reprinted in many variant forms after its first (suppressed) printing in the mid-1550s. The first extant edition is dated 1559. Despite its very uneven literary quality it was enormously popular.

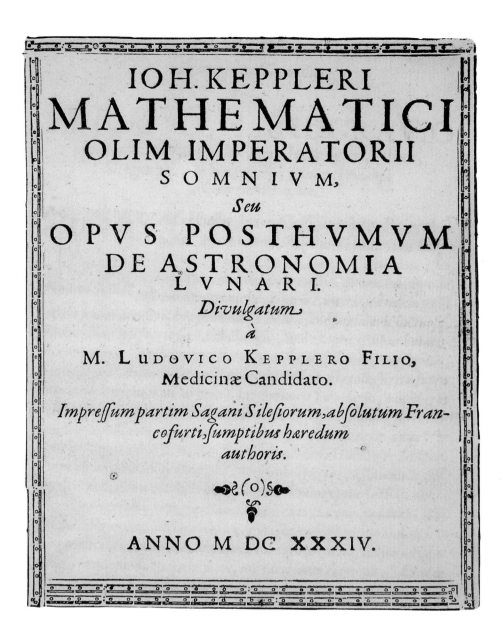

IOH. KEPPLERI
MATHEMATICI
OLIM IMPERATORII
SOMNIVM,
Seu
OPVS POSTHVMVM
DE ASTRONOMIA
LVNARI.
Divulgatum
à
M. LUDOVICO KEPPLERO FILIO,
Medicinæ Candidato.

Impressum partim Sagani Silesiorum, absolutum Francofurti, sumptibus hæredum
authoris.

ANNO M DC XXXIV.

Kepler, Johannes, 1571–1630

Ioh. Keppleri mathematici olim imperatorii Somnivm, seu opvs posthvmvm de astronomia lvnari. Divulgatum à M. Ludovico Kepplero filio, medicinæ candidato. Impressum partim Sagani Silesiorum, absolutum Francofurti, sumptibus hæredum authoris, 1634.

2 p. l., 182, [2] p. diagrs. 19 x 15.5 cm.

1. Astronomy—Early works to 1800. I. Kepler, Ludwig, 1607–1663. II. Title: Somnivm. III. Title: De astronomia lvnari.

QB41.K38 1634

Kepler's *Somnium* is a dream-story (sometimes a nightmare-story) of a trip to the moon. Although containing supernatural elements, it is in many respects a fictionalized autobiography in which Kepler's mother figures as a white witch who knows how to transport the dreamer to the moon. Not printed until four years after the death of the author, the *Somnium* had already been circulating widely in manuscript and had caused the family much trouble: Kepler's mother was almost burned at the stake. The story is important in the history of science fiction. Although a journey to the moon had long been a standard narrative episode, Kepler's differed from most in combining an imaginative tale involving magical potions and strange events with a description of the moon and its inhabitants based on scientific observation and measurement. The *Somnium* comments on the lessening of the force of gravity as one moves away from the surface of earth and on the difficulty of breathing in rarefied air. Kepler speculates that there is life on the moon, but he does not assume that the inhabitants have humanoid characteristics. Instead, they are akin to dinosaurs and lack any form of civilization.

[Wilkins, John, bp. of Chester] 1614–1672

...A discourse concerning a new world & another planet. In 2 bookes. London, Printed for Iohn Maynard, 1640.

2 v. in 1. illus., diagrs. 17.5 cm.

Engraved t.-p. Each volume has also special t.-p.

Pages 221–222 wanting in v. 2.

CONTENTS.—[v. 1] The first book. The discovery of a new world. Or, A discourse tending to prove, that 'tis probable there may be another habitable world in the moone. With a discourse concerning the possibility of a passage thither. The third impression. Corrected and enlarged.—[v. 2] A discovrse concerning a new planet. Tending to prove, that 'tis probable our earth is one of the planets. The second booke, now first published... 1. Astronomy—Early works to 1800. I. Title.

QB41.W68 1640

STC 25640.5; [Gamble 5075].

Other copies and editions in the Gimbel collection: QB41.W68 1638: *The discovery of a world in the moone,* [1st ed.] London, 1638; QB41.W68 1684: 4th ed. "corrected and amended," London, 1684; QB41.W68 1684a: 5th ed., London, 1684; QB41.W68: *Le monde dans la lvne,* trans. le Sr de la Montagne, Rouen, 1655, with engraved t.-p.; QB41.W68 1656: another ed. of the previous item, Rouen, 1656.

A man of wide general learning, Wilkins was made Master of Wadham College, Oxford, in 1648, presiding over the university's Philosophical Society. Later he was to be an important member of the Royal Society. A writer of elegant prose, he was keen to remain in touch with the latest discoveries in science and was well equipped to write works of "high popularization" such as his *Discovery*. Appearing at a time when fictional accounts of the moon were growing common, this book turns to (probable) realities. Soon after its first publication in 1638, Wilkins revised the book, adding a substantial final chapter on the proposition that "'tis possible for some of our posteritie, to find a conveyance to this other world." Having read Kepler's *Somnium* and other contemporary moon-journeys, Wilkins attempts to answer the scientific questions raised by them. Confident that human flight was possible, even though "it may seeme a terrible and impossible thing ever to passe through the vaste spaces of the aire," he commented that future ages would take flight for granted. He discussed problems related to gravity, to the density of the air, to the cold of the upper atmosphere, and to the probable distance of the moon from the earth. He calculated that distance as 179,712 miles, which is of the right order of magnitude. The figure was repeated as established fact by many later writers. A practical scientist, Wilkins also gave serious thought to the physical circumstances of life during the journey: as there are no airborne inns, how will the travelers eat, how will they overcome the intolerable boredom of the trip, when will they sleep?

ATHANASII KIRCHERI

FVLDENSIS BVCHONII, E SOC. IESV.

MAGNES

siue De

ARTE MAGNETICA

OPVS TRIPARTITVM

Quo

PRÆTERQVAM QVOD VNIVERSA MAGNETIS
Natura, eiusque in omnibus Artibus & Scientijs vsus noua,
methodo explicetur, è viribus quoque & prodigiosis effe-
ctibus Magneticarum, aliarumque abditarum Naturæ
motionum in Elementis, Lapidibus, Plantis
& Animalibus elucescentium, multa huc-
usque incognita Naturæ arcana per
Physica, Medica, Chymica, &
Mathematica omnis ge-
neris experimenta,
recluduntur.

Sumptibus Hermanni Scheus sub signo Reginæ.

ROMAE, ExTypographia Ludouici Grignani. MDCXLI.
SVPERIORVM PERMISSV.

Kircher, Athanasius, 1602–1680

...Magnes, siue De arte magnetica opvs tripartitvm...
sumptibus Hermanni Scheus..., Romae, Ex
typographia Ludouici Grignani, 1641.

15 p. l., 916, [16] p. illus. 25 cm.

1. Magnetism—Early works to 1800. I. Title.
Q155.K58

**Other copies and editions in the Gimbel
collection:** Q155.K58 1654: 3rd ed. "ab ipso authore
recognita," Romæ, 1654.

A voluminous writer who combined true
scientific curiosity with credulity and a vivid
imagination, the Jesuit priest Kircher caught
the imagination of many readers with his
book on magnetism (reprinted in 1643 and
1654). Writing first of the natural, observable
qualities of the magnet, he then proceeds to
more recondite matters, including magnetic
hydromancy and oneiromancy. In an
engraving opposite p. 358 he illustrates his
explanation of the wooden dove of Archytas.
According to Aulus Gellius (second century
C.E.), Archytas of Tarentum, a friend of Plato
(fourth century B.C.E.), built and flew a
wooden dove, "so nicely balanced was it, you
see, with weights and moved by a current of
air enclosed and hidden within it" (*Noctium*

atticarum libri xx, X.12.8–10; see Appendix).
Writers of the Renaissance frequently
discussed the true means by which this bird
might have flown. Kircher says that it must
have been propelled by hidden magnets and a
wire so fine as to escape detection. The Latin
caption beneath the engraving says, "Neither a
wheel, nor a wind but a magnet enables the
device to move." Scientists were often
fascinated by the practical uses to which they
thought the somewhat mysterious power of
the magnet might be put.

The wooden dove of Archytas continued
for centuries to encourage inventors to build
flying models. Among the most interesting is
a design by Erasmus Darwin, grandfather of
Charles, for a model goose (1777).

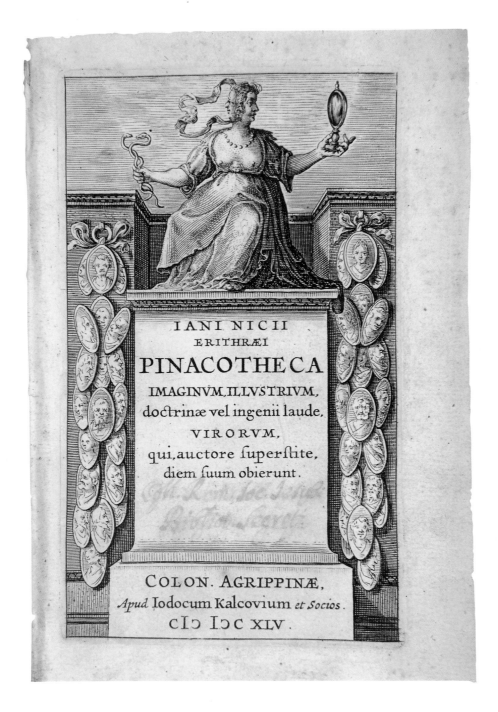

IANI NICII
ERITHRÆI
PINACOTHECA
IMAGINVM, ILLVSTRIVM,
doctrinæ vel ingenii laude,
VIRORVM,
qui, auctore superstite,
diem suum obierunt.

COLON. AGRIPPINÆ,
Apud Iodocum Kalcovium *et Socios.*
CIↃ IↃC XLV.

Rossi, Gian Vittorio, 1577–1647

Iani Nicii Erithræi Pinacotheca imaginvm, illvstrivm, doctrinæ vel ingenii laude, virorvm, qui, auctore superstite, diem suum obierunt. Colon. Agrippinæ, Apud Iodocum Kalcovium et Socios, 1645.

2 v. in 1. port. 15.5 cm.

1. Biography—17th century. I. Title: Pinacotheca imaginum, illustrium.

CT93.R82

One of Rossi's "illustrious men" is the painter, sculptor, and architect Paolo Guidotti, who was born in Lucca in 1569. Guidotti was a man of many talents: in addition to being a skilled visual artist he was a musician, poet, and doctor of laws. Toward the end of the sixteenth century he decided to try to add human flight to his other achievements. He accordingly made wings from whalebone held in shape with springs and covered with feathers. These he fixed under rather than on top of his arms, thus ensuring further rigidity.

With this equipment he threw himself from a height and seems to have managed a short glide, which one sober-minded witness described as more like a controlled fall than a flight. The attempt ended when he crashed through a roof and landed on the floor of the room below, breaking his thigh. The date of this attempt is unknown. One account says that is was as late as 1628, but Guidotti was then 59 years old and unlikely to have engaged in such vigorous activity at that age.

Effigies Reverendi admodum viri
Johannis Wilkins nuper Episcopi
Cestriensis

Mathematicall
MAGICK.
OR,
THE VVONDERS
That may be performed by
Mechanicall Geometry.

In two Books.

CONCERNING
Mechanicall { POVVERS.
             { MOTIONS.

BEING ONE OF
The moſt eaſie, pleaſant, uſefull,
(and yet moſt neglected} part of
MATHEMATICKS.
Not before treated of in this language.

By I. W. M. A.

Τέχνη κρατᾆμεν ὧν φύσει νικώμεθα.

LONDON,
Printed by M. F. for Sa: Gellibrand at the
braſen Serpent in Pauls Church-yard. 1648.

Wilkins, John, bp. of Chester, 1614–1672

Mathematicall magick. Or, The wonders that may be performed by mechanicall geometry. In two books. Concerning mechanicall powers [and] motions. Being one of the most easie, pleasant, usefull, (and yet most neglected) part of mathematicks. Not before treated of in this language. By I.W., M.A. London, Printed by M.F. for S. Gellibrand, 1648.

7 p. 1., 295 p. illus., diagrs. 16.5 cm.

1. Mechanics.

QC123.W68 1648

[Brockett 12900]; [Gamble 5076]; Wing W2198

Other copies and editions in the Gimbel collection: QC123.W68 1680: rev. ed. with frontispiece portrait, London, 1680; QC123.W68 1691: 4th ed., London, 1691.

Throughout his life Wilkins puzzled over ways in which manned flight might be achieved. Reconsidering, in this new book, the ideas that he had set out at the end of the revised edition of *The Discovery of a World in the Moone*, he arranged possibilities into categories, deciding that there were "four severall ways whereby this flying in the air, hath beene or may be attempted. Two of them by the strength of other things, and two of them by our owne strength." These he lists as "By spirits or Angels…By the help of fowls…By wings fastned immediately to the body…By a flying chariot" (*Mathematicall Magick*, pp. 199–200). He considers each of these in turn. The first is of no help to those who wish to achieve things by rational means; the second he thinks not impossible, given sufficient skill in training birds; the third he

believes to have been tried already with some success by several men; though difficult, the fourth seems to him to be the most likely to succeed and also potentially the most useful. He then proceeds to devote a chapter to a discussion of the difficulties. Like many others in his day, Wilkins believed that gravity fades away a few miles above the earth's surface and that the flier would need to expend only enough energy to reach that height. Equally interested in the matter, the secretary of the Royal Society, Robert Hooke, consulted him on a number of occasions with designs for a primitive helicopter and techniques for attaching wings to the body.

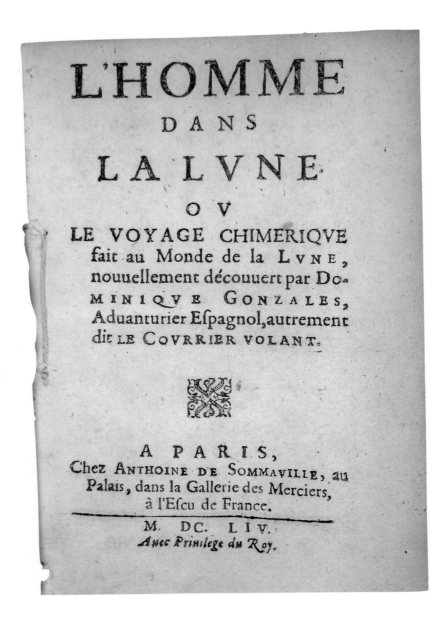

L'HOMME
DANS
LA LVNE
OV
LE VOYAGE CHIMERIQVE
fait au Monde de la LVNE,
nouuellement découuert par Do-
MINIQVE GONZALES,
Aduanturier Espagnol, autrement
dit LE COVRRIER VOLANT.

A PARIS,
Chez ANTHOINE DE SOMMAVILLE, au
Palais, dans la Gallerie des Merciers,
à l'Escu de France.

M. DC. LIV.
Auec Priuilege du Roy.

[Godwin, Francis, bp. of Hereford] 1562–1633

L'homme dans la lvne, ov Le voyage chimeriqve fait au monde de la lvne, nouuellement découuert par Dominiqve Gonzales [pseud.], *Aduanturier Espagnol, autrement dit le Covrrier volant.* A Paris, Chez Anthoine de Sommaville, 1654.

8 p. l., 176 p. illus. 16.5 cm.
1. Voyages, Imaginary. I. Title.
TLE1041.G59

Other copies and editions in the Gimbel collection: TLE1041.G59s 1708:...*an account of the admirable voyage of Domingo Gonsales...to the world in the moon...*, in [Nathaniel Crouch], *The English acquisitions in Guinea & East-India...*London, 1708; TLE1041.G59s 1768: *The strange voyage and adventures of Domingo Gonsales to the world in the moon,...*, 9th ed., London, 1768.

Godwin's *The Man in the Moone* was first published, anonymously, in 1638. The date of composition is uncertain but may have been *ca.* 1628. Immensely popular, it was frequently reprinted and translated into four languages. This abridged French translation by Jean Baudoin first appeared in 1648 and was reissued several times. Despite its popularity (or perhaps because of it: popular books are quickly worn out), the first English edition is extremely rare. After a series of adventures, the hero, Domingo Gonsales, is put ashore on a distant island where he finds wild swans, a flock of which he tames. It occurs to him to use these to lift him from the earth. After a number of experiments, he eventually succeeds in being raised by twenty-five of

them. After further adventures he uses his "gansas," as he calls them, to escape from danger but finds to his surprise that they take him in an unexpected direction: the birds hibernate on the moon. Before they arrive, he finds that he and the birds escape from the effects of the earth's gravity. Like a modern space rocket, the birds no longer need to use power but sail on through the air at great speed, moving their wings only rarely. Not only is physical gravity left behind, but Gonsales feels that he has escaped from all the spiritual heaviness of mortality. Once arrived at the moon, he describes it in great detail. The book had an enduring influence on subsequent writers of science fiction.

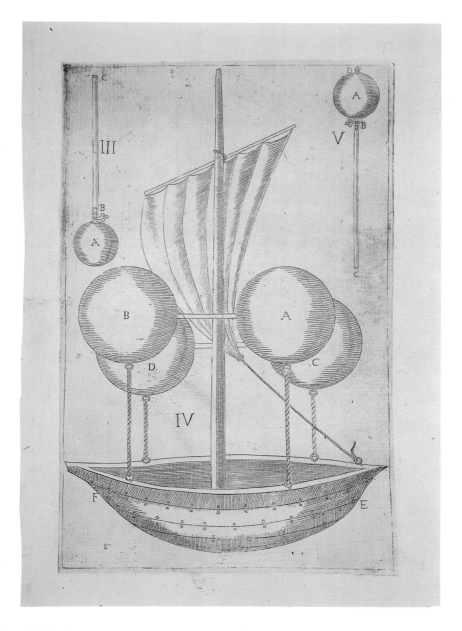

Lana de Terzi, Francesco, 1631–1687

Prodromo; ouero, Saggio di alcune inuentioni nuoue premesso all'Arte maestra, opera che prepara il P. Francesco Lana Bresciano della Compagnia di Giesv. Per mostrare li piu reconditi principij della naturale filosofia, riconosciuti con accurata teorica nelle piu segnalate inuentioni, ed isperienze sin'hora ritrouate da gli scrittori di questa materia & altre nuoue dell'autore medesimo. Dedicato alla Sacra Maesta Cesarea del imperatore Leopoldo I. In Brescia, Per li Rizzardi, 1670.

4 p. l., 252 p. 20 pl. (incl. music) 33 cm.

Contents (in part).—Proemio, in cui l'autore dichiara qual sia per essere l'opera che'promette (Magisterium naturae, et artis. Brescia, 1684) p. 1–17.—cap. 1. Nuoue inuentioni di scrivere in cifera.—cap. 2. In qual modo un cieco nato possa imparare a scriuere [e] nascondere sotto cifera i suoi segreti.—cap. 3. In qual modo si possa parlare senza mandar ne lettere, ne messagiere.—cap. 4. Come si possa insegnare a parlare ad uno che per esser nato sordo sia muto—cap. 6. Fabricare una naue, che camini sostentata sopra l'aria a remi, & à veli, p. 52–61 e pl. [2] fig. III, IV, V. At end of volume a French manuscript translation of this chapter (20 p.) preceded by a manuscript table of contents to the Prodromo in French.—cap. 16. L'Arte maestra d'agricoltura.—cap. 20. L'Arte maestra di chimica.—cap. 21. L'Arte maestra di medicina.—

cap. 22. L'Arte maestra di aritmetica. L'Arte maestra sopra l'arte della pittura (4 chap.) L'Arte maestra: regole per fabricare molte sorti di cannocchiali, e microscopij (8 chap.)

Ex libris: Gaston Tissandier. Vellum binding. Spine title. Plate sheets divided, tipped in, recto, at end.

1. Mechanical engineering—Early works to 1800. 2. Science—Early works to 1800. 3. Aeronautics. 4. Flying-machines. 5. Deaf and dumb—Means of communication. 6. Blind—Printing and writing systems. 7. Telescope. 8. Microscope and microscopy. I. Lana de Terzi, Francesco, 1631–1687. Magisterium naturae, et artis. II. Title.

TJ144.L24

Brockett 7107; Gamble 1134

Other copies in the Gimbel collection: five complete copies.

1: Vellum binding. Spine title. Each double sheet of plates bound between gatherings. 2: Vellum binding. Spine title. Plates sewn and bound at end. Bookseller's advertisement. 3: Vellum binding. Spine title. Bookplate of Mr. Howard A. Scholle. Library card of Williams College. 4: Vellum binding. Spine title, with cataloguer's label. Plate sheets divided, tipped in, recto, at end. Bookseller's typed note. 5: Modern binding. Plates loose, sewn as gathering. Bookplate of Theodore von Karman Memorial Collection. Bookseller's typed note.

The *Prodromo* of the Jesuit priest Francesco Lana de Terzi is among the most frequently cited early books on aviation. Although his proposal for an airship began as little more than a scientific *jeu d'esprit*, it rapidly became very famous and was often taken seriously. It was frequently copied, embellished, and plagiarized. Lana surmised that large globes emptied of air would rise. He proposed that, on the basis of his calculations, the four globes, of thin copper or bronze (about 0.1 mm in thickness), should be twenty feet in diameter. He was aware of the experiments with the "Magdeburg spheres" (1654) that had so dramatically demonstrated the strength of air pressure (see Appendix, Guericke, *Experimenta nova*, 1672) and hoped—in vain, of course—that a purely spherical form would prevent the globes from collapsing. In a later treatise he suggested that the globes could be made of very light wood, such as is used for musical instruments. (Lana de Terzi, *Magisterivm natvrae, et artis* II, Brixiæ, 1686, pp. 293–294. See Appendix.) Such a structure should be strengthened with thin wooden laths bonded to it, and the whole might need to be varnished to keep it airtight. His calculations showed that globes so made need be only ten feet in diameter. In the last paragraph of his description in the *Prodromo*, Lana commented that the greatest difficulty confronting anyone who might try to build such a machine would be insurmountable: God would not permit men to have at their disposal something so readily capable of destroying the fabric of society by immoral and violent methods. He concluded by describing explicitly what he meant. His aerial ship could be used as a new weapon of war. It could carry soldiers to attack cities, private dwellings, and vessels at sea; iron weights, bombs, and fireballs could be dropped on ships and their crews; houses, fortresses, and cities could be destroyed with impunity since the aerial ship could operate from beyond the reach of defensive fire. This reads in part as a serious warning and in part as conventional self-protective rhetoric—withdrawal from personal involvement in a dangerous proposal.

Lana's proposal is akin to a much older idea. That a ship filled only with the "ether" that used to be thought to lie above the atmosphere could float on the surface of the air, just as an air-filled ship floats on water, was the basis of a thought experiment by Nicole Oresme as early as 1377. Repeated several times by later writers, the idea was mentioned in 1640 by Bishop Wilkins.

La terre me fut importune,
Ie pris mon essort vers les Cieux,
Iy vis le soleil, et la lune,
Et maintenant Iy vois les Dieux.

LÉS OEUVRES DIVERSES DE MONSIEUR DE CYRANO BERGERAC.

TOME PREMIER

Enrichi de Figures en taille douce.

A AMSTERDAM,

Chez DANIEL PAIN, Marchand Libraire
Sur le Voorburgwal proche du Stilfteeg.

M. DC. XCIX.

Cyrano de Bergerac, Savinien, 1619–1655

Les oeuvres diverses de Monsieur de Cyrano Bergerac. A Amsterdam, Chez Daniel Pain. 1699.

2 v. 16 cm.

With front. (port.) in each volume; and other illus.

PG1793.A1 1699

[Brockett 3234]; [Gamble 48]

Other copies and editions in the Gimbel collection:
PQ1793.A1 1709: *Les oeuvres de Monsieur de Cyrano Bergerac,* illus., Amsterdam, 1709; PQ1793.A1 1710: another ed. of the previous item, Amsterdam, 1710; PQ1793.A2A 1899: *A voyage to the moon,* an edition by C. H. Page of Lovell's translation, New York, 1899; PQ1793.A2A 1899: another copy of the previous item; PQ1793.A2K: *L'autre monde...*preface by Steffi Kiesler, Paris, [194–]; PQ1793.A2Sc: *Mondstaaten und Sonnenreiche,* trans. Martha Schimper, Leipzig, 1913; PQ1793.A2Al: *Voyages to the Moon and the Sun,* trans. Richard Aldington, London [n.d.]

Following its first publication in 1650, new editions of *Histoire comique des estats et empires de la lune* (included in vol. 1 of this collection) continued to appear throughout the century. This high-spirited work of the imagination is a series of outrageous scientific spoofs. Cyrano's fictionalized alter ego made several attempts to fly to the moon. For the first he attached phials of dew to his body so that when the dew began to rise because of the sun's warmth he would be carried with it. By this means he flew high but mismanaged the balance of gravity and upward force and failed to reach the moon. A second attempt with an ornithopter also failed. He had better success, though inadvertently, when soldiers attached rockets to the wreck of his machine, which carried him up with it. The machine fell away beneath him and as he approached the moon he turned over, the lesser gravity of the moon having replaced that of the earth. He crash-landed on his feet. Another flight followed, this time a return journey made by the magical power of his attendant spirit. His next and most imaginative journey was undertaken with an ingenious and still more incredible machine. Cyrano traveled past all the planets using a large, frail box with holes drilled in the top and bottom. Over the upper hole he placed a crystal vessel in the shape of an icosahedron, also with holes drilled in it, the one at its bottom coinciding with the upper hole in the box. The sun's rays filled the space in the crystal vessel, heating the air, which was driven out through its top hole. A "great abundance of Air" then rushed up through the hole in the bottom of the box and the energy of the air's movement carried the whole thing aloft. Once again Cyrano eventually lost his machine, which fell unharmed to Poland while he continued to the surface of the sun. Although, naturally enough, no one believed a word of this, Cyrano's sparkling imagination encouraged inventors to develop yet further ideas for motive force.

Happel, Eberhard Werner, 1647–1690

...*Grösseste Denkwürdigkeiten der Welt, oder so genandte Relationes curiosæ*...Hamburg, Thomas von VViering, 1689.

600 p. illus. 20 cm.
At head of title: E. G. Happelii. Vierter Theil. [Issued in 5 v., 1683–1690. *Cf.* BL 446.b.3–6.] Partial contents: Das in der Luft seeglende Schiff, p. 308. Plate (Lana).
1. Geography. 2. History, Universal. 3. Natural history. I. Title.
G114.H25

This book of natural "wonders"—an early encyclopedia—is one of many to copy Lana's design, with imaginative improvements. One of the crew steers the airborne ship by means of a rudder, which evidently needs little effort to manipulate. As in Lana's original, and in innumerable designs for steerable balloons and airships well on into the nineteenth century, the sail is falsely shown filled out by the wind and carrying the ship along. An awareness of the truth about relative speeds in the air was slow to develop. The earthbound onlookers, including the dogs, are astonished. The detail of the upward-leaping dog is borrowed from representations of the shepherd-boy Ganymede, carried aloft by Jupiter, of which one of the best known is by Correggio (*ca.* 1530) in the Kunsthistorische Museum, Vienna. The skills of the modern scientist and engineer are shown to have surpassed the forces of pagan divinity.

Hooke, Robert, 1635–1703

Philosophical collections, containing an account of such physical, anatomical, chymical, mechanical, astronomical...experiments and observations as have lately come to the publishers hands...
[London, Printed for John Martyn, 1679–1682].

   210 p. illus. 23 cm.
   Issued in 7 numbers; continuous paging;
     imprint varies.
   1. Science—Early works to 1800. I. Title.
   Q155.H78

Hooke, the irascible secretary of the Royal Society, showed a lifelong interest in flight. In the first issue of *Philosophical Collections* he reports on the abortive trials of a Mr. Gascoyn, carried out sometime around 1640 but about which nothing is known. Hoping to succeed where Gascoyn had failed, Hooke sketched many ideas for equipment to supplement human muscle power and once designed a helicopter, the details of which have not survived. He is also credited with having invented a model bird powered by "springs and wings," which "rais'd and sustain'd it self in the Air." Although like many other inventors in the period he looked first to birds for his ideas, he was unusual in also considering the wings of bats and even those of flying fish. Along with a sketch of Lana's airship, the illustration includes a design for a flying machine which had been published in

Amsterdam only a few months before and was the nominal subject of Hooke's note. It shows Besnier, a locksmith of Sablé, flying with hinged wings made of taffeta stretched over frames and flapped by both arm and leg power. Besnier did not claim to have been able to rise from the earth, but he did allege that, starting from a height, he could sustain himself in a glide for long enough to be able to cross a river. The illustration, representing Besnier in classically nude style, is highly schematic. If he were indeed able to remain airborne at all, his equipment must have been very different from that shown. The wings must have been much larger and would not, of course, have flapped alternately as is sometimes shown in other illustrations (see, for example, Cambridge, *The Scribleriad*, 1751).

Nachricht
Von dem
Fliegenden
Schiffe /
So aus
Portugal /
Den 24. Junii in Wien mit seinem
Erfinder /
Glücklich ankommen.

Von neuen nach dem allbereit gedruckten Exem=
plar in die Naumburger Meß gesandt.
ANNO 1709.

Nachricht von dem fliegenden Schiffe / so aus Portugal / den 24. Junii in Wien mit seinem Erfinder / glücklich ankommen...[n.p.,] 1709.

[4] p. 27 cm.
English tr. (ts.) laid in.
1. Gusmão, Bartholomeu Lourenço de, 1685–1724.
TLB154.N2 1709

In 1709, the Brasilian Bartholomeu Gusmão managed to persuade the king of Portugal to grant him a patent for a flying machine that would be capable of covering distances of more than 200 miles a day. He called the machine a *Passarola* (great bird). Drawings of the *Passarola*, with a bird-shaped fuselage, feathered wings, and a sail-like canopy over the top, circulated rapidly and were frequently reproduced. There is some evidence that Gusmão had successfully built small hot-air balloons, and it is possible that he also demonstrated some form of glider. Many people were persuaded that he had achieved complete success with a man-carrying machine. This account, based on an imaginary news report from Vienna, tells of Gusmão's demonstration of manned flight before an awe-struck audience of the inhabitants. Gusmão is said to have started from Lisbon at 6 A.M. the day before and to have passed by the moon on the way. Before he reached the city, some of the citizens, not knowing what was going on, thought that perhaps the Day of Judgment was beginning. The *Passarola* arrived, preceded and surrounded by a great flock of birds, like a celestial chariot encircled by angels. The landing, however, was less than divine: a sudden gust caused the canopy to be snagged on the spire of Saint Stephen's Cathedral, in the center of the city, where Gusmão hung for a couple of hours. As no one was willing to help, he had to free himself before landing a short distance away near the Hofburg. He related how, during the journey, he had frequently to fight off the attentions of strange celestial birds.

Fron. III. del Volo

P. Aquila Incid.

Martello, Pierjacopo, 1665–1727

Versi, e prose, di Pierjacopo Martello. In Roma, Per Francesco Gonzaga, 1710.

16 p. l., 324 p. front., pl. 20.5 cm.

Title vignette. Initials.

Contents—*Degli occhi di Gesù, libri sei, ad Amarilli.—Del volo.—Della poetica, sermoni.*

At the end of book IV of *Degli occhi di Gesù* (first published Bologna, 1707) Martello describes an airship and its imaginary voyage. When this edition of the poem was published, he added the four prose dialogues entitled "Del volo"; in later editions the fourth dialogue ("Mattina ultima") was suppressed. *Cf.* Boffito, G., *Biblioteca aeronautica italiana*, 1929, p. 276; Venturini, G., *Da Icaro a Montgolfier*, 1928, I.272–298.

1. Jesus Christ—Poetry. 2. Airships. 3. Aeronautics.

TLB154.M37 1710

[Brockett 8072]

Other copies and editions in the Gimbel collection: TLB154.M37 1729: 2nd ed., expanded, Bologna, 1729.

Poets as well as satirists frequently focused on the growing interest in manned flight. Martello's long poem *Degli occhi di Gesù* describes a journey to the earthly paradise, guided by the great aeronautical charioteer of the Bible, Elijah (2 Kings 2:11). The prophet's flying machine is, however, supplanted by a new one based on a simplified version of Gusmão's *Passarola.* Martello's ship, vastly bigger than Gusmão's, has landing gear: a set of grapples to hold the earth. He is also more explicit than Gusmão about the method of propulsion—so explicit, indeed, as to show that he treats the whole thing as an amusing fiction. The wings are attached to oars manipulated by a hundred galley slaves, all of whom are apes. Evidently aware of the real needs of eighteenth-century galleys, Martello describes two shifts of rowers who relieve

each other by turns. He evidently has no faith in the common idea that flight in the regions above the lower atmosphere was effortless.

In the third part of the tract *Del volo,* attached to *Degli occhi di Gesù,* Martello discusses flight in general and comments on the flying machine that he described in the poem and which he assures the reader was only a poetic invention. He discusses problems of stability, pointing out that any lack of coordination among so many rowers would have worse consequences than in a ship on water and would lead to the machine's crashing to the earth. He therefore suggests a mechanism for keeping the oars synchronized. Martello gives a full description of the *Passarola,* this time much closer to Gusmão's, shown coming to grief in the second illustration along with a version of Lana's flying ship.

Tome 1er p. 1.

Crespy Scul.

GOMGAM,
OU
L'HOMME PRODIGIEUX,
TRANSPORTÉ
DANS L'AIR, SUR LA TERRE,
ET SOUS LES EAUX.
Livre veritablement nouveau.
TITETUTEFNOSY.
SECONDE EDITION.

Augmentée du dénouëment de l'histoire du
Docteur Dirto, de ses sentences & juge-
gemens, de ses bons mots, d'une maniere
extraordinaire inventée pour punir un Sa-
tyrique, d'une Figure qui en represente
l'éxecution, & de plusieurs autres.

TOME PREMIER.

✦✦✦

A PARIS,
Chez PIERRE PRAULT, en la Boutique de la
Veuve Saugrain, sur le Quay de Gesvres, du côté
du Pont au Change, au Paradis.

M DCCXII.
Avec Approbation & Privilege du Roy.

Einnahmebuch Nr.: 41. 28

[Bordelon, Laurent] 1653–1730

Gomgam, ou l'homme prodigieux, transporté dans l'air, sur la terre, et sous les eaux. Livre veritablement nouveau. Titetutefnosy. Seconde édition. A Paris, Chez Pierre Prault, 1712.

2 v. illus. 16.5 cm.
Tissandier, p. 7.
1. Voyages, Imaginary. I. Title.
PQ1957.B67A64 1712
[Brockett 2039]

Other copies and editions in the Gimbel collection: PQ1957.B67A64 1713: new ed., Paris, 1713.

First published in 1711, this fantasy is a loose adaptation of the tale of Abaris, a legendary Scythian servant of Apollo who, in some Greek accounts, is said to have flown around the world on a golden arrow (see, for example, Origen, *Contra Celsum,* III.31). If there is any truth behind the story, it is probable that Abaris merely carried with him the golden arrow that is a symbol of Apollo's authority. The flying legend is explicitly mentioned toward the end of Bordelon's first volume, where it is said to be nothing but a fable; by contrast, the aerial power of Gomgam's golden arrow, which he acquires about halfway

through the story, is alleged to be a reality. Despite a few passing comments about the nature of the physical universe, the frivolous tone of the book is in sharp contrast with aeronautical fiction of the previous century based on the imaginative development of scientific theories. One of Gomgam's journeys does nevertheless take him to examine and theorize about a rainbow.

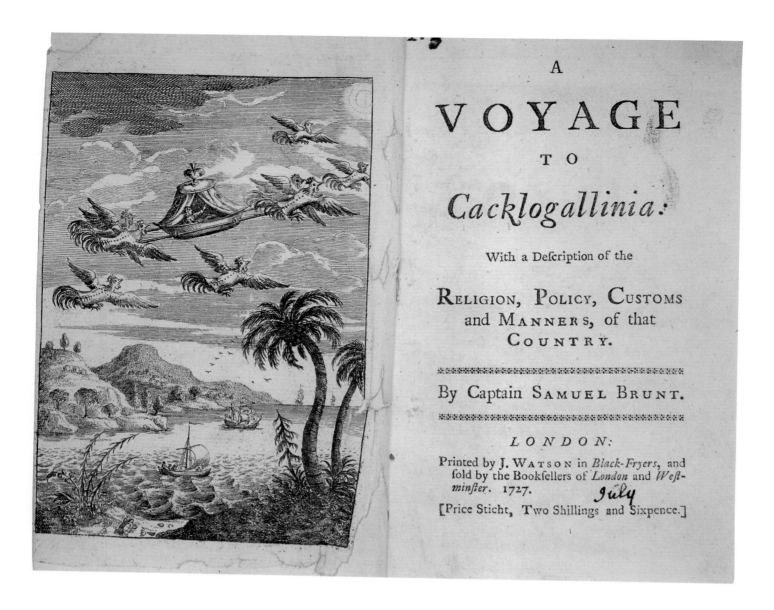

A

VOYAGE

TO

Cacklogallinia:

With a Defcription of the

RELIGION, POLICY, CUSTOMS
and MANNERS, of that
COUNTRY.

By Captain SAMUEL BRUNT.

LONDON:

Printed by J. WATSON in *Black-Fryers,* and
fold by the Bookfellers of *London* and *Weft-
minfter.* 1727. *July*

[Price Sticht, Two Shillings and Sixpence.]

Brunt, Samuel [pseud.]

A voyage to Cacklogallinia: with a description of the religion, policy, customs and manners, of that country. By Captain Samuel Brunt. London, J. Watson, 1727.

167 p. front. 18 cm.

"A journey to the moon," pp. 122–167.

1. Voyages, Imaginary. I. Title.

PR3328.B38 1727

Other copies and editions in the Gimbel collection:
PR3328.B38 1751: *Captain Samuel Brunts Reise...aus dem Englischen übersetzt,* Leipzig, 1751.

A lively Robinsonade, this satire on contemporary mercantilism is indebted in many respects to the last book of Swift's *Gulliver's Travels,* which had appeared the previous year. "Captain Brunt" (who remains unidentified) finds a country inhabited not by talking horses but by talking birds, whose language he learns. His description of their society bears directly on that of England. The birds conceive a project of traveling to the moon to discover gold in its mountains. Brunt demurs, using arguments from previous writers, including, in particular, those of Wilkins (see above, Wilkins, *A discourse,* 1640), which focused on the difficulty of getting to the moon. He loses the argument and reluctantly agrees to head the expedition. In this, Brunt's story differs from many of its predecessors, whose heroes are only too keen to get to the moon. Brunt flies, but only in the sense that the birds bear him along with them in a specially constructed aerial carriage. The journey having been made, the moon is found to be an idyllic place where "chrystal Rivulets" seemed "so many Mirrors reflecting the various Beauties of those odoriferous flowers which adorn'd their Banks" (p. 135). Contact is established with the idealistic moon-dwellers, who are of "neither a corporeal nor an aerial Substance, but...between both" (p. 142). Brunt also finds that the moon is a place of dreams, partly inhabited by the souls of sleeping humans acting out their fantasies. These passages return the reader to some of the earliest myths about the relationship of moon and earth. Thereafter the satire continues for a time until Brunt is flown back—to Jamaica. In telling his story, Brunt quotes many scientific facts and theories, some taken directly from Godwin, Wilkins, and Cyrano; others are more up to date.

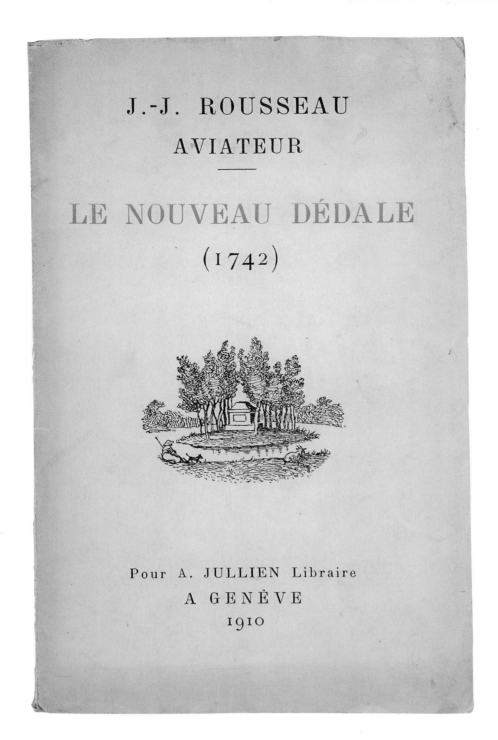

J.-J. ROUSSEAU

AVIATEUR

———

LE NOUVEAU DÉDALE

(1742)

Pour A. JULLIEN Libraire
A GENÈVE
1910

Rousseau, Jean-Jacques, 1712–1778

Le nouveau Dédale (1742). A Genève, A. Jullien, 1910.

25 p., 1 l. 23 cm.

At head of title: J.-J. Rousseau, aviateur.

With reproduction of original t.-p.: *Le nouveau Dédale; ouvrage inédit de J.-J. Rousseau, et copié sur son manuscrit original daté de l'année 1742.* A Paris, Chez Mᵐᵉ. Masson, [1801].

Introduction signed: Pierre-Paul Plan.

"Extrait du Mercure de France 16-x-1910 et tiré à cent soixante-quinze exemplaires."

With this is bound a copy of the original edition: A Paris, Chez Mᵐᵉ· Masson...[1801].

1. Aeronautics. I. Plan, Pierre-Paul, ed. II. Title.

TLB154.R86 1742

Gamble 100

Other copies and editions in the Gimbel collection: TLB154.R86a 1742: facsimile of 1st ed. (1801), Pasadena, [1950].

In 1742 a highly eccentric Frenchman called Jean-François Boyvin de Bonnetot, who falsely styled himself Marquis de Bacqueville, announced that he would fly across the Seine from his house on the quai des Théatins (now the quai Voltaire) and land in the Tuileries. At that date he was about 60 years old. A crowd gathered to watch as Bacqueville, with wings attached to his arms and legs, threw himself from a window. Exaggerated accounts say that he flew for "100 fathoms" (600 feet) before falling into a laundry boat where, as is so often related in accounts of such attempts, he broke his thigh. He nevertheless survived his ordeal and did not die until 1760—and then only in a fire that burned down his house. Rousseau, who had been among the crowd of onlookers at the attempt to cross the Seine, was prompted by the event to write a speculative essay on the possibility of human flight, which he found an intriguing puzzle. (He plays on the meaning of *dédale* as a common noun: maze, or labyrinth.) Taking up the idea of aerial navigation, he points out that a flying machine will not sail on the surface of the air, as does a ship on water, but will be immersed in it. He focuses also on the difficulty of maintaining control over the altitude of any machine dependent on lighter-than-air principles.

L. P. Boitard Invᵗ et Sculp.

According to Act of Parliament 1751.

[Cambridge, Richard Owen] 1717–1802

*The Scribleriad: an heroic poem. In six books...*London, Printed for R. Dodsley...and sold by M. Cooper..., 1751.

6 pt. in 1 v. front., 6 pl. 26 cm.
Title vignette.
Each part has separate t.-p. and paging.
Preface signed.
I. Title.
PR3339.C125
[Gamble 45]

Other copies and editions in the Gimbel collection:
PR3339.C125L: *An aerial race between a Briton and a German...*[extracts, illus.], London, 1918.

Cambridge's *Scribleriad* is written in imitation of Pope's *Dunciad.* Among its several mock epic events is a race between a German and a Briton, both equipped with artificial wings. The illustration (frequently reproduced) shows the German using modern technology—the flapping wings of Besnier, but without the harness that enabled Besnier to use leg power. Although, like Besnier, the German is essentially naked, he wears a loincloth suitable for a public ceremonial occasion before an elegantly dressed audience. He is a fine, athletic, young man. His opponent is fully naked and more rugged, to suggest more primitive origins. The Briton's wings, damaged because, like Icarus, he has flown too high, do not depend, as do those of the German, on up-to-date technology but resemble those

described in very early accounts of manned flight. Cambridge makes the comparison explicit: the Briton falls because of his excessive ambition. Having flown too high, he finds that the air will no longer support his weight. He plunges to the earth, catching the German's foot and treacherously carrying him down as he passes. To describe the Briton's fall, Cambridge translates Ovid:

> His naked arms in yielding air he shook:
> His naked arms no more support his weight,
> But fail him sinking from his airy height.
> (IV.148–149)

As compensation for his ill fortune, the German is ironically rewarded with a statue of Icarus.

Tab. VI

Boitard Fecit

Nasgigs Engagement with Harlokins General.

[Paltock, Robert] 1697–1767

The life and adventures of Peter Wilkins, a Cornish man...Taken from his own mouth, in his passage to England, from off Cape Horn in America, in the ship Hector...Illustrated with several cuts...presenting the...wings of the Glums and Gawrys...By R. S., a passenger in the Hector...London, Printed for J. Robinson and R. Dodsley, 1751.

2 v. illus. 17 cm.
First ed.
I. Title. II. Title: Peter Wilkins.
PR3615.P5p 1751
[Gamble 93]

Other copies and editions in the Gimbel collection:
PR3615.P5p 1783: another ed., London, 1783;
PR3615.P5p 1783a: another copy of the previous item;
PR3615.P5p 1784: another ed., Berwick, 1784, Gamble 93; PR3615.P5p 1828: first American ed., Boston, 1828, R-P 13; PR3615.P5p 1828a: "improved" ed. (i.e., bowdlerized and abridged), Boston, 1828; PR3615.P5p 1830: reprint of the previous item, Boston, 1830; PR3615.P5p 1832: another abridged ed., Boston, 1832; PR3615.P5p 1833: abridgement of 1828 with col. ill., Boston, 1833; PR3615.P5p 1839: reprint of an ed. originally prepared for children by Robert Dodsley, London, 1839; PR3615.P5p 1840: reprint of the abridged ed. of 1828, Boston, 1835 [i.e., 1840]; PR3615.P5p 1843: another abridged ed., Hartford, 1843; PR3615.P5p 1847: abridged ed., Boston, 1847; PR3615.P5p 1848: abridged ed., Philadelphia, 1848; PR3615.P5p 1854: abridged ed., Philadelphia, 1854; PR3615.P5p 1856: dramatized version in two acts, 22 p., 2 copies, New York, 1856?, R-P 34; PR3615.P5p 1884: reprint, with t.-p. of 1st ed., London, 1884; PR3615.P5p 1915: modern ed. (Everyman), London and New York, 1915; PR3615.P5L5 1925: modern ed., London, 1925; PR3615.P5pa: abridgement (39, [1] p.) and satire, London, [1802]; PR3615.P5pf: *Les hommes volants...*, French trans., illus., Paris, 1763, Brockett 12901.

Beginning as another Robinsonade, Paltock's book also adapts material from Swift's *Gulliver's Travels*. Remaining extremely popular throughout the eighteenth and nineteenth centuries, it was translated into several languages. Peter Wilkins finds himself in a strange subterranean world inhabited by Glums and Gawries—male and female creatures who are almost exactly like human beings except that they can fly by the use of a ribbed membrane, which grows with them as they mature and which they can detach when they desire. In vol. 1, chap. 20, Paltock gives a description of the wings and their structure so detailed as to suggest that he might have envisaged someone's trying to make a pair. Peter Wilkins lives among these people for many years and marries one of the Gawries, producing seven children. The popularity of Paltock's book owes much to the deep-seated wish, felt by many people, to fly by natural means rather than by the use of a machine. The book helped to encourage experiments with ornithopters.

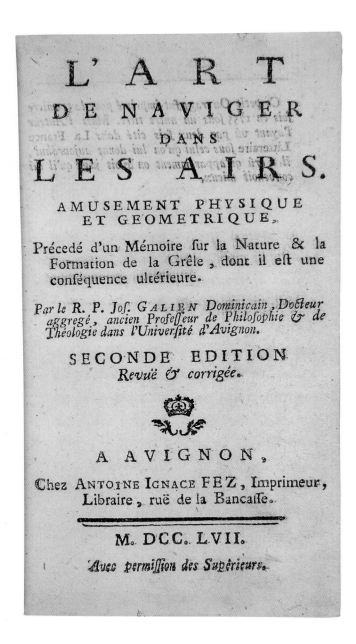

L'ART
DE NAVIGER
DANS
LES AIRS.

AMUSEMENT PHYSIQUE
ET GEOMETRIQUE.

Précedé d'un Mémoire fur la Nature & la
Formation de la Grêle, dont il eft une
conféquence ultérieure.

Par le R. P. Jof. GALIEN Dominicain, Docteur
aggregé, ancien Profeffeur de Philofophie & de
Théologie dans l'Univerfité d'Avignon.

SECONDE EDITION
Revuë & corrigée.

A AVIGNON,

Chez ANTOINE IGNACE FEZ, Imprimeur,
Libraire, ruë de la Bancaffe.

M. DCC. LVII.

Avec permiffion des Supérieurs.

Galien, Joseph, 1699?–1762

L'art de naviger dans les airs. Amusement physique et geometrique, précedé d'un Mémoire sur la nature & la formation de la grêle, dont il est une conséquence ultérieure. Par le R. P. Jos. Galien . . . 2. éd., rev. & cor. A Avignon, Chez Antoine Ignace Fez, 1757.

2 p. l., 87, [1] p. 14.5 cm.

First edition published anonymously, 1755, under title: *Mémoire touchant la nature et la formation de la grêle et des autres météores qui y ont rapport, avec une conséquence ultérieure de la possibilité de naviger dans l'air à la hauteur de la région de la grêle.*
Bookplate of Albert Tissandier.
1. Aeronautics. 2. Hail. I. Title.
TLB397.G15

Although suggestions for airships or balloons filled with "ether," or air of superfine nature found at high altitude, were made as early as the Middle Ages, Father Galien's proposed airship is probably the most grandiose ever imagined. As a spin-off from a serious discussion of the formation of hail—a recurrent problem for agriculture in the south of France—Galien describes his idea for a flying machine filled with light air, the volume of which would be the equivalent of a cube on a side of 6,000 feet. Longer and wider than the city of Avignon, the ship would be capable of carrying 4 million people, plus their baggage, together with a cargo of 58 million hundredweight. He speculates that such a ship, an order of magnitude larger than the Ark, could provide refuge from another flood or perhaps from a new danger: a world engulfed in pestilential air. The crew would manage the ship from little skiffs suspended from the sides with ropes and pulleys. Although based on sober calculations, Galien's airship is little more than a semiscientific amusement. In concept it is not, however, even semitechnological. Galien gives no thought to the engineering problems that would confront anyone trying to build such a structure from the materials he suggests: skins, cables, cords, and strong double cloth, waxed or treated with pitch. He says nothing at all about the means of propulsion, nor does he suggest how his ship might be used to alleviate the thunderstorms with which he began.

Morghen, Filippo, b. 1730?

Raccolta delle cose più notabili vedute dal cavaliere Wild Scull, e dal Sig.ʳ de la Hire nel lor famoso viaggio dalla terra alla luna che sono spiegate nella storia di detto viaggio descritta dall'istesso Wild Scull nell'ordine seguente, e disegnate dal detto Sig.ʳ de la Hire. Esposte in nove rami incisi appresso Filippo Morghen Fiorentino. Numero 1°. Rappresenta un selvaggio montato sopra un serpente alato che combatte con una fiera somigliante ad un porco spino. N. 2°. Vna nuova macchina per fendere da capo a coda le fiere. N. 3°. Le carozze che si vsano nella luna e che vanno alla vela. N. 4°. Maniera di navigare a forza di mantici praticata in quel globo. N. 5°. Maniera di trasportare le merci sopra zattere tirate da un mantice. N. 6°. Zucca che serve per barca da pescare. N. 7°. Zucche che servono d'abitazioni per garantirsi dalle fiere. N. 8°. Barca che ha per vela le ali d'un grandissimo vccello. N.9°. Abitazione dentro l'aqua, e nuova maniera di chiamare l'oche a suon di tamburo. Dedicata a. s. e. il signor Guglielmo Amilton, inviato di S. M. B.ᶜᵃ alla corte di Napoli. [Naples? *ca.* 1760].

1 p. 1., 9 pl. 40 x 54 cm.

Engraved t.-p. showing the Cavalier Wild Scull and Signor de la Hire descending from their flying machine on the moon and introducing themselves to its inhabitants.

Plates in first state.

Another issue has title: *Raccolta delle cose più notabili vedute da Giov. Wilkins erudito vescovo inglese nel suo famoso viaggio dalla terra alla luna con i disegni di animali e machine a noi incognite e dal medesimo descritte nella sua celebre Istoria, esposte in nove rami incisi appresso Filippo Morghen Fiorentino. N. 1°. Rappresenta un selvaggio montato sopra un serpente alato che combatte con una fiera somigliante ad un porco spino...N. 9°. Abitazione dentro l'acqua, e nuova maniera di chiamar l'oche a suon di tamburo. Dedicata a s. e. il signor Guglielmo Amilton, inviato di S. M. C.ʳᵉᵃ alla corte di Napoli. 1764.*
The plates have no connection with the text of John Wilkins' *Discovery of a world in the moone* (London, 1638) to which the title apparently refers.

1. Voyages, Imaginary. I. Wilkins, John, bp. of Chester, 1614–1672. The Discovery of a world in the moone. TLE1041.M86

The title announces that this is a collection of "the most noteworthy things seen by the Cavalier Wild Scull and Signor de la Hire during their famous voyage from the earth to the moon." A set of engravings without text, it is prompted in part by Bishop Wilkins. While the name "Wild Scull" suggests an imaginary adventurer, "Signor de la Hire" refers to a well-known scientist, Phillippe de la Hire (1683–1768), who did not believe that the moon was habitable. As is indicated in the catalog entry, de la Hire's name was replaced in later editions by that of the more imaginative Wilkins. The illustration on the title page shows the two adventurers shortly after their arrival on the moon, respectfully greeting the inhabitants. Their flying machine is like a low wooden house or shed equipped with a pair of wings. It may owe something of its conception to the legend of the transport of the Virgin's house to Loreto. There is no indication as to how the wings were operated. Other engravings in the set show details of life in a charming, zany, lunar world like something out of Lewis Carroll or, even, in some cases, Roald Dahl.

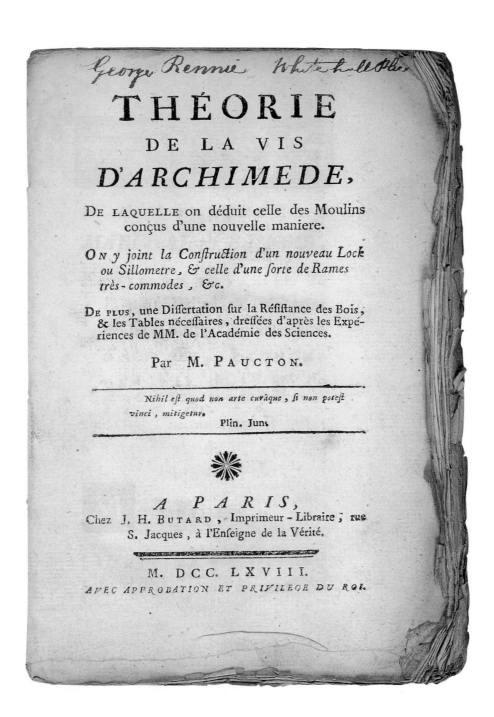

Paucton, Alexis Jean-Pierre, 1732–1798

Théorie de la vis d'Archimede, de laquelle on déduit celle des moulins conçus d'une nouvelle maniere. On y joint la construction d'un nouveau lock ou sillometre, & celle d'une sorte de rames très-commodes, &c. De plus, une dissertation sur la résistance des bois, & les tables nécessaires, dressées d'après les expériences de MM. de l'Académie des sciences. Par M. Paucton... A Paris, Chez J. H. Butard, 1768.

xx, 6 p. l., 214, [10] p. 7 fold. pl. 18 cm.
1. Archimedean screw.
TLB397.P32

At the end of this dissertation on the properties and uses of the Archimedean screw, Paucton suggests its application to the building of a helicopter (pp. 210–214). Although he protects himself from ridicule by alleging that he is writing only for amusement, it is clear that he has an entirely serious, practical idea in mind. Following much calculation based on the primitive hydro- and aerodynamic theories of his day, he states that since a man can support his own weight on his arms, he should be able to lift himself into the air by turning rotor blades fitted to a suitable chair and operated by a handle, everything being built lightly and with care to minimize friction. As the movement is simple, friction would in any case be low. The rotor blades would be sectors of a full circle. For

directional control a second, horizontal rotor should be added. When the aeronaut needed to rest, he could move a lever that would turn the blades of the upper rotor, reducing their pitch to zero and thus form a closed canopy. With this parachute above him, he would sink gently to the ground. Paucton's calculations indicated that the necessary total surface of the upper rotor blades would be 144 square feet. Paucton's book, which contains many detailed arithmetical tables but no drawings, was read by many later theorists of aviation. Illustrated variants of his design turn up frequently, some even in patents of the nineteenth century. A similar suggestion by Robert B. Taylor (1842) is discussed in Charles H. Gibbs-Smith, *Sir George Cayley's Aeronautics, 1796–1855* (London: HMSO, 1962), pp. 102–108.

Zamagna, Bernardo, 1735–1820

Bernardi Zamagnae s.j. Navis aeria et Elegiarum monobiblos. Excudebat Romae Paullus Giunchius, 1768.

xvj, 151, [1] p. 1 illus. 18.5 cm.
Engraved title vignette: tail-pieces.
"Navis aeria," a poem written in honor of F. Lana de Terzi and his airship project, describes an imaginary trip by airship to various parts of the world.
"Idyllium I–IV" p. 131–151.
1. Lana de Terzi, Francesco, 1631–1687. 2. Voyages, Imaginary. 3. Aeronautics—Poetry. I. Title: Navis aeria. II: Title: Elegiarum monobiblos.
TLE1041.Z2
[Gamble 35]

Thoroughly versed in classical literature, the Jesuit father Bernardo Zamagna celebrated the invention of his countryman and fellow priest Francesco Lana de Terzi by writing an epic poem in Latin hexameters describing an imaginary voyage around the world. In the second canto, he describes the takeoff and the airship's 24-hour circumnavigation of the globe. Although far from being a great circle, Zamagna's imaginary route is generally westward. Written in conscious imitation of

Virgil, the verses are accomplished, if far from truly Virgilian in tone and movement. Just as Virgil—and Lucretius before him—enjoyed making poetry out of technicalities, Zamagna writes at length about the structure of the flying ship and about the scientific theories that lay behind it. He is largely successful in his project of combining modern science and technology with the classical arts and in bringing the ancient epic journey not only into the modern world but into what, for him, was the future.

THE LIFE AND ASTONISHING ADVENTURES OF JOHN DANIEL,

A Smith at Royston in Hertfordshire, For a Course of Seventy Years.

CONTAINING,

The melancholy Occasion of his Travels, His Shipwreck with one Companion on a desolate Island. Their way of Life. His accidental discovery of a Woman for his Companion. Their peopling the Island.

ALSO

A Description of a most surprising Eagle, invented by his Son Jacob, on which he flew to the Moon, with some Account of its Inhabitants. His return, and accidental Fall into the Habitation of a Sea Monster, with whom he lived two Years. His further Excursions in Search of England. His Residence in Lapland, and Travels to Norway, from whence he arrived at Aldborough, and further Transactions till his Death, in 1711. Aged 97.

The SECOND EDITION.

LONDON:
PRINTED for T. PARKER, at No. 17, West - Smithfield.

M. DCC. LXX.

Daniel, John, of Royston [pseud.]

*The life and astonishing adventures of John Daniel... containing the melancholy occasion of his travels... also a description of a most surprising eagle...on which he flew to the moon...*2nd ed. London: Printed for T. Parker, 1770.

319 p. illus. 17 cm.
Attributed to Ralph Morris.
1. Morris, Ralph. II. Title.
TLE1041.D17 1770

Other copies and editions in the Gimbel collection: TLE1041.D17: reprint of the 1751 ed., London, 1926, Gamble 88; TLE1041.D17 1848: *Flying and no failure! or, Aerial transit accomplished more than a century ago...*, reprint of 1751 ed., Totham, 1848, Gamble 87.

First published in 1751, a rich year for aeronautical literature, this entirely fictional account of a journey to the moon acts as a vehicle for a serious (if impractical) suggestion for a real flying machine, which is illustrated and described in detail. The concept is entirely original for its period. The machine is a flapper of generally rectangular shape operated by the vigorous working of a handle like that of a water pump. Its frame is built mostly of iron "thin, light, and taper," and of "several pieces of wood." A set of levers and hinges, carefully thought-out, allows the ribs of the parasol-like structure to be simultaneously bent downward. After the downstroke on the handle is released, the ribs automatically bend back to the horizontal. The propulsive power thus comes from jet action like that of a jellyfish. Directional control is achieved by variations in the center of gravity, the flier standing on the appropriate side to cant the machine. The total lifting surface is of the order of 500 square feet. The idea for the flying machine was lampooned in 1769, immediately before this reprint, by an anonymous writer who, not having read the original, misunderstood the illustration. His version led many to believe that the machine stayed aloft because air was pumped from above to below.

THE

PRINCE

OF

ABISSINIA.

A TALE.

THE FIFTH EDITION.

LONDON:

PRINTED FOR W. STRAHAN, J. DODSLEY,
AND E. JOHNSTON.

MDCCLXXV.

Johnson, Samuel, 1709–1784

The Prince of Abissinia, a tale. 5th ed. London: Printed
for W. Strahan, J. Dodsley, and E. Johnston, 1775.

viii, 304 p. 17 cm.
I. Title.

PR3529.A1 1775

Other copies and editions in the Gimbel collection:
PR3529.A1 1803: new ed., London, 1803; PR3529.A1
1810: new ed., Frederick-Town [Md.], 1810;
PR3529.A1 1812: new ed., London, 1812; PR3529.A1
1819: new ed., illus., London, 1819; PR3529.A1 1826:
new ed., Boston, 1826; PR3529.A1 1829: new ed.,
Chiswick, 1829; PR3529.A1 1831: new ed., Boston, 1831;
PR3529.A1 1844: new ed., Boston, 1844; PR3529.A1
1850: new ed., Hartford [Conn.], 1850; PR3529.A1
1864: new ed., New York, 1864; PR3529.A1 1875: new
ed., Philadelphia, 1875; PR3529.F8 1832: the English
text with a French translation, English and French
on facing pages, Paris, 1832.

First published in 1759, this popular tale went
through many editions. It is usually referred
to as *Rasselas,* the name of the prince of the
tale. The sixth chapter consists of a "Dissertation on the Art of Flying," a satirical discussion between the prince and a mechanic who
believes he has invented wings for human
beings. Rasselas takes a special interest
because he wishes to escape from a "Happy
Valley," where life is idyllic but bland, to
encounter a more bracing world. Wings will
not, however, be of service to him. At the end
of the chapter the mechanic "appeared
furnished for flight on a little promontory: he
waved his pinions a while to gather air, then
leaped from his stand, and in an instant
dropped into the lake. His wings, which were

of no use in the air, sustained him in the
water, and the prince drew him to land, half
dead with terrour and vexation" (p. 43).
Deeply pessimistic about all human endeavor,
Johnson was probably responding to the
many books about imaginary flight published
a few years earlier; he may have read some of
the many sarcastic accounts of the flight
undertaken in Paris by the Marquis de
Bacqueville. The idea that before takeoff a
flier might need to "gather air" in the wings
was frequently mentioned. By waving the
feathers back and forth for a time, the flier
would gather air in the interstices. Because air
was thought to be naturally "light," this action
would give the wings added buoyancy.

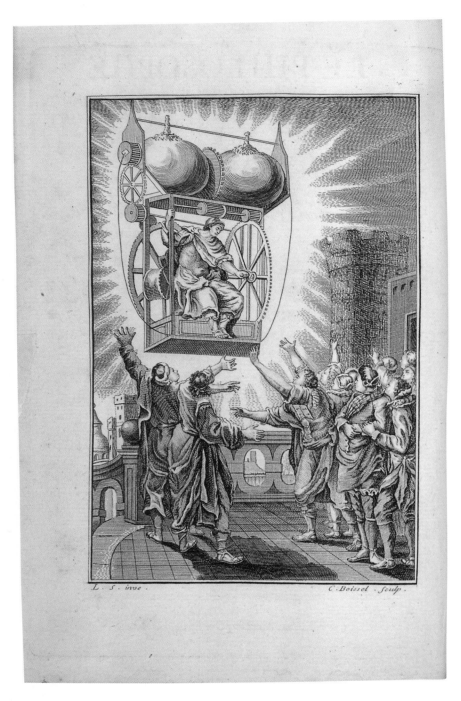

L. S. *inve*.   C. Boissel *sculp*.

[La Follie, Louis Guillaume de] 1733?–1780

Le philosophe sans prétention, ou L'homme rare.
Ouvrage physique, chymique, politique et moral, dédié
aux savans. Par M. D. L. F. A Paris, Chez Clousier, 1775.

349, [1] p. front. 19.5 cm.
Engraved title vignette, frontispiece, and head-piece.
Incomplete: p. 337–338 wanting.
1. Physics—Early works to 1800. 2. Chemistry—
    Early works to 1800. I. Title.
Q157.L16
Brockett 4686

This work, another that explores flight in unusual ways, belongs both to science fiction and to the class of imaginary voyages that brings an exotic traveler to us rather than sending a familiar hero to strange lands. The machine shown in the illustration is flown by an inhabitant of the planet Mercury. Written by a practicing chemist, the book explores the possibilities of flight by the use of static electricity. Having expected to see a flying chariot with wings, the narrator is surprised to find a strange and apparently unaerial piece of scientific machinery. Two glass globes each 3 feet in diameter are held on wooden members that are themselves covered with glass plates. Springs between the wooden members allow the globes to turn. The platform at the base is rubbed with camphor and covered with gold leaf. Metal wires surround the whole thing, which thus suggests some kind of primitive dynamo. The

spinning globes produce a powerful beam of light shining in a downward direction. The light causes the machine to rise by reducing the air pressure above it, so that it can be made to travel in any direction at the pilot's discretion. The description of the mechanism and its effects, which occupies only a small part of the book near its beginning, is a piece of technobabble surpassing the propositions of the Projectors in *Gulliver's Travels*, Book III. La Follie's analysis of the relationship of air, fire, and static electricity, presented in a tone of total seriousness, reads like a forerunner of a speech from *Dr. Who*. The account of scientific discussions in the Mercurian academy is a thinly disguised parody of intellectual life in the French Academy and the Royal Society.

Victorin prenant son vol.

[Restif de la Bretonne, Nicole Edme]
1734–1806

*La Découverte australe par un Homme-volant, ou
Le Dédale français; Nouvelle très-philosophique:
suivie de la Lettre d'un Singe, &c. . .* Imprimé à
Leïpsick: Et se trouve à Paris, [1781].

4v. fronts. (v. 1, 2, 3) pl. (1 fold.) 16.5 cm.

Title vignette.

Half-title, prefixed to v.1: *Oeuvres posthumes de
N. ******. Oeuvre S. ^de, La découverte australe,
ou Les Antipodes: avec une estampe à chaque
Fait principal,* 1781.

Paged continuously throughout the first, second,
and part of the third volume (624 p.) where a
new pagination begins, continuing through
the fourth volume (422 p.).

Illustrated by Binet? *Cf.* Cober, *Guide de l'amateur
de livres à gravures du XVIIIᵉ siècle* (1886), p. 503.

"Ouvrages du même auteur, dont on trouve des
exemplaires à Paris, chés la veuve Duchêne...";
2 p. at end.

Imperfect; plate to follow p. 357 (v. 2) and list of
plates and contents (at end of v. 4) are wanting.

Book-plate (in v. 1): Ex libris Gaston Tissandier.

1. Voyages, Imaginary. I. Binet, Louis, 1744–*ca.*
1800, supposed illus.

II. Title. III. Title: Homme volant.

PQ2025.D4

Brockett 10313

Other copies and editions in the Gimbel collection:
PQ2025.D4 1818: *Avventure e viaggi di un uomo
volante. Traduzione dal Francese,* 2 v., Milano, 1818.

Restif's long novel brings together two themes
often connected in the visual arts: flight and
love. The hero longs to pay court to a girl whose
social station is too far above his own to permit
him to approach her. He decides to carry her off
by force to a place inaccessible except by flight.
For some years he studies the flying action of
every winged creature, the details of which
Restif explores in leisurely fashion. Like many
aspiring birdmen before him, including
Leonardo, the hero makes trials in secret. He
feels dizzy during his first successful flight but
rapidly accommodates to the experience. When
he is satisfied with his equipment, he prepares a
small settlement on a mountaintop, sowing
seeds for a farm and carrying off the assistants
he will need in order to lead a civilized life there:
a group of astonished servants and a priest. The
basket in the illustration is laden with some of
his provisions. Finally he flies away with his
beloved, who is content to be with him. There
follows a long series of adventures, including
scenes in the Antipodes of the half-title. The
hero's flying machine consists of large wings
made of oiled boxwood, leather, silken cords,
and a small quantity of steel, operated by both
arm and leg power. The parasol-like structure
over the head can be rapidly opened and closed
to provide lift and propulsion in a way similar to
that described a generation earlier in the flying
machine of Ralph Morris. As in the work
attributed to Morris, a serious attempt to
suggest a practical means of flight is given a
fictional setting. The book was long popular,
especially with female readers.

L'Expérience faite à Versaille, en présence de leurs Majestés et de la Famille Royale,
par M. Montgolfier, le 19. Sept. 1783.
La Machine Aérostatique avoit 57. Pieds de haut, sur 41. de Diamètre.

DESCRIPTION
DES EXPÉRIENCES
DE LA MACHINE
AÉROSTATIQUE
DE MM. DE MONTGOLFIER,
Et de celles auxquelles cètte découverte a donné lieu ;
SUIVIE

DE RECHERCHES sur la hauteur à laquelle est parvenu
le Ballon du Champ-de-Mars ; sur la route qu'il a tenue ;
sur les différens degrés de pesanteur de l'air dans les couches
de l'atmosphère ;

D'UN MÉMOIRE sur le gaz inflammable & sur celui qu'ont
employé MM. de Montgolfier ; sur l'art de faire les Machines
aérostatiques, de les couper, de les remplir, & sur la manière
de dissoudre la gomme élastique, &c. &c. ;

D'UNE LETTRE sur les moyens de diriger ces Machines,
& sur les différens usages auxquels elles peuvent être em-
ployées.

OUVRAGE orné de neuf planches en taille-douce, représentant les diverses Machines qui ont été construites jusqu'à
ce jour, particulièrement celle de Versailles, & celle dans
laquelle des hommes ont été enlevés jusqu'à la hauteur de
324 pieds, &c. &c.

Par M. FAUJAS DE SAINT-FOND.

A PARIS,
Chez CUCHET, rue & hôtel Serpente.

M. DCC. LXXXIII.
Avec Approbation & Privilège du Roi.

Faujas de Saint-Fond, Barthélemy, 1741–1819

*Description des expériences de la machine aérostatique
de MM. de Montgolfier, et de celles auxquelles cette
découverte a donné lieu. Suivie de recherches sur la
hauteur à laquelle est parvenu le ballon du Champ-de-
Mars. . . A Paris, Chez Cuchet, 1783–1784.*

2 v. illus. 20 cm.
Vol. 2 has title: *Première suite de la Description des
expériences aérostatiques.*
1. Balloons, 2. Montgolfier, Joseph, 1740–1810.
3. Montgolfier, Étienne, 1745–1799.
TLB273.F25
Brockett 4376, 4378; Gamble 563
Other copies and editions in the Gimbel collection:
TLB273.F25 1784: 2nd ed., Paris, 1784, Brockett 4377;
TLB273.F25 1784a: another ed., Bruxelles, 1784;
TLB273.F25 1784d: *Beschryving der proefneemingen...,*
Dutch trans. by Martinus Houttuyn, Amsterdam,
1784, Brockett 4375; TLB273.F25 1784d2: *Vervolg
der proefneemingen...,* [=continuation of the
experiments..., preceded by *Beschryving der
proefneemingen...*], Dutch trans. by Martinus
Houttuyn, Amsterdam, 1784; TLB273.F25 1784g:
Beschreibung der Versuche..., German trans.,

Leipzig, 1784–1785, Brockett 4374; TLB273.F25
1784g2: *Der Herren Stephan und Joseph Montgolfier
Versuche...,* 7 p., 8 pl., extract by C. G. von Murr,
Nürnberg, 1784; TLB273.F25 1784i: *Descrizione delle
esperienze...,* Italian trans., Venezia, 1784.

A long period of preparation preceded the first
manned flight in a free balloon, which took
place on November 21, 1783. Among the many
enthusiasts keen to assist the experimenters
was Faujas de Saint-Fond, a geologist then in
his early forties. An ebullient and energetic
man, he organized a subscription on behalf of
the inventor of the hydrogen balloon, Jacques
Alexandre César Charles — although
characteristically without first asking for
Charles' agreement—and helped with the work
that culminated in the first unmanned flight.
He was equally enthusiastic about the
subsequent successes of the Montgolfier
brothers and wrote this very circumstantial

account of the events throughout the period.
Each of the flights is described in detail, with
tables of weights, dimensions, and so on. The
text is accompanied by excellent engravings
showing the apparatus used both for hydrogen
and for hot-air balloons. The illustration here
shows the balloon in which a sheep, a cock,
and a duck were flown during the experiment
with a montgolfière, 57 feet high and 41 feet in
diameter, at Versailles in the presence of Louis
XVI and his entourage, September 19, 1783.
After the landing the animals were found to be
in good shape, although half an hour before
takeoff the sheep had kicked and damaged the
cock's right wing, an accident that some
reports falsely attributed to the rigors of the
flight. Faujas complains about the sensational
and inaccurate accounts that circulated after
each experiment.

REPRÉSENTATION DU GLOBE AÉROSTATIQUE
QUI S'EST ÉLEVÉ DE DESSUS L'UN DES BASSINS DU JARDIN ROYAL DES THUILLERIES
Le 1.er Décembre 1783. a 1. heure 40. min.tes

Cette Machine merveilleuse montée par M.M. Charles, et Robert le jeune, s'étant élevée majestueusement
à une hauteur considérable, a pris sa direction au Nord-Ouest, et l'on remarque la suite, et la fin de son
voyage aérien, dans le Récit de M. Charles prononcé à l'Ouverture de son Cours de Physique, qui ac-
compagne cette Estampe.

Charles, Jacques Alexandre César, 1746–1823

Représentation du globe aérostatique qui s'est élevé de dessus l'un des bassins du jardin royal des Thuilleries le 1er. décembre 1783, à 1. heure 40. min.tes. Avec le récit de son voyage aérien...[Paris, 1783?].

xv p. 2 fold. col. pl. 26 x 20 cm.
Author's name appears in note on t.-p.: the ascension was undertaken by the author and M. N. Robert.
French and Spanish in parallel columns.
"Article du Journal de Paris du 13 & 14 décembre 1783."
1. Balloon ascensions. 2. Robert, M. N. I. Title.
TLB276.C4R42

Other copies and editions in the Gimbel collection: TLB276.C4R42a: French and Italian in parallel columns, [Venezia, 1783].

Some three months after the first ascent of a hydrogen balloon, Charles and his assistants, A. J. and M. N. Robert (brothers who developed the gas-producing apparatus), announced a free manned flight to rival that of the montgolfière that had taken place on November 21, 1783. After some delay the flight was successfully made before a huge crowd on December 1, 1783. Charles, a scientist and the inventor of the hydrogen balloon, was accompanied by one of the Robert brothers. The strong netting over the

upper half of the balloon was intended to prevent its bursting as it rose into the thinner atmosphere. After a first landing, some 24 miles from Paris, Robert was left behind while Charles continued alone, rising to an altitude of 9,000 feet and making observations as he did so. The first balloon ascents coincided with, and were of course to a large extent the consequences of, the intense interest in science—and especially in chemistry—which characterized the final decades of the eighteenth century.

PREMIERE EXPÉRIENCE
DE
LA MONTGOLFIÉRE
CONSTRUITE PAR ORDRE DU ROI,

Lancée en présence de Leurs Majestés, de la Famille
Royale, et de Monsieur le COMTE D'HAGA,

Par M. PILATRE DE ROZIER, Pensionnaire du Roi, Intendant des Cabinets
de Physique, de Chimie, d'Histoire Naturelle de MONSIEUR Frère du Roi,
Secrétaire du Cabinet de MADAME, membre de plusieurs Académies nationales
& étrangères ; Chef du premier Musée autorisé par le Gouvernement, sous la
protection de MONSIEUR & de MADAME, &c. &c.

Le 23 Juin 1774.

IMPRIMÉ AUX FRAIS DU GOUVERNEMENT;

Et se distribue au Musée.

A PARIS,
DE L'IMPRIMERIE DE MONSIEUR.
M. DCC. LXXXIV.

Pilâtre de Rozier, Jean-François, 1754–1785
*Premiere expérience de la Montgolfiére construite par
ordre du roi, lancée en présence de Leurs Majestés...
par M. Pilatre de Rozier...le 23 juin 1774. Imprimé aux
frais du gouvernement...*
A Paris, De l'imprimerie de Monsieur, 1784.

   20 p. 26 cm.
   Head-piece.
   Name originally: Jean-François Pilastre
     Desroziers.
   1. Balloon ascensions. I. Title.
   TLB276.P6A34
   Brockett 9754

**Other copies and editions in the Gimbel
collection:** TLB276.P6A34 1784: 2nd ed., with date
on t.-p. corrected, Paris, 1784.

A young man in his twenties, with some
scientific experience, Pilâtre de Rozier was
keen to be involved in the early balloon
experiments and offered his services. Apart
from the likelihood that Jacques-Étienne
Montgolfier allowed himself to be raised
some days before him, Pilâtre was the first to
be lifted free of the earth in a tethered
balloon. On November 21, 1783, he was
accompanied by the Marquis d'Arlandes on
the first demonstration of free flight. In this
account of a flight in the following year,
Pilâtre, who was accompanied by the chemist
Joseph-Louis Proust (1754–1826), writes almost
ecstatically, focusing especially on the peace
experienced by those suspended beneath a

free balloon: "it seemed, from the tranquillity
with which we sailed, that we were carried
along by the diurnal rotation of the earth." By
his own account, they reached an altitude of
11,732 feet. Twenty minutes after landing, the
sense of peace was dissipated when strong
winds pushed the balloon over, causing the
brazier to damage it.

Pilâtre subsequently made many more
flights before the first air crash on June 15, 1785,
when he and a companion fell to their deaths
from a height of about 1 mile in a burning
balloon. Their vehicle on that occasion was
inherently dangerous: a compound structure
consisting of a montgolfière with a hydrogen
balloon coupled above it.

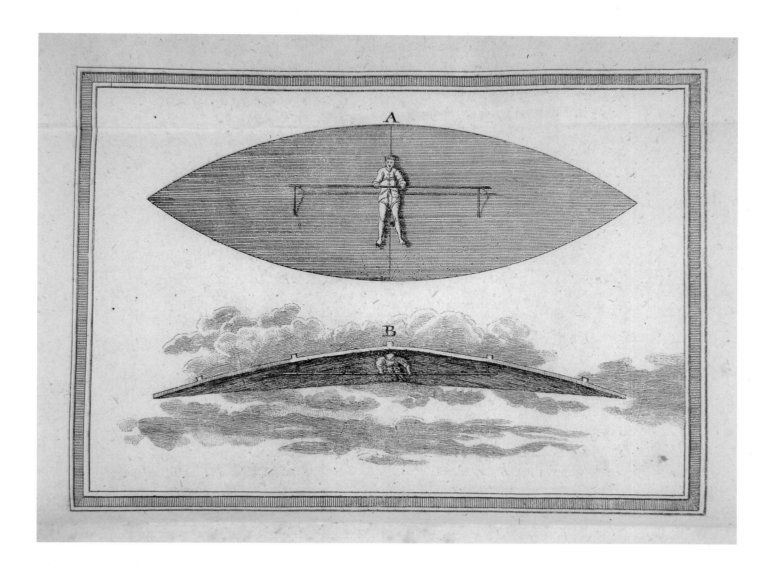

Meerwein, Karl Friedrich, 1737–1810

L'art de voler à la manière des oiseaux, par Charles Frédéric Meerwein...A Basle, chez J. J. Thourneysen, fils, 1784.

48 p. 2 fold. pl. 18.5 cm.

First published in German.

"Lettre de m. de G*** à m. Meerwein": p. 36–44.

"Response à cette lettre, sous le nom de m. Merrwein *[sic], par un ennemi juré des voleurs*": p. 45–48.

1. Ornithopters. I. Title.

TLD624.M49 1784

Brockett 8311

Other copies and editions in the Gimbel collection:
TLD624.M49 1784: a second copy, wanting t.-p.;
TLD624.M49 1785: 2nd French edition, Basle, 1785;
TLD624.M49 1785: a second copy.

Meerwein, who lived in a small town in western Germany, began experiments with ornithopters in 1781. He published his suggestions in a series of articles, in German, in January 1783. An expanded and improved version, which was widely read, was published as a book in 1784. This French translation, published in the same year, is a modified version of the German original with the addition of two facetious letters. A Portuguese translation appeared in 1812. The span of Meerwein's ornithopter wing is 30 feet, and the maximum cord 10 feet. The mechanism is a simple up-and-down flapper operated by pushing down on the rod which the pilot is shown holding. The fully raised wings lie at an anhedral angle of about 9°. Although the diagram does not show it, Meerwein specifies

a fan-shaped tail: between the legs of a specially made pair of trousers reaching to below the feet is to be sewn a piece of cloth sufficiently wide to allow the legs to be spread. Meerwein envisages the use of this tail not for stability but as an aid to directional control—a common belief about the primary function of a bird's tail. There is no undercarriage, and the only provision for the pilot's safety and comfort is a face mask to enable him to breathe while speeding through the air. Together with the practical attempts at flight being made in France at the same time by Jean-Pierre François Blanchard (*cf.* below, Blanchard, *An exact and authentic narrative*, 1784) this exercise in primitive aeronautics helped to encourage other experiments, both serious and facetious.

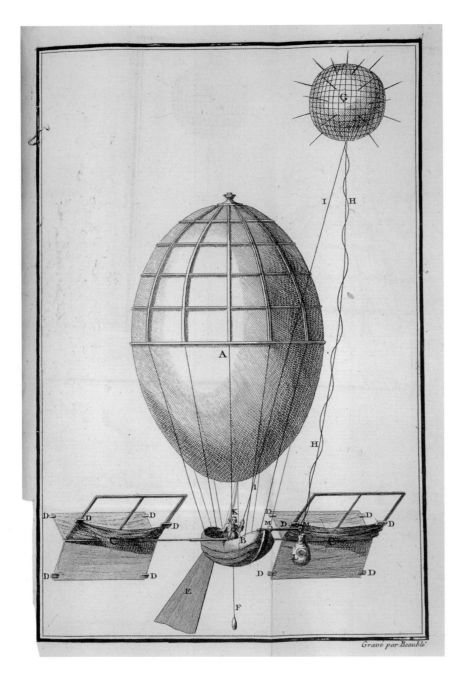

Gravé par Beaublé

Bourgeois, David

Recherches sur l'art de voler, depuis la plus haute antiquité jusqu'à ce jour; pour servir de supplément à la Description des expériences aérostatiques de M. Faujas de Saint-Fond. Par M. David Bourgeois... A Paris, Chez Cuchet, 1784.

viii, 143, [1] p. 20.5 cm.

1. Aeronautics—Hist. 2. Balloons.

TLB273.D44 no. 1

Other copies and editions in the Gimbel collection:

Two other identical copies, TLB398.B77; TLB155.A247 no. 1

Brockett 2071

One of the scores of books published in the year or two following the successful balloon flights of 1783, this work counts as one of the earliest extended attempts to write a history of aviation. Although Bourgeois' "researches" are anything but rigorous, he summarizes a substantial body of material about early flying stories, beginning with Abaris, continuing with other classical and mythological figures, including Daedalus and Archytas, and summarizing the theories of early scientists. In all, he discusses twenty-eight writers and experimenters, including Bacon,

Albert of Saxony, Leonardo, della Porta, Cyrano, Kircher, Lana, Gusmão, and Galien. In the middle of the book, Bourgeois passes on to the principles of aerostation, the achievement of a practical balloon, and the problem of directional control. In his concluding pages he quotes passages from Lana and from Giovanni Alfonso Borelli, who, in his *De motu animalium* (2 v., 1680–1681, see Appendix), had demonstrated the impossibility of flying by the use of human muscle power alone.

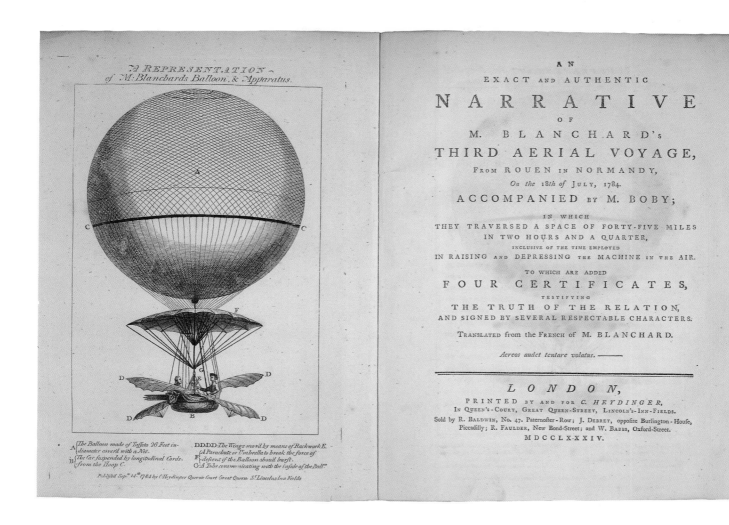

A REPRESENTATION of M: Blanchards Balloon, & Apparatus.

A [The Balloon made of Taffeta 26 Feet in diameter cover'd with a Net.
B [The Car suspended by longitudinal Cords from the Hoop C.
DDDD. The Wings mov'd by means of Rackwork E.
F [A Parachute or Umbrella to break the force of descent if the Balloon should burst.
G A Tube communicating with the inside of the Ball"

Published Sep.r 14th 1784 by C Heydinger Queens Court Great Queen S.t Lincolns Inn Fields

AN

EXACT AND AUTHENTIC

NARRATIVE

OF

M. BLANCHARD's

THIRD AERIAL VOYAGE,

FROM ROUEN IN NORMANDY,

On the 18th of JULY, 1784.

ACCOMPANIED BY M. BOBY;

IN WHICH

THEY TRAVERSED A SPACE OF FORTY-FIVE MILES
IN TWO HOURS AND A QUARTER,

INCLUSIVE OF THE TIME EMPLOYED

IN RAISING AND DEPRESSING THE MACHINE IN THE AIR.

TO WHICH ARE ADDED

FOUR CERTIFICATES,

TESTIFYING

THE TRUTH OF THE RELATION,
AND SIGNED BY SEVERAL RESPECTABLE CHARACTERS.

TRANSLATED from the FRENCH of M. BLANCHARD.

Aereos audet tentare volatus.

LONDON,

PRINTED BY AND FOR C. HEYDINGER,
IN QUEEN'S-COURT, GREAT QUEEN-STREET, LINCOLN'S-INN-FIELDS.
Sold by R. BALDWIN, No. 47. Paternoster-Row; J. DEBRET, opposite Burlington-House,
Piccadilly; R. FAULDER, New Bond-Street; and W. BABBS, Oxford-Street.
MDCCLXXXIV.

Blanchard, Jean-Pierre, 1753–1809

An exact and authentic narrative of M. Blanchard's third aerial voyage, from Rouen in Normandy, on the 18th of July, 1784. Accompanied by M. Boby; in which they traversed a space of forty-five miles in two hours and a quarter, inclusive of the time employed in raising and depressing the machine in the air. To which are added four certificates, testifying the truth of the relation, and signed by several respectable characters. Translated from the French of M. Blanchard...London, Printed by and for C. Heydinger, 1784.

2 p. l., [iii]–viii, 17 p. front. 28 x 22.5 cm.
TLB276.B6A15

1. Balloon ascensions.

Other related books in the Gimbel collection:
The collection also holds accounts of his
fourth voyage (English: TLB276.B6A25),
fifteenth voyage (French: TLB276.B6A258),
sixteenth voyage (French: TLB276.B6A26),
forty-fifth voyage (English: TLB276.B6A29 1793,
with two later copies: photocopy
TLB276.B6A29; reprint TLB276.B6A29 1918),
forty-fifth voyage (French: TLB276.B6A29f).
For the forty-fifth voyage, see below,
Blanchard, *Journal*, 1793.

Brockett 1888; Gamble 468

Born on July 4, 1753, in Normandy, Blanchard (who became a skilled mechanic) was a man of relatively humble birth and an egotist of almost ruthless determination. In the early 1780s he made several attempts to build heavier-than-air machines, one of which had four wings, fore and aft, for lift, with another four, intended to provide forward propulsion, placed at the center. Despite failures, he persisted for some time before allying himself with the balloon experimenters. In 1784 he built a hydrogen balloon which, for safety, had a parachute placed under the bag on the top of the rigging and a pair of double-ended paddles worked by a treadle mechanism. Just before the launch, on March 2, 1784, an unfortunate quarrel led to Blanchard's being wounded in the hand; at the same time the

balloon and some of its equipment were damaged. Blanchard nevertheless undertook the flight, reaching an altitude of something like 12,500 feet. In his account of his third flight, on July 18, 1784, he alleges that he was able to exercise some control over the balloon by the use of the paddles. In the years that followed, he made a precarious living from demonstrations of balloon flights, including one across the English Channel and others in the United States. In 1809 he died—remarkably enough, of natural causes—having made either 59 or 60 flights. His widow then took over, making 67 flights in all before falling to her death after having set fire to her balloon by indulging her showman's habit of setting off fireworks while aloft.

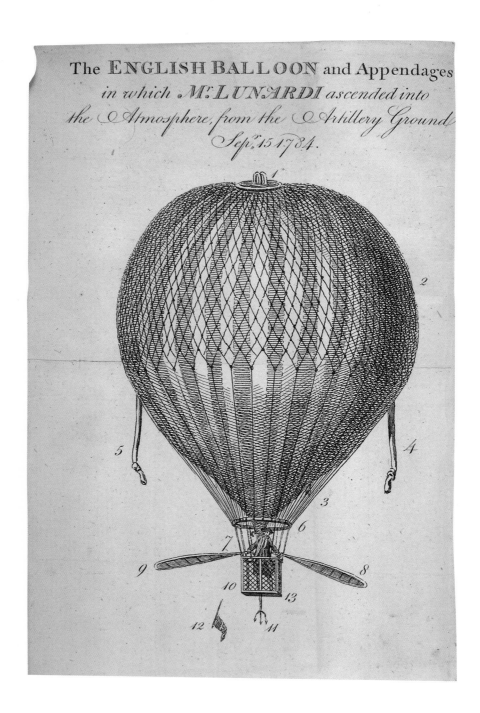

The ENGLISH BALLOON and Appendages in which Mr. LUNARDI ascended into the Atmosphere, from the Artillery Ground Sep.r 15 1784.

Lunardi, Vincent, 1759–1796

An account of the first aërial voyage in England, in a series of letters to his guardian, Chevalier Gherardo Compagni, written under the impressions of the various events that affected the undertaking, by Vincent Lunardi...London, Printed for the author, sold...by J. Bell [etc.], 1784.

2 p. l., 66, [1] p. front. (port.) fold. pl. 21.5 cm.

1. Balloon ascensions.

TLB276.L8A16

Brockett 7816; Gamble 695

Other copies and editions in the Gimbel collection:
TLB276.L8A16 1784: 2nd ed., London, 1784.

An attaché of the Neapolitan embassy in London, Lunardi had the temperament of a showman. Determined to arrange the first real balloon ascent to take place in England, he constructed a hydrogen balloon, which he first exposed to view in the Strand to an estimated attendance of 20,000 visitors. On the afternoon of September 15, 1784, in the presence of George III, his Prime Minister William Pitt, the Younger, and a huge crowd, he flew from the Artillery Ground. (The best seats cost 5 shillings.) Written in the form of an epistolary novel, consisting of a series of letters to his guardian, his book provides a vivid account of the day-to-day difficulties he encountered in bringing his project to fruition. He had intended to fly in the company of another aeronaut, George Biggin, but the impatience of the crowd caused him to take off when the balloon had been sufficiently filled with gas to allow only one man to rise: "hesitation and delay, would have been construed into guilt" (p. 30). He did, however, take with him a pigeon (which escaped), a dog, and a cat. As is shown in the illustration, the balloon, 33 feet in diameter, was (pointlessly) equipped with a pair of oars one of which almost immediately broke and fell off, narrowly missing a spectator. Although the flight had no special technological significance, it contributed greatly to public sympathy for such exploits. In his account, Lunardi writes amusingly, if also with some edge, about the volatile reactions of the public and of the officials with whom he had to deal. Once success was evident, the flight was enthusiastically received and commemorated in a flood of verse, pamphlets, and decorated ceramic ware.

Plate II.

Cavallo, Tiberius, 1749–1809

The history and practice of aerostation. By Tiberius Cavallo, F. R. S. London, Printed for the author and sold by C. Dilly [etc.], 1785.

viii, 326, [7] p. 2 fold. pl. 21.5 cm.

1. Aeronautics—Hist.

TLB273.C16

Brockett 2610; Gamble 499

Other copies and editions in the Gimbel collection:
TLB273.C16 1786: *Histoire et pratique de l'aérostation...*, French trans., Paris, 1786.

An Anglo-Italian electrician and mathematician, Cavallo was born in Naples but came to England in 1771. He wrote several scientific treatises, mainly related to electricity and gas. A practical man, Cavallo experimented with the most suitable envelopes for balloons. He was among the first to make soap bubbles rise by filling them with hydrogen. Cavallo's history focuses almost exclusively on recent events. Of the twenty-three chapters in his book, all but the first part of Chapter 1 treat the history of ballooning during the two or three years following the experiments of Charles and the Montgolfiers. Although brief,

his remarks on the thoughts and achievements of earlier centuries are in general well judged. He considers, but rejects the notion that the dove of Archytas might have been filled with "inflammable air" (hydrogen). If such a thing had been built, he says, it must have been so vast that it could hardly have passed into oblivion. In his summary of later commentators and experimenters, he makes his prejudices plain by dismissing the value of anything to do with heavier-than-air flight. The only earlier writer whom he respects, despite the impracticality of his proposal, is Lana.

SIC ITUR AD ASTRA.

45.ᵗʰ Ascention and the first made in America January 9.ᵗʰ 1793. at Philadelphia 39° 56′. N. Latitude by Mʳ. I. P. Blanchard.

45.ᵉ ascension et la premiere faite en Amerique Le 9 Janvier 1793 a Philadelphie. 39° 56′ Latitude N. par Mʳ. I. P. Blanchard.

[Blanchard, Jean-Pierre] 1753–1809

Journal of my forty-fifth ascension, being the first performed in America, on the ninth of January, 1793... Philadelphia, Printed by Charles Cist, 1793.

27 p. front. 21 cm.
Dedicated to George Washington. Signed: Blanchard.
1. Balloon ascensions. 1. Title.
TLB276.B6A29 1793
Brockett 1897; Gamble 470; R-P 5

Other copies and editions in the Gimbel collection: TLB276.B6A29f: *Journal de ma quarante-cinquieme ascension, la premiere faite en Amérique, le 9. janvier, 1793...,* Philadelphie, de l'imprimerie de Charles Cist, 1793, 27 p. front. 20 cm. R-P 4. This is the very rare French edition published by the same printer in the same year. As Blanchard spoke no English, it is presumably the original text. See also above, Blanchard, *An exact and authentic narrative...,* 1784.

Prompted mainly by a desire to find a new audience for his well-organized "balloon show," Blanchard decided, in December 1792, to try his luck in the United States, which, "so interesting by its situation, offered to my emulation an attraction which I could not resist." His first flight was an immediate popular success. On January 9, 1793, using a hydrogen balloon, he flew from the jail in Philadelphia—a choice of site dictated largely

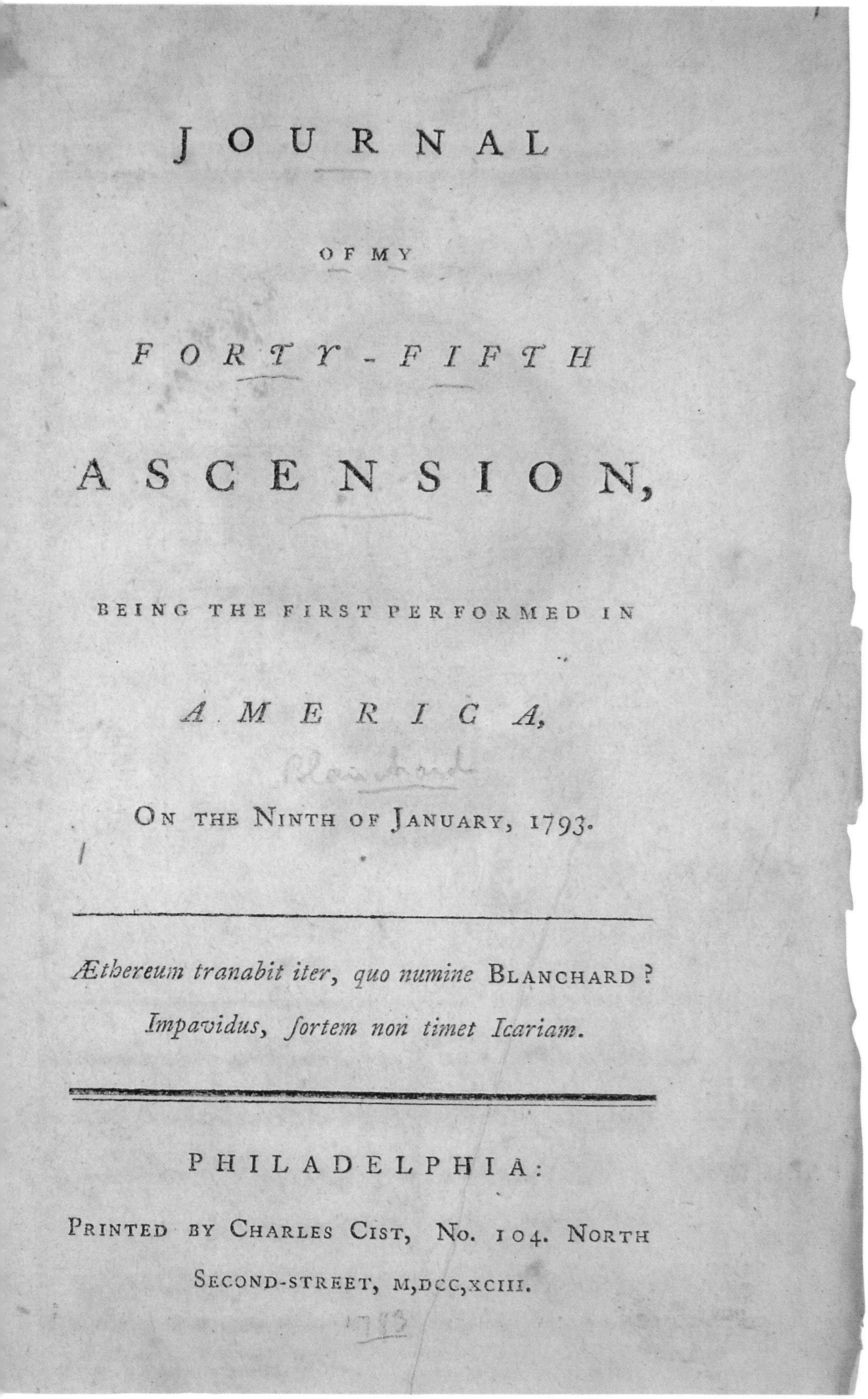

J O U R N A L

OF MY

F O R T Y - F I F T H

A S C E N S I O N,

BEING THE FIRST PERFORMED IN

A M E R I C A,

ON THE NINTH OF JANUARY, 1793.

Æthereum tranabit iter, quo numine BLANCHARD?

Impavidus, fortem non timet Icariam.

PHILADELPHIA:

PRINTED BY CHARLES CIST, No. 104. NORTH

SECOND-STREET, M,DCC,XCIII.

---

by practical considerations, though not without political implications. The ascent was watched by George Washington and a large number of other notable individuals. Blanchard reports that on the way he encountered and frightened a flock of birds and that when he had reached his maximum altitude (a little over a mile), a small black dog which a friend had entrusted to him as a companion showed signs of airsickness. He bottled samples of air and checked his own pulse rate (which had risen from an already high 84 to 92). He ate a little biscuit, drank a little wine, and prepared to descend. After the landing a frightened local assisted him—once Blanchard had persuaded him to try some of his wine—and was soon joined by others. By Blanchard's reckoning, this ascent was his forty-fifth, which he described in an almost euphoric manner. Although it made him famous in America, the flight was a financial disaster. He stayed on for another five years but with no greater success and in 1798 returned to France, saying that the visit had ruined him.

LA MINERVE *vaisseau aërien destiné aux découvertes par le professeur Robertson*
Die Minerva, ein Luftschiff welches durch Professor Robertson zu einer Entdeckung bestimt ist.
man sehe die Erklärung nach.

Robertson, Étienne Gaspard, 1763-1837

*La Minerve, vaisseau aërien destiné aux découvertes,
et proposé à toutes les académies de l'Europe; par le
physicien Robertson...2. éd., rev. et cor.* Vienne, De
l'imprimerie de S. V. Degen, 1804; réimprimé à
Paris, chez Hocquet, 1820.

iv, [5]–36 p. pl. (1 fold.) 20.5 cm.

"Ex libris Gaston Tissandier."

1. Balloons. I. Title.

TLD932.R65

Brockett 1042; Gamble 781

Related holding in the Gimbel collection:

TLB276.R64A24: *Extrait du rapport fait à
l'Académie des Sciences de Saint-Petersbourg, par
M. Robertson, de son voyage aérostatique avec M.
Sacharoff,* [n.p.], 1804]. Extract from *Annales de
Chimie,* v. 52, [121]-142.

This remarkable design for a vast airship is a
spin-off from the early interest in the
potential value of balloons for scientific
investigation. In 1803 the Saint Petersburg
Academy of Science arranged to have a series
of experiments made at altitude. These
included gathering samples of air and
measuring magnetic dip. The observations, of
doubtful value, were made in January 1804 by
Robertson, accompanied by Sacharoff, a
member of the Academy. The list of items
taken on the flight provides an interesting
insight into the methods used: chronometer,
barometer, thermometer, pigeons, other birds,
megaphone, telescopes, firearms, chemicals,
quick-lime, gas-jars, money, water, wine,
bread, cooked chicken, and other food. (For
his first flight in England, Lunardi was also
provided with wine, bread, and chicken.)
Although styling himself a physicist,

Robertson was not altogether dedicated to the
sciences but enjoyed playing the role of part-
time entertainer.

The *Minerve* is among the largest balloons
ever conceived. A charlière (a hydrogen
balloon named after its inventor, the physicist
J. A. C. Charles) with a diameter of 150 feet, it
was designed to carry a load of 161,000
pounds including a company of 60 scientists.
As the illustration makes clear, it is imagined
as a true flying ship, complete with dinghy, or
jolly-boat (in the form of a smaller balloon),
an anchor, and ample accommodation for the
travelers, including a full-size church, a
library or study (on the gallery), and a
gymnasium (under the prow). The main hull
could be used as a conventional ship in the
event of a mishap over water. (The propor-
tions of the diagram are not, of course, always
well worked out.) As the ship is not normally
immersed in water, other accommodation
and provisions could be slung below. The
suspended accommodation at the rear is
intended for a small number of female
observers, who would be kept apart from the
men for fear of distracting them (perhaps a
disguise for a brothel). Despite the pointless
provision of a log at the rear, Robertson is
aware that a technique for directing the
horizontal movement of a balloon had not
then been developed. The forward sail is
intended only to show whether the balloon is
rising or descending. The *Minerve* is neither
designed for the benefit of an idyllic society
nor intended, as were some earlier imaginary
flying machines, to enable mankind to get
away from it all. It is equipped with cannons
and a strong military presence: outside the
church and on the upper equatorial gallery,
guards may be seen on duty, one of them
standing by a gas-lamp standard—a recent
invention. Named for the goddess of wisdom,
the *Minerve* was intended to make possible
scientific study of the whole globe as the
vehicle drifted from place to place. Wherever
it goes, says Robertson, there will be things of
interest. The banner at the top bears the
inscription *Scientiarum favore:* "By the grace
of knowledge."

Already to some degree a scientific joke,
Robertson's concept was several times
parodied by later artists and commentators.

Merkwürdige Begebenheiten
alter und neuer Zeit.

1) Auch fliegen kann der Mensch. Dazu die Abbildung des fliegenden Jacob Degen.
2) Der Hussitenkrieg. (wird fortgesetzt)
3) Kriegsbegebenheiten seit dem Tilsiter Frieden.
   Bombardement Coppenhagens. Eroberung Finn-
   lands. Thronveränderung in Spanien.

4) Der Eingang vom Sund. (nebst Kupfer)
5) Joseph Napoleon, König von Spanien. (nebst
   Bildniß)
6) Gustav Adolph, König von Schweden. (nebst
   Bildniß)
7) Erzählungen und Anecdoten.

Der fliegende Mensch, Jacob Degen.

Dresdner Chronicken, und Geschichts, Calender 1809. Dresden, Christian August Otto, [1809].

> [56] p. illus. 21 x 17.5 cm.
> Cover title.
> Imperfect: back cover wanting.
> Partial contents: *Auch fliegen kann der Mensch...* Jacob Degen, p. [29–32]. Illus.
> 1. Almanacs, German. 2. Degen, Jacob, 1750–1848.
> AY854.D7

A Swiss, and by profession a clock-maker, Jacob Degen lived in Vienna. Between about 1807 and 1817 he spent much of his time experimenting with flying machines, some of which he tested in public in Vienna's Prater Park. The most celebrated of his inventions, illustrated here, was misrepresented in press reports and in some drawings, winning for Degen an unjustified reputation as a charlatan. As shown, Degen hoped to be able to fly with a pair of flappers operated, like those of Meerwein, by a depressible rod. Unlike Meerwein's, Degen's wings were fully trussed and were made not of a single unbroken surface but of 3,500 flap valves cut from varnished paper. The valves closed on the downstroke and opened on the upstroke. When he tried the apparatus indoors, he was able to obtain some lift but could raise himself from the floor only when he partially counterbalanced himself and his machine with a pulley-and-weight system. Taking advice from a visiting journalist, Degen decided to replace the pulley and weight with a small balloon and to try the combination out of doors. With this apparatus he gave demonstrations not only in Vienna but also in Berlin and Paris. It was in Paris that a crowd, disappointed by the quality of his display, mobbed him and caused him serious injury. Reports of Degen's experiments, widely circulated, stimulated many other experimenters, including in particular one of the most important figures in early aviation history, Sir George Cayley. They also caught the attention of a less fortunate man, Albrecht Berblinger, the so-called tailor of Ulm who, in the presence of King Frederick of Württemberg, tried to fly across the Danube in 1811 using a copy of Degen's wings but without taking the precaution of making prior tests. He fell into the river from which he had to be fished out by passing sailors. A replica of the tailor's apparatus can be seen in the Rathaus at Ulm.

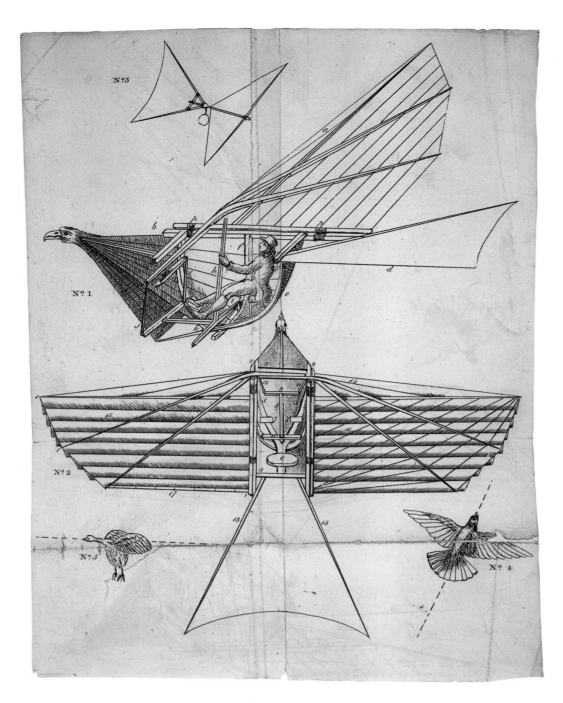

Walker, Thomas, portrait painter

A treatise upon the art of flying, by mechanical means, with a full explanation of the natural principles by which birds are enabled to fly; likewise instructions and plans for making a flying car with wings, in which a man may sit, and, by working a small lever, cause himself to ascend and soar through the air with the facility of a bird...By Thomas Walker, portrait painter, Hull. Printed by Joseph Simmons, and sold by Longman, Hurst, Rees, & Orme, London, 1810.

x, [5]–67 p. fold. col. front. 22.5 cm.

1. Flight. 2. Ornithopters. I. Title: The art of flying.
TLD209.W17

Brockett 12618; Gamble 2229; [R-P 7, 8]

Other copies and editions in the Gimbel collection:
TLD209.W17 1814: first American ed., New York, 1814, Brockett 12616; TLD209.W17 1910: reprint with facsimiles of t.-p.s of first ed. (1810) and of 2nd ed. (1831), [London], 1910.

The true mechanism of bird flight was not understood until recent times, and indeed some aspects of the matter are still undergoing investigation. Leonardo's ornithopters were fundamentally flawed in conception, as indeed were virtually all those proposed in later centuries, including Thomas Walker's. Although he does not make the old mistake of thinking that birds strike their wings down and back, his theory of flight, based on the elasticity of air, is wholly mistaken. (He drew false conclusions from the flight of the small paper glider drawn at top-left of the illustration.) His book, especially in the revised edition of 1831, was nevertheless influential. Using calculations based on published studies of the condor, Walker proposed a rather heavy structure in which the flier sits in something akin to the cockpit of a light airplane. He operates the wings by pushing the stick-like lever backward and forward through a very wearying total distance of 3 feet. Control of ascent, descent, and turns would come from shifting the pilot's center of gravity. After having observed birds landing, he suggested a quick nose-up pitch immediately before touchdown. In the revised edition published in 1831, Walker moved away from his focus on a bird-like configuration and proposed a tandem-wing structure foreshadowing that of Samuel Pierpont Langley's machines.

CLIVE HART

A

FLIGHT

TO

THE MOON;

OR,

THE VISION OF RANDALTHUS.

———◆———

BY GEO. FOWLER,

AUTHOR OF THE WANDERING PHILANTHROPIST.

———◆———

BALTIMORE:

PRINTED AND SOLD BY A. MILTENBERGER,
No. 10. *NORTH HOWARD STREET.*

••••••••••••

1813.

Fowler, George

*A flight to the moon; or, The vision of Randalthus.
By Geo. Fowler.* Baltimore: Printed and sold by A.
Miltenberger, no. 10. North Howard Street, 1813.

185 p. 18 cm.

1. Moon. 2. Voyages, Imaginary. I. Title.
TLE1041.F78

An early American example of the moon-
journey, Fowler's little-known book is
indebted to Swift and to Cyrano de Bergerac,
from whom he took, among other things, the
idea that the hero would turn over halfway
between the earth and the moon as gravity
was reversed. He is also indebted to the many
representations of Diana, Luna, or Selene,
goddesses of the moon, who were often
imagined as surrounded by a fine white haze
or mist. Fowler's hero, Randalthus, is led to
the moon by a beautiful woman enveloped in
a milk-white cloud. She announces to him
that he is "destined to visit the moon!":

> She here vanished in a vivid flash of light,
> but I was greatly astonished when I found
> myself encompassed apparently in the very
> cloud in which she had appeared, and
> swiftly advancing above the confines of the
> earth. I hardly had time to look down and
> behold the gradual disappearance of the

earth before every part of it seemed involved
in confusion. (p.7)

In some respects the book's opening pages
present a variant of the myth of Endymion,
the beautiful young shepherd with whom the
goddess of the moon fell in love. The imagery
of those pages sometimes anticipates that of
Keats' treatment of the theme in his long
poem *Endymion* (1818). Writing the bulk of
the book in the style of early pedagogic
dialogue-treatises, Fowler has his hero
instruct the Lunarians, and thereby the reader,
in basic physical matters such as the nature of
the tides and the reflection of earth-light by
the moon. Following a familiar and well-
established convention, he also uses the
journey to exotic places as an excuse for
offering moral and satirical comments about
the state of society on earth.

I Nuovi Abitatori della Luna
Disegnato al Capo di buona Speranza dal Sig.ᵣ Herschel

[Locke, Richard Adams] 1800–1871

Great astronomical discoveries lately made by Sir John Herschel...at the Cape of Good Hope. [n.p., 1835].

28 p. 25 cm.

First published in the *New York Sun,* from the Supplement to the *Edinburgh Journal of Science.*

A hoax.
1. Herschel, Sir John Frederick William, 1792–1871.
   I. Title.
QB52.L81 1835g

Other copies and editions in the Gimbel collection:
QB52.L81 1835: *Grandes descubrimientos astronómicos hechos recientemente por Sir John Herschel...,* trans. Francisco de Carriou *[sic],* Habana, 1835; QB52.L81 1835d: *Découvertes dans la lune..., traduit de l'Américain,* Turin, 1836; QB52.L81 1835f: *Delle scoperte fatte nella luna dal Dottore Herschel,* Firenze, 1836, Italian trans., with front.; QB52.L81 1836: *Grandes descubrimientos...,* 2nd ed., Madrid, 1836; QB52.L81 1836b: *Découvertes dans la lune...,* another ed., with ms. notes by A. Baron (1864), Lausanne, 1836; QB52.L81 1836d: another ed. of the Italian version, Livorno, 1836; QB52.L81 1836e: another ed. of the Italian version, [n.p., 1836]; QB52.L81 1836g: *Neuste Berichte...,* German trans., Hamburg, 1836; QB52.L81 1836i: *Intorno alle scoperte fatte nella luna,* [perhaps = the first Italian edition], [Ravenna, 1836]; QB52.L81 1836p: *Publication complète des nouvelles découvertes de Sir John Herschel...,* another version of the French ed., Paris, 1836; QB52.L81 1852: *The celebrated "moon story," its origin and incidents,...*by William N. Griggs [with the original articles], New York, 1852; QB52L81 1859: *The moon hoax...,* another reprint, New York, 1859; QB52.L81 1975: a reprint of the previous item, Boston, 1975.

This entertaining spoof was first published in the *New York Sun* in 1835. It caught the public imagination, increased the paper's circulation fivefold (or so claimed the proprietors), and was quickly reissued as a pamphlet. In the following months it also appeared in French and Italian. The hoax alleged that the Herschel telescopes had been able to detect wonders on the moon's surface, including a numerous race of batmen. The illustration (which is from the frontispiece to the Italian translation, Firenze, 1836) shows a curious mixture of ballet-dancer and primitive warrior, with wings derived both from Paltock's Glums and from Restif's inventive hero. About 4 feet tall, the Lunarians had glossy, copper-colored hair and prominent mouths giving them a generally simian appearance. Their bat-like wings (not accurately represented in the illustration) could be spread very wide or folded neatly against the back. Locke concludes his account of these creatures by making an oblique allusion to unseemly sexual behavior about which he declines to elaborate: "they are doubtless innocent and happy creatures, notwithstanding some of their amusements would but ill comport with our terrestrial sense of decorum." As in Paltock and Restif, flight and eroticism are readily combined in the imagination. In the last paragraph of his account, Locke returns to the batmen, inventing a virtuous breed of them to set alongside their amoral and unenlightened fellow creatures. Elsewhere on the moon the observers discovered, he says, a "very superior species of the Vespertilio-homo," as beautiful as angels and wonderfully skilled in the arts. As so often, a parable of good and bad flight emerges. The whole is couched in flat, pseudo-scientific language intended to allay doubts. For a time many people were persuaded that this work was indeed a serious report of findings by famous astronomers.

A

SYSTEM OF AERONAUTICS,

COMPREHENDING ITS

EARLIEST INVESTIGATIONS,

AND

MODERN PRACTICE AND ART.

DESIGNED AS A HISTORY FOR THE COMMON READER, AND
GUIDE TO THE STUDENT OF THE ART.

IN THREE PARTS.

CONTAINING AN

Account of the various attempts in the Art of Flying by Artificial Means,
from the Earliest Period down to the Discovery of the Aeronautic
Machine by the Montgolfiers, in 1782, and to a later Period.

WITH A BRIEF HISTORY OF THE AUTHOR'S FIFTEEN YEARS'
EXPERIENCE IN AERIAL VOYAGES.

ALSO, FULL INSTRUCTIONS IN THE ART OF MAKING BALLOONS, PARACHUTES,
ETC. ETC., AS ADAPTED TO THE PRACTICE OF AERIAL NAVIGATION,
AND DIRECTIONS TO PREPARE EXPERIMENTAL BALLOONS.

BY JOHN WISE,

AERONAUT.

"There are more things in heaven and earth, Horatio,
Than are dreamt of in your philosophy."

PHILADELPHIA:
JOSEPH A. SPEEL,
96 CHERRY STREET ABOVE SIXTH STREET.
1850.

Wise, John, 1808–1879

A system of aeronautics, comprehending its earliest investigations, and modern practice and art. Designed as a history for the common reader, and guide to the student of the art. In three parts. Containing an account of the various attempts in the art of flying by artificial means, from the earliest period down to the discovery of the aeronautic machine by the Montgolfiers, in 1782, and to a later period. With a brief history of the author's fifteen years' experience in aerial voyages. Also, full instructions in the art of making balloons...By John Wise...Philadelphia, Joseph A. Speel, 1850.

xvi, [17]–310 p. front. (port.) pl. 22.5 cm.
An enlarged edition was issued in 1873 under the
   title *Through the Air,* Brockett 12948.
1. Aeronautics—Hist. 2. Balloons.
TLB251.W81

Brockett 12945; Gamble 849; R-P 28

Other copies and editions in the Gimbel collection:
five other copies of this edition.

Born in Lancaster, Pennsylvania, in 1808, John Wise was probably the most celebrated of all American balloonists. Although his attempt to fly across the Atlantic in 1859 ended in failure, it established a world record for distance—about 809 miles—which stood until 1910. With three companions he had flown from St. Louis, Missouri, to Henderson, Jefferson County, New York, in 20 hours and 40 minutes. Among the most substantial to have been published by 1850, his book opens with a brief history of aviation written in the spirit of a practically minded up-to-date thinker. Showing little interest in the remote history of his subject, Wise passes quickly on to the experiments in France leading to the first free manned flight. Viewing the events from more than half a century later, he was able to make a cool assessment of the overzealous imaginings which that success had at first stimulated. Not only were many of the plans for future development impractical, but they were often, in his view, morally and socially suspect. Despite these reservations, Wise celebrates the invention of the balloon, which, in the hands of the sober-minded, he believes to be a potential boon for the future advancement of civilization. In the second of the book's three sections he gives detailed instructions, based on fifteen years' experience, as to how to make and fly a balloon. The book ends with the words: "It would seem as though nature itself cried aloud to us upon this subject, inviting us to its elysian fields to drink in the fluid of life and relieve poor enervated humanity."

Printed Books, 1851–1914

Tom D. Crouch

T HE TASK OF SELECTING FIFTY TITLES from among the thousands of printed books in the Colonel Richard Gimbel Aeronautical History Collection is a daunting challenge. My goal has been to illustrate the depth and breadth of the Gimbel collection while describing some of the critically important books that both shaped and recorded the early history of flight.

The list includes significant works of science and engineering that played a key role in the development of flight technology, along with works of fiction that have inspired generations of flight enthusiasts. Solid histories of aeronautics share the list with items that explore the social and cultural impact of aviation. Otto Lilienthal's report of his pioneering glider experiments is included, as is the novel with an aviation theme that Sinclair Lewis wrote for boys. Whether science, fiction, or history, each of these books had an impact on history.

"In 1898 I read your *War of the Worlds*," Robert Hutchings Goddard wrote to H. G. Wells in April 1932:

> I was sixteen years old, and . . . the compelling realism of the thing made a deep impression. . . . I decided that what might conservatively be called "high altitude research" was the most fascinating problem in existence. . . . How many more years I shall be able to work on the problem, I do not know; I hope as long as I live. There can be no thought of finishing, for "aiming at the stars," both literally and figuratively, is a problem to occupy generations, so that no matter how much progress one makes, there is always the thrill of just beginning.

Such is the power of the printed word to touch a life and through that life to shape a future. Housed in a library that serves the intellectual needs of America's future aerospace leaders are the precious volumes that provided a firm foundation for the age of flight. We owe Colonel Gimbel a great debt.

Detail of page from
*Through the Air: A
Narrative of Forty Years'
Experience as an Aëronaut,*
John Wise (Page 106)

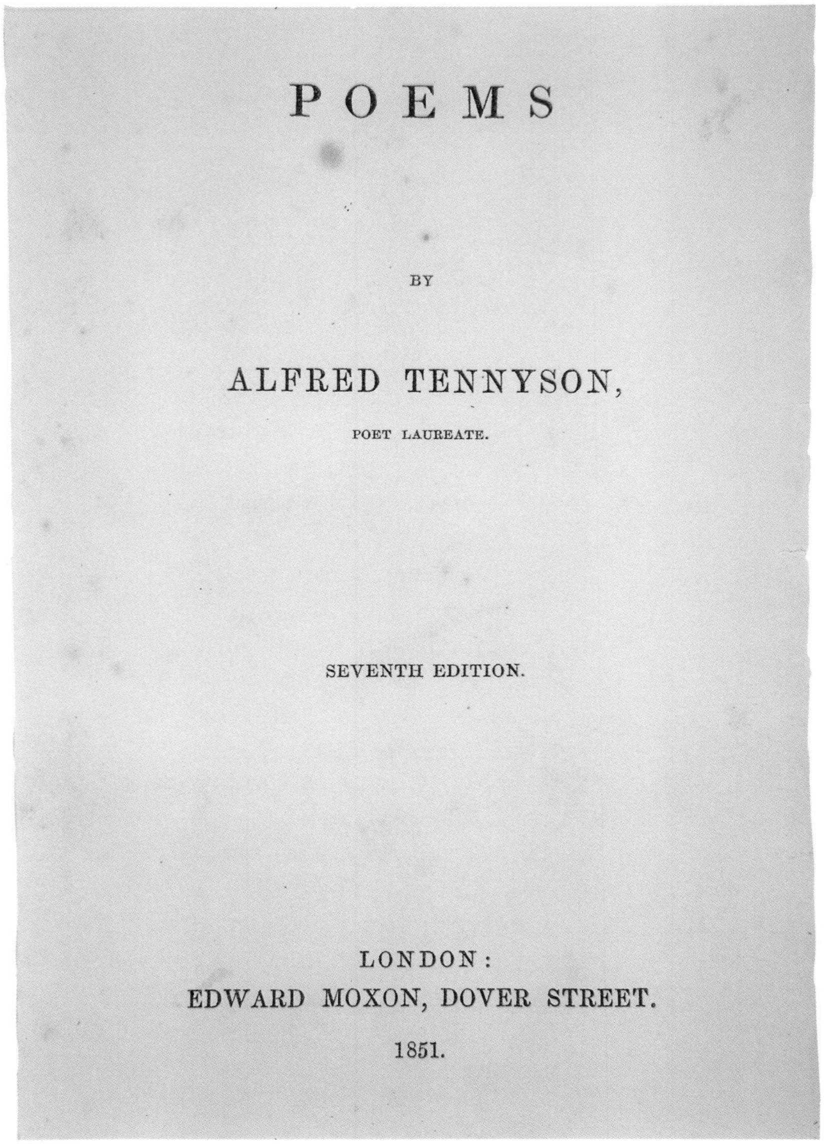

POEMS

BY

ALFRED TENNYSON,

POET LAUREATE.

SEVENTH EDITION.

LONDON:
EDWARD MOXON, DOVER STREET.
1851.

Tennyson, Alfred, Baron
Poems.

> 7th ed. London: Edward Moxon, 1851. xii, 375 p.
> 17 cm.
> PR5551.E51

Alfred Tennyson (1809–1892) earned high marks for prescience with the publication of "Locksley Hall." The poem is a long monologue in which a young man, disappointed in love and depressed by contemporary social problems, still expresses a solid Victorian faith in progress and the ability of human beings to shape their own destiny. Although the benefits of aerial commerce may be temporarily offset by the terrible vision of "airy navies grappling in the central blue," for example, the battle flags will eventually be "furl'd" and international disputes adjudicated "in the Parliament of man, the Federation of the world."

Tennyson returned to this theme in "Locksley Hall Sixty Years After" (1886). The narrator of the first poem, now an embittered old man, is comfortable with his own lot but no longer hopeful about the future.

TOM D. CROUCH

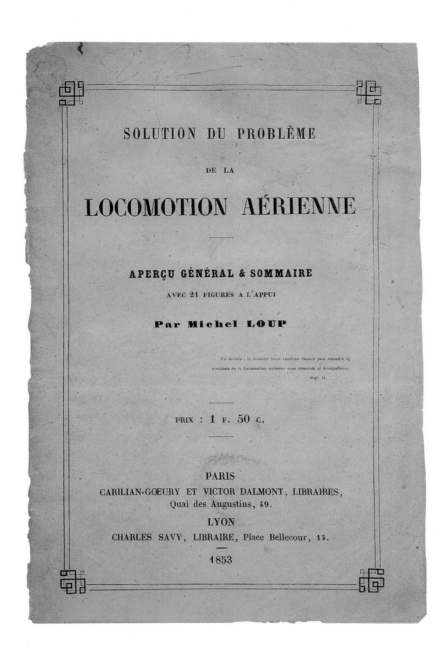

Loup, Michel

Solution du Problème de la Locomotion Aérienne: Aperçu Général & Sommaire, Avec 21 Figures à l'Appui, par Michel Loup.

Paris: Carilian-Goeury et Victor Dalmont [etc.], 1853. 2 p. l., 75, [3] p. 2 fold. pl. 19.5 cm.

TLB399.L88

Brockett 7713

Bibliographic note: The copy held by the Gimbel collection is ex libris Gaston Tissandier.

Michel Loup produced the first well-considered French proposal for a powered airplane. The craft was a bird-like monoplane with fixed tandem wings, a tricycle undercarriage, and a large cruciform rudder and elevator. An engine powered twin propellers mounted between each triangular pair of wings.

Charles Harvard Gibbs-Smith, the eminent English authority on the prehistory of flight, remarks that Viscount Carlingford, in 1856, designed a tractor monoplane similar to Loup's machine, although it was to be powered by a single tractor propeller mounted on the nose. He apparently constructed a full-scale, unpowered version of this "aerial chariot," which was tested as a kite in Ireland.

SETTING OUT.   p. 14.

[Goodrich, Samuel Griswold]
The Balloon Travels of Robert Merry and His Young Friends over Various Countries in Europe.

Ed. by Peter Parley [pseud.]. . . New York: J. C. Derby, 1856. viii, [9–312 p.] illus. 19 cm.

D980.G65 1856

[Randers-Pehrson 33]

Bibliographic note: The Gimbel collection holds fourteen Goodrich volumes. Six of these are editions of the volume described. Two of those editions, including the volume cited, are 1856 copies. The others date to 1855, 1857, 1860, and 1866.

A native of Connecticut, Samuel Griswold Goodrich (1793–1860) devoted himself to providing reading material that would entertain, educate, and communicate moral lessons to young people.

Griswold entered the publishing business in 1816 and issued the first of what would become a series of 116 Peter Parley titles *(The Tales of Peter Parley About America)* in 1827. Peter Parley was the pseudonym adopted by Goodrich and used for all the authors, including Nathaniel Hawthorne, whom he hired to produce books for the series.

Goodrich, who also served as a Whig member of the Massachusetts legislature and as U.S. Consul to Paris (1851–1853), was a publishing phenomenon who had sold as many as 7 million books by the time of his death in 1860. In addition, he published two successful children's magazines: *Parley's Magazine* (founded 1833) and *Robert Merry's Museum* (founded 1841).

The Balloon Travels of Robert Merry. . . is typical of the Parley volumes. Merry, the central character, leads a group of inquisitive youngsters on an adventurous balloon journey across Europe, during which he provides his young charges with information on history, geography, science, and other matters. Ballooning, the fictional editor explains in the preface, "provides an easy mode of traveling—that of gliding along in the air—and the opportunity it affords to move rapidly from country to country, looking down upon each and studying it like a map—surely must prove an effective mode of impressing their form and appearance upon the mind and memory."

"It is hoped too," Goodrich comments, "that the occasional passages of moral instruction given in the conversations of Robert Merry may be useful, by imparting sound morals and good manners. At all events, it is believed the work may contribute to the innocent pleasure of youthful readers, and for this object it is mainly intended."

TOM D. CROUCH

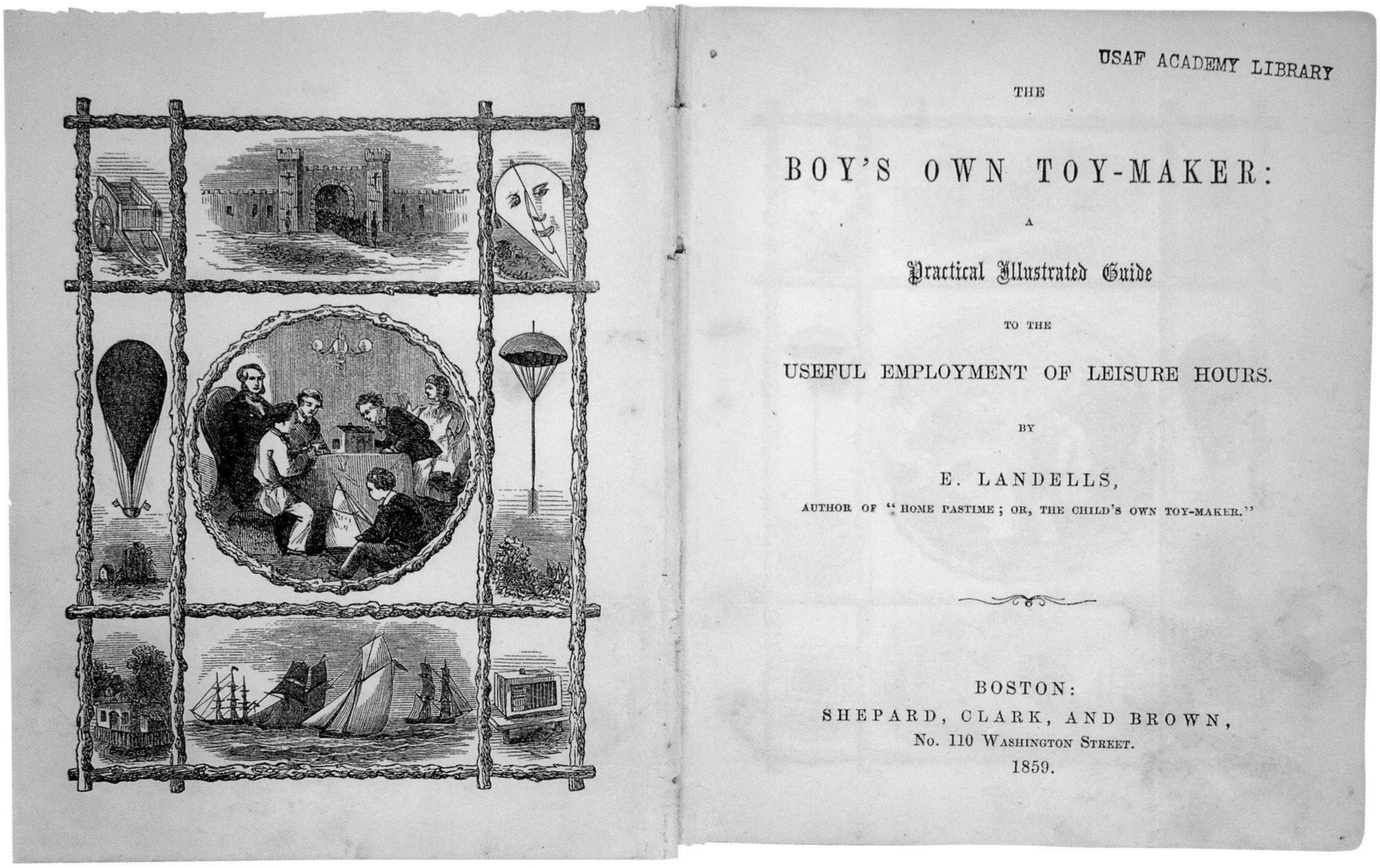

THE

BOY'S OWN TOY-MAKER:

A

Practical Illustrated Guide

TO THE

USEFUL EMPLOYMENT OF LEISURE HOURS.

BY

E. LANDELLS,

AUTHOR OF " HOME PASTIME ; OR, THE CHILD'S OWN TOY-MAKER."

BOSTON:
SHEPARD, CLARK, AND BROWN,
No. 110 WASHINGTON STREET.
1859.

Landells, E.
The Boy's Own Toy-Maker: A Practical Illustrated Guide to the Useful Employment of Leisure Hours. . .

Boston: Shepard, Clark, and Brown, 1859. viii, 153 p. illus. 16 cm.

GV1201.L25

Books describing magic tricks and scientific experiments that could be performed or interesting toys that could be constructed using commonly available household items were great favorites with nineteenth-century youngsters. Some discussion of the scientific or technical principles involved in the individual projects was often included as a means of underscoring the educational value of the activity. No such book was worth its salt without a sampling of flight-related projects. Landells' book, typical of the genre, provides step-by-step instructions for the construction of a fire balloon, two kinds of parachutes, and four varieties of kites.

Although the kites and parachutes were harmless enough, the paper fire balloons described by the author, kept aloft by bits of cotton soaked in turpentine, were genuine fire hazards. When Henry James senior, the future father of Henry and William James, was a 13-year-old student at the Albany Academy, he lost a leg after being badly burned attempting to extinguish a fire started by one of his own fire balloons.

PROF. T. S. C. LOWE,
AERONAUT OF THE AIR-SHIP "CITY OF NEW YORK."

Lowe, Thaddeus S[obieski]
C[onstantine]

*The Air-Ship City of New York: Full
Description of the Air-Ship and the
Apparatus to be Employed in the Aerial
Voyage to Europe; with a Historical
Sketch of the Art of Ballooning, and the
Aeronaut's Address to the Public.*

New York: Baker and Godwin, Printers, 1859.
24 p. incl. front. (port.) pl. 19.5 cm.

TLD921.C58L8

Brockett 7736; Randers-Pehrson 36

Bibliographic note: In addition to this
pamphlet, the Gimbel collection contains the
following items by T.S.C. Lowe: "Balloon
Operations in the Civil War," in *The War of the
Rebellion: A Compilation of the Official Records
of the Union and Confederate Armies*, series III,
v. iii, pp. 252–319. Washington, D.C., 1899. 23
cm., Gamble 3672; T.S.C. Lowe, *Early
Aeronautic and Meteorological Investigations.*
Los Angeles: B. R. Baumgardt, 1895. 31 p. 23 cm.;
T.S.C. Lowe, *The Latest Development in Aerial
Navigation.* [Los Angeles: Aerial Publishing
Co., 1910?] 52 p. illus. facsim. 23 cm.

Six feet tall with broad shoulders, clear
penetrating eyes, and a sweeping mustache,
T.S.C. Lowe (1832–1913) emerged as a leading
American aeronaut immediately prior to the
Civil War. Born in Jefferson Mills, New
Hampshire, he took an early interest in
science and, from the age of twenty, earned
his living as an itinerant lecturer. He made

his first balloon ascent in 1856 and gained
experience in a series of flights in the United
States and began work on the balloon that
was to be known as the *City of New York* in
July 1859.

The huge aerostat, designed to fly the
Atlantic, had a diameter of 130 feet and stood
200 feet tall from the gas valve on top of the
envelope to the keel of the lifeboat dangling

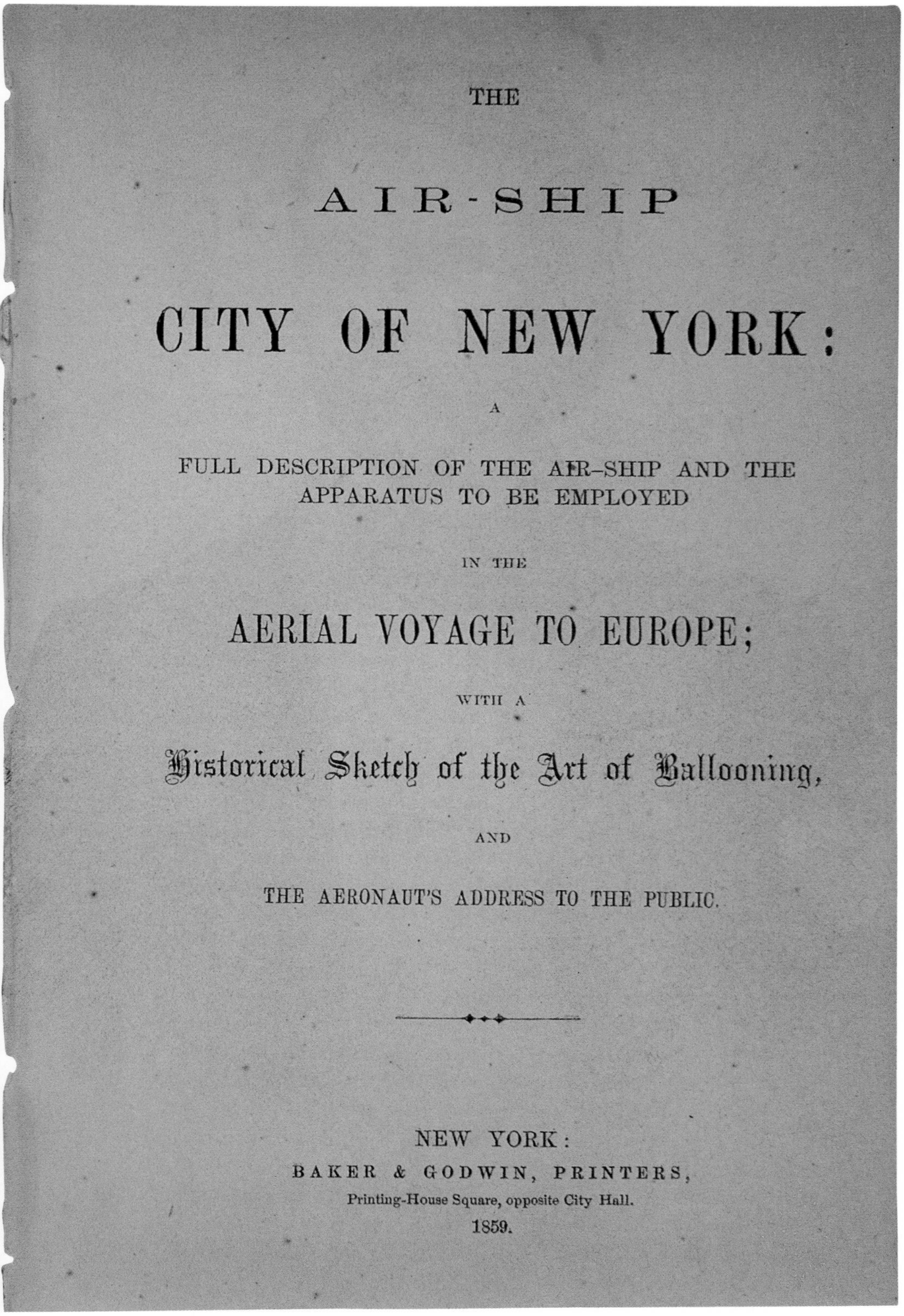

THE

AIR-SHIP

CITY OF NEW YORK:

A

FULL DESCRIPTION OF THE AIR-SHIP AND THE
APPARATUS TO BE EMPLOYED

IN THE

AERIAL VOYAGE TO EUROPE;

WITH A

Historical Sketch of the Art of Ballooning,

AND

THE AERONAUT'S ADDRESS TO THE PUBLIC.

———◆◆◆———

NEW YORK:
BAKER & GODWIN, PRINTERS,
Printing-House Square, opposite City Hall.
1859.

beneath the basket. When filled with 725,000 cubic feet of coal gas or city illuminating gas, the balloon would lift an estimated 11.25 tons. Lowe began to inflate the balloon inside New York City's Crystal Palace Exhibition Hall in the fall of 1859. It soon became apparent, however, that the city gas works was not up to the task. Disappointed, Lowe shifted his operation to Philadelphia—and renamed the balloon *Great Western*. The envelope burst during a renewed attempt at inflation in October 1860. Undaunted, Lowe flew another balloon (named *Enterprise*) from Cincinnati to the Atlantic coast of South Carolina in April 1861. With the Civil War looming on the horizon, Lowe traveled to Washington, where he lobbied for a balloon reconnaissance effort.

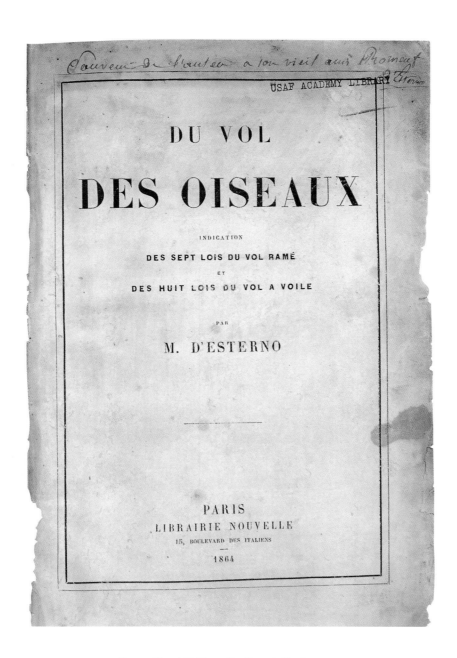

DU VOL

DES OISEAUX

INDICATION

DES SEPT LOIS DU VOL RAMÉ

ET

DES HUIT LOIS DU VOL A VOILE

PAR

M. D'ESTERNO

PARIS
LIBRAIRIE NOUVELLE
15, BOULEVARD DES ITALIENS
1864

Esterno, Henri Philippe Ferdinand, Comte d.'

Du Vol des Oiseaux; Indication des Sept Lois du Vol Ramé et des Huit Lois du Vol à Voile, par M. d'Esterno.

> Paris: Librairie Nouvelle, 1864. 61 p., 1l. illus. 2 pl. (1 fold.) 20.5 cm.
>
> TLD181E7
>
> Brockett 4192; Gamble 5212

Count Henri Philippe Ferdinand Charles Honoré d'Esterno (1805–1883) was one of the most significant figures in mid-nineteenth-century aeronautics. Esterno was the first to underscore the notion of soaring, the ability of a bird to maintain or even gain altitude without beating its wings. Moreover, the Count called attention to alterations in the shape of a bird's wing as a means of controlling its attitude in the air. It should be noted, however, that Esterno did not fully understand the torsion of the wings as a means of effecting lateral control.

Moreover, in the interesting and advanced aircraft design presented in *Du Vol des Oiseaux,* the Count provided a moveable seat for the pilot, clearly suggesting that weight shifting would be a key element of the control system. There is little substance to the notion suggested after the invention of the airplane that Esterno was the first to describe the wing torsion control system pioneered by the Wright brothers. Esterno's general impact was, however, considerable.

TOM D. CROUCH

THE FALL OF ICARUS.

Photo-zincographed at the Ordnance Survey Office, Southampton, under the superintendence of Capt.[?] *H. Bolton, Major R.E. 2nd Col. Sir H. James R.E. F.R.S. &c Director.*

1884

Turnor, Christopher Hatton
Astra Castra; Experiments and Adventures in the Atmosphere...

> London: Chapman and Hall, 1865. xxiii, 530 p. front., illus., plates, ports. 31.5 cm.
>
> TLB2511.T95
>
> Brockett 12110; Gamble 373
>
> **Bibliographic note:** The Gimbel collection contains an additional uncatalogued copy of the same edition of this book.

Christopher Hatton Turnor (1840–1914), who listed himself on the title page of *Astra Castra* as an officer in the Prince Consort's Own Rifle Brigade, was a founding member of the Aeronautical Society of Great Britain (1866), later the Royal Aeronautical Society, and an original member of the governing council of that organization. He is best remembered, however, as the author of this volume, a chronological history of aeronautics from the earliest times to 1864.

Turnor provides a wide range of extracts and translations of flight-related documents, from the myths, legends, and poetry of classical times through the introduction and spread of ballooning, all knit together in a loose fashion with his own prose. The volume is, for its time, very well illustrated. The appendices range from speculative essays on meteorology and astronomy to a bibliography of books on flight and a list of the first 500 balloonists and the dates of their first ascents. For all of its eccentric quality, the book would remain for many years the most comprehensive and accurate treatment of the subject available in English.

The title is drawn from the motto of the Lindsay family: "Astra, Castra, Numen, Lumen." James Fairbairn, *Fairbairn's Crests of the Leading Families of Great Britain and Ireland* (Baltimore: Genealogical Publishing Co., 1963), confirms that a literal translation of the motto—"Star, Camp, God, Light"—is correct but offers no clue as to its meaning in the context of this volume.

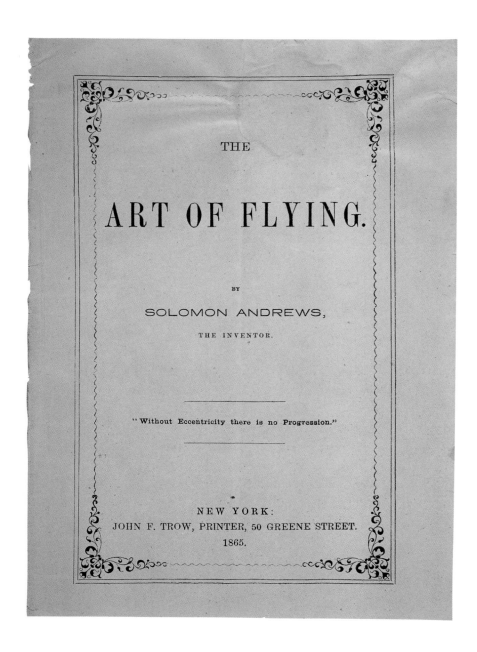

THE

ART OF FLYING.

BY

SOLOMON ANDREWS,

THE INVENTOR.

" Without Eccentricity there is no Progression."

NEW YORK:
JOHN F. TROW, PRINTER, 50 GREENE STREET.
1865.

Andrews, Solomon
Aerial Navigation and a Proposal to Form an Aerial Navigation Company, by Solomon Andrews, M.D., The Inventor.

> (Cover title: *The Art of Flying*) New York: John F. Trow, 1865. 32 p. 25 cm.
>
> TLD902.A56
>
> Gamble 3535; Randers-Pehrson 41
>
> **Bibliographic note:** The Gimbel collection contains a second facsimile copy of this work, bound with a facsimile of Solomon Andrews, *The Aereon, or flying ship, invented by Solomon Andrews.* New York: John F. Trow & Co. Publishers, for the Aerial Navigation Company, 1866. 16 p. 32 cm. An illustration of "The First Aereon of 1863" is included, apparently as the back cover sheet of the original.

Solomon Andrews, a classic inventor-mechanic, and one-time mayor of Perth Amboy, New Jersey, was one of the most persistent of all mid-nineteenth-century American experimenters with dirigible airships. His earliest plans for the navigation of the air dated to the 1840s, but it was not until he returned from a tour of duty as a surgeon with the Union army that he began construction of the first "aereon."

The craft consisted of three 80-foot-long cigar-shaped balloons constructed by aeronaut John Wise. Andrews planned to employ a sort of aeronautical perpetual motion to propel the craft. The force of the air on the top or bottom of the gasbags, which could be angled nose up or down from an operator's car suspended 16 feet beneath the balloons, would cause the vehicle to climb or descend. The momentum built up in a descent could be used to power a climb.

A series of apparently successful flights beginning in 1862 led to initial efforts to interest government officials in the project. When funds were not forthcoming, Andrews established a joint stock venture, which funded work on a second craft in 1866. Additional flights with the new machine were impressive but did not result in the increased funding required to sustain the effort; Andrews was forced to abandon the work.

TOM D. CROUCH

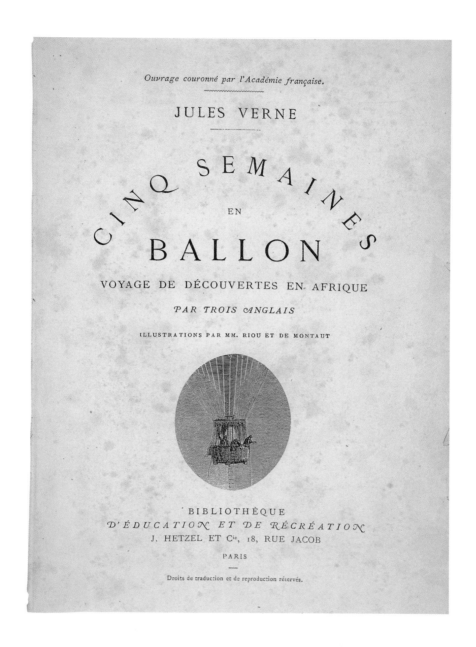

Verne, Jules

Cinq Semaines en Ballon, Voyage de Découvertes en Afrique par Trois Anglais; Illustrations par MM. Riou et De Montaut.

Paris: J. Hetzel, [186?]. 2 p. l., 267 p. incl. front., illus., double map. 28.5 cm.

PQ2469.C5

Bibliographic note: The Gimbel collection also holds a second Hetzel edition of this novel dated 1885. In addition, there are eight American editions: two copies of *Five Weeks in a Balloon; or, Journeys and Discoveries in Africa, by Three Englishmen.* Compiled in French by J. Verne, from the original notes of Dr. Ferguson [pseud.] and done into English by W. Lackland. New York: D. Appleton & Co., 1869. 1 p. l., 345 p. plates. 12 cm., Randers-Pehrson 47; same title, New York: R. Worthington, 1882. [2], 345 p. illus. 19 cm.; same title, New York: Pollard & Moss, 1887. [2], 345 p. illus. 19 cm.; same title, New York: Mershon Co. [n.d.]. 265 p. 19 cm. "Arundel edition"; . . . Five Weeks in a Balloon; an Abridged Translation. . . by Charles J. Finger. Girard, Kansas: Haldeman-Julius, [ca. 1923]. 64 p. 12.5 cm. (Little Blue Book No. 482) Text ends on p. 57. "Pocket Series no. 482."

Jules Verne (1828–1905) was, with Herbert George Wells, the most influential contributor to the literary genre that would be known as science fiction. Born at Nantes, France, the young Jules Verne earned his living as a stockbroker but loved literature and the theater. He produced a string of unpublished stories and unproduced plays prior to 1862, when he began his association with J. Hetzel, a successful author and publisher of children's literature. Anxious to obtain new material for a children's magazine, Hetzel encouraged Verne to try his hand at producing a novella with an adventurous theme.

The result was *Cinq Semaines en Ballon. . .* a tale in which three companions cross Africa in a balloon. The plot is less complex and dramatic than later and more famous novels like *Twenty Thousand Leagues Under the Sea, Journey to the Center of the Earth,* or *From the Earth to the Moon.* Still, it fits the pattern of the classic Verne *Voyages extraordinaires*— an adventurous tale with strong didactic elements in which a group of individuals make imaginative use of technology to undertake a dangerous and exciting journey. It was the book that launched an extraordinary literary career.

LES VOYAGES EXTRAORDINAIRES
couronnés par l'Académie française.

DE LA TERRE A LA LUNE

TRAJET DIRECT

EN 97 HEURES 20 MINUTES

PAR

JULES VERNE

41 DESSINS ET UNE CARTE PAR DE MONTAUT

BIBLIOTHÈQUE
D'ÉDUCATION ET DE RÉCRÉATION
J. HETZEL ET Cⁱᵉ, 18, RUE JACOB
PARIS

Tous droits de traduction et de reproduction réservés.

Verne, Jules

*De la Terre à la Lune; Trajet Direct en 97
Heures 20 Minutes, par Jules Verne; 41
Dessins et une Carte par de Montaut.*

Paris: J. Hetzel et Cie, [1866]. 2 p. l, 170 p. illus.
27.5 cm.

PQ2469.D3 1866

Bibliographic note: The Gimbel collection
holds two copies of the edition cited. In
addition, the collection features: same title,
Nouvelle éd. Paris: Collection Hetzel, [1867].
[1]–305 p. illus. 19.5 cm. The collection holds
only two English-language translations of the
book: Miller, Walter James, *The Annotated Jules
Verne: From the Earth to the Moon, Direct in
Ninety-Seven Hours and Twenty Minutes. . .* New
York: Crowell, 1978. [168]–171 p. and *From the
Earth to the Moon*. London: Lock and Tyler,
[1876?]. (Bound with a translation of the sequel,
Round the Moon and a copy of *A Journey into
the Interior of the Earth*. 3 vol. in 1. illus. 18 cm.)

The Gimbel collection includes only one
French edition of the sequel: . . . *Autour de la
Lune, par Jules Verne . . .* Paris: J. Hetzel, [1867?].
180 p. illus. 28 cm. The collection boasts a
considerable number of English-language
editions in which the two volumes are
presented as a single book: *From the Earth to
the Moon, Direct in 97 Hours 20 Minutes; and a
Trip Round It . . . Tr. from the French by Louis
Mercier. . . and Eleanor King. . .* London:
Sampson Low, Marston, Low, and Searle, 1873.

viii, 323 p. illus. 20.5 cm.; another copy by the
same press dated 1874; 111; same title, New York:
Scribner, Armstrong and Co., 1874. viii, 323 p.
illus. 20 cm.; a second edition from the same
publisher, vi, 323 p. illus. 19 cm.; same title,
London: Ward, Locke and Tyler, [1876?]. 3 vol.
in 1. illus. 18 cm; same title, New York: Lowell,
[1876?]. 3 vol. in 1. illus. 18 cm.; same title, New
York: Lowell, [1888?]. 125, 151 p. 19 cm.
(Hawthorn series); same title, New York: C.
Scribner's Sons, 1893, viii, 323 p. illus. 21 cm.;
*From the Earth to the Moon and Round the
Moon, by Jules Verne. . .* New York: A. L. Burt
Company, [190?]. 1 p. l., 330 p. 19 cm.
(Publisher's lettering: The Home Library);
Miller, Walter James, *The Annotated Jules Verne;
From the Earth to the Moon, Direct in Ninety-
Seven Hours and Twenty Minutes,* New York:
Crowell, 1978. [168]–171 p.

De la Terre à la Lune. . . is one of the best
and most influential of Jules Verne's *Voyages
imaginaires*. The second of the author's
adventure tales, it recounts the journey of
artillery expert Impey Barbicane and two
companions *From the Earth to the Moon*.
The three make the trip in a hollow artillery
shell weighing 30,000 pounds, fired from
"The Columbiad," a 68,000-ton, 9,000-foot-
long cannon buried up to the muzzle in the
soil of Florida. At the end of the book, and
a 97-hour, 20-minute trip through space, the
three voyagers are left orbiting the moon.
Anxious readers had to wait for the rescue
in the sequel, *Autour de la Lune* (1870).
Unlike most Verne tales, the real purpose
of the two novels is to outline some of the
problems barring the way to spaceflight and
to describe the technology that might make
such a trip possible, or at least thinkable.
Konstantine Tsiolkovskii and Hermann
Oberth, who, along with the American Robert
Goddard, offered the first mathematical
proofs of the possibility of spaceflight and
outlined some of the key technological steps
that would lead to eventual success, dated
their own early fascination with the subject
to a reading of *From the Earth to the Moon*.

TOM D. CROUCH

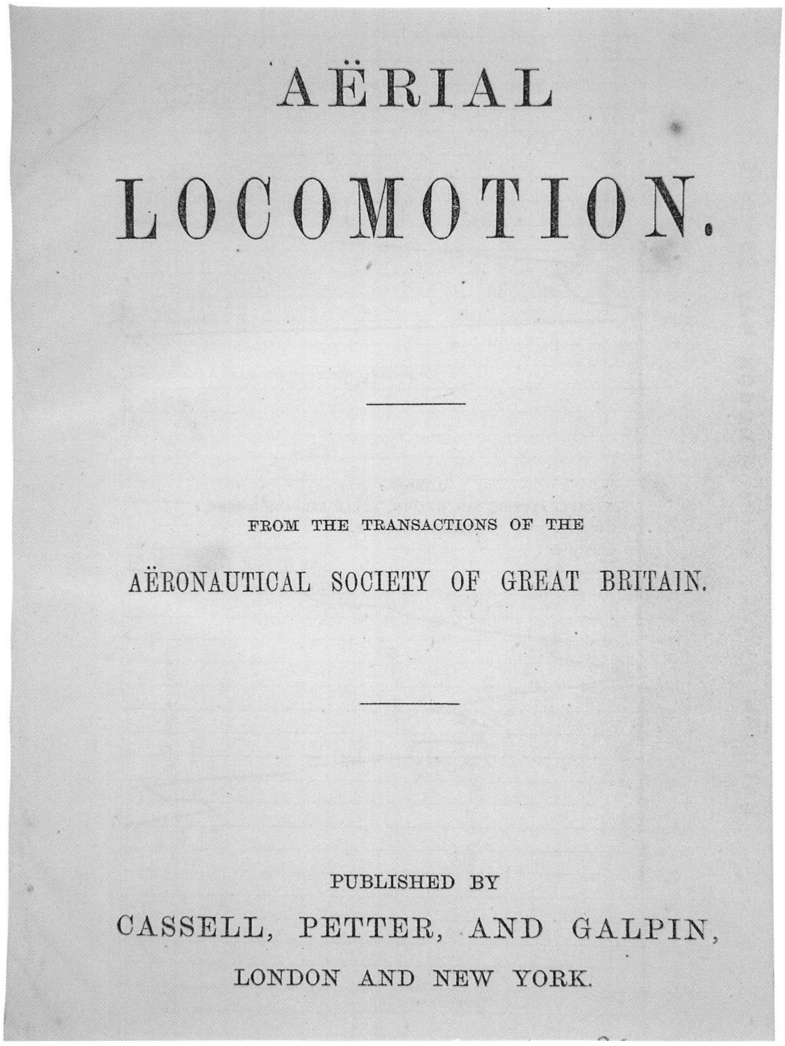

AËRIAL LOCOMOTION.

FROM THE TRANSACTIONS OF THE

AËRONAUTICAL SOCIETY OF GREAT BRITAIN.

PUBLISHED BY

CASSELL, PETTER, AND GALPIN,

LONDON AND NEW YORK.

Aëronautical Society of Great Britain
[Royal Aeronautical Society]

Report 1–8 [1866–1873]; 9–15 [1874–1880];
16–23 [1881–1893].

London and New York: Cassell, Petter, and
Galpin, [1866]; Greenwich: Henry S.
Richardson, [1867–1893]. 23 vol. in 3. illus.,
plates, diagrs. 18 cm.

TLB14.R88

[Brockett 197; Gamble 4578]

The Aeronautical Society of Great Britain was
not the first organization of its kind in the
world, but it was certainly the most significant
and influential. Founded in 1866, the Society
attracted both talented amateur experimenters and distinguished professional engineers
interested in the subject. The leaders of the
group arranged informative lectures and
technical meetings, and sponsored the first
public exhibition of aeronautical technology.
The published series of annual reports proved
to be the organization's most important
contribution, however.

The best of the papers published in the
early reports were marked by a determination
to extend the power of contemporary engineering theory and practice into aeronautics.
Francis Herbert Wenham's description of the
wind tunnel experiments that he and John
Browning conducted at Penn's Engineering
Works, Greenwich, for example, opened
a new era in the history of flight research.
(See "Concluding Remarks," *Sixth Annual
Report of the Aëronautical Society of Great
Britain for the Year 1871*, pp. 73–81.) Today, the
wide-ranging technical materials published
by the Royal Aeronautical Society continue a
tradition established in 1866.

Tissandier, Gaston
*En Ballon! Pendant le Siège de Paris.
Souvenirs d'un Aéronaute par Gaston
Tissandier, Professeur de Chimie,
L'Association Polytechnique, Directeur du
Laboratoire de l'Union Nationale, etc.*

Paris: E. Dentu, 1871. 3 p. l., xv, 318 p. 18.5 cm.

DC313.T61

Brockett 11883

Bibliographic note: Ex libris Horace Oswald
Short, with decorated book-plate. The Gimbel
collection contains a much better known
account by the same author, Gaston Tissandier,
*Souvenirs et Récits d'un Aérostier Militaire de
l'Armée de la Loire, 1870–1871.* Paris: Maurice
Dreyfous, 1891. x, 356 p., incl. front. illus., plates,
facsim. 28.5 cm., Brockett 11874; Gamble 3771.
The collection also contains a copy of another
standard account: G. de Clerval, *Les Ballons
Pendant le Siège de Paris; Récits de 60 Voyages
Aériens, Réunis et mis en ordre par G. de Clerval
. . .* Paris: F. Wattelier, 1871. 148 p. 20 cm.,
Brockett 2821. Colonel Gimbel collected a wide
range of additional items relating to the
Franco-Prussian War, including manuscripts,
medals, newspapers, and prints.

The French army marched off to battle in July
1870, confident of its ability to defeat Prussia.
Within weeks, however, the cream of the
army was besieged at Metz, while Emperor
Napoleon III was defeated at Sedan. By early
September, panic and the spirit of revolution
were sweeping through the streets of Paris.
A new Government of National Defense
began taking shape as two Prussian armies
moved toward the capital. The Siege of Paris
was under way.

During the long months of isolation,
which ended with the armistice and surrender
in January and February 1871, the sight of
balloons bobbing above the skyline or flying
to safety carrying mail and official news to the
outside world provided a source of hope and
pride for thousands of Parisians. During the
course of the siege, more than 65 balloons
carried 164 passengers and 11 tons of paper,
ranging from government dispatches to an
estimated 2.5 million letters to the outside
world. All but 8 of the balloons succeeded in
carrying their cargo to friendly hands. Carrier
pigeons were also pressed into service by this
first official airmail operation.

In addition to their involvement with
the Paris post, French aeronauts served with
military units continuing to operate in the
field. Gaston Tissandier recounts his experience as one of the aeronautical heroes of the
Franco-Prussian War. In addition, he provides
an early account of the famous aerial post
in which balloons and pigeons carried mail
out of Paris and Metz.

TOM D. CROUCH

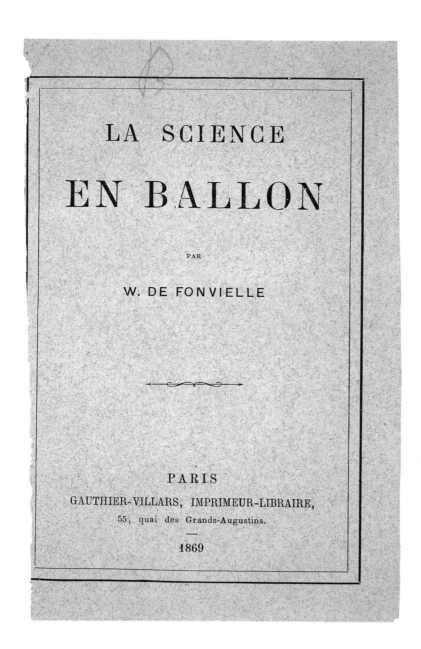

LA SCIENCE

EN BALLON

PAR

W. DE FONVIELLE

PARIS
GAUTHIER-VILLARS, IMPRIMEUR-LIBRAIRE,
55, quai des Grands-Augustins.
—
1869

Fonvielle, Wilfrid de
La Science en Ballon...

Paris: Gauthier-Villars, 1869. 3 p. l., xvi, 141 p.
11. 18 cm.

TLB273.F68s

Bibliographic note: This copy is marked: "A. F.
Zahm, Notre Dame, Ind." Zahm was a
controversial aviation pioneer who taught
physics for a time at Notre Dame. In addition
to the single edition of the volume noted, the
Gimbel collection includes the following
volumes by Fonvielle: *Les Ballons-sondes et
les Ascensions internationales, précédé d'une*

Introduction par J. Bouquet de la Grye... 2nd
ed. Paris: Gauthier-Villars, 1899. ix, 148 p. 11.
illus. (incl. maps), diagrs. 19 cm. (Gimbel copy
is ex libris Albert Tissandier); *Notre Flotte
aérienne, par Wilfrid de Fonvielle et Georges
Besançon...* Paris: Gauthier-Villars, 1908. 2 p. l.,
234 p. illus. (incl. ports.) 22 cm., Brockett 4863A;
*Falempin, ou l'espion aérien: Roman patriotique
du Siège de Paris...* Paris: E. Gaillard, [1910?].
270 p. illus. 29 cm. The collection also contains
several copies of James Glaisher, *Voyages aériens*
to which Fonvielle contributed.

Wilfrid de Fonvielle (1826–1914), a scientist
who had been exiled to Algeria for a time as a
result of his liberal political views, was the
author of works on a variety of popular
scientific topics, including human fossils,
insects, and meteorology. He was best known,
however, as a scientific balloonist, a historian
of ballooning, and one of the aeronaut-heroes
of the Siege of Paris.

He first came to public attention as a
balloonist in 1867, when he accompanied Jules
Godard on a flight above the clouds to
observe a meteor shower. It was the first in a
long series of scientific flights described in *La
Science en Ballon.* One of the great aeronauts
of the era, well known as both a scientific and
sport balloonist, Fonvielle was elected the first
president of the Aéro-Club de France in 1893.

THE TRANSATLANTIC BALLOON.

Wise, John

Through the Air: A Narrative of Forty Years' Experience as an Aëronaut. Comprising a History of the Various Attempts in the Art of Flying by Artificial Means from the Earliest Period Down to the Present Time. With an Account of the Author's Most Important Air-Voyages and His Many Thrilling Adventures and Hairbreadth Escapes.

Also an Appendix, in which are Given Full Instructions for the Manufacture and Management of Balloons. By John Wise.
Philadelphia, New York, Boston and Chicago: To-day Printing and Publishing Co., 1873. 630 p. incl. col. front., plates, ports, facsim. 24 cm.

TLB273.W81

Brockett 12948; Gamble 850; Randers-Pehrson 57

Bibliographic note: *Through the Air* is a revised and enlarged edition of an earlier Wise volume: TLB251.W81. *A System of Aeronautics, Comprising its Earliest Investigations, and Modern Practice and Art. Designed as a History for the Modern Reader, Account of Various Attempts in the Art of Flying by Artificial Means, from the*

Earliest Period Down to the Discovery of the Aeronautic Machine by the Brothers Montgolfier, in 1782, and to a Later Period, with a Brief History of the Author's Fifteen Years' Experience in Aerial Voyages. Also, full instructions in the art of making balloons. . . Philadelphia: J. A. Speel, 1850. xvi, [17]–310 p. front. (port.), plates. 22 cm., Brockett 12945; Gamble 849; Randers-Pehrson 28. The Gimbel collection contains only one copy of *Through the Air* and two copies of *System of Aeronautics* (cited here) and a second edition: Fairfield, Wash.: Ye Galleon Press, 1979. 310 p. illus. 28 cm. In addition, the collection contains a copy of John Wise, *Lightning and the Lightning Rod; Use and Abuse of the Rod, Thunder and Thunderstorms, Thirty Years in the Clouds.* Lancaster, Pa.: Pearsol, 1870. 39 p. 23 cm.

Born in Lancaster, Pennsylvania, John Wise (1808–1879) became nineteenth-century America's best known aerial voyager. Trained as a cabinet and piano maker, he made over 450 balloon ascents between his first flight in 1835 and his death while attempting to fly across Lake Michigan. A leading balloon

builder, Wise pioneered the use of new materials for the construction of envelopes, new sealing varnishes, and technological innovations like the ripping panel, which enabled an aeronaut to empty the envelope immediately after landing.

Wise carried the first air mail officially sanctioned by the U.S. Post Office, popularized the notion of aerial photography, and argued forcefully for the use of aerial reconnaissance as early as the Mexican War. Unlike most other aeronauts of the period, Wise was genuinely interested in science, particularly meteorology, which he defined as "the geology of the atmosphere." He built his reputation on his extraordinary skill as an airman, however.

Wise was involved in some of the great long-distance flights undertaken in antebellum America, notably an 809-mile flight from St. Louis, Missouri, to Henderson, New York, in June 1859. He was perhaps best known for his unrealized dream of flying the Atlantic. *Through the Air* remains one of the classic American aeronautical autobiographies.

TOM D. CROUCH

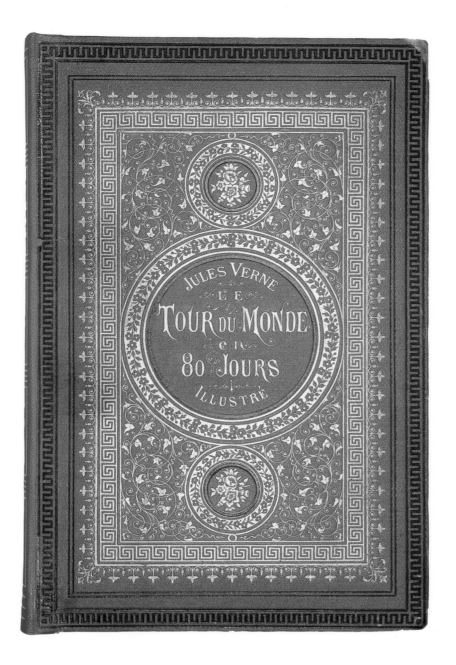

Verne, Jules
Le tour du monde en quatre-vingts jours, par Jules Verne...

> Paris: J. Hetzel, [1874]. 2 p. l., 217, [3] p. incl. front., illus., maps. 27.5 cm.
> PQ2469.T7 1874

Bibliographic note: In addition to the single French volume cited, the Gimbel collection contains two English-language editions: *The Tour of the World in Eighty Days*, by Jules Verne ... Translated by George M. Towls. Boston: J. R. Osgood, 1874. 291 p. front. 15 cm. (The Santerer's Series); same title, Chicago and New York: Belford Clarke, 1884. 320 p. illus. 19 cm.

Compared to Jules Verne's more complex novels, *Around the World in Eighty Days* is a relatively straightforward adventure tale with a simple point. By the last quarter of the nineteenth century, the advent of the steamship and transcontinental railroad travel had drastically reduced the time required to travel to the far corners of the world. Verne's hero, a London clubman, wagers that he can girdle the globe in eighty days. Restricted to modes of locomotion that were actually available, the free balloon was Verne's only opportunity to launch his circumnavigating heroes into the skies.

Throughout his career, Verne based one story after another on lighter-than-air flight technology. As far as we know, however, the author made only one flight, a short ascent from Amiens in 1873 with aeronaut Eugène Godard.

WASHINGTON H. DONALDSON,
AERONAUT.

Amick, M. L.
*History of Donaldson's Balloon Ascensions,
Laughable Incidents, Frightful Accidents,
Narrow Escapes, Thrilling Adventures,
Bursted Balloons. . . Comp. and Arranged
by M. L. Amick, M.D. Illustrated from the
original drawings of Donaldson.*

Cincinnati News Company, 1875. 199, [1] p.
front. (port.), plates. 22.5 cm.

TLB276.D66A6

Brockett 564; Gamble 535; Randers-Pehrson 61

Washington Harrison Donaldson (1840–1875),
born in Philadelphia in 1840, earned early
fame as a gymnast, acrobat, tightrope walker,
and aerialist. At the time of his first ascent in
1871, he employed the balloon as little more
than a flying acrobatic platform. Donaldson
performed his feats of aerial derring-do on
the load ring of the balloon or dangling from
a trapeze bar that substituted for the basket.

As Donaldson gained experience in the
air, he came to share the desire of an older
generation of American balloonists to fly the
Atlantic. He reached the height of his fame in
1873, as a result of the publicity surrounding
an abortive attempt to conquer the ocean

with an enormous balloon, the *Daily Graphic*,
funded by the newspaper of the same name.
Like John Wise, Donaldson died as a result
of an unsuccessful attempt to fly across
Lake Michigan.

M. L. Amick, a Cincinnati physician and
an acquaintance of Donaldson, provided a
classic portrait of the career of a leading aerial
showman, complete with delightfully primitive woodcut illustrations.

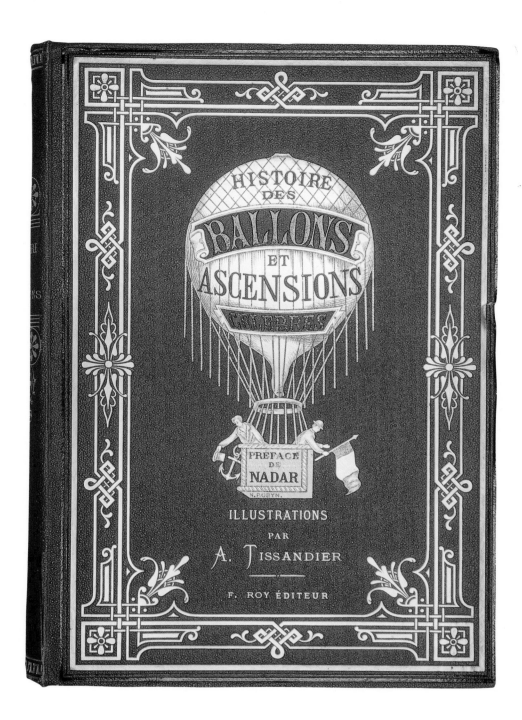

Sircos, A. [Alfred] and Pallier, Th.
*Histoire des Ballons et des ascensions
célèbres; [avec une] préface de Nadar:
Dessins de A. Tissandier et des meilleurs
artistes.*

> Paris: F. Roy, 1876. 2 p. l., 476 p. front., illus.
> (incl. ports.) 29 cm.
>
> TLB273.S61
>
> Brockett 11263; Gamble 803

With an introduction by Gaspard-Félix
Tournachon (Nadar), the great French
photographer-aeronaut, and illustrations
by aeronaut Albert Tissandier (1839–1906)
and other artists, *Histoire des Ballons . . .*
is one of the best of several classic histories
of ballooning that appeared in the late
nineteenth century. The text is generally
accurate but offers a much stronger coverage
of the early history of ballooning than of the
prehistory of flight. The illustrations are
worthy of special note.

Tissandier, Gaston

Le Grand Ballon Captif à Vapeur de M. Henri Giffard. Cour des Tuileries—Paris, 1878. Avec de Nombreuses Illustrations, par M. Albert Tissandier.

Paris: G. Masson, 1878. 67, [1] p. incl. front., illus., plates (part double) 22.5 cm.

TLB276.G4T61

Brockett 11942; Gamble 820

Bibliographic note: This volume is ex libris Gaston Tissandier. The Gimbel collection also contains a second copy of this edition; and a Nouvelle édition, also 1878 and ex libris Gaston Tissandier. In addition to those volumes by Gaston Tissandier specifically cited here and elsewhere in this book, the Gimbel collection contains the following items: …*Application de l'Électricité à la Navigation Aérienne; l'Aérostat Électrique à Hélice de MM. Albert et Gaston Tissandier…Notre Présentée à la Société d'Encouragement le 11 janvier 1884…*Paris, Imprimerie J. Tremblay, 1884. 16 p. illus., fold. pl. 26.5 x 22.5 cm.; *Les Ballons dirigeables. Application de l'électricité à la navigation aérienne, par Gaston Tissandier…Ouvrage accompagné de 35 figures et de 4 planches hors texte.* Paris: Gauthier-Villars, 1885. 2 p. l., [vii]–xii, 108 p. incl. front. illus., plates, map. iv double pl. 19.5 cm., Brockett 11871; Gamble 1350; *Les Ballons dirigeables; Expériences de M. Dupuy de Lôme en 1872, par Gaston Tissandier…* Paris: E. Dentu, 1872. vii, 62 p. illus. 18 cm.; *Deux Conférences sur les aérostats et la navigation aérienne, par Gaston Tissandier; 1st La Météorologie en ballon; Conférence faite au Congrès scientifique de Lille, le 21 août 1874. 2nd la Direction des Aérostats; Conférence faite à la Sorbonne, le 3 mai 1883. Suivies du catalogue des projections relatives aux aérostats.* Paris: A. Molteni, [1884]. 87, [1] p. incl. front. 19 cm.; *Histoire de mes ascensions; Récit de Quarante-cinq Voyages aériens (1868–1888) par Gaston Tissandier…* Paris: M. Dreyfous, [pref. 1888]. 2 p. l., ii, [ix]–xxiv, 308 p. incl. front., illus., plates, diagrs. 26.5 cm.; *La Navigation aérienne;*

l'Aviation et la direction des aérostats dans les temps anciens et modernes, par Gaston Tissandier…Ouvrage illustré de 99 Vignettes. Paris: Hachette et Cie, 1886. 2 p. l., ii, 334 p., 1l. incl. illus., plates, front. 18.5 cm.; *Les Martyrs de la Science. Ouvrage Illustré de Trente-quatre Gravures sur Bois, Compositions de Camille Gilbert.* Paris: M. Dreyfous, [1879]. 334 p. illus. 25 cm.; *Le Présent et l'avenir de l'aéronautique, par Gaston Tissandier…le 19 septembre 1889.* 39 p. 20 cm.; *La Photographie en ballon, par Gaston Tissandier…*Paris: Gauthier-Villars, 1886. vii, 45 p., 1l. incl. illus., plates, front. (mounted phot.) 21 cm.; *Science, Patrie; Conférence faite par… le 29 novembre 1889, au siège de l'Association des Dames françaises…*Amiens: Delattre-leNoel, 1889. 15 p. 21 cm.; *Simples Notions sur les ballons et la navigation aérienne par Gaston Tissandier, avec un Frontispice par Albert Tissandier et 36 vignettes par G. Mathieu.* Paris: Librairie illustrée, [1876]. viii, [9]–125 p., 1l. incl. front., illus. 16.5 cm. (ex libris Gaston Tissandier).

LE BALLON CAPTIF DANS LES NUAGES, VU DE TERRE.

The huge captive balloon that operated as a central attraction at the Paris World's Fair of 1878 was perhaps the largest aerostat ever constructed. With a capacity of 883,000 cubic feet of hydrogen, the balloon was capable of lifting 17 tons. Fifty passengers at a time would be admitted into the circular car. Allowed to rise high above the Paris skyline, the balloon was pulled back down to earth by a powerful steam winch. An estimated 35,000 individuals took advantage of the opportunity to obtain a spectacular view of the City of Lights during the course of the exhibition.

Henri Giffard, the brilliant engineer who designed and supervised construction of the huge craft, had also built and flown the world's first genuinely successful powered airship. A 144-foot-long, spindle-shaped craft powered by a 3 h.p. steam engine, Giffard's dirigible balloon flew for the first time in 1852. Giffard built his first very large tethered balloon, a 176,500-cubic-foot aerostat, for the Paris Exposition of 1867. Two years later, he provided a similar balloon for a London exhibition. Wilfrid de Fonvielle and Gaston Tissandier, the author of this account, made a series of flights with the London aerostat, now the world's largest free balloon, in an effort to raise money for an aerial expedition to the North Pole.

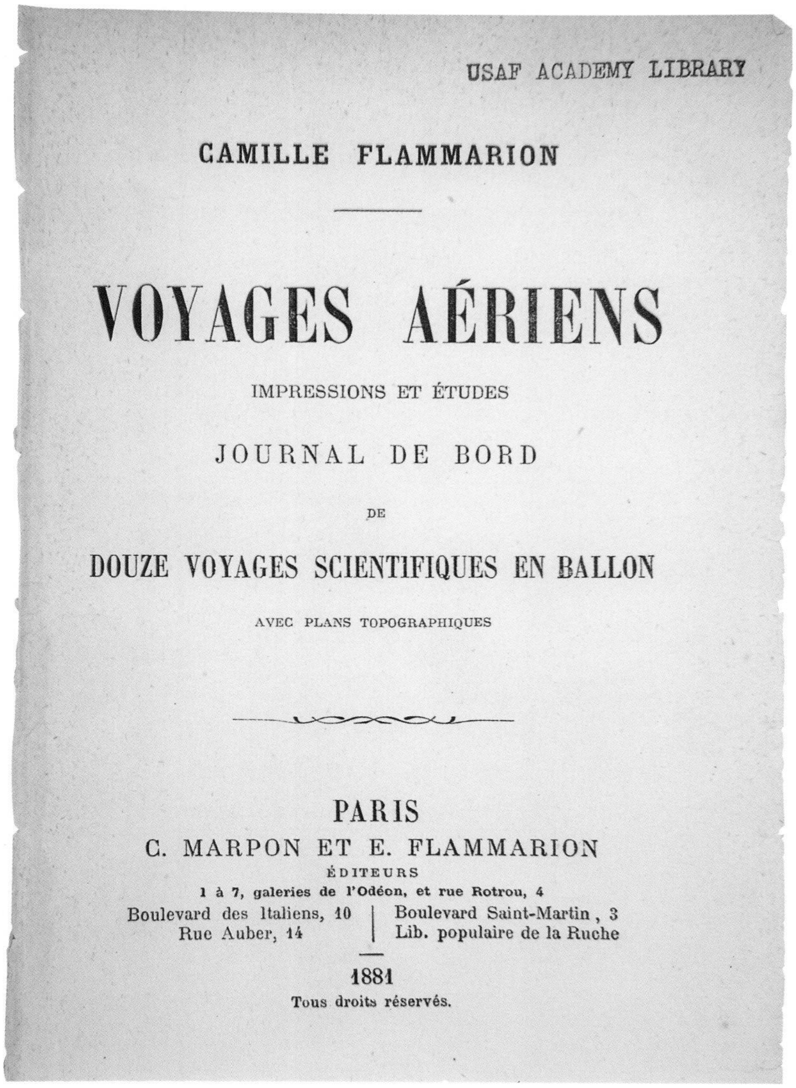

CAMILLE FLAMMARION

VOYAGES AÉRIENS

IMPRESSIONS ET ÉTUDES

JOURNAL DE BORD

DE

DOUZE VOYAGES SCIENTIFIQUES EN BALLON

AVEC PLANS TOPOGRAPHIQUES

PARIS

C. MARPON ET E. FLAMMARION

ÉDITEURS

1 à 7, galeries de l'Odéon, et rue Rotrou, 4

Boulevard des Italiens, 10 | Boulevard Saint-Martin , 3
Rue Auber, 14 | Lib. populaire de la Ruche

1881

Tous droits réservés.

Flammarion, Camille
*Voyages aériens; Impressions et études;
Journal de bord de douze voyages
scientifiques en ballon; avec plans
topographiques.*

Paris: C. Marpon et E. Flammarion, 1881. 2 p.
l., 384 p. illus. (maps) 19 cm.

TLB273.F58

Brockett 4604

Bibliographic note: This copy is inscribed: "A
Mademoiselle Marie Levy-Bing—sympathique
hommage—C. Flammarion, Mois des Fleurs,
1881." The Gimbel collection contains a second
copy of this edition, ex libris Albert Tissandier.

An astronomer with the Paris Observatory,
Camille Flammarion (1842–1925) made
a dozen scientific ascents with aeronaut
Eugène Godard, 1867–1870. In this report
of those flights, the author focuses on
meteorology, reporting on the temperature,
humidity, clouds, and air currents encountered aloft. Flammarion also conducted
aerial experiments involving optics, acoustics,
and astronomy.

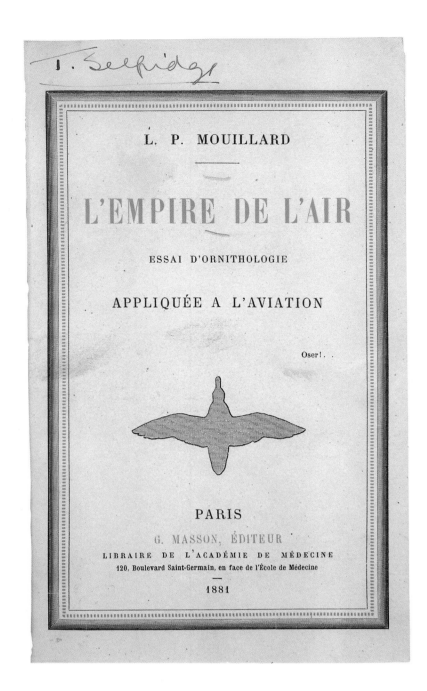

Mouillard, Louis Pierre
*L'Empire de l'Air: Essai d'Ornithologie
appliquée à l'aviation.*

> Paris: G. Masson, 1881. 284 p. illus. 26.5 cm.
>
> TLD181.M92
>
> Brockett 8837; Gamble 5270

Louis Mouillard (1834–1897), a native of Lyons, abandoned a promising career in art to emigrate to Algeria; he farmed there until 1865 when he fled to Cairo as a result of political problems. His interest in flight was initially aroused by observing the birds. Some of his most important publications, including *L'Empire de l'Air,* focused on bird flight rather than on his own aeronautical experiments or glider designs.

Mouillard built three gliders in the 1850s, in one of which he succeeded in making at least one significant flight. He corresponded with the leading aeronautical enthusiast Octave Chanute in the 1890s. Chanute funded a glider constructed by Mouillard in Cairo during the mid-1890s, and arranged for an English translation of *L'Empire de l'Air* and its re-publication by the Smithsonian Institution. Chanute was convinced that his friend's description of aerodynamic control in bird flight represented the earliest technical explanation of the lateral control technique developed by the Wright brothers.

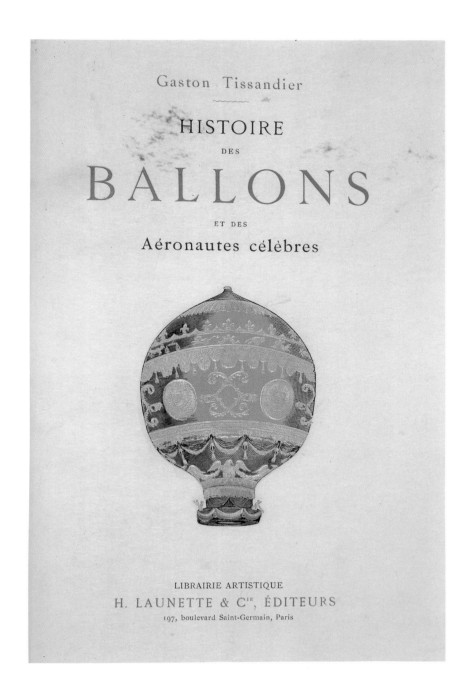

Tissandier, Gaston
Histoire des Ballons et des Aéronautes célèbres, Volume 1, *1783–1800*; Volume 2, *1801–1890*.

> Paris: H. Launette, 1887, 1890. 2 v. fronts., illus., plates (part col., 2 double) ports. 20 cm.
>
> TLB273.T61
>
> Brockett 11925, 11926; Gamble 821
>
> **Bibliographic note:** "Il a été fait une édition spéciale de grand luxe à vingt-cinq exemplaires numérotés sur papier du Japon, avec une double suite de toutes les planches en photogravure." N° 25.

Gaston Tissandier (1843–1899), a research chemist and one of the leading sport and scientific balloonists of nineteenth-century France, made some 40 ascents during an active career that stretched from 1868 to 1886. His most famous flight was an ascent from Paris on April 17, 1875, aboard the balloon *Zénith.* Accompanied by scientists Theodore Sivel and Joseph Croce-Spinelli, and equipped with an experimental oxygen apparatus, Tissandier was determined to break an altitude record established by Henry Coxwell. Tissandier lost consciousness at 22,800 feet. He recovered to find his companions dead on the bottom of the basket and the balloon dropping very rapidly toward the earth. He was the only survivor. Gaston Tissandier, who had written his name large in the annals of flight, was fascinated by the development of aeronautics and produced a classic history of ballooning.

HENRY COXWELL.

[From a Photograph by Messrs. Negretti & Zambra.]

MY LIFE

AND

BALLOON EXPERIENCES,

WITH

A SUPPLEMENTARY CHAPTER

ON

MILITARY BALLOONING.

BY

HENRY COXWELL.

London:

W. H. ALLEN & CO. 13 WATERLOO PLACE, S.W.

1887.

Coxwell, Henry
My Life and Balloon Experiences, with a Supplementary Chapter on Military Ballooning.

> London: W. H. Allen and Co., 1887, 1889. 2 v. front. (v. 1) 13 plates. 19 cm.
> TLB290.C87
> Brockett 3157; Gamble 514

Henry Tracey Coxwell (1819–1900), one of the most colorful and experienced of all British aeronauts, made his first flight in 1844, his 500th in 1863, and his 1,000th (and last) in 1885. Throughout his long career, he developed a reputation for both courage and hairbreadth escapes. On July 6, 1847, Coxwell ascended from Birmingham with several passengers and 60 pounds of fireworks. Caught in a thunderstorm, the balloon burst at 4,000 feet. Coxwell allowed the lower portion of the envelope to invert into the upper netting, forming a parachute that returned the party safely to earth.

Coxwell made one of the most famous ascents of all time on September 5, 1862, when he set out from Wolverhampton with scientist James Glaisher to study atmospheric and physiological conditions at high altitudes. Passing through 30,000 feet, the expanding balloon pulled the valve line out of reach. With Glaisher unconscious, Coxwell, his hands frozen, climbed up onto the load ring and pulled the valve line with his teeth. Both men survived.

In addition to his well-publicized scientific ascents, Coxwell experimented with aerial reconnaissance, bomb dropping, and other aspects of military aeronautics. In 1870 and 1871 he conducted a series of important flights at Cologne and Strasbourg and helped to organize and train a balloon unit for the German army.

BIBLIOGRAPHIE

AÉRONAUTIQUE

CATALOGUE

de livres d'histoire, de science, de voyages et de fantaisie,
traitant de la Navigation aérienne ou des Aérostats

PAR

Gaston Tissandier

PARIS

H. LAUNETTE ET Cie, ÉDITEURS

197, boulevard Saint-Germain, 197

1887

Tissandier, Gaston
*Bibliographie aéronautique: Catalogue
de livres d'histoire, de science, de voyages
et de fantaisie, traitant de la Navigation
aérienne ou des Aérostats…*

Paris: H. Launette, 1887. 2 p. [5]–62 [2] p. 29 cm.

Z5063.T61

Brockett 11919; Gamble 32

Bibliographic note: "Il a été fait une édition
spéciale de grand luxe à vingt-cinq exemplaires
numérotés sur papier du Japon." This copy
was annotated by Col. Richard Gimbel.

In addition to being a leading aeronaut,
designer of aerostats, and historian of
aeronautics, Gaston Tissandier was also an
important collector of books and manuscripts
on aeronautics and artifacts relating to the
history of flight. His *Bibliographie* lists over
800 items covering all aspects of the subject.
With illustrations reproduced on high-quality
Japanese paper, the book remains a classic
guide to early aeronautica.

Der Vogelflug

als Grundlage der Fliegekunst.

Ein Beitrag

zur

Systematik der Flugtechnik.

Auf Grund

zahlreicher von O. und G. Lilienthal ausgeführter Versuche

bearbeitet von

Otto Lilienthal,

Ingenieur und Maschinenfabrikant in Berlin.

Mit 80 Holzschnitten, 8 lithographierten Tafeln und 1 Titelbild in Farbendruck.

Berlin 1889.

R. Gaertners Verlagsbuchhandlung

Hermann Heyfelder.

SW. Schönebergerstraße 26.

KREISENDE STORCHFAMILIE.

Lilienthal, Otto
*Der Vogelflug als Grundlage der
Fliegekunst: Ein Beitrag zur Systematik der
Flugtechnik. Auf Grund zahlreicher von O.
und G. Lilienthal ausgeführter Versuche
bearbeitet von Otto Lilienthal…Mit 80
Holzschnitten, 8 lithographierten Tafeln
und 1 Titelbild in Farbendruck.*

Berlin: R. Gaertners, 1889. viii, 187 p. col. front.,
illus. VIII fold. diagr. 23.5 cm.

TLD181.L72v

Brockett 7557; Gamble 5239

Germany's Otto Lilienthal (1848–1896), the
author of this work whose title translates to
"Birdflight as the basis of aviation: a contribution toward a system of flight technology,"
began his serious work in aeronautics with
engineering tests conducted during the years
1866–1870, 1873–1874, and 1885–1889. His basic
goal was to measure the lift and drag produced by different airfoil shapes at various
angles of attack. Working with his brother
Gustav, Lilienthal began by demonstrating
that cambered, or curved, wings produce
greater lift than a flat plate and then pro-
ceeded to identify what he believed to be the
most efficient airfoil shapes.

Having published his results in *Der
Vogelflug*, Lilienthal turned from theory to
practice. Between 1890 and 1896, he completed
some 2,000 glides in 18 distinct glider designs.
Photographs and eyewitness descriptions of
his flights convinced the readers of magazines
and newspapers that the age of winged flight
was at hand.

Otto Lilienthal died on August 10, 1896,
as a result of injuries suffered in a glider
crash. He inspired the generation of experimenters who would take the final steps
toward the invention of the airplane.
The technical information in *Der Vogelflug*
provided subsequent experimenters with
a starting point; they, in turn, corrected
Lilienthal's data and improved on his research.

TOM D. CROUCH

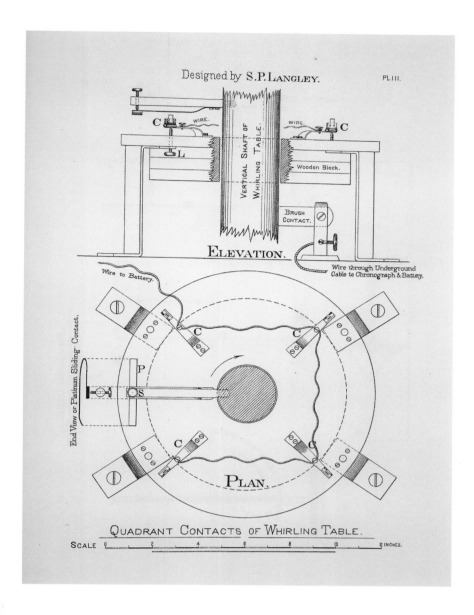

Designed by S. P. LANGLEY.

PL. III.

ELEVATION.

PLAN.

QUADRANT CONTACTS OF WHIRLING TABLE.

SCALE

Langley, S[amuel] P[ierpont]
Experiments in Aerodynamics.

Washington, D.C.: Smithsonian Institution, 1891. iii, 115 p. incl. tables, diagrs. x plates (part fold.) 33.5 cm. (Smithsonian Contributions to Knowledge) [v. 27, n. 1] Smithsonian Institution publication 801.

TLD209.L28

Brockett 7166; Randers-Pehrson 82

Bibliographic note: This volume is an account of Langley's earliest experiments. The design, construction, and testing of several models and full-scale aerodromes are covered in: *Langley Memoir on Mechanical Flight,* Parts 1 and 2. Washington, D.C.: Smithsonian Institution, 1911. 1 v. illus., plates (part double) diagrs. 33.5 cm. (Smithsonian Contributions to Knowledge, v. 27, n. 3), Smithsonian Institution publication 1948.

The third secretary, or director, of the Smithsonian Institution, Samuel Langley (1834–1906) earned fame as a pioneer astrophysicist and an administrator of science. Interested in flight since childhood, he began a series of aerodynamic experiments in 1886–1887, while he was still director of the Allegheny Observatory at the Western University of Pennsylvania (now the University of Pittsburgh). His goal was to answer the basic question: Is it possible to design and build a successful mechanical, heavier-than-air flying machine? "The most important general inference from these experiments," Langley reported in *Experiments in Aerodynamics,* "is that…mechanical flight is possible with engines we now possess."

Having demonstrated to his own satisfaction that the basic problem could be solved, Langley would spend the last decade of his life attempting to develop a practical flying machine. He began by testing small flying models powered by strands of twisted rubber, then moved on to steam-powered "aerodromes" with wingspans of up to 15 feet. In 1896, after five years of effort, Langley's team achieved sustained flight with two of these models. The final step, which came between 1898 and 1903, involved the design and construction of a full-scale aerodrome. The craft was destroyed during a final unsuccessful attempt at a test flight in December 1903.

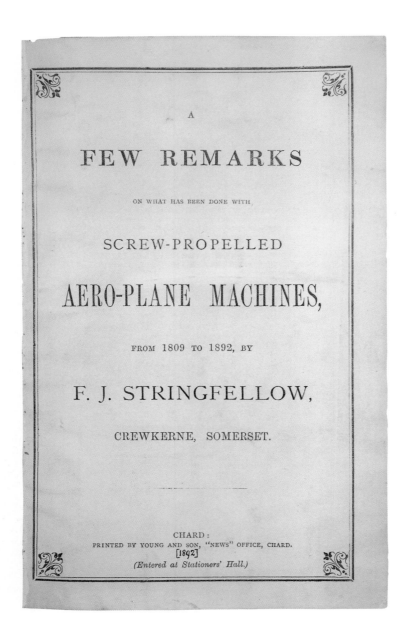

Stringfellow, F[rederick] J[ohn]
A Few Remarks on What Has Been Done with Screw-Propelled Aero-Plane Machines, from 1809 to 1892.

> Chard, England: Young and Son, 1892. 14 p. 6 mounted illus. 21.5 cm.
>
> TLB252.S91.A2
>
> Brockett 11592

Frederick John Stringfellow (1832–1905) was a native of Chard, England. His father, John Stringfellow (1799–1883), was an aeronaut, amateur scientist, and brilliant engineer who had developed light steam engines for industrial applications. In 1840, Stringfellow and William Samuel Henson (1805–1888) began a collaborative effort to solve the problems of powered, heavier-than-air flight. Two years later, Henson patented the design for a high-wing, passenger-carrying mono-plane with a 150-foot span. Over the next decade, the *Aerial Steamship* as it became known, inspired a series of both serious and comic graphic prints that spread the fame of Henson and Stringfellow throughout Europe and America.

The collaboration ended in 1848, when Henson emigrated to the United States. In later years, Frederick Stringfellow claimed a short, sustained free flight for a steam-powered model with a 10-foot wingspan developed by his father during this period. Stringfellow and son were awarded a £100 prize for a lightweight steam engine designed to power a triplane model displayed at the Aeronautical Society of Great Britain exhibition in 1868. Frederick, who developed a series of multiplane models following his father's death, sought to ensure that the contributions of W. S. Henson and two generations of Stringfellows would not be forgotten.

TOM D. CROUCH

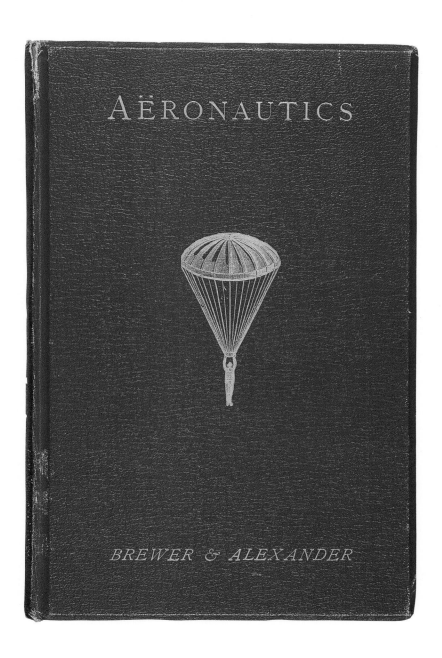

Brewer, Griffith, and Alexander, Patrick Y.
*Aëronautics: An Abridgment of
Aëronautical Specifications Filed at the
Patent Office from A.D. 1815 to A.D. 1891.*

London: Taylor and Francis, 1893. vi, 160, [16] p.
illus. 21.5 cm.

TLD38.B84

Brockett 505; Gamble 166

In May 1891, Patrick Y. Alexander (1867–1943),
a wealthy English balloonist and technological
enthusiast, accompanied Griffith Brewer
(1867–1948), a patent agent and amateur
aeronaut, on a flight from Chelsea. Striking
up a friendship, the two men decided to
collaborate on a digest of existing British
aeronautical patents. Her Majesty's Patent
Office had already issued an annual index
of all patents, but Brewer and Alexander did
not believe that it was particularly useful
to flying machine experimenters. "Many of
the specifications," they noted in the preface,
"describe inventions which are impractical…
ridiculously absurd…and probably the result
of dreams."

The two collaborators were determined
to produce an annotated compendium
of existing patents that would help serious
investigators separate the wheat from the
chaff. Brewer conducted most of the basic

patent research, while Alexander evaluated
the designs and identified key features.
The resulting volume is still of interest and
value to historians of flight technology.

Griffith Brewer (who eventually became a
close friend, student, business associate, and
supporter of the Wright brothers) was one of
the great figures in the early history of British
aviation. Although considerably less influential than Brewer, Patrick Alexander would
remain a well-known figure in aeronautics
during the years prior to World War I.

If, for instance, the possible soaring angle were 4°, we should have for the position of the center of pressure, back from the front edge, a distance of $0.2 + 0.3\ sin.\ 4° = 0.22$ per cent. So that it seems probable that if its load had been applied at 22 per cent. instead of 33 per cent. back from the front edge, the flat plane would have soared at a flatter angle than 15°, and would have shown less "thrust," because the effect of placing the weight so far

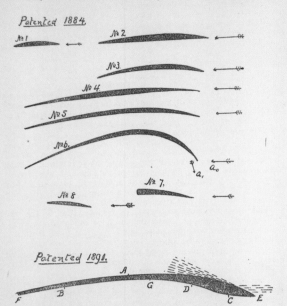

FIG. 65.—PHILLIPS—1884–1891.

back was to tilt the plane unduly, and thus to increase both the angle of incidence and the thrust.

It is not known whether Joëssel's formula applies to curved surfaces ; but be this as it may, it is reasonable to believe that it would be but little modified, so that perhaps the error in locating the center of pressure operated to the disadvantage of the curved forms nearly as much as to that of the plane. We may, therefore, accept the general

---

Chanute, Octave
Progress in Flying Machines by O. Chanute, C.E.

New York: *American Engineer and Railroad Journal,* [1894].

iv, 1l., 308 p. illus. 22.5 cm.

TLB251.C45 1894

Gamble 1585; Randers-Pehrson 99

A native of Paris, France, Octave Chanute (1832–1910) immigrated to the United States with his father in 1838. At the age of 17 he took a position as an apprentice with a railroad construction crew and rose through the professional ranks to become one of the leaders of American civil engineering during the years following the Civil War.

In the early 1870s, Chanute became fascinated by the aeronautical experiments undertaken by French and English engineers. He immersed himself in the literature of the field and began to correspond with virtually every major experimenter of flying machines in the world. In 1886, Mathias Forney, editor of the *American Engineer and Railroad Journal,* invited Chanute to publish a series of articles on aeronautics. Twenty-seven installments of the series "Progress in Flying Machines" were published in the journal beginning in October 1891. Forney published the entire series, revised and expanded by the author, as a book of the same title in 1894. This volume, combined with Chanute's lectures, his support of promising young experimenters, and his involvement in

the design and testing of hang gliders, established the engineer and author as one of the world's leading authorities on flight.

The most important association of Chanute's life began in May 1900, when he received a letter from Wilbur and Orville Wright, the owners of a small bicycle shop and manufacturing facility in Dayton, Ohio. Over the next decade, Chanute served as an important sounding board for the Wright brothers, introduced them to the larger international circle of aeronautical experimenters, and generally publicized their work. In spite of a general cooling in their relationship with Chanute after 1905, the Wrights never doubted the value of his friendship and support. "By the death of Mr. O. Chanute the world has lost one whose labors had to an unusual degree influenced the course of human progress," Wilbur Wright noted in January 1911. "No one was too humble to receive a share of his time. In patience and goodness of heart he has rarely been surpassed. Few men were more universally respected and loved."

TOM D. CROUCH

Plate I.

LEONARDO DA VINCI.
1452–1519.

From a drawing in red chalk by himself. In the Royal Library, Turin.

No. I.

The
Aeronautical Annual.

1895.

DEVOTED TO THE ENCOURAGEMENT OF EXPERIMENT WITH
AERIAL MACHINES, AND TO THE ADVANCEMENT
OF THE SCIENCE OF AERODYNAMICS.

EDITED BY

JAMES MEANS.

This publication will be sent, postpaid, to any
address on receipt of one dollar.

BOSTON, MASS.:
W. B. CLARKE & CO.,
340 WASHINGTON STREET.

Means, James, ed.
The Aeronautical Annual ... Devoted to the Encouragement of Experiment with Aerial Machines, and to the Advancement of the Science of Aerodynamics. Edited by James Means. no. 1–3; 1895–1897.

Boston: W. B. Clarke & Co., 1894–1897. 3 v. illus. TLB237.A25

Brockett 8288, 8289, 8290; Randers-Pehrson 102, 105, 112

Bibliographic note: The Gimbel collection also contains a copy of *The Epitome of the Aeronautical Annual...Ed. by James Means...*Boston: W. B. Clarke Company, 1910. 4 p. l., 5–220 p. front., illus., plates, ports. 23.5 cm. The epitome includes reprints from the original three volumes together with some new material. Additional Means items in the collection

include: James Means, *Manflight, by James Means.* Boston: James Means, 1891. 29 p. diagrs. 23.5 cm., Brockett 8285; Randers-Pehrson 83; James Means, *The Problem of Manflight, by James Means.* Boston: W. B. Clarke & Co., 1894. 20 p. incl. diagrs. 23 cm., Brockett 8292; Gamble 2443; Randers-Pehrson 97; James Means, *Five Patents Relating to Aviation.* Boston, [1909?]. [7] p. 22 cm.; James Means, *The James Means Control for Flying Machines.* Boston, 1913. [12] p. illus. 18 cm.; James Means, *Twentieth Century Energy: A Pamphlet which Treats Briefly of an Unseen Yet Potent Form of Matter, by James Means.* Boston: W. B. Clarke & Co., 1896. 19 p. 23 cm.

James Howard Means (1853–1920), a native of Massachusetts who had made a fortune in the shoe business, became a center for aeronautical enthusiasm in the Boston area and a major publicist in the cause of heavier-than-air flight. Convinced that rivalries and miscommunications between experimenters were retarding the search for a successful airplane, Means was determined to establish a publication that would offer useful and trustworthy information to the entire aeronautical community.

The first volume of the *Aeronautical Annual* focused on figures from the relatively distant past: Leonardo da Vinci, Sir George Cayley, F. W. Wenham, Thomas Walker, and Benjamin Franklin. In the second and third volumes, however, Means featured articles by the leading experimenters of the day: Otto Lilienthal, Octave Chanute, S. P. Langley, Hiram Maxim, and others. Although the publication was relatively short-lived, it did become a forum for the presentation of the latest research, as Means had hoped.

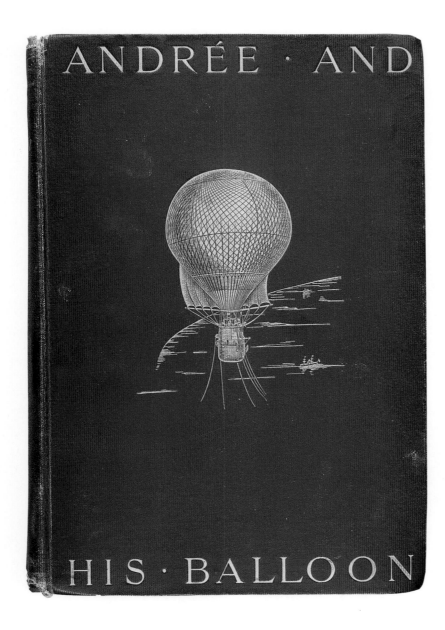

Lachambre, Henri, and Machuron, Alexis
Andrée and His Balloon.

Westminster: A. Constable, 1898. 305 p. illus. 20 cm.
G700.L13 1898

Bibliographic note: In addition to this volume
on the construction of the balloon *Ornen* and
the early history of the Andrée expedition, the
Gimbel collection also contains books
published after the discovery of the remains on
White Island. The most important of these is
Svenska sällskapet för antropologi och geografi
(Swedish Society for Anthropology and
Geography), *Andrée's Story: The Complete
Record of His Polar Flight, 1897, from the Diaries
and Journals of S. A. Andrée, Nils Strindberg, and
K. Fraenkel, found on White Island in the
Summer of 1930. Translated from the Swedish by
Edward Adams-Ray.* New York: Viking Press,
1930. Gamble 4507

Henri Lachambre and his associate and
nephew, Alexis Machuron, were among the
leading balloon builders of *fin de siècle* Paris.
During the winter of 1895–1896, the firm won
the contract for the construction of a very
large balloon designed to carry a crew of three
from the Norwegian island of Spitsbergen to
the North Pole and on to a safe landing.
Salomon August Andrée, chief engineer of
the Swedish Patent Office, was to head the
expedition, accompanied by Nils Strindberg
and Knut Fraenkel. The project was privately
funded and attracted the support of both
Alfred Nobel and King Oscar of Sweden.

The finished balloon, named the *Ornen*
(Eagle), had a volume of 170,000 cubic feet.
It was constructed of 3,360 individual pieces of
silk sewn together with 8.4 miles of thread.
Fifteen miles of Italian hemp made up the
net that supported the large closed basket,
or gondola. The expedition was well equipped
to deal with any emergency encountered aloft

or on the ice. The intrepid explorers would
report their progress to a waiting world via
carrier pigeon.

At 1:43 P.M. on the afternoon of July 11,
1897, the *Ornen* rose slowly to an altitude of
some 300 feet over Dane Island, Spitsbergen,
then began to move in a northeasterly
direction over Virgo Harbor. The first serious
attempt to reach the North Pole by air was
under way at last. The balloon dipped so low
that the basket touched the water, then rose
rapidly to an altitude of 1,950 feet. Observers
on shore noted that the huge craft was still
moving to the northeast when it vanished
into the clouds and into history at 1:56 P.M.

The disappearance of the *Ornen* and its
three passengers, Salomon August Andrée,
Nils Strindberg, and Knut Fraenkel, was one
of the first great mysteries of the air age.
Thirty-three years later, on August 5, 1930, the
Bratvaag, a sealing vessel chartered by a
Norwegian scientific expedition, sent a party
ashore to explore White Island, a remote spot
of land east of Spitsbergen. To their astonish-
ment, members of the party stumbled into
the last camp of the Andrée expedition. In
addition to the remains of the three explorers, the crew of the sealer found cameras,
diaries, logbooks, letters, maps, and diagrams
that chronicled the expedition from takeoff
until October 7, 1897. Developed more than
three decades after they had been taken, the
photographs provided a ghostly visual record
of the final days of the Andrée expedition.
The old mystery was solved.

The records revealed that the *Ornen* had
crashed on the ice far to the northeast of
Spitsbergen just three days after takeoff. Their
dream of reaching the pole dashed, the three
explorers had then started back toward the
Arctic coast on foot, dragging what equipment and supplies they could salvage. Their
goal was to reach Spitsbergen before winter.
Instead, they were forced to pitch their final
camp on White Island. All three men died
within a few days of reaching the island.
Death came as a result of exposure to the
elements, although other factors, notably the
consumption of tainted polar bear meat, have
also been cited as possible causes of death.

TOM D. CROUCH

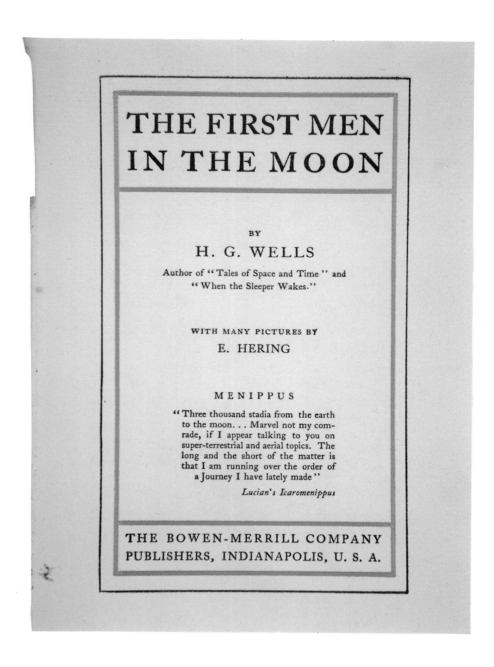

THE FIRST MEN
IN THE MOON

BY

H. G. WELLS

Author of "Tales of Space and Time" and
"When the Sleeper Wakes."

WITH MANY PICTURES BY

E. HERING

MENIPPUS

"Three thousand stadia from the earth
to the moon. . . Marvel not my comrade, if I appear talking to you on
super-terrestrial and aerial topics. The
long and the short of the matter is
that I am running over the order of
a Journey I have lately made"

Lucian's Icaromenippus

THE BOWEN-MERRILL COMPANY
PUBLISHERS, INDIANAPOLIS, U. S. A.

Wells, H. G. [Herbert George]
*The First Men in the Moon…With Many
Pictures by E. Hering.*

Indianapolis: Bowen-Merrill Company, [1901].
4 p. 312 p. front, plates. 20 cm.

PR5774.F5 1901a

H. G. Wells (1866–1946) was, with Jules Verne, the most important and influential early contributor to the literary genre that would become known as science fiction. Although the best of his early novels (*The Time Machine* [1895], *The Island of Dr. Moreau* [1896], *The Invisible Man* [1897], *The War of the Worlds* [1898]) are more concerned with the impact of science on society than with technical detail, he clearly had a gift for inspiring dreams.

By 1915, Robert H. Goddard, the American spaceflight pioneer, was already deeply involved in his early rocket experiments. His diary records that he read H. G. Wells' *The First Men in the Moon* on July 19, 1898. Ten days later, after a morning spent working on rocket nozzles and pumps, he looked the book over a second time. Then, on August 8,

Goddard had a vivid dream in which he flew to the moon.

"In 1898 I read your *War of the Worlds*," Goddard informed Wells in 1932. "I was sixteen years old…and I decided that what might conservatively be called 'high altitude research' was the most fascinating problem in existence." Like Verne, Wells delighted millions of general readers and inspired a handful of geniuses to transform the dream into reality.

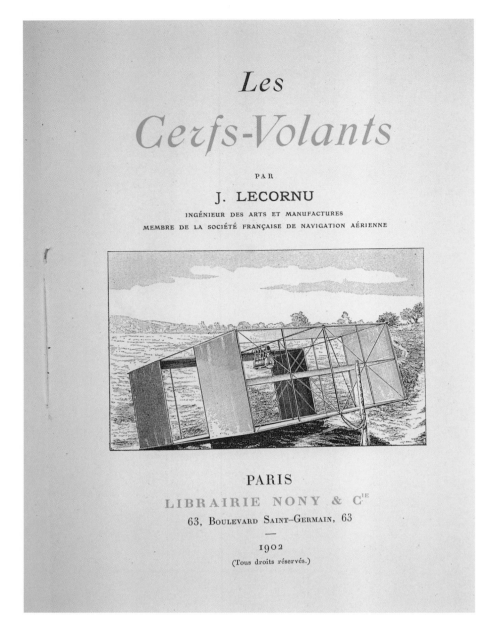

Les

Cerfs-Volants

PAR

J. LECORNU

INGÉNIEUR DES ARTS ET MANUFACTURES
MEMBRE DE LA SOCIÉTÉ FRANÇAISE DE NAVIGATION AÉRIENNE

PARIS

LIBRAIRIE NONY & Cie

63, BOULEVARD SAINT–GERMAIN, 63

—

1902

(Tous droits réservés.)

Lecornu, Joseph
Les Cerfs-Volants…

> Paris: Librairie Nony et Cie, 1902. 2 p. l., [iii]–
> 240 p. illus., diagra. 22.5 cm.
>
> TLD951.L46
>
> Brockett 7362; Gamble 2652

Experience with kites, the oldest flying objects constructed by human beings, played a critically important role in the invention of the airplane. Joseph Lecornu, a graduate engineer and member of the French Aerial Navigation Society, produced the best introduction to the theory, practice, and history of kites that was available to the engineers who designed and built the first airplanes.

The book opens with a useful introduction to the theory of kite design and proceeds to a discussion of materials, construction techniques, and similar practical matters. Over half of the volume is devoted to aspects of kite history and to a discussion of specialized topics, including man-lifting kites, kite photography, meteorological kites, and the use of kites for scientific research. A careful and detailed treatment of the subject, *Les Cerfs-Volants* remains as useful and interesting an account as it was at the time of publication almost a century ago.

Santos-Dumont

Santos-Dumont, Alberto
My Air-Ships, by A. Santos-Dumont.

> New York: The Century Co., 1904. ix, 356 p. incl. plates, ports., diagrs., front. 19.5 cm.
>
> TLB290.S23
>
> Brockett 10808
>
> **Bibliographic note:** The Gimbel collection has a second copy of this volume: *My Air Ships,* New York: Dover, 1973. xviii, 122 p. 22 cm. In addition, the collection has other volumes by Santos-Dumont: Alberto Santos-Dumont, *Dans l'Air,* Paris: Charpentier et Fasquelle, 1904. 2 p. l., 343 p. 21. incl. illus., plates, port., front. 21 cm.; Alberto Santos-Dumont, *O que eu vi.* São Paulo: Typ. Piratininga, 1918. 100 p. illus. 22 cm.; Alberto Santos-Dumont, *Os meus balões,* [Rio de Janeiro]: Biblioteca do Exército, 1973. 260 p. illus. 23 cm. (Coleção General Benício, vol. 109.)

Alberto Santos-Dumont (1873–1932) was one of the most colorful figures in the early history of powered flight. Le Petit Santos weighed only about 110 pounds and stood 5 feet 5 inches tall in his shiny patent leather shoes fitted with lifts. Dark hair, parted sharply in the center and plastered in place with pomade, capped a cadaverous face. Those who knew him assure us that his faintly comic appearance masked a cold patrician manner. His enthusiasm for flight was so all-encompassing that he ate at a table and chair suspended 6 feet above the floor of his dining room.

The son of a wealthy Brazilian coffee planter, Santos-Dumont came to Paris in 1897 to acquire an engineering education. He acquired a balloon instead, but quickly tired of operating at the mercy of the winds. Prior to the turn of the century he ordered the first in what would become a series of 15 small, one-man airships. One of the great moments of his career came on October 19, 1901, when he won the 100,000-franc Deutsch de la Meurthe Prize for a flight from the Aéro-Club de France hangar at Saint-Cloud to the Eiffel Tower and back in less than half an hour.

The sight of the little Brazilian chugging along just above the rooftops of Paris epitomized the spirit of the *Belle Époque,* but Santos-Dumont soon grew as dissatisfied with pressure airships as he had with the free balloon. Inspired by news of what the Wright brothers were accomplishing in the United States, and armed with an imperfect understanding of Wright technology, Santos-Dumont began work on an airplane. On the afternoon of October 23, 1906, that aircraft, *14-bis,* flew for roughly 164 feet at an altitude of 9 to 16 feet. For the first time, an airplane had made a publicly announced flight.

A second aircraft developed by Santos-Dumont, *La Demoiselle,* established him as one of the preeminent designers of the era. Diagnosed as suffering the early stages of a debilitating disease, however, he retired from active involvement in aeronautics prior to World War I. Depressed by his own failing health, by a series of air disasters that had taken a heavy toll of human life, and by an outbreak of violence in Brazil in which air power was a factor, Alberto Santos-Dumont took his own life on July 23, 1932, three days after his fifty-ninth birthday.

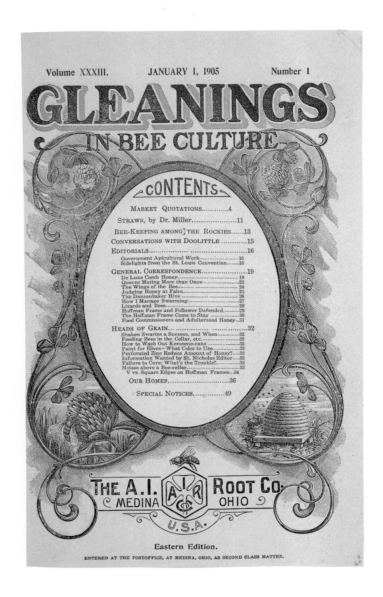

Root, A. I. [Amos Ives]
"Our Homes, By A. I. Root," in *Gleanings in Bee Culture*

v. 33, no. 1, January 1, 1905, pp. 36–38.

SF521.G4 33

By September 20, 1904, Wilbur and Orville Wright had been flying from Torrence Huffman's cow pasture, some 8 miles east of Dayton, Ohio, for some time. They had made their first powered flight at Kitty Hawk, North Carolina, on December 17, 1903, and returned home to Dayton determined to find a local site where they could continue to practice flying and perfect their machine in relative seclusion. After a less than impressive demonstration flight in the spring of 1904 that discouraged curious local reporters, the pair settled on Huffman Prairie.

The world was still not aware of the fact that the Wright brothers had invented the airplane, but Amos Root was determined to correct the situation. A resident of Medina, Ohio, Root operated a very successful bee-keeping supply house and edited *Gleanings in Bee Culture,* a trade journal. For some weeks he had been hearing vague rumors about two minister's boys who were emulating the birds

in a field near Dayton. Fascinated by all things mechanical, he drove south in his automobile to investigate for himself:

> Imagine a locomotive that has left its track, and is climbing up in the air right toward you…. Well, now, imagine this white locomotive, with wings that spread twenty feet each way, coming right toward you with a tremendous flap of its propellers, and you will have something like what I saw. The younger brother bade me move to one side for fear it might come down suddenly; but I tell you friends, the sensation that one feels in such a crisis is hard to describe.

For the first time in history, an airplane had turned in full circles, and Amos Root had been there to see it. *Gleanings in Bee Culture* had scooped the great newspapers of the world on the story of the century.

TOM D. CROUCH

Erfahrungen

beim

Bau von Luftschiffen.

Vortrag

gehalten auf der 49. Hauptversammlung des
Vereines deutscher Ingenieure zu Dresden
am 29. Juni 1908

von

Dr.-Ing. Graf Zeppelin.

Berlin.
Verlag von Julius Springer.
1908.

Zeppelin, Ferdinand Adolf August
Heinrich, Graf von
Erfahrungen beim Bau von Luftschiffen.
Vortrag gehalten auf der 49.
Hauptversammlung des Vereines deutscher
Ingenieure zu Dresden am 29. Juni 1908.
> Berlin: Verlag von Julius Springer, 1908. 23 [1]
> p. 22 cm.
> TLD901.Z5e
> Brockett 13167; Gamble 1417

Count von Zeppelin (1838–1917), the single most important figure in the history of the rigid airship, served as an officer in the German army between 1861 and 1891. The first flights of *La France* in 1884, along with the publication of several key papers, fired Zeppelin's imagination and convinced him that Germany should develop an airship of its own. When a prestigious state commission rejected his initial impractical design, Zeppelin turned to Professor Muller-Breslau, who assisted in the development of the classic cigar-shaped craft.

After Zeppelin organized a joint stock company in 1894, work began on the design and construction of the *LZ1*, which made its

first flight over Lake Constance on July 2, 1900. In spite of their impressive size, the early zeppelins were woefully underpowered and difficult to control. Not until the *LZ3* (1906) did the Count begin to taste genuine success. During the period between 1906 and 1913 zeppelin enthusiasm was rampant, as the huge airships seen cruising over the cities of the Reich became the very symbol of German strength and technological achievement.

Girard, E., and Gervais, A. de Rouvelle
Les Ballons dirigeables: Théorie—Applications; avec 143 figures dans le texte.

> Paris: Berger-Levrault & Cie, 1907. 2 p. l., 307 p. illus., diagrs. 22.5 cm.
>
> TLD901.G51
>
> Gamble 1069

From the last half of the nineteenth century until 1906–1908, with the full emergence of the German rigid airships, France dominated the field of large navigable airships. Henri Giffard (1852) and Gaston and Albert Tissandier (1883) built and flew the earliest steam and electrically powered dirigibles, neither of which was able to exceed 10 miles per hour in still air. It remained for Paul Renard and Arthur Krebs, of the French military balloon facility at Chalais-Meudon, to produce the first marginally practical airship, *La France,* in 1884. Even after the initial success of the early zeppelins, Chalais-Meudon and other French manufacturers continued to produce large airships, including Lebaudy (*Le Jaune,* 1902), Astra (*Ville de Paris,* 1906/1907; *La Patrie,* 1907), and Clement-Bayard (*Clement-Bayard,* 1908).

Unlike the zeppelins, rigid airships in which gasbags were located inside a rigid, fabric-covered framework, all of the pre-World War I French craft were semirigids, or pressure airships, in which a single large gasbag was attached to an external keel. *Les Ballons dirigeables,* a review of the leading French airships, is a reprint of articles originally published in the *Revue du Génie militaire* from July 1906 to January 1907.

Ostoya, Victor E.
Vole, Wright!

Paris, 1908. 642–656 p. illus. 31 cm. (*L'Assiette au Beurre*, no. 405, Janvier 1909)

TLB290.W95

There was simply no precedent for the incredible wave of incredulity, excitement, and enthusiasm that gripped first France, then all of Europe, following the first public demonstration flight of a Wright aircraft at a Le Mans racetrack on August 7, 1908. Periodically over the next century, one aerospace figure after another would emerge as the next great hero of the hour—Louis Blériot, Charles Lindbergh, Amelia Earhart, Jean Mermoz, Italo Balbo, Yuri Gagarin, the Apollo astronauts. None of them, however, would match the extent to which Wilbur and Orville Wright would stun the world.

Between 1903 and 1908, there was little proof that the Wrights had flown. The brothers had purposely not made any public flights, and they had not released many photographs of their aircraft in the air. When the

Americans refused to try for the rich prizes being offered to would-be aviators, most French aviation experimenters assumed that the Wrights were *"bluffeurs."* The first flights at Le Mans swept all of those doubts away and instantly established Wilbur Wright as the most famous man in Europe. Caricatures of "Veelbur Reet," with a bird-like beak and a soft, peaked cap, were everywhere, as this typical collection of comic sketches and text demonstrates.

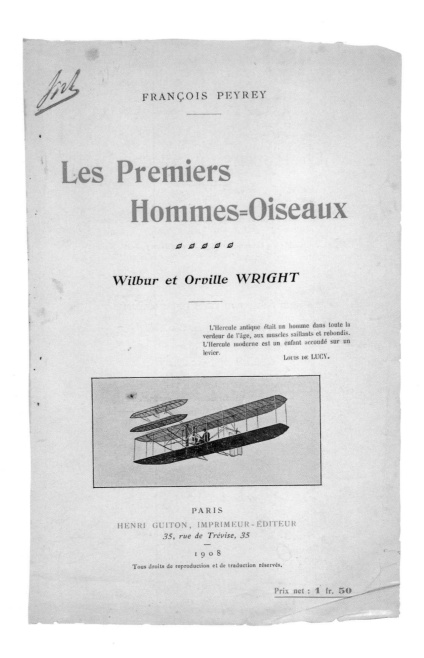

Peyrey, François
Les Premiers Hommes-Oiseaux, Wilbur et Orville Wright.

> Paris: H. Guiton, 1908. 2 p. l., [9]–78 p. 1l. illus. (incl. plan) plates, ports., map, 24 cm.
>
> TLB290.W95P

Bibliographic note: The Gimbel collection holds a good selection of Peyrey's books on the birth of aviation. In addition to the first edition cited, the collection contains ...*Les Premiers Hommes-Oiseaux; Wilbur et Orville Wright...Édition Nouvelle, Relatant Toutes les Expériences des Frères Wright en France et aux États-Unis d'Amérique...* Paris: H. Guiton, 1909. 3 p. l., [9]–151 p. 21 illus. (incl. maps, plans) plates, ports. 24.5 cm. (cover signed by the author); ...*Au Fils du vent; avec une préface du comte Henri de la Vaux...* Paris: H. Guiton, 1909. 2 p. l., [9]–303 p. illus., plates, ports. 28.5 cm.; *L'oeuvre de l'Aéro-Club de France et l'Aéronautique contemporaine.* Paris: H. Dunod et E. Pinat, [1910]. 2 p. l., 149 p. illus. (incl. ports.) 22.5 cm.; ...*Les Oiseaux artificiels; avec une préface de Santos-Dumont.* Paris: H. Dunod et Pinat, 1909. 3 p. l., [v]–xiv, 667 p. illus., diagrs. 23 cm.

There can be no doubt that François Peyrey (1873–1934) was *le premier historien des frères Wright en France.* He provided French readers with the first full and trustworthy accounts of the brothers, from their roots in Dayton, through their experiments in America (1900–1905), to their first spectacular public flights in 1908. At the time, Peyrey's books were fuller and more accurate than any accounts of the Wrights available in English.

F. FERBER

L'AVIATION

SES DÉBUTS — SON DÉVELOPPEMENT

De Crête à Crête

De Ville à Ville

De Continent à Continent

BERGER=LEVRAULT & Cⁱᵉ, ÉDITEURS

PARIS	NANCY
RUE DES BEAUX-ARTS, 5 -- 7	RUE DES GLACIS, 18

JUILLET 1908

Ferber, Ferdinand
L'Aviation; ses Débuts—son Développement; de Crête à Crête, de Ville à Ville, de Continent à Continent.

Paris, Nancy: Berger-Levrault & Cⁱᵉ, 1908. xii, 250 p. illus., diagrs. 23 cm. ("Les Calculs," p. [107]–248 is a revision of the author's: *Les Progrès de l'aviation par le vol plané; les calculs.* 1907.)

TLB251.F34 1909

Bibliographic note: The Gimbel collection contains a second copy of this edition (Cinquième tirage) and a 1910 Nouvelle édition. Other holdings by Captain Ferber include: *Les Progrès de l'aviation par le vol plané; les calculs, par F. Ferber…avec 26 figures dans le texte.* Paris, Nancy: Berger-Levrault & Cⁱᵉ, 1907. 85 [1] p. illus. diagrs. 23 cm.; *Les Progrès de l'aviation depuis 1891 par le vol plané, par F. Ferber…avec 44 figures dans le texte.* Paris, Nancy: Berger-Levrault & Cⁱᵉ, 1905. 53 p. 1l. illus. 22 cm. "Deuxième édition."; "Extrait de la Revue d'artillerie-mars 1904." …*Die Kunst zu Fliegen…* Berlin: R. C. Schmidt & Co.; New York: Steiger & Co., 1910. 215 p. illus. (incl. ports.) diagrs. 22.5 cm.

Ferdinand Ferber (1862–1909) was primarily responsible for the rebirth of French interest in aviation after 1900. A native of Lyons and a professional artillery officer, Ferber was something less than the ideal soldier. He was overweight, walked with a slouch, and was apparently a less than dashing horseman. Although chronically nearsighted, he refused to wear spectacles. Legend has it that he once failed to spy the approach of a general officer, missed giving a salute, and was thus doomed to remain a captain.

Ferber became interested in flight in 1898, while serving as an instructor at the *École d'application.* He corresponded with aviation pioneers, including both Clément Ader and Otto Lilienthal's brother, Gustave, and, by 1900 had built and flown a variety of craft, from a kite to a rather crude copy of a standard Lilienthal glider. A letter to Octave Chanute in 1901 led to his discovery of the work of the Wright brothers.

Ferber built and flew a very crude biplane glider, inspired by the early Wright aircraft, at Beuil in 1902. From that point, until the time of his death in a flying accident seven years later, Captain Ferber remained in the forefront of French experimenters. As this volume, and the others listed in the bibliographic note, demonstrate, he was also a leading publicist and historian of early aviation in Europe.

LES JOURNÉES HISTORIQUES DE LA NAVIGATION AÉRIENNE

VOYAGE DE LA « FRANCE » AU-DESSUS DE PARIS (25 SEPTEMBRE 1885).
Cliché communiqué par le Command. P. Renard.

VOYAGE DE L'AÉROPLANE « BLÉRIOT » DE TOURY A ARTENAY,
ET RETOUR AVEC ESCALES (31 OCTOBRE 1908). Photo Rol.

La Route de l'air.   Pl. 1, Frontispice.

ALPHONSE BERGET
DOCTEUR ÈS SCIENCES
PROFESSEUR A L'INSTITUT OCÉANOGRAPHIQUE

LA ROUTE DE L'AIR

AÉRONAUTIQUE
AVIATION

HISTOIRE — THÉORIE — PRATIQUE

82 DIAGRAMMES EXPLICATIFS
66 GRAVURES TIRÉES HORS TEXTE

NUL ne peut dès maintenant prévoir
les conséquences de l'Aviation
sur les mœurs humaines.

LIBRAIRIE HACHETTE ET CIE
79, BOULEVARD SAINT-GERMAIN, PARIS · 1909

Berget, Alphonse, i.e., Thomas Claude Xavier Alphonse

…La route de l'air; Aéronautique, Aviation, Histoire—Théorie—Pratique. 82 diagrammes explicatifs, 66 gravures tirées hors texte…

Paris: Librairie Hachette et Cᵢₑ, 1909. 3 p. l., vi, 311, [1] p. front., illus., plates. 25.5 cm.

TLB251.B49r 1909

Brockett 1593b

Bibliographic note: This volume is ex libris Horace Oswald Short, with his book-plate. The Gimbel collection contains another copy of this edition, ex libris Aero Club of America.

The collection also contains several editions of the English translation: *The Conquest of the Air: Aeronautics, Aviation, History, Theory, Practice, by Alphonse Berget…* New York: G. Putnam's Sons; London: Heinemann, 1909. xxiv, 295 p. illus. (incl. maps) xxxii (i.e., 36) pl. (incl. front.) 23.5 cm. The collection has twin copies of the 1911 editions: "New and revised edition," New York: G. Putnam's Sons; London: Heinemann, 1911. xx, 249 p. illus. 22 cm. In addition, the collection holds: Alphonse Berget, *Ballons, Dirigeables et Aeroplanes.* Paris: Librairie Universelle, 1908. 3 p. l., (i.e., iii) 276 p. incl. illus. (incl. ports.) plates (2 double) 19 cm.; *L'Aviation, Ballons, Dirigeables, Avions.* [Paris]: Hachette, 1924. 64 p. incl. front., illus., diagrs. 24 cm.; *L'Air…Illustré Sous la Direction de Lucien Rudaux.* Paris: Librairie Larousse, [c. 1927]. 310 p. illus. 32 cm.

Alphonse Berget (1860–1934) was one of the leading historians of early aviation. His work remains useful for its insight into the personalities and events of *fin de siècle* aeronautics.

A Professor Filling, & Explaining to an Audience, the Nature of a Baloon.

Bruel, François-Louis
Histoire aéronautique par les monuments peints, sculptés, dessinés et gravés des origines à 1830. Deux cents reproductions en noir et en couleur, texte par François-Louis Bruel du Cabinet des Estampes de la Bibliothèque Nationale.

Paris: André Marty, 1909. 4 p. i., [5]–93, [2] p. l. plates (part col., part fold.) ports., facsim., 37.5 cm. x 29 cm.

TLB258.B84

Gamble 170

François-Louis Bruel's (1881–1912) lavishly illustrated *Histoire* remains one of the great treasures in the history of aeronautical publishing. Covering the period from antiquity to 1830, the volume is filled with a wealth of illustrations, ranging from full-color reproductions of eighteenth- and nineteenth-century prints to a wide variety of other historic works of art. Printed on special papers, using colored inks, and tipped or specially bound into the volume, many of the images are reproduced as virtual facsimiles of the originals. In addition to the thoughtful and very informative text, the *Histoire* is a masterwork of the printer's art.

Le possibilità dell'aereonavigazione

PER

l'Ing. GIULIO DOUHET

Capitano di Stato Maggiore

Non vorrei che, dalla prima impressione di questo mio articolo, mi si giudicasse un misoneista; non lo sono, anzi, adoro tutto quello che ha sapore di novità e di progresso, ma mi piace guardare ogni novità con occhio sereno e tranquillo, senza lasciarmi trasportare dalla fantasia, perchè credo che questo sia il metodo migliore per rimanere nel vero e per provare il minor numero di disillusioni.

L'aereonavigazione è, si può dire, l'ultima novità del giorno; essa è giovanissima; non dico in fasce per non offender nessuno; la gioventù, non è un difetto, tutt'altro, è l'età delle speranze, dell'entusiasmo e dei sogni, e noi dobbiamo considerare un fenomeno che si verifica tutte le volte che una novità si affaccia sulla scena del mondo. Questo fenomeno si manifesta con la successione delle seguenti quattro fasi:

1° Si cerca di adattare la novità alla guerra;

2° Si esagera la portata della novità;

3° Si provano delle disillusioni;

4° La novità si adatta automaticamente ai vari bisogni ai quali è capace soddisfare.

Questo fenomeno noi l'abbiamo visto svolgersi, nelle quattro fasi ora distinte, per quanto ha tratto con la trazione meccanica su strada ordinaria. Non appena le prime vetture automobili incominciarono, fra numerose e frequenti *pannes*, a sollevare la polvere delle soleggiate strade di diverso ordine, parve, alle menti più ricche di fervida immaginazione, che i futuri campi di battaglia, più che all'odor della polvere, dovessero esser profumati all'idrocarburo; sembrò che le ferrovie dovessero in breve, per vendetta, ridurre in chiodi le loro rotaie; parve insomma che l'automobile fosse capace di compiere anche quello che non è dato al Parlamento inglese, il quale, come tutti sanno, può tutto, eccetto che mutare una donna in un uomo.

Si scrissero durante questo periodo, prima e seconda fase del fenomeno, una quantità enorme di corbellerie che potrebbero, ora, venire usate come cura risanatrice del sangue, poi, poco alla volta, vennero le disillusioni; la ferrea realtà delle cose ricondusse a terra i sognatori e l'automobile, diventando pratico, s'impose ai bisogni che poteva realmente sod-

---

Douhet, Giulio
Le possibilità dell'aereonavigazione.

758–771 p. 26 cm. (In *Revista delle Comunicazioni*. Anno III, Fasc. VIII Roma: Ministero delle Poste e dei Telegrafi, 1910.)

TLB400.D73

Giulio Douhet (1869–1930) was the earliest and most influential of the military officers who came to be identified as "Prophets of Air Power." Born into a family with a tradition of service to the House of Savoy, Douhet developed an early reputation as an officer who was willing to say what he thought and fight for what he believed. Already an authority on mechanized warfare, he emerged as the principal Italian spokesman for the military airplane with the publication of this article in 1910. Although he had not yet flown, and had seen only one or two airplanes in the air, Douhet was already expressing the major elements of his airpower theory in the most forceful terms. Command of the air, he argued, would prove just as important as command of the sea.

Italy was the first nation to explore the military role of the airplane. Nine aircraft supported the Italian invasion of Turkish Libya in 1911. This small air unit conducted some of the earliest coordinated reconnaissance and bombing missions in history.

Named to command the provisional Italian air battalion prior to the outbreak of World War I, Douhet placed an order for an advanced trimotor Caproni bomber without authorization. In spite of the fact that the big Caproni would eventually become the pride of both Italian and American air units battling Austro-Hungarian forces during World War I, Douhet was removed from his post and sent to an infantry unit. Undaunted, he continued his outspoken attacks on Italian air policy, for which he was court-martialed and imprisoned.

Following his release from prison, Colonel Douhet published a prophetic novel, *Come Fini la Grande Guerra—la Vittoria Alata* (How the Great War Ended—the Winged Victory). His most important book, *Il Domino dell'Aria* (Command of the Air), appeared in 1921, with a second edition in 1927. Translated into other languages, the book played an important role in shaping a debate on the potential of the air weapon during the years between the wars.

TOM D. CROUCH

DARIUS GREEN
AND HIS
FLYING-MACHINE

By J. T. TROWBRIDGE

WITH ILLUSTRATIONS BY
WALLACE GOLDSMITH

HOUGHTON MIFFLIN COMPANY
BOSTON AND NEW YORK ▼ THE
RIVERSIDE PRESS CAMBRIDGE
MDCCCCX

1910

Trowbridge, John
Darius Green and His Flying-Machine,
by J. T. Trowbridge; with illustrations
by Wallace Goldsmith.

Boston and New York: Houghton Mifflin
Company, 1910. 53, [1] p. incl. front. plates, 16 cm.
PS3097.D21

Bibliographic note: The Gimbel collection also
contains *The Vagabonds, and Other Poems.*
Boston: J. R. Osgood, 1875. Includes *Darius
Green . . .* iv, 172 p. 17.5 cm.

During the years following the Civil War,
most Americans came to regard the flying
machine as the ultimate in foolish dreams.
John Townsend Trowbridge (1827–1916)
provided a classic statement of this attitude
in his poem "Darius Green and His Flying-
Machine," which may have appeared as a
magazine piece as early as 1869. Like many
another "country dunce," young Darius
was convinced that "the air was also man's
domain." Determined to conquer the sky,
he sets to work

> …with thimble and thread and wax and
> hammer and
> buckles and screws,
> and all such things as geniuses use,
> Two bats for a pattern, curious fellows!
> A charcoal pot and a pair of bellows, some
> wire and
> several old umbrellas;
> A carriage cover, for tail and wing, a piece of
> harness, and straps and strings,
> …these and a thousand other things.

Encased in his contraption, the inventor
leaps from the hayloft and falls straight down
into the barnyard, surrounded by "a wonderful whirl of tangled strings, broken braces
and broken wings, shooting stars and various
things." To the thousands of readers who
chuckled over poor Darius' plight, the meaning was perfectly clear: "If God had intended
for humanity to fly, he would have given
them wings."

67. CASE II.—Single plane without tail or rudder.—
This case may be deduced from the preceding one by
putting S_2 and $l = 0$. But where the stability is entirely
dependent on the shifting of the centre of pressure, it
is really easier to start afresh and use the complete

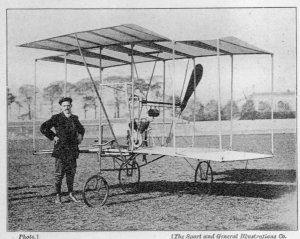

[*Photo.*]   [*The Sport and General Illustrations Co.*]

FIG. III.—EDWARD MINES BIPLANE AT DONCASTER.

An aeroplane having no auxiliary tail planes or vertical fins. *Longitudinal
stability* could only be attained by means of the shift of the centre of pressure
with varying angle of attack (§ 67), and the stability condition would thus
impose a superior limit to the speed. There is no *lateral stability*, all the
coefficients in the biquadratic except the first two vanishing.

discriminant $\mathfrak{H} > 0$ instead of the approximate substitute
$\mathfrak{CD} - \mathfrak{CB} > 0$. We have

$$\frac{\mathfrak{A}}{W^3} = k^2, \qquad \frac{\mathfrak{B}}{W^3}\left(\frac{W}{KUg}\right) = S'k^2(1 + 2\mu^2) \qquad \frac{\mathfrak{C}}{W^3}\left(\frac{W}{KUg}\right)^2 = \frac{W}{Kg}S'e\mu$$

$$\frac{\mathfrak{D}}{W^3}\left(\frac{W}{KUg}\right)^3 = \frac{2W}{Kg}S^2e\mu^3\left(1 + \frac{\tan\theta}{2\mu}\right)$$

$$\frac{\mathfrak{E}}{W^3}\left(\frac{W}{KUg}\right)^4 = \frac{2W^2\cos\theta}{K^2U^2g}S^2e\mu^2(1 + \mu\tan\theta) \quad . \quad . \quad . \quad . \quad . \quad . \quad (119)$$

Bryan, George Hartley
*Stability in Aviation; An Introduction to
Dynamical Stability as Applied to the
Motions of Aeroplanes, by G. H. Bryan…*

London: Macmillan and Co., Ltd., 1911. x, 1l.,
192 p. illus., diagrs. 22.5 cm.

TLD491.B91 1911

Gamble 1564

George Hartley Bryan (1854–1928), a professor
at the University College of North Wales, was
a major first-generation contributor to flight
science and technology. The inventors of the
airplane were engineers of genius, but they
had left a great many questions unanswered.
During the first two decades of the twentieth
century, German researcher Ludwig Prandtl,
based at Göttingen University, addressed fundamental aerodynamic problems and developed the core of a circulation theory of lift.
Other pioneering contributors to aerodynamic
theory included Wilhelm Kutta, Nikolai
Zukovskii, Frederick Lanchester, and a host
of Prandtl's students and associates, notably
Max Munk and Theodore von Karman.

    G. H. Bryan was the most important early
contributor to the study of another set of
theoretical problems relating to stability and
control. Bryan published his earliest article
in this field in 1903. *Stability in Aviation*
provided a generation of airplane designers
with a solid understanding of issues related
to aircraft and control.

Grahame-White, Claude, comp.

The Aeroplane, Past, Present, and Future, by Claude Grahame-White (Winner of the Gordon Bennett International Aviation Cup, 1910) and Harry Harper; with ninety-three illustrations.

London: T. W. Laurie, 1911. 2 p. l., vii–xv, 310. [1] p. front. plates, ports., fold. tab. 23.5 cm.

TLB251.G74 1911

Bibliographic note: The Gimbel collection contains two copies of this edition and a third copy marked: "This edition de luxe consists of 100 copies, numbered and signed. This is No. 21." As noted, the volume is signed and differs slightly from copies of the standard first edition: xv, 319 p. illus. 23 cm. The collection also contains a copy of the first American edition: Philadelphia: J. B. Lippincott, 1911. vii–xv, 319 p. illus. 24 cm.

Other volumes by Grahame-White represented in the Gimbel collection include: *The Story of the Aeroplane, by Claude Grahame-White.* Boston: Small, Maynard and Company, [c. 1911]. xii, 390 p. illus. 21 cm.; *Aviation, by Claude Grahame-White.* London, Glasgow: Collins's Clear Type Press, (pref. 1912). 262 p. front. (port.) 18 cm.; *The Invisible War-Plane. A Tale of Air Adventure in the Great Campaign, by Claude Grahame-White and Harry Harper…* London: Blackie and Son Ltd., [1915]. v, 1l., 272 p. front. plates. 19 cm.; *Learning to Fly; a Practical Manual for Beginners, by Claude Grahame-White and Harry Harper…* London: T. W. Laurie, Ltd., [c. 1916]. 111, [1] p. front., plates. 19 cm.

Claude Grahame-White (1879–1959) was one of the great English aviators of the first generation, and Harry Harper one of its first great publicists. Grahame-White earned fame in March and April 1910 when he competed with the French aviator Louis Paulhan for the £10,000 *Daily Mail* prize for the first flight from London to Manchester. Grahame-White lost the race, but he made the first recognized night flight in Europe during the course of the contest and won the affection and admiration of his countrymen.

Grahame-White toured the United States as well. In spite of being targeted by the Wright brothers for competing for prize money with a machine covered by their American patent, Grahame-White emerged as the star of the Harvard-Boston Meet in September 1910 and won the 1910 James Gordon Bennett International Aviation Cup, staged as part of the great Belmont Park flying meet the following month.

In 1910, Grahame-White and his friend, the aviation enthusiast and publicist Harry Harper, published one of the most popular of all early books on winged flight. *The Aeroplane* is as much a compendium of essays as an authored work. Among the featured sections are a chronology of aviation and a list of records; short biographies of the first aviators; a description and analysis of the earliest aircraft fatalities; a discussion of aircraft engines; a discussion of "the constructional future of aeroplanes" by Henri Farman; C. G. Grey's notes on aircraft safety; and the thoughts of Col. J. F. Capper on the future of military aviation.

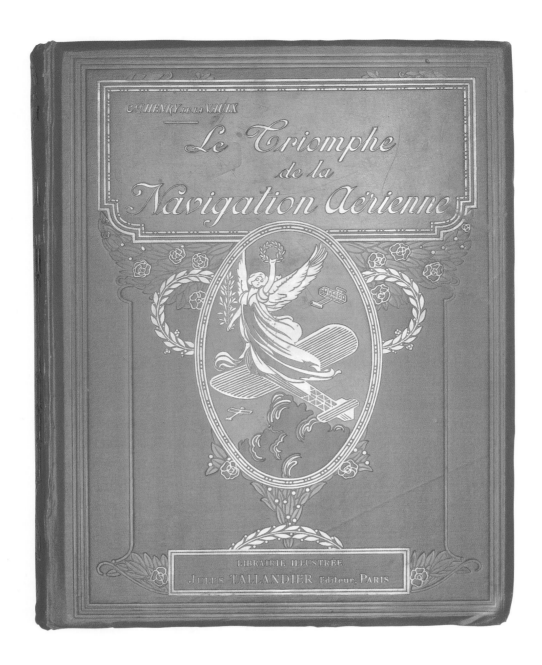

La Vaulx, Henri, Comte de
Le Triomphe de la Navigation Aérienne;
Aéroplanes, Dirigeables, Sphériques.

Paris: J. Tallandier, [1910]. 2 p. l., 3–392, [4] p.
incl. illus., plates. double pl. 33.5 cm.

TLB251.L39

One of the wealthy sport balloonists who
founded the Aéro-Club de France (1898), the
Comte Henri de la Vaulx (1870–1930) was a
confirmed nationalist who worked to ensure
that France, the nation of the Montgolfiers,
would lead the world into the air age. As
president of the Aéro-Club during the critical
year of 1904, he presided over a renaissance
of French interest in winged flight following
the revelation of what the Wright brothers
had accomplished.

The Comte de la Vaulx encouraged
experiments with winged aircraft, established
prizes to encourage aeronautical achievement, and commissioned the construction
of a monoplane based on a design by the
nineteenth-century pioneer Victor Tatin,

which left the ground on two occasions in
1907. In addition, Comte de la Vaulx produced
Le Triomphe de la Navigation Aérienne, a
volume that the English authority Charles
Harvard Gibbs-Smith regarded as "one of the
most authoritative of the early histories of
flying" *(The Rebirth of European Aviation*
[London: PRO, 1974], p. 9).

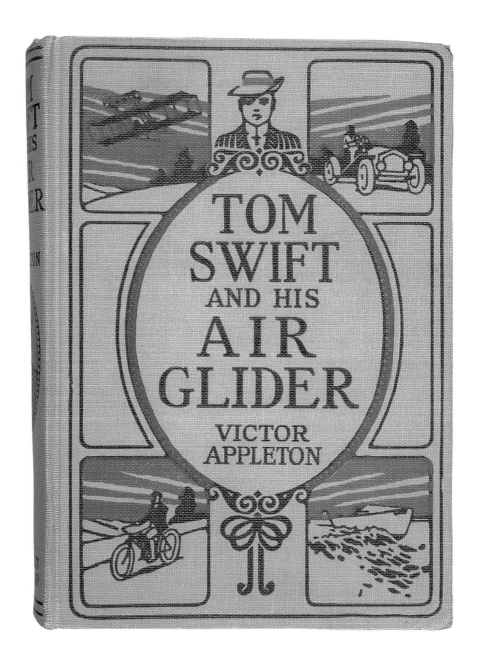

Appleton, Victor [pseud.]
Tom Swift and His Air Glider, or Seeking the Platinum Treasure.

>New York: Grosset & Dunlap, [1912]. iv, 209 p. front. 19.5 cm.
>
>TLB418.A65

Once upon a time in America, Tom Swift was a name to conjure with. Edward Stratemeyer (1862–1930), the publishing giant and "king of the juveniles" who inaugurated the Motor Boys, Rover Boys, and Bobsey Twins series of juvenile novels, also set the Tom Swift saga in motion. As had been the case with earlier book series back to the time of Samuel Goodrich, Stratemeyer conceived the character, established the basic formula, and farmed out the writing chores. All of the Tom Swift volumes appeared under the name of Victor Appleton, although author Howard Garis wrote most of the books.

The formula seldom varied. Tom, the son of a widowed inventor, with the assistance of a standard group of friends, supporters, and comic foils achieves yet another technological triumph in order to defeat the latest scheme of the "Happy Harry Gang," rival inventor Addison Berg, or Andy Foger, "a red-headed, squint-eyed rich bully" determined to steal Tom's latest invention.

The most successful of all Stratemeyer's creations, Tom Swift books continued to appear for over a decade after his death. The forty titles published between 1910 and 1941 sold an estimated 6.5 million copies. In spite of the best efforts of school librarians who decried their literary shortcomings, the books had an enormous impact. The indomitable young hero, ever ready to overcome the most daunting problem with yet another breakthrough, helped to inspire generations of American youngsters with faith in the power of the machine.

Copyright, 1910, by The Pictorial News Co.
CURTISS' HUDSON RIVER FLIGHT—OVER THE STATUE OF LIBERTY

Curtiss, Glenn Hammond
The Curtiss Aviation Book, by Glenn H. Curtiss and Augustus Post; with chapters by Captain Paul W. Beck, U.S.A., Lieutenant Theodore G. Ellyson, U.S.N., and Hugh Robinson; with numerous illustrations from photographs.

New York: Frederick A. Stokes Company, [c. 1912]. 3 p. l., v–x, 307 p. front., 1 illus., plates, ports., diagrs. 20 cm.

TLB400.C98

Glenn Hammond Curtiss (1878–1930) loved speed above all things. As a young man, he raced bicycles, then built and raced motorcycles. The sale of a motorcycle engine to power an airship operated by Thomas Scott Baldwin (1864–1923) marked Curtiss' entry into aeronautics. In 1908, he provided the power plant for the *SC-1*, the first U. S. Army airship, designed and built by Baldwin.

As early as 1907–1908, Curtiss joined forces with Alexander Graham Bell, Lt. Thomas E.

Selfridge, J. McCurdy, and F. W. Baldwin to form the Aerial Experiment Association (AEA). The AEA produced a series of machines, culminating in the *June Bug*, which won the *Scientific American* trophy for the first public flight in the United States of about half a mile or more (July 4, 1908).

In the summer of 1909, Curtiss won the first James Gordon Bennett International Aviation Cup, which was awarded for a speed contest staged at the great flying meet at

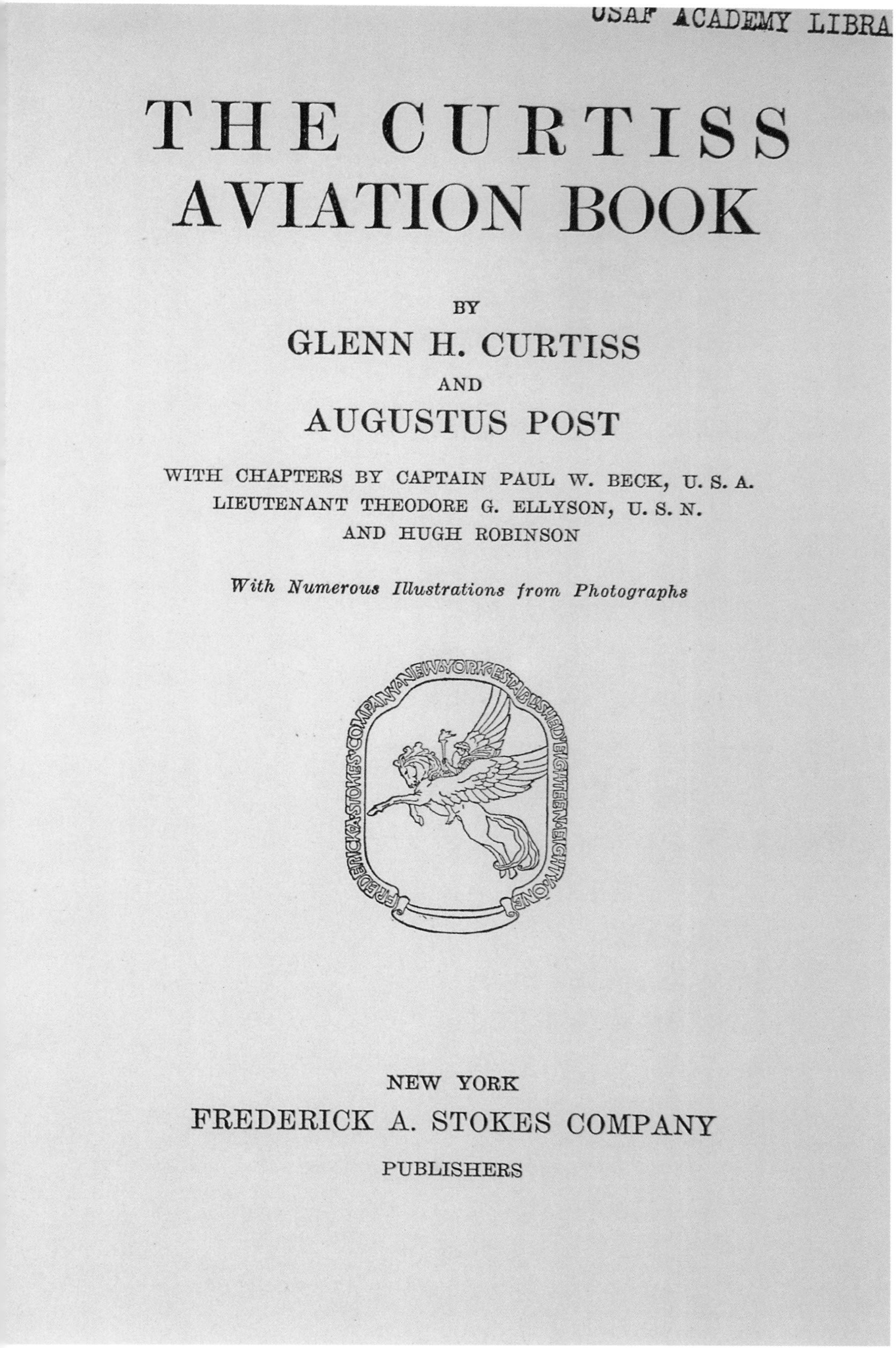

THE CURTISS AVIATION BOOK

BY

GLENN H. CURTISS

AND

AUGUSTUS POST

WITH CHAPTERS BY CAPTAIN PAUL W. BECK, U. S. A.
LIEUTENANT THEODORE G. ELLYSON, U. S. N.
AND HUGH ROBINSON

With Numerous Illustrations from Photographs

NEW YORK

FREDERICK A. STOKES COMPANY

PUBLISHERS

Reims, France. Curtiss was not the first to fly off water, but he did become the world's best-known and most successful builder of flying boats. Curtiss aircraft were also the first to take off from and land on ships. Moreover, the early successes chronicled in the *Curtiss Aviation Book* were achieved while Curtiss was the target of the most important of the lawsuits brought by the Wright brothers against those whom they regarded as having infringed their patent.

Within two years of the publication of this volume, the Curtiss Aeroplane and Motor Company would become the most successful of all U. S. aircraft manufacturers. The firm was the leading supplier of flying boats to the navies of the world, the designer and builder of a flying boat thought capable of flying the Atlantic, and the leading U. S. supplier of aero engines and training aircraft. Curtiss had become one of the great names in American aviation, and so it would remain.

Photo. G. Cooke.

André Beaumont [signature]

Conneau, Jean Louis Camille
My Three Big Flights, by André Beaumont (Lieut. J. Conneau) with a sonnet by Edmond Rostand and sixty illustrations.

New York: McBride, Nast & Company, 1912. XI, 150 p. front., plates, ports. 23.5 cm.

TLB290.C75

During a three-month period in the summer of 1911, Jean Conneau, an ensign in the French navy who flew (and wrote) under the name of André Beaumont, won three of the great aerial competitions of the prewar era: the Paris-Rome Race (May 28–31); the Circuit of Europe (June 18–20); and the Circuit of Britain (July 22–24). Conneau immediately began work on a series of lectures and a book, both of which would be illustrated with his photographs.

Conneau's book, which includes a poem by Edmond Rostand, is one of the great personal accounts of the period. The aviator offers considerable insight into the problems of operating the aircraft of the time, including the difficulties of point-to-point navigation. Having made his name as a racing pilot, Conneau returned to duty with the French navy, where he pioneered operations with the Donnet-Leveque biplane, a Curtiss-style flying boat.

[Lewis, Sinclair]
Hike and the Aeroplane, by Tom Graham
[pseud.]*; with illustrations in two colors*
by Arthur Hutchins.

    New York: Frederick A. Stokes & Company,
    1912. 6 p. l., 275 p. col. front., col. plates. 19.5 cm.
    TLB418.L676h

"You're damn right," Sinclair Lewis (1885–1951)
explained to Chauncey Tinker in 1938, "I wrote
Hike and the Aeroplane for the sole and not
very commendable purpose of getting from
the firm of Frederick A. Stokes & Company,
who paid outright for the book at salary rates,
a long vacation to do a few words on my first
novel, *Our Mr. Wren*." Although the first
American Nobel laureate in literature may
not have been especially proud of the fact,
Hike and the Aeroplane, not *Our Mr. Wren,*
was his first published novel.

    Written during a three-week stay at
Provincetown, Massachusetts, in 1911, the
book is a straightforward boy's adventure
story of the Tom Swift variety in which Hike,
the 16-year-old hero, makes use of an airplane
to triumph over the evil Captain Welch.
Fascinated by aviation, Lewis had already

published a short story ("Captains of Peace")
based on an aeronautical theme. Lewis
informed his friend Gene Baker that three
well-known aviation pioneers—Glenn H.
Curtiss, J.A.D. McCurdy, and U.S. Army pilot
Capt. Paul Beck—had read and approved
the manuscript of the novel. "But that ain't
no sign," he concluded. "Since when were
aviators established as the perfect court of
literary judgment?"

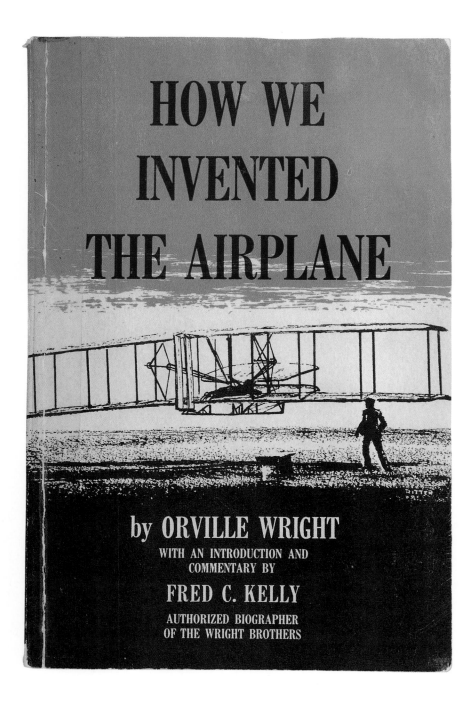

HOW WE INVENTED THE AIRPLANE

by ORVILLE WRIGHT

WITH AN INTRODUCTION AND
COMMENTARY BY

FRED C. KELLY

AUTHORIZED BIOGRAPHER
OF THE WRIGHT BROTHERS

Wright, Orville
How We Invented the Airplane.

> Edited and with commentary by Fred C. Kelly.
> Drawings by James MacDonald. New York:
> McKay, 1953. 78 p. illus. 18 cm.
> TLB251.W95h

Neither Wilbur nor Orville Wright was ever able to write a detailed account of their work in aeronautics. During their lifetimes, the full story of what they had achieved remained locked away in their letters, diaries, and notebooks. Both men did tell their story in several major court depositions, however. Orville Wright offered a particularly clear and concise account on January 13, 1920, when he testified as a government witness in the case of *Montgomery v. The United States.* The suit was brought by individuals who argued that in supporting the patent claims of the Wright brothers and others the government had unfairly ignored the prior claims of John Joseph Montgomery, a California aeronautical pioneer. The Montgomery heirs lost their case, but Fred Kelly, a journalist and official biographer of the Wrights, edited the testimony that Orville offered on that occasion and published it as a short book that remains the best first-person account of the invention of the airplane.

Wilbur Wright, 1867–1912

Orville Wright, 1871–1948

McFarland, Marvin W., ed.
The Papers of Wilbur and Orville Wright, including the Chanute-Wright letters and other papers of Octave Chanute.

New York: McGraw-Hill Co., 1953. 2 v. 1 v., 1,278 p. illus., ports., facsims., 24 cm.

TLB290.W95

Few, if any, major episodes in the history of technology are as well documented as the invention of the airplane. The letters, diaries, notebooks, photographs, and other original documents preserved by the Wright brothers represent a remarkably complete record of their achievement. In crafting an agreement transferring the priceless Wright manuscript collection to the Library of Congress in 1949, the executors of Orville Wright's estate suggested that "it would be desirable" to compile and publish the most important documents in order to produce "a comprehensive record of the Wright brothers and their work."

Wisely, the leadership of the Library of

Congress placed Marvin W. McFarland in charge of the project. McFarland, who had served as a U.S. Army Air Forces historian in uniform during World War II, decided to follow the example of those who handled presidential papers, publishing the most important documents in the collection in a scholarly edition complete with extensive notes, appendices, and illustrations. McFarland and the members of his small team began work in the late spring of 1950. The result, nothing less than a masterpiece of historical scholarship and editing, was published on the occasion of the fiftieth anniversary of powered, heavier-than-air flight.

OFFICE OF

MT. CARMEL AERONAUTIC NAVIGATION CO.

MANUFACTURERS OF

AEROSTATIC MACHINES.

AUTHORIZED CAPITAL $20,000,000

WOODWARD & TIERNAN, PRTG. CO. ST. LOUIS.

Mt. Carmel, Illinois, _____ Nov 8 _____ 1890.

Mr Wm Harrison Riley

Townsend Center Mass.

Dear Sir:-your favor of

Nov 4 received,your letter was of great interest to us,and we

would be happy to have the pleasure of meeting you and to ex-

amine in to any of your plans,and if we find that we can use

them in connection with ours we will be willing to pay you for

their use, we of course understand the spirit of ridicule which

is prevalent in regard to aerial navigation and it seems to us

 that the U S government in stead of discouraging the efforts

of the inventive genius in that line should encourage it,it is a

rich country and prides itself on her progressive ideas and with

the large surplis of money in the treasury we think a million

dollar appropriation for the purpose mentioned would be of in-

calculable benifit,but as you say in your letter when anything

of that kind is mentioned''insane crank''is all one gets for

their efforts and their comunications are wastebasketed,France

has so far taken the lead in aerial navigation and fosters a

Manuscripts

CLIVE HART

A S WITH THE PRINTED BOOKS, the strength of the Gimbel collection's 324 manuscripts and typescripts lies in their diversity. Together with letters from many of the most significant figures in the history of aeronautics since the late eighteenth century—the Montgolfiers, Pilâtre de Rozier, Gaston Tissandier, Otto Lilienthal, Octave Chanute, Count von Zeppelin, Alberto Santos-Dumont—it includes material helping to reveal the scientific, social, and personal contexts in which aeronautical experiments were carried out. Letters from the loquacious Faujas de Saint-Fond, who did so much to publicize the early balloon flights, tell us much about his personality. In addition to notes and letters from Wilbur and Orville Wright, several personal letters from their father, Milton, provide insights into the familial atmosphere in which the brothers lived and worked. Letters from Samuel Pierpont Langley reveal details of his dealings with others. Although most of the manuscripts are private communications, there is a complete, two-volume anonymous novel including a passage on a balloon flight, an Italian manuscript that relates what seems to be an imaginary account of the construction and inflation of balloons, and several manuscript drafts of material that was subsequently printed and published.

The choice of items to which special attention is given illustrates that diversity. Their authors range from the highly sophisticated to the barely literate, from scientists and technologists to practitioners of the arts, from the foremost aeronautical experimenters to the humblest onlookers. Although most of the letters were written in English (including several charming notes by a Francophone Brazilian) there are examples in French and German.

In addition to the holographs and typescripts, the collection holds a number of photocopies and facsimiles. Although the text of these items is often of importance, none has been included in the selection. In keeping with the overall cut-off date of this catalogue, manuscripts later than 1914 have been excluded.

✳ ✳ ✳

Where available, bibliographical information for the manuscripts is given in the following order: author, type of manuscript (letter, note, etc.), where written, name of recipient, location of recipient, date as given, pagination, size, other relevant information, and the Gimbel collection call number. All manuscripts are pen/paper. (AL-autograph letter; ALS-autograph letter, signed; TL-typescript letter; TLS-typescript letter, signed.)

Detail of lettter from
R. H. Butler, to
Wm. Harrison Riley,
Nov. 8, 1890 (Page 157)

De notre Monastaire de la visitation Ste marie
de villefranche Ce 26 decembre 1783

Voiture aërienne
partant de Villefranche
proprieta ...

Mon pere

je vois toûjours venir avec empressement Le tems ou je puis vous
donner de nouveau temoignage de mon Respect ainsi que de mon
tendre et Sincere attachement, Mon plaisir Seroit bien plus Sensible
Si moins éloigné de vous je pouvois vous voir, et vous faire part, d'une
maniere plus particuliere, des voeux que j'adresse au très haut dans Cette
nouvelle année, pour tout ce qui peut Contribuer a vous la Rendre
heureuse, daignez être persuadé que C'est une pratique journaliere que je
me fais un devoir de ne pas manquer.

S'il m'étoit possible d'avoir une des nouvelle voiture aërienne et
que Sans manquer a la Cloture je pu voler traverser les airs j'en
dirigerois la Route du Coté de provence j'irois a toulon vous —

Michel, Soeur. Letter (ALS) from the Convent of the Visitation of Saint Mary, Villefranche [Alpes-Maritimes?], to Père Michel of the Oratory at Toulon.

Dated le 26 decembre 1783

4 p. 22 cm.

XF-2-1 2394 1783/DEC. 26

Sister Michel writes to her priest to tell him of her religious devotions and to express her strong desire to see him again:

> If it were possible to have one of the new aerial carriages, and if, without being missed in the convent, I could travel through the air, I should make my way toward Provence, I should go to Toulon to embrace you, to tell you what my heart would tell me to say and should return from that content to savor the happiness of my solitude.

Immediately after the first free balloon flights, people began speculating about the balloon's potential for travel. Plays, poems, novels, and vaudeville acts explored the possibilities, sometimes seriously, often with irony. Philosophers and others often saw in the idea of manned flight the potential end of civilization. Not everyone would use flying machines for such benign purposes as Sister Michel had in mind and in any case her letter touches on one of the dangers: people in closed religious orders might escape, break their vows, and bring about the collapse of moral order. Thieves would find their work much easier and lovers could secretly fly through their mistresses' windows. A correction that Sister Michel made as she wrote shows that she was sensitive to this moral question. For *traverser* (travel through) she had first written *voler* (fly) but had immediately corrected herself. *Traverser* is much less sharply focused. In addition, *voler* means both fly and steal. The double sense of the word (not a pun) is the basis of a somewhat tiresome play on words in one of the letters appended to the French translation of Karl Meerwein's *Die Kunst zu fliegen.*

CLIVE HART

Londres le 18. May 1802.

Citoyen,

J'ai différé jusqu'à ce jour de vous faire part d'aucune de mes opérations dans cette ville parceque je chargeois mon épouse qui étoit à Paris de vous faire part de ce qui pourroit vous intéresser par-rapport à moi; elle vient d'arriver en bonne santé.

Les affaires qui me concernent ne peuvent s'arranger ici que fort lentement: la chose qui m'a été la plus difficile ce fut de trouver un local à peu près convenable pour faire mes expériences; ce n'est que depuis deux jours que j'ai réussi à cet égard. mon ballon et mon parachute sont en exposition au Panthéon: c'est une salle de bal aussi grande que l'opéra de Paris. ma première expérience qui sera celle du parachute, est fixée au 2. juin, la seconde aura lieu le 8. la 3e le 14, et le 20. je repartirai pour Paris où j'aurai sûrement l'honneur de vous voir le 27.

Il seroit difficile de vous faire ici une esquisse de la ville de Londres appellée à juste raison l'abrégé de ...

Garnerin, André Jacques, 1769–1823. Letter (ALS) from 65 Poland Street, London, to M. Amaury Duval, rue de Grenelle, Paris.

> Dated le 18. May [sic] 1802
> 4 p. 23 cm. Address on p. 4
> XF-2-1 2404 1802/MAY 18

On October 22, 1797, Garnerin made the first significant parachute descent. His umbrella-shaped canopy, about 30 feet in diameter with a small basket beneath, was folded and attached to a hydrogen balloon, which he flew to a height of 3,000 feet. He then cut the line to the balloon and allowed the basket to fall free. Although the parachute was unstable, causing the basket to oscillate violently, Garnerin landed safely. Subsequently he made many more descents. Exactly two years later Jeanne-Geneviève Labrousse, who shortly afterward became his wife, was the first woman to make a parachute descent. His niece also gave professional demonstrations.

During a visit to England Garnerin began experimenting with parachute descents at night, when the air was more stable. Before hostilities resumed in the Napoleonic wars, he returned to France and continued night descents. In this letter Garnerin writes in a business-like manner, mentioning his forthcoming schedule and his fee, asking to be employed for the July 14 celebrations, and advertising the fact that his balloon and parachute are on display in the Panthéon. (See also Appendix, Printed Books: 1489–1850, *Air Balloon*, TLB273.A29 [1802].)

Cincinnati May 10th 1835
I take the opertunity to write a few lines to let you
know that I am well I received a letter from Thomas
a few weeks since he is in New orleans he writes that he is
in good health and will be up the last of June and
would like to have a letter from you time are a
geting pretty brisk in this place a good many buildings
going on there is a grat many curiosites to be seen in
the west Mr Clayton ascended in a beloon the 8th
of April and landed in virginia 400 miles
from cincinnati in 9 hours he took a dog up in
a parachute one mile and let the dog dowon
safe he will take another trip the 13th of may
and calculates to land in the vicinity of new york
thirsday the 7th of may all the fire men
turnd out in cincinnati 1500 men
I am driving a furniture car I was going out to the
lane seminary the other day to bring in s
things for a young man I was asking
if he knew a fellow by the of Dresser
he said he did and he was the very Dresser that
I was enquiring for hes studing physick
he sends his best wishes to you
I wrote home some time a go and have
had no answer I would like to have some
of you write as soon as you Receive my letter
Robert W Dresser

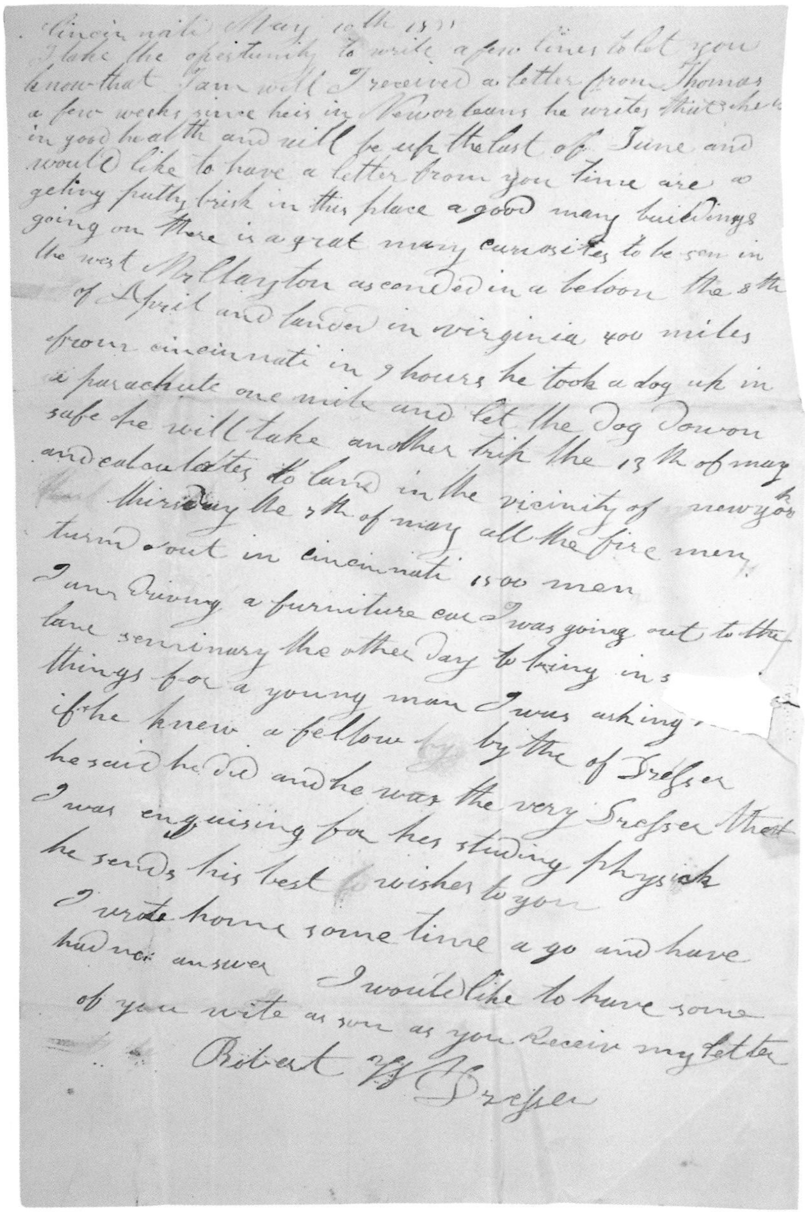

Dresser, Robert W. Letter (ALS) from Cincinnati, [Ohio,] to Comfort C. Dresser, Chester, Vt.

Dated May 10th 1835
1 p. 30.7 cm.
XF-2-1 2421 1835/MAY 10

In a letter commenting on familial matters and describing the circumstances in which he finds himself while in Cincinnati, Robert Dresser mentions a recent notable event: a flight by Richard Clayton from Cincinnati to Virginia. Dresser's prose is unpunctuated and idiosyncratically spelled:

> there is a grat many curiosites to be seen in the west Mr Clayton ascended in a beloon the 8th of April and landed in virginia 400 miles from cincinnati in 9 hours he took a dog up in a parachute one mile and let the dog dowon safe he will take another trip the 13th of may and calculates to land in the vicinity of new york . . .

An English immigrant born in 1811, Clayton had settled in Cincinnati in 1831, where he set up as a watchmaker. Captivated by the flights of Thomas Kirkby in late 1834 and 1835, he announced that he would himself undertake a long balloon voyage. He accordingly constructed the *Star of the West*, which, when inflated, was nearly 50 feet high. On April 8, 1835, he took off from Cincinnati and after remaining airborne all night landed in Monroe County, Virginia, 350 miles away, creating a world record for distance.

At the start of his journey, Clayton attracted additional attention when he released a dog by parachute. As revealed in several of the books described above (see the section Printed Books, 1489–1850), early balloonists often took animals with them, sometimes for serious scientific purposes, sometimes, as in this case, for showmanship.

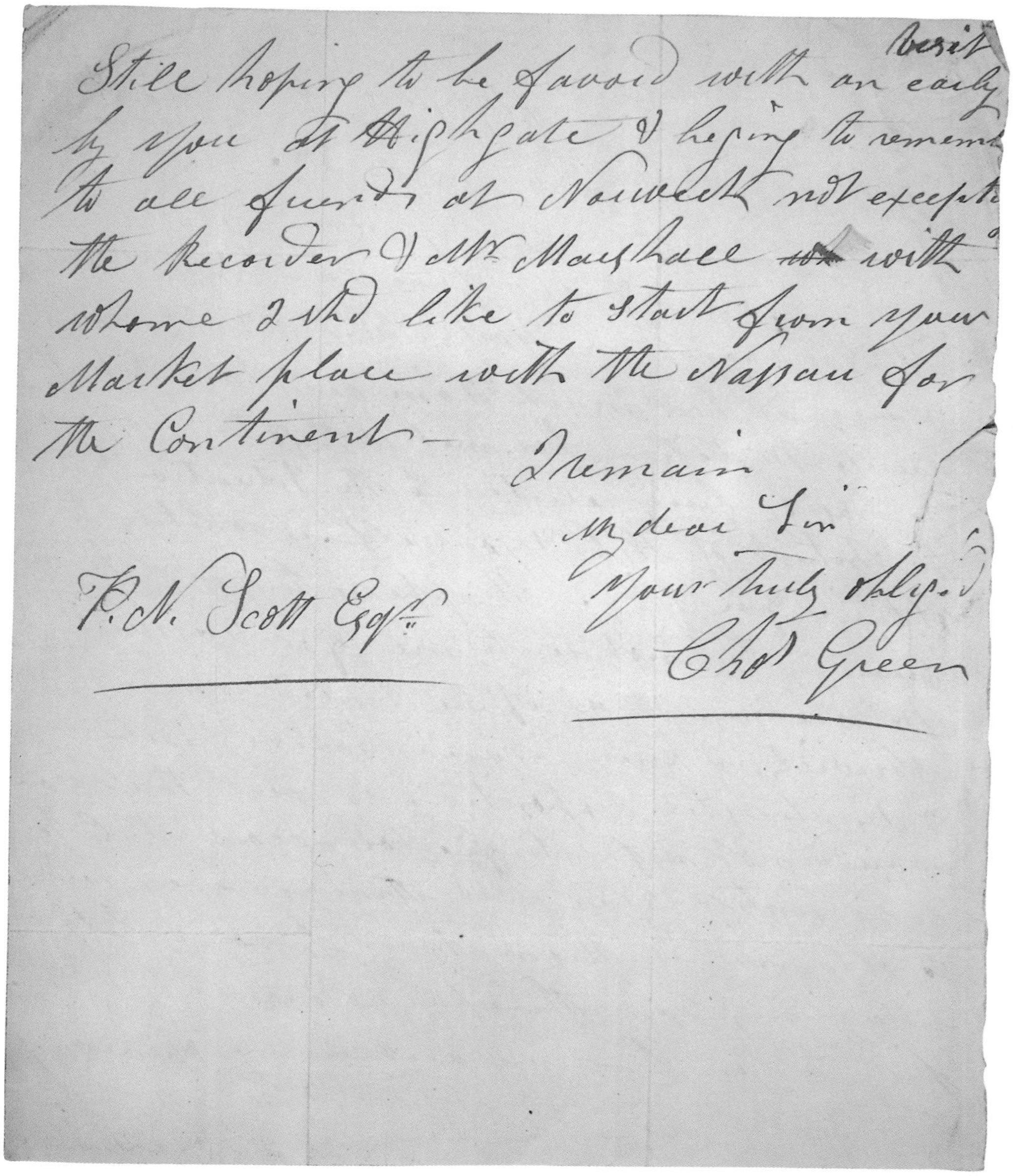

Still hoping to be favoured with an early by you at Highgate & hoping to remember to all friends at Norwich not excepting the Recorder & Mr Marshall with whome I shd like to start from your Market place with the Nassau for the Continent —

P. N. Scott Esqr.

I remain My dear Sir Your Truly oblg.d Chas Green

Green, Charles, 1785–1870. Letter (ALS) from Highgate to Page Nicol Scott (surgeon), [Norwich].

Dated 26 May [18]41

2 p. 22.8 cm.

XF-2-1 2424 1841/MAY 26

Charles Green was one of the most remarkable balloonists of all time. On November 7, 1836, together with Robert Holland, M.P., and Thomas Monck Mason, he ascended from Vauxhall Gardens, London, in a huge hydrogen balloon of about 85,000 cubic feet, which he had constructed and later owned. After a flight of some eighteen hours, the balloon landed near Weilburg, in the duchy of Nassau, having covered a distance of about 380 nautical miles. The balloon was thereafter known as the *Nassau*. Green had already flown many times and went on to make ascents well into his old age. In all he flew over 520 times. In 1828 he had flown from the Eagle Tavern, London, seated on his favorite pony, a feat later copied by others, including George Gale (see letter from Thackeray, XF-2-1 2441 [1858?] below).

In this letter Green expresses his thanks to Scott for having helped Mr. Nelson to secure a position. In his concluding lines he asks to be remembered "to all friends at Norwich not excepting the Recorder & Mr Marshall with whome I shd like to start from your Market place with the Nassau for the Continent."

To J. Chapman, Esq.

167 ½ Drury Lane,
18 May, 1843

Sir.   I have been honoured by Mr ——— with a sight of your Letter to him on the subject of the aërial inventions. I thank you for your examination of my roughdraft MS.; your expressions as to my essays encourage me. This broad field for discovery seemed unoccupied, and open to my ambition; for I knew then but of Dante's success with Wings, of Icarus, and the fable in Rasselas: it has been to me an excitement of pleasure, that in two years from the date of my Essay, men devoted to practical sciences have enthusiastically set about this enterprise. It is of similar interest with the happy theory of Columbus, and the encountering of the stormy perils of the north-west passage. I shall add to my History two inquiries in scien=tific investigation: in the new theory there is the great problem to solve, how to sail on in air in opposition to fluctuating currents, either directly, or on side tacks, imitating the old and the improved science of seamen. To go down the wind has been perfectly done by balloonists. — We see a boy with a good kite & string bidding his comrade lift high the paper kite, he himself runs it up against the wind: if idle he ceases and keeps it floating in the air; if active he causes the kite to aspire to an angle of 75 degrees, approximating to the vertical line. If he reverts his course & walks after his kite, she falls down wind to the ground. The principle is here explained of converting atmospheric resistance into an auxiliary. — Attach a kite of 10 feet (raising it, as usual, but with a stout line) to a steam-engine on a straight line of railroad, having a steady head wind all the dis=tance intended; she will sail gallantly in the wind's teeth above 36 miles an hour. — I have, in print, reported the fact that a man has flown with Wings. I will endow an intrepid young man with my membranaceous wings or my fan-shaped wings, the materials whereof I invented for such purpose by first applying such combinations to the construction of wings. I am propounding an imaginary argument for theoretical deductions in an increasing series. With these wings I know he

---

Hamilton, Charles Claude. Letter (ALS) from 167 ½ Drury Lane, London, to J. Chapman, 6A Lisson Grove, London.

Dated 18 May, 1843
4 p. 26 cm.
XF-2-1 2426 1843/MAY 18

Hamilton was characteristic of the many loquacious enthusiasts who, believing that they saw clearly what was needed for success in the air, based their ideas on mistaken physical theories. He writes with great energy of "an *aërial royal road*" that he wishes to see "firmly paved with great principles." His own "great principle" is the harnessing of wind power. He describes the lifting of a kite by running into wind with the line but wholly misunderstands how the forces are applied. He does not say that he himself will fly but makes an offer: "I will endow an intrepid young man with my membranaceous wings or my fan-shaped wings, the materials whereof I invented for such purpose by first applying such combinations to the construction of wings." The youth will fly into wind with a large kite tethered above him, and helping to sustain him aloft. Hamilton then sketches in a progressive development toward increasingly sophisticated flying machines, all based on his false principles. Very insistent, with many words underlined, his prose is al-most an unconscious parody of the scientific speculators who are made to look so ridiculous in *Gulliver's Travels* and *Le philosophe sans prétention*. Entirely confident that he knows the route to success, he exaggerates: "I have, in print, reported the *fact* that a man *has* flown with Wings." Earlier in his letter he had nevertheless claimed to know only of Dante (i.e., Giovanni Battista Danti, *ca.* 1477–1517, who is said to have crashed onto the roof of a church in Perugia), Icarus, and the abortive flight of the mechanic in *Rasselas*. Two years earlier Hamilton had published his *Essay on the Art of Flying, with an Indication of the Materials Best Adapted for Wings* (dated by the author 1839), Finchley, 1841. A second edition appeared in London in 1842.

The letter from Chapman which Hamilton here answers is listed in the Appendix (XF-2-1 2425 1843/MAY 15).

CLIVE HART

This Mr. Gale was appointed to a situation as inspector in the coast blockade service in Ireland. This post was not suited to him, and he again embraced the stage at the City of London Theatre. The altered state of the dramatic profession, however, induced him to turn his thoughts to scientific pursuits, and, having had a balloon manufactured at the Montpelier Grounds, Walworth, he made his first ascent from the Rosemary Branch Tavern in 1848. From that period, he had made a great number of ascents in all parts of the kingdom, and his last fatal ascent, which took place on the 9th of September eight years ago was the 114th, wh: took place from the Hippodrome of Vincennes, at Bordeaux, seated for the first time on the back of a pony. He attempted to descend at a place called Anquielles. When the animal had been released from his slings, the peasants, who held the ropes of the balloon, misunderstanding the directions, let go, and the balloon having still sufficient gas in it to give an ascensional force after losing the weight of the beast, rose ~~suddenly~~ suddenly. Mr. Gale, however, clung to the ropes, and pulled the string to cause the gas to escape. The ascent of the balloon was checked, and it was thought that Mr. Gale had been enabled to get into the car. This was not the case, as on the morning of the next day the balloon was discovered on the ground some miles from the spot where the pony was liberated: the ~~dead~~ dead body of Mr. Gale was found in a wood with his limbs all broken.

Very faithfully yours

Wm Thackeray

Thackeray, W[illiam] M[akepeace], 1811–1863. Letter (ALS) from Onslow Square, Brompton, to [the actor] Charles Kean, Stage Door, Royal Princess's Theatre, Oxford Street, W[est] [London].

Dated "Wednesday" [1858?]

2 p. 16 cm.

3d p. blank; address on p. 4. Above address "Please send answer by Bearer"

XF-2-1 2441 [1858?]

Evidently in response to a request from the actor Charles Kean, Thackeray agrees to relate "all I know about poor Gale." Born in May 1794, in Fulham, London, George Burcher Gale (1794–1850) began his career as an actor playing small parts on the London stage. In 1831 he visited America, where, after acting in New York, he traveled west and joined a tribe of Indians; on his return to London, he brought back six of the Indians and their chief. After a further burst of work on the stage and a spell as a coast blockade inspector in Ireland, he became a professional balloonist, making his first ascent in 1848. As balloons quickly disappeared from the sight of the watching crowd, something eye-catching and dangerous was frequently arranged for the first minutes of the flight. Mme. Blanchard died as a consequence of her aerial fireworks displays, and Gale's overambitious decision to fly while seated on the back of a pony suspended below his *Royal Cremorne* balloon indirectly caused his death near Bordeaux on September 8, 1850. Thackeray gives a plain account of the events:

> When the animal had been released from his slings, the peasants, who held the ropes of the balloon, misunderstanding the directions, let go, and the balloon having still sufficient gas in it to give an ascensional force after losing the weight of the beast, rose suddenly. Mr. Gale, however, clung to the ropes, and pulled the string to cause the gas to escape. The ascent of the balloon was checked, and it was thought that Mr. Gale had been enabled to get into the car. This was not the case, as on the morning of the next day the balloon was discovered on the ground some miles from the spot where the pony was liberated: the dead body of Mr. Gale was found in a wood with his limbs all broken.

The ascent had been Gale's one hundred fourteenth. After his death, his widow, emulating Mme. Blanchard, took over from Gale and continued to earn a living from ballooning.

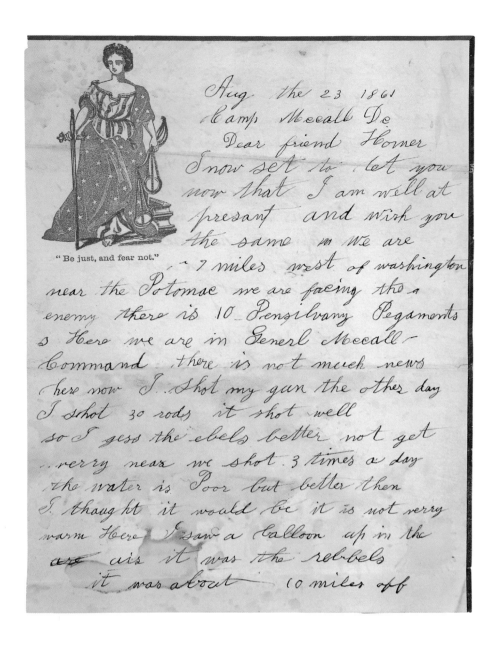

"Be just, and fear not."

Aug the 23 1861
Camp Mccall De
Dear friend Homer
I now set to let you
now that I am well at
presant and wish you
the same we are
7 miles west of washington
near the Potomac we are facing the
enemy there is 10 Pensilvany Pegaments
Here we are in Generl Mccall
Command there is not much news
here now I Shot my gun the other day
I shot 30 rods it shot well
so I gess the ebels better not get
verry near we shot 3 times a day
the water is Poor but better then
I thaught it would be it is not verry
warm Here I saw a Balloon up in the
air it was the rebbels
it was about   10 miles off

Chapman, C. D. Letter (ALS) from Camp McCall, D.C., to Homer Card.

Dated Aug. the 23 1861

2 p. 17.5 cm.

XF-2-1 2445 1861/AUG. 23

During the first two years of the Civil War hydrogen balloons were often used for reconnoitering. The Union forces had a regular balloon staff under the command of General McClellan. Although the balloons proved valuable for gathering information around the area of Richmond, in particular, a variety of problems, disagreements, and misunderstandings in the later stages of the war led to the corps' being disbanded by August 1863.

C. D. Chapman, a Union soldier, wrote to his friends appealingly, if with shaky spelling. At night he had seen an observation balloon flown by the Confederates:

> Dear friend Homer. I now set to let your now that I am well at present and wish you the same we are 7 miles west of washington near the Potomac we are facing the enemy there is 10 Pensilvany Regaments Here we are in Generl Mccall Command there is not much news here now I shot my gun the other day I shot 30 rods it shot well so I gess the [r]ebels better not get verry near

we shot 3 times a day the water is Poor but better then I thought it would be it is not verry warm Here I saw a balloon up in the air it was the rebbels it was about 10 miles off I saw it in the night I saw it by the light we went out on Picket gard 5 miles west we got 2 ducks 2 hens some green Corn some Potatoes we got them on the farms of the rebels they left there homes and joined the sotherns army we are digging a trenchments here now we have to work 1 day in a week we dont drill but a little we expect an attact every day Homer I rote 3 letters to you since I got any sow I will have to stop writing any more letters.

The use of balloons during the Civil War is described in Frederick Stansbury Haydon, *Aeronautics in the Union and Confederate Armies* (Baltimore: Johns Hopkins Press, 1941). See also Joseph Jenkins Cornish III, *The Air Arm of the Confederacy* (Richmond: Richmond Civil War Centennial Committee, 1963).

Appareil volant.

La propulsion dans les airs, ce problème de la plus haute importance, qui, résolu, produirait inévitablement des conséquences incalculables dans les relations et dans les forces sociales, a résisté, depuis un siècle près, à tous les efforts de l'esprit humain, au point qu'on proclamait généralement cette solution comme impossible.

Cependant, la nature, en créant l'oiseau, avait bien prouvé que ce problème de la mécanique n'était nullement absurde.

Voici cette solution tant désirée, aussi obstinément recherchée que repoussée d'autre part, et réputée illusoire par des autorités scientifiques imposantes, qui modifièrent enfin leurs opinions par l'impérieuse nécessité des moyens nouveaux dont la France a besoin.

Imaginons un ballon principal B (voir le dessin annexé), qui porte la nacelle N et la charge.

Sous la nacelle traverse l'axe tournant EE, muni à ses extrémités des bras DD tournant en même temps.

Aux extrémités se trouvent attachés deux ballons beaucoup moindres PP, qui subissent des évolutions rotatives et constituent de véritables propulseurs de l'appareil.

Des deux côtés de la nacelle se trouvent placés deux chassis CC, s'inclinant à volonté vers l'horizon, et formant en quelque sorte les ailes de l'appareil.

En arrière se trouve un gouvernail G, espèce de queue d'oiseau; et l'appareil est complet.

Voyons comment il fonctionne.

De notre nacelle, forçons les propulseurs à descendre dans leur position la plus basse. Ils opposeront naturellement une résistance, et pousseront tout l'appareil vers le haut, qui ne pourra monter que suivant le plan incliné des ailes; et la propulsion s'en suit nécessairement. Pour empêcher qu'on ne retombe pas au retour des propulseurs, il suffit d'étendre les ailes horizontalement.

Rien de plus facile que le calcul de la hauteur à laquelle on pourra s'élever par ce moyen mécanique.

Soit notre appareil, de force à soutenir le poids de 2000 K., quelque peu au dessus de l'horizon; et nos deux propulseurs, de force de 10 K. ensemble, et leur rayon rotatif de $4^m.00$; admettons que la pression atmosphérique soit de $0^m.80$. Puisque tout l'appareil se trouve en équilibre, les propulseurs descendront de $4^m.00$, et l'appareil s'élèvera de $4^m.00$, et y sera retenu par la résistance des ailes, tandis que les propulseurs, laissés libres, retourneront à leur place forcément de 4^m plus haut. Tel sera l'effet du premier tour qui peut s'effectuer en une seconde. L'action du second tour sera à peu près la même, parce que le changement dans la gravitation sera insensible. Mais, en nous élevant continuellement, nous arriverons à la hauteur

où la

Bukaty, A. Letter (ALS) from 54 rue Mazarine, Paris, to Comfort C. Dresser, Chester, Vt.

Dated le 21. 9bre 1870

3 p. 26.5 cm.

XF-2-1 2447 1870/SEP. 21

Styling himself *ingénieur civil*, Bukaty writes to Dresser in formal style, heading his letter *Appareil volant* (Flying Machine) as if he were writing a short article. Beginning by focusing on the problem of controlled movement through the air, considered for centuries to be virtually impossible, he then proposes an ingenious and highly original (if entirely impractical) method of propulsion dependent on action and reaction. Below an aerostat a transverse rotating rod is mounted; at the two ends arms are fixed at right angles. Two small balloons are attached to the extremities of the arms. There is also provision for two independent wing-like surfaces which can be extended horizontally or turned at an angle. With the wings held at a positive angle of attack, the transverse rod is rotated so that the two small balloons are lowered, the reaction thus causing the main balloon to climb and move forward. The angle of attack of the wings is then reduced to zero while the rotation brings the small balloons back up to top dead center, the horizontal position of the wings inhibiting the machine's descent before the cycle is repeated. The ingenuity of Bukaty's idea is compromised by his having failed (among other things) to take full account of the horizontal components of the reactive effects.

Bukaty continues with some specious calculations of the speed of which his machine will be capable and ends by commenting on its value as a weapon of war during the Siege of Paris. Bombs could be dropped on the enemy while "the importance of the solution of such a problem would be sufficient to make them highly respectful."

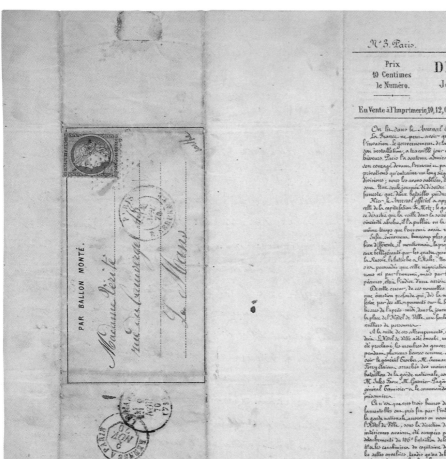

[The Siege of Paris; a collection of contemporary journals and manuscripts. 1870–1871]

    1 v. (album) 37 cm.

    DC311.A2

    Includes 16 issues of *Lettre-Journal de Paris*; 4 issues of *Dépêche-Ballon*; 2 issues of *La Cloche*; 1 issue of *Journal-Poste*; 1 issue of *L'Indépendant*; 3 ALS "par ballon monté"; 2 original [?] microprints

    1. Paris (France)—Siege, 1870–1871—Sources.

During the Franco-Prussian War of 1870–1871, Paris was twice besieged. At the start of the first siege (September 19, 1870), Chancellor Bismarck believed the city to be completely cut off from the rest of the world and therefore sure to capitulate quickly. Using their ingenuity, the French, who had a small number of balloons at their disposal, rapidly overcame their isolation. Instead of setting up captive observation platforms, as they had at first intended to do, they allowed the balloon *Neptune*, piloted by Jules Duruof, to rise in free flight on September 23. Three hours later it landed at Évreux, some 60 miles away to the west. The 275 pounds of military dispatches and mail that Duruof had carried with him were then forwarded from Évreux by conventional surface transportation. Mass production of balloons at the Gare d'Orléans and the training of more pilots enabled the world's

first regular airmail service to continue for more than four months. By January 28, 1871, when the last sortie was made, more than 60 balloons had flown out of the city.

    Messages were sent back to Paris by carrier pigeons that had been taken with the pilots; the number of letters that a single bird could carry was greatly increased by photo reduction of the texts. The enterprise was very successful: more than 2 million letters reached destinations outside Paris—some of them outside France altogether—and more than 50,000 messages were carried back by the pigeons. Small journals were published in Paris with the specific intention of conveying information about the siege to the outside world. Individuals often added private messages to copies that they sent to friends and relatives.

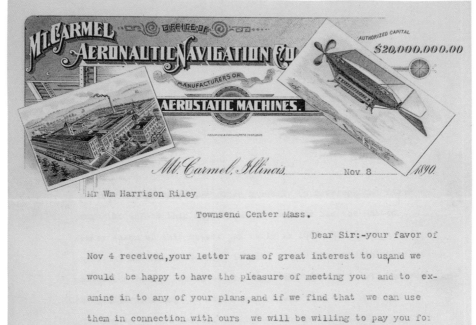

Mt. Carmel
AERONAUTIC NAVIGATION CO

OFFICE OF

MANUFACTURERS OF

AEROSTATIC MACHINES.

AUTHORIZED CAPITAL
$20,000,000.00

Mt. Carmel, Illinois,_____ Nov. 8 ___ 1890.

Mr Wm Harrison Riley

Townsend Center Mass.

Dear Sir:-your favor of

Nov 4 received,your letter was of great interest to us,and we

would be happy to have the pleasure of meeting you and to ex-

amine in to any of your plans,and if we find that we can use

them in connection with ours we will be willing to pay you for

their use, we of course understand the spirit of ridicule which

is prevalent in regard to aerial navigation and it seems to us

that the U S government in stead of discouraging the efforts

of the inventive genius in that line should encourage it,it is a

rich country and prides itself on her progressive ideas and with

the large surplis of money in the treasury we think a million

dollar appropriation for the purpose mentioned would be of in-

calculable benifit,but as you say in your letter when anything

of that kind is mentioned''insane crank''is all one gets for

their efforts and their comunications are wastebasketed,France

has so far taken the lead in aerial navigation and fosters a

Butler, R. H. Letter (TLS) from Mt.
Carmel, Ill., to Wm Harrison Riley,
Townsend Center, Mass.

Dated Nov 8 1890

2 leaves. 28 cm.

On the letterhead of Mt. Carmel Aeronautic
Navigation Co., Manufacturers of Aerostatic
Machines

XF-2-1 2457 1890/NOV. 8

Prompted by a letter from his correspondent,
Butler, secretary of his company, writes in a
spirit of outrage at the lack of support given
by the U.S. government to the inventors of
flying machines. As his anger increases, his
spelling and punctuation grow ever worse.
Butler was by no means alone. Complaints
were frequently made about lack of official
support from the governments of many countries at a time when experiments with flying
machines were flourishing in France. Creating
the impression of someone who lives in a
dream world, Butler alleges that his company

has already "developed a speed of 200 miles
an hour on our ship"—doubtless referring to
the fantastic airship on the letterhead. By 1890
small rigid airships had been successfully
flown in America and there were many plans
for larger machines. Although U.S. officials
had occasionally shown some interest, there
was little enthusiasm in Congress. A few years
later the Wright brothers fought a protracted
and unsuccessful struggle to win practical
support from central authorities.

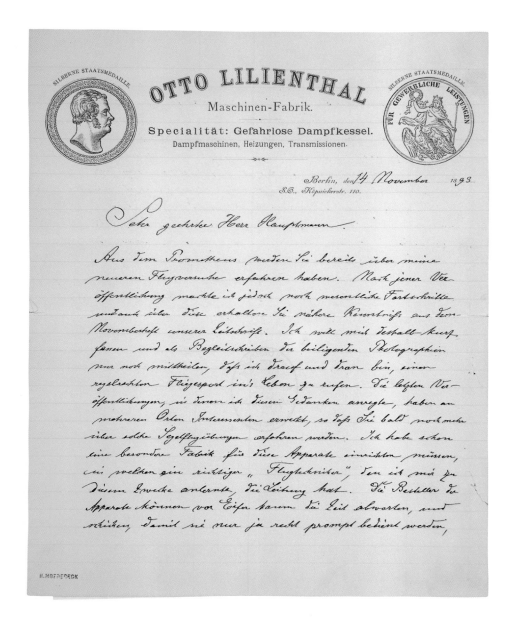

Lilienthal, Otto, 1848–1896. Letter (ALS) from 110 Köpnickerstrasse, Berlin, to "Herr Hauptmann" [a name? or merely "Captain"?]

Dated 14 November 1893

2 p. 28 cm. On his letterhead "Otto Lilienthal | Maschinen-Fabrik" and a reproduction of the "Silberne Staatsmedaille" given for progress in industry. Letter stamped "Moedebeck Archiv" (with balloon design)

XF-2-1 2462 1893/NOV. 14

This letter was written at an important period in the work of the great German experimenter who was killed when flying one of his gliders less than three years later. Having become proficient in passive hang-gliding, Lilienthal was working on plans for the powered machine to which he briefly alludes. To the usual fixed wings of his earlier gliders he added, on each side, six movable slats to act as flappers. He intended eventually to power these by a 2-horsepower carbonic acid motor. In 1894 he tested the machine first without the motor and then with it in place but not functioning, using the combination as a glider.

> Next year should bring me a good deal of further progress since the flight which now occasionally shows an angle of 1:10 without wing-beats is to be fitted out with powerful beating wings. The aircraft that I shall use

for this purpose is basically finished and I believe that this winter I shall be able to demonstrate it in a flying session, equipped with movable wings though not flying freely.

On August 9, 1896, when Lilienthal was flying one of this standard gliders, a gust caused him to stall. He could not get the nose down in time and in the crash his spine was broken. He died the next day.

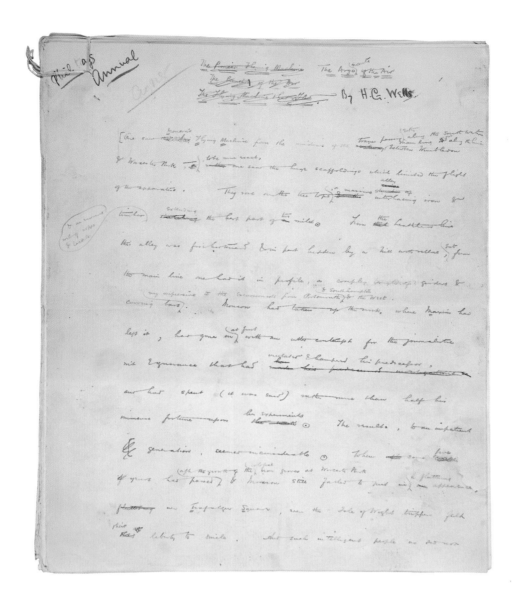

[Wells, Herbert George, 1866–1946.] Early holograph draft, in pen, of his short story "The Argonauts of the Air." 1895

22 p. 26 x 21 cm.

Some ms. notes in another hand, including "By H. G. Wells," on p. 1

XF-2-1 900 [1895]

Even the most visionary of science fiction writers commonly underestimate the speed of technological progress. As late as 1901, Wells suggested that a practical flying machine would "probably" be achieved by 1950. This story, written in his late twenties, tells of a brave failure. Monson, an inventor, has designed an aircraft that combines ideas from Maxim and Lilienthal, both of whom are acknowledged. Wells nevertheless shows little awareness of aeronautical principles and especially of stability. Monson's machine is powered by a pusher propeller "in place of a tail; and so hovering, which needs an almost vertical adjustment of a flat tail, was rendered impossible." The angle of incidence of the wings can be varied either together, for control of pitch, or separately, for control of roll and (presumably) yaw. Wells also says that the leading edge can be moved back to reduce the wing area, although he explains neither the mechanism nor the purpose of this. The machine is initially tested on a trolley running on a captive-rail structure derived from Maxim. On the first, premature free flight Monson overcontrols the wings, which leads to his death and to that of his engineer. A year later Lilienthal was killed.

Wells wrote "The Argonauts of the Air" in 1895 for publisher Grant Richards, who was the editor of *Phil May's Christmas Annual*. The story was delivered in typescript in mid-July. The manuscript is close to being a heavily emended first draft. Before settling on the published title, Wells tried five others: "The Pioneer Flying Machine," "The Pioneers of the Air," "The Pioneer of the Air," "The Flying Machine that Flew," and "The Argo of the Air."

Zeppelin, Graf Ferdinand von, 1838–1917.
Letter (ALS) from 19 Kepler Street,
Stuttgart, to [an unnamed captain].

Written at two periods, dated 15 Januar 1900
and 22 Januar 1900
6 p. 17.7 cm.
XF-2-1 2466 1900/JAN. 15

Count Ferdinand von Zeppelin (1838–1917) made his first balloon ascent in America, where for a time he had acted as an observer moving freely among the Union forces during the Civil War. On August 17, 1863, he accompanied German-born John Steiner on a tethered ascent in St. Paul, Minnesota. Interested in aeronautics thereafter, he was the inventor of the fully practical rigid airship, the first version of which, the *LZ1*, he began constructing in June 1898. In July 1900, he and his crew flew it over Lake Constance, managing to keep it airborne for 18 minutes. It achieved a top speed of about 17 miles per hour but because the sliding-weight mechanism used to control pitch had broken, it was thought advisable to terminate the flight about 4 miles from the starting point. The airship was slightly damaged on landing. Although the *LZ1* was barely successful, Zeppelin learned much from its flight.

Zeppelin wrote this letter during what for him was a very depressing period. Funding was proving difficult, commentators in the press were alleging that success was impossible, officials and old friends alike were warning him that his plans would come to nothing and that he should give up. (Before the initial trials, morale was further damaged by the defection of Zeppelin's engineer and technical director, Kübler, who declined to fly because the count had been unable to obtain insurance.) Zeppelin writes that he is very busy trying to rescue the project; although he refuses to despair, he is in urgent need of a pilot.

2)

of little value—remain, as they are
paying a large percent on the
money invested.

I got home the 8th, and found
Katharine and Lorin and family
well; but Wilbur and Orville are away
in an outing of several weeks to
Kitty Hawk, Currituck Co., North
Carolina; Wilbur partly to make
some experiments concerning
his improvement in the construction and control of a flying machine—the winds being favorable there.

I came out here Sat. the 13th, and
preached Sunday at 10:30 at Hopewell U. B. Church, in Leach, adjoining
my farm, and made an address at a
S.S. rally at Salem M. P. Church, 1½ miles
n.e. of Hopewell, the best M. Protestant
society I ever knew, its surviving old
members being warm friends of ours before
and since we lived there in 1860–1862.
I have not heard of you, or your health,
since I left home August 13th. I will be here
till Monday the 22nd, then go to Dayton. Over
I have a nephew here, and cousins near Hopewell.

Wright, Milton, 1828–1917. Letter (ALS)
from Fairmount, Ind., to "Dear Sister"
[Mrs. B. Mosier?].

Dated Oct. 18, 1900

2 p. 20.4 cm.

XF-2-2 2490 1900/OCT. 18

An obsessive concern with money and property was a major contributing factor to the
ultimate failure—much to be regretted—of
the Wright brothers' attempts to dominate the
early days of powered flight. This letter to
their aunt from their father, Milton—a
preacher who had become a bishop of the
United Brethren Church—reveals that a
strong focus on financial matters was a family
characteristic. Always a firm supporter of his
sons' work, Milton mentions their first visit to
North Carolina where they tested their No. 1
glider, a biplane structure with warping control fitted to wings of 17-foot span and an area
of 165 square feet. This craft had the now familiar forward elevator that the Wrights used
in all their aircraft until 1910, but no tail surfaces. On most occasions it was flown as a
kite, the controls being operated from ground
level. As winds were lighter than expected,
only a few pilot-controlled tethered flights
were made, together with a few pilot-controlled glides. These experiments marked the
first important stage in their successful development of a powered craft. Milton's letter
reflects his sons' paramount concern with
control: "Wilbur and Orville are away in
an outing of several weeks to Kitty Hawk,
Currituck Co., North Carolina; Wilbur partly
to make some experiments concerning his
improvement in the construction and control of a flying machine—the winds being
favorable there."

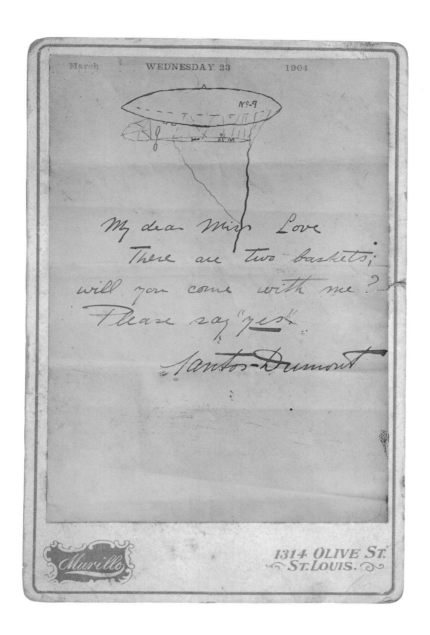

Santos-Dumont, Alberto, 1873–1932. Note
(ALS) from 1314 Olive St., St. Louis, Mo.,
to Miss Love.

> Dated March Wednesday 23 1904
>
> 1 p. 13.5 cm.
>
> XF-2-1 2468 1904/MAR. 23

The energetic and determined Brazilian-born
Alberto Santos-Dumont delighted Paris in the
late 1890s with his exploits in small powered
airships roughly similar to the one he sketched
on his note to Miss Love. During a visit to
the United States in 1904, he attended the
Saint Louis Exhibition where he met Octave
Chanute (1832–1910), re-established his
acquaintance with Samuel Pierpont Langley
(1834–1906), whom he had met in Paris in
1900, learned of the Wright brothers' recent
successes, and began to turn his attention
to heavier-than-air flight. Two years later
that new interest resulted in the creation
of one of the most famous airplanes of all
time—if also one of the ugliest—his canard-
configured no. *14-bis*. Something of his
engaging character may be judged from
the simplicity of his invitation to Miss Love.
He offers her the security of a separate basket.
Did she accept?

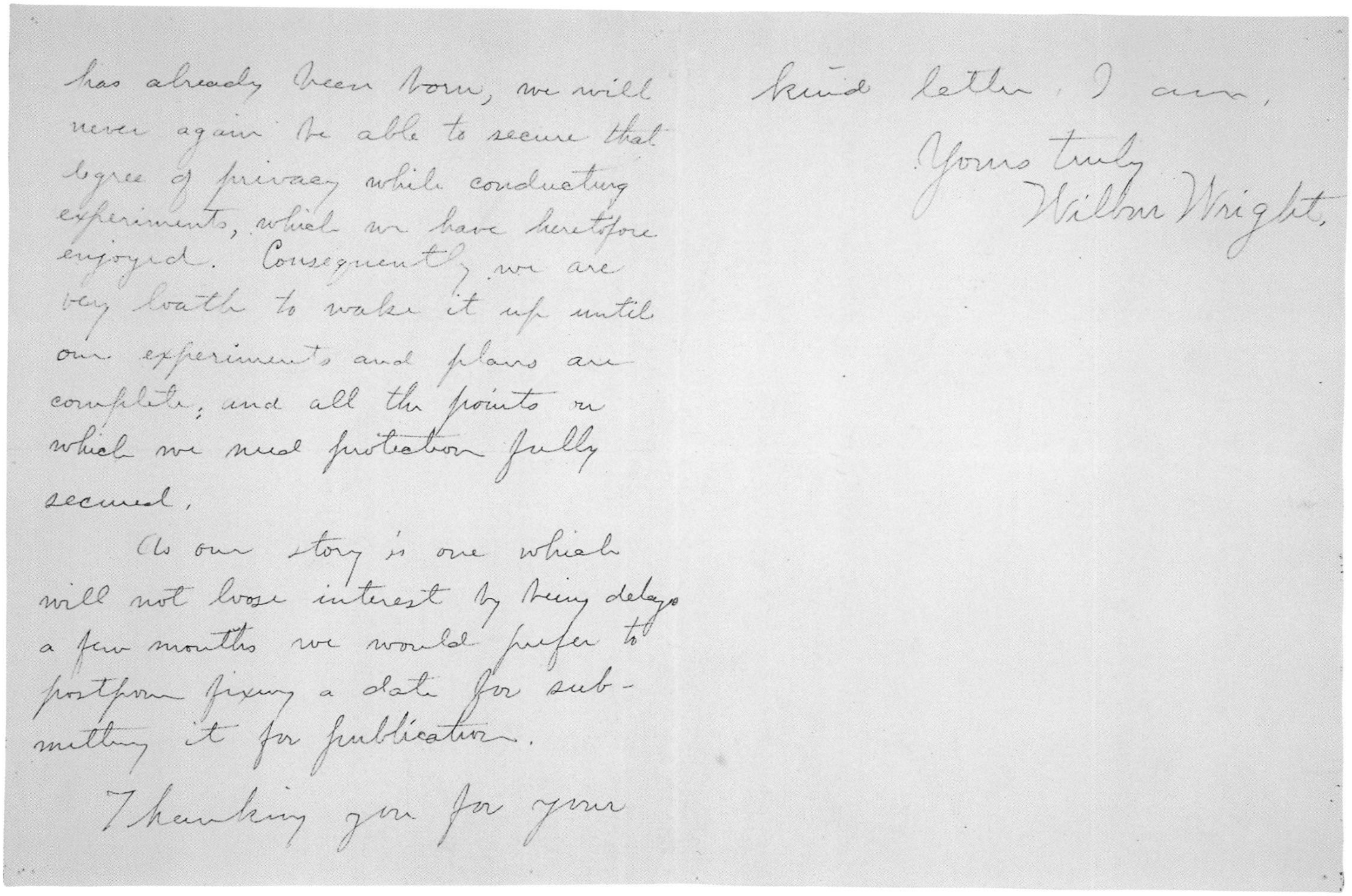

has already been born, we will never again be able to secure that degree of privacy while conducting experiments, which we have heretofore enjoyed. Consequently, we are very loath to wake it up until our experiments and plans are complete, and all the points on which we need protection fully secured,

As our story is one which will not loose interest by being delayed a few months we would prefer to postpone fixing a date for submitting it for publication.

Thanking you for your

kind letter, I am,

Yours truly,

Wilbur Wright,

Wright, Wilbur, 1867–1912. Letter (ALS) from Dayton, Ohio, to Mr. R. U. Johnson, New York.

> Dated Oct. 16, 1904
> 3 p. 16.4 cm.
> XF-2-2 2524 1904/OCT. 16

Throughout their experiments the Wrights insisted on secrecy. By nature private, taciturn, and confident that they were ahead of the competition in the early years of the century, they zealously protected rights that they believed they could sell for large sums of money:

> We realize that when once the world really wakes up to the fact that the flying machine has already been born, we will never again be able to secure that degree of privacy while conducting experiments, which we have heretofore enjoyed. Consequently we are very loath to wake it up until our experiments and plans are complete, and all the points on which we need protection fully secured.
>
> As our story is one which will not lose interest by being delayed a few months we would prefer to postpone fixing a date for submitting it for publication.

In later years, when their financial hopes were largely disappointed, Wilbur's courtesy as a correspondent gave way to a somewhat sharper tone.

At the time of this letter, the brothers were hard at work transforming their successful but barely practical machine of ten months earlier into an aircraft that could be reliably flown for extended periods. The outcome of these efforts was the *Flyer III,* finished in June 1905. It was the first truly practical airplane ever flown.

Prints

Paul Maravelas

COLONEL GIMBEL began to amass his aeronautical collection during World War II, a decade after author Lockwood Marsh had lamented that early aeronautical prints were becoming difficult to find. Yet Gimbel was able to assemble an unsurpassed private collection of images, including one important print (Vuë d'Annonay en Vivarais), which I believe is one of two copies in the United States. At the end of his life Gimbel owned approximately 2,000 prints, which he organized into about 40 groups according to theme. Aside from a handful of prints that were framed and exhibited in Gimbel's New Haven home, the collection was kept in semi-rigid boxes.

Such an extensive archive allows one to compare a variety of illustrations that depict a single aeronautical event; one soon concludes that we cannot view these prints literally. The variations are not surprising when we reflect that a commercial medium was used to generate commemorative images of scenes that were often momentary or, in fact, had yet to occur; in either case they presented particular challenges to the artist.

Flight, throughout its history, appeared to be less promising to some people than to others, and one sees (especially in the eighteenth century) a large number of satirical prints in which the balloon is used to symbolize folly or the balloon itself is characterized as the contrivance of misguided enthusiasts. The subject is well addressed in Melvin Waldfogel, François-Louis Bruel (De Vinck), and by Burkhard Leismann in a chapter of *Leichter als Luft*. Without ignoring this phenomenon altogether, I have selected largely from the prints produced for aeronautical enthusiasts. I have tried to emphasize in the text the perspective of the audience for which the prints were intended, with the hope that we might consider how these prints were regarded by those who first enjoyed them.

❊ ❊ ❊

Measurements of the prints are given in centimeters measured from the edges of the plate with intaglio prints and the edges of the images for others. In the descriptions the wording is recorded as it appears on the prints, incorporating the irregular spellings and apparent disregard for accents sometimes found on the originals. Many of the artisans or artists who created these works could not be located in documentary sources, and their names appear simply as given on the prints. The publishers are indicated only when their prominence or association with the world of aeronautics seemed to dictate it. The numbering system maintained in the Gimbel collection (the "X" number identifying each print) is based on Gimbel's grouping. Finally, the full citations to the catalogues and other works (e.g., Bruel, Caproni, George, *Leichter als Luft*, Liebmann and Wahl, March) mentioned in the descriptions are included in the "Prints" section of the Bibliography at the end of this catalogue.

Detail of etching *Vue de la Terrasse de Mr. Franklin à Passi* by P. G. Tavenard (Page 177)

165

Dædalus & Icarus, in the Salon at
Houghton

> Johann Gottlieb Facius & George Sigmund
> Facius, after Charles Le Brun (1619–1690)
>
> Etching, stipple engraving, 27.5 x 40 cm.
>
> XP-XL-1 (1018)

Charles Le Brun profoundly influenced French
art while serving in various official positions,
including first painter to Louis XIV. Le Brun's
"Dædalus & Icarus," which measures over
4 x 6 feet, shows the mythological pair preparing their escape from the Island of Crete,
where they were imprisoned for offending
King Minos. Icarus and Dædalus fashioned
wings for the escape, but Icarus flew too near
the sun (which melted the wax that held the
wings together) and fell into the sea. The
myth suggests the importance of remember-
ing one's place in the cosmos; the painting
emphasizes fatherly dedication and the
recklessness of youth. Most of Le Brun's
paintings were published as engravings.
At the time this print appeared (November
1779), Le Brun's painting was part of the

collection at Houghton Hall in Norfolk,
England, which had been built between 1722
and 1735 by Sir Robert Walpole. After Sir
Robert's death in 1745 the house passed in
succession to two sons who let Houghton Hall
deteriorate. A third son, the famous Horace,
noted in 1773 that the house was "half a ruin,
though the pictures, the glorious pictures,
and furniture were in general admirably
well preserved." The painting is now in the
Hermitage, St. Petersburg.

L'Uom Volante

[After 1781]. Etching, sheet trimmed to
8.2 x 14.3 cm.
XP-XL-27 (2223)

This design formed the frontispiece to a
fantasy in four volumes: *La Découverte
australe par un homme volant* written by
Restif de la Bretonne and published in Leipzig
and Paris in 1781. The parachute-like device
strapped to the flier's head is an intriguing
innovation, as the print appeared years before
the parachute was developed. *(This is a copy of
the original; in the original, the figure faces left.)*

European Magazine.

Fig. XLII.

An AIR BALLOON
invented in the last Century.
Publifhd by J. Sewell.Cornhill.1ªMarch 1789.

An Air Balloon invented in the last
Century

    London, 1789. Etching, 18.6 x 12.3 cm.
    XB-8-3B (1052)

This etching pictures the aircraft designed by
Francesco Lana de Terzi, which incorporated
four copper spheres devoid of air. Originally
published in 1670, this articulation of the
aerostat is the earliest we know of, although it
was never built and it appears that since the
spheres would need to resist the pressure of
the atmosphere, they would be too heavy to
float in the air. Although Lana's concept had
no direct effect on the invention of the
balloon, his craft received a new bout of
publicity when the balloon was introduced
in 1783. It would appear that the English,
however, were not paying very close attention,
as this plate appeared in *European Magazine
and London Review* in February 1789, six years
after similar images had been exhumed and
published in France and four years after
Tiberius Cavallo had devoted several pages to
it in his *History and Practice of Aerostation*,
published in London. The two-page article

that accompanies this plate in *European
Magazine* begins: "A correspondent has
obliged us with the following quotation from
a scarce book, incontrovertibly proving that
the subject of BALLOONS had been investi-
gated long before the FRENCH AERONAUTS
and LUNARDI entertained the public with
the practical succession of these useless
phænomenon." The article consists of
passages from Johannes Sturmis' *Collegium
Experimentale*, a book that presented, in 1701,
the idea of Lana's aerostat without acknowledging the source. (*An exact predecessor of this
print was published [in reverse] in Michael
Bernhard Valentini's* Museum Museorum,
Th. 3 tab. xxvii, Frankfurt am Main, 1714.)

PAUL MARAVELAS

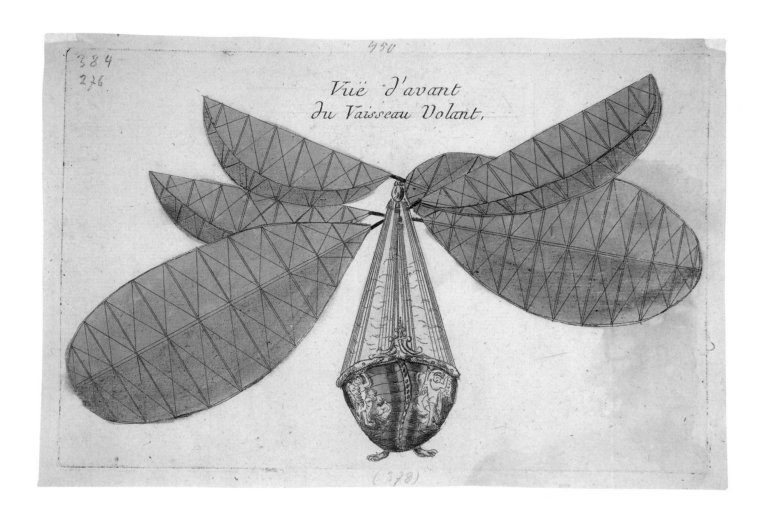

Vuë d'avant du Vaisseau Volant

Etching, 23.8 x 16 cm.

XP-XL-6 (1214)

Jean-Pierre Blanchard constructed this ornithopter in 1782 and promised to fly it in May of that year. The attempt was postponed because of rain, and despite continuous promises, it never occurred. Blanchard's reputation suffered greatly. This print forms a part of a series of four images illustrating the machine, which used a series of pulleys and ropes operated by the pilot with his arms and legs. *(The print is a copy of the original series of four views published by François-Nicolas Martinet, probably issued after Blanchard began his career as a balloonist in 1784.)*

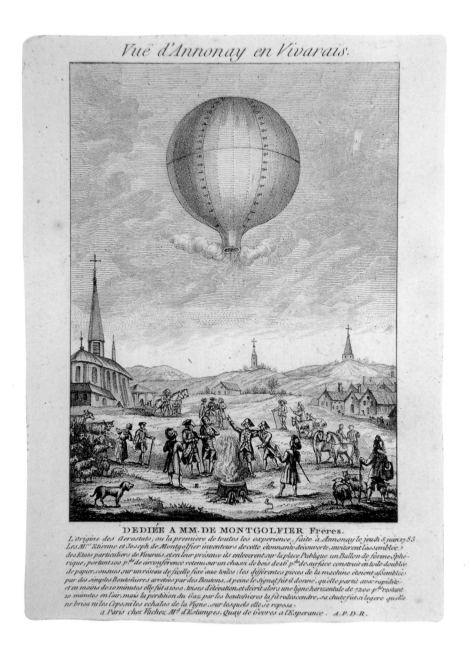

Vuë d'Annonay en Vivarais

DEDIÉE A M.M. DE MONTGOLFIER Freres.

L'Origine des Aérostats, ou la premiere de toutes les experience, faite à Annonay le jeudi 5 juin 1783
Les M.rs Étienne et Joseph de Montgolfier inventeurs de cette étonnante découverte, invitérent l'assemblée
des États particuliers de Vivarais, et en leur présence ils enleverent sur la place Publique un Ballon de forme sphe-
rique, portant 100 p.ds de circonference retenu sur un chassis de bois de 16 p.ds de surface construit en toile doublée
de papier, cousues sur un réseau de ficelle fixé aux toiles : les differentes pieces de la machine étoient assemblées
par des simples Boutonieres arretées par des Boutons. A peine le Signal fut il donné, qu'elle partit avec rapidité,
et en moins de 10 minutes elle fut a 1000 toises d'élévation, et décrit alors une ligne horizontale de 7200 p.ds restant
10 minutes en l'air, mais la perdition du Gaz par les boutonieres la fit redescendre, sa chute fut si legere qu'elle
ne brisa ni les Cepans ni les echalas de la Vigne, sur lesquels elle se reposa.
a Paris chez Vachez M.d d'Estampes, Quay de Gevres a l'Esperance. A.P.D.R.

Vuë d'Annonay en Vivarais. Dediée a M.M. de Montgolfier Frères

Paris, [1785?]. Chez [Le] Vachez. Etching,
15 x 10.3 cm.

XC-10-2M (2878)

This small print supposedly depicts the first public launch of a balloon by Joseph and Étienne Montgolfier in June 1783 before an audience of the regional government, *Les États particuliers de Vivarais*. Several features signal that this depiction is inexact. The desolation of the surroundings is especially odd since this launch took place in the middle of a modest town before a multitude of people. It is improbable that a hot-air balloon would possess so fine a mouth, and there is no depiction of what Étienne Montgolfier described as a "carriage" below the envelope. The print *does* depict the method of fastening the parts of the balloon together, which involved the use of buttons. According to the caption this method allowed the balloon to

be rapidly assembled, presumably so that the Montgolfiers could transport the paper and canvas aircraft in parts. The many lines around the envelope may be meant to depict the net mentioned in the caption. The date of this print's appearance is curious, for one would presume it to be some time proximal to the event depicted; instead, the print was announced in the *Journal de Paris* on December 26, 1784, although the plate had yet to be prepared. No other eighteenth-century depiction exists of this first public display, although later artists address the event. The print shown here was widely copied in the nineteenth century. It has been attributed to P. G. Tavenard by Liebmann and Wahl (#175), and to Nicolas de Launay (engraver) and Étienne Chevalier de Lorimier (artist) by Marsh; no artist's marks appear on the print. *(This is probably the rarest aeronautical print known, and the Gimbel copy is thought to be one of two examples in the United States. It was issued as part of a series of prints by Nicolas-François Le Vachez, all of which were schematically similar and the same size. The*

series included XC-10-2C 3390, "Vue de la prairie de Nesle, situé à 9 lieus de Paris"; XC-10-2M 2882, "Vuë de Versaille, prise du coté de la çhapelle"; XC-10-2M 2893, "Vue de la Terrasse de Mr. Franklin à Passi"; and XL-6 4622, "Vue du Château de Douvres." The Journal de Paris *of October 8, 1784, mentions the series, "all five and a half inches in height and four wide," for sale at 12 sous colored and 8 plain. The series was reported to be complete with the publication of a print depicting the "third trial of the Robert Brothers . . . on the 19th of September," which had already been issued in a larger format [print XP-XL-4 1159 below]. On the 26th of December, 1784, two additional prints were announced. Mondin identifies nineteen prints in the series. The Tissandier collection in the Library of Congress in Washington, D.C., holds a copy of the "Vuë d'Annonay" bound into a rare [and possibly unique] collection of fifteen of the prints titled:* Suite complète des estampes représentant les expériences aérostatiques, *undated, with the imprint: "A Paris, Chez le Vachez.")*

Expérience de la Machine Aréostatique de Mᵐᵉ de Montgolfier, d'Anonai en Vivarais.

Reppetée à Paris le 27 Aoust 1783. au Champ de Mars, avec un Balon de Taffetas enduit de Gomme élastique, de 36. pieds 6 pouces de Circonférence.

Ce Balon plein d'Air Inflamable a été éxécuté par Mᵉˢ Robert, en vertu d'une Souscription Nationale sous la direction de Mᵐᵉ Faujas de Saint Fond.

Se vend à Paris chez Le Noir Mᵈ d'Estampes au Louvre et rue du Coq S.ᵗ Honoré.

Expérience de la Machine Aréostatique de Mrs. de Montgolfier, d'Anonai en Vivarais. Reppetée à Paris le 27 Aoust 1783 au Champ de Mars.

Paris, [1783?]. Chez Le Noir. Engraving, 27.2 x 40 cm.
XP-XL-3 (1100)

The small fabric balloon that was launched on August 27, 1783 from the Champ de Mars was intended to repeat the demonstration in Annonay and introduce the balloon to the French capital. Faujas de Saint-Fond, a geologist, was responsible for raising the money for the 36-foot balloon; physicist J.A.C. Charles was responsible for its design and launch; and the Robert brothers built it. Charles could assume that the Montgolfiers had used hydrogen for their Annonay balloon, or at least that hydrogen would work well for the purpose of repeating the Annonay trial. This print is famous for its recycled foreground. As historian François-Louis Bruel first pointed out, the plate had previously been used for the print "Aux incrédules de Paris," a satirical treatment of Blanchard's "flying machine" over Paris. There are two states of the "balloon" version, with differences in the foreground and middle ground to more accurately reflect the circumstances of the launch. In this version, the valve is still attached to the mouth of the balloon, whose small size (or possibly closed position) caused the explosion of this balloon in flight. *(This is the "third state" of the plate, published by Le Noir, showing new environs but retaining some of the foreground figures. The print was quickly ready for distribution, since parts of the plate existed as explained above; the* Journal de Paris *announced publication on August 29; the price was 12 sous. Benjamin Franklin mentions the print by title in a September 2 postscript to a letter of August 30, addressed to Sir Joseph Banks. Franklin noted that, in the caption of the print, Faujas de Saint-Fond had been credited with the organization of a national subscription in support of the balloon and that Charles had been added as an organizer, although his name "is wrote with pen, not engraved." Aside from Franklin's mention, the author has not noted this addition on any other copies of the print. Le Noir, whose first name is not known, was either the father or the brother of the engraver Rose Le Noir, who engraved print XL-41 3237 below.)*

A MESSIEURS LES SOUSCRIPTEURS.

ALLARME GÉNÉRALE DES HABITANTS DE GONESSE, occasionée par la chûte du Ballon Aréostatique de M. De Montgolfier .

Ce Ballon, de 38. pieds de circonference, fait en Taffetas enduit de gomme Elastique et plein d'Air Inflamable, tiré du Fer au moyen de l'acide Vitriolique, s'eleva de lui même au Champ de Mars à Paris, le 27 Aoust 1783. à 5. heures du Soir en présence de plus de 300 mille personnes . La pluie d'Orage qui survint dans l'instant ou on l'abandonna, ne l'empê- cha pas de s'elever avec un mouv.t accelleré jusqu'au dela des Nuës . On présume qu'il fut porté à plus de vingt mille pieds de hauteur ou il creva par la réaction du Gaz Inflam- mable sur l'air Atmosphérique . Il tomba à 6. heures 3. quarts près de Gonesse à 10. milles du Champ de Mars. Les Habitans accoururent en foule, et deux Moines leur ayant assuré que c'etoit la peau d'un Animal monstreux, ils l'assaillirent à coups de Pierres, de Fourches et de Fléaux ; le Curé du lieu fut obligé de se transporter près du Ballon pour rassurer ses Paroissiens epouventés . Il attacherent enfin à la queue d'un Cheval l'Instrument de la plus belle expérience de Physique qui ait jamais été faite, et le trainerent à plus de mille toises à travers Champs .   Se vend à Paris chez Le Noir M.d Fournisseur des Estampes du Cabinet du Roi, demeurant au Louvre .

A messieurs les souscripteurs. Allarme générale des habitants de Gonesse

> Paris, [1783?]. Chez Le Noir. Etching, 31.4 x 21.4 cm.
> XP-XL-3 (1101)

Issued by Le Noir, this intriguing plate suggests the ignorance of the provincials, who were reportedly so alarmed by the balloon as it descended on August 27, 1783 near the village of Gonesse that they destroyed it. As the caption states, 300,000 Parisians had watched the balloon launch 45 minutes prior to this scene; the reaction of the provincials illustrates the lack of communication and the disparity of technologies at the time. The same device could enlighten the people of one city and cause panic in a village 12 miles away. This print was clearly intended for the upper classes of Paris and was sold by "Le Noir, M[archan]d Fournisseur des

Estampes du Cabinet du Roi, demeurant au Louvre" (Le Noir, merchant and purveyor of prints to the Cabinet of the King, residing at the Louvre). We can contrast it to many other satirical prints of the balloon that were intended for the general public. *(The Gimbel collection includes five different prints of this scene, all schematically similar.)*

Expèrience faite à Versailles en presence de S. M. le Roy par le Sieur Montgolfier le 19 Septembre 1783.

Expèrience faite à Versailles en presence de S. M. le Roy par le Sieur Montgolfier le 19 Septembre 1783

> [After Étienne Chevalier de Lorimier (1759–1813)]
>
> 1783? Painting, with ink details, on paper, 13.1 x 18.2 cm.
>
> XC-10-2M (2884)

On September 19, 1783, Étienne Montgolfier "proved" the invention before the king of France at Versailles and a multitude of curious Parisians. Unlike the balloon of August 27, this aircraft carried a payload and captivated all of Paris. This event provided an extremely popular image, and numerous decorated objects feature this scene. (*Clément [p. 46] shows a similar painting on a box, as does Jackson [p. 38]. The Gimbel collection includes two boxes: one [Misc. 25] of 7 cm. diameter with the image painted on the top and signed by Y. Capelle [1746–1800]; another [Misc. 24] shows the launch from a different perspective.*)

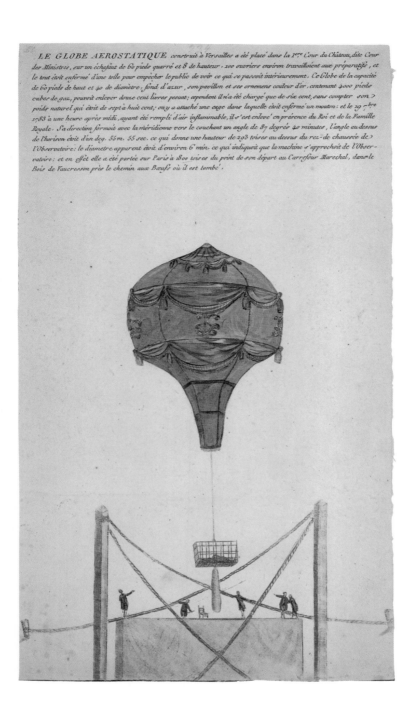

Le globe aërostatique construit à Versailles a été placé dans la 1ere. Cour du Château

Etching, with roulette, 33.7 x 19.2 cm.
XP-XL-2 (1066)

The demonstration on September 19, 1783, not only revealed the workings of the hitherto mysterious hot-air balloon, but established the safety of flight—at least for sheep and fowl. This straightforward version of the ascent ignores the mass of Parisians before whom this invention was unveiled, emphasizing instead the technology involved. The payload included a cage containing three animals, while a long cylinder housing a crude recording barometer is given special prominence by the artist. The print's caption explains that the balloon's lift is 1,200 pounds, its size is 60 feet high by 40 wide, and its coloration is gold detail on a blue background. "About 100 workers helped to ready it, and the whole area was enclosed with canvas to prevent the public from seeing what went on inside." This caution was typical of the Montgolfiers, and in fact the caption

erroneously reports that this hot-air balloon was inflated with "inflammable air." Close examination of this print reveals what appear to be buttons along the seams, which suggests the repetition of the technique used in the balloon of June 5, shown in print XC-10-2M 2878 above. *(An English version, "The Original Air Balloon" [XC-10-2M 2903], is a direct copy of this print.)*

Expérience faite à Versaille, en présence de leurs Majestés et de la Famille Royale, par M. Montgolfier, le 19. Sept.1783

Nicolas De Launay (1739–1792), after a design by the Chevalier de Lorimier (1759–1813)

Paris, [1783]. Etching, 15.5 x 10 cm.

XC-10-2M (2880)

This masterful sketch of the September 19 ascent of a sheep, cock, and duck appeared as the frontispiece in the *Description des expériences aérostatiques* by Faujas de Saint-Fond. The nine prints in the book are known for their accuracy as well as their beauty; in fact, the publisher of the work boasted of its precise depictions, which were created at the events. Twenty-four-year-old Étienne Chevalier de Lorimier (1759–1813) designed all nine of the prints, which were executed by the well-known engravers François Noël Sellier (1737 – ?), Pierre Gabriel(?) Bertault (1748–ca. 1819), and Nicolas De Launay (1739–1792). Intended for a position within the book, this print was labeled plate 5 in the upper right. When the book was finalized, this print, "more ornate than the others," was placed instead opposite the title page. The 53-year-old De Launay prepared the plate shown here and three others included in the book's 1784 sequel, *Première suite de la description.* Lorimier's drawing is in the Musée Carnavalet in Paris.

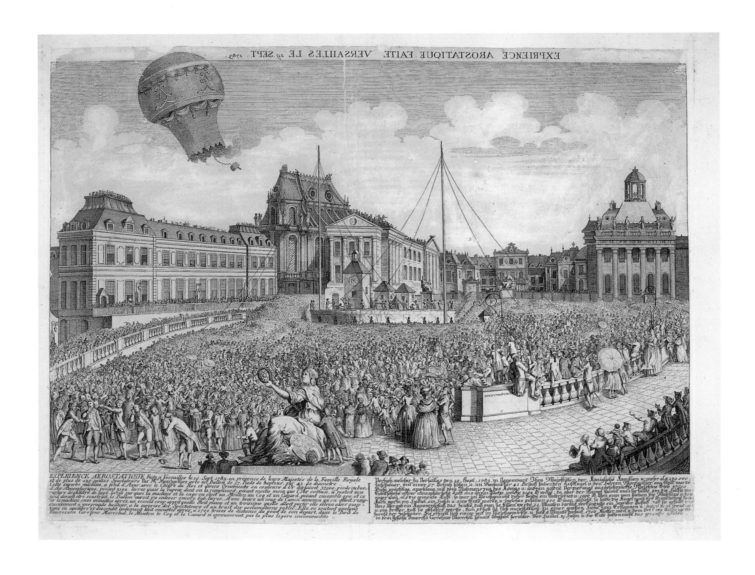

Exprience arostatique faite Versailles le 19 Sept 1783

[sic; *title appears in reverse*]

Engraving, 29.3 x 37.8 cm. (sheet) (plate size indeterminate)

XP-XL-2 (1062)

The title of this print appears in reverse so that when the print is viewed through a *vue d'optique* device, the wording would read normally. Given in French and German, the caption explains the specifics of the balloon, including its size and coloration. The crowd, which is drafted in great detail that would be further enhanced by the *vue d'optique,* is described as numbering 130,000. Part of the inscription (in reverse) on the stone pediment in the foreground appears to read "monr. Vicvin." Liebmann and Wahl (#197) identify the sculpture in the foreground as a personification of Genius and suggest that the print was produced by the Augsburg printer Probst. *(This print appears to be a German copy of XP-XL-2 1064, issued by Le Noir, in which the inscription on the stone pediment in the foreground may include the artist's signature; it reads: "R M" or "II M" and "εργον εξ ημερων" ["six days' work"]. Other copies of the Le Noir plate are the colored prints XP-XL-2 1060 and XP-XL-2 1061.)*

VUE DE LA TERRASSE DE Mr. FRANKLIN A PASSI.

Premier voyage Aérien en présence de Monseigneur le Dauphin. Cette Expérience c'est faite sous la direction de Mr. Montgolfier, dans le jardin de la Muette, ce Globe portant 70 pieds de hauteur sur 46 de diamètre, le pouds qu'il a enlevé étoit d'environ 16 à 1700 livres, fut construit par Mr. le Marquis d'Arlande et Mr. Pilâtre des Rosiers, ces deux intrepides Voyageurs partirent le 21 Novembre 1783, a une heure 54 minutes après midi, ils s'élevèrent à 270 pieds de hauteur, ils arrivèrent à bon port sur la Butte aux Cailles entre le moulin de Merveilles et le moulin Vieux, ayant vogué dans l'air un intervalle de 400 toises en 20 ou 25 minutes sans avoir éprouvé la plus legere incomodité. A Paris chez Vachez, quai de Gevres, à l'Espérance. A.P.D.R.

Vue de la Terrasse de Mr. Franklin à Passi

P. G. Tavenard [after Étienne Chevalier de
Lorimier (1759–1813)]
Paris, [1784?]. Etching, 15 x 10.5 cm.
XC-10-2M (2893)

This view was seen by Lorimier from Benjamin Franklin's home, reportedly with Franklin at his side. Franklin's house in the suburb of Passy, where he had settled as a diplomat in 1776, was quite near to the Château de la Muette, where the balloon was launched on November 21, 1783, carrying the first two people to fly, the Marquis d'Arlandes and Pilâtre de Rozier. This print, a variant of which forms the frontispiece of Faujas de Saint-Fond's *Première suite de la description* of 1784, depicts the scene from an intriguing perspective of earthiness, to which the free flight of the balloon strikes a forceful contrast. Two observers atop a roof on the lower right watch the progress of the balloon. According to Préaud, the publisher of this print, Nicolas-François Le Vachez, moved his establishment from rue de Grenell-Saint-Honoré to quai de Gesvres in October 1784; as the latter address is given on the lower right, we can assume that this print appeared after this date. On this copy the ink has been effaced from parts of the envelope. *(This is undoubtedly part of a series by Le Vachez, discussed in the description of print XC-10-2M 2878 above: "Vuë d'Annonay en Vivarais," although the style of the title's lettering varies from others in the series, using roman capitals as in print XL-6 4622. For a view of quite another subject, but which shares the perspective of the rooftops, compare print XL-38 3167 below: "Thirty-six Views Around Fugaku.")*

[Montgolfière of November 21, 1783]

   Painting on wood, 29.5 x 21.4 cm.

   XP-XL-41 (3236)

The grounds of the Château de la Muette were crowded with thousands of people, yet the anonymous artist of this painting chose to present fewer spectators, giving a more casual impression. The coloration of this painting suggests a relatively modern origin, although its rapidly sketched style makes a charming statement.

La traversée de Paris par Pilâtre
de Rozier et le marquis d'Arlandes
(21 novembre 1783)

    Marcel JeanJean (1893–1973)
    Colored lithograph, 24 x 17 cm.
    XP-XL-14 (1500)

This dynamic view of the ascent of November
21, 1783, takes a perspective rarely exploited
before the twentieth century. JeanJean, a
World War I aviator and illustrator who was
appointed official painter to the French
minister of air in 1931, became known for his
books and drawings on aeronautical themes.
*(This print is part of a series by JeanJean,
including prints 1498–1500.)*

Décente de la Machine Aërostatïque dans la Plaine au de la des Nouveaux Boulevards près le petit Gentilly vis à vis le Moulin Crouleubarbe en cet endroit doit etre élevé une Piramide en mémoire éternelle a la gloire de M\. de Montgolfier auteur de cette découverte et de M\ le Marquis d'Arlandes et Pilatre du Rozier Premiers Voyageurs Aériens la Machine parti du Chateau de la Muette le 21 Novembre a une heure 54 Minutte, portant les deux voyageurs ci dessus. elle séleva à la hauteur de 3000 Pieds traversa paris et descendit à 2 heures 20 Minuttes.

Décente de la Machine Aërostatïque dans la Plaine au de la des Nouveaux Boulevards près le petit Gentilly . . . en cet endroit doit etre élevé une Piramide en mémoire éternelle a la gloire de M\r. de Montgolfier . . .

Etching, colored, 22.7 x 30.4 cm.

XP-XL-2 (3442)

This interesting print shows the landing of the Montgolfier balloon on November 21, 1783, an event witnessed by some who followed the balloon across Paris on horseback. There is a curious and probably inaccurate representation of the fire used to heat the balloon while aloft, and there is little trace of the chaotic conditions that prevailed at this landing. The author of this print suggests in the caption that a monument (which can be seen at right) be erected at this site, although the structure never materialized.

A study by Elisabeth Boselli in the magazine *Icare* (105, 1983/2) discusses the place of landing at length and again proposes that a monument be erected there. Historian Charles Dollfus was able to identify the place of departure by speaking to the gardeners of the Bois de Boulogne, who had preserved an oral tradition.

SECOND VOYAGE AÉRIEN.

Expérience faite dans le Jardin des Thuilleries par M.M. Charles et Robert, le 1er. xbre. 1783.
Le Globe en Taffetas gommé de 26 Pieds de diamètre était plein d'Air inflamable.

Second voyage aérien. Expérience faite
dans le Jardin des Thuilleries par M.M.
Charles et Robert, le 1er. xbre. 1783

Nicolas De Launay (1739–1792), after a design
by Étienne Chevalier de Lorimier (1759–1813)

[Paris, 1784]. Etching and engraving,
15.4 x 10.5 cm. (image)

XC-10-2C (3386)

A cult of sorts grew around J.A.C. Charles,
whose successful flight on December 1, 1783,
in the first man-carrying gas balloon seemed
to capture the intrigue of the Parisians more
than any other aeronautical event had done.
Perhaps his popularity was due to his personality and style, both said to have been power-
fully disarming. In any case, many thought
his method of inflating balloons to be superior to the methods of the Montgolfiers,
whose balloons were comparatively limited
in endurance.

Le moment d'hilarité universelle, ou le triomphe de MMrs. Charles et Robert au Jardin des Thuileries le 1er. xbre. 1783. Presenté à mon Pere pour son 89me. Anniversaire

> J.H.E. (i.e., Johann Heinrich Eberts) invenit et delinavit; H. G. Bertaux, sculpt.
>
> Paris, [1784]. Chez Le Noir. Etching, 15 x 20.3 cm.
>
> XP-XL-4 (1141)

A formal depiction of the balloon of December 1, 1783, this print is unusual (though not unique) for its portrayal of the balloon as it lifts off and again as it gains altitude. In addition, the artist shows the small pilot balloon released by Étienne Montgolfier in the upper left. The small vignette titled "Projet d'un monument" shows a tall pyramid surmounted by a small balloon, with two figures and a plaque at the base; the figures form part of a fountain. This design was no doubt intended for an unfinalized government competition to select a monument design in 1784 to commemorate the invention. In an unusually long notice which includes many interesting details, the appearance of this print was announced in the *Journal de Paris* of March 5, 1784. Without mentioning his name, the notice refers to the artist as an amateur who produced the print in homage to his father, 89 years old. The artist donated 100 copies to benefit octogenarians, about a fifth of which he wished to have bestowed on an 89-year-old man. Some copies of the edition were printed on fine "Holland paper," in order to reduce the weight for those who wished to send the print abroad. The print was available from Le Noir (*"sous le passage de la colonnade du Louvre"*) for 1 livre, 4 sous. The preparation of the plate is credited to Bertaux and Guttemberg le jeune, although only the former is mentioned on the print. The first four words of the title apparently refer to a phrase used by Charles in describing his flight in the *Journal de Paris* of December 13, 1783. (*The vignette is repeated on another print in the Gimbel collection, "Etienne et Joseph Montgolfier, freres, Nés à Annonay en Vivares" [XC-10-2M 2870] where the vignette is titled: "Projet d'un monument a elever a M. Charles." The vignette was cynically remembered in 1784 when it was parodied on print XP-XL-5 1188 below: "Les deux Midas."*)

Charles, aux Thuilleries, le 1ᵉ Decembre MDCCLXXXIII

Simon Charles Miger, 1736–1820
Paris, [1784]. Engraving, 25.2 x 19 cm.
XP-XL-20 (1821)

The physicist and balloonist J.A.C. Charles is shown before the image of a balloon (background, at top). Three lines of poetry suggest that Charles, personifying technology, has displaced a symbol of nature, the eagle:

> Until then without equal
> the King of the Air
> follows his rival there.

Miger was an expert and well-known engraver, who had been elected to the Académie in 1778. The *Journal de Paris* of March 31, 1784, as well as the *Gazette de France*

of April 6, announced this print, priced at 2 livres, 8 sous. *(Marsh [pl. 14] shows a crayon drawing upon which this print was no doubt based. Print XC-10-2C 3370 is the same work facing left, engraved by P. G. Tavenard. Compare XP-XL-20 1822, "Charles aux Thuileries le 1ᵉʳ December 1783" [another portrait]. The same three lines of poetry are repeated at bottom.)*

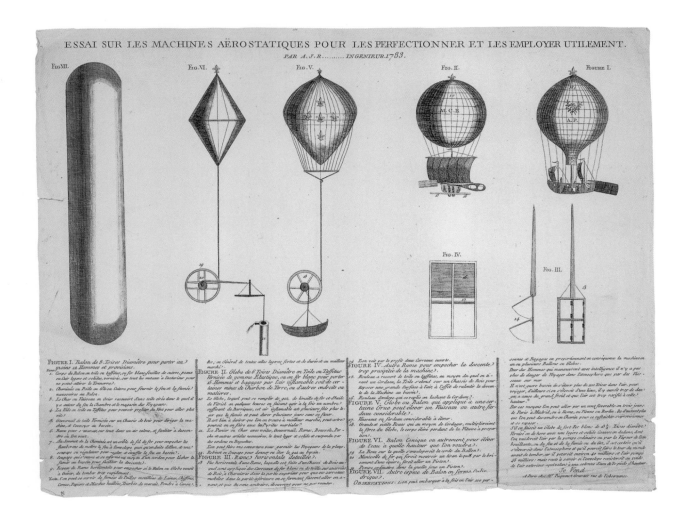

Essai sur les machines aërostatiques pour les perfectionner et les employer utilement. Par A.J.R........Ingénieur.1783.

> Paris, [1783?]. Etching, 37 x 46.5 cm. Letters on balloon at right: "M./A.P.," and second from right: "M.C.R."
>
> XP-XL-4 (1121)

The invention of the balloon brought forth many ideas for utilizing the new technology, and this print offers designs for a pump, a lift, and a semi-dirigible balloon. It suggests (in the left-most figure) a cylindrical shape for the carrying of "100 people and baggage," which is equipped with a chimney and stove to generate smoke and gas from wet straw, gunpowder, oiled paper, wool, rags, peat— "anything which can be cheaply had." The acronym "A.J.R." in the caption may refer to Anne-Jean Robert, who with his brother assisted J.A.C. Charles with his balloons and later constructed an elongated balloon which is shown in print XP-XL-4 1159 below.

LA COQUETTE PHISICIENNE.

Je suis, je crois, assez aimable ;   J'excelle dans l'air inflammable

Qui veut me suivre, vite, allons.   Point de chute avec mes Balons

La Coquette Phisicienne

Etching, 24 x 16.7 cm.

XP-XL-15 (4624)

The prints that survive of the balloon costume that was popular during the brief period of the "balloon craze" satirize the subject, so it is difficult to judge from them the exact nature of the style. No doubt exaggerated, they are consistent in showing hats, with sleeves, shoes, and skirts all enlarged with balloons. This print with its caption is apparently meant to suggest a moral lightness. *(The figure in XP-XL-15 4624, "La Coquette Phisicienne," is copied in reverse in print XP-XL-15 1564, "La phisicienne galante," where the hat is changed. Other prints depicting the balloon costume are XP-XL-15 3433, "L'homme Aux balons ou la folie du jour"; XP-XL-15 1563, "Le petit-maitre phisicien"; and XP-XL-15 1565, "Madame la Comtesse de M . . . devant aller voir la fameuse experience.")*

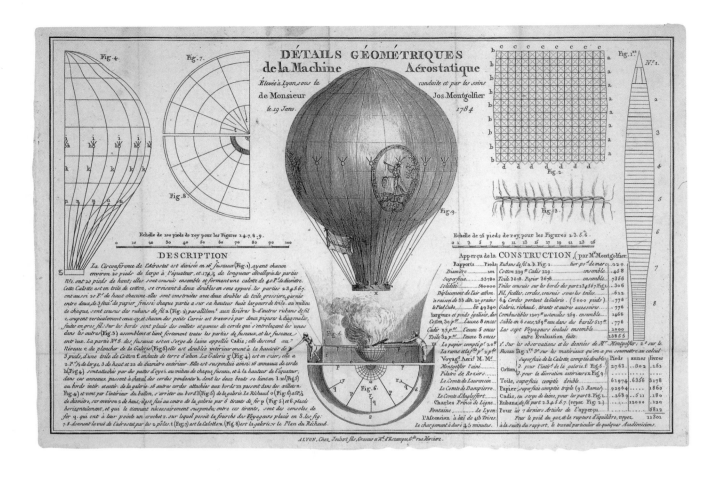

Détails géométriques de la Machine Aérostatique Élevée à Lyon

Lyon, [1784]. Engraving, 22 x 32.5 cm.
XP-XL-2 (1082)

In early December 1783, Joseph Montgolfier began to assemble this balloon, which was financed by a subscription. Despite a paternal prohibition against flying, Montgolfier hoped to make a long flight in the aircraft. The balloon was named for Jacques de Flesselles, Intendant of Lyon, and bore insignias symbolizing History and Fame. It was assembled with the help of Jean-François Pilâtre de Rozier, who arrived at Lyon on December 27. Progress was slowed by Pilâtre's commandeering style, by rain, by fire, and finally by snow. On the nineteenth of January 1784, the balloon was ready and six people (including Joseph Montgolfier and Pilâtre) took their places in the gondola—despite the evident frailty of the now-decrepit paper and cloth envelope. As the balloon left the ground, a seventh person jumped aboard. After a flight of about fifteen minutes, the envelope began to fail, and the balloon descended quickly to earth; it was the only time a Montgolfier ascended in a balloon. *(The section "Aperçu de la construction par Mr. Montgolfier" [a feature sometimes seen on prints of the period] gives enough detail to let the enthusiast construct a balloon. Many prints were published of this balloon, including some that show a continuous scene on the envelope, without the four medallions as here.)*

Comme il devoit partir. *Comme il est parti seul.*

EXPERIENCE DU VAISSEAU VOLANT de Mr Blanchard le 2 Mars 1784. ou il est monté a midi et demie On estime qu'il s'est elevé à la hauteur de 2500 toises ; Il devoit etre accompagné de Dom Pêche sans la faillie d'un jeune homme qui s'est elancé dans son Vaisseau, voulant absolument partir avec lui. Et fit un très grand domage à sa Machine. Et est descendu a 1 heur e 3 quarts dans la Plaine de Billancourt.

A Paris chez Basset rue St. Jacques. Avec Privilège du Roy.

Experience du Vaisseau Volant de Mr
Blanchard le 2 Mars 1784

> Paris, [1784?]. Chez Basset. Etching,
> 19.4 x 31.4 cm. (image)
> XP-XL-6 (1220)

The resurrection of the term *vaisseau volant* in a print apparently commissioned by Jean-Pierre Blanchard suggests that the inventor was hoping to salvage his reputation by modifying the ornithopter of the same name that he had constructed in 1782. This print shows two views of Blanchard's *vaisseau volant*, the center one with parachute, labeled "as it should have departed," and the view at right, labeled "as he departed by himself." The parachute visible on the left was arranged below the envelope, but not carried on the actual flight because of its weight, and one can see that the "wings," or oars, have been left behind as well. Apparently to explain why equipment central to the trial was abandoned, the caption relates that Blanchard was to be accompanied by aeronaut Dom Pêche, but a young man, who hoped to accompany the balloonists, threw himself into the basket, "heavily damaging the machine." After a very brief flight with Dom Pêche, Blanchard ascended for a flight of three hours leaving Dom Pêche, the parachute, and the wings that are shown on the ground. It was the fourth man-carrying flight of a balloon.

Aréostat des MM. Robert, Fait d'après
leur dessin

> Paris, [1784?]. Chez [Le] Vachez. Etching and
> engraving, 27.3 x 19.5 cm.
> XP-XL-4 (1159)

The elongated shape was immediately seen
as a practical way of making the balloon
aerodynamic, and as early as September 1784,
the brothers Robert (who had served as
technicians for J.A.C. Charles) had completed
this aircraft and readied it for trial. The inset
"Cartes des voyageurs" would no doubt have
amused those who saw the balloon from
afar and were curious as to the position and
course of the aircraft. *(On a related print
by the same publisher [Le Vachez] see XC-10-
2M 2878 above. The medallion: "Cartes des
voyageurs" is similar to other maps produced
of flights, for example Gimbel XP-XL-6 1212:
"Carte des marches aërographiques"; XP-XL-4
4604: "Rentrée du char triomphant"; and XC-
10-2M 2870: "Etienne et Joseph Montgolfier,
frères nés à Annonay" [with its "Cartes des
premiers voyages aërostatiques"].)*

Étienne et Joseph de Montgolfier frères,
Nés à Annonay en Vivarais.

> Roze (or Rose) Le Noir, after a bas-relief by
> Jean-Antoine Houdon (1741–1828)
> [Paris, 1783]. Color engraving, and stipple
> engraving, à la poupée, in sepia and brown.
> 15 x 9.5 cm.
> XL-41 (3237)

Sculptor Jean-Antoine Houdon produced
a large number of busts of contemporary
notables in various media between about
1771 and 1789. Houdon's 1783 relief of the
Montgolfiers appears in several prints of
the collection and on the medal of 1783
(XM-11 3506). This print was announced in
the *Journal de Paris* of December 18, 1783,
possibly "to be joined with Faujas de Saint-
Fond's work," the *Description des expériences
aérostatiques,* although in fact the book
appeared without it. Rose Le Noir was either
the daughter or the sister of the publisher
Le Noir, who produced a number of early
aeronautical prints. The eight lines of verse
by Gudin de la Brenelerie at the base of this
print promise that soon "the dangerous journey
will no longer seem a mere entertainment."

*(A print with a similar title [lacking the "de"
before "Montgolfier"] was designed and
engraved by Robert De Launay [1754–1814],
brother of Nicolas De Launay, and announced
in the* Journal de Paris *of October 17, 1783.
An advertisement for the De Launay print
appeared in Faujas de Saint-Fond's* Description *[page xl], offering the print at the book's
publisher [Cuchet] as well as the artist's, for
1 livre, 4 sous. The Gimbel collection includes
five prints based on Houdon's motif.)*

MONTGOLFIER IN THE CLOUDS

CONSTRUCTING OF AIR BALLOONS FOR THE GRAND MONARQUE

FOURTH SKETCH

O by gar! dis be de grande invention. — dis will immortalize my King, my Country, and myself.
We will declare de War against our ennemi; we will make des English quake, by gar;
We will inspect their Camp, we will intercept their Fleet, and we will set fire to their Dock-yards;
And by gar, we will take de Gibraltar in de air balloon. and when we have
Conquered d'English, den we conquer d'other Countrie, and make them all Colonie
to de Grand Monarque.

a Companion to this in a few day

Published as the act directs March 2 1784 by J. Foster N.º 3 Piccadilly

Montgolfier in the Clouds. Constructing of Air Balloons for the Grand Monarque. Fourth Sketch

[London], published March 2, 1784. Etching, 35 x 24.7 cm.

XP-XL-15 (1575)

In the monologue given as a caption, "Montgolfier" describes the ways in which the French will use the new invention to dominate the world. Clearly, the enthusiasm for Montgolfier and his useless balloons is seen as a trivial manifestation of French egotism. The bubbles are no doubt meant to suggest the insubstantial nature of the invention, relying upon a sense of the word "bubble" to connote a hoax. The caption makes mention of the British fortress of Gibraltar, whose siege by the Spanish and later the French from 1779 until February of 1783 is often cited as a motive for Joseph Montgolfier's invention of the balloon. *(Apparently part of a series, as the title mentions "fourth sketch" and promises "a companion to follow in a few days.")*

Montgolfier vole au Rang des dieux / et L'immortalité Ravie / avec approbation de L'academie de marseille

Fiere d'un nom Si glorieux / L'inscrit aux fastes du genie

Montgolfier vole au Rang des dieux

Louis-Alexandre de Buigne, after a painting by Jean Biard [Marseilles], 1784.

Etching, 24 x 19.5 cm.

XP-XL-2 (1089)

In this etching, the name of Montgolfier is being entered by Immortality into the *fastes du génie* (or the annals of genius) held by Time. The portrait bust on the pedestal is thought to be Louis XVI. The balloon pictured with three fleur-de-lis is a bit enigmatic as it does not appear in any other print of the 1780s; it is probably intended to represent the balloon in general. The zodiacal spectrum at top with its Arabic number "12" between Libra and Scorpio must represent some event (on October 12?), but its significance is unknown. Unlike previous schematic uses of ethereal vapors to suspend figures, here the figure of Immortality rests on vapors that emanate from a man-made sack found among a heap of scientific instruments in the foreground. *(A copy in the Bibliothèque Nationale in Paris has this addition to the last line:* "Se vend 24 s. à Marseille ché Briard rue Vacon hotel de Saxe.")

J^h. M^l. Montgolfier, Membre de la Légion
d'Honneur

>   *ca.* 1810. Stipple engraving, 38 x 28.5 cm.
>   XL-20 (1836)

Joseph Montgolfier, who invented the balloon
in 1782, was absentminded in the extreme.
It is said that, while traveling, he once forgot
his horse, and once, his wife. Best known for
his work with the balloon, he was perpetually
musing and experimenting. This memorial
print, issued after Montgolfier's death in 1810,
celebrates both the balloon (or aërostat)
and his *bélier hydraulique*, which worked to
capture the force of moving water and convert it to use in pumping. Although the
vignette ineptly shows a gas balloon rather
than a hot-air balloon, it does draw the

viewer's attention to a *bélier hydraulique*
lifting water high above a river. The scene
evokes the dramatic countryside near
Annonay, where Montgolfier was born in 1740.
A few lines from *The Odes* of Horace (II, 18)
serve as an epithet:

>   Non ebur neque Aureum . . . at fides et
>   ingeni Benigna vena est.
>   *(Neither ivory nor gold . . . but loyalty and a
>   kindly vein of genius.)*

L'HOMME AEROSTATIQUE ou MON PAUVRE ONCLE.

Un Physicien ayant construit un balon, employa pour le remplir d'air inflammable, deux seringues ordinaires ; Surpris d'une colique à la suite d'une dispute qu'il avoit eu avec un de ses amis aussi Physicien, on lui fit prendre pour le guerir, de l'eau de Cologne qui ne fit pas l'effet qu'on en devoit attendre ; Son neveu et la gouvernante récoururent de lui donner des lavemens, et se servirent des seringues qui lui injectèrent l'air inflammable dont elles étoient remplies ; Son ventre aussitôt s'enfla, il fit plusieurs sauts dans sa chambre, et finit par enfiler la fenêtre, la culotte sur les talons. On le perdit bientôt de vue : son bonnet a été trouvé à quelques lieues de Paris, et des Chasse-marée ont rapporté que sa perruque étoit tombée à Rouen. On peut croire qu'il est à present à caracoler vers le firmament, sans qu'on puisse avoir nouvelle de lui. Cela a été annoncé dans le Journal de Paris du 3 Octobre 1783, afin que si on le rencontre à l'endroit de sa chute, on le renvoye par la premier occasion à M. Borné son neveu, rue Neuve St. Marceau. Sa taille est petite, il est maigre, la tête et les épaules larges, les emboitures fortes ; son habillement est une robe de chambre d'ancien Damas couleur de rose sèche, culotte de velours canelle, des bas gris, il n'a qu'un soulier attaché d'une petite boucle d'argent, à jarretière.

L'homme aerostatique ou mon pauvre oncle

[Paris, 1784]. Etching, colored, 26 x 20.1 cm.
XL-15 (4628)

A letter in the *Journal de Paris* of October 3, 1783, describes the flight of the letter-writer's uncle, who, suffering from colic, accidentally received into his anus an injection of the "inflammable air" used in balloons, which caused him to fly from his bed and out the window. His nephew implored the *Journal* to publish his letter so the uncle might be found. Apparently this letter became something of a sensation as several prints appeared featuring the subject. On the door in the background one can read the words "Assemblé Dexperience"; on the corner of the building, above the window, one reads "R. Neuve, St. Morceaux." *(Related prints are XP-XL-15 1581, "The Day's Folly"; XP-XL-15 1582, "L'homme aérostatique"; XP-XL-15 3434, "Avis très important"; and XP-XL-15 3448, "Graces à Dieu, voila mon Oncle retrouvé." A print with this title was announced in the* Journal de Paris *of April 17, 1784.)*

AEROSTATION.

1. *Montgolfier's Balloon.* 2. *Blanchard's.* 3. *Charles & Robert's.* 4. *Lunardi's.*
5. *Baldwin's View over the City of Chester, from Lunardi's Balloon.*

Aerostation

J. Pass

London, published by J[ohn] Wilkes
[of Millard House, Sussex,] June 28, 1803.
Engraving, colored, 19.8 x 24.7 cm.

XP-XL-9 (1362)

This print shows two popular balloon flights: the ascent of Pilâtre de Rozier and the Marquis d'Arlandes on November 21, 1783, and Jean-Pierre Blanchard's ascent of March 2, 1784. At bottom is shown preparations for the launch by J.A.C. Charles and the brothers Robert on August 27, 1783, and Vincent Lunardi's balloon, which first flew on September 15, 1784. In the center appears the view of the city of Chester as recorded by Thomas Baldwin and first published in 1786. The publisher, John Wilkes, issued a number of specialized offprints based on the articles in his *Encyclopaedia Londinensis,* and this print may have been prepared to accompany one on aerostation, of which no record can now be found. *(A similar plate engraved by [Inigo] Barlow is dated 1796 and appears in the 1797 and 1810 editions of Wilkes' Encyclopaedia Londinensis. The Gimbel collection includes an earlier print in the same genre, print XP-XL-22 1867, "Representation of various balloons, with the methods of constructing and filling them.")*

L'expérience qui devoit avoir lieu ce jour la avoit attirés aux Luxembourg, et aux environs, une multitude innombrables de Spectateur après plusieurs tentatives inutiles pour élever la machine le feu y á pris. Les Spectateurs impatients ont murmurés hautement, la populace est entreé malgré la Garde et á détruit, Brulés, saccagé, tout ce qui s'est trouvés sous leurs mains.

A Paris chez J. Chereau, rue S.t Jacques au dessus de la Fontaine S.t Severin aux 2 Colonnes N.º 257.

Embrâsement déplorable de la Machine Aërostatique des S^rs. Miolan et Janinet le dimanche 11 Juillet 1784

Paris, [1784?]. Engraving, 25.5 x 38.2 cm. (image)
XP-XL-5 (1185)

The engraver Jean-François Janinet and the Abbé Miolan constructed a hot-air balloon in Paris with funds raised through subscription. Subscribers were entitled to watch the inflation and flight from within the confines of the Luxembourg Gardens; the event was regulated by the police who had dealt with trouble at other such events. Twenty thousand spectators packed the gardens on Sunday, July 11, 1784, suffering through long delays on a still, sweltering day. Janinet and Miolan (like all balloonists in all times) strongly felt their obligations to the crowd, and inflated their balloon despite the heat, the resulting lack of lift, and probable failure; when the balloon's crown caught fire, the ascent was postponed. The spectators in the garden left peacefully, but the crowd outside the garden entered and destroyed the balloon. On the lower left one can see Janinet and Miolan (depicted as an ass and a cat), together with the Marquis d'Arlandes, hurrying themselves from the scene. The ladders may have been provided to those who wished to climb into the nearby trees and walls to watch the ascent; certainly the chairs so prominent in this depiction were available only to the aristocrats who could afford to enter the enclosure. To the eighteenth-century eye this print symbolized a revolt upon the social hierarchy. *(Colonel Gimbel collected a number of prints satirizing this event or the characters of the proprietors including: 1181, "Un chat est un chat"; 1182, "Les phisiciens travaillants à l'observatoire dédié aux souscripteurs"; 1183, "Jugement définitif en faveur des Srs. Miolan et Janinet" (not in color); 1184, "La physique confond l'ignorance." All are in XP-XL-5. Grand-Carteret [p. xiii] shows an unusual print of this aircraft rising from the ground, titled "Machine aërostatique de MMrs. l'Abbé Miolan et Janinet.")*

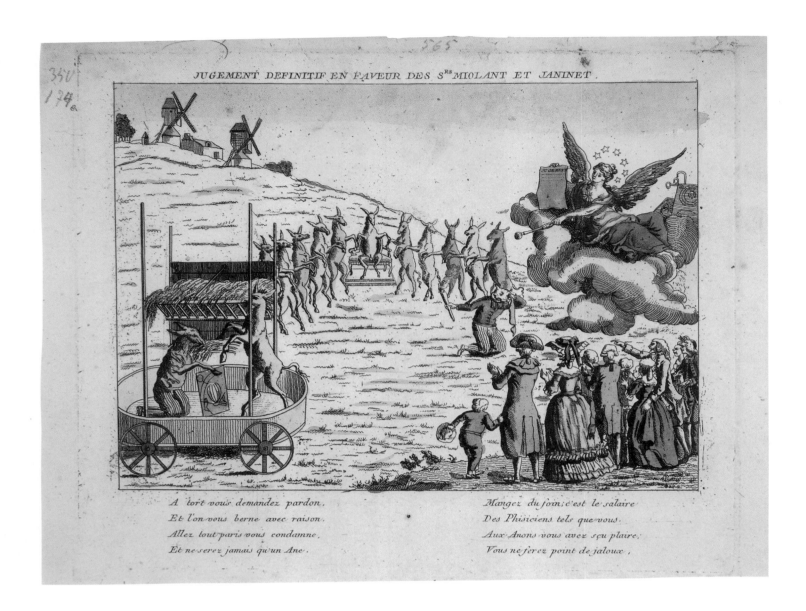

A tort vous demandez pardon,
Et l'on vous berne avec raison.
Allez tout paris vous condamne,
Et ne serez jamais qu'un Ane.

Mangez du foin; c'est le salaire
Des Phisiciens tels que vous.
Aux Anons vous avez sçu plaire,
Vous ne ferez point de jaloux,

Jugement définitif en faveur des S^{rs}. Miolan et Janinet

[1784?]. Etching, 20 x 24.5 cm.
XP-XL-5 (1186)

A murderous ocean of ridicule descended on the Abbé Miolan and Jean-François Janinet, manifested in numerous prints whose symbols, as in this etching, parodied their names. Miolan, whose name sonically resembled the French word *miaulement* (meowing), kneels before the same symbol of immortality that Jean Biard employed in the austere print XP-XL-2 1089 above, "Montgolfier vole au rang des dieux." Janinet, whose name suggested *âne*, or ass, is shown at the left, eating hay in a cart; the cart resembles the gondola of the balloon. Sued by one subscriber for the cost of the subscription, Miolan prevailed in court, having solicited the supporting opinions of Pilâtre de Rozier and Faujas de Saint-Fond. Intent on vindicating his name as a physicist, he later received an exonerating opinion from Étienne Montgolfier. The author of this print asserts in the text:

> You wrongly ask for pardon, and are justly derided.
> Come! all of Paris condemns you, you will never be but an ass.
> Eat hay [i.e., be a fool]; it's the wages of physicists like you.
> You knew how to please the young asses, and will excite no jealousy.

One historian has pointed out that it was not the paying subscribers who rioted but the spectators outside the walls; although the rioters had not lost money per se, they were enraged at waiting for what they came to consider a fraud. Miolan and Janinet were never able to overcome this perception with the populace of Paris, which no doubt counted among the asses described above the applauding aristocrats on the right of the print. The image held by the ass in the cart is based on the engraved admission ticket issued for this event, one of which is preserved in the Gimbel collection. It depicts the balloon before a rainbow and two small balloons (or spheres) on tethers above and below the main balloon. *(A less-detailed version of this print, in reverse, is the uncolored XP-XL-5 1183, which is an etching with aquatint in sepia. There has survived, to my knowledge, only one nonsatirical depiction of this balloon, which was to test vents in the envelope as a means of horizontal propulsion, at the suggestion of Joseph Montgolfier.)*

Les Deux Midas. Vue de l'Elévation du Globe Aërostatique faite par un détachement des Gardes Suisses, sous la direction des Messieurs Miolan et Janinet le 11 Juillet 1784

[1784?]. Etching, 22 x 25.6 cm.

XP-XL-5 (1188)

Full of insults, this print represents the unprecedented assault on Miolan and Janinet in the popular culture of Paris. The two balloonists are shown at right and left, both with the ears of an ass, and Miolan with the head of a cat. Their buttocks are bared in the manner of other satirical prints that play upon the contemporary association of human gas and the "air inflammable" used in balloons. At the feet of the balloonists stand upturned hats full of coins, beneath which the two captions refer to the "elevation" attained by the balloon, the bottom-most claiming it to be "27 feet, 11 inches, 5 lines, with the help of a pole of like height." Around each balloonist's neck is a noose-like vine of oak leaves. The satirical vignette at bottom, titled "Projet d'un monument," is clearly based upon the vignette of the same title in print XP-XL-4 1141 above, "Le moment d'hilarité universelle" and represents either an upturned hat ready to receive the charity of the people or a barber's bowl, perhaps playing on the verb *raser* (to shave, to demolish). In colloquial use, the verb also

means "to bore." The proposed monument with its fetters is surrounded with the inscription: *Chacun son métier, et les vaches seront bien gardées* (Everyone to his craft, and the cows will be well tended). It appears that the central portion of this print may have been prepared as a formal depiction of the inflation, and the satirical borders added following the loss of the balloon on July 11. The title ("The Two Midas") evokes the mythological king who was given the gift of "the golden touch," and no doubt refers to the venality of the two balloonists. The central ornament at top prominently features a whistle (evoking the practice of hooting) and a pipe of Pan, sometimes used for disciplining dogs and cats. Viewers conversant with mythology might have recalled that after Midas had judged a musical contest between Apollo and Pan and decided against the former, Apollo changed Midas' ears into those of an ass.

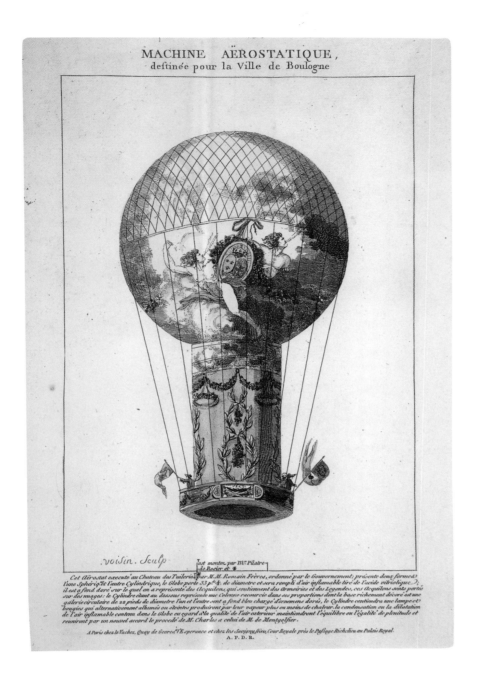

MACHINE AËROSTATIQUE,
destinée pour la Ville de Boulogne

Machine aërostatique, destinée pour la Ville de Boulogne

   Voisin, sculp.

   1785. Etching, 29.8 x 18.2 cm.

   XP-XL-5 (4623)

This balloon was launched from France on June 15, 1785, in an attempt to cross the Channel. It was the first balloon that combined hot air (in the long column) with hydrogen (in the sphere). Although technical information is vague, it appears that in order to provide lift, the heat from the burner was intended to rarefy the air in the column rather than the gas in the sphere. Like other prints, this one shows the two parts of the balloon as contiguous, although other descriptions and other prints indicate that a space of several yards separated the two parts. Flown by its builder, Jules Romain, and the famous Pilâtre de Rozier, this kind of balloon came to be called a "rozière." Using helium for a lifting gas and propane to heat it, the rozière became popular for long flights. *(The same print in Bruel [106] has Calais rather than Boulogne in the title, no doubt indicating a change of plans in the launch site. Print XP-XL-5 1199 is an imaginary view of the balloon setting out from Calais.)*

Monsieur Pilatre de Rosier qui avec le Marquis d'Arlandes avoit fait la premiere ascension dans les airs au Château de la Muette le [21 novembre] 1783

Aquatint, 40 x 27.5 cm.
XP-XL-25 (2015)

The title is not directly relevant to the event illustrated; taken from the first line of the caption, it describes Pilâtre de Rozier as the aeronaut who accompanied the Marquis d'Arlandes on the flight from the Château de la Muette in 1783. Depicted in this print is the world's first aeronautical disaster, which occurred when Romain and Pilâtre's balloon, shown in the previous print, caught fire and crashed to earth while still over France. The fire is usually attributed to sparks from the burner, which ignited escaping hydrogen; but another theory postulates that the valve line, which ran outside of the envelope to the top of the balloon, produced a spark while being worked against the gold-leaf decorations on the envelope. Pilâtre was dead when onlookers reached the balloon, and Romain died shortly after. It is said that Pilâtre's fiancée, Susan Dyer, was so shocked by the sight of the crash that she died soon afterward. *(The publisher of this print must have lacked reliable information about the date of the flight by Pilâtre de Rozier and the Marquis d'Arlandes [which was November 21, 1783]—a blank area in the caption has been left for it.)*

DOVER CASTLE,

WITH THE SETTING OFF OF THE BALLOON TO CALAIS, IN JANUARY 1785.

Painted by T. Rowlandson, & engraved by W. Birch, Enamel Painter.

Published Aug.t 1.1789 by Wm. Birch, Hampstead Heath & sold by T. Thornton, Southampton Str.t Cov.t Garden.

Dover Castle, with the setting off of the balloon to Calais, in January 1785

William Russell Birch (1755–1834), after a painting by Thomas Rowlandson (1756–1827)

London, 1789. Etching, 15 x 17.5 cm.

XP-XL-6 (1230)

Shown against the backdrop of Dover Castle is the balloon of Jean-Pierre Blanchard and his passenger, John Jeffries, an American physician who had moved with his family to London. Trained in both medicine and physics, Jeffries financed the flight to conduct his own scientific research. Their two-hour flight carried them across the Channel to France on January 7, 1785. During the voyage the two balloonists had to jettison nearly everything, including some of their clothing, in order to avoid landing in the Channel. Then, as they flew over France near Calais, they jettisoned their urine to slow their descent. Despite the calmness permeating this print, the relationship between the two men was poor; Tom Crouch in *The Eagle Aloft* characterized the preparations for the flight as a time of "constant bickering."

(Print XP-XL-6 1229, an etching with simple lines, is based upon the same painting. The event was a popular subject for painters. Liebmann and Wahl [#48] show a similar painting, "The balloon leaving Dover 1785 from the oil painting by E. W. Cocks, in the possession of Sir Mortimer Singer." Leichter als Luft [p. 83] shows the Cocks painting [p. 179] as well as an oil attributed to the early nineteenth century, which is in the Science Museum, London.)

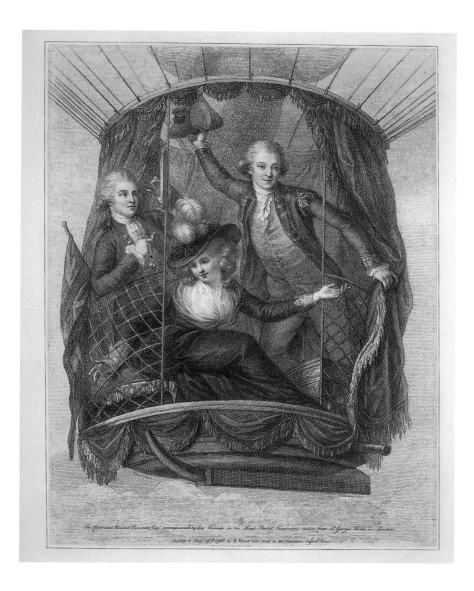

The Celebrated Vincent Lunardi Esqr. accompanied by two friends in his third Aerial Excursion, taken from St. George's Fields, near London.

Published June 25, 1785, by E. Wyatt next door to the Pantheon, Oxford Street.

The celebrated Vincent Lunardi Esqr. accompanied by two friends in his third aerial excursion

> Francesco Bartolozzi (1728–1815), after a painting by J. F. Rigaud (1742–1810)
>
> London, 1785. "Published June 25, 1785 by E. Wyatt next door to the Pantheon, London."
> Etching, 33.5 x 25 cm.
>
> XP-XL-7 (1263)

This elaborate print, which emphasizes the dash of the aeronauts more than the flight, was published on June 25, 1785, to commemorate a planned flight on June 29. We see that the balloon was to be readied for three people. A memoir written by "Mrs. Sage," the woman depicted in the print, records that five people crowded into the basket when the balloon was inflated; their weight proved too much for the available lift. Three, including Lunardi, left the gondola, and Mrs. Sage and the 25-year-old George Biggin ascended, making Sage "the first English female aerial traveller." Sage mused that Mr. Biggin thought it "no degradation to communicate his observations to a woman, of whose understanding, I am proud to think, he had not a contemptible opinion." While aloft, Biggin made various scientific observations, holding an electrometer with two pith balls at arm's length and "exposing it to a cloud we were then passing . . . he told me his conclusion, which was that the electricity of that cloud was negative." *(With the glass, one can see the ghost of an eradicated line of text that lies behind the last line of the caption in this print; the eradicated caption appears to include the word "Oxford." This print can be found in three states: one with the title: "V. Lunardi Esqr. Mrs. Sage G. Biggin Esqr.," published May 13, 1785, by "Mr. Bovi . . . Oxford Market"; one with the title as above ["The celebrated Vincent Lunardi . . . "]; and one with the title: "The three favorite aerial Travellers." In the last state, the artist has added a hat and improved the collar and tie of the figure on the left, which is no doubt George Biggin. This change might have resulted from the wealthy Biggin's objection that without these accessories he would appear as the social inferior of Lunardi, although in fact Biggin had provided substantial monetary support to the balloonist. Gibbs-Smith describes Lunardi's dress as "the uniform of the Honourable Artillery Company." The cannon-like device below the basket may be intended to represent and publicize Lunardi's poorly documented experiments with cannons. What seems to be the original drawing for this print is shown in Alvin Josephy,* Adventure of Man's Flight, *p. 52. This plate reportedly existed and was being used in the twentieth century. The engraver, Francesco Bartolozzi [whose life dates have also been given as 1748–1815], engraved Lunardi's portrait in 1784 [Gimbel XC-10-2A 3261].)*

A BALLOON ASCENT A CENTURY AGO.

A balloon ascent a century ago

Maurice Leloir (1853–1940)
1889. "Chromotypogravure," 52.5 x 38 cm.
XP-XL-6 (1255)

Large, fanciful, and striking, this "chromo-typogravure" shows two aeronauts aloft in an ornate car adorned with French symbols. The artist, a specialist in historical costume and known for book illustration and theatre-set design, seems to have borrowed from the print that shows Lunardi, Sage, and Biggin (XP-XL-7 1263 above). It is possible that Jean-Pierre Blanchard is the male figure, although it is difficult to determine who the woman is meant to be (Marie Madeleine Sophie Blanchard did not make her first ascent until 1804). The large flags bear Virgil's phrase, which is used repeatedly in connection with ballooning: *Sic itur ad astra* (thus immortality [or the heavens] is/are gained); the same motto was given to Pierre Mont-golfier's family when ennobled in 1783 by Louis XVI. This is romantic art fit for a cereal box, shown for its artistic rather than historic properties. The print is signed and dated in the scene at lower right. *(In Neidhardt-Jensen [p. 103] this same print appears titled: "Une ascension, il y a cent ans.")*

The New Mode of Picking Pockets

London, published by E. Hodges, September 14, 1784. Etching, 32.5 x 22.5 cm.

XL-5 (3431)

This British print was published while the moneyed were still within the throes of *balloonmania*, but it evokes a growing suspicion regarding the balloon and its increasingly venal promoters. In a style like that of "Aerostation out at Elbows" (see print XP-XL-7 1264 below), it depicts a well-manicured balloonist as a pickpocket and knave. The print is rather crudely crafted, and within the caption for London on the right, the wording has been reworked to correct an error with little attempt to erase the old lettering. This print no doubt was inspired by the balloonist Chevalier de Moret, who had built a balloon and prepared to launch it from a garden in Chelsea, London, on August 11,

1784. Although he claimed to be an associate of the Montgolfiers, "Count" Moret apparently knew little of ballooning, and his balloon failed to ascend despite three hours of preparations. The balloon finally collapsed into the fire, at which point part of the crowd of 50,000 rioted, entered the enclosure, robbed the subscribers, and destroyed benches, windows, and equipment. Hodges published this print the day before the first successful ascent in England by Vincent Lunardi. *(George [vol. vi, p. 166] lists this print without showing publisher and with the attributed date of August 1784, suggesting that another state of this print [or a copy] appeared without this information.)*

All on Fire —
Or the Doctors disappointed
A view taken in Lord Foleys Garden Sep. 29. 1784

London Published Oct. 20. 1784
by E. Wyatt N. 360 Oxford Street.

1 The principal Figure.
2 Companion to ditto

All on Fire, or the Doctors disappointed; a view taken in Lord Foley's garden
Sep. 29, 1784

London, published by E. Wyatt, October 20, 1784.
Mixed method intaglio, etching with mezzotint,
27.5 x 36.5 cm.

XP-XL-5 (1195)

The printmakers of London had another aeronautical attempt to caricature after the hot-air balloon of Allen Keegan caught fire before launch. Associated with the anatomist Dr. John Sheldon (who later ascended with Blanchard on October 12) and possibly Jean-Pierre Blanchard, Keegan inflated the large balloon at least once in mid-August before a free-flight was announced in late September. A tradesman dealing in umbrellas and water-proof items, Keegan made his envelope of coarse varnished linen. Two numbers in lower right (1: principal figure; and 2: companion) refer to figures in the foreground, whom Marsh identifies as Blanchard (left) and

Sheldon (right). Four fire engines were on hand as a precaution when the balloon was engulfed. *(George [6703] reports publication on October 20, 1784, by E. Wyatt, No. 360 Oxford St., London. She tentatively attributes this print to the famous Paul Sandby [1725–1809], who designed numerous prints using balloons and flight as a motif.)*

AEROSTATION OUT AT ELBOWS.
OR THE ITINERANT AERONAUT.

Behold an Hero comely tall and fair!
His only Food Phlogisticated Air!
Now on the Wings of Mighty Winds he rides!
Now torn thro' Hedges — Dash'd in Oceans tides!

Now drooping roams about from Town to Town
Collecting Pence t'inflate his poor Balloon;
Pity the Wight and something to him give,
To purchase Gas to keep his Frame alive.

Aerostation out at Elbows, or the Itinerant Aeronaut

> [Thomas Rowlandson, 1756–1827]
>
> [London, 1785]. Etching, colored, 23.5 x 21.2 cm. (image)
>
> XP-XL-7 (1264)

This caricature of Vincent Lunardi shows him in rags with an outstretched hand. After conducting the first successful ascent in London in 1784, Lunardi made many ascents in Great Britain. This print appears somewhat providential because during December 1785, Lunardi—then on the road with his balloon—lost it at sea after an ascent from Edinburgh. He was rescued by fishermen, and his balloon was later recovered; but Britain had apparently tired of the balloon craze. After a botched ascent in Newcastle that ended with the death of an assistant, Lunardi turned his attention to a maritime life-saving apparatus. He resumed ballooning in 1788 when he returned to Italy. Eight lines of verse on the print suggest his fall from popularity, so that he, "now drooping, roams about from town to town." Various authorities attribute this work to Thomas Rowlandson, the famous satirist. *(Print XP-XL-7 1264a is an uncolored copy, and both it and XP-XL-7 1264 are trimmed; neither shows publisher or date. George [6858] reports publication on September 5, 1785, by T. Cornell, Bruton Street, London, with a second issue [6858A] on March 24, 1786, by E. Jackson, No. 14 Marylebone Street, Golden Square, London.)*

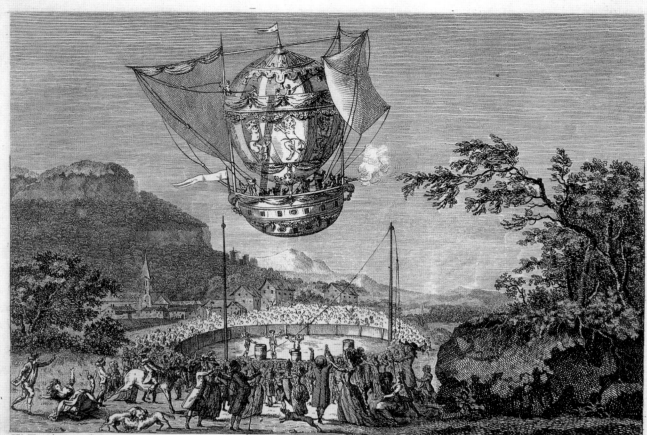

Ire. Expérience de la Machine Aérostatique avec les moyens de la diriger à volonté par le Docteur Jonathan, et la Vue du Village Deß eßebruc-que, au Pays de Galles d'ou est partie, cette machine le 22. Dec^bre 1783 à 9 heures du matin laquelle après avoir parcouru environ l'espace de 10. lieues est revenue tomber proche l'endroit d'ou elle s'étoit enlevée, cette machine est construite de fil de laiton très fin laminé arangé en forme de toile ordinaire et couvert d'une toile de Coton enduite d'un mastic, le Gouvernail est aussi de laiton couvert d'une toile de coton, et la Voile de toile ordinaire). ... Dessiné d'après Nature et Gravé par Waulstaine et se Vend chez lui au N.º 122 . en la Cité à Londres .

Ire. Expérience de la Machine Aérostatique avec les moyens de la diriger à volonté par le Docteur Jonathan

[c. 1785? Paris?] "Dessiné d'après Nature & Gravé par Waulstaine et se Vend chez lui au No. 122 en la Cité à Londres." Copy 2 is uncolored.

Etching, 13.7 x 18 cm.

XP-XL-25 (2010)

This fantastic depiction of a dirigible balloon may have inspired the well-known *Minerve* of Étienne Robertson, although some students of the period (Bruel [De Vinck] #985; Liebmann and Wahl #257) have mistaken it for a representation of an actual flight. The print is probably a sarcastic response to grandiose schemes like the airship shown in print XP-XL-4 1121 above. The artist "Waulstaine" does not appear in any of the standard references, and it is curious that his prints would be captioned in French while supposedly published in London. Perhaps the name is a thinly veiled recasting of "wall stain" and represents a publisher working discreetly in Paris. *(Another print [XP-XL-25 2011] shows this airship leaving the ground; showing "Waulstain" as publisher, the print purports to represent the second trial of the aircraft on January 10, 1784. The aircraft is similar to that depicted in XP-XL-16 1627, XP-XL-16 1628, XP-XL-25 2014, and others.)*

Si vende in Roma al

Negozio di stampi a Pasquino

Globo Aereostatico
di Diametro pal. 40. Romani inalzato in Roma dal Sig.ʳ Vincenzo Lunardi
nell'Anfiteatro Correa il di 8 luglio 1788.

Globo Aereostatico di Diametro pal. 40.
Romani inalzato in Roma dal Sig.ʳ
Vincenzo Lunardi

Rome, [1788]. Etching, 18.8 x 26.4 cm.
XP-XL-7 (1274)

In 1784 Vincent Lunardi attempted to use airborne oars, whose operation can be pretty easily surmised from this depiction of 1788. The oars were intended to move the aircraft both vertically and horizontally, but in fact could do nothing to move the great mass of the balloon. Lunardi first tried his oars very briefly during his London flight of September 15, 1784, when he claimed some effect from their use; like other devices of the period, Lunardi's oars were designed to let air flow through them on the backstroke and to provide useful resistance during the stroke. As with other prints celebrating the ascents of Lunardi and probably initiated by him, this print of his ascent in Rome on July 8, 1788, was no doubt prepared prior to the event. The circumstances of this launch were difficult, and records of it are confusing. Apparently Lunardi had some trouble with the quality

or quantity of lifting gas, and near midnight he substituted the lighter Carlo Lucangeli for himself. Lucangeli endured a short flight, unable because of fright to release his grip on the support ropes and compelled to take the valve line in his teeth in order to descend. The substitution of Lucangeli was a disappointment to the people of Rome, and Lunardi, accused of cowardice, was ordered by the governor of Rome to refund his proceeds to the subscribers. It was Lucangeli, rather than Lunardi, who ascended that day. *(Another print issued of this ascent, "Globo Aereostatico di diametro pal. 40 Romi inalzato in Roma," copies this one for its depiction of the balloon, which is shown in reverse, with Lunardi looking left and his dog on the right, but it was later reworked to show Lucangeli in a cage-like basket.)*

L'ascension de la Nymphe aérienne s'est faite le 1er. Janvier 1787 sur la place du quartier des Buisses à Lille par le Sr. Enslen.

L'ascension de la Nymphe aérienne s'est faite le 1er. Janvier 1787 sur la place du quartier des Buisses à Lille par le Sr. Enslen

[1787?]. Etching, 18.5 x 23.5 cm.
XP-XL-8 (1282)

"Special shape balloons" are so common today that congregations of them are popular spectacles. They date to 1783, however, and were readily available from makers in Europe's larger cities. Karl Enslen and his unnamed brother reportedly made a specialty of balloons shaped like people, and various prints exist of these dating from 1784 to 1795. The pronounced headpiece of the *Nymphe* may be an exaggerated representation of a balloon hat or it may be a ridiculous characterization of the period's coiffures. Another balloon, rather

difficult to discern, can be seen above and to the right of the *Nymphe*. (Leichter als Luft *[p. 64] shows a print depicting the flight of the Nymphe on July 12, 1784, in Strasbourg, with its filling apparatus below; here the headpiece can be seen to be in the form of a Montgolfier balloon. In addition, Gimbel XP-XL-22 1867: "Representation of various balloons, with the methods of constructing and filling them," depicts an aerostatic horse and rider, "which was exhibited at the Pantheon by the brothers Enslen.")*

Les Jacobins allant révolutioner la lune en ballons

LES JACOBINS ALLANT RÉVOLUTIONER LA LUNE EN BALLONS.
Ah ca ira, ca ira, ca ira.

Les Jacobins allant révolutioner la lune
en ballons

> Mixed method intaglio, engraving with
> aquatint, 34.8 x 25 cm. (image)

> XP-XL-15 (1586)

A banner hanging from the balloon at center
reads: *A la lune, chers amis* (to the moon,
good friends). Other balloons can be seen in
the sky. The artist seems to be suggesting that
the French Revolution had been reckless in
overstepping France's borders and is attempting an improbable task. The caption ends
with the words from a popular revolutionary
song: *Ah! Ça ira, ça ira, ça ira* (Ah! It will work
out, it will work out, it will work out), which
was the main anthem of the Revolution until
the introduction of *La Marseillaise* in 1792.
The undocumented monogram "J. S." appears
in a circle below the image on the lower right.

'AMERICA'S FIRST SUCCESSFUL AIR FLIGHT—PHILADELPHIA, JANUARY 1793

America's First Successful Air Flight—
Philadelphia, January 1793

Roland F. Harper (?–ca. 1958)

[1954]. Lithograph, from a scratchboard
drawing, 27.8 x 18.4 cm.

XP-XL-28 (2281)

This modern drawing depicts the launch
of Jean-Pierre Blanchard in Philadelphia in
January 1793, considered the first ascent in
America. No doubt Blanchard, who was
fleeing the chaotic conditions of the French
Revolution in Europe, planned to continue
his practice of touring an uninitiated country
and providing the spectacle of a balloon ascent
in some of the larger cities. (His last ascent
had been in the Tyrolean mountains of Austria
in July 1792, where he had been imprisoned for
disseminating revolutionary ideas.) The Philadelphia flight, which was his forty-fifth, was a
financial failure. He attempted to raise interest
in further ascents by exhibiting his large balloon and by sending animals aloft with small
balloons. He made stops in Charleston, Boston, and finally New York, where a tornado
destroyed the balloon and killed Blanchard's
16-year-old son on September 14, 1796. When
he left New York in May 1797 the *New York
Diary* reported sarcastically, "Blanchard has
at last taken his flight," a witticism reminiscent

of the response to Blanchard's *bateau volant*,
when popular French songs exploited the
double meaning of *voler* (to fly, to steal).
His next ascent was in Rouen, France, in 1798.
This print was issued as a Christmas greeting
from the Ajax Electric Company in Philadelphia in 1954; from 1935 to 1970, the company,
which manufactures furnaces for industrial
heat treating, issued a series of Christmas prints
emphasizing Philadelphia history. Harper, a
commercial artist known for his scratchboard
work, was commissioned for at least seven of
the prints between 1948 and 1957. (*This print
can be compared to the work of Philadelphian
Charles R. Gardner [1901–?], who produced a
woodcut or wood engraving in 1931 of this ascent;
the print appeared in the 1943 edition of* The
First Air Voyage in America, *published by the
Penn Mutual Life Insurance Co. of Philadelphia,
whose office occupies the site of the 1793 ascent.*)

PAUL MARAVELAS

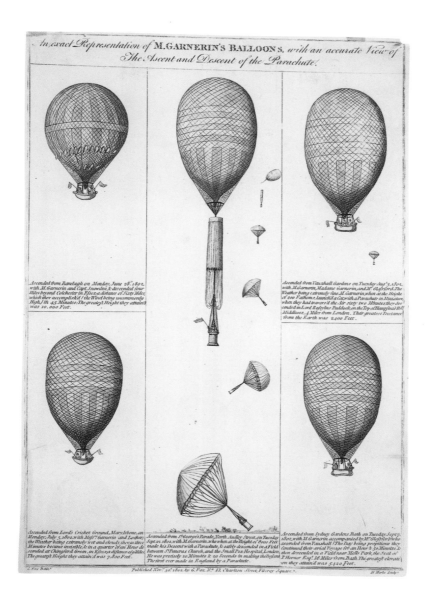

An exact Representation of M. Garnerin's Balloons, with an accurate View of The Ascent and Descent of the Parachute

An exact Representation of M. Garnerin's Balloons, with an accurate View of The Ascent and Descent of the Parachute

H. Merke, after a drawing by G. Fox

London, 1802. Softground etching, 35.7 x 24.8 cm.

Published November 30, 1802. Upper left: flight June 28, 1802, from Ranelagh to Essex, 60 miles in 45 minutes. Center: descent by parachute over London; first parachute descent in England, 10 minutes 20 seconds from 8,000 feet, September 21, 1802. Upper right: descent of cat by parachute. Lower left: July 5, 1802. Lower right: September 7, 1802.

XP-XL-24 (1992)

These depictions chronicle some of the work of balloonist André Jacques Garnerin, who came to England in 1802 and ascended from various parks and pleasure gardens. In 1802, the year this print was issued, the parachute was still a novel invention that had not been perfected and remained to be proved. Its origins are not positively known, although we can see the concept expressed much earlier than the technique was tried (for example, in the long-obscured work of Leonardo da Vinci and in *L'uom volante* of 1781 [see print XP-XL-27 2223 above]). A parachute appears on some of the views of Blanchard's *vaisseau volant*, as well as on his balloon of February 27, 1784, and Blanchard began parachuting animals from balloons on June 3, 1784. Generally the invention of the parachute is credited to Joseph Montgolfier or Blanchard (both in 1777) or to Sébastien Lenormand in 1783. The center panel of this print shows Garnerin himself descending from his balloon, "the first ever made in England by parachute." The life dates of engraver Merke are unknown, but he is known to have been born near Zurich in the late eighteenth century; he worked in London from 1800 to 1820. *(Another work [Gimbel XP-XL-11 3446] is a watercolor depiction titled "Ascent of three Persons with a Balloon from Vauxhall Gardens 1802." It shows a small parachute descending from the balloon.)*

[Garnerin's descent by parachute]

Étienne Chevalier de Lorimier (1759–1813)

Gouache over graphite, 18.5 x 13 cm.

XB-9-3A (4603)

This handsome painting shows what is thought to be the descent by André Jacques Garnerin on October 22, 1797. On that day, Garnerin launched his hydrogen balloon from Parc Monceau in Paris and descended by parachute from 3,000 feet. His descent was successful except that the parachute, which had no provision for spilling air, developed violent oscillations. The painting bears the signature "L. M.," which is that of Étienne Chevalier de Lorimier.

Caricatures Parisiennes.

Ascension de Madame Garnerin, le 28 mars 1802.

Le Goût du Jour n°. 8.

A Paris chez Martinet, Libraire, Rue du Coq S. Honoré.

Le Goût du Jour n°. 8.

Paris, [1802]. Captioned "Ascension de Madame Garnerin le 28 mars 1802." At top is the phrase: "Caricatures Parisiennes."

Lithograph, colored, 16.4 x 23.7 cm.

XP-XL-11 (1399)

This plate emphasizes the new clothing fashion of the early nineteenth century, with its high-waisted styles. The men sport exaggerated beaver hats and coats, which are cut dramatically away at the waist with long tails; the woman at left carries a fan, and she is draped with a colorful wrap. Jeanne-Geneviève Garnerin, wife of André Jacques, is considered the first female pilot and the first woman to descend in a parachute. In addition, their niece, Elisa Garnerin, considered the first professional female parachutist, made about forty descents between 1815 and 1836.

BATAILLE DE FLEURUS.

Les plaines de Fleurus, où, cent quatre ans auparavant, le maréchal de Luxembourg avait battu le prince de Waldeck, devinrent, le 26 juin 1794, le théâtre d'une action non moins glorieuse pour les armes françaises. — Jourdan, général en chef de l'armée de Sambre-et-Meuse, après divers succès balancés, était parvenu à s'emparer des hauteurs de Fleurus. Voulant reconnaître, avant de livrer bataille, les positions de l'ennemi, il avait fait monter dans un ballon un de ses officiers qui, planant au-dessus des deux camps, pût les observer en détail. — L'armée alliée, commandée par Cobourg et le prince d'Orange, s'avança avec 90,000 combattants, pour reprendre ce point important défendu par 76,000 Français. Dès l'aurore du 26 juin, elle se mit en mouvement sur neuf colonnes. Cette affaire allait être décisive : Jourdan ordonne de ne tirer qu'à bout

Propriété de l'Éditeur. (Dépôt.)

portant, et bientôt l'artillerie fait des ravages épouvantables dans les rangs ennemis. Les deux armées combattirent avec un acharnement incroyable. Enfin une dernière attaque, simultanément ordonnée sur tous les points, fut partout victorieuse. Le prince de Cobourg opéra sa retraite, laissant, sur le champ de bataille, 7,000 morts et 5,000 prisonniers. — La conquête de la Belgique devint le résultat de cette victoire.

Napoléon livra à Fleurus, le 16 juin 1815, une nouve de bataille, où les Français furent encore victorieux, malgré trahison de quelques lâches : mais le lendemain, à Waterloo, le drapeau tricolore devait tomber avec Napoléon, dans mêmes plaines d'où, vingt-un ans auparavant, il était parti pour faire la conquête de l'Europe ! ! !

Fabrique de PELLERIN, Imprimeur-Libraire, à ÉPINAL.

Bataille de Fleurus.

Fabrique de Pellerin . . . à Epinal

Epinal (France), [after 1815]. Wood engraving, 32 x 53.3 cm. (image)

XP-XL-25 (2019)

One of the first uses of the balloon in war was at the battle of Fleurus on June 26, 1794. The balloonists made important observations and relayed information that provided a real advantage to the French army, which faced 52,000 Austrian and German troops. Information from the airborne observers allowed Gen. Jean-Baptiste Jourdan (commander, Armée du Nord) to monitor the rather unorganized movements of his enemy and repulse them in a battle of six hours; the battle is considered pivotal in the War of the First Coalition, which ended in 1797. After making repeated attempts to advance into the region around Fleurus during 1794, Jourdan and his army were very much discouraged by the time of the battle, but the general was urged on and even threatened by the civil commissioners of France. The publisher of this print, the Fabrique de Pellerin, produced rather simple images for the general public; it was named for its founder, Charles Pellerin (1756–1836), who produced many celebratory works such as this in the town of Epinal, famous as a center for popular images.

Bataille de Fleurus gagnée par l'Armée Française, le 8 Messidor, de l'An 2

Commandée par les Généraux Jourdan, Le Fevre, et Hatre: Contre l'Armée Imperiale: Commandée par Cobourg, et Beaulieu.

Bataille de Fleurus gagnée par l'Armée Française, le 8 Messidor, de l'An 2

Pierre Adrien Le Beau (1748– ?), after a drawing by Naudet

Engraving, 33.4 x 48.6 cm.

XL-25 (2020)

Another view of the battle of June 26, 1794, shows the coalition troops on the left and the French on the right, with the balloon aloft above the battle. The French balloon company, organized in April 1794, has been called "the first air corps in history," and its objectives were threefold: to provide reconnaissance, to relay signals between units on the ground, and to spread propaganda from the air. By June 10, 1794, the French balloon company had joined Gen. Jean-Baptiste Jourdan's army at Maubeuge and began to provide reconnais-

sance from the air. A second company was formed on June 23 but was not deployed until 1795. Both units were active until the first company and its balloon were captured at the battle of Würtzburg on September 3, 1796. Despite some success, the French balloon corps was troublesome to maintain, and it was disbanded in 1799.

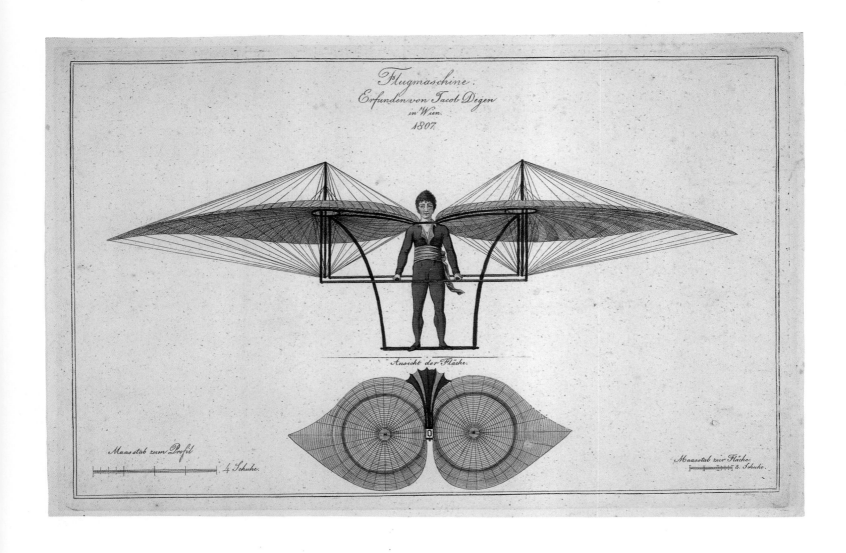

Flugmaschine. Erfunden von Jacob Degen in Wien, 1807

Etching, colored, 28.2 x 43 cm.

XP-XL-18 (1780)

Swiss watchmaker Jacob Degen constructed this ornithopter and began trials with it in 1806, first using a counterweight to help hoist it and keep it aloft, and then employing a small balloon. He gave demonstrations in Vienna and then came to Paris, where in 1812 the aircraft was destroyed by a mob. Degen rebuilt it, trying it again in Paris in 1813 and in Vienna in 1817. He is known to have experimented with a small helicopter in 1816. It is said that Degen's trials were the motive for Sir George Cayley to publish his famous paper "On Aerial Navigation," which appeared in the *Journal of Natural Philosophy* in three parts in 1809 and 1810.

EXPÉRIENCE ARÉOSTATIQUE.

Exécutée dans le Champ-de-Mars à Paris le 2 7ᵇʳᵉ 1812 par Mʳ Degen mécanicien de Vienne en Autriche.
L'aéronaute s'est élevé au moyen de deux ailes de 22 pieds d'Envergure, dont il occupe le centre, et qui sont adaptées à un Ballon dont la force ascensionnelle n'est que de 90ᵉ

Expérience aréostatique. Exécutée dans le Champ-de-Mars à Paris le 2 7ᵇʳᵉ 1812 par M.ʳ Degen, mécanicien de Vienne en Autriche

Foursny

"Gravé sur verre et Imprimé par Foursny. Deposé à la direction gᵃˡᵉ de la Librairie." Etching or engraving on glass, colored, 24.1 x 19.6 cm.

XB-8-3B (1049)

The text of this print emphasizes the success of Degen's ornithopter in its trial of September 2, 1812, and makes it clear that the mechanical wings were the important part of the aircraft, since the attached balloon provided only "90 pounds of ascensional force." As the phrase "engraved on glass" at lower left relates, this image is printed from a glass plate—an uncommon and a relatively short-lived intaglio technique. *(Gimbel XB-8-3B 1004 shows the mob destroying the ornithopter on October 5, 1812.)*

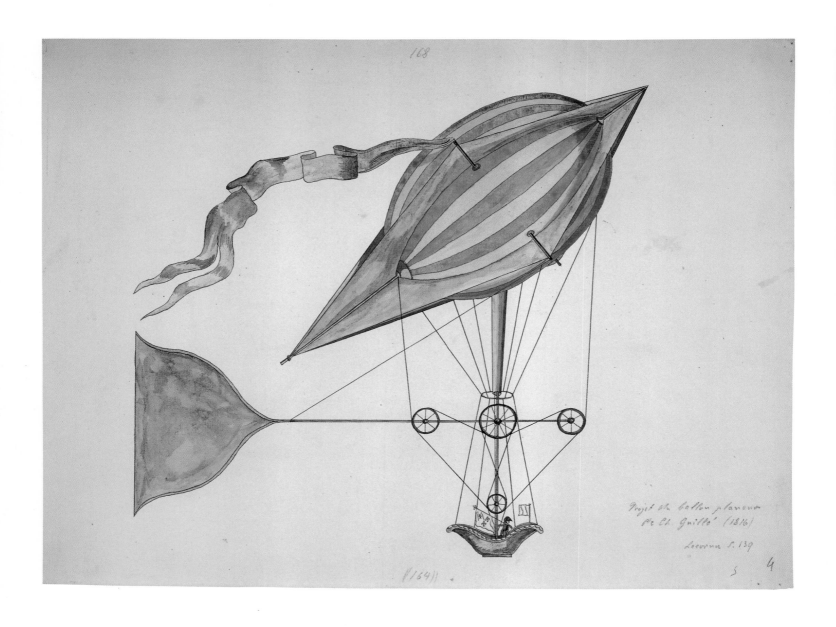

Projet de ballon planeur de Ch. Guillé (1816)

Ink and water color on (hand-made) paper, with manuscript annotation: "Projet du ballon planeur de Ch Guillé (1816) Lecornu p. 139," 29.6 x 41 cm.

XL-11 (1387)

Louis Charles Guillé made this elongated envelope with long stabilizing surfaces, which were meant to guide the balloon forward while it ascended and descended. On November 13, 1814, Guillé demonstrated this unsuccessful craft in the Champ de Mars in Paris. The design enjoyed continued life when Jules François Depuis-Delcourt published it (as plate 5) in his *Nouveau manuel complet d'aérostation* of 1850. The inclined plane is a fairly common concept for guiding balloons; for example, in 1851 it

was advocated by Constantino Cernuschi and in 1859 by John Wise. Guillé made the first parachute descent in the United States when he dropped from a balloon over New York on August 2, 1819.

M. S. Blanchard Célèbre Aéronaute, au
moment de son ascension aérienne suivie
à Turin, Le Soir du 26 avril 1812

Etching and engraving, 28 x 17.8 cm.

XP-XL-20 (1819)

The professional aeronaut, Marie Madeleine
Sophie Blanchard, was the wife of Jean-
Pierre Blanchard, whom she married in 1798.
She was well known for her night ascents.
Her sixty-seventh ascent, in July 1819, was her
last. Although the accounts of her last flight
are contradictory, it appears that after fireworks were lit below her basket, the balloon
caught fire; she extinguished the fire and
arrested the descent of the balloon but finally
collided with a roof and was thrown from
the basket to the ground and killed. Marie

Blanchard was Jean-Pierre's second wife
(he had married Victoire Le Brun in 1774 and
abandoned her in 1779). *(Bruel [no. 143] repro-
duces another version, dated 15 August 1811,
celebrating Marie Blanchard's ascent in Milan,
which is signed at lower left "N.H.G." and at
lower right "L. Rados." This print can also be
found with the date 19 April 1812; Caproni shows
the two prints [15 August 1811, and 19 April 1812]
side by side [no. 73].)*

FÊTE DU 14 JUILLET AN IX.

Vue du Temple eleve dans le Grand Carré des champs Elysées dans lequel le Concert Fut Exécuté.

A Paris chez Basset M.d d'Estampes et Fabriquant de Papiers peints, rue St Jacques au coin de celle des Mathurins N.º 670

Fête du 14 Juillet an IX.

[Paris? 1801?] Engraving, colored, 23.7 x 41.4 cm. (image)

XP-XL-9 (1300)

Numerous prints celebrate the commemorative use of the balloon in official functions, especially in the Napoleonic era. This print represents a celebration on July 14, 1801, which commemorated the formation of the French republic, a day then referred to as the "Anniversary of the Federation" by the French and now referred to as Bastille Day by English-speakers. It memorialized the taking of the small state prison and fortress, the Bastille, on July 14, 1789, by Parisian citizens after a four-hour battle; to the revolutionaries, the prison represented the arbitrary power of the king, who could imprison without trial. In 1801 the Anniversary of the Federation began at six in the morning with thirty rounds of cannon fire and included displays of statuary, pantomime exhibitions, skits, balls, orchestras, and the balloon ascension depicted here. In the evening, the theatres were opened to the public without charge, and fireworks decorated the sky. This view of the Champs Elysées shows the scene

of the festivities, and the caption relates that a "temple has been constructed in the square of the Champs Elysées, in which the concert was held." The balloon in the background is shown dropping a parachute; it probably is that of André Jacques Garnerin. In the upper left a small, unmanned balloon can be seen. *(The Gimbel collection includes numerous examples of this genre, including: XP-XL-9 1318: "The Chinese Pagoda and bridge . . . for the Grand Jubilee of the 1st of August"; XP-XL-9 1319: "Coronation procession of his Majesty George the Fourth 19 July 1821"; XP-XL-9 1321: "London Bridge opened by King William IV and Queen Adelaide, August 1, 1831"; XP-XL-9 1330: "Révolution Française 1848, fête de la Concorde"; XP-XL-11 1369: "Vue perspective du Champ de Mars le jour de la fête donnée le 24 Juin 1810"; XP-XL-11 1386: "Entrée triomphante de S. M. Louis xviii dans sa capitale.")*

XII FRIMAIRE AN XIII (5 Decembre 1804).

FÊTE DU SACRE ET COURONNEMENT DE LEURS MAJESTÉS IMPÉRIALES.

Vue de la Place de la Concorde, ornée des quatre Salles de danse et du Piedestal élevé au milieu, à l'instant ou la fête commence par la distribution de
Médailles, le départ des Chars remplis de Musiciens et l'Ascension des 5 Balons qui s'élevèrent majestueusement a une certaine hauteur ou ils détonnerent.

Fête du sacre et couronnement de leurs
Majestés Impériales. Vue de la Place de la
Concorde

Jacques Marchand (1769– ?), engraver, and
Jean-Baptiste Gautier, etcher, after a drawing
by Louis Le Coeur

Paris, [1804?]. Etching and engraving, colored,
35.7 x 45.8 cm.

XP-XL-9 (1305)

On December 2, 1804, Napoleon and Josephine were crowned emperor and empress of the French, and the public celebrations included a parade of musicians and the launch of balloons. This view is taken from the Place de la Concorde on December 3. Five balloons were launched that day, including the one shown here, which carried a massive eagle, surrounded by flags and surmounted by a garland. The balloons were designed to be consumed by fire while aloft, adding to the spectacle. Another balloon, carrying an imperial crown, flew all the way to Rome, where part of it is said to have been deposited on the tomb of Nero. André Jacques Garnerin, who executed the coronation event, reportedly lost his job over this incident and was replaced by Marie Blanchard. The life dates of the artist, Le Coeur, are not recorded, but he was born during the second half of the eighteenth century and is known for his prints of the French Revolution.

FÊTE DONNÉE PAR LA VILLE DE PARIS A LOUIS XVIII LE 29 AOUT 1814.

Cortège du Roi Louis XVIII se rendant du palais des Tuileries par les quais à l'Hôtel de Ville, pour assister à la fête qui lui fut donnée par la ville de Paris, en réjouissance du rétablissement du Trône des Bourbons.

Fête donnée par la ville de Paris à Louis XVIII le 29 Aout 1814.

Paris, [1814?]. Etching, colored, 26 x 40.5 cm. XP-XL-9 (1320)

In 1814 the allied armies of Europe at last overcame Napoleon and entered Paris. Napoleon, no longer the hero of France, was exiled to Elba. In the vacuum that ensued after Napoleon's abdication, the allied powers agreed that a restoration of the Bourbons was the safest and best choice. This scene shows the return of Louis XVIII to Paris; the procession of the king was accompanied by the launch of a series of aerostatic animals and riders on horses. *(An English print [XP-XL-9 1310] shows the same event but depicts a full-sized and manned balloon.)*

[New Hungerford Market, London;
Graham's balloon on opening day,
2 July 1833]

Watercolor, 15 x 20 cm.

XP-XL-9 (1323)

This scene depicts the New Hungerford Market and the celebration that opened it in 1833. The old Hungerford Market had been established in 1680 but had never prospered and was rebuilt in 1833 as a meat and vegetable market. It was demolished about 1860, when the Charing Cross Railway Station was constructed nearby. George Graham was active as a balloonist from 1823 to 1851; his wife, Margaret Graham, was active from 1824 to 1853. *(Gimbel XP-XL-9 1324 is a print showing three people in the basket at lift-off. Marsh [plate 80] shows another print by M. O'Connor, London, "View of the New Hungerford market as it appeared at the opening on the 2nd of July 1833.")*

NORTH FRONT OF THE HEATH.

As it appeared, Nov.ʳ 25.ᵗʰ, 1836 in celebration of the Birth of a Son and Heir, to J. Ackers, Esqʳᵉ,

by his humble Servant.

E.Hodson del.ᵗ

North Front of the Heath. As it appeared Nov.ʳ 25.ᵗʰ, 1836 in celebration of the Birth of a Son and Heir to J. Ackers, Esq.ʳᵉ

E. Hodson

[1836?]. Lithograph, 20.3 x 29 cm.

XP-XL-9 (1328)

A spirited celebration with cannon fire, marching band, roasted viands, and a balloon ascension commemorated the birth of James Ackers, Jr., born on November 18, 1836. Beyond the information provided by the print, we know only a few biographical details concerning the family. James Ackers' parents were married in 1832. His mother, Mary Williams Ackers, died in 1848. His father, James Ackers (1811–1868) was a Member of Parliament for Ludlow in Shropshire, England, from 1841 to 1847. It is unclear where this scene occurred, as the family did not acquire Prinknash Manor southeast of Gloucester, until 1847. James Ackers, Jr., died in December 1859 at the age of twenty-three.

THE VAUXHALL ROYAL BALLOON,

Formed of 2000 yards of Silk and capable of ascending with Twenty Eight Persons, beside Ballast and Apparatus. Circumference 157 Feet. — Height, with Car attached, 80 Feet. First Ascent, with 9 Persons, made from Vauxhall September 9th 1836.

London, Published by William Spooner, 377 Strand.

The Vauxhall Royal Balloon, Formed of 2000 yards of Silk

F. Alvey, after W. S. (William Spooner?)

London, [1836?]. Published by William Spooner. Signed lower left (in image): "W.S."

Lithograph, colored, 30.5 x 23 cm.

XP-XL-12 (1406)

Charles Green designed this balloon, which had its first flight on September 9, 1836. The crowded car was reportedly capable of carrying 28 people. The *Vauxhall Royal Balloon,* which was about 70,000 cubic feet in capacity, was built under the auspices of London's Royal Vauxhall Gardens as an attraction.

A. BUTLER. LITH. FROM A SKETCH BY   MONCK. MASON. ESQ.

[Environs of Liège, seen from the balloon at night]

A. Butler, after a sketch by Monck Mason
[1836?]. Lithograph, 11.5 x 16.5 cm.
XP-XL-12 (1410)

This innovative sketch shows the *Vauxhall Royal Balloon* as it flies over Liège, Belgium, with blast furnaces visible below. The creator of this sketch, Monck Mason, accompanied Robert Holland with Charles Green as pilot on a voyage of about 380 nautical miles from London to a place near Weilburg, Germany. Mason described the flight through darkness as "clearing our way through an interminable mass of marble." It was a flight of eighteen hours, beginning on November 7, 1836. A broadside advertising the balloon (see "Grand new balloon, to be called the *Vauxhall Royal Balloon*," XP-XL-12 1404 , in "Other Holdings" section below) describes the many virtues of this aircraft, first flown in September 1836; its large capacity would allow it to ascend to hitherto unattained heights and seek out

"currents of air proceeding in one direction for several months together." For the flight pictured here almost 100 pounds of food and 2 gallons each of sherry, port, and brandy were carried. The journey received much publicity, and the *Vauxhall Royal Balloon* was renamed the *Great Balloon of Nassau* to honor the Duchy of Nassau, where the balloon landed. It remained in service for 35 years and was purchased by the balloonist Henry Coxwell who used it for the famous ascent shown in print XP-XL-14 1508 below.

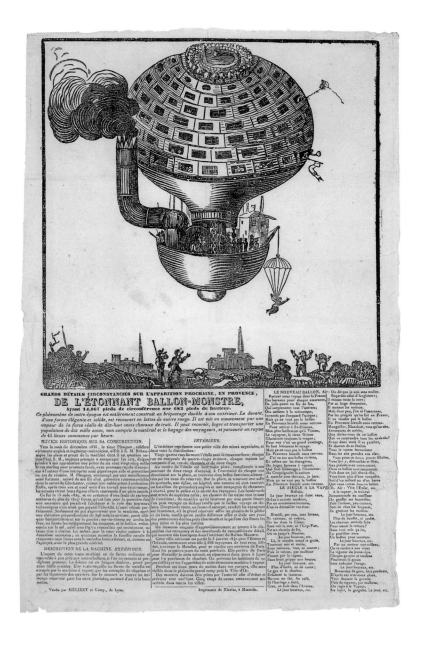

Grands détails circonstanciés sur
l'apparition prochaine, en Provence, de
l'étonnant ballon-monstre

Marseille, [1839?]. Letterpress with woodcut,
Imprimerie de Nicolas, à Marseille, 25.8 x 24.2 cm.
XP-XL-16 (1646)

This simply executed print parodies the beginnings of the Chartist Movement in England,
which called for egalitarian reforms. In 1839
more than a million Englishmen signed a
"monster petition" stating six demands, including annual meetings of Parliament and
universal male suffrage. The monster petition
was presented to Parliament on July 12, 1839,
and rejected the same day. On July 22, the
Chartists called for a "sacred month"—a
general, month-long srike to begin on August
12. A week before the strike was to begin, the
movement's leaders acknowledged a lack of
support for a prolonged protest and called
instead for a strike from August 12 to 15, predicting that the government would collapse
by the latter date. Equating the events in
England with this obviously unwieldy scheme
for a flying town, the text of this French print
reports the flight of the *ballon-monstre* on
August 15. Elaborating on Étienne Robertson's

Minerve of 1804, the print depicts a balloon
with a railroad that runs around the exterior
of the envelope, 24 streets containing 80 houses
each, boulevards with cafés and a comple-
ment of soldiers. The text advertises a flight
from England to France for 4,568 passengers
on January 3, 1840.

VOLO DELL' AEREONAUTA FRANCESCO ORLANDI

eseguito nei pubblici Giardini di Bologna l'anno 1839

Applaudi o Patria alla sua impresa ardita   Sol per renderti onor spregia la vita

Volo dell' aereonauta Francesco Orlandi
eseguito nei pubblici Giardini di Bologna
l'anno 1839

    G. Meloni

    Lithograph, colored, 28 x 41.2 cm.

    XP-XL-12 (1423)

Despite the death in June 1785 of Pilâtre de Rozier and Jules Romain in their combination hot-air and hydrogen balloon, experimenters continued to build balloons that combined these elements. The aeronaut Francis Olivari lost his life in one on November 25, 1802, at Orléans, as did Francesco Zambeccari on September 21, 1812, near Boulogne. Francesco Orlandi, whose balloon is shown in this print, seems to have been the most successful with these aircraft. Orlandi published a treatise on ballooning, suggesting his new design, in 1800. His first flight did not occur until August 30, 1825, after which he made 40 flights. This print commemorates his flight on July 22, 1839, when he ascended from the public gardens in Bologna. His work was furthered in print, although not in practice, by his son Guido as late as 1871. Others, including Pascal Andreoli and Phillipe Silvestrini, experimented with combination balloons in Italy during the first decades of the nineteenth century.

ALTRE SCOVERTE FATTE NELLA LUNA DAL SIG.ʳ HERSCHEL

Altre scoverte fatte nella Luna dal Sig.ʳ Herschel

Naples, 1836. Lithograph, colored 50 x 41 cm.
XP-XL-27 (2251)

The *New York Sun* temporarily boosted its circulation in August 1835 with reports by astronomer John Herschel of "man bats" that roamed the "pebbly beaches" of the moon. The story, ostensibly copied from the *Edinburgh Journal of Science* but actually written in New York by Richard A. Locke, became quickly known around the world, in part because the *Sun* sent the report abroad in the form of a generic pamphlet. The *Sun* ran Locke's detailed observations daily from August 25 to August 31, while "the almost universal impression and expression of the multitude was that of confident wonder and insatiable credence." Edgar Allan Poe, who had just begun the publication of his own serial story describing Hans Pfaal's voyage to the moon, later wrote that people should have known better, especially since the description of the wings in Locke's report "was but a literal copy of the the wings of his flying islanders"— a reference to the hero of *The Life and Adventures of Peter Wilkens* by Robert Paltock, published in 1751. The *Sun* lauded itself for

"diverting the public mind, if only for a while, from that bitter apple of discord, the abolition of slavery," yet skepticism spread more tardily than the hoax had, and as late as 1852 it was reported that the story was still believed in parts of Germany. This Italian print, designed by Leopoldo Galluzzo and published by Gatti e Dura, was part of a series of six published in 1836. Locke's hoax made a considerable impact in Italy where, according to Caproni, twelve pamphlets and twenty prints relating to it were issued in 1836. *(In addition to the account in his newspaper,* Sun *publisher Benjamin H. Day also issued print XP-XL-27 2233, "Lunar animals and other objects discovered by Sir John Herschel," which was reportedly ready for sale when the story's run was completed on August 31, 1835. The Gimbel collection includes all of the six prints in the Gatti and Dura series: XP-XL-27 2251–2256.)*

The Great Nassau Balloon . . . accompanied by the Parachute in which the late unfortunate Mr. Cocking made his fatal descent, July 24th, 1837.

London, [1837?]. T. Pewtress. Lithograph, 33 x 22 cm.

XP-XL-24 (1991)

Robert Cocking, a 61-year-old watercolor painter, had long mused upon the perfection of the parachute. In 1837, he convinced the proprietors of the Royal Vauxhall Gardens to permit their *Great Nassau* balloon to carry him aloft for a trial. *(Print XP-XL-24 1990 is colored, showing a balloon with gores of green, purple, and blue, although this famous balloon was actually red and white. Some of the caption is trimmed off.)*

The Ascent of the Royal Nassau Balloon
with the Parachute attached, 24th July 1837

Lithograph, 28.4 x 45 cm.

XP-XL-24 (1993)

Robert Cocking had apparently watched a famous parachute descent by André Jacques Garnerin on September 21, 1802, during which the violent oscillations of the 23-foot parachute greatly fatigued the parachutist. Then 24 years old, Cocking resolved to improve the device and apparently mused upon it for years. He saw the inverted shape as the means to obtain stability during the descent, and he tested his design with small parachutes dropped from diminutive hydrogen balloons. His work-

ing model was a heavy contraption, 107 feet in circumference and 10 feet in height, with three metal hoops connected by spars of wood. Weighing 223 pounds, it provided a surface of 124 square yards. *(Garnerin's descent is represented by print XP-XL-24 2000, "Expérience du parachute.")*

The fatal Descent of the Parachute by which Mr. Cocking lost his life

The fatal Descent of the Parachute by
which Mr. Cocking lost his life

    Lithographs, colored, 21 x 15.5 cm. (each image)
    XP-XL-24 (1996)

Robert Cocking tested his parachute on July 24,
1837. Charles Green, the pilot of the *Great
Nassau* balloon, which lifted the parachute,
wanted Cocking to be responsible for his own
release, so a "liberating iron" was designed
and mounted on the balloon and controlled
by Cocking from the basket of the parachute.
The parachute descended for only three or
four seconds before collapsing and then
Cocking fell precipitously, dying shortly after
contacting the ground. The tragedy generated much attention in the press and among
England's printmakers.

G. Meloni disegnò, e inv.ᵗ   Bologna. Lit. Zannoli, e Cᵒ.

[Volo del Bolognese Muzio Muzzi nell'aereonave rettiremiga]

G. Meloni

Bologna, [1838]. Zannoli. Lithograph, 28.4 x 42 cm.

XP-XL-12 (1414)

Muzio Muzzi of Bologna, son of Professor Luigi Muzzi of the Papal University of Bologna, developed dirigible designs in the 1830s and 1840s. The "aereonave rettiremiga" shown in this print relied on rotating vanes for propulsion and a narrow, disc-shaped envelope for speed. This airship was scheduled to fly on November 4, 1838, but the envelope's failure during inflation prevented the attempt. Another design of Muzzi's, a "Nave Aerortoploa," which called for forward motion given by inclined planes while the airship ascended and descended,

was patented in Europe and the United States. The airship was never built, but a model was exhibited in New York in 1844, and a pamphlet cataloging support for his ideas was published in 1845. Muzzi, born in Bologna in 1809, died in Cuba in 1846. *(Another depiction: XP-XL-31 2729 shows two images of this aircraft, one with paddles mounted on the equator of the balloon, the other with the paddles mounted on the basket.)*

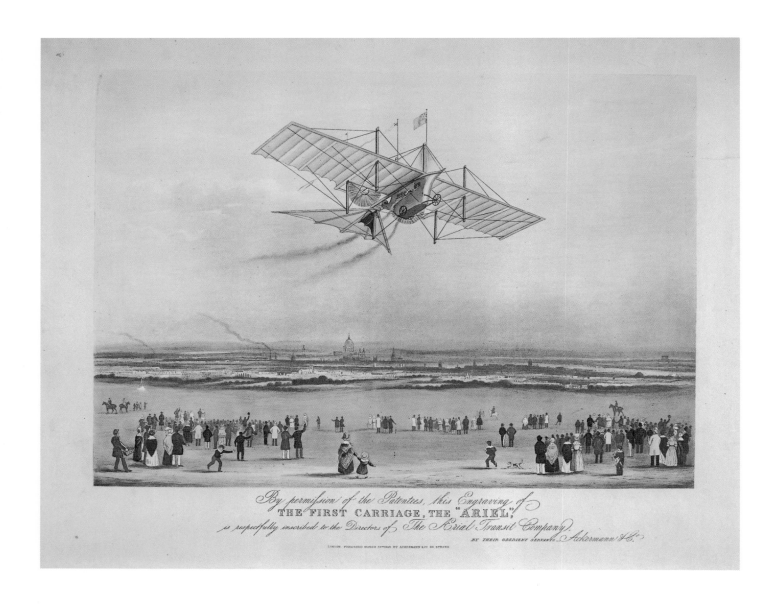

By permission of the Patentees, this Engraving of
THE FIRST CARRIAGE, THE "ARIEL",
is respectfully inscribed to the Directors of The Arial Transit Company,
BY THEIR OBEDIENT SERVANTS, Ackermann & C°.

LONDON, PUBLISHED MARCH 26TH 1843, BY ACKERMANN & C° 96, STRAND.

The First Carriage, the "Ariel"

London, 1843. Colored lithograph, 23.3 x 33 cm.
XP-XL-19 (4682)

John Stringfellow and W. S. Henson worked together to produce what became well known as "Henson's aerial steam carriage," an airplane that certainly resembles the machine that was invented fifty years later. The Aerial Transit Company, in which the inventor Frederick Marriott was involved, heavily publicized the steam carriage and issued a number of promotional prints showing the aircraft in flight over various landmarks around the world. Both the *Illustrated London News* (April 1, 1843) and the Parisian *L'Illustration* (April 8) published views of the machines with drawings of the workings, although in other forums the plans met with ridicule. In 1847 a model of the steam carriage, with a 20-foot wingspan, failed in trials, and the discouraged Henson abandoned the invention. Stringfellow, however, pursued it and prepared a working model in 1848, followed by a less successful model triplane,

which he exhibited at the Aeronautical Exhibition in the Crystal Palace, London, in 1868. *(The full caption reads: "By permission of the Patentees this Engraving of the First Carriage, the "Ariel," is respectfully inscribed to the Directors of The Aerial Transit Company by their obedient servants. . . ." Another print depicting the "Aerial" in the Gimbel collection is 1788: ". . . The first carriage, the 'Ariel'." London, 1843 [XP-XL-19]. Another copy, XP-XL-19 1788c, is not colored.)*

Lehmann's Luftfahrt mit seinem Riesen
Ballon, der "Adler von Wien" . . . 23 Mai
1846

Andreas Geiger

Wien, [1846?]. At head: Besondere Bilder Beilage
zur Theaterzeitung. Engraving, 39 x 27.7 cm.

XP-XL-12 (1431)

Shown in the basket are Christian Lehmann,
his daughter Caroline, and the Viennese
scientist Dr. Johann F. Natterer. Caroline
is throwing handbills from the basket, while
the two men are involved in the customary
waving of hats and flags. The wings on
either side of the basket are presumably
meant for propulsion.

ROUEN EN BALLON

VUE PRISE AU DESSUS DE LA COTE S^TE CATHERINE.

Rouen en ballon. Vue prise au dessus de la Cote Ste. Catherine

Jules Arnout (1814–1868)

Paris, 1846. Top: "Excursions aériennes." Lithograph, 29 x 44.8 cm. "Impression par Lemercier, à Paris." "Drawn from nature and lithographed by Jules Arnout. London. Published 25 March 1846."

XP-XL-10 (1340)

Jules Arnout, a student of Jean Sebastian Rouillard (1759–1850), was known for his landscapes of Italy, France, and Great Britain. The symbol "1" at bottom center may indicate that this is first in a series. *(Print XP-XL-10 1341 is the same with black and brown only. Compare, from the same series, XP-XL-10 1342: "Brighton. View taken in balloon. Brighton. Vue prise en ballon." The Gimbel collection includes nine of Arnout's aerial views of English and French cities, numbered XP-XL-10 1341–1349, about half dated 1846 and half undated. Included are views of Paris, Versailles, Blois, St. Cloud, Windsor, and Brighton. Print XP-XL-20 1843 is a view of Alameda, Mexico.)*

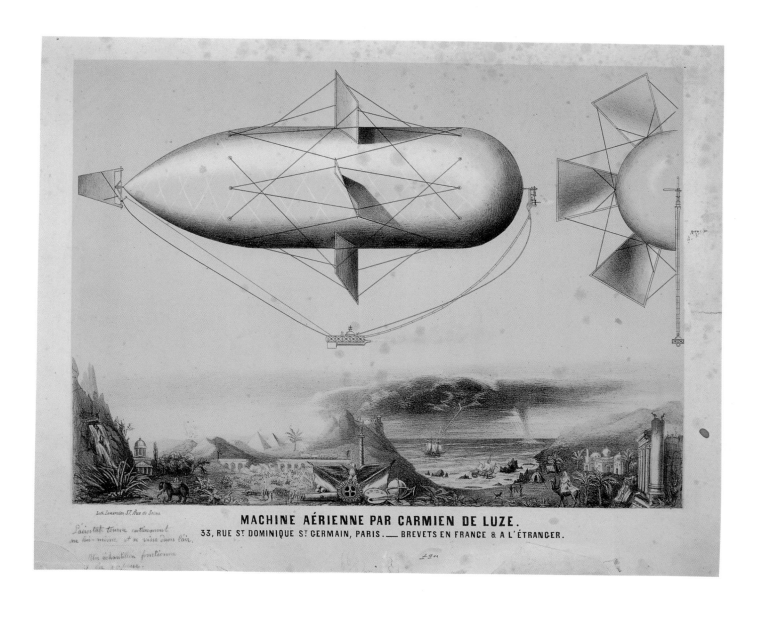

MACHINE AÉRIENNE PAR CARMIEN DE LUZE.
33, RUE ST DOMINIQUE ST GERMAIN, PARIS.— BREVETS EN FRANCE & A L'ÉTRANGER.

Machine aérienne par Carmien de Luze

Lithograph, 36.5 x 49 cm.

XP-XL-18 (1756)

Carmien de Luze designed this airship, in which the envelope rotates on its longitudinal axis and propulsion is provided from the vanes striking the air. According to John Grand-Carteret, the design was patented in 1862, and the airship itself was to appear in 1864. The design evokes both an earlier and later manifestation of the rotating envelope scheme: Pierre Ferrand's plan using a helical arrangement of planes around the envelope in 1835;

and the Cyclocrane introduced in Oregon in 1984, which rotated its envelope in order to provide lift from airfoils fixed longitudinally around its periphery. Below the ship is a bizarre scenario of disaster and ruin, including a battle, a safari with elephants, a shipwreck, a ship struck by lightning, and a waterspout.

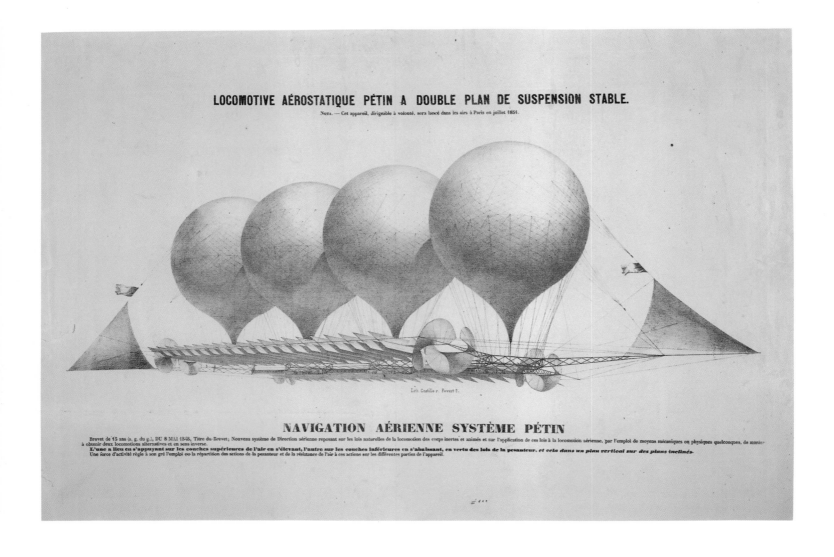

LOCOMOTIVE AÉROSTATIQUE PÉTIN A DOUBLE PLAN DE SUSPENSION STABLE.

Nota. — Cet appareil, dirigeable à volonté, sera lancé dans les airs à Paris en juillet 1851.

Lith. Castille r. Fevret 2.

NAVIGATION AÉRIENNE SYSTÈME PÉTIN

Brevet de 15 ans (s. g. du g.), DU 8 MAI 1848, Titre du Brevet; Nouveau système de Direction aérienne reposant sur les lois naturelles de la locomotion des corps inertes et animés et sur l'application de ces lois à la locomotion aérienne, par l'emploi de moyens mécaniques ou physiques quelconques, de manière à obtenir deux locomotions alternatives et en sens inverse.
L'une a lieu en s'appuyant sur les couches supérieures de l'air en s'élevant, l'autre sur les couches inférieures en s'abaissant, en vertu des lois de la pesanteur, et cela dans un plan vertical sur des plans inclinés.
Une force d'activité règle à son gré l'emploi ou la répartition des actions de la pesanteur et de la résistance de l'air à ces actions sur les différentes parties de l'appareil.

Locomotive aérostatique Pétin à double
plan de suspension stable . . . Navigation
aérienne système Pétin

> [1850?], [Paris]. "Lith. Castille." Lithograph, 29.5
> x 55 cm. (image) on a sheet 40.4 x 59.8 cm.
> XP-XL-18 (1769)

Ernest Pétin, the designer of this aircraft,
announces in the caption that it "will be
launched into the air at Paris in July, 1851."
Several methods are possible: the helical
screws could be turned "by hand or by some
other mechanical means" or the inclined
planes could convert the vertical movement to
forward motion, as in the design of Charles
Guillé. A patent was issued for this aircraft on
May 8, 1848. *(What may be the original design
for this large lithograph is an uncatalogued
watercolor painting [16.5 x 22.5 cm.] in the
Gimbel group "uncataloged matted prints.")*

[Le Ballon dirigeable de Mr. Giffard—1852]

> (Title in manuscript on mounting.) Pen and ink drawing with wash, 19 x 22.7 cm.
>
> XP-XL-18 (1766)

A 3-horsepower steam engine powered this dirigible designed and flown from Paris by the renowned engineer Henri Giffard on September 24, 1852. Emile Cassé witnessed the flight and was struck by "the strange feeling we felt as we saw the brave inventor rise up in his machine to the whistling noise of the steam, replacing in these circumstances the usual waving of a flag." The aircraft was able to develop a speed of about 5 miles per hour. "Not for a single moment did I dream of struggling against the wind; the power of the engine would not have permitted it," Giffard reported. "That had been thought of in advance and proved by calculations; but I carried out various manoeuvres of circular and lateral movement successfully." Giffard built a second machine that was launched in 1855; it was similar to this one, but 230 feet long as opposed to 144. It failed during the initial flight. (*This drawing shows a car with solid walls rather than the open nacelle of the actual machine.*)

Scientific Ascent of Mr. H. Coxwell's
Mammoth Balloon from the Crystal
Palace, Sept. 1, 1862

> C. Robinson, after a drawing by J. Taylor
>
> London, September 13, 1862. "C. Robinson,
> Litho." Tinted lithograph, colored. 37 x 60 cm.
>
> XP-XL-14 (1508)

This flight was part of a series made famous
by the publication of James Glaisher's *Voyages
Aériens* and *Travels in the Air.* Glaisher claimed
that during a scientific ascent a few days after
the flight depicted here, on September 5, the
valve line was lifted out of reach, the balloon
went into an uncontrolled ascent, and rose to
36,000 feet before one of the balloonists
regained control of the valve. The claim is
rather incredible, as the balloonists could not
have survived this altitude; it is thought that
24,000 feet is a more probable altitude. The
caption asserts that the balloon "attained the
elevation of six miles, the greatest height
ever reached."

THE BATTLE OF FAIR OAKS, VA MAY 31ST 1862.

General McClellan having advanced "The Army of the Potomac" to near Richmond, the Rebels took advantage of a terrible storm which had flooded the Valley of the Chickahominy, and at 1 O'Clock P.M. attacked the advanced lines on the right bank of the river, and succeeded in forcing them back; but Generals Heintzelman & Kearney gallantly brought up their troops and checked the enemy, while Genl Sumner by great exertions succeeded in bringing across the river, Genls Sedgewicks and Richardson's divisions; when the Rebels were driven back at the point of the bayonet, leaving over 1200 of their dead on the field. The next morning June 1st they attempted to renew the conflict but were at every point repulsed with great slaughter.

The Battle of Fair Oaks, Va. May 31st, 1862.

New York, 1862. Currier and Ives. Lithograph, colored. 20 x 31.4 cm.

XP-XL-25 (2034)

Bruce Catton described the Civil War battle at Fair Oaks as "bloody enough, with five or six thousand casualties on each side, but . . . indecisive. The diaries of the men who fought in it cannot be put together to make a picture of anything but a series of savage combats in wood and swamp. . . . there seemed to be no tactical plans other than a simple urge to get the men up into places where they could shoot at each other." Above this scenario, balloonist Thaddeus Lowe attempted to keep the Union army informed of enemy activity by ascending in three different captive balloons on the day of the battle. He claimed that this scouting was the most significant of his wartime service, as he was able to prepare the Union army for the attack with which the battle began. It was the most severe action that Lowe witnessed. Currier and Ives, the famous New York firm, which issued over 7,000 different images from 1857 to 1907, made three versions of this print, all titled as above and issued in 1862. Such scenes were standard fare for the firm, which

published more than 70 prints whose title began with the word "battle." The Union army ceased using balloons after June 1863. *(Included in the Gimbel collection is the uncolored version XP-XL-25 2034 [sic]; the two prints are very similar and are the same size. The uncolored has, as the first word in the last line of the caption, the word "bajonet," where the colored has "point of the bayonet." The principal difference in the two images is the position of the horseman's sword at upper right, which is pointed backward on the colored and forward on the uncolored.)*

Jeu du ballon, Le Géant

Paris, [1863?]. Published by Rousseau, printed by Destouches, Paris. Lithograph, colored, on paper, 60 x 44 cm.

XP-XL-22 (1875)

This board game is inspired by the huge balloon *Le Géant,* built by the famous photographer and aeronautical enthusiast Nadar (or Félix Tournachon). *Le Géant* held 212,000 cubic feet of gas and produced a lift of more than four tons; below this massive envelope was a two-story wicker car with a balcony, passenger compartments, a photographic lab, and a printing press. The balloon made two flights in 1863 from the Champ de Mars, on October 4 and 18. The first flight, with Nadar in command and two of the Godard brothers as assistants, carried twelve additional passengers. It ended only fifteen miles from Paris, probably because of a badly seated gas valve at the crown. The second flight was an overnight voyage of 400 miles, with Nadar and the Godards accompanied by six

passengers; it ended with a spectacular crash landing in Germany. This flight was sensationalized by the press, and this board game was probably inspired by it. The game is played with dice, and the players advance from the twelve spaces at bottom (the "Champ de Mars") up the tether lines and net to the crown of the balloon. Players suffer penalties if they land on "accident" or "broken rope." Landing on "valve" requires descent to the bottom of the basket, or car. Nadar flew *Le Géant* from various European cities until 1867.

AU BASTION

Siège de Paris, Au Bastion

Draner (i.e., Jules Renard, 1833– ?), artist and lithographer

Paris, [*ca.* 1870]. Tinted lithograph, 54 x 34.2 cm.

XP-XL-14 (1506)

Sixty-six manned (and one unmanned) balloons departed from Paris during the siege of 1870–1871, bringing out large quantities of mail and dispatches and, occasionally, political leaders needed for the war effort outside the besieged capital. This scene from the Franco-Prussian War appears to be apocryphal—the bastion shown, "No. 95," never existed. Renard, whose pseudonym consisted of his name spelled backward, also published a series of colored views on the siege in book form, including *Souvenirs du siège de Paris: les soldats de la République; Souvenirs du siège de Paris: les défenseurs de la Capitale;* and *Paris assiégé.*

THE NEW DYNAMITE BALLOON.—From the Inventor's Sketches—[See Page 331.]

The New Dynamite Balloon—from the inventor's sketches

Wood engraving, 23.5 x 34.5 cm.

XP-XL-18 (1755)

This print appeared in *Harper's Weekly* of May 23, 1885. A short accompanying article discusses the proposal of Russell Thayer, who designed the 185-foot-long "dynamite balloon" and suggested its use to the U.S. Navy. The airship was to drop "huge bombs" of dynamite, a material invented almost twenty years earlier but only recently embraced by the military. Although the article concedes that a satisfactory method for propelling airships was not at hand, it noted that "new methods hold out new possibilities." Predicting that recently developed engines would provide a solution,

the article compares the advent of the airship to that of the marine screw propeller, concluding that the airships' "value in peace might overshadow their war uses." In France, in 1883 and 1884, Albert and Gaston Tissandier and Charles Renard and Arthur Krebs had launched electrically propelled airships that were only moderately successful. In the print, the artist dramatically shows discharged smoke, suggesting the use of steam. Two men are shown standing in the car, from which a bomb has just been dropped.

BALLON CAPTIF DU TROCADÉRO
88, Avenue Klóber, 88

LOUIS GODARD

A. Liébert, Phot.   6, Rue de Londres. — Paris

Ballon captif du Trocadéro . . .
Louis Godard

> Alphonse J. Liébert
> Paris, [1889]. Photograph, 21.5 x 16.9 cm.
> XP-XL-14 (1514)

Dated 1889, this photograph shows the large captive balloon managed by Louis Godard, nephew of the famous Eugène Godard, a pioneer in the genre of the large balloon. Both were balloon builders, and the family included numerous balloonists, led by Eugène: Pierre, father of Eugène, and Eugène's brothers and sister—Louis (son of Louis who managed the pictured balloon), August, Jules, and Eugénie. In fact the Godard name became so closely associated with the balloon that in 1960 historian Charles Dollfus claimed he could still find people in the French countryside who referred to any spherical balloon as a "godard." This view was no doubt taken during the Paris Exposition of 1889, which was visited by 32 million people, and during which the Eiffel Tower opened. Liébert, known for applying electric lighting to indoor photography, ran a concession at the Exposition to photograph balloon passengers. In the photograph, ten people fill the basket, which is draped by flags, including, curiously, that of Turkey, which was officially absent from the Exposition. Seen on the right, attached to the basket, is a heavy dragline and anchor, so the balloon is prepared for free flight should it sever its tether. In the background at lower left a wheeled hydrogen generator can be seen. This photograph evokes the famous *grands ballons captifs* of Henri Giffard, the last of which rose above Paris for the Exposition of 1878 and could carry fifty people; Giffard built his first great tethered balloon for the Exposition of 1867.

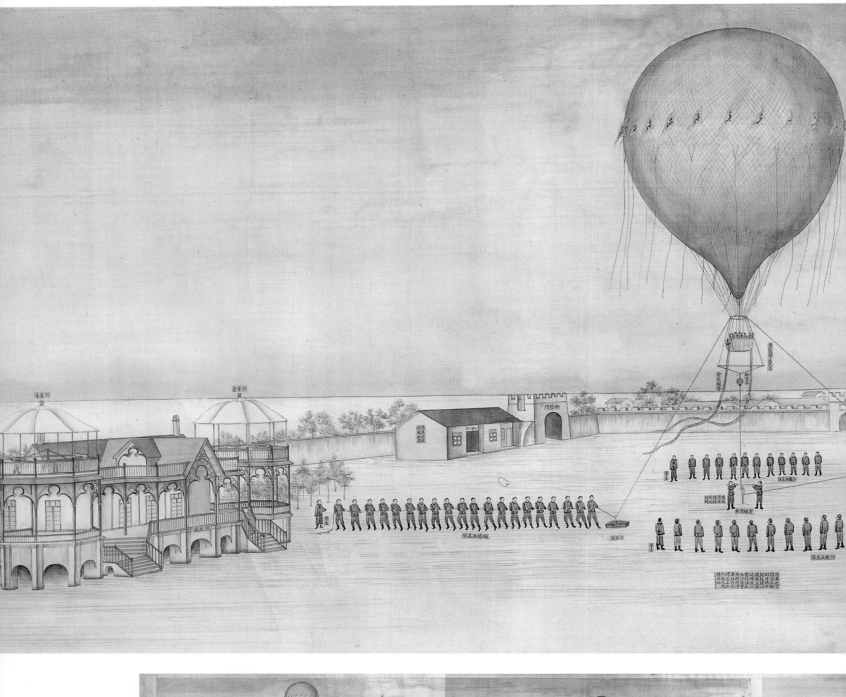

[Ascension of a balloon at the Tientsin military academy]

[1887?]

Scroll, with watercolor on silk; five panels: three 53.5 cm. x 101.5, one 53.5 x 132, and one 53.5 x 310.

This scroll's numerous written captions simply name the technical apparatus and other features, but it likely illustrates the activities of the summer of 1887, when the French introduced the first balloon into China. Two balloons were brought from France to the Tientsin military academy near Peking, including one of 3,000 cubic meters that could carry ten people. Though the balloons arrived in early April, the aeronaut Pillas-Panis worked until September instructing the academy's

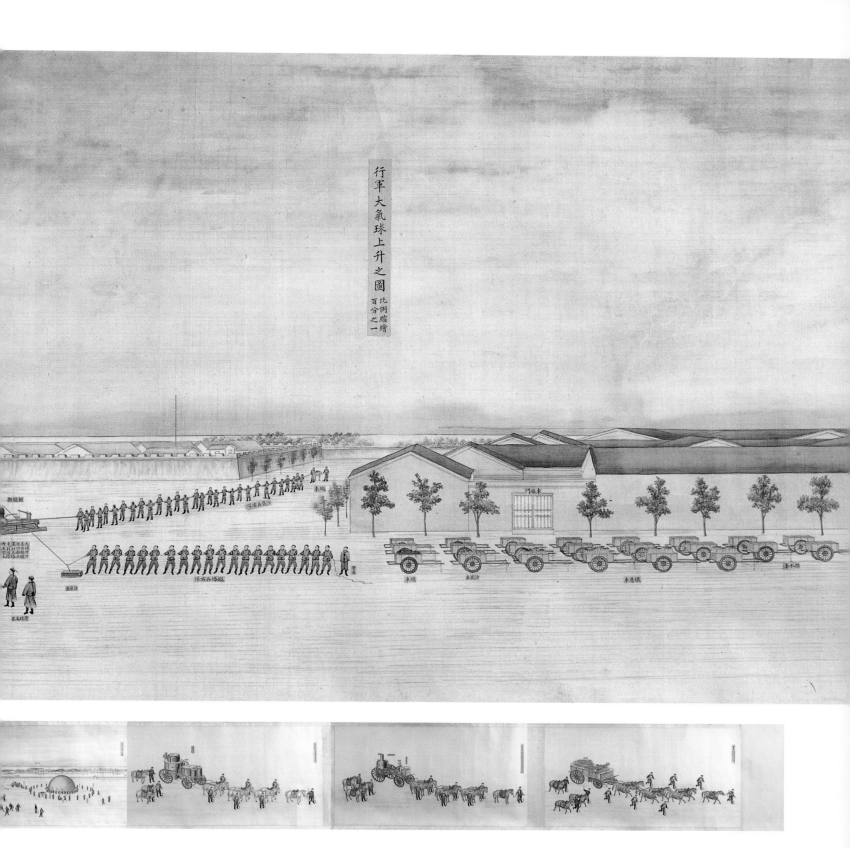

行軍大氣球上升之圖

此例縮繪
百分之一

students and staff in balloon history, technique, and maneuvers. On October 2, 1887, Pillas-Panis ascended before a crowd he estimated to contain 200,000 people. By the end of November Pillas-Panis was able to entrust the operation to his students; the improvements to the grounds, including the corrugated metal balloon shed, suggest that the balloons were intended as permanent additions to the Chinese army.

Kites over Sakura District Viewed from the Emperor's Castle

    Hiroshige (1797–1858)

    Woodcut, 33.7 x 22 cm.

    XP-XL-38 (3153)

In this woodcut, part of a series of 100 views around Tokyo produced between 1853 and 1856, Hiroshige, one of the most prominent of Japanese printmakers, shows a number of kites being flown. Presumably the scene is a breezy New Year's Day, since the game *hagoita,* with its shuttle in the center and paddles shown in the foreground, is generally played then. Kites, which came to the West from the Orient centuries ago, have their origins in ancient times, apparently around 200 B.C.E. They played an important role in the development of the airplane because experimenters extensively used kites to perfect wing structures.

Thirty-six Views Around Fugaku

> Hokusai (1760–1849)
>
> Woodcut, 24.7 x 36.8 cm.
>
> XP-XL-38 (3167)

This view is part of a famous series of 46 prints of Fugaku (Mount Fuji) produced by Hokusai between 1825 and 1831, although 36 prints are cited in the title. Above a bustling scenario, with workmen repairing the Hongan Temple in the foreground, the kite at center commands the scene, including the clouds that partially obscure the dwellings. This print might be compared to early French balloon prints and especially to Tavenard's "Vue de la Terrasse de Mr. Franklin à Passi," which includes the motif of an observer atop a roof. Hokusai was one of the most prominent of printmakers; his "Wave" (also a part of "Thirty-six Views"), which shows a distant Mount Fuji framed by large seas, is familiar to many Westerners.

[Woman on balcony looking at balloon]
    Dry point, in sepia ink, 15.2 x 9.9 cm.
    XP-XL-16 (1621)

This *fin de siècle* image is without extraneous words; *L' Avant Garde*, which serves as the title to the newspaper, also suggests the meaning of the print. The clothing, iron railing, the swept-back hair, and the balloon all contribute to the modernism of the scene, elaborated by the artist's stylistic liberty.

CAPTURE OF EL CANEY, EL PASO & FORTIFICATIONS OF SANTIAGO.
CHARGE OF THE ROUGH RIDERS.

Capture of El Caney, El Paso, and Fortifications of Santiago. Charge of the Rough Riders. At lower left: "July 1 & 2, 1898. General Shafter commanding 15,000 troops."

Copyright 1898 by Kurz and Allison, Chicago. Colored lithograph, 44.8 x 60.2 cm.

XP-XL-25 (2017)

Under the command of the 300-pound Civil War hero, Gen. William R. Shafter, American troops landed in Cuba on June 20, 1898, to continue the Spanish-American War; the conflict lasted about ten weeks and established Theodore Roosevelt as a national hero. In the battle of El Caney, near Santiago, Lieutenant Colonel Roosevelt ordered his Rough Riders to attack fortifications on the hills above the battleground. During the battle, balloonist Ivy Baldwin ascended several times to observe the action in an antiquated balloon that the U.S. Army had purchased in France in 1892. The

intelligence gained from the flights was of great value, but the balloon attracted a great deal of enemy fire onto the surrounding area, and many derided the role of the balloon, pointing out that it allowed enemy gunners to locate the army's position. General Shafter, incidentally, had been awarded the Medal of Honor in 1867 for his heroism in the Battle of Fair Oaks, which is represented in print XP-XL-25 2034 above.

[Wright glider in flight]

Photograph (modern silver print), 29.2 x 37.2 cm.
XP-XL-29 (2314)

This photograph shows one of the Wright brothers in flight during their Kitty Hawk trials of October 1902, after the twin-surface, fixed rudder had been replaced by a single-surface, adjustable one. The new rudder was designed to add much-needed stability, but the Wrights feared it was also going to add to the complexity of flying the aircraft. In Orville Wright's words, the pilot "would now not only have to think, and think quickly, in operating the front elevator . . . he would also have to think so as to operate this rudder." To simplify the pilot's task, the control of the rudder was made automatic and linked to the control for warping the wings and rolling the aircraft; it was later made independent. "With the machine as now constituted," wrote Orville,

"we began a long series of gliding flights. The disastrous experiences which we had when the fixed vanes [i.e., the rudders] were used now seemed to be entirely avoidable." The Wright brothers made just over 300 photographs of their aeronautical work, partly to further and partly to document their own research. Their negatives were bequeathed to the Library of Congress in 1949.

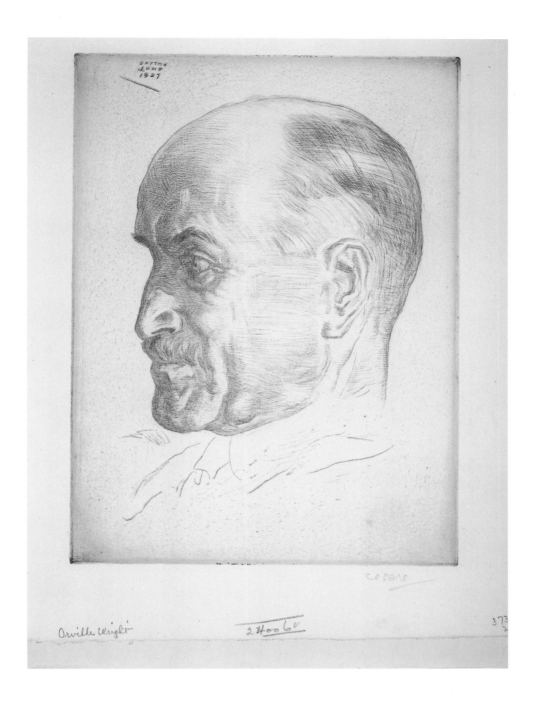

Dayton June 1927 [Orville Wright]

Oscar Edward Cesare (1883–1948)
(Bracketed portion in pencil at lower edge.)
Drypoint, 27.7 x 20.4 cm.
XP-XL-29 (2304)

The Swedish-born Cesare was well known for his cartoons and portraits published in the United States and Europe from World War I until World War II, and after 1920 he was a regular contributor to the *New York Times*. Although Cesare developed the novel technique of portraying and interviewing his subject, this print was published as an illustration to an article by Lester J. Maitland ("Knights of the Air: The Immortal Wrights") which appeared in the September 1928 issue of *The World's Work*, a periodical that often featured news and commentary on flying. The print shown here was created about the time that Orville Wright met Charles Lindbergh at Wright Field just after Lindbergh had flown the Atlantic alone, and the two had dinner in Wright's home. *(A drawing by Cesare featuring a full view of the face of Orville Wright appeared in the August 1925 issue of* The World's Work.*)*

Zeppelin über dem Bodensee

Michael Zeno Diemer (1807–?)

München, 1909. Reichold and Lang. Colored lithograph, 55 x 75 cm.

XP-XL-C (3099)

This poster was created in 1909, a significant year for Count Ferdinand von Zeppelin and his dirigibles. An airship *(LZ5)* was completed in the spring, funded largely by contributions from the German people, and on May 29 Count Zeppelin undertook an ambitious flight from his base at Friedrichshafen almost to Berlin. The airship was damaged when it struck a tree at Goppingen while returning to Friedrichshafen, but completed the flight of 850 miles in 36 hours. Another ship *(LZ6)* was completed in August, and after a flight to Berlin, gave a series of sightseeing tours over the Bodensee, or Lake Constance, situated between Switzerland and Germany. Zeppelin's airships achieved notoriety in 1909, the same year that one was first accepted for military service by the German army. In November, Count Zeppelin founded the famous Deutsche Luftschiffahrts-Aktien-Gesellschaft (or "Delag"), which historians have called the "first commercial airline."

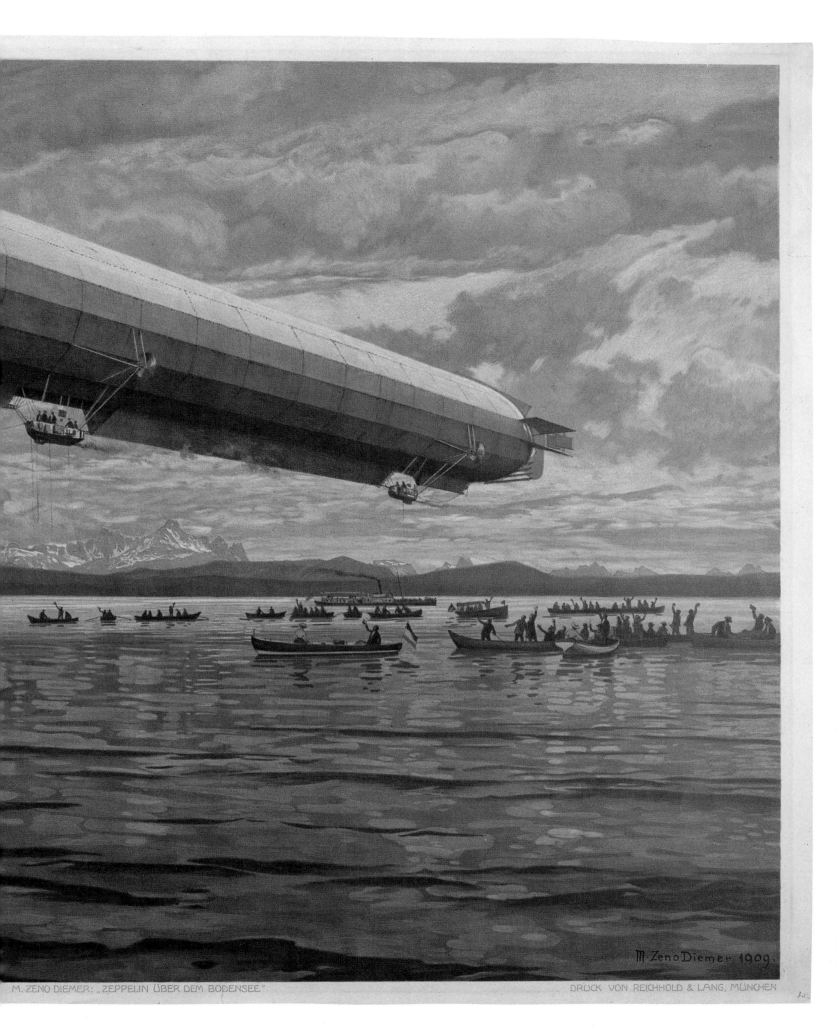

M. ZENO DIEMER: „ZEPPELIN ÜBER DEM BODENSEE". DRUCK VON REICHHOLD & LANG, MÜNCHEN

[*Octavie No. 3* biplane of 1909]

Chromolithograph, 13.6 x 18.6 cm.

XP-XL-41 (3226)

Gimbel's notes for this print, found on a separate card, read: "This pictures the Voisin Biplane of 1908 when Farman carried [the] first passenger, Leon Delagrange." But Gimbel was in error: the print depicts an aircraft somewhat different from Henri Farman's as it appeared on the flight of March 28, when it made a hop of 600 feet. That aircraft did not have a wheel under the nose, and it had not yet been fitted with the side-curtains between the planes, both of which are evident in the print. The number "20" on the empennage is certainly for the Reims aviation meet, held August 22 to August 29, 1909, from which we can conclude that the plane is the *Octavie No. 3* built for Louis Paulhan and first flown on June 7, 1909. Among the 38 aircraft and 22 pilots entered at the Reims meet, the pictured plane distinguished itself by establishing a new duration record of 2 hours 43 minutes, and took third place for distance by covering about 80 miles. The print is in a carved frame decorated with a balloon and kite.

TRAVERSÉE DE PARIS par EM. DUBONNET

VUE DE L'ARC DE TRIOMPHE

Traversée de Paris par Em. Dubonnet

M. Branger

Collotype, 25.7 x 37.5 cm.

XP-XL-19 (1792)

The first overflight of a major city by airplane is attributed to the Count de Lambert (Wilbur Wright's first pupil), who excited the Parisian populace on October 18, 1909, by circling the Eiffel Tower in a Wright airplane. But when Emile Dubonnet "aeroplaned" across the city on the afternoon of April 24, 1910, there was an even greater sensation. In a flight of about 42 miles Dubonnet crossed over the Place de la Concorde and flew down the Champs Elysées, all at an altitude of 200 feet, occasionally rising to 300. At such a height he was affected by eddies from the buildings, which he sometimes found "difficult to negotiate." Dubonnet was a pilot for Tellier Works, makers of speedboats and constructors of the monoplane shown in this print. (*Lambert's flight is commemorated in print XP-XL-19 1801, "de Lambert im Wrightflieger über Paris."*)

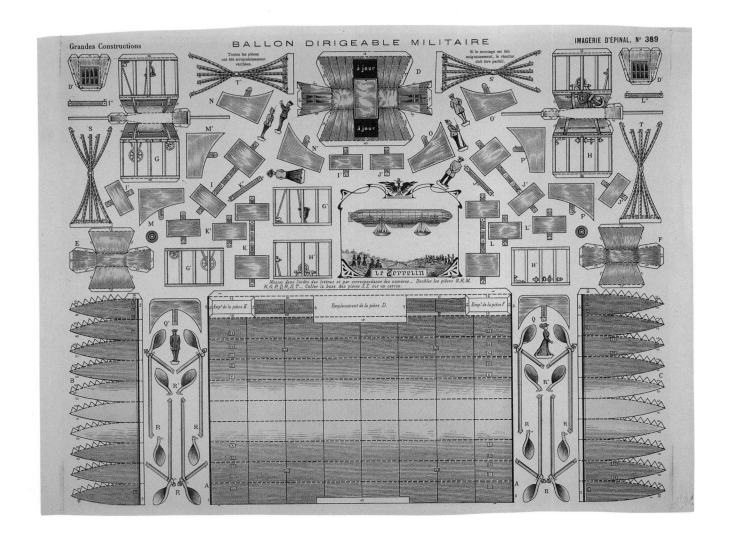

Ballon dirigeable militaire

(Paper cut-out model.) Above: Grandes
constructions. Imagerie d'Épinal, no. 389.
Lithograph, colored, 36 x 44.6 cm. (image)
XP-XL-19 (1782)

"Le Zeppelin" is one of a series of paper cut-
out models collected by Gimbel. When
assembled, the model would be about 13 inches
long; at center can be seen a small vignette
showing the airship in flight. The model
probably dates from about 1910, as it emulates
the zeppelins made between 1905 and 1910.
In 1910 five zeppelins began to be used for a
tourist service in Germany that carried over
35,000 passengers until the beginning of the
World War in 1914.

THE CHANNEL FLIGHT
BLÉRIOT – JULY 25TH 1909

The Channel Flight: Blériot—July 25th, 1909

H. Delaspre

London, [1909?]. Chromolithograph, 33.7 x 44.7 cm.

XP-XL-19 (1803)

The wealthy Louis Blériot began dabbling in airplanes in 1906; committed to monoplanes, he built three during 1907, the last of which included most of the features we associate with the modern airplane, although neither wing-warping nor ailerons were used with the main wings. Two years later, in July 1909, he won the *Daily Mail* prize of £1,000 by flying across the English Channel from France to England in his monoplane No. XI, an aircraft with a wing span of about 25 feet, powered by a 25-horsepower engine. The event attracted wide attention and the reputation of Blériot as an airplane builder was assured.

Other Holdings

DOMINICK A. PISANO

THE COLONEL RICHARD GIMBEL AERONAUTICAL HISTORY COLLECTION is especially rich in what is termed "other holdings"—so-called ephemera that reflect Colonel Gimbel's wide-ranging interest in things aeronautical. In addition, these items reveal the breadth of the popular arts—advertising, journalism, popular music, and popular reading material—with which aeronautics came into contact in the eighteenth, nineteenth, and early twentieth centuries. This part of the collection demonstrates that aeronautics has always been shared with the public. Moreover, it shows that public response to flying dictated that various forms of the popular arts reflect aeronautical events.

Among the Gimbel collection's aeronautical ephemera that I have included here are advertisements, dime novels, excerpts from newspapers and periodicals, handbills, circulars, leaflets, postcards, programs, sheet music, tickets, a cartoon, a stock certificate, stereograph slides, and an aeronautical supplies catalogue. The Appendix lists additional representative selections of ephemera from the collection. It was difficult to decide which items to describe because the uniform excellence and representativeness of the materials bear witness to Colonel Gimbel's skill as a collector. Finally, I have included a descriptive note for the advertisement, dime novel, and sheet music sections. These notes provide contextual information for each of those sections and explain the place of aeronautics within them.

Detail of postcard (Man and woman sitting in airship gondola), 1909 (Page 288)

ADVERTISEMENTS

Advertising became modern, as Roland Marchand points out, when "a few advertisers had begun to appreciate the advantages of selling the benefit instead of the product—illumination instead of lighting, prestige instead of automobiles," and so on. Some of the early examples of advertising media in the Gimbel collection that use aeronautical themes presage this advertising strategy by using balloons, airships, and aircraft to sell commercial products that have no connection with aviation. Perhaps advertisers thought that by identifying a product with flying, consumers would be transported out of the everyday world into one that represented freedom and escape—sensations associated with flying. The pleasant associations would induce them to buy products. This trend continued into the 1920s and 1930s, as aviation became more popular and advertisers attempted to exploit the glamour and speed of the airplane and the celebrity status of famous aviators to sell everything from cigarettes to motor oil.

Excelsior Standard Screw Fastened
Boots & Shoes

> Date unknown
>
> Advertisement, 9.5 x 17.5 cm.

This advertisement is an early example of how aeronautical themes were used to sell manufactured products in the United States. Shoes and balloons may seem dissimilar, but the advertisement successfully integrates the two. It depicts a Standard Screw Fastened Shoe going aloft in a balloon, while another with "clinching screw nails" plummets to earth. The reverse advertises "James Shannahan, dealer in Boots, Shoes, Slippers, and Rubbers . . . Milford, N. H."

Soapine Rises Above Everything

Date unknown
Advertisement, 7 x 10.5 cm.

This advertisement is another example of
the use of aeronautical themes to advertise
commercial products. A box of Soapine, a
laundry product made by Kendall Mfg. Co. in
Providence, R.I., rises in a balloon over a town
surrounded by mountains, trees, and a lake.
The reverse of the ad reads: "For Washing and
Cleaning Everything, No Matter What, Soapine
Works, Quicker, Easier, Cheaper and Better
Than Soap or Anything Else."

High Flyers from Coast to Coast Use
Lash's Bitters, The Great Tonic Laxative

ca. 1911
Advertisement, 8.5 x 13.5 cm.

After the first successful powered heavier-than-air flight by the Wright brothers in December 1903, manufacturers began to use aircraft to advertise their products. This advertisement postcard depicts what looks like a Wright Model A in flight over Manhattan, carrying a bottle of Lash's Bitters. Although barely visible, numbers on the front of the postcard refer to early twentieth-century Manhattan landmarks like the Woolworth Building, Bankers' Trust Building, and the Brooklyn Bridge.

A SHELL FROM THE CONFEDERATE MORTAR EXPLODED DIRECTLY BENEATH THE BALLOON.

DIME NOVELS

"The dime novel," as Russel Nye has observed, "sprouted in the eighteen-forties and fifties, flowered in the sixties and seventies, and drooped and died at the turn of the century." Nevertheless, this form of popular fiction had a strong attraction for young men during the half-century of its popularity. Although many stories were Westerns, others, Nye points out, "covered the Revolution, the War of 1812, the Mexican War, and the Civil War; they used pirate stories, sea stories, city stories of high and low life, crime stories, bandit stories, stories of exploration, adventure, history, love, romance." The writing was formulaic and the characters often coarse, but the stories stressed virtuous behavior. As time went on, however, the emphasis turned to "sensationalism, violence, and overwrought emotionalism." Some stories included balloons, airships, and imaginative flying machines as drama-heightening devices, and the colorful cover art focused on these situations. It is quite possible that the adventures of dime-novel heroes like Frank Reade, Jr., motivated the first generation of pilots. The situations in these stories presaged the use of aviation in films, pulp novels, and radio serials. The editions presented were published between 1897 and 1910.

Beverly Kennon. "Phil in the Balloon Corps; or, A Flight Above the Clouds." *Red, White and Blue: A Patriotic Weekly Story Paper.* May 15, 1897. Vol. 1, No. 28. New York: Street & Smith, [c. 1897].

Dime novel, 27 p. illus.

XA-2-2D

The exciting cover text ("A shell from the Confederate mortar exploded directly beneath the balloon") and illustration announce another number in the *Red, White and Blue Library* of Street & Smith. In his book on Street & Smith, Quentin Reynolds observes that the *Red, White and Blue Library* was "designed to cater to the spirit of patriotism presumably inherent in the breast of every red-blooded American boy. The stories were alternately about two boys, Ralph in the navy and Phil in the army. These two youngsters performed military and naval feats never dreamed of by the experts, and they were at all times ready to cry, 'Hurray for the Red, White and Blue.'" The *Red, White and Blue Library* began in 1896 and lasted a year.

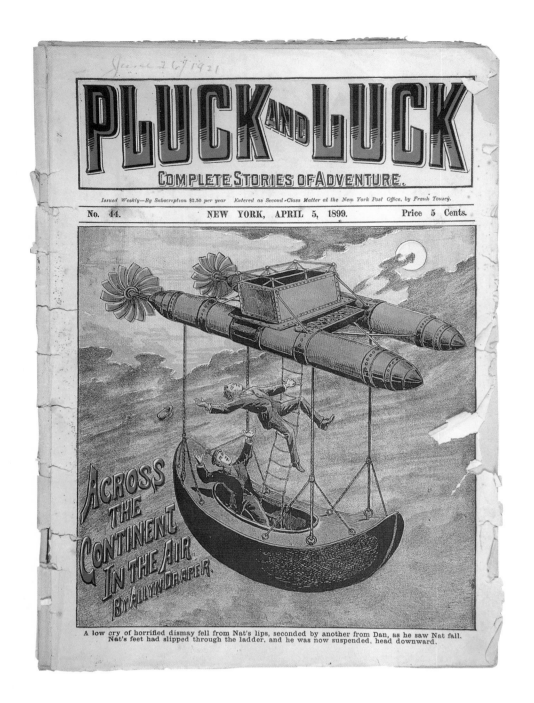

A low cry of horrified dismay fell from Nat's lips, seconded by another from Dan, as he saw Nat fall. Nat's feet had slipped through the ladder, and he was now suspended, head downward.

Allyn Draper. "Across the Continent in the Air." *Pluck and Luck: Complete Stories of Adventure.* April 5, 1899. No. 44. New York: Frank Tousey, [c. 1899].

Dime novel, 31 p. illus.

The heroes of the story, Nat Nimmo and Dan Taylor, undertake a cross-country odyssey in an aerial conveyance, which Nat has invented. The flying vehicle, with an upper part shaped like a catamaran and a lower part shaped like a canoe, is driven by a "powerful, reciprocating electrical engine" and is called the "Rocket." In dime-novel fashion, the cover depicts a typical hair-raising scene. One character dangles head downward from the rope ladder that connects the two parts of the vehicle, while the other stands by helplessly. The boys free themselves from this dilemma, but more adventures await them on their journey.

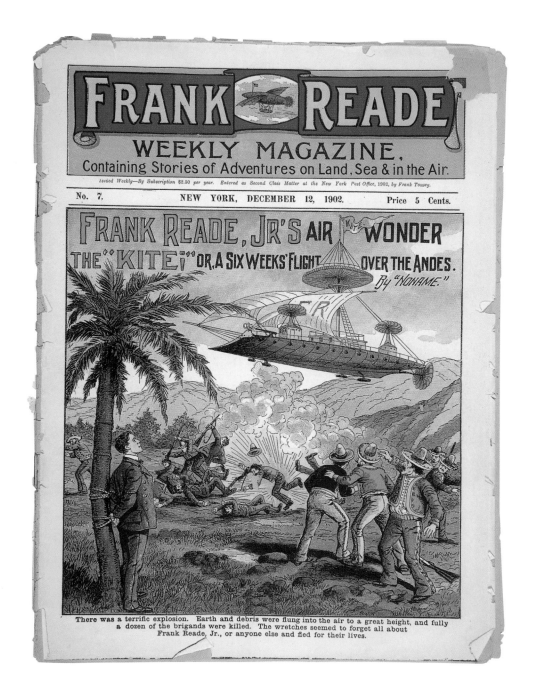

There was a terrific explosion. Earth and debris were flung into the air to a great height, and fully a dozen of the brigands were killed. The wretches seemed to forget all about Frank Reade, Jr., or anyone else and fled for their lives.

"Noname." "Frank Reade, Jr.'s Air Wonder, 'The Kite'; or, A Six-Weeks' Flight over the Andes." *Frank Reade Weekly Magazine* [Containing Stories of Adventures on Land, Sea and in the Air]. December 12, 1902. No. 7. New York: Frank Tousey, [c. 1902].

Dime novel, 28 p. illus.

XA-3-3A

The colorful cover illustration depicts the hero, Frank Reade, Jr., tied to a tree somewhere in the Andes, while an airship called the "Kite" flies overhead. The cover text ("There was a terrific explosion. Earth and debris were flung into the air to a great height, and fully a dozen of the brigands were killed . . .") alerts the reader to the exciting climax when the hero is rescued by the airship. At the end of the story, Frank Reade, Jr., drops bombs from the Kite onto his enemies, driving them "like sheep from their hiding places" and scattering them "like chaff before the wind."

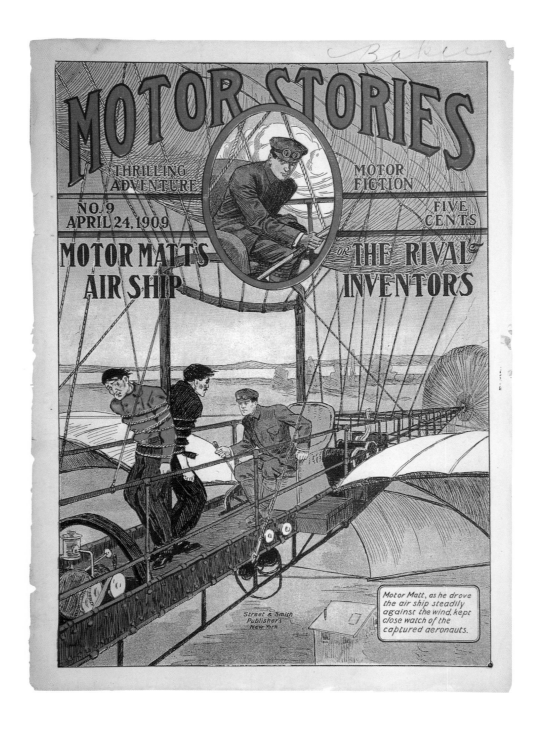

"Author of 'Motor Matt.'" "Motor Matt's Air Ship, or The Rival Inventors." *Motor Stories* [Thrilling Adventure Motor Fiction]. April 24, 1909. No. 9. New York: Street & Smith, [c. 1909].

Dime novel, 31 p. illus.

"Motor Matt," the hero of this *Motor Stories Library,* "is simply a youth who has considerable training in a machine shop where motors of all kinds were repaired, and who is possessed of a genius for mechanics." The titles of the other editions in the series suggest that Matt's adventures involve automobiles, but here, he and the villains use an airship to heighten the dramatic effect of the story.

DOMINICK A. PISANO

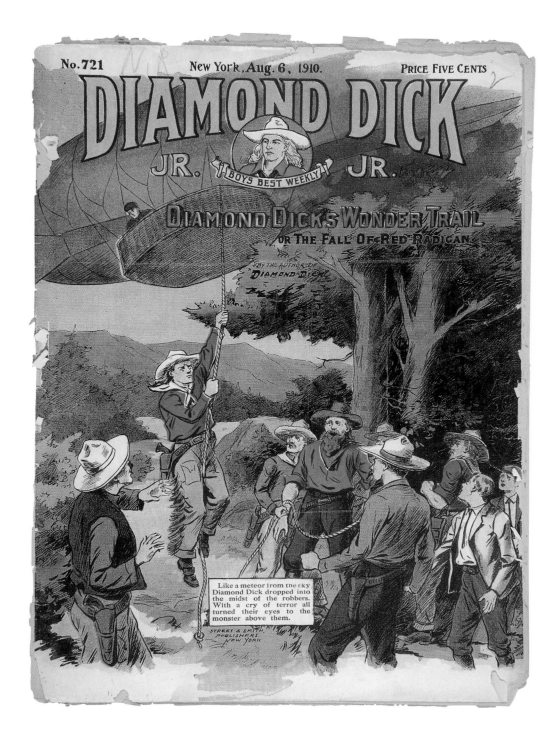

Like a meteor from the sky Diamond Dick dropped into the midst of the robbers. With a cry of terror all turned their eyes to the monster above them.

"Author of 'Diamond Dick.'" "Diamond Dick's Wonder Trail or, The Fall of Red Radigan." *Diamond Dick, Jr.: Boys Best Weekly.* August 6, 1910. No. 721. New York: Street & Smith, [c. 1910].

Dime novel, 31 p. illus.

Diamond Dick, Jr., ostensibly a Western hero, was the fictional son of Diamond Dick, one of the most successful characters in the Street & Smith dime-novel empire. On occasion, Diamond Dick, Jr., used aerial vehicles of one kind or another to thwart his antagonists. In this 1910 adventure, the hero's flight in a balloon sends "thrills through his being" and is "the most wonderful of all" his adventures. In the story's climax, he drops from the sky to frustrate the highwaymen's attempts at robbery.

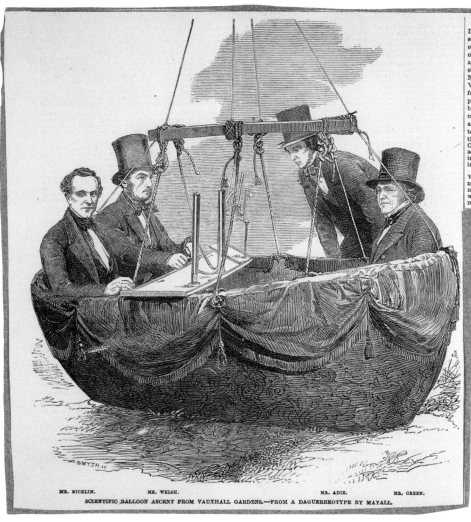

SCIENTIFIC BALLOON ASCENT.

IN our Journal of last week, we detailed the first balloon ascent for scientific objects, under the direction of the Kew Committee of the Council of the British Association. The ascent took place at Vauxhall Gardens, on the 17th ult., and the second of the series, on Friday (last week), at 44 minutes past 4 P.M., from Vauxhall, under very favourable circumstances of wind, weather, and freedom from cloud. Mr. Welsh and Mr. Nicklin were, as before, the aëronauts, under the guidance of Mr. Green. Various re-arrangements and adaptations of the instruments had been found desirable by the experience of the first ascent. The descent took place with great ease at Latimer, near Boxmoor, at 7.35 P.M., the balloon not having travelled more than 25 miles in two hours fifty-one minutes; the rate in the previous ascent having been about 40 miles an hour. The greatest height attained was about 19,200 feet; the temperature of the air being 7 degrees Fahrenheit, or 25 degrees below the freezing point. One of the dew points was 17 degrees below zero. Clouds were not seen above the aëronauts, although cumuli were observed around, below the level of the balloon. No difficulty of breathing was experienced. Air was brought down from the greatest height in tubes previously exhausted, for future analysis.

Previous to the first ascent the two experimentalists, Mr. Welsh and Mr. Nicklin, together with Mr. Green, the aëronaut, and Mr. Adie, of 395, Strand, the maker of the instruments taken up in the balloon, were daguerréotyped by Mr. Mayall, which has enabled our artist to engrave the group, in illustration of this memorable ascent.

MR. NICKLIN.　　MR. WELSH.　　MR. ADIE.　　MR. GREEN.

SCIENTIFIC BALLOON ASCENT FROM VAUXHALL GARDENS.—FROM A DAGUERREOTYPE BY MAYALL.

EXCERPTS FROM NEWSPAPERS AND PERIODICALS

Scientific Balloon Ascent. Poss. from *London Illustrated News,* [1852?] with engraving

Clipping, 25 x 18.5 cm.

The illustration, adapted from a daguerreotype by a "Mr. Mayall," depicts a scientific balloon ascent from Vauxhall Gardens in Charles Green's balloon, the *Nassau*. The figures are, from left to right, Mr. Nicklin, Mr. Welsh, Mr. Adie, and Charles Green himself, one of Great Britain's most famous balloonists. This was the second in a series of four balloon ascents undertaken by Green "for scientific objects, under the direction of the Kew [Observatory] Committee of the Council for the British Association." Mr. Welsh and Mr. Nicklin, presumably of the Kew Committee, were the aeronauts, under Green's direction. Mr. Adie made the scientific instruments taken on the voyage. The ascents attained heights of 12,640 to 22,930 feet.

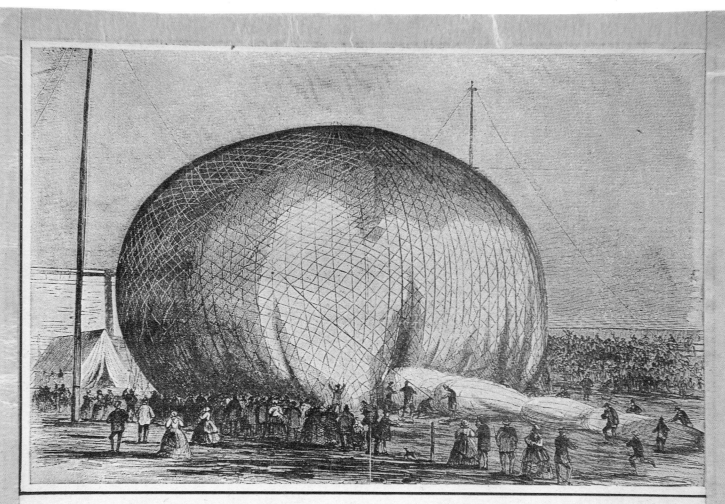

A GREAT AERONAUTIC EVENT OF HALF A CENTURY AGO.

THE MONSTER BALLOON OF MR. LOW, AN INTREPID AERONAUT OF THE LAST CENTURY, IN TH
CRYSTAL PALACE GROUNDS AT NEW YORK—PICTURE SHOWS THE BALLOON IN THE PROCESS
OF INFLATION—THE DIAMETER OF THE BAG WAS 130 FEET, AND IT WAS 200 FEET HIGH,
WEIGHING ABOUT THREE AND A HALF TONS, WITH A LIFTING POWER OF TWENTY-TWO
AND A HALF TONS—ITS CAPACITY OF GAS WAS 725,000 CUBIC FEET

A great aeronautic event of half a century ago. 1909

> Clipping, 8 x 11 cm.
>
> XF-1-1 2375

The clipping depicts Thaddeus Lowe's "monster balloon," the *City of New York* (later called the *Great Western*), being inflated on the grounds of the Crystal Palace in New York in 1859. Lowe had constructed the balloon, which had a diameter of 130 feet, weighed 3.5 tons, and could hold 725,000 cubic feet of gas, for the purpose of crossing the Atlantic. Tom Crouch, in *The Eagle Aloft,* observes that the inflation of such a gigantic balloon was not without problems and that at the slow rate at which gas was being pumped into it "the *Great Western* would never be inflated." The gas, Crouch writes, "was now escaping from the envelope faster than the gasworks could pump it without blacking out the city." Lowe accepted an offer to take the airship to Philadelphia, "but realized that the season was now too far advanced to attempt a crossing before spring." Finally, he put the large balloon in storage and went to Charleston, South Carolina, where he "spent the winter in ascending and studying various air currents" using his smaller lighter-than-air craft.

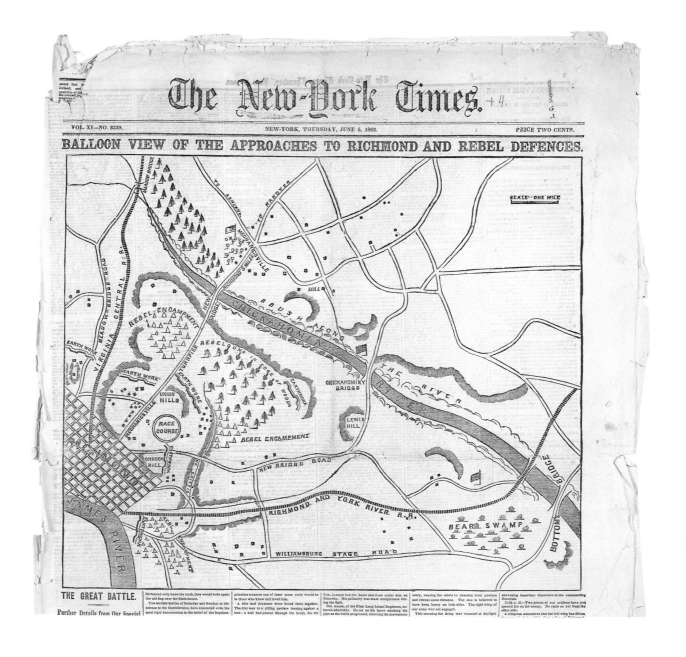

Balloon view of the approaches to Richmond and Rebel defences. Front page with map from the *New York Times* for June 5, 1862.

Clipping, 30 x 34.5 cm.

This aerial map, which appeared on the front page of the *New York Times* for June 5, 1862, was presumably drawn in an observation balloon launched by Thaddeus Lowe during the Peninsular Campaign of the Civil War. It shows the approaches to Richmond, capital of the Confederacy, and the rebel encampments between the Chickahominy River (runs diagonally from top left to bottom right) and the city. The account discusses Lowe's role in observing the area and relaying that intelligence to Washington: "Prof. Lowe has made two ascensions since sunrise, and made minute reports of his observations, which have been telegraphed to headquarters, the apparatus for that purpose having been brought upon the ground and put into operation yesterday. Notwithstanding the telegraph facilities, orderlies are continually arriving at the balloon headquarters, for the purpose of conveying important dispatches to the commanding Generals."

DOMINICK A. PISANO

THE PILCHER FLYING MACHINE.

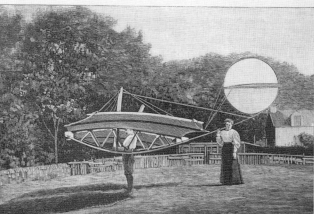

THE LATEST FORM OF FLYING MACHINE.

New flying machine [of Percy S. Pilcher], 1895. *Scientific American*, October 19, 1895, p. 249.

Clipping, 41 x 28.5 cm.

XE-2-1 3282

Scientific American, founded by Rufus Porter (a famous American airship pioneer), was the first periodical in the United States to take seriously the efforts of the aerial experimenters. In the October 19, 1895 issue, the magazine featured the work of the English experimenter Percy S. Pilcher, Otto Lilienthal's leading disciple. Pilcher's work was also influenced by Octave Chanute, a colleague of the Wright brothers. The article contains two illustrations of the Pilcher machine. "Mr. Pilcher's machines," the article points out, "are light structures of wood and steel supporting a vast spread of wing and braced with piano wire. The wings themselves, which are made of nainsook—a sort of muslin originally manufactured in India—have an area of 150 square feet; and each machine, as our pictures indicate, possesses a vertical and horizontal rudder of circular shape, the one cutting the other at right angles. The former, which is rigid, serves to keep the machine's head to the wind, while the latter arrests an inclination to pitch sideways—a common vice in all like inventions."

Nouvelle Série. N° 292. — 5 Septembre 1908

20 centimes.

UN AN
Paris et Départements, 10 fr.
Étranger, 14 fr.

SIX MOIS
France, 5.50 — Étranger, 7.50

RÉDACTION
122, rue Réaumur, 122
PARIS

VENTE ET ABONNEMENTS
9, rue Saint-Joseph, 9

Le Rire

JOURNAL HUMORISTIQUE PARAISSANT LE SAMEDI

L'AVIATEUR WRIGHT

LES GENS DU MANS. — Il vole presque aussi bien qu'une de nos poulardes, mais il doit être plus coriace.

Dessin de LÉANDRE.

L'Aviateur Wright. *Le Rire: Journal humoristique Paraissant le Samedi,* 5 Septembre 1908.

Magazine cover (with illustration), 23.5 x 30.5 cm. TLB157.G8

The cover illustration from *Le Rire* illustrates the public's fascination with Wilbur Wright during his demonstration flights in France in 1908. The form depicted suggests that the French ascribed bird- or bat-like and machine-like qualities to Wilbur for his exceptional displays of flying. As Robert Wohl has pointed out, the French public "read about his exploits and flocked by the thousands to see his flights. They bought postcard images of his profile, rendered appropriately bird-like, and replicas of his green cap. . . . They sang songs about or inspired by him. They consumed an unending stream of newspapers and magazines that bore his portrait and recounted anecdotes about his eccentricities. . . . They quoted with delight his outrageously un-Gallic statement . . . 'The only birds who speak are parrots; they can't fly very high.'"

DOMINICK A. PISANO

Philip W. Wilcox. "The New Sport of Flying; the First Flight of an Amateur Aviator." *Country Life in America,* January 1911, p. 265.

> Clipping (with cover illustration), 35 x 25 cm.
> XE-6-3 3360

Wilcox's remarkably candid article illuminates the sport-flying movement in the United States before World War I. The author provides the reader with vivid impressions of the "sensation of unlimited space and freedom, which is never more impressive than during an aeroplane flight." "Space," he writes, "seems to be without limit as the machine plunges up and down at the will of the operator. The swerving from side to side at the slightest movement of the rudders; the tipping sidewise of the planes at every cross current and gust of wind, and finally the variation of the forward velocity of the machine, as it goes up or down, all add to this sensation." But Wilcox does not dismiss the danger: "The strain on the nerves [during the flight] had been tremendous, and although everything had turned out about as expected, the suddenness with which things took place was most alarming." Wilcox goes on to say that perfect weather gave him ample time to react to situations and saved him from injury.

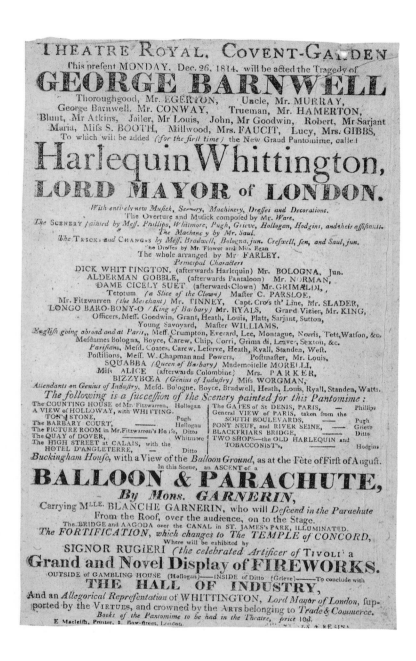

HANDBILLS, CIRCULARS, AND LEAFLETS

Ascent of a Balloon & Parachute, by Mons. Garnerin, Carrying Mlle. Blanche Garnerin, who will Descend in the Parachute From the Roof, over the audience on to the Stage. E. Macleish, Printer, London

Handbill, 24 x 15.3 cm.

XL-21 2104a

André Jacques Garnerin, a Frenchman, was the first aeronaut to make a parachute jump from a balloon. He also made the earliest significant ascents in England during the early nineteenth century, the first of which took place on June 28, 1802, in London. The handbill refers to an ascent in 1814 made by Garnerin and a parachute jump made by his wife at Covent Garden. In attendance was Harlequin Whittington, Lord Mayor of London.

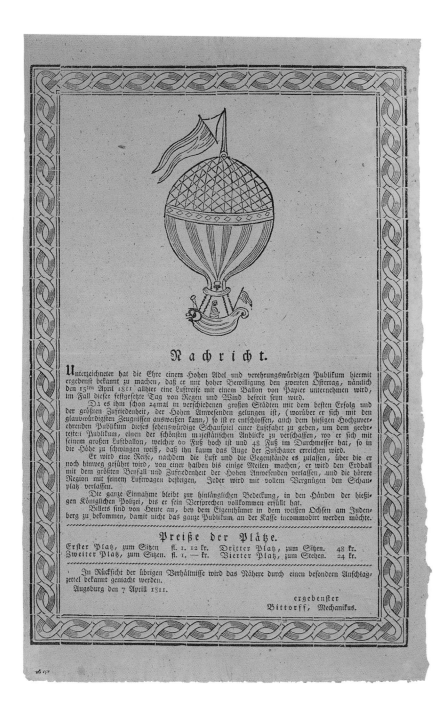

Nachricht [Notice]. Unterzeichneter hat
die Ehre . . . Augsburg, 1811

> Letterpress on blue paper, 36 x 21.5 cm.
> XL-21 2116

This broadside advertises the ascent of H. (or
Sebastian) Bittorf (sometimes "Bittdorf," here
"Bittorff") from Augsburg. On July 16, 1812,
Bittorf perished during his thirtieth ascent,
from Mannheim, his hometown. A Madame
Bittorf, no doubt connected to him, also made
ascents in Germany.

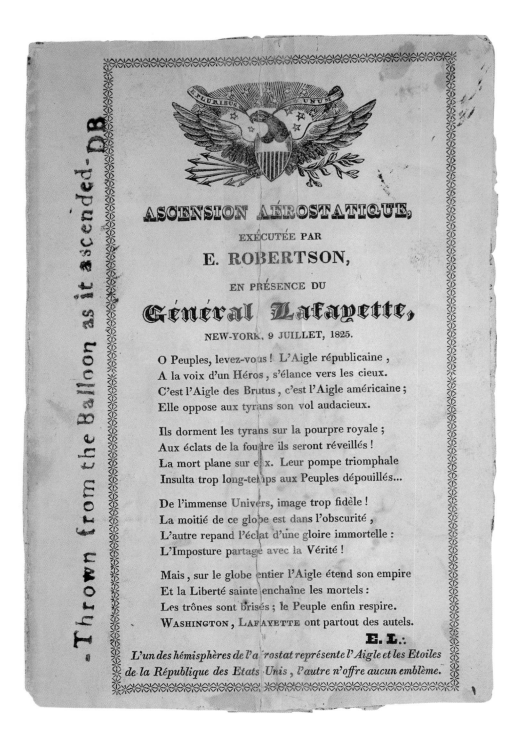

Ascension Aérostatique, Exécutée par E. Robertson en Présence du Géneral Lafayette . . .

Handbill, 12.5 x 18.5 cm.

This handbill announces a flight in honor of the Marquis de Lafayette on July 9, 1825; Eugène Robertson flew from Castle Garden, a pleasure garden located on a small island west of the Battery in New York City. According to Tom Crouch, in *The Eagle Aloft,* Robertson, a Frenchman, and member of one of the great ballooning families of Europe, "planted the seed of an American aerostatic tradition" during his tours of the United States. The poem speaks of flight and democracy, the overthrow of tyrannical government, and the heroism of Lafayette and George Washington.

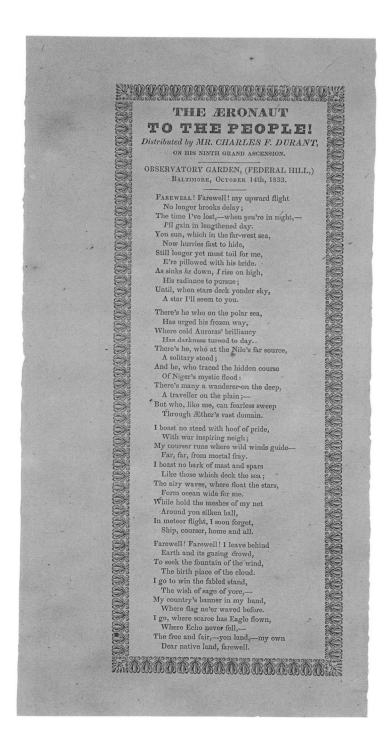

THE ÆRONAUT
TO THE PEOPLE!
Distributed by MR. CHARLES F. DURANT,
ON HIS NINTH GRAND ASCENSION.

OBSERVATORY GARDEN, (FEDERAL HILL,)
BALTIMORE, OCTOBER 14th, 1833.

FAREWELL! Farewell! my upward flight
  No longer brooks delay;
The time I've lost,—when *you're* in night,—
  I'll gain in lengthened day.
Yon sun, which in the far-west sea,
  Now hurries fast to hide,
Still longer yet must toil for me,
  E're pillowed with his bride.
As sinks *he* down, *I* rise on high,
  His radiance to pursue;
Until, when stars deck yonder sky,
  A star I'll seem to you.

There's he who on the polar sea,
  Has urged his frozen way,
Where cold Auroras' brilliancy
  Has darkness turned to day.
There's he, who at the Nile's far source,
  A solitary stood;
And he, who traced the hidden course
  Of Niger's mystic flood:
There's many a wanderer on the deep,
  A traveller on the plain;—
But who, like me, can fearless sweep
  Through Æther's vast domain.

I boast no steed with hoof of pride,
  With war inspiring neigh;
My courser runs where wild winds guide—
  Far, far, from mortal fray.
I boast no bark of mast and spars
  Like those which deck the sea;
The airy waves, where float the stars,
  Form ocean wide for me.
While hold the meshes of my net
  Around yon silken ball,
In meteor flight, I soon forget,
  Ship, courser, home and all.

Farewell! Farewell! I leave behind
  Earth and its gazing crowd,
To seek the fountain of the wind,
  The birth place of the cloud.
I go to win the fabled stand,
  The wish of sage of yore,—
My country's banner in my hand,
  Where flag ne'er waved before.
I go, where scarce has Eagle flown,
  Where Echo never fell,—
The free and fair,—yon land,—my own
  Dear native land, farewell.

The Aeronaut to the People! Distributed by Mr. Charles F. Durant . . . October 14, 1833

Letterpress, 30 x 12.2 cm.
XP-XL-26 2183

This handbill was designed to be dropped from the balloon in which Charles Ferson Durant made his ninth American ascent from Baltimore on October 14, 1833. It contains a long poem in which the poet (uncredited) reflects on leaving earth behind and traveling on the ocean of air. After training in France, Durant had begun making ascents from New York in 1830. He was on the road in 1833 and made ascents in Baltimore on September 26 and October 14. Though Durant retired in 1834 after only thirteen flights, he was important in the history of American ballooning. According to Tom Crouch in *The Eagle Aloft,* Durant "fixed the image of the daring aeronaut in the minds of the American public."

The Aerial Ship! An Interesting Account of the above Stupendous Balloon called "The Eagle" . . . [1835]

Letterpress with wood engraving, 35.6 x 25.5 cm.

Comte de Lennox created this dirigible, which he constructed in 1835 and hoped to fly to Paris from London in six hours, an event that the text of the article announces for the coming August. The dirigible was to be "a direct communication between the several Capitals of Europe." The design includes a bladder contained within the envelope, which would be filled with compressed air and serve as ballast—an idea dating almost to the invention of the balloon but probably reinvented by the Count. The paddles on the sides of the envelope were to be worked by "machinery" contained within the central cabin, although we can assume that the motive force was provided by the arms of the ten crew members. The Count's tenacity is to be lauded, for in the previous year (1834) he had built another airship, which had been destroyed by the crowd when, following a mishap, the ascent was postponed. The 1835 aircraft was built and exhibited but never flown. Gimbel apparently purchased the item already mounted with two other advertisements for *The Eagle*.

DOMINICK A. PISANO

GRAND

NEW BALLOON,

TO BE CALLED

THE VAUXHALL ROYAL BALLOON,

WHICH WILL, WHEN INFLATED WITH COAL GAS, ASCEND WITH

FROM EIGHT TO TEN PERSONS;

AND IF INFLATED WITH PURE HYDROGEN GAS, WITH

28 PERSONS, besides BALLAST & APPARATUS.

The Proprietors of VAUXHALL have the great satisfaction to announce, that after many months of anxiety and labor, this wonderful Machine is at length completed, and will make its FIRST ASCENT

On FRIDAY, the 9th of SEPTEMBER, 1836,

AT FOUR O'CLOCK IN THE AFTERNOON.

This beautiful and stupendous Balloon has been constructed under the immediate superintendance of MR. GREEN, to whom, on account of his great experience and success in Aerostation, (he having made 220 ascents) the Proprietors have, with the utmost confidence, entrusted the sole direction. The Balloon is 157 Feet in circumference; and the extreme height of the whole, when inflated, and with the car attached, will be 80 Feet. It is formed of 2000 yards of crimson and white silk, imported in the raw state from Italy, expressly for the purpose; and is dyed by Messrs. Jaques, and manufactured by Messrs. Soper, of Spitalfields. The method of uniting the gores (the invention of Mr. Green) is by a cement of such a tenacious nature, that when once dry, the joint becomes the strongest part. It contains 70,000 cubic feet of gas. The weight of atmospheric air sufficient to inflate it, is about 5,346 lbs.; and that of the same quantity of pure hydrogen gas, about 364 lbs; the Machine would consequently, if inflated with that gas, have an ascending power of 4,982 lbs.; and allowing 700 lbs. for the weight of silk and apparatus, and 362 lbs. for ballast, would be capable of ascending with 28 persons of the average weight of 140 lbs. each. But Mr. Green in his first experiments in Aerostation, seeing the great expense, difficulty and inconvenience of using pure hydrogen gas, conceived the possibility of substituting carburetted hydrogen or coal gas, such as is used for illumination; and proved the truth of his assertion by ascending with his Balloon inflated with it from the Park, on the day of the coronation of his late Majesty George IV. From that time the use of pure hydrogen has been almost, if not entirely, discontinued, the expense of generating it being six times greater than that of coal gas. The specific gravity of coal gas being considerably greater than that of hydrogen, it gives a Balloon a much smaller ascending power; and the quality of coal used, and the methods employed by different gas companies in its manufacture are so various, (the specific gravity having been found to vary from 340 to 790) that it is impossible to ascertain exactly what would be the power of a Balloon inflated with it. It is, however, calculated that the new Balloon will ascend with from 8 to 10 persons, besides ballast and apparatus; the power varying according to the quality of the gas, the state of the atmosphere, and a variety of causes. As a matter of curiosity, it may be stated, that the inflated silk will sustain an atmospheric pressure of 20,433,600 lbs., or 9,122 tons. The net which entirely envelopes the silk is of hemp, and the car of basket work; the grapple or anchor, is of wrought iron, and will be attached to an elastic Indian rubber cord from the factory of Mr. Sievier. This will prevent in a very great measure, any sudden jirk in stopping the Balloon in rough weather, whereby so many accidents have occurred.

Among the many advantages to be gained from the enormous increase in the dimensions of this Aerostatic Machine, are the following:—A much greater elevation will be attained than hitherto has been, and the long-agitated question decided as to whether there are, at a great altitude, currents of air proceeding in one direction for several months together. This, Mr. GREEN, from many observations he has made, believes to be the case at an altitude where the atmosphere is not acted on by the reflection of the sun's rays from the earth, or dense masses of clouds. Should this theory be found correct, a grand step in the progress of Aerostation will be made. The great power of the Machine, even when inflated with coal gas, will enable scientific gentlemen to ascend with philosophical apparatus, for the purpose of making experiments on Electricity, Pneumatics, Magnetism, &c. or Astronomical Observations, which from the small dimensions of all other Balloons, has been impossible; and this circumstance has caused them to be regarded by scientific men as mere objects of public exhibition. A small chamber to be attached, in place of the car, is about to be constructed for the above purpose, in which from three to six persons can ascend, with ample room and every convenience for experimental apparatus.

It having appeared in a public print that the Proprietors of Vauxhall were about constructing an Aerial Ship, which was intended to be guided through the air, it is proper to state such a plan was never contemplated, the opinion of Mr. Green, and indeed of all other experienced aeronauts, being that that grand desideratum is totally impracticable to any extent.

Gentlemen or Ladies wishing to ascend will be pleased to apply personally at the Gardens.

The Doors will be opened at One o'Clock, and the following Amusements given during the Afternoon:—A CONCERT—THE RAVEL FAMILY'S PERFORMANCES—M. JAVELIE ON THE TIGHT ROPE—THE COLDSTREAM AND QUADRILLE BANDS—DIORAMIC PICTURE OF THE NEW HOUSES OF PARLIAMENT, &c. &c.

DOORS OPEN AT ONE O'CLOCK.   ADMISSION, 2s. 6d.

The Voyages of the ROYAL VAUXHALL BALLOON will not be confined to Ascents in this Country; but arrangements are in progress to visit with it the principal Capitals of Europe.

[Balne, Printer, 38, Gracechurch Street.

Grand New Balloon, to be called Vauxhall Royal Balloon . . . first ascent on Friday, the 9th of September, 1836. Printed by Balne, 38 Gracechurch Street, [London]

Letterpress, 37.4 x 34.2 cm.

XP-XL-12 1404

This broadside describes the many virtues of the *Vauxhall Royal Balloon*, whose large capacity would allow it to ascend to hitherto unattained heights and seek out "currents of air proceeding in one direction for several months together." If such currents were discovered, "a grand step in the progress of Aerostation will be made." The text disclaims the rumor that the balloon would be steerable: "Such a plan was never contemplated . . . the opinion of Mr. Green . . . being that great desideratum is totally impracticable to any extent." The operator of the *Vauxhall Royal*, Charles Green, was one of the most famous of the Victorian-era English balloonists.

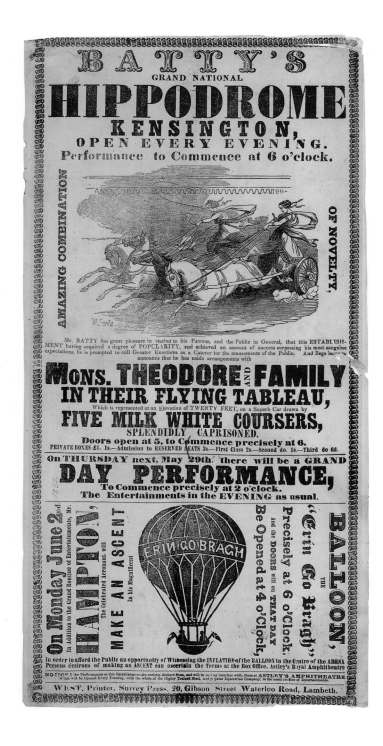

Batty's Grand National Hippodrome, Kensington. With woodcut of balloon, 11 cm., printed by West, 20 Gibson Street, Waterloo Road, Lambeth, London

Handbill, 49.5 x 24.1 cm.

XP-XL-11 1372

This handbill illustrates how the word "flying" was used to attract customers to circus entertainment in the nineteenth century. Conversely, it shows how balloon ascents in a setting like the Hippodrome in the Kensington section of London could become part of the entertainment fare of the day. The hippodrome, an arena for equestrian performance in nineteenth-century parlance, was fashioned after the oval stadium in ancient Greece, which was used for horse racing and chariot racing.

The upper part of the handbill depicts "Mons. Theodore and family in their flying tableau, Which is represented at an Elevation of TWENTY FEET, on a Superb Car drawn by Five Milk White Coursers Splendidly Caprisoned." The lower part announces, "On Monday June 2nd. In Addition to the Grand Routine of Entertainments, Mr. Hampton, The Celebrated Aeronaut, will Make an Ascent in his Magnificent Erin Go Bragh."

Alhier zijn verkrijgbaar: bewijzen van
toegang tot het terrein der opstijging van
den Heer Nadar, met den monsterballon
Le Géant, te Amsterdam . . . 11 Sept. 1865.
[Amsterdam, 1865?]

> Letterpress with line block illustration,
> on yellow paper, 47.8 x 31.8 cm.
>
> XP-XL-13 1467

This poster advertises the flight of *Le Géant*
from Amsterdam in September 1865. *Le Géant*
was constructed by the photographer Nadar
(Gaspard-Félix Tournachon) to finance
research into heavier-than-air flight, which he
believed to be the only viable way of navigating the air. He organized a society (which
included Victor Hugo, Alexander Dumas, Sr.,
Alexander Dumas, Jr., and Jules Verne),
published a *Manifesto* in 1863, and began the
publication of the periodical *L'Aéronaute*. On
October 9, 1863, *Le Géant* ascended from Paris

with fifteen people; its large car was equipped
with a lavatory and carried a printing press
and photographic darkroom. The first flight
ended abruptly at Meaux, about 30 miles from
Paris. The next flight—on October 18—
transported nine people to Hanover in 16
hours. This trip was noted for its disastrous
landing, in which the balloon was dragged
across the country for 6 or 7 miles. Nadar later
made ascents at Brussels, Lyons, Amsterdam,
and Paris but never succeeded in raising any
money with the balloon.

GRAND BALLON CAPTIF
A VAPEUR
DE LA COUR DES TUILERIES
PARIS 1878

Départ d'un Ballon ordinaire de comparaison dans l'enceinte du Ballon captif.

Volume du Ballon captif : 25,000 mètres cubes. — Diamètre de la sphère : 36 mètres. — Hauteur totale de l'aérostat : 55 mètres. — Longueur du câble : 600 mètres. — Poids du treuil où il s'enroule : 42,000 kilogrammes. — Nombre de voyageurs : 35 à 45. — Force des machines à vapeur : 300 chevaux. — Appareil à gaz hydrogène produisant 1,000 à 2,000 mètres cubes de gaz à l'heure.

TOUS LES JOURS ASCENSIONS CAPTIVES DE 10 HEURES A 6 HEURES
EXCEPTÉ LES JOURS DE PLUIE OU DE VENT
Gonflement et Ascension d'un Ballon de comparaison les Dimanches et Jeudis, de 3 heures à 5 heures, si le temps le permet.

22 024. — Typ. Lahure, rue de Fleurus, 9, à Paris.

Grand Ballon captif à vapeur de la Cour des Tuileries Paris 1878. Paris, Typ. Lahure, [1878?]

Handbill, 24 x 19.2 (borderline) on 41 x 26.6 cm. sheet

XE-5-3 3294

This handbill was a souvenir from a 1,300-to 1,800-foot-high flight of a gigantic tethered balloon designed and constructed by Henri Giffard, during the Paris World's Fair. Giffard, a brilliant engineer, had built and flown the world's first successful powered dirigible balloon on September 24, 1852. The enormous *Grand Ballon* held 883,000 cubic feet of hydrogen and could lift 27 tons. It was raised above the city and brought back to earth by means of a steam winch. The balloon's particulars were recorded by Gaston Tissandier, himself a well-known balloonist, in *Le grand ballon captif à vapeur de M. Henri Giffard,* a rare item in the Gimbel collection.

T. S. Baldwin, practical aeronaut, will make one of his grand balloon ascensions in his mammoth air-ship "City of Quincy," Tuesday, August 23 [1887?]. New York. Richard K. Fox, Show Printer and Engraver, Franklin Square, New York

> Handbill, 55 x 20.5 cm.
>
> XL-30 2699

This handbill advertises T. [Thomas] S. Baldwin's balloon, the *City of Quincy,* as "the largest and best gas balloon now in use" and explains that it is "Specially constructed under the immediate supervision of MR. BALDWIN, whose personal attention to detail guarantees that every precaution to insure perfect safety has been attended to." The *City of Quincy* was 72 feet from basket to dome, had a diameter of 46 feet, and could hold 50,000 cubic feet of gas. The flight, which took place on August 23, 1887, was one of a series that Baldwin made at Rockaway Beach in Queens, New York City,

and included a parachute jump from 5,000 feet. A few months earlier, on January 30, at Golden Gate Park in San Francisco, before a crowd of 30,000 people, Baldwin had made the first successful parachute jump on record from a height of 1,000 feet. Baldwin was one of America's most famous aeronauts.

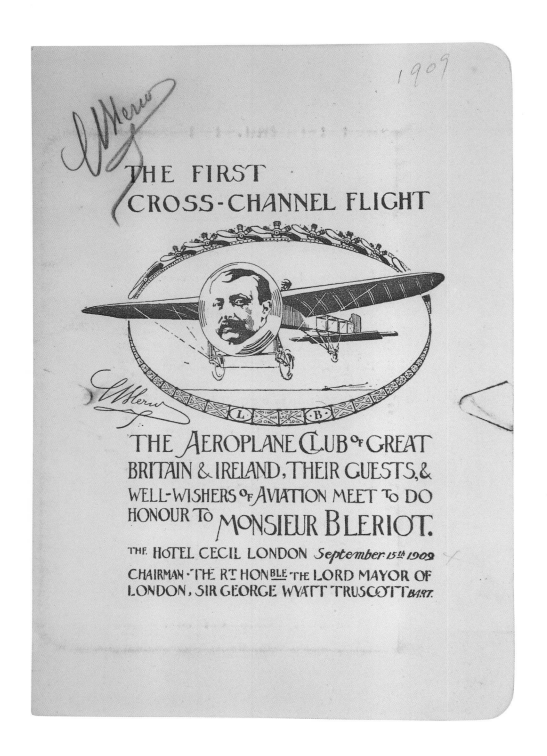

1909

THE FIRST
CROSS-CHANNEL FLIGHT

THE AEROPLANE CLUB OF GREAT
BRITAIN & IRELAND, THEIR GUESTS, &
WELL-WISHERS OF AVIATION MEET TO DO
HONOUR TO MONSIEUR BLERIOT.
THE HOTEL CECIL LONDON September 15th 1909
CHAIRMAN · THE RT HONBLE THE LORD MAYOR OF
LONDON, SIR GEORGE WYATT TRUSCOTT BART.

The Aeroplane Club of Great Britain &
Ireland . . . meet to do honour to Monsieur Bleriot . . . September 15, 1909

Handbill, 9 x 13 cm.

TLB157.G8

A few months after Louis Blériot's historic flight over the English Channel in July 1909, the Aeroplane Club of Great Britain & Ireland met at London's Hotel Cecil to honor Blériot and celebrate his accomplishment. Underneath such typical shows of enthusiasm, however, lay another reality. Blériot's flight brought with it the recognition that England's vaunted insularity could be breached. The French realized this too. Gaston Calmette, editor of *Le Figaro,* observed, "What will become of men's laws, their customs barriers, the vain efforts of their industrial protectionism, their commercial exchanges, their defenses, their relations, their intercourse, on the day when man can, by the action of his will alone, pass in a few hours beyond all horizons across all the oceans and above all the rivers. . . ." Before long, Lord

Northcliffe, whose *Daily Mail* had sponsored the prize money for the Channel crossing, began a campaign to convince the British government of the necessity for the speedy development of a military air arm, an action Alfred Gollin has called "the beginning of air power politics in Britain."

DOMINICK A. PISANO

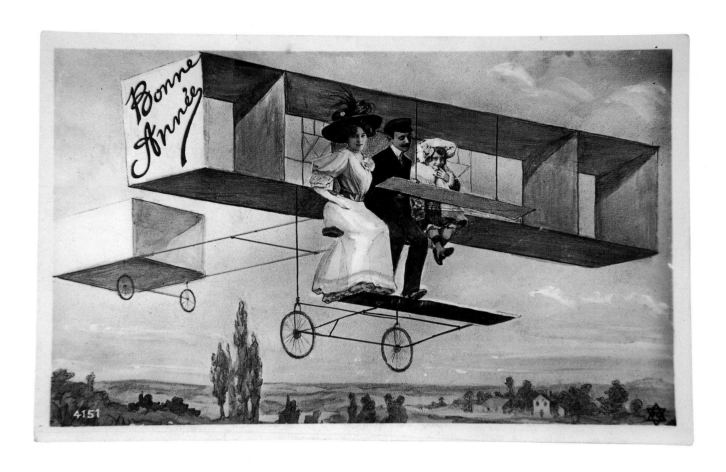

POSTCARDS

[Woman, man, and child sitting in
airplane with greeting "Bonne Année"]
[1908?]

    Postcard, 9 x 14 cm.

This postcard reflects popular European
interest in aeronautics in the early twentieth
century. The greeting is in French ("Happy
New Year"); the man, woman, and child are
sitting in a Voisin-like aircraft.

[Man and woman sitting in airship gondola] Postmark, New York, N.Y., June 25, 1909

Postcard, 8.5 x 13.5 cm.

This postcard reflects popular American interest in aeronautics in the early twentieth century. The couple sits in an airship gondola above New York City. The Brooklyn Bridge is at bottom left.

DOMINICK A. PISANO

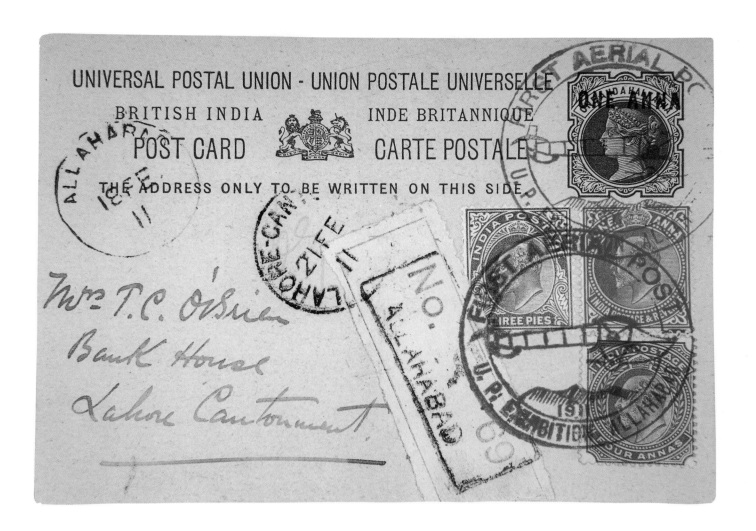

Universal Postal Union, British India, Post Card, February 18, 1911, First aerial post, U.P. Exhibition, Allahabad

Postcard, 8.5 x 12 cm.

This postcard was carried on the world's first official airmail flight by airplane—from Allahabad, India, as part of the United Provinces Industrial and Agricultural Exhibition held in February 1911. After a short flight from Allahabad (postmark February 18, 1911) to Naini, the postcard was conveyed to Lahore (postmark February 21, 1911).

DAS FRANZÖSISCHE LUFTSCHIFF

Das französische Luftschiff [The French airship]. Postmark, Brooklyn, New York, June 28, 1911

Postcard, 9 x 14 cm.

This postcard depicts the Lebaudy-type airship *La Patrie,* built for the French army in 1906. The airship was the largest of its time, more than 200 feet long, with a capacity of 111,250 cubic feet. On maneuvers at Verdun in 1907, while the airship was tied to the ground, a tremendous windstorm arose. Two hundred men labored unsuccessfully to hold the ship down and keep it from being blown away. The giant airship broke free, sailing over France, England, Wales, and part of Ireland, and disappeared over the Atlantic.

DOMINICK A. PISANO

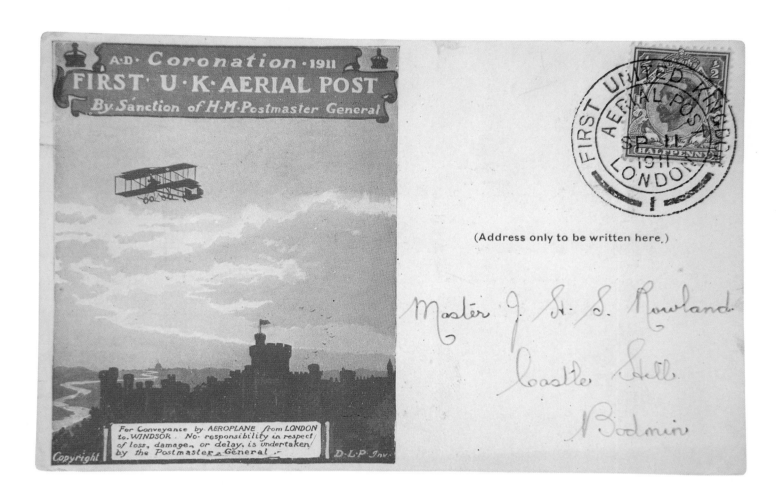

First U.K. Aerial Post, Coronation, A.D. 1911, By Sanction of H.M. Postmaster General

Postcard, 9 x 14 cm.

This postcard (postmark September 11, 1911) was carried on the airpost flights between London and Windsor as part of a celebration of the coronation of H.M. King George V. These airmail flights are commonly known as the British Coronation Aerial Post.

REVOLVING AIR SHIP TOWER
STEEPLECHASE PARK, CONEY ISLAND, N. Y.

Revolving Air Ship Tower, Steeplechase Park, Coney Island, N.Y., undated and unaddressed

Postcard, 8.75 x 14 cm.

This postcard depicts an amusement park ride—a revolving air ship tower constructed at Steeplechase Park—that reflected popular interest in aeronautics at the end of the nineteenth century and beginning of the twentieth. Steeplechase Park was one of three amusement areas that opened between 1897 and 1905 at Coney Island in Brooklyn, New York.

DOMINICK A. PISANO

PROGRAMS

Harvard-Boston Aero Meet. Harvard Aero
Field, Atlantic, Mass. Sept. 3rd to 13th, 1910

Program, 12.4 x 22.7 cm.

TLC71.H 33 1910

The Harvard-Boston Aero Meet took place
September 3–13, 1910, in the village of
Squantum, southeast of Boston. It was the first
large air meet in the eastern United States;
more than $90,000 in prizes and appearance
fees were offered. Ten thousand dollars of that
sum was paid to the British aviator Claude
Grahame-White for winning a 33-mile race
over land and water around Boston Light, an
event that Wilbur Wright and Glenn Curtiss
thought too dangerous to compete in.

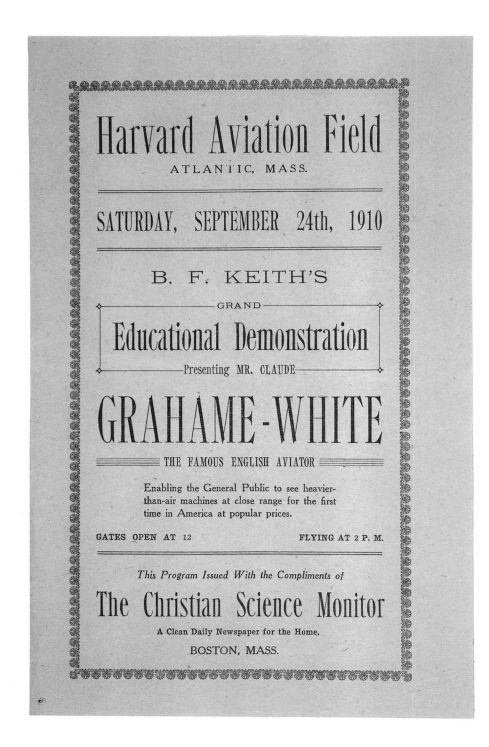

Educational Demonstration Presenting
Mr. Claude Grahame-White, The Famous
English Aviator, Harvard Aviation Field,
Atlantic, Mass., September 24, 1910. Issued
with the compliments of the *Christian
Science Monitor*

Program, 24 x 14.5 cm.

A group of Bostonians offered Claude
Grahame-White, one of Great Britain's foremost early aviators, $50,000 plus expenses to
come to the United States to participate in the
Boston-Harvard Aero Meet (September 3–13,
1910). After the meet, B. F. Keith, a showman,
sponsored a special demonstration on September 24, 1910, in which Grahame-White flew
a Blériot monoplane and a Farman biplane.
The program featured aerial stunts, including
Grahame-White's attempts to dive from 4,000
feet with a dead engine and to beat the world
altitude record of 8,000 feet.

Sheet Music

Early twentieth-century American popular music, a product intended for commercial mass market distribution, often reflects its social and cultural surroundings. Because this was a time when new inventions and discoveries were having a profound effect on society, it is not surprising that popular music of the day would use the airplane as thematic material. Many aeronautical songs written in the early twentieth century are concerned with the airplane's mobility (especially compared with other forms of transportation like the automobile) and escape (for example, the fanciful notion that the flying machine can carry passengers into outer space). The titles presented are primarily early twentieth-century American compositions. However, *Icare,* a French sonnet set to music, and *Aeroplane, or flying machine,* a British waltz dedicated to Samuel F. Cody, reflect popular European interest in the subject.

Won't You Come Up and Spoon in Coey's Balloon. Words by Victor H. Smalley. Music by Bernie Adler. Chicago: Smalley & Adler, 1908.

> Sheet music, 5 p., 28 x 35.5 cm.
> XK-24-2 3420

The title of the song refers to the balloon *Chicago,* which belonged to Charles Andrew Coey, president of the Federation of American Aero Clubs and the Aeronautique Club of Chicago. According to Tom Crouch in *The Eagle Aloft,* the *Chicago* "stood ten stories tall and was perhaps the largest envelope flown in the United States" during the first decade of the twentieth century.

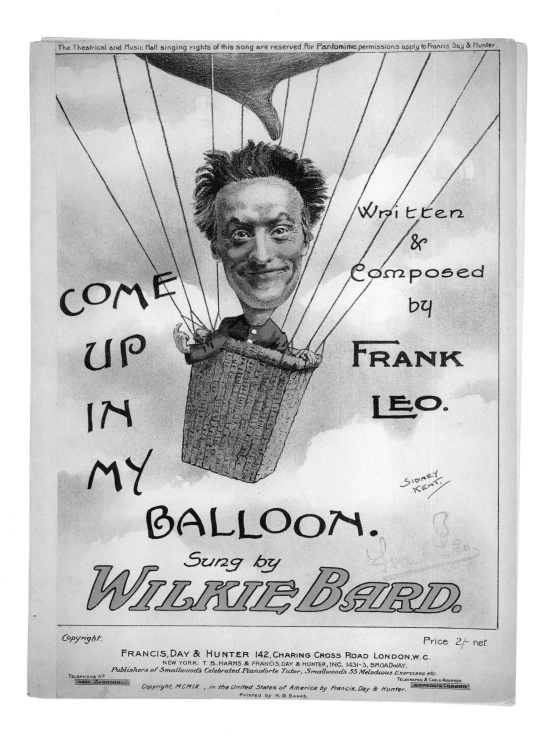

Come Up in My Balloon. Written and composed by Frank Leo. Sung by Wilkie Bard. London: Francis, Day and Hunter, 1909.

Sheet music, 4 p., 26 x 36 cm.

XK-24-2 3427

Come Up in My Balloon is an early twentieth-century song that compares aerial conveyances with other forms of transportation (motors, sailing yachts and floaters, and electric omnibuses) but opts for the joy of flying ("Give me aer-ial nav-i-ga-tion, I am caus-ing a sen-sa-tion With my cheap bal-loon excursions up to Mars").

Up in My Flying Machine. Words by Charles Saxby. Music by Phil Kaufman. Los Angeles: Southern California Music Co., 1910.

> Sheet music, 5 p., 27 x 36 cm.
> XK-24-2 3686

This 1910 song was dedicated to Dick Ferris, originator of the Los Angeles Aero Meet at Dominguez Field in 1910. Like other aeronautical songs of the period, it begins with lyrics about the automobile ("with a chauf-feur smart and a gas go cart and a coup-le of extra ti-res") but quickly focuses attention on the airplane, which enables one to escape earth's boundaries and leave the clouds far below as "on the trails of air we go."

Come Josephine in My Flying Machine (Up She Goes!). Words by Alfred Bryan. Music by Fred Fischer. New York: Maurice Shapiro, 1910.

Sheet music, 5 p., 26 x 34.5 cm.

XK-24-2 1536

Come Josephine in My Flying Machine (Up She Goes!) has been called the most popular aeronautical song ever written and often appears as background music in films about early aviation. Its connection with popular songs about the telephone (*Hello Central, Give Me Heaven* by Charles K. Harris) and the automobile (*In My Merry Oldsmobile* by Vincent P. Bryan and Gus Edwards) indicates that late nineteenth and early twentieth-century technologies were favorite topics for tunesmiths.

A Hundred Years from Now. By Caddigan, Brennan and Story. Boston: O. E. Story, 1914.

Sheet music, 5 p., 27 x 34 cm.

XK-24-2 1539

This 1914 sheet music cover depicts a gnome-like figure gazing through a spyglass at a fanciful city beyond. The city, a projection of what life might be like in 2014 (as the song's title suggests, "A Hundred Years from Now"), shows more than a dozen flying machines, including what looks like a huge aerial yacht. Although there is no mention of flying machines in the song's lyrics, there is speculation about the pace of life a century into the future: "I won-der what kind of a life they'll lead A hun-dred years from now? I won-der what's go-ing to be the speed A hun-dred years from now."

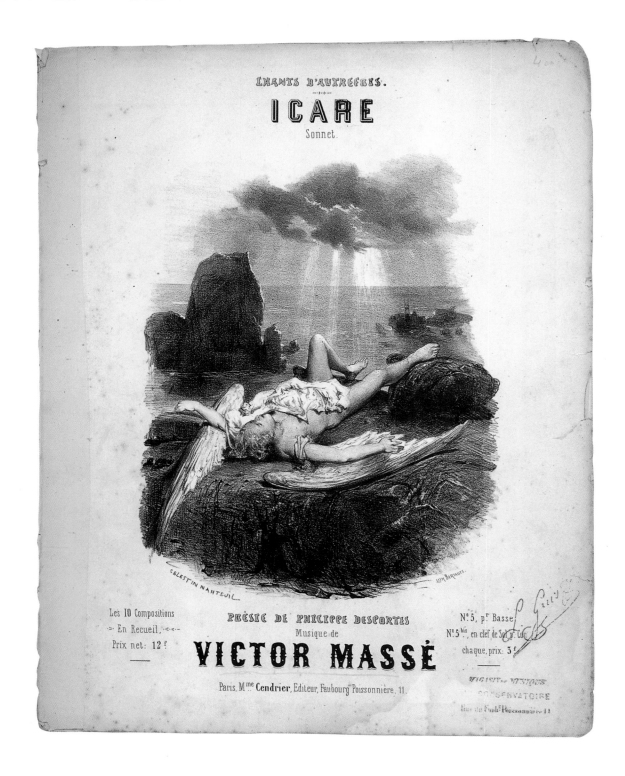

Icare. Poésie de Philippe Desportes. Musique de Victor Massé. Paris: Cendrier, [*ca.* 1840?].

> Sheet music 5 p., 27 x 35 cm.
> XK-24-2 1556

This French sonnet (literally, "little song") is based on the Greek legend of Daedalus and Icarus. It is, as Charles Gibbs-Smith has pointed out in *Aviation: An Historical Survey,* "the modern airman's legend par excellence." Having constructed the Cretan labyrinth for King Minos, Daedalus, an inventor and patron of craftsmen and artists, incurred the king's wrath. To escape from Crete, he constructed wings fastened with wax for his son Icarus and himself. Daedalus warned Icarus not to fly near the sun. Icarus disobeyed, and the sun melted the wax that anchored his wings, causing him to plunge to his death in the sea. The sonnet is an Italian verse form consisting of fourteen lines, typically of iambic pentameter in English, or *alexandrine* (iambic hexameter) in French, rhyming to a determined scheme. The illustration shows the dead or dying Icarus lying on rocks, while streams of light pass through ominous dark clouds.

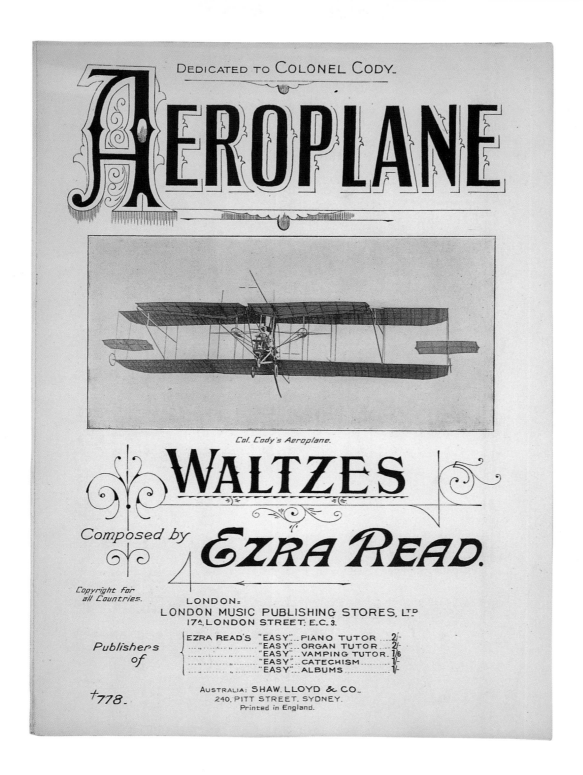

Aeroplane. By Ezra Read. London: Music Publishing Stores, Ltd., no date.

Sheet music, 7 p., 26 x 35.5 cm.

XK-24-2 1555

This waltz-tempo composition is dedicated to Col. Samuel F. Cody, a photograph of whose aircraft is on the cover. Cody was a flamboyant Texan who had been a cowboy, gold prospector, and Wild West showman. On October 16, 1908, he made the first officially recognized heavier-than-air flight in Great Britain in his British Army Aeroplane No. 1 at the Farnborough Balloon Factory.

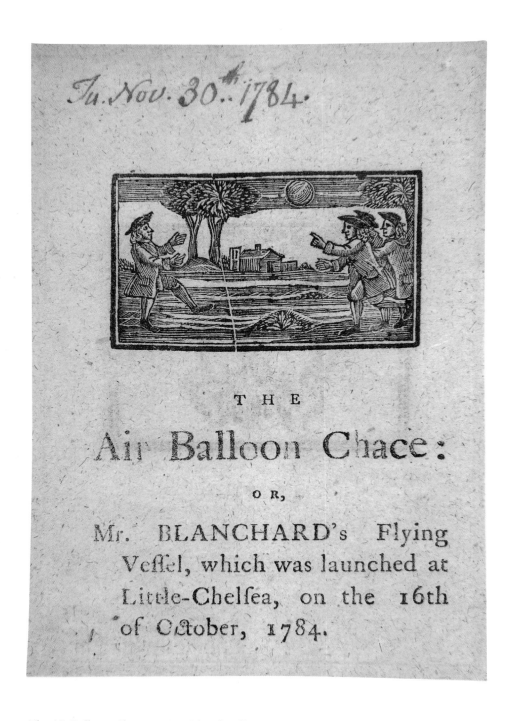

The Air Balloon Chace: or, Mr. Blanchard's
Flying Vessel, which was launched at Little-
Chelsea, on the 16th of October, 1784

    Engraving, 9.5 x 13.5 cm.

    TLB 276.B6

The illustration and text on the ticket refer to a
balloon flight made by Jean-Pierre Blanchard
and Dr. John Sheldon, an anatomist, on
October 16, 1784. This flight, which took place
at Lochee's Military Academy, was attended by
250,000 spectators, some of whom arrived in
approximately 2,000 carriages. Blanchard and
Sheldon made three attempts before ascending
successfully. J. E. Hodgson described the voyage
in *The History of Aeronautics in Great Britain:*
"Having cleared the neighbouring buildings, a
north-westerly breeze carried the balloon . . .
over Hammersmith, Chiswick, and Twicken-
ham, from which point the descent was gradual,
until a landing was made near the seat of Lord
Vere at Sunbury." Here Sheldon got down from
the balloon, and Blanchard continued alone,
landing at Romney, 73 miles from London. The
handwriting on the ticket refers to a balloon
flight made by Jean-Pierre Blanchard and John
Jeffries on Tuesday, November 30, 1784.

Vincenzo Lunardi Lucchese, Anfiteatro Corèa, Viglietto de' Sig.[ri] Contribuenti, pè l globo aereostatico, 8 Luglio 1788

Ticket with engraving, 11.5 x 7.5 cm.

XB-7-11 2806

This engraved ticket, which contains a portrait of Lunardi, was issued for a July 8, 1788 ascension, although there is no indication as to where the flight took place. Lunardi, an Italian reportedly born in Lucca on January 11, 1759, was secretary to the Neapolitan ambassador to the Court of St. James. He made the first manned balloon flight in Great Britain on September 15, 1784, and quickly established himself as one of Europe's most famous aeronauts. He died on a tour of Portugal on July 31, 1806, at the age of forty-seven.

Grande Semaine Aéronautique de la Champagne [The Champagne region's great aviation week], Reims, du 22 au 29 Août 1909

> Ticket, 7 x 9 cm.
> TLB157.G8

This cork-shaped ticket admitted the bearer to the world's first air meet held at Reims, France, from August 22 to August 29, 1909. Sponsored by the city of Reims and France's most renowned champagne houses, each of whom contributed 200,000 francs for prizes in speed, distance, altitude, and passenger carrying. James Gordon Bennett, American sportsman, expatriate, and publisher of the *New York Herald* and its European edition, the Paris *Herald,* donated the most prestigious award, the Coupe Internationale d'Aviation (International Aviation Cup, or Gordon Bennett Cup), a silver trophy that was presented along with 25,000 francs in cash.

Although marred by rain and mud, the Reims meet played host to the most famous names in French aviation manufacturing, including Voisin, Blériot, Farman, Antoinette, and the American aviator Glenn Curtiss, and was attended by the elite society of France and America. On the next-to-last day of the meet, Curtiss thrilled the crowd of spectators by beating Louis Blériot for the Gordon Bennett Cup by 6 seconds.

DOMINICK A. PISANO

International Aviation Tournament, 1910, Belmont Park, Long Island, U.S.A., Good for One Admission to Field [October 26, 27, 29, 30]

> Ticket, 11 x 6.5 cm.
>
> XB-7-11 2830, 2831, 2832, 2833

These tickets admitted the holder to the air meet held at Belmont Park Race Track on Long Island in October 1910. The meet's main event was the 100 kilometer (60-mile) Gordon Bennett Cup Race on October 29, won by Britain's top pilot Claude Grahame-White, with a time of 61 minutes, 4.74 seconds. This was the second time the trophy would be awarded (the first was at Reims in 1909) and the first time it was given in America.

The final event of the meet, a 33-mile race across New York City to the Statue of Liberty and back, evoked a bitter dispute. John Moisant was declared the winner although he had begun the race 21 minutes after the starting deadline. An angry Grahame-White lodged a complaint with the Fédération Aéronautique Internationale (F.A.I.) in Paris. Later, the F.A.I. overturned the judges' decision and awarded Grahame-White the $10,000 prize plus interest.

Engraved for the European Magazine.
The Descent of the Air Balloon.

Monsieur de Montgolfiers Air Balloon, after having Ascended an Amazeing heighth above the Clouds & being Carried in the Air 45 Leagues, fell down near a Cottage, where the poor Country People were exceedingly frightend & Astonishd, the Cock, Sheep, & the Duck, came out of the Basket which had been tyed to it unhurt.

Published Decr 1. 1783 by J. Fielding. Pater Noster Row.

OTHER ITEMS OF INTEREST

The Descent of the Air Balloon. A cartoon representation of the sheep, duck, and cock coming out of the basket. Engraving by J. Lodge, 1783

Engraving, 17.8 x 12.7 cm.

At Versailles, on September 19, 1783, before a large crowd that included King Louis XVI of France, Étienne Montgolfier launched a balloon that contained the first air travelers— a sheep, a duck, and a rooster. The balloon rose to a height of 1,700 feet. While it was descending, the cage containing the animals caught the branch of a tree. The door of the cage was jarred open and the animals escaped. The sheep and duck were unharmed, but the rooster had injured its wing during the journey, prompting some to question the future safety of humans in flight.

The text of the cartoon engraving seems to take no notice of the injury to the rooster: "Monsieur de Montgolfier's air balloon, after having ascended an amazing height above the clouds and being carried by the wind into the air 45 leagues, fell down near a cottage, where the poor country people were exceedingly frightened and astonished. The cock, sheep and the duck came out of the basket which had been tyed to it unhurt."

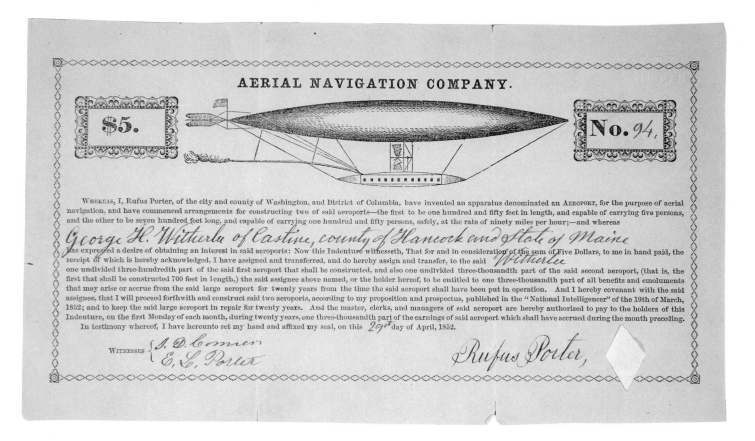

AERIAL NAVIGATION COMPANY.

$5.

No. 94.

Whereas, I, Rufus Porter, of the city and county of Washington, and District of Columbia, have invented an apparatus denominated an AEROPORT, for the purpose of aerial navigation, and have commenced arrangements for constructing two of said aeroports—the first to be one hundred and fifty feet in length, and capable of carrying five persons, and the other to be seven hundred feet long, and capable of carrying one hundred and fifty persons, safely, at the rate of ninety miles per hour;—and whereas

George H. Witherlee of Castine, county of Hancock and State of Maine

has expressed a desire of obtaining an interest in said aeroports: Now this Indenture witnesseth, That for and in consideration of the sum of Five Dollars, to me in hand paid, the receipt of which is hereby acknowledged, I have assigned and transferred, and do hereby assign and transfer, to the said *Witherlee* one undivided three-hundredth part of the said first aeroport that shall be constructed, and also one undivided three-thousandth part of the said second aeroport, (that is, the first that shall be constructed 700 feet in length,) the said assignee above named, or the holder hereof, to be entitled to one three-thousandth part of all benefits and emoluments that may arise or accrue from the said large aeroport for twenty years from the time the said aeroport shall have been put in operation. And I hereby covenant with the said assignee, that I will proceed forthwith and construct said two aeroports, according to my proposition and prospectus, published in the "National Intelligencer" of the 19th of March, 1852; and to keep the said large aeroport in repair for twenty years. And the master, clerks, and managers of said aeroport are hereby authorized to pay to the holders of this Indenture, on the first Monday of each month, during twenty years, one three-thousandth part of the earnings of said aeroport which shall have accrued during the month preceding. In testimony whereof, I have hereunto set my hand and affixed my seal, on this 29th day of April, 1852.

WITNESSES { I. D. Commen / E. L. Porter

Rufus Porter,

Aerial Navigation Company. Stock certificate, April 29, 1852, Washington, D.C., issued to George H. Witherlee

Stock certificate, 12 x 20 cm.

XF-2-1 2433

Rufus Porter's career was varied to say the least. For fifty years, after he abandoned school teaching in 1813, he was, according to Tom Crouch, in *The Eagle Aloft*, "a poet, dancing master, shoemaker, machinist, printer, and journalist." In 1845, he founded *Scientific American*. His career as an aeronautical entrepreneur, however, included the design of an "aeroport," a cigar-shaped balloon with a gondola slung underneath that would carry crew and passengers. In 1852, optimistic that he could turn his idea for the aeroport into a practical aerial conveyance, he issued stock in the Aerial Navigation Company. The Gimbel collection has certificate number 94 for $5.00, issued to George H. Witherlee of Maine.

Reims Air Meet, 1909

Stereograph slides, b&w

This stereograph (photographic images designed to produce a three-dimensional effect when used with a stereoscopic viewer) of the 1909 air meet at Reims is one of forty in the Gimbel collection.

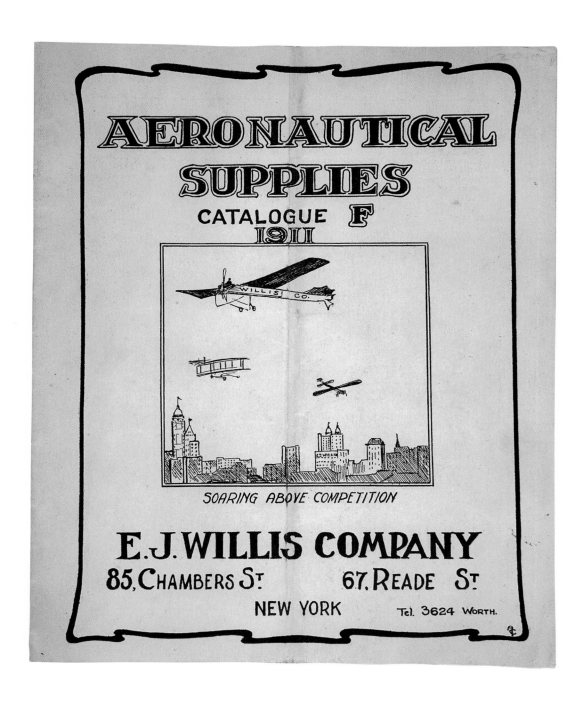

Aeronautical Supplies Catalogue F 1911

Catalogue, 18 x 22 cm.

The E. J. Willis Company, which had two locations (85 Chambers Street and 67 Reade Street) in New York City, sold aeronautical supplies of various kinds. Willis accepted only cash and C.O.D. and offered to pay transportation charges on items priced at $10 or more ("exclusive of Woodwork, Oils and Greases") to places within 5 miles of New York and on items priced at $50 or more to places within 100 miles. Willis sold everything from ailerons to wheels, including aviators' apparel, and complete Blériot, Farman, or Curtiss-type aircraft.

1

2

1. Wine Taster
The Montgolfier brothers are commemorated on the medallion enclosed in this French silver wine taster.

2. Watch
Engraving on the back of this silver watch case honors the May 4, 1814 balloon flight of Madame Marie Blanchard.

3. Box
Five miniature watercolor paintings adorn the top and sides of this pewter box. The largest, on the top, depicts the September 1783 Montgolfier balloon flight which carried a sheep, a duck, and a rooster.

4. Box
The September 1783 Montgolfier balloon flight is also depicted in a Capelle watercolor, mounted in an exquisitely crafted cylindrical wood box.

5. Cream Pitcher
A whimsical depiction of two bears escaping from a balloon graces this 1906 china cream pitcher. The caption reads, "They slid down ropes and hit the ground | And landed in Chicago safe and sound."

6. Ornament
A 15 watt "Kentucky" brand light bulb was transformed into a doll-carrying balloon ornament by an imaginative early twentieth-century crochet artist.

5

6

DOMINICK A. PISANO

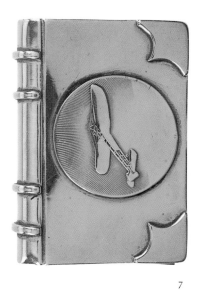

7

8

9

7. Cigarette Lighter

The Blériot Model X1 monoplane, in 1909 the first powered flying machine to cross the English Channel, graces this silver cigarette lighter.

8. Earthenware Plate

The unsuccessful 1784 attempt by Guyton de Morveau and the Abbé Bertrand to steer a balloon by the use of sails is depicted on this earthenware plate by an unknown artist.

9. China Plates (pair)

In 1840, on this rare pair of gilded china plates, the French painter, J. Siquier, captured the flights of the Robert brothers, Jean and Noel, and M. Colin; and Jean-Pierre Blanchard with Dom Pêche.

10. Fan

Romance and ballooning are paired on this nineteenth-century ivory and paper fan.

10

Cylinder seal picturing a
winged genius dominating two
mixed beings (Page 320)

Seals

ELLEN MORRIS AND HOLLY PITTMAN

LTHOUGH MOST OF THE MAJOR MONUMENTS of architecture and visual arts of the ancient civilizations of the Near East have long been buried under vast piles of melted mud brick, cylinder and stamp seals record for us in images and in texts some of the details of the lives of individuals who lived millennia ago. Because seals are small and made of durable materials, a good number of them have survived. The earliest seals, dating to around the sixth millennium B.C.E. (before the invention of pottery), were shaped stones whose flat surface was engraved with figures of animals or abstract designs. Seals are also referred to as glyptic art because their imagery is carved or engraved. In each seal, a hole was drilled for suspension. The engraved design was impressed many times on clay masses that had been put over strings that were used to close boxes, baskets, and leather bags.

We do not know for certain what specific meaning the engraved images carried, but we think that they were part of an administrative system that helped ancient people to monitor the exchange and the production of things necessary for survival—foodstuffs, clothes, raw materials. The cylindrical shape of seals was invented somewhere in the cradle of civilization in southern Mesopotamia in the land of Sumer lying between the Tigris and the Euphrates Rivers, which is today known as Iraq. The cylinder seal was invented around 3400 B.C.E. along with that seminal creation of humanity—writing. Like the stamp seals, designs were carved around the vertical edges of cylinder seals and these designs were impressed on clay locks and clay tablets inscribed with cuneiform sign. They served for more than 3,000 years much as a seal or a signature does today: a guarantee that the content of a document has been accepted or that the contents of a package passed inspection. These designs were most often images of gods in the Sumerian and Akkadian pantheon and images of rulers and military leaders. Frequently seals would be inscribed with the name and the title of the seal owner, and in some cases the political authority to which he was responsible. In addition to their administrative importance, seals were potent magical amulets that protected the owner from harm.

The Colonel Richard Gimbel Aeronautical History Collection at the Air Force Academy Library has a fine selection of more than a dozen cylinder seals and two stamp seals from the civilizations of Sumer, Akkad, Babylon, and Assyria. Colonel Gimbel was surely drawn to these ancient stones because they are engraved with images of both real and mythical flying creatures. Indeed, the first seal described in this section depicts an Anzu bird, the mythical eagle that flew to the heavens with a man on its back. The seals range in date from the early part of the third millennium B.C.E. through the seventh century C.E. The catalogue entries describe the imagery carved on the seals and recorded in the photograph of the modern clay impression. In addition, the entries attempt to set those pictorial stories into the wider context of the civilizations that made them.

Cylinder seal with hero dominating caprids

Southern Mesopotamia: *ca.* 2700 B.C.E.
Chalcedony quartz. h: 15.5 mm. d: 12 mm.
For comparison: Frankfort Xc; Ashmolean 157

A kneeling bald male figure, nude except for his belt, suspends two horned caprids by their hind legs. Separating this repeating motif on the rolled-out impression is an eagle with wings and legs outstretched. In the Early Dynastic period (*ca.* 2900–2350 B.C.E.) of Sumerian culture, depictions of a naked hero subduing various beasts are frequent. Heroes who wear belts, as does the figure in this seal, may have represented a recognizable mythic individual or perhaps category of individuals to the ancient audience. It is significant that nude, belted men are likewise represented in three-dimensional media at this time.

The eagle, frequently found in Early Dynastic glyptic art, is also a popular personality in Sumerian and Akkadian mythology—often cast in the role of a haughty and ambivalent character. It was the Anzu bird, described and depicted as an eagle or, more frequently,

as a lion-headed eagle, who stole the tablets of life from the god Enlil. In the myth of Etana, a quarrelsome eagle assists the hero in his search for a fertility-inducing plant. Both myths apparently served as subject matter for a small number of Akkadian seals some 200 years later. Whether the eagle in Early Dynastic glyptic art is related to the eagles of Sumerian and Akkadian mythology remains unknown.

Parallel interior hatching, such as is employed here on the caprids and the eagle, is characteristic of an Early Dynastic II artistic style. The summary treatment of the human head, with its primary emphasis being the eye, and the lack of definition within the body are other markers of the period. Significant, too, are the bent legs of the eagle, which are rarely found represented in such a fashion after the Early Dynastic period.

ELLEN MORRIS & HOLLY PITTMAN

Cylinder seal with a hero and lions attacking a caprid

Southern Mesopotamia: *ca.* 2500 B.C.E.
Pale limestone. h: 35 mm. d: 18 mm.
For comparison: Collon 83; Frankfort XIIc

Two rampant lions bite into the haunch of a suspended caprid. To the left of this group is a bird, which, by analogy to its contemporary parallels, should likely be restored with a lion's head. Crossing behind the lion to the right is a more immediately fortunate caprid who is grasped by a naked hero, probably originally possessing flame-like curls. This character was thought by several scholars at the beginning of the century to represent Gilgamesh, but this theory is too speculative to gain much currency in modern discussion.

Seals of the Early Dynastic III period (*ca.* 2500–2350 B.C.E.) frequently depicted the contest scene. At this time, many Sumerian city-states had developed into small kingdoms. The names of rulers are deciphered in contemporary script, and at Ur an extremely rich royal cemetery was discovered in the 1920s. When the names of royal males occur

on seals, it is almost always the contest scene that is presented, the banquet scene being most frequently associated with royal women. Indeed, examples of these two genres are among the best modeled seals of the period and are occasionally found carved in lapis lazuli—a stone almost certainly imported from Afghanistan. Limestone and shell are also used for this style of glyptic.

This sophisticated version of the theme of the nude hero with animals stems from an earlier tradition, as may be appreciated when this seal is compared to the preceding one. The patterning of the suspended caprid and the upturned legs of the bird are artistic holdovers from the glyptic style of the Early Dynastic II period. The frontal view of the lions' faces and their tufting manes, however, are new developments and are significant for dating the scene.

Two-register cylinder seal with lions, birds, and a scorpion

Southern Mesopotamia: *ca.* 2500 B.C.E.

Black serpentine. h: 29 mm. d: 10 mm.

For comparison: Collon 911; Buchanan 239

On the upper register of this seal, two peculiar schematic birds hover above lions whose heads are raised and turned to look behind. Separating the repeating pairs is a scorpion, which faces downward, its pincerlike claws nearly brushing the ground-line and its tail extending in an arc above. In the narrower register below, four birds walk in a line. Crescent moons float above three of the birds.

The creatures selected by the artist were certainly not random. As two of the most fearsome and regal beasts of ancient Mesopotamia, the lion and the eagle served as potent talismans for the seal owner. Scorpions shared this dangerous and protective potential and possessed, as well, connections both to healing and to celestial forces. The depiction of the creature that hovers above the lion is

unusual. Although there are renderings of two-headed eagles and lion-headed eagles that may serve perhaps as parallels, none is entirely convincing. Whether the neck of this animal commences in two separate heads facing in opposite directions or whether the head is to be understood as schematized into two gigantic eyes remains unclear.

Dividing the glyptic field into registers was common in the later Early Dynastic period, while the use of the animal file as subject matter harkens back to the Late Uruk and Jemdet Nasr traditions of *ca.* 3200–2900 B.C.E. This type of compact and highly stylized art served as the inspiration for some regional styles as late as the beginning of the Ur III period, around 2100 B.C.E.

ELLEN MORRIS & HOLLY PITTMAN

Cylinder seal with a suppliant goddess leading a worshipper before storm god

Southern Mesopotamia: *ca.* 2000 B.C.E.

Black hematite. h: 26 mm. d: 15 mm.

For comparison: Tessier 109; Collon 153

A worshipper in a fringed gown is led by a suppliant goddess Lama into the presence of the storm deity, Adad, or Ishkur, who stands in the "ascending position" with one leg bare and rests his foot upon a symbolic mountain. The god holds a lion-headed scepter. This lion motif is further emphasized in the decoration of the cultic stand separating the god from his visitors; the creatures at the base of the stand are winged lion-dragons, totems of the god, and symbolic forms of the storm. A rectangular frame, enclosing an inscription too faint to be read, is positioned behind the storm god. Above the goddess Lama hangs a crescent moon. The popularity of the latter deity, in her role as mediator between the gods and humankind, is attested by her frequent manifestation in the visual arts.

During the Ur III period, after Sumerian rulers had regained control of southern Mesopotamia from the mountain tribes of the east, artistic themes became exceedingly pious.

The presentation scene, in which a worshipper is led before a deity (or perhaps its cult statue) by a goddess (or a priestess in the guise of a goddess), developed in the Akkadian period, became dominant in the Neo-Sumerian period, and survived to succeeding ages. In this particular seal, the worshipper's hatched headgear and beard betray his non-Sumerian character. Likewise, the weather god's pose and attributes are not traditional in the Ur III repertoire. The fact that the goddess still stands before the mortal, instead of behind him with arms raised, however, is evidence that the Ur III kingdom is not long fallen. This seal appears to date to the early Isin-Larsa period of competing, often Amorite, dynasties.

Hematite first became popular as a material for seals in the Ur III period and later became almost ubiquitous. According to an Assyrian dream book, "a man shall lose what he has acquired" if he dreams of a hematite seal.

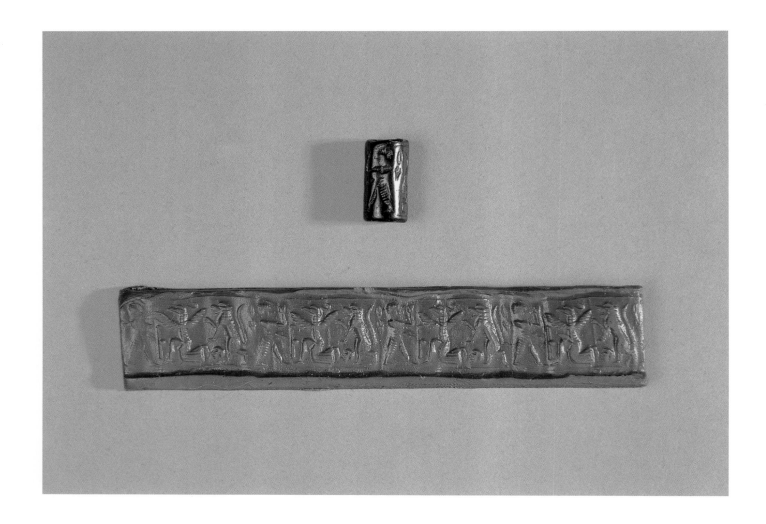

Cylinder seal with a man and Old Syrian creatures

Syria: *ca.* 1920–1840 B.C.E.

Black serpentine. h: 13 mm. d: 6.5 mm.

For comparison: Buchanan 1182; Ashmolean 899a

A robed male figure with right arm raised faces a kneeling, bird-headed griffin. The latter possesses wings instead of arms, but exhibits fully human legs and wears an open garment. A curling feathered lock may be seen on its head. Free-floating between this pair is a "ball-and-staff," and low in the register, behind the left foot of the griffin, is an isolated lion's head. A full-bodied rampant lion stands behind, facing in the same direction. The last element in the design is either the disembodied head of a hare or a motif of unknown significance.

The Old Syrian and the Syro-Cappadocian glyptic styles of the early nineteenth century coincided with the emergence of Old Assyrian presence in northern Syria. At this time Assyria became involved in long-distance trade with Anatolia, exchanging textiles and tin for silver and gold. Due to far-flung trading contacts, the Old Syrian style became widespread, and elements of its iconography are

still to be traced in the Neo-Assyrian art of the seventh century B.C.E. Indeed, the winged, eagle-headed genius, so ubiquitous in the palaces of Nimrud and Khorsabad, has its prototype in the griffin portrayed here. In later times this figure is a markedly benevolent force who seems particularly concerned with the tending and purification of the king and the sacred tree. The "ball-and-staff" is a filler motif, which was very popular in the Old Babylonian period (*ca.* 1800–1600 B.C.E.). It seems to be especially connected in glyptic art with the "nude goddess" and the "man with the mace"—both presumably Amorite imports to the Babylonian pantheon.

Stylistically, this glyptic period is characterized by curvilinear forms, a high degree of modeling, and many filling devices of unknown meaning. The armless griffin in his robe and the rampant, leaning lion are frequently represented in this art.

Cylinder seal with two winged bulls frolicking

Assyria: *ca.* 8th century B.C.E.

Black serpentine. h: 32.5 mm. d: 15 mm.

For comparison: Frankfort 35h; Pittman 63

Two winged bulls are glimpsed in mid-gallop as they gambol through a cosmic landscape. Although the linear style in which they are defined is fairly schematic, details such as the rib cage and the individual wing feathers are clearly defined. The tails of the bulls curve downward, and the horns are seen in side view—a naturalistic solution not always followed in ancient Near Eastern art. Seven stars, a common representation of the Pleiades, hover protectively over one bull, while two crescent moons are suspended above the second. Separating this repeating image is a star and a rhomb; a linear border frames the scene top and bottom.

As an artistic motif, the winged bull became especially popular in the Middle and Neo-Assyrian periods. During these periods the bulls may have been viewed as the wilder cousins of the beneficent *lamassu,* human-headed winged bulls who guarded the entranceways of Neo-Assyrian palaces. More importantly, however, in Middle Assyrian and early Neo-Assyrian art, winged bulls are frequently connected with celestial elements, particularly with the Pleiades. This association is not surprising as the second month of the Babylonian year (our mid-April to mid-May) shared both the winged "Bull of Heaven" (later known as Taurus) and the Pleiades as its marked constellations. Because a knowledge of the stars was thought to allow the ancient astronomers access to divine messages, astrology was of utmost importance to official and popular religion in the first millennium.

Originating in Middle Assyrian glyptic, this linear style was common in the ninth and eighth centuries B.C.E. The arched necks and curved tails of the bulls may indicate the later date is to be preferred. The dark serpentine stone, the linear bordering, and the seal's relatively tall and thin shape are further evidences of Neo-Assyrian date of manufacture.

Cylinder seal picturing a winged genius dominating two mixed beings

Assyria: *ca.* 8th–7th century B.C.E.
Pink carnelian. h: 22 mm. d: 12 mm.
For comparison: Frankfort 36e; Forte 50

A supernatural personage with four wings and a partially open robe grasps the forelegs of two rampant mixed creatures whose faces are turned in opposite directions. Standing just to the left of the scene, as if observing it, is a small man in a full robe. Above this figure is what appears to be a winged sun disc. A star and crescent moon hang suspended in the firmament.

The winged male figure in this scene is perhaps to be identified with the *apkallu,* a category of semi-divine, antediluvian sages who are particularly connected with magic and arcane knowledge. *Apkallu* are variously represented as anthropomorphic and winged, as eagle-headed, or as garbed in the skin of a fish. The former category of being is closely associated with the Assyrian king in palace relief.

In this period the winged sun disc perhaps indicates Assur, patron deity of the empire.

Neo-Assyrian and Neo-Babylonian glyptic styles are often difficult to distinguish because they often tend to draw upon a shared corpus of artistic themes and motifs. Although the four wings of the anthropomorphic figure are Babylonian-inspired, we think Neo-Assyrian artists represented the upper set of wings as being shorter than the lower—as is the case in this seal. The pose of the central male is dubbed "master of the animals" and finds its origins in the protohistoric times of the mid-fourth millennium B.C.E.

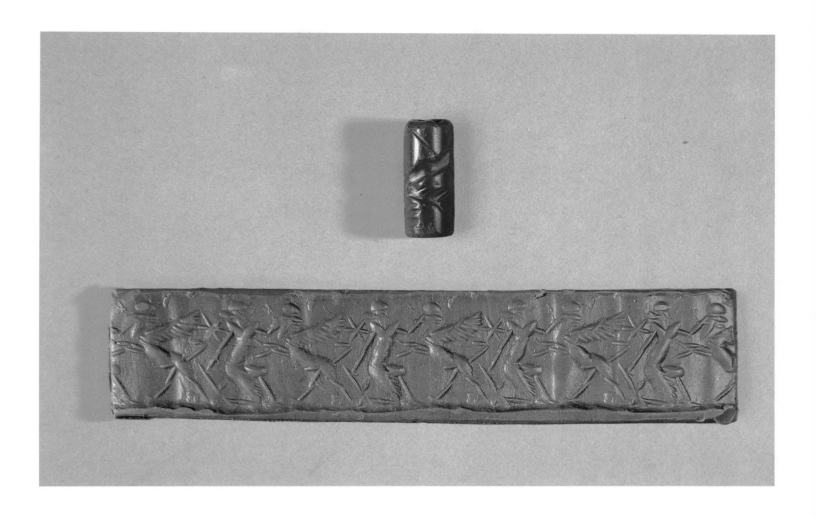

Cylinder seal with a man facing a mixed being

Babylon: *ca.* 7th century B.C.E.
Pink carnelian. h: 19 mm. d: 8 mm.
For comparison: Frankfort 36c; Collon 370

A bearded, kneeling man wearing a fringed robe faces a rampant mixed creature. The man grasps a stick or a weapon of some sort in his right hand and raises his left arm. When the seal is rolled out to create an impression, the repetition of the schematic star between the shoulder of the man and the wing of the beast serves to border the scene.

The fantastic creature of this seal and the two like it in the preceding seal share in common their general composition (a human head combined with the body of a winged, hoofed quadruped) even down to the angular twist of the tail. This type of creature shares affinities with depictions of bullmen, centaurs, and ibex-men. Although the bull-man had an extremely long tenure in Mesopotamian art, centaurs and ibex-men were relatively late developments, stemming out of Middle Assyrian tradition. The latter creature was

particularly popular with Neo-Babylonian glyptic artists. Unfortunately, because the nature of these creatures has barely been illuminated by textual references, whether their characters were essentially protective or malevolent remains a mystery.

The use of the cutting wheel at this late date is characteristic of both Neo-Babylonian artists and their Assyrian counterparts. Carnelian was favored by both as well, although the relative thinness of this particular seal may indicate that a previous design had been erased. Recutting was a not uncommon practice of seal cutters once seal designs became out-moded or a seal changed ownership.

Cylinder seal depicting a fabulous beast
and its earthly relative

Assyria: *ca.* 7th century B.C.E.

Alabaster onyx. h: 20.5 mm. d: 10 mm.

For comparison: Tessier 247; Collon 334

In this highly schematic seal, a winged
quadruped confronts its earthly counterpart—
identical save for its wings and mane. The
latter animal, perhaps a caprid or an equid,
appears to be on the descent from a sharp
leap. Drill points, a schematized star, and a
crescent moon further enhance the
otherworldly atmosphere of the scene.

Neo-Assyrian art owes much to Syrian
and especially to Mitannian art of the mid-
second millennium B.C.E. These earlier
traditions perfected the art of creating
composite beasts of the type that are well
known from their borrowings by Egypt and
the Aegean. The Assyrians adopted many of
these creations into their artistic repertoire

and developed a predilection for pairing
the fabulous with the mundane. Thus, it is
not uncommon in Assyrian glyptic to find
eagles hovering above griffins, lions sparring
with lion-demons, and creatures such as
those depicted in this seal interacting with
one another.

The use of a cutting disc and drill was
responsible for the schematic nature of this
drilled-style seal. Although presumably this
method of fashioning a seal was comparatively
economical, it seems to have constituted an
aesthetic taste in its own right in the ninth to
seventh centuries B.C.E.

Stamp seal with various animals pictured

Near East: *ca.* unknown period C.E.

White chalcedony. h: 26 mm. d: 18 mm

The central figures on this seal appear to be dogs or dog-like creatures personified. The dog to the left rides an animal, which is perhaps to be understood as a donkey, and is hailed by the dog to the right who stands upon two legs. To the upper left of the group is a rooster, and the sun appears at the top of the seal.

This ring bezel, in opposition to the two following stamp seals, does not draw upon any known ancient Near Eastern official or court style. It possibly was fashioned in a region peripheral to the major spheres of artistic and political activity or it is an example of folk art. The lively arrangement and personification of the two major figures make it quite likely that the subject matter was drawn from a popular tale of the day.

Stamp seal with a standing, human-headed winged bull

> Sasanian: *ca.* 5th century C.E.
> Chalcedony. h: 20 mm. d: 17 mm.
> For comparison: Bivar EJ 5 and EJ 7

Stamp seal with a kneeling, human-headed winged bull

> Sasanian: *ca.* 5th century C.E.
> Dark brown jasper. h: 14 mm. d: 14 mm.
> For comparison: Bivar EH 4-7

Human-headed winged bulls had been present in Mesopotamian art since the Early Dynastic period (3000–2350 B.C.E.) and became especially popular during the Neo-Assyrian era. At this time they were known as *lamassu* and were frequently carved in stone at palace doorways to guard the building from evil, both mundane and supernatural. Following the Neo-Assyrian monumental tradition, the Persian king Xerxes carved a winged, human-headed bull on his gateway at Persepolis. This prototype was very likely adopted by the Sasanians, later Iranian rulers who like the Persians practiced the Zoroastrian religion. It is thought that during the Sasanian period the winged, human-headed bull may have represented Gopatshah, a mythological being mentioned in the Menog-i Khrat and the Bundahisin, religious Pahlavi texts dealing with Zoroastrian themes.

Stamp seals began to replace cylinder seals as early as the eighth century B.C.E. when Aramaic, written on perishable materials as

ELLEN MORRIS & HOLLY PITTMAN

opposed to clay, largely superseded Akkadian
as the lingua franca of the ancient Near East.
As documents following this transition were
commonly sealed with dollops of clay or
wax, a smaller, more discrete impression than
that of the cylinder seal became practical.
Stamp seals such as these were placed in rings
and used as signets.

Numismatics

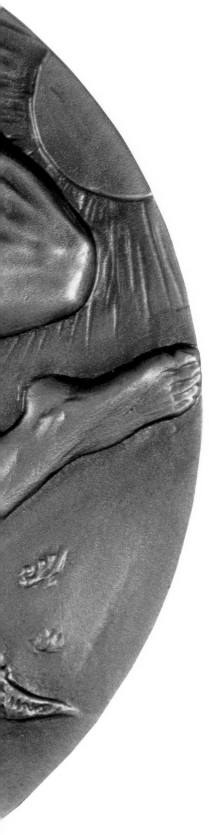

EDWARD ROCHETTE

COINS AND MEDALS provide a tangible link to civilization's past. They enable us, so to speak, to hold history in our hands. Although coins and medals are similar in appearance and method of manufacture, they are worlds apart in the eyes of a collector. Both may be created for the purpose of commemorating historical events, but medals are not intended to circulate as money. Coins and medals both trace their origins to the sixth century B.C.E. Medals, which give artists freedom from the constraints posed by circulating coins, are often sculptures-in-miniature. However, collectors of historical medals will seek with equal enthusiasm specimens that are prized more for their record of historical events than for their artistic merit, as evidenced in the Gimbel collection.

The items selected to best represent the numismatic section of the Gimbel collection are, for the purpose of this book, listed by subject rather than by date of issue. Thus, we first examine items from antiquity—those that relate to the dream of flight; second, we look at post-Renaissance items that commemorate lighter-than-air devices; and third, we regard specimens that honor the modern era and power-assisted mechanized flight. The vast majority of numismatic issues are commemorative and as such they mark anniversaries rather than being contemporary to the events portrayed. There are exceptions and these are the pieces that help make the Gimbel collection unique.

Man's dream of flight is best retold through modern issues; the twentieth-century art-medals of French Mint manufacture and the commissioned works of the Society of Medalists serve this purpose satisfactorily. Because the catalogue depicts but a small percentage of the numismatic issues in the Gimbel collection, the issues illustrated were selected to represent (1) the dream—the mythological legend of Daedalus and Icarus; (2) the concept—the genius of Leonardo da Vinci; and (3) the imagination—the scholarship of Jules Verne.

On June 15, 1783, the Montgolfier brothers, Joseph and Étienne, gave their first public demonstration of an ascension by hot-air balloon at Annonay, France. The 10-minute flight was the first real step in man's daring attempt to be free of the power of the earth's gravity. Other pioneers soon followed. The Gimbel collection is rich in the numismatic issues commissioned by or issued on behalf of these early aeronauts. Some pieces were issued as commemorative medals; others were token souvenirs of early events. The French Mint's issues created to commemorate the achievements of the Montgolfier brothers, the memorial pieces to honor early fatalities, and the medals ordered by the early balloonists to satisfy the desires of those wanting tangible mementos of the events witnessed are only some of the contemporary examples of medallic art to be found in the Gimbel collection.

Wilbur and Orville Wright made the first sustained and controlled takeoff in a gasoline-powered aircraft. Their historic achievement at Kitty Hawk, North Carolina, on December 17, 1903, marked the true beginning of the realization of the age-old dream of flight. There are items in the Gimbel collection that depict the hectic and daring pioneering days through and including the journey into outer space, fulfilling the prophecy made and noted in another medallic issue—that of Jules Verne.

The numismatic items comprising the Gimbel collection continue to grow in number and in scope, matching man's record of aeronautical accomplishment and man's dream of finding ever newer horizons to discover.

Detail of Medal *Flight of Icarus,* 1992 (Page 328)

FLIGHT OF ICARUS

Medal [Icarus, 1992]

Obverse: The beginning of the flight, Icarus in the foreground, his father below. No legends. Designer's name, SHEPPARD, SC incused near lower left edge.

Reverse: The fall of Icarus, father above, land and sea below.
No legends.

Issuer: Society of Medalists (US), 124th issue. 1992.

Diameter: 63 mm. Bronze.

XM-1 3908

The mythological legend of Daedalus and Icarus represents one of man's earliest dreams of flight. Daedalus saw flight as the sole means of escape from Crete. Fashioning wings from feathers and wax, Daedalus admonishes his son, Icarus, to follow him closely and not to set his own course. Impetuously, Icarus disregards his father's advice and flies too close to the sun.

In this myth, sculptor-medalist Joseph Sheppard saw the freedom represented by new invention tempered by the need to exercise caution. On this high-relief bronze art medal, prepared by Sheppard to be the 124th issue of the Society of Medalists, the artist depicts the beginning of the legendary flight on the obverse and the inevitable fall of Icarus on the other side of the medal.

LEONARDO DA VINCI

Medal [Leonardo da Vinci, 1983]

Obverse: Man suspended from glider designed by Leonardo da Vinci.
To right, VOL LIBRE
Designer's name: JP. RETI to lower right.
Reverse: Bust of Leonardo da Vinci flanked by his designs. Legend above:
"...L'HOMME DOIT RES- / TER LIBRE DE LA CEINTURE EN / HAUT, POUR POUVOIR S'EQUILIBRER, / COMME IL LE FAIT DANS UNE BARQUE / AFIN QUE LE CENTRE DE GRAVITE DE / L'ENSEMBLE QU'IL / FORME AVEC L'INSTRU- / MENT PUISSE SE DEPLACER..." / LÉONARD DE VINCI
Issuer: Paris Mint. From the general collection, 1983.
Diameter: 72 mm. Bronze.
XM-1 3667

Had Leonardo da Vinci (1452–1519) restricted his thoughts solely to the study of aerodynamics, he would still have secured a prominent place in the history of man's dream of flight. Leonardo's understanding of air pressure and wind currents enabled him to envision and design instruments now in common use: the windspeed indicator and the inclinometer capable of helping an aviator enveloped in clouds tell whether his plane is flying level. His genius brought forth the concepts of the parachute, the helicopter, and the modern aircraft propeller. His actual aircraft, however, remains to this day mere flight of fancy.

JOSEPH MONTGOLFIER

ÉTIENNE MONTGOLFIER

Medal [Montgolfier, 1783]

Obverse: Profiles to left, Montgolfier brothers superimposed one over the other.

Legend around: JOSE. ET ETIEN. MONTGOLFIER above; POUR AVOIR RENDU L'AIR NAVIGABLE below.

Designer's name: N. GATTEAUX on truncation of bust.

Reverse: Woman with two lions on ground, angel on cloud with torch under balloon in center.

Legend above: ATTONIUS ORBIS TERRARUM, below in exergue, ITINERE PER AERA FELICITER / TENTATO ANNO / MDCCLXXXIII.

Issuer: Paris Mint. Dies remain extant. Restrike of 1783 issue.

Diameter: 42 mm. Silver.

XM-1 3501

Historians often cite June 5, 1783, as the date of the first ascension of a hot-air balloon. In reality, it was the first *public* demonstration and the event occurred at Annonay, France. It is certain that the Montgolfiers, who were paper manufacturers, had occasion to send trial balloons aloft before this date. The brothers, Joseph (1740–1810) and Étienne (1745–1799), had been experimenting ever since they had discovered that when hot air was collected inside a paper bag, the bag became buoyant. Working with small balloons at first, they later tried steam and then hot air.

By the date of their first public display, the pair had built a paper balloon, sectionalized and held together with buttons, measuring 110 feet across, and weighing nearly 1,000 pounds when inflated. To the awe of spectators, the

balloon reached an altitude of 6,000 feet and stayed aloft for about 10 minutes. With that demonstration the age of flight had indeed dawned. The successful launch led to an invitation from King Louis XVI to conduct another on September 19 before the king and his court at Versailles. The Montgolfiers intended to send people aloft on a tethered flight, but the king ruled against human cargo. Three farm animals were substituted for human cargo and a free flight was allowed. The balloon remained aloft for 8 minutes and covered a distance of about 2 miles.

The First Manned Flights

Medal [Montgolfier, 1784]

Obverse: Two manned balloons in clouds, the Montgolfier hot-air balloon in the foreground; the Charles-Robert hydrogen balloon in the background.

Legend: AUDACIA FELIX above: AERA PERMEARUNT XXI. NOV. / L.F. DARLANDES ET F. PILATRE / I. DEC. J.A.C. CHARLES / ET M.N. ROBERT / ANNO MDCCLXIV in exergue.

Reverse: Text circumscribed within a ring of stars.

Legend: PATEFACTO / PER AERA ITINERE / A JOSEPHO ET STEPHANO / MONTGOLFIER / V. JUNII MDCCLXXXIII. / REI MEMORIAM / POSTERITATI TRADT / JUSSIT / LUDOVICUS XVI. / ANNO MDCCLXXXIV.

Issuer: Paris Mint. Dies remain extant. Restrike of 1784 issue.

Diameter: 49 mm. Bronze.

XM-1 3902

After successfully sending animals aloft, the Montgolfier brothers were ready for the next logical step: to send man aloft. At first the king refused to let any citizen, save convicts, participate in a flight. But having viewed the experiment at Versailles, he acquiesced and on November 21, 1783, Jean-François Pilâtre de Rozier and the Marquis d'Arlandes ascended from the Dauphin's Garden within the Bois de Boulogne. The pair flew high above Paris for nearly a half-hour, spending most of their time between tending to the fire of burning straw that supplied the hot air needed to stay aloft and sponging the sparks their fire created to keep them from setting fire to the paper-lined balloon.

Ten days later, on December 1, 1783, Professor Jacques Alexandre César Charles (1746–1823) and a companion, Marie-Noel Robert, took off in the first piloted hydrogen balloon. The pair flew from Paris to Nesle, a distance of 27 miles. The flight so unnerved Charles, who was the pilot, that he never flew again.

THE FIRST FLIGHT IN ENGLAND

THE FIRST FLIGHT IN ENGLAND

Medal [Lunardi, 1784]

    Obverse: Profile bust of Lunardi facing left.

    Legend around: VINCENT LUNARDI / FIRST AERIAL TRAVELLER IN ENGLAND.

    Reverse: Balloon with wings protruding from cabin.

    Legend above: ET SE PROTINIES AETHEREA TOLLIT INASTRA VIA; in exergue; below, SEPTEMBUS 15 / MDCCLXXXIV.

    Issuer: Unknown

    Diameter: 35 mm. Silver wash.

    XM-1 3519

An Italian by birth, Vincent Lunardi (1759–1806) made his aeronautical mark in England. He was secretary to the Neapolitan ambassador to London when the news of aerial flights in France reached the city; the events inspired him to design and build a balloon of his own. On September 15, 1784, at Moorfields, he made the first hydrogen balloon ascent in England. The flight drew enough attention for King George III to break from a council meeting to watch the ascent via telescope. The king is reported to have commented, "We may resume our deliberations on the subject before us at our pleasure, but we may never see poor Lunardi again."

England did see more of Lunardi. The secretary-cum-aeronaut quit his diplomatic post to pursue a career as a professional balloonist, but was later forced to flee England after a British citizen became the victim of a balloon accident.

JEAN-PIERRE FRANÇOIS BLANCHARD

Medal [Blanchard, 1788]

Obverse: Profile bust of Blanchard to right.

Legend above: IOANNES PETRUS BLANCHARD.

Designer's name: F. LOOS, below.

Reverse: A landscape of Warsaw in the distance; above the city is Blanchard's balloon.

Legends above: IMPAVIDUS NON SORTEM TIMET ICARIUM / VARSOVIE / MDCCLXXXVIII.

Issuer: Unknown

Diameter: 28 mm. Silver.

XM-1 3574

He had all the attributes to succeed as the world's first professional aeronaut. Jean-Pierre François Blanchard (1753–1809) had the imagination to envisage what others could not, the daring to try what seemed impossible, the showmanship to draw attention to his endeavors, and the touch of a charlatan to raise the funds to underwrite his efforts.

Even before the Montgolfier brothers launched their first manned balloon, Blanchard had conducted experiments with parachutes and ornithopters. His parachute designs were tested by dropping sheep from tall buildings. Within a year of the Montgolfiers' first success, Blanchard headed for England to demonstrate lighter-than-air flight. An early passenger, Dr. John Jeffries, proposed that the two make the first England-to-France flight and offered a fee of £800. Blanchard accepted but had little intention of sharing honors. At the weighing-in before the flight, Blanchard claimed that they were overweight and that the balloon could only carry one person. Dr. Jeffries noted that it was Blanchard who seemed "overweight." Close examination revealed that Blanchard was wearing lead weights under his coat. Because an estimated 250,000 people had gathered to watch their liftoff, Blanchard reluctantly shed the weights. The flight was a success and much heralded in Europe, with Louis XVI awarding Blanchard a prize of 12,000 *livres* and a lifetime pension, but extending a mere royal thank you to Jeffries. Blanchard went on to make a career of being the first to fly in several countries, including the United States.

ANDRÉ JACQUES GARNERIN

Medal [Garnerin, 1797]

Obverse: Facing bust of Garnerin.

Legend around: ANDRE JACQUES GARNERIN 1769–1823.

Reverse: Shows man descending in parachute.

Legend: In the field to the left, PREMIERE / DESCENTE / EN PARACHUTE; to the right, PARC / MONCEAU / 22 OCTOBRE / 1797.

Designer's name: VIC DAUMAS at lower right edge.

Issuer: Paris Mint. From the general collection, No. M-4212.

Diameter: 68 mm. Bronze.

XM-1 3903

Despite medallic issues to the contrary, André Jacques Garnerin (1769–1823) neither invented the parachute nor was the first to make a successful jump. Credit for the concept should go to Leonardo da Vinci. Credit for the first recorded jump from an appreciable height belongs to another Frenchman, Sébastien Lenormand who, in 1783, fourteen years earlier than Garnerin, jumped from the tower of the Montpellier Observatory in southern France. He might have earned more recognition for his feat had he not promoted the parachute as a practical means of evacuating a tall building in case of fire.

In 1785, two years after the Montgolfier

brothers' first ascent, J.-P. Blanchard placed a dog in a basket, attached a parachute, and dropped it from a balloon. The dog landed safely, but it was not until 1793, eight years later, that Blanchard made the attempt himself. He survived, albeit with a broken leg.

André Jacques Garnerin made his first jump over Paris in 1797 and then gained fame for his daring by making a profession of jumping. Unfortunately, the designs of his parachutes were such that they swayed so violently that each descent left him violently airsick, a problem he failed to overcome throughout the remainder of his showman days.

CHARLES GREEN AND ISAAC E. SPARROW

Token [Sparrow, 1823]

   Obverse: Profile bust of Sparrow facing left.

   Legend around: ISAAC EARLYSMAN SPARROW.

   Reverse: Sparrow and Green in balloon.

   Legend around: IRONMONGER BISHOPSGATE LONDON.

   Issuer: Unknown

   Diameter: 23 mm. Copper.

   XM-1 3594

Charles Green (1785–1870) is recognized as England's greatest balloonist. In his lifetime, he made over 500 successful ascents, including a 480-mile overnight flight from London to Germany. Green pioneered the use of coal gas, which he found cheaper than hydrogen and which he obtained by tapping into London's recently installed gas lines that supplied the city's new street lamps.

   In the field of numismatics, Green's greatest contribution was accommodating a paying passenger named Isaac Earlysman Sparrow. The flight inspired an interesting series of

farthing-sized tradesman's tokens commemorating Sparrow's ascent on June 23, 1823, and promoting Sparrow's business of manufacturing nails. The flight so impressed the young manufacturer that he named his company's storage facilities Balloon House and bought and wore a "pilot's cap" for the rest of his days.

City of New York

Medal [City of New York, 1859]

> Obverse: *City of New York* balloon in center.
>
> Legend: GREAT AIR SHIP to left; CITY OF NEW YORK to right.
>
> Reverse: Text only. DIAMETER, / 130 FEET. / HEIGHT, 200 FEET. / WEIGHT WITH OUTFIT / 3 1/2 TONS. / LIFTING POWER / 22 TONS. / CAPACITY / OF / GAS ENVELOPE, / 375,000 CUBIC FEET.
>
> Issuer: Unknown
>
> Diameter: 34 mm. Dull silver finish.
>
> XM-1 3589

Thaddeus Sobieski Constantine Lowe (1832–1913) was America's latter-day J.-P. Blanchard—a showman first and aeronaut second. Dubbing himself Professor Lowe, he began his career as a traveling medicine man. During his travels he met several balloonists and became interested when he recognized ballooning's financial potential. By 1858, Lowe had learned to fly and began a subscription campaign to fund the first west-to-east, trans-Atlantic crossing by balloon. Sufficient funds were raised to construct the *City of New York*, a massive balloon 130 feet in diameter. It was the largest balloon built to date. Unfortunately, the New York Gas Company was unable to deliver hydrogen gas with sufficient pressure to fully inflate the balloon. At that point, a storm arose that materially damaged the balloon. Hasty repairs led to an explosion on the next attempt to fill it; Lowe then abandoned the project.

To help with expenses, Lowe ordered a medal to be issued and sold. He then turned to cross-country exhibitions. One unfortunate day, soon after the outbreak of the Civil War, Lowe unintentionally landed behind Confederate lines and was held as a Union spy. Convincing the Confederates of their error, Lowe was released. He returned north to immediately offer his services to the Union army. During the war, five of Lowe's craft saw service as observation balloons. After the war, he turned his attention in another direction, from up to down. He proposed a submarine to the U. S. Navy for use during the Spanish-American War, but was rebuffed.

JULES VERNE

Medal [Verne, 1972]

Obverse: Portrait, three-quarter left, Verne.

Legend: JULES VERNE 1828–1905 to left; SCIENCE-GEOGRAPHIE-FICTION to right.

Designer's name: R. B. BARON at right.

Reverse: Superimposed over globe, the balloon from *Five Weeks in a Balloon;* below, submarine *Nautilus* entwined in the tentacles of a giant octopus; to left, portion of the map of Africa; to right, portion of a map of the moon's surface.

Legend: LE TOUR DU MONDE EN 80 JOURS. 5 SEMAINES EN BALLON. VOYAGE DE LA TERRE A LA LUNE. 20 MILLE LIEUES SOUS LES MERS, prominent works of the author.

Issuer: Paris Mint. From the general collection, No. M-1813. 1955.

Diameter: 68 mm. Bronze.

XM-1 3659

The Man of Prophecies, Jules Verne (1828–1905), has also been called the Father of Science Fiction. A lawyer by education, Verne enjoyed writing. At age thirty-five, he achieved immediate recognition with his first novel, *Five Weeks in a Balloon,* a tale of an aerial journey across the African continent. The book established the formula for his successful later works, including the most popular of all, *Around the World in Eighty Days.* Although the genre preceded Verne by centuries, no one can deny that time has given fact to what many considered sheer fantasy during his day. Verne envisaged submarines in *20,000 Leagues Under the Sea,* heavier-than-air-flight in *The Clipper of the Clouds,* and even earth satellites in *The Begum's Fortune.* During his 77-year life, Verne witnessed the advent of the heavier-than-air flight he had predicted.

Medal [Siege of Paris, 1870–1871]

Obverse: Pigeon in flight.

Legend around: CORRESPONDANT PENDANT LE [SIC] ARRIVEE DES PIGEONS / SIEGE DE PARIS 1870–1871.

Reverse: Text in six straight lines: LE 22 8BRE / ARRIVEE DE / 5 PIGEONS MEDAILLES / APPORTANT / DES NOUVELLES / DE TOURS.

Issuer: Unknown

Diameter: 29 mm. Copper.

XM-1 3493

Following the French defeat at Sedan the previous day, Napoleon surrendered on September 2, 1870, along with 80,000 of his troops. Two weeks later, two German armies began a 135-day siege of Paris. Playing a defensive role during the siege, balloons were used primarily for communications with French forces outside of Paris. No fewer than 66 balloons left Paris, carrying 164 persons, 381 carrier pigeons, and mail. Most got through safely, although six were captured by the enemy and a few became caught in strong wind currents and landed far from their intended destinations. One, the *Ville d'Orléans,* came down in Norway after a fifteen-hour flight;

another was not found until three years later near Port Natal in Africa.

Enterprising Frenchmen issued at least eighty-three different copper or lead medallions commemorating the various balloons. The pieces were offered for sale and proceeds were used to help finance the costs of constructing the balloons in various railway station factories throughout the city. In addition, as small change started to disappear, the provisional government ordered trial and proof strikes of siege coinage that depicted the balloons. The need failed to materialize and the coins were never placed into circulation.

Otto Lilienthal

Medal [Lilienthal, 1914]

Obverse: Profile bust of Lilienthal facing left.

Legend: 1848 OTTO LILIENTHAL 1896 to left; NON OMNIS MORIAR to right.

Reverse: Man with experimental wings attached; blacksmith's tools in foreground; birds and mountains in background.

Legend: OSTMARKENFLUG / 1914 above; WELAND / DER SCHMIED to left below; U.Z. / [ERINNERUNG] to right below; and FUR-VERDIENSTE at base.

Issuer: Unknown

Diameter: 72 mm. Bronze.

XM-1 3553

At the close of the nineteenth century, man and his flying machines had advanced to the glider stage, thanks in particular to one man, a German named Otto Lilienthal (1848–1896). He built his craft in the manner few dreamers of manned flight had patience for. Lilienthal constructed his aircraft after long and careful study of the then-known principles of aerodynamics. He held to the idea that mastering the skill of gliding was the primary step toward achieving success with manned flight.

For all his studies, however, Lilienthal was overly influenced by the flight of birds. He believed that to achieve the dream of powered flight, man would have to emulate the feathered creatures. Lilienthal built two ornithopters, both failures, before turning his thoughts toward fixed-wing aircraft. On August 9, 1896, Otto Lilienthal logged his final flight. Taking off from the crest of a hill, his glider gained an altitude of approximately 100 feet when a sudden gust of wind caused his craft to stall and plummet to the ground. The one who had become known as the Flying Man sustained a broken back and died less than twenty-four hours later.

Count Ferdinand von Zeppelin

Medal [Graf Zeppelin, 1929]

Obverse: Bust of Graf Zeppelin toward right.

Legend: ZIEL ERKANNT—KRAFT GESPANNTI above; GRAF / ZEPPELIN to left.

Reverse: Graf Zeppelin passing the Cathedral at Friedrichshafen.

Legend: GEPRAGT AUS DEN RESTEN DES LUFTSCHIFFS Z.4. above; 4. U. 5. AUG. 1908 to left: DAUERFAHRT / FRIEDRICHSHAFEN - / MAINZ / 583 KLM at bottom.

Issuer: Unknown

Diameter: 33 mm. Satin silver finish.

XM-1 3525

The man whose name remains synonymous with rigid airships became interested in ballooning as a young German military observer during the American Civil War. A visit by Count Ferdinand von Zeppelin (1838–1917) to St. Paul, Minnesota, in August 1863, coincided with a commercial tour being conducted by John H. Steiner. Steiner had served in the balloon corps and pioneered balloon reconnaissance. By late 1863, he had quit the U. S. Army in a dispute over payment. He supported himself by touring the country and taking on paying passengers. Zeppelin was one of Steiner's passengers and he was to write to his father afterward, "While I was above St. Paul, the idea of aerial navigation was strongly impressed upon me, and there it was that my idea of zeppelins came to me."

Throughout his lifetime, von Zeppelin continued to promote his idea of an airship capable of directed flight. After failing to interest his own government in building a rigid airship, the count turned to private enterprise and founded his own company. In 1900, his first rigid airship was launched. By 1911, he had arranged for regular passenger flights between major German cities. In a short time, 32,250 passengers on 1,500 flights had flown on one of his four dirigibles—without a fatality. In 1928, his *Graf Zeppelin* inaugurated the first scheduled trans-Atlantic air service only to be replaced in 1937 by the larger, more luxurious *Hindenburg*. The latter met its end when it exploded and burned at Lakehurst, New Jersey, on May 6, 1937, bringing the brief era of commercial air service by dirigible to an end.

Alberto Santos-Dumont

Medal [Santos-Dumont, 1932]

    Obverse: Facing portrait in center.

    Legend: name SANTOS DUMONT above. Terminal dates 1873 and 1932 left and right.

    Reverse: Montage of early Santos-Dumont aircraft superimposed over Eiffel Tower and outline of Brazilian coastline. Depicted are: the balloon BRASIL, upper left; the airship *S. O. No. 6*, top center; the plane LA DEMOISELLE, captioned at right; and the airplane *14 BIS*, bottom center. In the field, above PRIX / DEUTSCH DE LA MEURTHE / 19 OCTOBRE / 1901; at lower right PRIX ARCHDEACON; at bottom BAGATELLE / 23 OCTOBRE 1906.

    Designer's name: Claude Lesot.

    Issuer: Paris Mint. From the general collection, No. M-4809, 1973.

    Diameter: 77 mm. Bronze.

    XM-1 3673

Claimed by Brazil as a native son, by France as an adopted one, Alberto Santos-Dumont (1873–1932) was one of the most colorful of the early aviators. Fearless to the point of being foolhardy, he had as much showmanship in his soul as innovation. The son of a rich coffee plantation owner, Santos-Dumont emigrated to Paris in 1891. Had he not become involved in aviation, history might still have remembered him as the man who conceived the idea of the wristwatch. Santos-Dumont had a genius for mechanics. He raced motorcycles before looking up, first toward ballooning, then to dirigibles. In all, he built a total of fourteen airships; not all became successfully airborne.

    On July 23, 1906, Santos-Dumont planned to attach one of his planes to the belly of a dirigible and test a revolutionary control system while both craft were airborne. Fortunately, the plane was damaged while it was being transported to a field for the test. It was later found that the aircraft was too underpowered to have flown successfully. Equipping the plane with a more powerful engine, Santos-Dumont became airborne for a distance of 722 feet in just over 21 seconds, the longest powered flight recorded in Europe at that date.

THE WRIGHT BROTHERS

Medal [Wright Brothers, 1908]

Obverse: Conjoined busts of brothers Wilbur, left, and Orville Wright, right.

Legend: AERO CLUB OF AMERICA above; W. WRIGHT / SEP. 21, 1908 / LE MANS / FRANCE to left; O. WRIGHT / SEP. 9, 1908 / FORT / MYER, VA / U.S.A. to right.

Reverse: Wright biplane above logo for Aero Club of America dividing date 19 05.

Issuer: Unknown

Diameter: 76 mm. Bronze.

XM-1 3531

Success four flights thursday morning all against twenty one mile wind started from Level with engine power alone average speed through air thirty one miles longest 57 seconds inform Press home Christmas. Orevelle [*sic*] Wright

Word that the age of heavier-than-air flight had finally dawned reached the world outside of Kitty Hawk, North Carolina, via a Western Union telegram dispatched at 5:25 P.M. on December 17, 1903. The message was addressed to Bishop M. Wright and had been sent by his son Orville, who piloted the world's first sustained, manned flight in a gasoline-powered aircraft. Legends to the contrary, the press was informed and more than one newspaper featured the Wrights' historic achievement on the front page of the following morning's edition.

Wilbur Wright (1867–1912) and his brother, Orville Wright (1871–1948), are recognized as the first to have flown in a heavier-than-air machine. Bicycle mechanics by trade, the brothers achieved their inaugural success in *Flyer I,* a plane they designed and built. Powered by a chain-driven, aluminum-cast motorcycle engine, the first flight attained an airborne distance of 120 feet and was followed by a second of 852 feet. Encouraged, the pair quit the cycle business in 1909 to form a company to produce aircraft.

Captain Ferdinand Ferber

Medal [Ferber, 1909]

Obverse: Bust of Ferber.

Legend around: CAPITAINE FERBER 1862–1909. Designer's name MICHEL FERBER, below.

Reverse: Ferber's biplane No. 6 in flight; two ground observers below.

Legend: LE PREMIER VOL STABLE A MOTEUR EFFECTUE EN EUROPE / MAI 1905 CHALAIS-MEDON AEROPLANE No 6 DECLENCHE EN LIBERTE.

Issuer: Paris Mint. From the general collection, No. M-3521. 1969.

Diameter: 68 mm. Bronze.

XM-1 3666

Captain Ferdinand Ferber (1862–1909) wished to be the first to fly a heavier-than-air-craft. He, too, shared the dream of the Wright brothers. A contemporary, Ferber wrote and did much of his research under the pseudonym Monsieur de Rue, a name chosen so as not to jeopardize his military career. His superiors saw the future of flight solely in the form of the balloon or dirigible. The airplane, they believed, was just a waste of his time.

In 1898, Ferber helped found the Aéro-Club of France. Four years later he built a glider similar to that designed by the Wright brothers.

Ferber equipped it with a 6-horsepower engine, which was suspended from an arm extending out from a tall tower. He spent many months conducting "routine" tests, all without success. In 1905, Ferber became the first man to pilot an airplane in Europe and is recognized as the father of French aviation. He lost his life in a crash at Boulogne four years later.

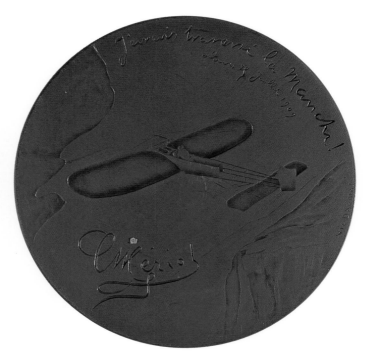

Louis Blériot

Medal [Blériot, 1909]

Obverse: Profile facing left.

Legend in the field at right: LOUIS / BLERIOT / 1872 / 1936.

Reverse: Blériot's airplane seen over the English Channel on the first flight from Calais to Dover.

Legend in script: J'AVAIS TRAVERSE LA MANCHE..../ DOUVRES 25 JUILLET 1909. Below is his signature. Designer's name VIC-DAUMAS to right.

Issuer: Paris Mint. From the general collection, No. 3653. 1970.

Diameter: 68 mm. Bronze.

XM-1 3901

The French have their heroes of early aeronautical achievement—from Montgolfier to Ferber, but no list may exclude Louis Blériot (1872–1936). By 1909, Blériot was building his eleventh airplane, each progressively developed from an earlier lesson. By this date, Blériot had spent more than $150,000 on his experiments and was badly in need of additional funding. When he learned that a prize of $5,000 awaited the first man to fly the English Channel by plane, Blériot made that his goal, not for the glory but for the money that would allow him to continue his experiments.

Facing both competitors and an engine that had never run for more than 20 minutes without overheating, Blériot took off from near Calais on the morning of July 25, 1909 for the estimated 22-minute flight to Dover. He had to ask a bystander the approximate direction of his destination. His engine ran as he feared—hot—as he neared the English coast. Just as his overheated engine began to falter, Blériot encountered a chance rainstorm; the rain solved the problem of overheating and the Frenchman won his needed prize.

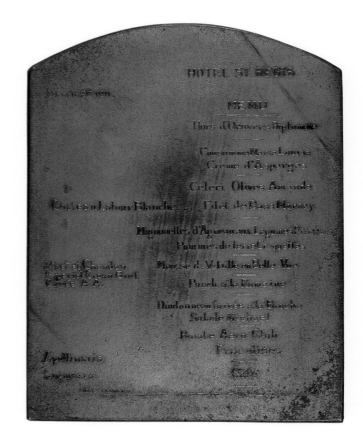

Coupe Aéronautique

Medal [Bennett, 1911]

Obverse: Likeness of trophy with dirigible, winged woman with torch.

Legend: COUPE AERONAUTIQUE / J. GORDON BENNETT above; WON BY AERO CLUB OF AMERICA/FRANK P. LAHM 1906/ EDGAR W. MIX 1909/ALAN R. HAWLEY 1910, below.

Reverse: Text of banquet menu

Issuer: Unknown

Dimensions: 85 mm. x 65 mm. Bronze.

XM-1 3529

In 1909, six years after the Wright brothers had first achieved liftoff at Kitty Hawk, James Gordon Bennett (1841–1918), publisher of the *New York Herald,* sponsored the inaugural Coupe Aéronautique, an international air race based on speed. (The 1906 race had been a national contest.) Twenty-eight pilots participated in an 8-day aerial extravaganza at

Reims, France. They competed for thousands of dollars in prizes, a 25,000-franc grand prize, a solid silver loving cup, and fame. As a souvenir of the race awards banquet, a medal inscribed with the menu of the evening was presented to all eligible to attend. Today, a Gordon Bennett Cup competition continues as an annual balloon race.

Chronology of Flight

852 B.C.E.	King Bladud of England allegedly killed attempting to fly
1250 C.E.	Roger Bacon theorizes about mechanical flight
1326–27	Kite and aerial bomb first illustrated in the Western world
1495–97	First powered airplane designed by Leonardo da Vinci
1638	Bishops Godwin and Wilkins publish fictional accounts of moon travel
1670	Lana's *Prodromo* published
1680	*De Moto Animalium* published by Borelli
1709	Glider version of Gusmão's flying machine designed and possibly tested
1782	The Montgolfiers fly their first model hot-air balloon
1783	First unpiloted public demonstration of a Montgolfier hot-air balloon
	Montgolfier hot-air balloon carries animals aloft, Versailles
	Hot-air jet propulsion from a balloon suggested by Joseph Montgolfier
	Pilâtre de Rozier and d'Arlandes make the first hot-air balloon ascent in history, Paris
	First ascent in a hydrogen balloon, Paris
1784	Lunardi makes first hot-air balloon flight in Britain
	Blanchard makes first attempt to propel a balloon with an airscrew, London
1785	Blanchard and Jeffries make the first crossing of the English Channel by balloon
1794	French army makes first military aerial reconnaissance from a balloon
1799	Cayley designs the first airplane with a modern fixed-wing configuration
1809–10	Cayley paper on aviation lays the foundation for modern aerodynamics
1837	Dihedral parachute, designed by Cayley, kills Cocking
1847	Henson tests first steam-powered, airscrew-propelled, fixed-wing airplane
1848	Steam-powered model airplane tested by Stringfellow
1849	First bombing raid by hot-air balloons against Venice
1852	Giffard flies first manned full-size airship powered by steam engine
1853	First man-carrying flight by glider
1857–58	Du Temple flies first successful clockwork-powered model airplane
1858	Nadar takes first aerial photo from balloon over Paris
1861	First use of balloons in U.S. Civil War
1863	*Five Weeks in a Balloon* published by Jules Verne
1864	*L'Aeronaute* journal founded by Nadar
1868	Stringfellow tests first powered model triplane
1870	Twisted rubber power for models introduced by Pénaud
	First balloon sent aloft during Siege of Paris
1871	Pénaud flies stable, powered model monoplane
1872	Airship first powered by internal combustion engine using envelope's gas
1874	First powered man-carrying airplane takes off but does not fly
1881	*L'Empire de l'Air* published by Mouillard
1883	Tissandier's airship propelled by electric motor in flight

1888	Wolfert's airship powered by petrol engine in flight
1889	*Der Vogelflug als Grundlage der Fliegekunst* published by Lilienthal
1891	First steam-driven, tandem-wing model aircraft tested in U.S. by Langley
1891–96	Lilienthal makes several piloted glider flights, including first biplane
1894	*Progress in Flying Machines* published by Chanute
1895–97	First three editions of the *Aeronautical Annual* published in U.S. by Means
1896	Lilienthal killed gliding
1898	Aéro-Club de France founded
1899	Glider crash kills Pilcher
1900	First Wright glider flown at Kitty Hawk, N. C.
1901	Second Wright glider flown at the Kill Devil Hills, near Kitty Hawk, N.C.
	Airship flown around the Eiffel Tower by Santos-Dumont
1903	Full-sized Langley *Aerodrome* crashed on takeoff
	Wright brothers make the first powered, sustained, and controlled airplane flights
1904	Wilbur Wright makes the first circular route flight
1905	Voisin incorporates the box-kite concept in an airplane
	Wright *Flyer III*, the first fully-practical airplane, flies
	Orville Wright makes the first flight of over half-an-hour
	La Vaulx founds the Fédération Aéronautique Internationale
1906	Vuia tests the first tractor monoplane
	First powered hop-flights made in Europe by Santos-Dumont
1907	Farman makes the first flight in Europe of over one minute
	First man-carrying helicopter rises vertically in free flight
1908	*Scientific American* trophy for first U.S. public flight goes to Glenn Curtiss
	Wilbur Wright flies first practical two-seat airplane in public
	Orville Wright flies in public for the first time at Ft. Myer, Va.
	The first person killed in a powered flight accident, Thomas Selfridge, is killed flying with Orville Wright
1909	Blériot flies across the English Channel
1910	First flights made in Spain, Switzerland, Argentina, Brazil, Indo-China, China
	Zeppelin airship passenger service begins in Germany
	Grahame-White makes the first night flight in Europe
	Glenn Curtiss makes the first bombing tests in the U.S.
	Belmont Park aviation meet; first in the U.S.
1911	First airmail flights by airplane in several countries
	U.S. Army conducts the first live bombing tests
	First takeoff and landing on a ship in the U.S.
1914	First zeppelin raid of World War I on Antwerp

Appendix

Printed Books: 1489–1850
(in order of publication year)

This additional selection of books gives special emphasis to the strength of the Gimbel collection in four main areas: scientific works of the Renaissance with some bearing on aviation; creative writing reflecting the mythology and iconography of flight; comic and satirical responses to the first balloon ascents; and practical manuals about flying and building balloons.

Albertus Magnus, Saint, bp. of Ratisbon, 1193?–1280. [Physica] Diui Alberti Magni phisicorum siue De phisico auditu libri octo. [Colophon: Impressum Uenetijs per Ioānem de Forliuio & Gregorium fratres. Anno dñi. M.CCCC.XCIIIJ. die vltimo Ianuarij [=n.s. January 31, 1495.] 128 leaves, 5–128 numbered 1–124. 31 cm. Hain 519. AC10.A3 1494.

Albertus Magnus, Saint, bp. of Ratisbon, 1193?–1280. [De caelo et mundo] Incipit liber primus [-quartus] de celo & mundo Alberti magni . . . [Colophon: Impressum Uenetijs per Ioānem & Gregorium d' Gregorijs fratres. Anno dñi. M.CCCC.LXXXXV. die vj. Iulij.] 73 [1] leaves. 31 cm. Hain 512. Bound with his Physica, 1494. AC10.A3 1494.

Albertus Magnus, Saint, bp. of Ratisbon, 1193?–1280. [De generatione et corruptione] Incipit Liber de generatione & corruptione. [Colophon: Impressum Uenetijs per Ioānem & Gregoriū de Gregorijs fratres. Anno dñi. M.CCCC.LXXXXV. die decima Iunij.] 23, [1] leaves. 31 cm. Hain 517. Bound with his Physica, 1494. AC10.A3 1494.

Albertus Magnus, Saint, bp. of Ratisbon, 1193?–1280. [De mineralibus] Alberti Magni . . . de mineralibus liber primus [-quintus] incipit. [Colophon: Impressum Uenetijs per Ioānem & Gregorium de Gregorijs fratres. Anno dñi. M.CCCC.LXXXXV. die xxij. Iunij.]. 21, [1] leaves. 31 cm. Hain 522. Bound with his Physica, 1494. AC10.A3 1494.

Ptolemaeus, Claudius, 2nd cent. C.E. [Epytoma in Almagestum] Cl. Ptolemei alexandrini Astronomorum principis [eis megalin syntaxin [transliterated]] id est in Magnam Constructionē: Georgij purbachij: eiusque discipuli Iohannis de Regio monte Astronomicon Epitoma [Ed. by J. B. Abiosus.] [Colophon: Opera . . . & arte . . . Iohannis hāman de Landoia: dictus hertzog . . . 1496 currente: Pridie Caleñ. Septembris Uenetiis.] [110] leaves. illus. 30 cm. Hain 13806. AC10.P9 1496.

Gellius, Aulus, ca. 130–180 C.E. Avlii Gellii Noctivm atticarvm libri vndeviginti. [Colophon: Venetiis in aedibvs Aldi, et Andreae soceri mense septembri. M.D.XV.] 31 p. l., 289 numb. l., [102] p. 16.5 cm. PA6390.A2 1515.

Alciati, Andreas, 1492–1550. . . . Emblematum libellus. Parisiis, Ex officina C. Wecheli, 1540. 119 [1] p. illus. 17 cm. PN6349.A34 1540.

Scaliger, Julius Caesar, 1484–1558. . . . exotericarvm exercitationvm liber qvintvs decimvs, De svbtilitate, ad Hieronymvm Cardanvm. Lvtetiae, Ex officina typographica Michaelis Vascosani, 1557. [4], 476, [31] numb. leaves. illus. 24 cm. Q155.S27.

Fulgentius, Fabius Planciades, 5th–6th cent. C.E. . . . opera, quae scripsit omnia . . . Basileae, [Ex officina Henric. Petrina, 1566]. 33 p. l., 850 p., 1 leaf. 15 cm. TLB154.F8 1566.

Cardano, Girolamo, 1501–1576. . . . Commentarii, in Hippocratis de aere, aqvis et locis . . . Accedvnt praeterea ante quoque non impressa . . . Basileae, Ex officina Henric. Petrina [Colophon: 1570, mense avgvsto.] 28 p. l., 338, [2] p. 32 cm. Q155.C26a.

Leslie, John, bp. of Ross, 1527–1596. De origine, moribvs, et rebvs gestis Scotorvm libri decem . . . Romae, in aedibus populi romani, 1578. 20 p. l., 588, [32] p. incl. 1 illus. (coat of arms) 11 pl. double map. 22 cm. DA775.L63.

Hero, of Alexandria, (date uncertain). Heronis Alexandrini Spiritalivm liber. A Federico Commandino vrbinate, ex graeco nvper in latinvm conversvs. Apud aegidium Gorbinum, 1583. 163 p. illus. 20 cm. QC142.H55.

Wecker, Johann Jacob, 1528–1586. Les secrets et merveilles de natvre. Recueillis de diuers autheurs, & diuisez en XVII liures, par Jean Jacqves Uvecker . . . Traduit en François . . . A Tovrnon, 1606. 8 p. l., 1246, [49] p. illus. 17 cm. AG103.W38.

Du Bartas, Guillaume de Salluste, seigneur, 1544–1590. Du Bartas His Deuine Weekes and Workes Translated: And Dedicated to the Kings most excellent Maiestie by Josuah Syluester. Now thirdly corrected and augm. . . . London, [1611]. 17 p. l., 819, [31] p. illus. (incl. port.) 18 cm. PQ1616.E2S8 1611.

Bate, John. The mysteries of nature and art, in 4 severall pts. The 2d ed. with many additions unto every pt. London, 1635. 288 p. illus. (incl. port.) 19 cm. STC 1578. Q155.B32.

Heywood, Thomas, d. ca. 1650. . . . The hierarchie of the blessed angells. Their names, orders and offices. The fall of Lucifer with his angells. . . . London, 1635. 5 p. l., 622, [8] p. incl. illus., 4 pl. 27.5 cm. First edition. STC 13327. PR2574.H6 1635.

[Schwenter, Daniel], 1585–1636. Deliciæ physico-mathematicæ. Oder Mathemat: und philosophische erquickstunden . . . am tag gegeben durch m. Danielem Schwenterum. Nürnberg, 1636–1692. 3 v. illus. (incl. music), pl. (1 fold.) diagrs. 19 x 16 cm. Q155.S41.

Kircher, Athanasius, 1602–1680. . . . Itinerarivm exstaticvm qvo mvndi opificivm . . . exponitur ad veritatem . . . Romæ, 1656. 4 p. l., 464, [24] p. 25 cm. QB41.K58 1656.

[Boyle, Hon. Robert], 1627–1691. Occasional reflections upon several svbiects, whereto is premis'd a discourse about such kind of thoughts. London, 1665. 80, 161–264, 229 p. 17 cm. Wing B4005. PN6330.B79.

Hooke, Robert, 1635–1703. Micrographia: or, Some physiological descriptions of minute bodies made by magnifying glasses . . . [2nd ed.] London, 1667. 18 p. l., 246 [10] p. XXXVIII fold. pl. 28.5 cm. Wing H2621. QH271.H78 1667.

Caramuel Lobkowitz, Juan, 1606–1682. . . . Mathesis biceps. Vetus et nova . . . In omnibvs, et singvlis veterum, & recentiorum placita examinantur . . . Lugduni, 1670. 2 v. illus., LII pl., diagrs. 31 cm. Added t.-p., engraved; initials; head and tail pieces. Paged continuously. Q155.C25.

Kircher, Athanasius, 1602–1680. . . . Ars magna

lucis et umbræ, in x. libros digesta . . . Editio altera priori multò auctior . . . Amstelædami, 1671. 16 p. l., 810 [*i.e.,* 710], [9] p. illus. 2 pl. (1 fold.), port., 2 tab., diagrs. 39.5 cm. Brockett 6731; Gamble 4889. Q155.K58 1671.

Guericke, Otto von 1602–1686. . . . *Experimenta nova . . . magdeburgica de vacuo spatio . . .* Amstelædami, 1672. 8 p. l., 244, [4] p., 1 l. illus. 2 double pl., port., diagrs., 33 cm. Q155.G93.

Fuente la Peña, Antonio de, 17th cent. *El ente dilucidado: discurso unico novissi[m]o que muestra ay en natural[ez]a; animales iraci-onales invisibles y quales sean . . .* Madrid, 1676. [18], 486, [19] p. 21 cm. TLB154.F9 1676.

Galatheau, de, *fl.* 1662–1674. *Dissertation touchant l'empire de l'homme, sur les autres animaux, & sur toutes les creatures sublunaires . . .* Paris, 1676. 3 p. l., 87, [1] p. 16 cm. BD450.G14.

Lohmeier, Philipp, *d.* 1680, praeses. . . . *Exercitatio physica de artificio navigandi per aerem . . .* Rinthelij, [1676]. 28 p. 20 x 16 cm. [Brockett 7674]. TLD902.L83.

Sturm, Johann Christoph, 1635–1703. *Collegium experimentale, sive Curiosum, in quo primaria hujus seculi inventa & experimenta physico-mathematica . . . quodqe nunc . . . adspicere voluit Johannes Christophorus Sturmius . . .* Norimbergae, 1676–1685. 3 v. in 1. illus. 21 cm. [Gamble 1336]. Q155.S92.

Borelli, Giovanni Alfonso, 1608–1679. *De motv animalivm . . . Opvs posthumum . . .* Romae, 1680–1681. 2 v. 18 fold. pl., 22 cm. [Brockett 2040]; Gamble 519. QP301.B72.

Bernoulli, Jacques, 1654–1705. . . . *Dissertatio de gravitate ætheris.* Amstelædami, 1683. 260 p. illus. 17 cm. QC17.B52.

Major, Johann Daniel, 1634–1693. . . . *See-farth nach der neuen welt / ohne schiff- und segel; anno 1670 zu erst / und nu wiederumb / der gelehrten welt vorgestellet.* Hamburg, 1683. 11 p. l., 258, [5] p. front. 18 cm. AE4.M3.

Lana Terzi, Francesco, 1631–1687. *Magisterivm natvræ, et artis. Opvs physico-mathematicvm . . .* Brixiæ, 1684–1692. 3 v., pl., 41.5 cm. Gamble 1133. Q155.L24.

[Fontenelle, Bernard le Bovier de], 1657–1757. *A plurality of worlds. Written in French . . . Translated into English by Mr. Glanvill.* London, 1688. 6 p. l., 152 p. 16 cm. First French edition 1686. QB54.F68p 1688.

Pasch, Georg, 1661–1707. . . . *De novis inventis, quorum accuratiori cultui facem prætulit antiquitas, tractatus . . .* Editio secunda . . . Lipsiæ, 1700. 8 p. l., 812, [125] p. front. 21.5 x 17.5 cm. Q155.P27 1700.

[Saunders, Richard], *d.* 1692. . . . *A discourse of angels: their nature and office, or ministry. Wherein is shewed what excellent creatures they are, and that they are the prime instruments of God's providence . . .* London, 1701. 4 p. l., 314 p. 21 cm. BT965.S25.

[Stübel, Andreas], 1653–1725. *Der neu-bestellte Agent von Haus aus, mit allerhand curieusen Missiven, Brieffen, Memorialien . . . Correspondencen . . . nach Erforderung der heutigen Staats- und gelehrten Welt.* Freyburg, 1704–1709. 3 v. illus. 16.5 cm. AC33.S94.

[Defoe, Daniel], 1661?–1731. *The consolidator: or, Memoirs of sundry transactions from the world in the moon. Tr. from the lunar language, by the author of The true-born English Man.* London, 1705. 2 p. l., 300 p. 19 cm. PR3404.C75 1705.

Becher, Johann Joachim, 1635–1682. . . . *Närrische Weisheit und weise Narrheit . . .* [n.p.], 1707. 39 p. l., 208 p. front. 14 cm. T44.B39.

[Bordelon, Laurent], 1653–1730. *L'histoire des imaginations extravagantes de Monsieur Oufle, causées par la lecture des livres qui traitent de la magie, du grimoire, des démoniaques, sorciers . . . des fées, ogres . . . phantômes & autres revenans . . .* Amsterdam, 1710. 2 v. front. pl. 17.5 cm. BF1410.B72.

Hauksbee, Francis, *d.* 1713? *Physico-mechanical experiments on various subjects . . .* 2d ed. London, 1719. 8 p. l., 336 p. VIII fold. pl. 20 cm. QC19.H37 1719.

Vanossi, Antonio, 1683–1757. *Placita physica de sympathia, & antipathia deprompta ex P. Francisco Tertio de Lanis . . .* Viennae, [1724?]. 3 p. l., 319, [12] p. 13 cm. BF110.V27.

Fabricius, Hieronymus, ab Aquapendente, *ca.* 1533–1619. . . . *Opera omnia anatomica et physiologica . . .* Lugduni Batavorum, 1738. 24 p. l., 452, [22] p. front., pl. 32 cm. QL803.F12.

La curiosité fructueuse; ouvrage dédié aux curieux intéressés . . . Paris, 1739. 14 [*i.e.,* 41], [2] p. 17 cm. Brockett 3222. TLB154.C97 1739.

[Worcester, Edward Somerset] 2d. Marquis of, 1601–1667. *A century of the names and scantlings of such inventions, as at present I can call to mind . . .* London, 1746. 94 p. 16 cm. First ed. 1663. [Gamble 113–114]. T44.W91 1746.

Baroni Cavalcabò, Clemente, 1726–1796. *L'impotenza del demonio di trasportare a talento per l'aria da un luogo all'altro i corpi umani . . .* Rovereto, 1753. xxiv, 141, [1] p. 23 cm. Brockett 1413;Gamble 4685. BF1524.B26.

Bingfield, William [pseud.]. *The travels and adventures of William Bingfield, Esq;*

containing, as surprising a fluctuation of circumstances, both by sea and land, as ever befel one man . . . London, 1753. 2 v. front. (v. 1) 16 cm. PZ3.B6126.

[Charbonnet, Pierre Mathias], *d.* 1815. *Éloge prononcé . . . devant les habitans des petites-maisons . . .* Avignon, 1760. 48 p. 17 cm. TLB154.C47 1760.

Caputi, Antonio. *Estasi e rapimento sopra la luna . . . Poema diviso in tre parti.* Napoli, 1763. 290, 8 p. 26 cm. Title vignette. PQ4215.C31.

Plets, Martin. *Den Engelske Flyveres Reisebeskrivelse, under hvilken Digt den naturlige Lovs og Folke-Rettens Grundfoetninger ungdommen til Nytte forestilles . . . Oversat af Svensk i Dansk . . . af Andreas Christian Krog . . .* Kiøbenhavn, 1774. 5 p. l., 142 p. 17 cm. PT9706.P72.

Cailhava d'Estendoux, Jean-François, 1730–1813. *Théâtre de m. Cailhava . . .* Paris, 1781–. v. 20.5 cm. PQ1959.C23A19.

[Bodard de Tezay, Nicolas Marie Félix], 1757–1823. *Le ballon, ou La physicomanie, comédie en un acte et en vers; représentée, pour la première fois . . . le 13 novembre 1783 . . .* Paris, 1783. 40 p. 20.5 cm. TLB154.B66 1783.

The balloon jester; or, Flights of wit and humour . . . with a diverting account of the adventures and reception of the air balloon . . . London, [1783]. 72 p. front. 18 cm. TLB154.G73 1783.

[C, M]. *The sheep, the duck, and the cock: a dramatic fable, written at Paris soon after the ascension . . . of the famous air balloon . . . at Versailles, Sept. 19, 1783.* Bath, [1783?]. 32 p. illus. 21 cm. Tr. of "Le mouton, le canard, et le coq, par M. C. . . ." TLB154.S54 1783.

[Thomson, William], 1746–1817. *The Man in the moon; or, Travels into the lunar regions, by the Man of the people.* London, 1783. 2 v. 16 cm. PZ3.T484m.

Arlandes, François Laurent, *Marquis* d', 1742–1809. *Les voyageurs aëriens, ou Relations des courses faites . . . par M. le major d'Arlande . . . le 22 novembre 1783 . . . & par M. Charles . . . le 2 décembre 1783 . . .* [n.p.], 1784. 20 p. illus. 17 cm. TLB273.A72.

Bertholon, Pierre, 1742–1800. *Des avantages que la physique, et les arts qui en dépendent, peuvent retirer des globes aërostatiques.* Montpellier, 1784. vj, [7]–82 p. 19.5 cm. TLB273.B54.

Brisson, Mathurin Jacques, 1723–1806. *Observations sur les nouvelles découvertes aërostatiques, et sur la probabilité de pouvoir diriger les ballons.* Paris, 1784. 63 p. 21 cm. Brockett 2213a. TLB273.B85.

Carra, Jean Louis, 1743–1793. *Essai sur la nautique aérienne, contenant l'art de diriger les ballons aérostatiques à volonté* . . . Paris, 1784. 23, [1] p. fold. pl. 20.5 cm. Brockett 2565; Gamble 949. TLB273.C31.

Duchosal, Marie Émilie Guillaume, 1763–1806. *Blanchard, poeme en deux chants* . . . Rouen et Paris, 1784. 13 p. 19.5 cm. TLB276.B6D82.

[Gérard, Laurent Gaspard], *Essai sur l'art du vol aérien* . . . Paris, 1784. 2 p. l., 178, xv p. fold. pl. 18 cm. Brockett 5199. TLB273.D44 no. 8.

Huber, Jean, 1721–1786. *Observations sur le vol des oiseaux de proie.* . . . Genève, 1784. 51 p. 7 fold. pl. 25.5 x 20.5 cm. Brockett 6294; Gamble 5221. QL698.H87.

Kratzenstein, Christian Gottlieb, 1728–1795. *L'art de naviguer dans l'air* . . . Copenhaven & Leipzig, 1784. 2 p. l., 90, [1] p. 2 pl. (1 fold.) 20.5 cm. Brockett 6879; Gamble 1127. TLD902.K9.

Martyn, Thomas, *fl.* 1760–1816. *Hints of important uses, to be derived from aerostatic globes. With a print of an aerostatic globe, and its appendages. Originally designed in 1783.* London, 1784. 16 p. fold. front. 35 cm. Brockett 8089. TLB274.M38.

The modern Atalantis; or, The devil in an air balloon. Containing the characters and secret memoirs of the most conspicuous persons of high quality, of both sexes, in the island of Libertusia, in the western ocean. Tr. from the Libertusian language. . . . London, 1784. iv, 135 p. 20 cm. TLB154.M68 1784.

Robert, Anne Jean, 1758–1820. *Mémoire sur les expériences aérostatiques faites par MM. Robert frères* . . . Paris, 1784. 1 p. l., 20 p. 28 x 21.5 cm. Brockett 10412. TLD902.R64.

Bibliothèque physico-économique, instructive et amusante, année 1784, ou troisième année . . . Paris, 1785. viii, 421 p. 3 fold. pl. 17 cm. AC20.B58.

Baldwin, Thomas, *aeronaut. Airopaidia: containing the narrative of a balloon excursion from Chester, the eighth of September, 1785, taken from minutes made during the voyage* . . . Chester, 1786. iiii–viii, 3 p. l., 360 (*i.e.,* 361) p. incl. tables. fold. pl. (part col.), fold. map. 22 cm. Brockett 1203. TLB273.B186.

Jeffries, John, 1745–1819. *A narrative of the two aerial voyages of Doctor Jeffries with Mons. Blanchard; with meteorological observations and remarks.* London, 1786. 60, [13] p.: ill. 29 cm. Includes ill. and ts. of trans. of French not included in original. [Brockett 6577]; [Gamble 4878]. TLB276.J4A31 1786b. (See also Appendix, Manuscripts, Jeffries, *Narration*, 1830, TLB159.J47.)

Lunardi, Vincent, 1759–1806. *An account of five aerial voyages in Scotland, in a series of letters to his guardian* . . . London and Edinburgh, 1786. 6, 114 p. 1 l. front. (port.) 2 pl. 20.5 cm. Brockett 7813; Gamble 696. TLB276.L8A18.

The Balloon, or Aerostatic spy; a novel, containing a series of adventures of an aerial traveller; including a variety of histories and characters in real life . . . London, 1786. 2 v. 19 cm. TLB154.B19 1786.

Blumhofer, Max. *Die Luftschiffer, oder der Strafplanet der Erde. Ein komisch, satirisches original Singspiel in 3. Aufzügen.* Leipzig, 1787. 80 p. 15.5 cm. TLB154.B65 1787.

[Resnier, André Guillaume], 1729–1811. *République universelle, ou, L'humanité ailée, réunie sous l'empire de la raison* . . . [Genève, 1788]. viii, 398 p. 2 fold. pl. 23 cm. TLB154.R42 1788.

Olivari, Francis. *An essay on aërostation: wherein is exhibited the easiest method of constructing and directing aerostats, a plan for reconnoitering balloons, and a new hint for aerostatical telegraphs* . . . Dublin, 1797. v, 26 p. 3 pl. 21 cm. [Brockett 9368]. TLB274.O47.

Barthez, Paul Joseph, 1734–1806. *Nouvelle méchanique des mouvements de l'homme et des animaux.* Carcassonne, [1798]. xv, 1 p. l., 246, [2] p. 26 x 20.5 cm. [Brockett 1429]. QP301.B28.

[Zambeccari, Francesco, *conte*], 1752–1812. *Saggio sopra la teoria e pratica delle macchine aereostatiche* . . . Bologna, 1800. xiv p. 23.5 x 18.5 cm. Brockett 13111. TLB276.Z2A54.

Air Balloon. A full and accurate account of the two aërial voyages made by Mons^R. Garnerin, on Monday, June 28, and Monday, July 5, 1802; including the interesting particulars communicated by Captain Sowden and Mr. Locker, who accompanied M. Garnerin. As written by themselves. To which is prefixed, The origin of balloons . . . [Sommers Town, 1802]. 37 p. incl. col. front. 18.5 cm. TLB273.A29.

Zachariae, August Wilhelm, 1769–1823. *Die Elemente der Luftschwimmkunst.* Wittenberg, 1807. vi, 282 p. fold. pl. (diagrs.) 22.5 cm. Brockett 13112; Gamble 5307. TLB398.Z14e.

Kraskovitz, M. G. *Skizzirte Darstellung der vorzüglichen Versuche der Luft zu durchschiffen, und Blicke, auf ihren Zweck, Werth, und Vortheile.* Wien, 1810. 78 p. 18.5 cm. TLB398.K91.

Sadler, James, 1751–1828. *Balloon. An authentic account of the ærial voyage of Messrs. Sadler and Clayfield, who ascended in a most magnificent balloon from a field in the neighbourhood of Stoke's-Croft, Bristol, on Monday, September 24th, 1810.* . . . Bristol, [1810]. 11, [1] p. front. (fold. map) 20.5 cm. TLB276.S14B3.

Zachariae, August Wilhelm, 1769–1823. *Fluglust und Fluges Beginnen.* Leipzig, 1821. 40 p. 18.5 cm. Brockett 13113. This copy includes additional material (pp. 41–60): . . . *und Fluges Fortgang* . . . , 1822. TLB398.Z14.

Zachariae, August Wilhelm, 1769–1823. *Geschichte der Luftschwimmkunst, von 1783 bis zu den Wendelsteiner Fallversuchen.* Leipzig, 1823. xviii, 1 p. l., [3]–199, [1] p. 18.5 cm. Brockett 13114. TLB398.Z14g.

Dupuis-Delcourt, Jules François, 1802–1864. *Mémoire sur l'aérostation et la direction aérostatique.* Paris, 1824. v, [7]–37 p., 1 l. 27.5 cm. Brockett 3815. TLB273.D94.

[Pocock, George], . . . *The aeropleustic art, or Navigation in the air, by the use of kites, or buoyant sails* . . . [London, 1827]. 1 p. l., 51 p. col. pl. 30.5 x 24 cm. Brockett 9861. TLD951.P7423b 1827.

Forster, Thomas Ignatius Maria, 1789–1860. *Annals of some remarkable aërial and alpine voyages, including those of the author; to which are added observations on the affections to which aerial and mountain travellers are liable* . . . London, 1832. xv, [1], 120 p. illus. 21.5 cm. Brockett 4944. [With his *Researches about atmospheric phenomena.* London, 1923. Copy 2.] TLB251.F73.

Rainold, K. G. *Erinnerungen an merkwürdige Gegenstände und Begebenheiten, verbunden mit erheiternden Erzählungen* . . . Wien und Prag, 1832. 350, [4] p. illus. 26 cm. AC35.R16.

Dubochet, J. A. *Recherches sur le vol des oiseaux et l'art aéronautique* . . . Nantes, 1834. 1 p. l., 76 p. pl. 20 cm. Brockett 3766. TLD181.D81.

Mason, [Thomas] Monck, 1803–1889. *Account of the late aeronautical expedition from London to Weilburg, accomplished by Robert Holland, esq., Monck Mason, esq., and Charles Green, aeronaut* . . . London, 1836. 52 p. 21.5 cm. Brockett 8182; [Gamble 711]; [R-P 15]. TLB276.M3A2.

Costa, Marco Antonio. *Saggi sull'aerostatica e sull' aeronautica.* . . . Napoli, 1837. 8 p. l., [5]–116 p., 1 l., 96 p. fold. pl. 23 cm. Brockett 3117. With *Complemento della seconda parte del secondo saggio sull'aerostatica e sull'aeronautica.* [Napoli, 1838?] 32 p. 23 cm. TLB273.C83.

[Garibbo, Luigi], 1784–1869. *Cenni storici sull'aeronautica fino alle recenti ascensioni fatte dal sig. Green e compagni da Londra e da Parigi* . . . Firenze, 1838. 175, [1] p. 20.5 cm. "Avvertimento" signed: L. G. [*i.e.,* Luigi Garibbo]. Brockett 5137. TLB398.G23.

Argentati, Raffaele. *Descrizione di un apparecchio locomotore applicabile alla direzione de' globi aerostatici*. Senigallia, 1840. 15 p. fold. pl. 21 cm. Dedication dated 18 Jan. 1841. Brockett 784. TLB274.D44.

Davidson, Richard Oglesby. *A disclosure of the discovery and invention and a description of the plan of construction and mode of operation of the aerostat; or, A new mode of aerostation*. Saint Louis, Mo., 1840. 32 p. illus. 19.5 cm. Brockett 3300; R-P 18. TLB398.D26.

Sanson, A. J. *Notice explicative sur la navigation dans l'air, ou Premières notions d'aéronautique . . . 2. éd. rev. et augm. . . .* Paris, 1840. 7, [1] p. 23.5 cm. Brockett 10783. TLD902.S22n.

The great steam-duck: or, A Concise description of a most useful and extraordinary invention for aerial navigation. By a member of the L[ouisville] L[iterary] B[rass] B[and]. . . .
32 p. 13.5 cm. [Louisville], 1841. R-P 20. TLB398.G78.

Pennington, John H. *A system of aerostation; or, Steam aerial navigation. . . .* 2d ed. Washington, D.C., 1842. 16 p. 21.5 cm. Brockett 9589; R-P 22. TLD902.P41.

Airé, George [pseud.]. *Narrative of the ascent and first voyage of the aerial steamer*. Cambridge, 1843. 16 p. illus. 20 cm. A hoax. Brockett 460. TLB252.H52A29.

Tupper, Martin Farquhar, 1810–1889. *Heart: a social novel. Etc. . . .* London, 1844. iv, 289 p. 20 cm. PR5699.T9A646.

The Annualette. A Christmas and New Year's gift. Ed. by a lady. Boston, 1845. 141 p. illus. 15 cm. PN511.A61 1845.

Marey-Monge, Edmond, *b.* 1807. *Études sur l'aérostation . . .* Paris, 1847. xiv, 351 p. 1x fold.

pl. 21.5 cm. Brockett 8039; Gamble 1163. TLB274.M32.

Dupuis-Delcourt, Jules François, 1802–1864. . . . *Nouveau manuel complet d'aérostation; ou, Guide pour servir à l'histoire et à la pratique des ballons . . .* Paris, 1850. vi, 292 p. illus., 16 fold. pl. (incl. ports., map, plans) 18 cm. (Manuels-Roret). Brockett 3816; Gamble 538. TLB273.D94n.

Sheldon, William, *d.* 1871. *Aerial navigation and the patent laws. . . .* Boston, 1850. 46 p. illus., diagrs. 23.5 cm. Gamble 2798; R-P 27. TLC802.S54.

Zeise, Heinrich, 1793–1863. *Die Aëronautik früher und jetzt, nebst theoretischen und practischen Vorschlägen zu einer vervollkommneteren Luftschiffahrtskunst . . .* Altona, 1850. viii, 190, [2] p. fold. front. 22 cm. Brockett 13154. TLB273.Z5.

Printed Books: 1851–1914
(in order of publication year)

The following volumes from the Gimbel collection were selected not only to illustrate the depth and range of this extraordinary library of rare aeronautica and collection of rare books but also to call attention to a series of additional volumes of critical importance in the history of flight. As in the list of annotated items, these books cover a range of topics from serious engineering texts and detailed histories to works of the imagination that inspired past generations with the desire to fly. In many cases, it would be very difficult to justify the decision to treat one volume with a full annotation and another as a title on this list.

Dupuis-Delcourt, Jules François, 1802–1864. . . . *Nouveau Manuel complet d'Aérostation ou, Guide pour servir à l'Histoire et à la pratique des ballons. . . .* Paris: A la Librairie encyclopédique de Roret, 1850. vi, 292 p. illus., 16 fold. pl. (incl. ports., map, plans) 18 cm. Brockett 3818; Gamble 538. TLB273.D94n.

Sheldon, William, *d.* 1871. *Aerial Navigation and the Patent Laws. . . .* Boston: Thurston, Torrey, & Company, 1850. 46 p. illus., diagrs. 23.5 cm. Brockett 2798; Randers-Pehrson 27. TLC802.S54.

Wise, John, 1808–1879. *A System of Aero-nautics, Comprehending its Earliest Inves-tigations, and Modern Practice and Art. . . .* Philadelphia: J. A. Speel, 1850. xvi, [17]–310 p. front. (port.) plates. 22.5 cm. Brockett 12945; Gamble 849; Randers-Pehrson 28. TLB251.W81.

Michel, J.-B. *La Locomotion aérienne Démontrée Possible par la solution d'un problème mathématique et physique appliqué à une machine inventée par J.-B. Michel* Paris: Chez l'auteur, 1851. 24 p. fold. pl. 25 cm. Brockett 8423. TLD902.M62.

[Locke, Richard Adams, 1800–1871], *The Celebrated "Moon Story," its Origin and Incidents; with a Memoir of the Author, and an Appendix, Containing, I. An Authentic Description of the Moon; II. A New Theory of the Lunar Surface in Relation to that of the Earth. By William N. Griggs*. New York: Bunnell and Price, 1852. 143 p. 15 cm. QB52.L81 1852.

Coxwell, Henry Tracey, 1819–1900. *Balloons for Warfare; a Dialogue between an Aeronaut and a General, by Henry Coxwell. . . .* London: J. Wesley, [1854]. Cover title, 8 p. illus. 19 cm. Brockett 3152. UGH3157.C87.

Schele, De Vere, Maximilian, 1820–1898. *Stray Leaves from the Book of Nature . . .* New York: G. P. Putnam & Co., 1855. 291 p. 18.5 cm. Q163.S32.

Locke, Richard Adams, 1800–1871. *The Moon Hoax; A Discovery that the Moon has a Vast Population of Human Beings. . . .* New York: W. Gowans, 1859. vi, [7]–63 p. incl. front. 24.5 cm. QB52.L81 1859.

Arnoult, Eugène d', *Voyage du Géant; de Paris à Hanovre en Ballon, E. d'Arnoult . . .* Paris: E. Dentu, 1863. 125 p. incl. front. 14 cm. Brockett 818. TLB276.T7A76.

Hale, William, *Treatise on the Comparative Merits of a Rifle Gun and Rotary Rocket, Considered as a Mechanical Means of Ensuring a Correct Line of Flight to a Body Impelled Through Space. By William Hale, C.E.* London: W. Mitchell, 1863. 39 p. fold. pl. 21 cm. UD390.H16.

La Landelle, Gabriel de, 1812–1886. *Aviation ou Navigation aérienne, par G. de la Landelle. . . .* Paris: E. Dentu, 1863. 3 p. l., [3]–4, [9]–315 p. 17.5 cm. Brockett 7140. TLB399.L19.

Ponton d'Amécourt, Gustave, *Vicomte* de, 1825–1888. *La Conquête de L'Air par L'Hélice; Exposé d'un Nouveau Système d' Aviation, par le vte. de Ponton d'Amécourt . . .* Paris: Chez tous les libraires et chez l'auteur, [1863]. 40 p. 24 cm. TLD802.P81.

[Tournachon, Félix], 1820–1910. *Le Droit au vol, par Nadar [pseud.].* Paris: J. Hetzel, 1865. 2 p. l., iii, 115, [1] p. 19 cm. Brockett 8973; Gamble 2199. TLB399.T73.

Verne, Jules, 1828–1905. *Las Escursiones Aereostáticas, por Julio Verne. Primera Version Española por Don Felipe de Burgos.* Barcelona: Trilla y Serra, [1865?]. 71, [1] p. illus. 28 cm. TLB273.V52.

Ponton d'Amécourt, Gustave, *Vicomte* de, 1825–1888. *Collection de Mémoires sur la locomotion aérienne sans ballons, publiée par le vte. de Ponton d'Amécourt.* Paris: Gauthier-Villars, 1864–[1867]. 1 p. l., [v]–viii p., 1 l., 152 p. diagrs. 27.5 x 22 cm. Brockett 9898; Gamble 2063. TLB155.P81.

La Landelle, Gabriel de, 1812–1886. . . . *Pigeon Vole. Aventures en l'air. Aviation.* Paris: P. Brunet, 1868. 3 p. l., [3]–414 p. illus. 18.5 cm. Brockett 7148. TLB165.L19.

Simões, Augusto Filippe, 1835–1884. *A Invenção dos Aerostatos Reivindicada Exame Critico das Noticias e Documentos Concernentes ás Tentativas Aeronauticas de Bartholomeu Lourenço de Gusmão, por Augusto Filippe Simões* . . . Evora: Typographia da Folha do Sul, 1868. 116 p., 2 l., 2 pl. 19.5 cm. TLB290.G98S.

[Vaucheret,   ], 1821–1899. *Aventures de Paul enlevé par un Ballon, par Jean Bruno* [pseud.]. Paris: Bernardin-Béchet, [1869]. 32 p. col. front., col. plates. 31 x 24 cm. TLB418.B89.

Dagron, Pruden René Patrice, 1819–1900. *La Poste par pigeons voyageurs. Souvenir du siège de Paris. Spécimen identique d'une des pellicules de dépêches portées à Paris par pigeons voyageurs. Photographiées par Dagron . . . Notice sur le voyage du ballon le Niepce Emportant M. Dagron et ses collaborateurs et détails sur la mission qu'ils avaient à remplir.* Tours-Bordeaux: [Typographie Lahure]; Paris, 1870–1871. 24 p. 18 cm. Photographic film (5 x 3.5 cm.) attached to a folded slip of paper with descriptive letterpress laid in. Brockett 3248. DC313.D12 1944.

Balloon Post. . . . no. 1–6; Apr. 11–17, 1871. Boston, Mass., 1871. 60 p. 28.5 cm. Randers-Pehrson 53. AP2.B19.

Le Journal du Siège de Paris, publié par Le Gaulois. [1.–36. journée; 15 sept. 1870–28 jan. 1871] Paris, 1871. 2 p. l., 476 p. 26.5 cm. DC313.J8.

Haddock, John A., *Mr. Haddock's Narrative of his Hazardous and Exciting Voyage in the Balloon Atlantic with Prof. Jno. La Mountain.* . . . Philadelphia: Press of Haddock and Son, 1873. iv, 5–15 p. front., illus., plates. 23 cm. Randers-Pehrson 55. TLB276.H2A2.

Raymond, Rossiter Worthington, 1840–1918. *The Man in the Moon and Other People.* New York: American News Co., [1874]. 347 p. illus. 20 cm. PZ3.R271m 1874.

Pettigrew, James Bell, 1834–1908. *La Locomotion chez les animaux; ou Marche, natation et vol, suivie d'une dissertation sur l'aéronautique par J. Bell Pettigrew.* . . . Paris: G. Baillière, 1874. 3 p. l., 360 p. front. illus. 21.5 cm. Brockett 9653. TLD181.P51 1874f.

Fonvielle, Wilfrid de, 1826–1914. *De l'Aérostation militaire de Wilfrid de Fonvielle* . . . Paris: A. Ghio, 1876. 16 p. 21 cm. Brockett 4701; Gamble 361L. UGH903.F68.

Tissandier, Gaston, 1843–1899. *Simples Notions sur les ballons et la navigation aérienne par Gaston Tissandier, avec un frontispice par Albert Tissandier et 36 vignettes par G. Mathieu.* Paris: Librairie Illustrée, [1876]. viii

[9]–125 p., 1 l. incl. front., illus. 16.5 cm. Brockett 11909. TLD931.T61.

Brannon, Philip, *The Air-Boat for Arcustatic Air-Travel, Dispensing with the Use of Gas, Hydrogen, Hot or Vapor Air Balloons, and Making Aero-navigation Facile, Rapid, Safe & Certain. With sketch cuts by the author, and supplementary abstract of his inventions.* . . . London: The author; sold by E. & F. N. Spon; London and New York: E. W. Allen, London, 1879. 6 p. l., [9]–56 p. front., illus., plates (1 double) 22 cm. TLD902.B82.

[Savage, Minot J.], *The Back of the Moon: or, Observations of Lunar Phases. By A. Lunar Wray.* Boston: Lee and Sheppard Publishers; New York: Charles T. Dillingham, 1879. 130 p. 17 cm. PS991.W94.

Kress, Wilhelm, 1836–1913. *Aëroveloce; Lenkbare Flugmaschine, Erfunden und Beschrieben von Wilhelm Kress.* Wien: Im Selbstverlage des Verfassers, 1880. 26 p. III fold. pl . 25.5 cm. Brockett 693; Gamble 2342. TLB399.K9.

Yon, Gabriel, 1835–1894. *Note sur la Direction des aérostats par M. L.-Gabriel Yon.* Paris: Typographie G. Chamerot, 1880. 1 p. l., 35 p. 16 pl. 28 x 23 cm. Brockett 13101. TLD901.Y5.

Figuier, Louis, 1819–1894. . . . *Les Aérostats, par Louis Figuier, Ouvrage illustré de 53 gravures sur Bois.* Paris: Jouvet et Cie, 1882. 2 p. l., 268 p. illus. (incl. ports.) 18 cm. Brockett 4536; Gamble 567. TLB273.F47.

Goupil, Alexandre, *La Locomotion aérienne; Étude par A. Goupil.* . . . Charleville: Impr. de A. Pouillard, 1884. 112 p. illus. VII fold. pl., diagrs. 25 cm. Brockett 5403; Gamble 4832. TLB400.G71.

Renard, Charles, *Le Ballon dirigeable La France. Nouvelles expériences exécutées en 1885, par M. le capitaine Ch. Renard.* Paris: Gauthier-Villars, 1886. Cover title, 7 p. illus. (map) pl., diagrs. 29 x 23 cm. Brockett 10250. TLD921.L17R4.

Moedebeck, Hermann W.L., *Handbuch der Luftschiffahrt, mit Besonderer Berück-sichtichung Ihrer Militairschen Verwendung, von H. Moedebeck.* Leipzig: E. Schloemp, 1886. 2 v. in 1. illus. 4 fold. pl. 24.5 cm. (Ex libris Gaston Tissandier.) Brockett 8604. TLB400.M69.

Marey, Étienne-Jules, *Le Vol des oiseaux.* . . . Paris: G. Masson, 1890. xvi, 394 p. illus. 25 cm. Brockett 8035. TLD181.M32.

Tissandier, Gaston, 1843–1899. *Souvenirs et récits d'un aérostier militaire de l'armée de la Loire 1870–1871; Avec une lettre autographe du Général Chanzy et de nombreuses illustrations de V.-A. Poirson.* Paris: M. Dreyfous, 1891. x, 356 p. incl. front., illus., plates., facsim. 28.5 cm. Brockett 11874; Gamble 3771. UGH3157.T61.

Sibbet, Robert Lowry, *The Siege of Paris; by an American Eyewitness, Robert Lowry Sibbet.*

With illustrations. Harrisburg, Pa.: Meyers Printing and Publishing House, 1892. ix, 580 p. pl. ports., maps, plan. 24 cm. DC314.S56.

Godard, Eugène, *Vingt-cinq ascensions en Orient par l'aéronaute Eugène Godard (Extraits des journaux bulgares)* . . . Paris, 1893. Cover title, 32 p. illus. (incl. port.) 21.5 cm. Brockett 5309. TLB276.G6A4.

Astor, John Jacob, *A Journey in Other Worlds. A Romance of the Future.* . . . New York: D. Appleton and Company, 1894. vi p., 1 l., 476 p. front. pl. 19.5 cm. PZ3.A858.

Proceedings of the International Conference on Aerial Navigation, Held in Chicago, Aug. 1, 2, 3 & 4, 1893. New York: *American Engineer & Railroad Journal,* 1894. Brockett 9993; Gamble 4561; Randers-Pehrson 98. TLB61.I63 1893.

Wouwermans, Armand. *Contribution à la Bibliographie de la locomotion aérienne, par Armand Wouwermans.* Anvers, 1894. 43, [1] p. 1 l., front. 32 x 24.5 cm. Brockett 12986. Z5063.W93.

Griffith, George, *Olga Romanoff, of the Syren of the Skies; a Sequel to the Angel of the Revolution* . . . London: Tower Publishing Co., 1894. viii, 377 p. illus. 21 cm. PZ3.G853r.

Lowe, Thaddeus S.C., 1832–1913. *Early Aeronautic and Meteorological Investigations.* Los Angeles: B. R. Baumgardt, 1895. 31 p. 23 cm. TLB311.L91.

Marey, Étienne Jules, 1830–1904. *Movement, by E. J. Marey.* . . . London: W. Heinemann, 1895. xv, 323 p. illus. 19 cm. QP301.M31m.

Dickman, Joseph Theodore, 1857–1927. *Balloons in War; a Lecture Delivered Before the Class of Officers at the United States Infantry and Cavalry School, Fort Leavenworth, Kansas, March 27th, 1896, Class 1895–'97.* Leavenworth, Kans.: United States Infantry and Cavalry School, 1896. 14 p. photocopy. Gamble 3596; Randers-Pehrson 106. UGH3157.D55.

Proctor, Richard Anthony, 1837–1888. *Other Worlds than Ours; The Plurality of Worlds Studied Under the Light of Recent Scientific Researches, by Richard A. Proctor.* New York: D. Appleton and Company, 1896. 334 p. col. front., illus., plates (part col.) 20 cm. QB51.P96.

Cyrano de Bergerac, Savinien, 1619–1655. *A Voyage to the Moon.* . . . New York: Doubleday & McClure Co., 1899. xxx, 219 p., front. plates, port. 15 cm. Randers-Pehrson 133. PQ1793.A2A 1899.

Bacon, John Mackenzie, 1846–1904. *By Land and Sky, by the Rev. John M. Bacon* . . . London: Isbister, 1900. 275 p. illus. 23 cm. Brockett 1120; Gamble 433. TLB276.B2A2.

Serviss, Garrett Putnam, 1851–1929. *Other Worlds: Their Nature, Possibilities and Habitability in the Light of the Latest Discoveries, by Garrett P. Serviss* . . . New York: D. Appleton and

Company, 1901. xv, 282 p. front. (chart) illus., plates. 19.5 cm. QB601.S49.

André, M. H., *Les Dirigeables; Étude complète de la direction des ballons, des tentatives réalisées, et des projets nouveaux, par M. H André.* . . . Paris: [etc.] C. Béranger, 1902. 2 p. l., iii, 346 p. illus. 22 cm. Brockett 612; Gamble 869. TLD901.A55.

[Marquis, Raoul, 1863–], *Les Ballons dirigeables et la navigation aérienne, par Henri Graffigny* [pseud.] . . . *Nouvelle édition augmentée avec 48 figures intercalées dans le texte.* Paris: J.-B. Baillière et Fils, 1902. 2 p. l., [7]–380 p. incl. illus., tables, diagrs. 18 cm. TLD901.M35.

United States, War Department, *Act of the Hague Peace Conference, proclaimed Nov. 1, 1901; the 3d item prohibits the launching of projectiles and explosives from balloons.* General Orders No. 4, Washington, D.C., 1902. 40 p. 19 cm. UB502.A2 1900.

Lecornu, Joseph, . . . *La Navigation aérienne; Histoire documentaire et anecdotique. Les Précurseurs, les Montgolfier, les deux Écoles, le siège de Paris, les grands dirigeables et le sport aérien* . . . Paris: Nony & Cie, 1903. vii, 484 p. illus. (incl. ports., maps, facsims.) diagrs. 31 cm. Brockett 7364. TLB251.L46.

Wright, Wilbur, 1867–1912. *Experiments and Observations in Soaring Flight* [Preprint of Journal of the Western Society of Engineers, vol. 3, no. 4, August 1903] Chicago: Western Society of Engineers, 1903. 18 p. illus. 23 cm. Brockett 13015; Gamble 2281. TLD621.W95.

Haenlein, Paul, 1833–1904. *Über das jetzige stadium des lenkbaren luftschiffes.* . . . Leipzig: Grethlein & Co., [1904]. 48 p. illus., diagrs. 20 cm. Brockett 5655. TLB276.H3A1.

Ferber, Ferdinand, 1862–1909. *Les Progrès de l'aviation depuis 1891 par le vol plané.* . . . Paris, Nancy: Berger-Levrault & Cie, 1905. 53 p., 1l. illus. 22 cm. Deuxième édition. Brockett 4462; Gamble 2394. TLB400.F34m.

Ader, Clément, *La première étape de l'aviation militaire en France, par C. Ader.* Paris: J. Bosc et Cie, 1907. 67 [1] p. front. 2 pl. on 1l. 25 cm. UGB9.A23.

Aero Club of America, *Navigating the Air; A Scientific Statement of the Progress of Aëronautical Science up to the Present Time, by the Aero Club of America* . . . New York: Doubleday, Page & Co., 1907. 7 p. l., ix–xli, 259 p. front illus., plates, ports. 20.5 cm. Brockett 128; Gamble 117. TLB251.A25.

Baden-Powell, Baden Fletcher Smyth, 1860–1937. *Ballooning as a Sport, by Maj. B. Baden-Powell* . . . Edinburgh and London: W. Blackwood and Sons, 1907. xx, 135, [1] p. 3 pl. (incl. front.) 20 cm. Brockett 1145; Gamble 435. TLB275.B13.

Lanchester, Frederick William, 1868–?. *Aerodynamics, Constituting the First Volume of a Complete Work on Aerial Flight.* . . . London: A. Constable & Co., Ltd., 1907. xvi, 442 p. front., illus., diagrs. (1 fold.) 23 cm. Gamble 4904. TLD209.L24.

Bracke, Albert, *Les Hélicoptères Paul Cornu.* Paris: F. L. Vivien, 1908. Cover-title, 16 p. illus. 22 cm. TLD809.B79.

Fonvielle, Wilfrid de, *Notre Flotte Aérienne, par Wilfrid de Fonvielle et Georges Besançon.* . . . Paris: Gauthier-Villars, 1908. 2 p. l., 234 p. illus. (incl. ports.) 22 cm. Brockett 4863a; Gamble 1045. TLD901.F68.

Parseval, August von, *Motorballon und Flugmaschine.* . . . Wiesbaden: J. F. Bergmann, 1908. 39 p. illus. 24.5 cm. Gamble 1229. TLD901.P26m.

Tatin, Victor, *Éléments d'aviation, par Victor Tatin.* . . . Paris: Dunod & E. Pinat, 1908. 2 p. l., vi, 65 p., 1l. illus. (incl. port.) diagrs. 27 cm. Gamble 2182. TLB400.T21.

Weiss, Joseph Bernard, *The Problem of Flight . . . General Considerations. The Principle of Gliding Flight . . . The Present Position. By José Weiss.* . . . London: King, Sell & Olding, Ltd., 1908. 14 p., 2l. III fold. pl. (incl. diagrs.) 25 cm. TLC112.W42p.

Adams, Heinrich, *Flug, von Heinrich Adams. Unser Flieger, von Wilbur und Orville Wright.* Leipzig: C. F. Amelangs Verlag, 1909. viii, 144 p. illus. 24.5 cm. Gamble 1424. TLB400.A21.

Berget, Alphonse, i.e., Thomas Claude Xavier Alphonse, . . . *La Route de l'air; Aéronautique Aviation, Histoire—Théorie—Pratique. 82 Diagrammes explicatifs, 66 Gravures tirées hors texte* . . . Paris: Hachette et Cie, 1909. 3 p. l., vi, [2] 311, [1] p. front., illus., plates. 25.5 cm. (This volume is ex libris Horace Oswald Short, with his bookplate.) Brockett 1593b. TLB251.B49r 1909.

Das Zeppelinbuch für die deutsche Jugend. . . . Stuttgart: Union Deutsche Verlagsgesellschaft, [1909?]. 107 p. illus. 21 cm. TLD901.Z5.

Grey, Charles Grey, 1875– . *Flying, the Why and Wherefore, by "Aero-amateur."* London: "The Aero," [1909]. 96 [2] p. fold. front., illus. 18.5 cm. TLB400.G84.

Hildebrandt, Alfred, 1870– . *Die Brüder Wright; Eine Studie über die Entwicklung der Flugmaschine von Lilienthal bis Wright, von Hauptmann. a. d. A. Hildebrandt* . . . Berlin: O. Elsner, 1909. 63, [1] p. illus. (incl. ports.) 23 cm. Gamble 1790. TLB290.W95H.

Hoogh, Peter, *Zeppelin und die Eroberung des Luftmeeres; zur Erinnerung an die Begeisterung Grosser Tage, von Dr. Peter Hoogh.* Leipzig: Uranus-Verlag, [ca. 1909]. 236 p. illus. 21 cm. Brockett 6260. TLB273.H77.

Peyrey, François, . . . *Les Oiseaux artificiels; avec une préface de Santos-Dumont.* . . . Paris: H. Dunod et E. Pinat, 1909. 8 p. l., [v]–xiv, 667 p. illus., diagrs. 23 cm. TLB535.P51.

Renard, Paul, 1854–1933. . . . *L'Aéronautique; Ouvrage illustré de 68 figures.* Paris: E. Flammarion, 1909. 2 p. l., 368 p. diagrs. 19 cm. Brockett 1028b; Gamble 337. TLB400.R39.

Squier, George Owen, *The Present Status of Military Aeronautics . . .* , in Smithsonian Institution, Annual Report. 1908. Washington, D.C., 1909. p. 117–144. 23 pl. on 13 l. 23.5 cm. UGH3207.S77.

Zodiac; anciens établissements aéronautiques Maurice Mallet, fondés en 1896; fournisseur agréé des gouvernements français et étrangers; dirigeables, captifs, sphériques, parachutes, treuils et tenders d'aérostation. Puteaux, [1909]. 31 p. illus. 27 cm. TLF237.Z8.

André, Henri, *Moteurs d'aviation et de dirigeables, par H. André.* Paris: L. Geisler, 1910. 3 p. l., 190, [4] p. 1l. illus., diagrs. 24.5 cm. TLE21.A55.

Calderara, Mario, *Manuel de l'aviateur-constructeur, par M. Calderara . . . [et] P. Banet-Rivet . . .* Paris: H. Dunod et E. Pinat, 1910. viii, 290 p. illus., diagrs. 19.5 cm. TLD481.C14.

Collins, Francis Arnold, *The Boy's Book of Model Aeroplanes; How to Build and Fly Them; With the Story of the Evolution of the Flying Machine.* . . . New York: Century Co., 1910. xi, 308 p. incl. illus., plates. front. 20 cm. TLB417.C71 1910.

Das Flugproblem, [von] Major v. Parseval [et al.]. Berlin: E. Frowein, 1910. 77 p. 20 cm. TLB400.P26.

Ferris, Richard, *How to Fly; or, The Conquest of the Air; The Story of Man's Endeavours to Fly and of the Inventions by Which He Has Succeeded, by Richard Ferris . . . Illustrated by Over One Hundred and Fifty Half-Tones and Line Drawings, Showing the Stages of Development from the Earliest Balloon to the Latest Monoplane and Biplane.* London, New York, [etc.]: T. Nelson and Sons, [1910]. 3 p. l., 11-475 p. col. front., illus., diagrs. 19.5 cm. Gamble 204. TLB251.F39 1910.

Lanchester, Frederick William, *Aerodonetics, Constituting the Second Volume of a Complete Work on Aerial Flight, by F. W. Lanchester . . .* , 2nd Edition. London: Constable & Co. Ltd., 1910. xv 433 p. incl. illus., port., tables, diagrs. front, fold. diagr. 23 cm. Gamble 4904. TLD209.L24a 1910.

Lougheed, Victor, *Vehicles of the Air; a Popular Exposition of Modern Aeronautics with Working Drawings, by Victor Lougheed . . .* [2nd ed.—revised and enl.] Chicago: Reilly and Britton Co., [1910]. 514 p. incl. front., illus., diagrs., plates (part. double) 23.5 cm. Gamble 289. TLB535.L88.

Modèles d'appareils d'aviation de l'antiquité à

nos jours. Paris: F. Vivien, 1910. 36 p. illus. 22 x 27.5 cm. TLB258.M67.

Surcouf, Édouard, *L'Aéronautique militaire; les dirigeables français et les dirigeables étrangers, l'accident du "République," l'avenir; conférence faites par M. Éd. Surcouf . . . à l'Hôtel des ingénieurs civils, pour la Séance Solennelle de la Société française de Navigation aérienne le 13 janvier 1910.* Paris: L'Aéronaute, [1910]. Cover title. 16 p. illus. 27.5 cm. UGH3147.S72.

Goldschmidt, Robert, *Les Aéromobiles, par Robert Goldschmidt . . . préface de m. Ernest Solvay. . . .* Paris: H. Dunod et E. Pinat; Bruxelles: Ramlot frères et soeurs, 1911. 4 p. l., 422 p. illus. (incl. maps), diagrs. 24 cm. TLB400.G62.

Painlevé, Paul, *Theorie und Praxis der Flugtechnik, von Paul Painlevé . . . [und] Émile Borel. . . .* Berlin: R. C. Schmidt & Co.; New York: E. Steiger & Co., 1911. 251 p. illus., double tab. diagrs. 22.5 cm. TLB400.P15.

Popper, Josef, 1838– . *Der Maschinen- und Vogelflug. Eine historisch-kritische flugtechnische Untersuchung. Mit besonderer Hervorhebung der Arbeiten von Alphonse Pénaud, von Josef Popper-Lynkeus, mit Figuren im Texte. Erweiterter Sonderabdruck aus der automobil- und flugtechnischen Zeitschrift "Der Motorwagen."* Berlin: M. Krayn, 1911. 103, [1] p. diagrs. 25.5 cm. TLD181.P83.

Rodgers, Calbraith Perry, *Story of My Flying with Complete Technical Description of My Aeroplane; Flying from Coast to Coast.* Chicago: Vin-Fiz Co., [1911]. 8 p. illus., photos. 16 cm. TLB290.R68.

Rotch, Abbott Lawrence, 1861–1912. *Charts of the Atmosphere for Aeronauts and Aviators, by A. Lawrence Rotch . . . and Andrew H. Palmer. . . .* 1st ed., 1st thousand. New York: J.

Wiley and Sons; [etc., etc.], 1911. 96 p., 1l. incl. 24 charts. 24 x 30 cm. QC879.R84.

Simmonds, Ralph, *All About Airships, a Book for Boys, by Ralph Simmonds . . . with a colour frontispiece and a large number of illustrations from photographs.* London, New York, [etc.]: Cassell and Company, Ltd., [1911]. 5 p. l., 374 p. col. front., plates. 21.5 cm. TLB251.S59.

Stelling, August, *12000 Kilometer im Parseval, von A. Stelling.* Berlin: G. Braunbeck & Gutenberg druckerei aktiengesellschaft, 1911. 209, [1] p. illus. 25 cm. TLD921.P26S82.

Wellman, Walter, 1858–1934. *The Aerial Age; a Thousand Miles by Airship over the Atlantic Ocean; Airship Voyages over the Polar Sea; The Past, the Present and the Future of Aerial Navigation.* New York: A. R. Keller & Company, 1911. 448 p. front., plates, ports. 20.5 cm. Gamble 4513. TLB285.W45.

Hayward, Charles Brian, *Practical Aeronautics; an Understandable Presentation of Interesting and Essential Facts in Aeronautical Science, by Charles B. Hayward . . . with introduction by Orville Wright . . .* Chicago: American School of Correspondence, 1912. xv, [1], 769 p. incl. front., illus., diagrs., plates. 25 cm. TLB535.H42 1912.

Inauguration du nouveau laboratoire aérodynamique de M. G. Eiffel. 19 mars 1912. Paris: L. Maretheux, imprimeur, 1912. 2 p. l., [3]–24 p. illus. 27 x 21 cm. TLD103.E3I3.

Lougheed, Victor, *Aeroplane Designing for Amateurs; A Plain Treatment of the Basic Principles of Flight Engineering—Including Heretofore Unpublished Facts Concerning Bird Flight and Aerodynamic Phenomena, by V. Lougheed. . . .* Chicago: Reilly & Britton Co., [1912]. 176 p. front., illus., diagrs. 18 cm. TLD481.L88.

[Michelin, André], *Notre Avenir et dans l'air.* Sceaux: gravé et imprimé par Charaire, 1912. Cover-title, 40 p. illus. (ports.) 21.5 cm. UGH903.M62.

Mouillard, Louis Pierre, 1834–1897. *Le Vol sans battement; ouvrage posthume inédit de L.-P. Mouillard . . . reconstitué et précédé d'une étude sur l'oeuvre ignorée de L. P. Mouillard par André Henry-Coüannier.* Paris: Librairie aéronautique, 1912. 484 p. front. (port.) illus., fold. pl. 23.5 cm. Gamble 5272. TLB535.M92.

Riley, James Whitcomb, 1849–1916. *The Flying Islands of the Night. . . .* Indianapolis: Bobbs-Merrill Co., [1913]. 4 p. l., 3–124 p. 16 mounted col. pl. (incl. front.) 25.5 cm. PS2704.F5.

Garros, Roland, 1888–1918. *L'Aéronautique par Roland Garros, Brindejonc des Moulinais, Alfred Leblanc, Frank Barra, Jean Bielovucic, comte de la Vaulx, Jacques Mortane, Marc Gouvieux, Marcel Viollette, Henri Mirguet; préface du baron d'Estournelles de Constant. Ouvrage orné de 48 pages d'illustrations photographiques hors texte et de plusieurs schémas.* Paris: P. Lafitte & Cie, [1914]. 2 p. l., xii, 389, [1] p. incl. illus., plates, ports., diagrs. 20.5 cm. TLB400.G24.

Guide Michelin pour les Officiers aviateurs; dressé avec le concours de la ligue aéronautique de France de Mr. Blondel la Rougery, et de l'Aérophile. Paris, 1914. 48 p. illus., maps. 18.5 cm. TLD1137.G94.

Hamel, Gustav, *Flying; Some Practical Experience by Gustave Hamel and Charles C. Turner.* London: Longmans, Green and Co., 1914. xii, 341 p. front., illus., plates. 24 cm. TLB535.H21.

Lasswitz, Kurd, . . . *Auf Zwei Planeten; Roman in Zwei Büchern . . .* Leipzig: B. Elischer, [1914]. 421, 545, [2] p. 19 cm. TLE1041.L34.

Manuscripts

(in chronological order)

Montgolfier, Abbé Alexandre-Charles. Letter (ALS) 178?, to his sister Marguerite-Thérèse at the Convent of Boulieu, north of Annonay[?]. 2 p. 21 cm. Mostly personal; reference to having been shaken up by hurrying too fast on the previous day in humid conditions. XF-2-1 2382 178?

? An extract from a letter from Paris, 1783 Oct. 20, to [?]. 2 p. 32.5 cm. Facts and statistics on the first three balloon ascents: 1783/8/27, 1783/9/19, 1783? XF-2-1 2393.1783/OCT. 20.

Pilâtre de Rozier, 1754–1785. Letter (ALS) [1784] to someone in the French Government? 4 p. 21.5 cm. Letter of thanks setting out several ideas for future experiments. XF-2-1 2396 [1784].

Costruzione e gonfiamento ed ascensione degli aereostati. Ms. in Italian, [1784?]. 5 p. illus. 20 cm. Includes drawings of filling apparatus and tethered balloon. Vendor's ts. note: Molto probabilmente falsificazione. TLB159.C84.

Memoria fatta da me D. Pavolo Andreani [1763–1823] *li 28 febbraro 1784 da servire per li prossimi esperimenti aerostatici.* Ms. in Italian, 1784/2/28. 3 p. illus. 30 cm. With diagrs. of balloon and equipment. Vendor's ts. note: Molto probabilmente falsificazione. TLB159.M53.

Davesseur, Marquise. Letter (AL) 1784/11/19, to the Marquis de Fourquevaux, Bonrepos (near Aix-en-Provence). 4 p. 18.5 cm. P. 3 has

a 12-line discussion of balloon ascensions. XF-2-1 2398 1784/NOV. 19.

Montgolfier, Étienne, 1745–1799. Letter (ALS) 1786/10/27, from Annonay, to the administrators of the Compagnie des Indes, Paris. 2 p. 20 cm. Address on p. [4]. On a shipment of paper; hope to get more orders. XF-2-1 2400 1786/OCT. 27.

Montgolfier, Étienne, 1745–1799. Letter (AL) 1787/1/15, from Annonay to Antoine Boissy d'Anglas, Paris. 4 p. 21 cm. Address on p. [4]. References to Jean-Baptiste Réveillon, the wallpaper manufacturer, and to a mausoleum erected in honor of Pilâtre de Rozier. XF-2-1 2401 1787/JAN. 15.

Oliphant, C. & R. Letter (ALS) and financial account, [1805], from Cockspur Street, Charing Cross, London, to [Vincent] Lunardi. 1 p. 33 cm. References to an account for purchases of hats between 1784 and 1786, presented on his return to England in 1805: "we trust you will not hesitate to favor us with a Draft for the amount [four pounds, three shillings]." XF-2-1 2405 [1805].

Augustin, [?]. Letter (ALS) 1817/4/8, from Lyon, to the Comte de Chabrol, Préfet du Département du Rhône. 2 p. 31.5 cm. Request for permission to make an aerostatic ascension in Lyon. XF-2-1 2414 1817/APR. 8.

Dibdin, Thomas Frognell. Letter (ALS) 1817/7/30, to [?]. 1 p. 24 cm. Discusses the possibility of making a kite fly for three months. XF-2-1 2416 1817/JUL. 30.

Balloon. [n.p.], 1821. 2 v. 18 cm. Ms. fictional day-book with many corrections, deletions, and insertions. Following the introductory pages it describes preparations for flight, with witty (?) dialog and "songs" interspersed. There are passages of political and social commentary. The actual flight is covered in three pages. TLB159.B19.

Jeffries, Doctor John, 1745–1819. *Narration des deux voyages aëriens du docteur Jeffries & de Monsieur Blanchard, avec des observations météorologiques & des remarques* ... Par le docteur Jeffries ... A Londres ... 1786. Traduite par Sacleu père en 1830. Elegantly written ms. volume. 34 x 26 cm. TLB159.J47. (Trans. of item in the Appendix, Printed Books: 1489-1850; Jeffries, *A narrative,* 1786. TLB276.J4A31 1786b.)

The Aerial Ship. [1835] 17 leaves. Bound. 33 cm. Holograph. The original ms. of an essay on the Comte de Lennox's airship *The Eagle,* written on backs of letter-wrappers, mostly addressed to Capt. F. Beaufort. References to the European Aeronautical Society. Includes a detached copy of the text as printed in *Aerial Navigation.* Bookplate and signature of John Lee. TLB159.A24.

Green, Charles, 1785–1870. Letter (ALS) 1840/3/21, from Highgate, London, to Page Nicol

Scott (surgeon), Norwich. 4 p. 23 cm. P. 3 blank. Address on p. 4. Thanking him for a gift of aerial documents; invitation to go with him into the pure and serene air. XF-2-1 2423 1840/MAR. 21.

Chapman, J. Letter (ALS) 1843/5/15, from 6A Lisson Grove, London, to H. Luriss[?]. 2 p. 22.6 cm. Criticizes the essay by Hamilton, the 1st ed. of which had been published in 1841 and the 2nd in 1842. (See Hamilton, 1843/5/18.) XF-2-1 2425 1843/MAY 15.

Spencer, Edward. Letter (ALS) 1846/3/9, from [?] to Davison Turner. 4 p. 25.4 cm. Account of his balloon ascents. XF-2-1 2427 1846/MAR. 9.

Green, Charles, 1785–1870. Letter (ALS) 1846/10/9, from the Hôtel de Bavière, to I. G. Flügel, Leipzig. 4 p. 29 cm. In reply to a request for autograph, Green describes his fifteenth ascent (Leipzig); p. 2 is blank; p. 3 is a "Copy" of Flügel's letter, the copy dated Oct. 7, 1847 [*sic*]; below (in different hand): "Received Oct. 11, 1846. F." "Mr. Charles George Green"'s card attached to p. 3. Address on p. 4. XF-2-1 2428 1846/OCT. 9.

Andrews, Solomon. Letter (ALS) 1849/3/12, from Perth Amboy, N.J., to John F. Frazee (M.D., Prof., University of Pennsylvania). 1 p. 24.7 cm. Seeks advice on possible difficulties in "navigating the atmosphere." XF-2-1 2431 1849/MAR. 12.

Beschreibung des Luftschiffes, [von] Karl [?] Rosenfeld. Vienna, 1850/1/5. 2 p. 39 cm. With drawing of an airship on top of the first page. XF-2-1 2432 1850/JAN. 5.

Green, Charles, 1785–1870. Letter (ALS) 1852/11/2, from Holloway to Mr. [Robert] Hollond, Regents Park, London. 2 p. 18 cm. With envelope. P. 2: "Having now made 504 ascents I do not intend ascending again except for scientific purposes. . . ." XF-2-1 2435 1852/NOV. 2.

Seymour, J. [?]. Letter (ALS) [1853?], to the editor of the *New York Sun.* 3 p. 32.5 cm. On the airship and the future of flying. XF-2-1 2439 [1853].

Boyer, C. Letter (ALS) 1858/8/29, from Onondaga, N.Y., to G.C.M. 4 p. 31.5 cm. The third page has a number of expectancies for the future, including the airplane and the wireless. XF-2-1 2442 1858/AUG. 29.

Slocum, H. W. Letter (ALS) 1862/6/14, to General [?]. 4 p. 20.5 cm. P. 3 blank. General McClellan requests that "an intelligent officer make frequent ascensions in the baloon [*sic*]." (See Chapman, 1861.) XF-2-1 2443 1862/JUN. 14.

Craine, J. Letter (ALS) 1858/9/20, from Lockport, N.Y., to "Cousin Andrew." 2 p. 19 cm. Balloon flight over Lockport, N.Y. XF-2-1 2444 1858/SEP. 20.

Verne, Jules, 1828–1905. Letter (ALS) 1890/2/3, from Amiens to G. F. Griges [= Griggs?; a child or young man], 45 Lauriston Road, South Hackney, London. In answer to a question as to whether there will be a sequel to his novel *Robur le conquérant,* he comments that "one should never abuse aerial journeys." 1 p. 21 cm. With envelope. Letterhead: Société Industrielle d'Amiens. XF-2-1 2456 1890/FEB. 3.

Langley, Samuel Pierpont, 1834–1906. Letter (TLS) 1898/11/30, from Washington, D.C., to Dr. Cyrus Adler, Washington, D.C. 2 p. 20.3 cm. On "Smithsonian Institution" letterhead. Concerning an assistant for Adler. XF-2-2 2509 1898/NOV. 30.

Rathbun, Richard. Letter (TLS) 1903/9/19, from Washington D.C., to Dr. Adler, New York City. 5 p. 20.5 cm. Re: published reports about Langley's statements on his flying machine. XF-2-2 2515 1903/SEP. 19.

Langley, Samuel Pierpont, 1834–1906. Letter (ALS) 1904/7/23, Ontario, to Dr. Cyrus Adler. 2 p. 17 cm. Re: "the launch," "the houseboat," etc.; preparing the model for flight; letter from Richard Rathbun[?]. XF-2-2 2522 1904/JUL. 23.

Santos-Dumont, Alberto, 1873–1932. Letter (ALS) [1908?] to [?]. 1 p. 19.5 cm. "I may begin the trials of my no. 15 next week; may be on Monday about 4 o'clock." Printed initials above: A. S-D. XF-2-1 2469 [1908?].

Prints

(in serial order; symbol © signifies color print)

1009
[Woodcut by Albrecht Dürer] Utrecht. This is a modern reproduction. (XP-XL-1).

1010
[Woodcut by Albrecht Dürer] Utrecht. This is a modern reproduction. (XP-XL-1).

1049
[Le globe aërostatique construit à Versailles] (XP-XL-2).

1064
Expérience aérostatique faite à Versailles le 19 Septembre 1783. Issued by Le Noir; announced in the *Journal de Paris* of October 20, 1783. (XP-XL-2).

1076
Expérience aérostatique faite à Marseille avec un ballon de 50 pieds de diametre portant deux voyageurs aëriens. Depicts the launch of a Montgolfier balloon on May 18, 1784, ornamented with an eagle with outstretched wings at the base of the envelope. (XL-2).

1080
Expérience aérostatique faite à Lyon. Paris [1784]. (XP-XL-2).

1084
Aérostat construit par les soins du Marquis de Brantes, d'Avignon. (XP-XL-2).

1086
Le Chateau Royale de Versailles du côté de la grande avenue de Paris. Paris. (XP-XL-2).

1126
Globe aérostatique. De M.ʳˢ Charles et Robert au Moment de leur depart du Jardin des Tuileries. Paris, [1783?]. (XP-XL-4).

1128
A l'honneur de Mrs. Charles et Robert. Expérience célébre faites à Paris. Paris, [1783?] (XP-XL-4).

1137
Second voyage aérien. Expérience faite dans le Jardin des Thuilleries par MM. Charles et Robert, le 1ᵉʳ xbre, 1783. [Paris, 1783]. (XP-XL-4).

1155
Au balon. ["Charles and Robert over Nesle. Hypothetical identification, based on Gimbel's grouping." —Air Force Academy library catalogue. More likely Académie de Dijon/Guyton de Morveau and Abbé Bertrand flight of 25 April 1784.] Apparently the original design for 1288. (XP-XL-4). (Watercolor). ©

1177
Dedicada al Exmo. Señor D. Vicente Maria de Vera de Aragon. 1794. (XP-XL-5).

1199
Charles Echard, Dessiné et gravé. Tour de Calais. Nouvelle Machine Aërostatique construite par M[ʳˢ]. Romain. Paris, [1784]. Part of title shown in brackets is supplied in ms. This rather imaginative depiction of the balloon flown on June 15, 1785, shows the craft departing from the coast at Calais to cross the Channel to England; the balloon actually flew from near Boulogne. The *Journal de Paris* of December 26, 1784 (p. 1528) mentions the appearance of this print. (XP-XL-5).

1212
Carte des marches aërographiques, dediée à M. Charles par . . . Perrier. Paris, [1784?]. Shows routes of balloons launched and flown by Charles (August 27), Montgolfier (September 19, 1783), Pilâtre de Rozier and the Marquis d'Arlandes (November 21, 1783), Charles (December 1, 1783), and Blanchard (March 3, 1784). (XL-6).

1227
Troisième voyage aérien de M. Blanchard. Rouen, [1784?]. (XP-XL-6). ©

1229
[Dover Castle], Pub[lishe]d Jan[uar]y 1, 1794 by S. W. Fores. An etching with very simple lines, based on the Thomas Rowlandson painting represented in print 1230 in this catalogue. The print depicts the beginning of the flight across the Channel by Jeffries and Blanchard on January 7, 1785. (XP-XL-6).

1235
[La quatorzième experience aerostatique de M. Blanchard, faite à Lille en Flandre le 26 Août 1785.] Proof before letters. Lille, [1785?]. (XP-XL-6). Title taken from the more advanced print 1234, which is colored.

1236
Entrée de Mr. Blanchard et du Chevalier Lepinard, cinq jours après leur Ascension Aerostatique, dans la Ville de Lille, le 16 Août 1785. [Lille?, 1785]. (XP-XL-6).

1242
Dix-huitième voyage aërien. M. Blanchard, citoyen de Calais. [1786]. (XP-XL-6).

1267
Deeble, T. (sculpt.) View of the ascent of Mr. Lunardi's celebrated air balloon from the Artillery Ground Sept.r 15th 1784. 1784. The first flight in England is depicted here, at the moment when an oar, devised to row the aircraft through the air, fell to the ground. On Lunardi's oars see print 1274 in this catalogue. Two states of this plate were apparently issued before the event, as they show the balloon ascending without the falling oar. (XP-XL-7).

1288
Cartes. Vauthier Cartier tient toutes sortes de papiers de France et d'Hollande. [Label]. Image is identical to print 1155, showing Académie de Dijon/Guyton de Morveau/Abbé Bertrand flight of 25 April 1784. (XP-XL-8).

1307
Fete of the Emperor. Illumination and balloon ascent in the Champs Elysées. [1804?]. (XP-XL-9).

1308
Passage de S. M. Louis Dix-huit sur le Pont Neuf, le 3 Mai 1814. (XP-XL-9).

1310
The entrance of his Majesty Louis XVIII into Paris, 3rd May 1814. London, published 1st February 1820. (XP-XL-9).

1329
[Ballon de fête religieuse, lancé à Frascati en 1830.] ("Title supplied from Bruel no. 144."—Air Force Academy library catalogue.) (XP-XL-9). ©

1342
Brighton. View taken in balloon. Brighton. Vue prise en ballon. Paris, 1846. Top: "Excursions aériennes." Compare print 1340 in this catalogue, which is a view of Rouen. (XP-XL-9). ©

1364
Descente[?] en Angleterre. [1803?]. (XP-XL-9).

1390
[Discesa in paracadute della Garnerin all'Arena di Milano . . . 1824. "Title and date from Caproni plate 82." —Air Force Academy library catalogue.] (XP-XL-11). ©

1395
Projet d'un superbe ballon de 120 pieds de diamètre qui doit être enlevé à Dijon. Paris. (XP-XL-11). ©

1426
Montag den 20 Ap. 1846 wird mit dem neuen Gesellschafts LuftBallon. [1846—Air Force Academy library catalogue]. Broadside. (XP-XL-12).

1505
Pennington & Co.s aerial steam ship or composite balloon. Philadelphia, 1850. (XP-XL-14).

1560
Départ du Général Mephitique. (XP-XL-15).

1564
La phisicienne galante. Shows a woman in balloon costume, holding a balloon print, with two balloons in background. At upper left is a man borne aloft by his copious balloon hat. The figures are numbered, and keyed to text at bottom, part of which suggests the sexual utility of the new technology. (XP-XL-15).

1565
Madame la Comtesse de M . . . devant aller voir la fameuse expérience. Depicts a woman in balloon costume rising from the step of her dressmaker's shop. In the background is "the famous demonstration of the man who could endure an ardent fire without feeling the effects of the heat." Like print 1564, there is a hint of sexual metaphor. (XP-XL-15).

1581
The Day's Folly. Paris, 1783. Similar to print 4628 in this catalogue, but in a circular form. Attributed in Bruel (no. 17): "A Paris chez Tilliard graveur." Shows the "uncle" inside, passing through the window. (XP-XL-15).

1582
L'homme aerostatique: un Physicien ayant construit un bâlon . . . "A Paris chés Crepy rue S. Jacques . . . " Shows the "uncle" outside, in flight. (XP-XL-15).

1625
The national parachute, or John Bull conducted to Plenty & Emancipation. London, 1802. Shows Garnerin-style parachute descending. Basket labeled "sinking fund," top of parachute has banner: "national debt." (XP-XL-16). ©

1627
La Minerve, vaisseau aërien destiné aux découvertes par le professeur Robertson. Die Minerva, ein Luftschif velches durch Professor Robertson zu einer Entdekung bestimtist. Robertson-type balloon, with rooster on top, facing right; flag has: "Scientiarum Favore." (XL-16).

1635
Wir der—dies Jahr in Europa nicht mehr gefeyerte—Napoleons-Tag auf der Insel St. Helena. (XP-XL-16). ©

1749
[Aerial ship.] Signed: Pothéy, [?] sc. (XP-XL-18). ©

1801
De Lambert im Wrightflieger über Paris. Leipzig, Meissner & Buch. (XP-XL-19).

1838
Pilâtre de Rozier. Paris, [c. 1785]. (XP-XL-20).

1843
[Portrait of Gaston Tissandier.] (XP-XL-20).

1855
Aéroplane monoplan du genre dit "Système Antoinette." (Cardboard cut-out model.) Above: Petites constructions. Imagerie d'Epinal, no. 1376. (XP-XL-22). ©

1867
Representation of various balloons, with the methods of constructing and filling them. C. Cooke, [London], February 5, 1790. Similar to print 1362 in this catalogue, with additional figures, including four different oars, four illustrations of apparatus, and an aerostatic horse and rider "which was exhibited at the Pantheon by the brothers Enslen." (XL-22).

2000
Expérience du parachute. Paris. With small portrait of Garnerin at bottom. (XP-XL-24).

2002
Platz der Crossen Vorstellungen im Prattei. Wien. (XP-XL-25). ©

2011
2ᵉ. Expérience de la Machine Aérostatique par le Docteur Jonathan. Shows the airship leaving the ground, purportedly on January 10, 1784. "Dessiné d'après nature et gravé par Waulstaine et se Vend chéz lui au No. 122 en la Cité à Londres." An expertly engraved print, with an enigmatic authorship; see description of print 2010 in this catalogue. (XP-XL-25).

2014
Pro bono Publico. Robertson-type balloon, with rooster on top facing left; flag bears blank heraldic crest. (XL-15).

2025
Ant. Klauber, after Swebach Defontaines. Sieg bei Fleurus den 26ten Iuny 1794. Perhaps part of a series, numbered xvi on plate, lower right. Shows the battle of Fleurus from the Austrian perspective, with the balloon in background. (XL-25).

2192
Les accidents de l'aérostat. Metz, [1875?]. Nineteenth-century cartoon-style summary of dreadful accidents, through the Zénith tragedy in 1875. (XP-XL-26). ©

2808
Parc de Bellevue, ascension equestre de Tetu-Brissy, le 10 Brumaire an 7. [Date supplied in ms.] (XB-7-11).

2870
Etienne et Joseph Montgolfier, freres, Nés a Annonay en Vivares. Includes vignettes: Projet d'un monument a elever a M. Charles, and: Carte des premiers Voyages aërostatiques. (XC-10-2M).

2882
Vuë de Versaille, prise du coté de la Chapelle. Paris, chez [Le] Vachet. (XC-10-2M). Shows the ascent of the sheep, cock, and duck on September 19, 1783. Possibly part of a series; see note on print 2878 in this catalogue.

3152
[Montgohill airship ca. 1890.] (XL-38). ©

3216
Ascensions aérostatiques les plus remarquables. Text identifies 81 aircraft from Lana's to Darville's. Nine balloons appear to be in serious trouble. (XL-33).

3248
L'ascension de Vincent Lonardi venitien à Londres en 1784. Paris, 1790. Shows ascending balloon, with both oars on board. Engraved by Ch. Du Pont[?]; published by V. Levallois. It seems curious that this event would be commemorated six years after the event, when Lunardi was in Naples. Perhaps the print was prepared as propaganda for a failed attempt on March 14, 1790, in Palermo and a successful flight from the same town on July 31. (XL-41). ©

3261
Vincent Lunardi Esqr. Engraved by Francesco Bartolozzi. London, 1784. (XC-10-2A).

3370
Charles aux Thuileries. Le 1ᵉʳ Decembre 1783. Faces left; this is a copy of a print issued by Simon Charles Miger (see print 1821 in this catalogue). (XC-10-2C).

3371
The air balloon, as it ascended with Mr. Lunardi, from the artillery ground, 15th Sep. 1784. London, 1784. (XC-10-2A).

3382
Expérience du globe aërostatique de MM. Charles et Robert, devant le Château des Thuileries, le 1. xbre 1783. (XC-10-2C). ©

3390
Vue de la prairie de Nesle, situé à 9 lieus de Paris. Paris, chez [Le] Vachez. Shows the landing of the balloon of Charles and Robert on December 1, 1783. Possibly part of a series; see note on print 2878 in this catalogue. (XC-10-2C).

3394
Origineelle Afbeelding van de Lucht Bal, opgelaten in 's Gravenhage in de Tuin van 't Oude Hof den 11 December 1783. At head: "In de Mercurius December 1783 p. 220." Depicts small balloon with six sides, shaped like a building. (XC-10-2C).

3433
L'homme aux ballons ou la folie du jour. À Orleans, chex Le Tourmi. Woodcut. Shows a gentleman in "balloon" costume, similar to print 4624 in this catalogue. (XL-15).

3434

Avis très important. On avertit le Public que le Bureau des Diligences Aërienne à commencés ses opérations. Refers to the "Bureau général établit sur la Butte de Mont-martre." Shows aristocrats being injected with syringes and taking flight. (XL-15).

3441

Principale[s] machine[s] aérostatique[s] construite[s] à Paris, et enlevé[es] dans le courant de 1783. Paris, [1784?]. Part of title shown in brackets is supplied in ms. (XL-2). ©

3446

Ascent of three Persons with a balloon from Vauxhall Gardens 1802. Watercolor. (XL-11).

3448

Graces à Dieu, voilà mon Oncle retrouvé. Les dangers de la Physique. Depicts the outcome of the accidental voyage of the "Uncle" whose beginnings are shown in prints 1581 and 1582. The uncle is returned to the family in a miller's sack, having been removed from a windmill blade onto which he had fallen. (XL-15).

3482

The Grand Republican balloon, intended to convey the Army of England to the Gallic shore, for the purpose of exchanging French Liberty! for the English Happiness! London, 1798. Robertson-type balloon, with rooster at top facing right; flag has "Liberty." (XL-15).

4604

La Rentrée du Char Triomphant. Paris, 1784. Charles' balloon of December 1 is shown returning to Paris atop a cart, still partially inflated and surrounded by men on horseback illuminating the way with torches. The print includes a map of the aerial voyage, sometimes seen as a vignette on prints of the period. "A Paris chés Vachez . . . Quay de Gevres"; on this publisher's other work see the description to print 2878: "Vuë d'Annonay en Vivarais," in this catalogue. (XL-4).

4606

Denckmünze aufsteugnung des Luftballons ausgetheilt wurde. [Design for a medal commemorating Baron von Lutgendorf's ascent in Augsburg, August 24, 1786, which apparently never took place.] (XB-9-2B).

4612

Nouvelles Coëffures en 1785. Paris, 1785. (XL-8). ©

4622

Vue du Château de Douvres; Cinquième Voyage Aërien de M. Blanchard. Paris. Shows Blanchard and Jeffries just after leaving the ground at Dover, with a large crowd of people assembled. "Chez le Vachez, aux Colonnades du Palais Royal No. 206," an address sometimes used by [Le] Vachez in addition to the more regular "Quay de Gevres." This print is probably part of the series mentioned in the description of print 2878 with a title in roman capitals as in print 2893 (both prints in this catalogue). (XL-6).

Other Holdings

CARTOONS

Der Dichter Sperling macht einen Ausflug in das Gebirg. Etching, 20.5 x 17.5 cm. Undated.

The Flight of Intellect. Caricature of a cylindrical flying machine. Portrait of Mr. Golightly experimenting on Mess. Quick & Speed's new patent, high pressure Steam Riding Rocket. London [ca. 1825]. Colored lithograph.

Het Jaar 1804. Satirical prints published in 1794 representing probable events in the aeronautic world ten years hence. Plate I. Depicting the booking office of the famous aeronauts Hopman and Loude. Copyright 1794. Aquatint, 16.5 x 21.6 cm.

Het Jaar 1804. Satirical prints published in 1794 representing probable events in the aeronautic world ten years hence. Plate II. Animated scene, men endeavouring to fill and raise their balloon, "Lust tot Anderzoek." Copyright 1794. Aquatint, 16.5 x 21.6 cm.

The Ascent of the Aerial Balloon. The balloon rising with the Sheep, Duck and Cock in the Basket. Caricature engraving by Lodge. 1783. Engraving, 19 x 10 cm.

The draft / All other methods of evading the draft having failed, the above disgraceful scheme is to be attempted on the 10th [1862]. Engraving, 19 x 12 cm.

DIME NOVELS

"Noname." *Frank Reade, Jr. and His Electric Air Yacht; Or, The Great Inventor Among the Aztecs.* The Five Cent Wide Awake Library. January 3, 1891. Vol. II. No. 1020. New York: Frank Tousey, 1891. Dime novel, 32 p. illus.

"Noname." *Frank Reade, Jr.'s Greatest Flying Machine; Or, Fighting the Terror of the Coast.* Frank Reade Library. Vol. v. No. 118. New York: Frank Tousey, [c. 1895]. Dime novel, 16 p. illus.

Draper, Allyn. *Lost in the Air; Or Over Land and Sea.* Pluck and Luck: Complete Stories of Adventure. July 13, 1898. No. 14. New York: Frank Tousey, 1898. Dime novel, 32 p. illus.

Arnold, Allan. *The Diamond Island or Astray in a Balloon.* Pluck and Luck: Complete Stories of Adventure. March 20, 1901. No. 146. New York: Frank Tousey, 1901. Dime novel, 32 p. illus.

"Noname." "Frank Reade, Jr.'s Air Wonder The 'Kite;' Or, A Six Weeks' Flight over the Andes." *Frank Reade Weekly Magazine.* December 12, 1902. No. 7. New York: Frank Tousey, 1902. Dime novel, 32 p. illus.

"Noname." "Lost in the Mountains of the Moon; Or, Frank Reade, Jr.'s Great Trip With the 'Scud.'" *Frank Reade Weekly Magazine.* July 10, 1903. No. 37. New York: Frank Tousey, 1903. Dime novel, 32 p. illus.

Reid, Robert. *Dick Hardy's School Scrapes Or The Rivals of No. 21.* Brave and Bold. July 7, 1906. No. 185. New York: Street & Smith, 1906. Dime novel, 32 p. illus.

White, Lawrence, Jr. *Tracked Across Europe Or the Clue of the Moving Pictures.* Brave and Bold. July 28, 1906. No. 188. New York: Street & Smith, 1906. Dime novel, 32 p. illus.

Falconer, Kirk. *Cadet, Clyde Conner Or Life at the Military Academy.* Brave and Bold. May 11, 1907. No. 229. New York: Street & Smith, 1907. Dime novel, 32 p. illus.

EXCERPTS FROM NEWSPAPERS AND PERIODICALS

"A large, elegant Air-Balloon." *The Essex Journal and the Massachusetts and New-Hampshire General Advertiser,* July 9, 1784. Clipping, 43 cm.

"Respecting an Air Balloon." *The Independent Ledger and the American Advertiser,* August 2, 1784. Clipping, 37.5 cm.

"Balloon." *The Providence Gazette and the Country Journal,* February 19, 1785. Clipping, 37.5 cm.
11"Mr. Printer." *Columbian Centinel,* January 12, 1793. Clipping, 46.5 cm.

"Patent F[o]ederal Balloons." *The Connecticut Courant,* June 2, 1800. Clipping, 53 cm.

"Aerial Excursion." *The [Boston] Independent Chronicle and the Universal Advertiser,* November 24, 1800. Clipping, 50.5 cm.

"Origin of Balloons." *The Mercury and New-England Palladium,* September 24, 1802. Clipping, 55 cm.

"Ascent of Mr. Green's Balloon on Wednesday Night." *London Illustrated News*, August 25, 1849. Clipping, 40 cm.

Atmospherical phenomena in a balloon ascension. [1853]. Clipping, 15 cm.

"See! they are under the balloon. Good God! they are cutting the ropes!" [1857]. Engraving, 15 x 23.4 cm.

Drifting through the clouds. [1884]. Clipping (18 cm.) with engraving, 16.7 x 13.5 cm.

"Trial of Maxim's steam flying machine." *Scientific American,* September 15, 1894, p. 165. Clipping, 38.5 cm.

HANDBILLS, CIRCULARS, AND LEAFLETS

Mr. Blanchard and a lady. [1785]. Broadside, 20 x 17.4 cm.

Most grand and magnificent aerial experiment and diversion, with a parachute, or umbrella's [*sic*] July 13, 1785. The advertiser (an Italian gentleman) will launch himself from a prodigious altitude, at Mr. Blanchard's aerostatic academy. [London?]: G. Laidler, [1785?]. Handbill, 24 x 17.5 cm.

Grand fête champêtre by day. A race between two balloons conducted by Mr. [Charles] Green and Mrs. Green against Mr. W. Green, and Mrs. W. Green. [London?]: Balne, Printer, [18??]. Handbill, 18.5 x 15.5 cm.

Melancholy death of Madame Blanchard, at Paris, through her balloon taking fire. London: P. White for the Religious Tract Society, [1819]. Broadside, 45 x 27.5 cm.

Grand ascension. Fifth aerial voyage of Mr.

Eugène Robertson, on Saturday, the 9th of July, at Castle Garden [1825?]. Clipping (or handbill), 40 cm.

Castle Garden. Grand night ascension! of Mr. E. Robertson. September 20 [1826] [n.p.]: Joseph C. Spear, Printer, [1826?]. Handbill, 54.5 x 15 cm.

Abbildung des neuen Gesellschafts Ballon genant der Adler von Wien. Wien: H. Zimer [1846?]. Handbill, 28 x 19.3 cm.

Grand, sublime & novel entertainment in a splendid mammoth pavilion. Balloon ascensions by John Wise, the world-renowned aeronaut. Exhibitions of fireworks. Columbus: Maj. J. Burnell, Advertiser, [1852?]. Poster, 62 x 24 cm.

This circular was dropped from the largest balloon that ever ascended from Boston Common, on the 103rd anniversary of American Independence, July 4, 1879. Boston: Kiley, [1879?]. Handbill, 18 x 10.5 cm.

Grand mammoth balloon ascension. Holyoke, Mass., Monday, May 24, 1880. 16 mammoth balloons in the air at one time [n.p., 1880]. Handbill, 70 cm.

POSTCARDS

"Aviation Meet at Los Angeles, California." Dominguez Field Air Meet, January 28, 1912. Postcard, 9 x 14 cm.

SHEET MUSIC
Puss in a parachute, or A gape at the balloon. Written by G. Colman, Esq. Pall Mall, M. Kelly [18??]. Sheet music (2–3 p.), 30.5 cm.

Un flot de dentelles. Valse brillante pour le piano par Antonio Vicini. Paris: A. Vicini, [18??]. Sheet music [cover page], 34 cm.

Le voyage aérien. By Gustave Nadaud, written for Mr. Jules Lefort. Paris: Menestrel, [*ca.* 1840]. Sheet music (2–3 p.), 32 cm.

Three Polkas. Composed by A. Wallerstein. New York: Firth, Pond & Co., *ca.* 1850. Sheet music (3–5 p.), 32 cm.

Up in a balloon. By G. Operti. New York: Wm. A. Pond, [c. 1869]. Sheet music (2–7 p.), 33 cm.

Sailing in my balloon. Words by A. J. Mills. Music by Bennett Scott. New York: Francis, Day and Hunter, [c. 1907]. Sheet music (2–5 p.), 34.5 cm.

The Aviator. By James M. Fulton. Boston: Ernest S. Williams, [c. 1908]. Sheet music (3–5 p.), 35 cm.

TICKETS

Ascension à ballon perdu, et descente en parachute, de l'aéronaute Garnerin . . . [18??] Ticket, 6 x 9 cm.

Eintritts-Karte. [18??]. Ticket, 9 x 6.5 cm.

Tivoli. Ascension aérostatique et promenade à ballon captif. Des osages. Une Personne. [n.p., 18??]. Ticket, 10.5 x 13 cm.

Ballon dirigeable. Billet de souscription. Bon pour une entrée. Strasbourg, Imp. Manuaire [?] [1834]. Ticket, 11 x 13.5 cm.

The Balloon Society of Great Britain invite[s] . . . to a lecture entitled The parachute & aerial engineering, by Thomas Moy, C.E., to be given January 4th, 1889. Ticket, 7.5 x 11.5 cm.

Numismatics

The Gimbel collection currently holds over 300 items of prized numismatica. This supplementary listing highlights some issues of importance and interest in the Gimbel collection in addition to those described in the illustrated sections of the catalogue.

BALLOONS

Count Francesco Zambeccari (1752–1812) — To recognize an early aeronaut. Zambeccari's first flights were from England where citizens considered ballooning to be a French fad and were primarily disinterested. When one of Zambeccari's launches in England failed and spectators rioted, the

Count fled to Italy where he made several successful flights. He was killed in a ballooning mishap in September 1812. Obverse: bust of Zambeccari to left. Reverse: legends only. Legends: in Latin. Designer: P. Tadolini. Bronze, struck 53 mm. XM-1 3523.

Chevalier Paulo Andreani (1763–1823) — To commemorate the first balloon ascension made in Italy. From his estate near Milan, on February 25, 1784, Andreani became the first man outside of France to fly. Obverse: classical portrait facing to right. Reverse: balloon entering cloud above. Legends: in Latin. Designer: A. Guillemard. Bronze, struck, 43 mm. Restrikes made in 1934 by Stefano Johnson, medallist, Milan. XM-1 3520.

Gaspard-Félix Tournachon dit Nadar (1820–1910) — To recognize the man who took the world's first aerial photograph from a balloon, *ca.* 1868. He also patented a system of aerial cartography through photography and delivered the first mail via air. Obverse: portrait of Tournachon. Reverse: view of balloon from below. Legends: in French. Designer: Madeleine-Pierre Querolle. Bronze, struck, 77 mm. Restrike still available from Paris mint. XM-1 3675.

Henri Giffard (1825–1882) — Souvenir of an ascension in Giffard's Captive Grand Balloon. Passengers were able to purchase souvenir medallions of different sizes and prices. Giffard was well known for his steam-powered balloon flight from Paris to Trappes in 1852. Obverse: picture of tethered balloon over Paris, date 1878. Reverse: legends, in French, attesting to ascension with space for individual name and date. Loop at top for mounting. Designer: C. Trotin. Gold finish, struck, 51 mm. XM-1 3502.

Esposizione Nazionale in Milano (1881) — Souvenir of ascension in a tethered balloon at the National Exposition of 1881. Obverse: tethered balloon over city of Milan with cathedral in background. Reverse: legend in Italian identifying event, place, and date. Designer: C. Alvi. Satin silver finish, struck, 46 mm. XM-1 3588.

Dirigibles

Royal Engineers Balloon School (date unknown) — Royal souvenir issue of the witnessing by the king and queen of England of the flight, in October 1907, of the *Nelli Secundis,* an airship constructed by the British War Department. Sailing from Farnborough to London, around St. Paul's Cathedral and then to the Crystal Palace, the airship maintained a speed of 24 miles per hour. Obverse: conjoined busts of Edward VII and Queen Alexandra. Reverse: airship over London. Legends: in English. Designer: unknown. Copper, struck, 32 mm. XM-1 3495.

Louis Malécot (1871–1943) — To commemorate dirigible flight over Paris by inventor Malécot in 1908. Obverse: portrait of Malécot. Reverse: Malécot airship over Paris. Legends: in French. Designer: Jean-Philippe Roch. Bronze, struck, 68 mm. Restrikes available from Paris Mint. XM-1 3661.

Major August Von Parseval (1861–1942) — To commemorate long-distance dirigible flights 12 to 19 October 1909 between Frankfurt, Nurnberg, Augsburg, Munich, Stuttgart, Mannheim, and Koln. Obverse: portrait of Von Parseval. Reverse: eagle atop dirigible. Legends: in German. Designer: Karl Goetz. Bronze, cast, 65 mm. XM-1 3568.

Heavier-Than-Air Craft

Aviation Day, New Britain, Conn. (date unknown) — Typical souvenir medalet of early air shows. Sold to raise funds for early fliers. The collection has a number of these early mementos, both in pinback and medallic format. Obverse: pusher in center. Souvenir of Aviation Day, New Britain, Connecticut, July 2, 1910. Reverse: name of manufacturer, T. & H. Mfg., Co., New Britain, Conn. Designer: unknown. Copper, cast, 30 mm. XM-1 3507.

Bibliography

Printed Books, 1489–1850

Alden, John. *Wing Agenda and Corrigenda.* Charlottesville: University of Virginia Bibliographical Society, 1958.

Brockett, Paul. *Bibliography of Aeronautics.* Washington, D.C.: Smithsonian Institution, 1910.

Copinger, W. A. *Supplement to Hain's Reportorium bibliographicum.* 32 vols. in 3. London: Henry Sotheran, 1895–1902.

Gamble, William Burt. *History of Aeronautics: A Selected List of References in the New York Public Library.* New York: New York Public Library, 1938.

Hain, Ludwig. *Reportorium bibliographicum.* 4 vols. Stuttgart and Paris, 1826–1838.

Pollard, A. W., G. R. Redgrave, et al. *A Short-Title Catalogue of Books Printed in England, Scotland, and Ireland and of English Books Printed Abroad, 1475–1640* (1926), rev. ed. by W. A. Jackson, F. S. Ferguson, and Katherine F. Pantzer, 3 vols. London: The Bibliographical Society, 1986–1991.

Randers-Pehrson, Nils Henrik, and A. G. Renstrom. *Aeronautic Americana: A Bibliography of Books and Pamphlets on Aeronautics Published in America Before 1900.* New York: Institute of the Aeronautical Sciences, 1943.

Reichling, Dietrich. *Appendices ad Hainii-Copingeri Reportorium bibliographicum.* 8 vols. Munich: Rosenthal, 1905–1914.

Rogers, David Morrison. *English Recusant Literature, 1558–1640.* Menston, Engl.: Scolar Press, 1967–1979.

Wing, Donald. *A Gallery of Ghosts.* New York: Modern Language Association of America, 1967.

Wing, Donald. *Short-Title Catalogue of Books Printed in England, Scotland, Ireland, Wales, and British America and of English Books Printed in Other Countries, 1641–1700.* 3 vols. New York: New York Index Society, 1945–1961; revised 2nd ed.: New York: Columbia University Press, 1972–1988; 2nd ed. newly revised and enlarged, in progress, 1994–.

Printed Books, 1851–1914

Aldiss, Brian W. *Billion Year Spree: The True History of Science Fiction.* Garden City, N. Y.: Doubleday, 1973.

Anderson, John D., Jr. *A History of Aerodynamics and Its Impact on Flying Machines.* Cambridge, England: Cambridge University Press, 1997.

Chanute, Octave. *Progress in Flying Machines.* New York: American Engineer and Railroad Journal, 1894.

Crouch, Tom D. *A Dream of Wings: Americans and the Airplane, 1875–1905.* New York: Norton, 1981.

Crouch, Tom D. *The Eagle Aloft: Two Centuries of the Balloon in America.* Washington, D. C.: Smithsonian Institution Press, 1983.

Dollfus, Charles, and Henri Bouché. *Histoire de l'Aéronautique.* Paris: L'Illustration, 1932.

Gibbs-Smith, C. H. *Aviation: An Historical Survey from its Origins to the End of World War II.* 2nd ed. London: HMSO, 1985.

Gibbs-Smith, C. H. *The Invention of the Aeroplane, 1799–1909.* New York: Taplinger, 1966.

Gibbs-Smith, C. H. *The Rebirth of European Aviation, 1902–1908: A Study of the Wright Brothers' Influence.* London: HMSO, 1974.

Hart, Clive. *The Dream of Flight: Aeronautics from Classical Times to the Renaissance.* New York: Winchester Press, 1972.

Hart, Clive. *Kites: An Historical Survey.* New York: Praeger, 1967.

Kelly, Fred C. *The Wright Brothers.* London: G. Harrap, 1944.

Ley, Willy. *Rockets, Missiles, and Men in Space.* Newly rev. and expanded ed. New York: Viking Press, 1968.

Morrow, John H, Jr. *The Great War in the Air: Military Aviation from 1909 to 1921.* Washington, D. C.: Smithsonian Institution Press, 1993.

Nicolson, Marjorie H. *Voyages to the Moon.* New York: Macmillan, 1948.

Renstrom, Arthur G. *Wilbur and Orville Wright: A Bibliography Commemorating the Hundredth Anniversary of the Birth of Wilbur Wright.* Washington, D. C.: Library of Congress, 1968.

Renstrom, Arthur G. *Wilbur and Orville Wright: A Chronology Commemorating the Hundredth Anniversary of the Birth of Orville Wright.* Washington, D. C.: Library of Congress, 1975.

Rolt, L.T.C. *The Aeronauts: A History of Ballooning, 1783–1903.* London: Longmans, 1966.

Schlaifer, Robert, and S. D. Heron. *Development of Aircraft Engines; Development of Aviation Fuels.* Elmsford, N. Y.: Maxwell Reprint, 1970.

Villard, Henry S. *Contact! The Story of the Early Birds.* New York: Crowell, 1968.

Von Braun, Wernher and Frederick I. Ordway III. *History of Rockets and Space Travel.* 3rd rev. ed. New York: Crowell, 1975.

Prints

Boselli, Elisabeth. "Le premier vol humain: recherches sur des sites oubliés," *Icare* (Paris) 105 (1983/2), pp. 70–75.

Bruel, François-Louis. *Histoire aéronautique.* Paris: A. Marty, 1909.

Bruel, François-Louis. *Bibliothèque Nationale. Départment des Estampes. Un siècle d'histoire de France par l'estampe, 1770–1871. Collection De Vinck, inventaire analytique.* Tome 1: Ancien Régime. Paris, 1909.

Caproni, Timina (Guasti). *L'aeronavtica italiana nell'immagine, 1487–1875; bibliografia di Giuseppe Boffito con aggiunte di Paolo Arrigoni.* Milano: Museo Caproni, 1938.

Clement, Pierre-Louis. *Montgolfières* (Hot-air Balloons). Paris: Tardy, 1982.

Crouch, Tom D. *The Eagle Aloft: Two Centuries of the Balloon in America.* Washington, D.C.: Smithsonian Institution Press, 1983.

George, Mary Dorothy. *Catalogue of Political and Personal Satires Preserved in the Department of Prints and Drawings in the British Museum.* Vol. 5 (1771–1783), 1935; vol. 6 (1784–1792), 1938; vol. 7 (1793–1800), 1942; vol. 8 (1801–1810), 1947. London: British Museum.

Gibbs-Smith, Charles H. *A History of Flying.* London: Batsford, 1953.

Grand-Carteret, John, and Léo Delteil. *La Conquête de l'air vue par l'image (1495–1909).* Paris: Paris Librairie des annales, 1910.

Jackson, Donald Dale. *The Aeronauts.* Alexandria, Va.: Time-Life Books, 1980.

Josephy, Alvin. *Adventure of Man's Flight.* London, 1962.

Leichter als Luft: zur Geschichte der Ballonfahrt. Landschaftsverband Westfalen-Lippe, Westfälisches Landesmuseum für Kunst und Kulturgeschichte. Münster: Landschaftsverband Westfalen-Lippe, [1985].

Liebmann, Louis, and Gustav Wahl. *Katalog der historischen Abteilung der ersten internationalen Luftshiffahrts-Ausstellung (ILA) zu Frankfurt am Main 1909.* Frankfurt am Main: Wusten & Co., 1912.

Marsh, W. Lockwood. *Aeronautical Prints and Drawings.* London: Halton and Smith, Ltd., 1924.

Marsh, W. Lockwood. "Balloon Prints," *Print Collector's Quarterly* (London), vol. 15, no. 8 (1928), pp. 235–261.

Mondin, Gilbert. *Inventaire analytique du recueil "Histoire des Ballons," Bibliothèque Nationale, Cabinet des Estampes.* (Manuscript and microfilm, Cabinet des Estampes, Bibliothèque Nationale, Paris.) 1977.

Neidhardt-Jensen, Elske, and Ernst Berninger. *Katalog der Ballonhistorischen Sammlung Oberst von Brug in der Bibliothek des Deutschen Museums.* Nurenberg: Hans Carl, 1985.

Piola Caselli, Carlo. *Studi in onore di Carlo Lucangeli per il Bicentenario del suo volo a Roma.* Rome: Atena, 1992.

Préaud, Maxime, Pierre Casselle, Marianne Grivel, and Corrine Le Bitouzé. *Dictionnaire des éditeurs d'estampes à Paris sous l'Ancien Régime.* Paris: Promodis, 1987.

Waldfogel, Melvin, in *The Balloon: A Bicentennial Exhibition.* Minneapolis: University of Minnesota, University Art Museum, 1983.

Other Holdings

Crouch, Tom D. *A Dream of Wings: Americans and the Airplane, 1875–1905.* New York: W. W. Norton, 1981.

Crouch, Tom D. *The Eagle Aloft: Two Centuries of the Balloon in America.* Washington, D.C.: Smithsonian Institution Press, 1983.

Doherty, E. Jay. "Of Planes They Sang!" *Flying and Popular Aviation.* February 1942, pp. 29–30.

The Encyclopedia Americana. International Edition. Danbury, Conn.: Grolier, 1984.

Gibbs-Smith, Charles H. *Aviation: An Historical Survey from Its Origins to the End of World War II.* London: H.M.S.O., 1970.

Hodgson, J[ohn] E. *The History of Aeronautics in Great Britain, From the Earliest Times to the Latter Half of the Nineteenth Century.* London: Oxford University Press, 1924.

Jackson, Donald Dale. *The Aeronauts.* Alexandria, Va.: Time-Life Books, 1980.

Jackson, Donald Dale. *Flying the Mail.* Alexandria, Va.: Time-Life Books, 1982.

Kronstein, Max. *Pioneer Airpost Flights of the World, 1830–1935.* Joseph L. Eisendrath, ed. Washington, D.C.: American Air Mail Society, 1978.

Maggs Bros. *A Descriptive Catalogue of Books and Engravings Illustrating the Evolution of the Airship and the Aeroplane.* London: Maggs Bros., 1920.

Maggs Bros. *The History of Flight: A Descriptive Catalogue of Books, Engravings and Airmail Stamps Illustrating the Evolution of the Airship and the Aeroplane.* London: Maggs Bros., 1936.

Marchand, Roland. *Advertising the American Dream: Making Way for Modernity, 1920–1940.* Berkeley: University of California Press, 1985.

Nye, Russel. *The Unembarrassed Muse: The Popular Arts in America.* New York: Dial Press, 1970.

Prendergast, Curtis. *The First Aviators.* Alexandria, Va.: Time-Life Books, 1980.

Reynolds, Quentin J. *The Fiction Factory; Or, from Pulp Row to Quality Street: The Story of 100 Years of Publishing at Street & Smith.* New York: Random House, 1955.

Romance of Ballooning: The Story of the Early Aeronauts. Edita S. A. Lausanne. New York: Viking Press, 1971.

Villard, Henry Serrano. *Contact! The Story of the Early Birds.* Rev. ed. Washington, D.C.: Smithsonian Institution Press, 1987.

Wohl, Robert. *A Passion for Wings: Aviation and the Western Imagination, 1908–1918.* New Haven, Conn.: Yale University Press, 1994.

Seals

Bivar, A.D.H. *Catalogue of the Western Asiatic Seals in the British Museum. Stamp Seals II: The Sassanian Dynasty.* London: British Museum Press, 1969.

Black, Jeremy, and Anthony Green. *Gods, Demons and Symbols of Ancient Mesopotamia: An Illustrated Dictionary.* London: British Museum Press, 1992.

Buchanan, Briggs. *Catalogue of Ancient Near Eastern Seals in the Ashmolean Museum I: Cylinder Seals.* Oxford, England: Clarendon Press, 1966.

Buchanan, Briggs. *Early Near Eastern Seals in the Yale Babylonian Collection.* New Haven, Conn.: Yale University Press, 1981.

Collon, Dominique. *First Impressions: Cylinder Seals in the Ancient Near East.* Chicago: University of Chicago Press, 1987.

Forte, Elizabeth Williams. *Ancient Near Eastern Seals: A Selection of Stamp and Cylinder Seals from the Collection of Mrs. William H. Moore.* New York: Metropolitan Museum of Art, 1976.

Frankfort, Henri. *Cylinder Seals: A Documentary Essay on the Art and Religion of the Ancient Near East.* London: Macmillan and Co., 1939.

Pittman, Holly, and Joan Aruz. *Ancient Art in Miniature: Near Eastern Seals from the Collection of Martin and Sarah Cherkasky.* New York: Metropolitan Museum of Art, 1987.

Porada, Edith. *Corpus of Ancient Near Eastern Seals in North American Collections: The Collection of the Pierpont Morgan Library.* New York: Pantheon Books, 1948.

Teissier, Beatrice. *Ancient Near Eastern Cylinder Seals from the Marcopoli Collection.* Berkeley: University of California and Summa Publications, 1984.

Numismatics

BOOKS

Daniel Guggenheim Medal Fund, Inc. *The Daniel Guggenheim Medal for Achievement in Aeronautics: Biographies of Orville Wright, Ludvig Prandtl, Frederick William Lanchester, Juan de la Cierva.* New York, 1936.

Maggs Bros. *A Descriptive Catalogue of Books, Engravings and Medals Illustrating the Evolution of the Airship and the Aeroplane.* London, 1930.

Malpas, Evelyn. *Lighter Than Air: 200 Years of Ballooning in Numismatics.* London: British Art Medal Society, 1989.

Mattoi, Eduardo. *Aeronautica in Nummis, dai Fratelli Montgolfier a Santo Dumont, 1783–1901.* Milano, 1906.

PERIODICALS

Amann, A. P. "Vincent Lunardi's Aeronaut," *Seaby's Coin and Medal Bulletin* (London), no. 646 (June 1972), pp. 224–225.

Bergman, Allan R. "Gasbags to Glory," *TAMS Journal* (Token and Medal Society, Tecumseh, Mich.), vol. 17, no. 2 (April 1977), pp. 48–60.

Bergman, Allan R. "The Zeppelin Flights 1900–1908," *TAMS Journal*, vol. 13, no. 6 (December 1973), pp. 223–230.

Bergman, Allan R. "1909—The First International Air Meet (ILA)," *TAMS Journal*, vol. 11, no. 4 (August 1971), p. 147.

Johnson, Norris A. "More Than Daring Eagles," *Coins Magazine* (Iola, Wisc.), vol. 21, no. 3 (March 1974), pp. 63–66.

Johnson, Norris A. "The Saga of Flight—From Leonardo to Lakehurst," *Coins Magazine*, vol. 16, no. 7 (July 1969), pp. 26ff.

Johnson, Norris A. "Wings of the Past: The Epic of Powered Flight," *Coins Magazine*, vol. 16, no. 8 (August 1969), pp. 36–39.

Kienast, Gunter W. "German Flying Aces of World War I on Medals," *TAMS Journal*, vol. 9, no. 1 (February 1969), pp. 16–21.

Newman, Arthur L. "Medals Struck in Connection with Early Aeronautical Meets," *The Numismatist* (Journal of the American Numismatic Association, Colorado Springs), vol. 83, no. 12 (December 1970), pp. 1764–1772.

Newman, Arthur L. "Some Medals in Honor of the Wright Brothers," *The Numismatist*, vol. 81, no. 12 (December 1968), pp. 1575–1582.

Newman, Arthur L. "Some Pre–World War I Aviation Medals," *The Numismatist*, vol. 82, no. 12 (December 1969), pp. 1669–1678.

Parrish, Joy. "Aviation Tokens and Medals: Evolution of Aviation," *Calcoin News*, vol. 30, no. 3 (Summer 1976), pp. 100–104.

Whiting, J.R.S. "Aeronaut and Airship Commemorative Medals," *Coins*, vol. 9, no. 4 (April 1972), pp. 31–32.

Editors

ELLIOTT V. CONVERSE III

Dr. Converse is a retired U.S. Air Force colonel whose doctorate is in history from Princeton University. He is the principal author of *The Exclusion of Black Soldiers from the Medal of Honor in World War II* (1997) and the editor of *Forging the Sword: Selecting, Educating, and Training Cadets and Junior Officers in the Modern World* (1998).

RICHARD W. LEMP

Dr. Lemp is a retired U.S. Air Force lieutenant colonel and is a professor of English at the United States Air Force Academy. He received his Ph.D. in French literature from the University of Arizona in 1986, and has most recently translated Brig. Gen. Lucien Robineau's "French Military Aeronautics Before and During the Great War" in *Airpower: Promise and Reality* (2000).

ALICE LEVINE

Alice Levine began her publishing career in 1961. She was assistant to the editor of Ace Books and then a project editor in the College Division of Harper & Row. For nearly twenty years, she was copy chief for Westview Press. Her editing experience includes manuscript evaluation, substantive editing, and copyediting for authors, publishers, and institutions. She has lectured at the Denver Publishing Institute and at Denver University.

DANA LEVY

Dana Levy has designed hundreds of books for publishers and museums, including Simon & Schuster, George Braziller, the National Gallery of Art, The Smithsonian Institution, The Getty Museum, as well as the University Presses of Washington and California. He and his wife, writer and editor Letitia O'Connor, founded Perpetua Press in Los Angeles where they create and produce ten to twelve books a year.

SHENA L. REDMOND

Shena Redmond has worked in the publishing field for the past ten years and presently is a senior project editor for Lynne Rienner Publishers in Boulder, Colorado. She graduated from Illinois Wesleyan University in 1989 and lives in Westminster, Colorado, with her husband and son.

Index

Numbers in **boldface** indicate artwork on that page.

A

Abaris (mythological character), 78

An account of the first aërial voyage in England (Lunardi), **80**

Ackers, James Jr., 224

Ackers, Mary William, 224

"Across the Continent in the Air" (Draper), **266**

Adams, Robert, 27

Ader, Clément, 24, 131

Advertisements, aviation, 262–264

AEA. *See* Aerial Experiment Association

Aerial Experiment Association (AEA), 140

Aerial Locomotion (Aeronautical Society of Great Britain), **103**

Aerial Navigation (Andrews), 22, **100**

Aerial Navigation Company, 22, **307**

The Aerial Ship! (letterpress), **280**

Aerial Steamship (monoplane), 118

Aerial Transit Company, 234

Aéro-Club de France, 105

Aerodynamic theory, 136

The Aeronautical Annual (Means, ed.), **121**

Aeronautical Society of Great Britain, 50, 103

Aeronautical Supplies Catalogue, **309**

Aëronautics (Brewer and Alexander), **119**

The Aeronaut to the People! (letterpress), **279**

The Aeroplane, Past, Present, and Future (Grahame-White and Harper), **137**

The Aeroplane Club of Great Britain and Ireland...(handbill), **286**

Aeroplane (Read), **301**

Aérostat des MM. Robert (etching and engraving), **188**

Aerostation (engraving), **194**

Aerostation out at Elbows (etching), **205**

Aerostats, 96–97, 168, 192

    See also Balloons; Balloons, gas-filled; Balloons, hot-air

The Air Balloon Chace (ticket), **302**

An Air Balloon Invented in the Last Century (etching), **168**

Airplanes, 125

    first British flight, 301

    14-bis, 162

    as military force, 134

    monoplanes, 118, **257, 259**

    paper model of, **258**

    postcards of, **287**

    stunt flying, 294

    19th Century designs for, 93

    used in advertising, **264**

    Voisin biplane, **256**

        See also Flight, airplane; Wright, Orville; Wright, Wilbur

The Air-Ship City of New York (Lowe), 96–97, **97**

Airships, 55, 66

    Cyclocrane longitudinal airship, 237

    La Patrie, **290**

    pressure, 125, 128

    propelled, 244

    rigid, 128, 340 (*See also* Zeppelins)

    used in advertising, **262**

Alexander, Patrick Y., 119

Alexander the Great, 7–8, **39**

Alhier zijn verkrijgbaar (letterpress), **283**

All on Fire (intaglio), **204**

Altre scoverte fatte nella Luna dal Sig. Herschel (lithograph), **229**

Alvey, F., 225

American Bookman's Association, 4

American Civil War, 17, 153, 154, **241, 272,** 336

American Philosophical Society, 6

American Society of Medalists, 9

America's First Successful Air Flight (lithograph), **210**

Amick, M.L., 19, 108

Andreani, Paolo, 16

Andrée, Salomon August, 122

Andrée and His Balloon (Lachambre and Machuron), **122**

Andreoli, Pascal, 228

Andrews, Solomon, 22, 100

Angelology, 37–38

Animals, as balloon payload, 15–16, 173, 174, 175, 306, **306**

Annonay, France. *See* Montgolfier, Étienne; Montgolfier, Joseph

Apkallu (semi-divine sage), **320**

Apollonius of Tyana, 45

Appleton, Victor (pseud.), 139

Archimedean screw, 68

Archytas of Tarentum, 9, 51, 78, 81

Ariosto, Lodovico, **43**

Aristophanes, 44

Arlandes, Marquis de. *See* Laurent, François, Marquis d'Arlandes

Arnold, Henry Harley "Hap," 27, **28**

Arnout, Jules, 236

L'art de naviger dans les airs (Galien), 14, **66**

L'art de voler à la manière des oiseaux (Meerwein), **77**

The Art of Flying. See Aerial Navigation

Ascension Aérostatique (handbill), **278**

L'ascension de la Nymphe aérienne (etching), **208**

Ascension of a balloon at the Tientsin military academy (paneled scroll), **246–247**

Ascent of a Balloon & Parachute (handbill), **276**

The Ascent of the Royal Nassau Balloon (lithograph), **231**

Ascents. *See* Balloon ascents

Astra Castra (Turnor), **99**

Atlantic (balloon), 19

Autobiography, 106

L'Aviateur Wright (journal illustration), **274**

Aviation. *See* Aviation research; Balloon ascents; Flight, airplane; Moon travel; Space travel

Aviation: An Historical Survey (Gibbs-Smith), 300

L'Aviation (Ferber), **131**

Aviation research, 103, 121, 339

    aerodynamic theory, 136

    balloons used for scientific research, 84, 105, 111, 113, 114, **270**

    emulation of birds, 86, 98, 112, 116, 339

    kites, 124

    ornithological studies, 98, 112, 116

    See also Experimentation

B

Bacon, Roger, 9, 42, 78

Bacqueville, Marquis de. *See* Boyvin de Bennetot, Jean-François

Baldwin, F.W., 140

Baldwin, Ivy, 251

Baldwin, Thomas Scott, 140, 285

T.S. Baldwin, practical aeronaut... (handbill), **285**

Ballon captif du Trocadéro (photograph), **245**

Ballon diregeable militaire (lithograph), **258**

Le Ballon dirigeable de Mr. Giffard (drawing), **239**

Les Ballons dirigeables (Girard and Gervais), **128**

A balloon ascent a century ago (chromotypogravure), **202**

Balloon ascents, 79, 201

    American ascents, 82–83, **210,** 279

    Blanchard and Sheldon, 302

    Blanchard's parachute from balloon, 187

    Channel crossing, 197, 200, **259, 311,** 333

    first ascent with payload, 173, 174, 175, **306, 310**

    first British balloon ascent, **80,** 203, **303, 332**

    first gas-powered ascent, **181,** 182

    first manned ascent, 14–15, 177, **178, 179, 180,** 183, **194, 199,** 331

    first public balloon launch, 170

    Janinet–Miolan debacle, **195, 196, 197**

    manned ascent of Green and Sparrow, 335

    provincial ignorance of, 172

    transatlantic flight, 89, 108

Ballooning, 96–97

    in America, 295

    long-distance, 19, 89, 108, 150, 151

    military applications of (*See* Military aviation)

    night flight, **226**

popularity of, 282, **288**
practical applications of, 17–22, 106, 148
Balloons, 11–14, 74, 75, 76, 78, 95, 113
  advertising and, **262**, **263**
  elongated envelope design, **188**, 218
  flying towns, 227
  gas-filled (*See* Balloons, gas-filled)
    hot-air, 11–17, 174, 198, 228
  as light-bulb ornament, **310**
  postal service and, 19–21, 106, 156, 243, 338
    (*See also* Carrier pigeons)
  powered, 22–23, 284, **284**
  rozière (hybrid), 198, 228
  special shapes, **208**
  as symbol of folly, 165
  18th century designs of, **184**
  used for scientific research, 84, 105, 111, **270**
  See also Military aviation; Montgolfier,
    Étienne; Montgolfier, Joseph
Balloons, gas-filled, 82–83, 110, 151, 285
  City of New York, 96–97, **271**, **336**
  Le Géant, 18, **19**, **242**, **283**
  rozière (hybrid), 198, 228
  See also Lunardi
The Balloon Travels of Robert Merry
  (Goodrich), **94**
Banks, Joseph, 15, 171
Bard, Wilkie, 296
Bartolozzi, Francesco, 201
Bastille Day, **220**
Bataille de Fleurus (engraving), **214**, **215**
Bate, John, 10
Bateau volant (flying boat), 210
Battle of Fair Oaks, Va. (lithograph), **241**
Battle of Fleurus, **214**, **215**
Batty's Grand National Hippodrome,
  Kensington, **282**
Beadle, Erasmus, 27
Beadle, Irwin, 27
Beaumont, André (pseud.). *See* Conneau, Jean
  Louis Camille
Beck, Paul, 143
Bélier hydraulique (hydraulic pump), 192
Bell, Alexander Graham, 140
Belle Époque (pressure airship), 125
Berblinger, Albrecht, 85
de Bergerac, Cyrano, 29–30, **30**, **56**, 78, 87
Berget, Alphonse, 132
Bertault (engraver), 175
Bertaux, H.G., 182
Bertrand, Abbé, **311**
Biard, Jean, 191, 196
Bibliographie aéronautique (Tissandier), **115**
Biggin, George, 80, 201, 202
Bill Bruce and the Pioneer Aviators (Arnold), **28**
Birch, William Russell, 200
Birds, study of. *See under* Aviation research
The Birds (Aristophanes), **44**
Bittorf, Sebastian, 277
Black, Joseph, 13–14
Bladud, King of England, 10, 48
Blanchard, Jean-Pierre François, 16, **16**, 77, 194,
  202, 204, 211, **311**

ascent with Sheldon, 302
Channel crossing, 200
first American balloon ascent, **82–83**, 210
history of, **79**, **333**
ornithopter, **169**, 187
perfidy of, 333
Blanchard, Marie Madeleine Sophie, **17**, 18, 79,
  153, 202, **219**, 221, **310**
M.S Blanchard Célèbre Aéronaute (etching), **219**
Blériot, Louis, 26, **259**, **286**, 304, **344**
"The Bobbsey Twins" series, 27
Bordelon, Laurent, 61
Borelli, Giovanni Alfonso, 78
Boston-Harvard Aero Meet (September 3-13,
  1910), **293**, 294
Bourgeois, David, 78
Boxes, decorative, **310**
Boyle, Robert, 11–12
Boyle's law, 11
The Boy's Own Toymaker (Landells), 10, 26, **95**
Boyvin de Bennetot, Jean-François, 63, 71
Branger, M. (artist), 257
de la Brenelerie, Gudin, 189
Brewer, Griffith, 119
British Coronation Aerial Post, **291**
Browning, John, 103
Brueghel, Peter, **8**
Bruel, François-Louis, 133, 171
Bruno, Giordano, 29
Brunt, Samuel (pseud.), 62
Bryan, Alfred (songwriter), 298
Bryan, George Hartley, 136
de Buigne, Louis-Alexandre, 191
Bukaty, A., 155
Bulfinch, Thomas, **8**
Bulls, as glyptic symbols, **319**, **324–325**
Butler, A., 226
Butler, R.H., 146, 157

C

Cælestinus, Claudius, **42**
Calmette, Gaston, 286
Cambridge, Richard Owen, 64
Capture of El Caney, El Paso and Fortifications
  of Santiago (lithograph), **251**
Cardano, Girolamo, 9–10
Carlingford, Viscount, 93
Carrier pigeons, 21, 156, 338
  See also Postal service
Cartoons, **129**, 253
Cassé, Emile, 239
Cavallo, Tiberius, 12, 13–14, 81, 168
Cavendish, Henry, 13
Cayley, George, 10–11, 23–24, **24**, 47, 85, 216
The celebrated Vincent Lunardi Esqr. accom-
  panied by two friends (etching), **201**
Les Cerfs-Volants (Lecornu), 10, **124**
Cernuschi, Constantino, 218
Cesare, Oscar Edward, 253
Channel crossing, 137, 197, 200, **259**, 286, **311**, 333
The Channel Flight (chromolithograph), **259**
Chanute, Octave, **10**, 24–25, 112, 120, 131, 273

Chapman, C.D., 154
Charles, Jacques Alexandre César, 15, **15**, 16, 74,
  75, 84, 171, 181, 183, 184, 188, 194, 331
Charles aux Thuilleries (engraving), **183**
Chartist Movement, 227
Chez Basset (printers), 187
Chez Le Noir (printers), 171, **172**, 182
Chez Le Vachez (printers), 170, 188
Chicago (balloon), 295
China, ballooning in, 246
Christianity. *See* Religion
Christian Science Monitor, 294
Church. *See* Religion
Cigarette lighter, **311**
Cinq Semaines en Ballon (Verne), **101**, 337
Circulars, 276–286
Circumnavigation of the globe, 69
Circuses, **282**
City of New York (balloon), 96–97, **271**, **336**
City of Quincy (balloon), 285
Clayton, Richard, 19, 150
Clothing. *See* Fashion
Cocking, Robert, 230, 231, 232
Cody, Samuel F., 301
Coey, Charles Andrew, 295
Coins. *See* Numismatics
Colin, M., **311**
Collegium Experimentale (Sturmis), 168
Come Josephine in My Flying Machine (Bryan
  and Fischer), **298**
Come Up in my Balloon (Leo), 296
Conneau, Jean Louis Camille, **142**
Conte, N.J., 20
La Coquette Phisicienne (etching), **185**
Country Life in America magazine, **275**
Coupe Aéronautique. *See* Gordon Bennett Cup
Coutelle, Charles, 20
Coxwell, Henry Tracey, 20, 113, 114, 226
Crashes. *See* Disasters and accidents
Cream pitcher, **310**
Croce-Spinelli, Joseph, 113
Crouch, Tom D., ix, 1–32, 90–145, 200, 271, 278,
  279, 295, 307
Currier and Ives, 241
Curtiss, Glenn Hammond, 140–141, 143, 144, 293,
  304
The Curtiss Aviation Book (Curtiss and Post),
  140–141
Cyclocrane (longitudinal airship), 237

D

Dædalus and Icarus (painting), **166**
Daedalus. *See* Icarus and Daedalus
Daniel, John, of Royston, **70**
Darius Green and His Flying-Machine
  (Trowbridge), **135**
Darwin, Erasmus, 51
Daumas, V. (medalist), 334, **344**
Dayton, June 1927 (photograph), **253**
Décente da la Machine Aërostatique (etching),
  180
La Découverte australe par un homme volant
  (Restif de la Bretonne), **36**, 73, 167

Degen, Jacob, 23, 85
De his que mundo (Cælestinus), **42**
Delagrange, Leon, 256
Delaspre, H. (artist), **259**
De la Terre a la Lune (Verne), **102**
Della Porta. *See* Porta, Giovanni Battista della
La Demoiselle (airplane), 125
De motu animalium (Borelli), 78
Depuis-Delcourt, Jules François, 218
The Descent of the Air Balloon (cartoon), **306**
Description des Expériences Aérostatiques
    (Faujas de Saint-Fond), 16, **74**, 175, 189
Desportes, Philippe, 300
Détails géométriques de la Machine
    Aérostatique (engraving), **186**
Deutsch de la Meurthe, Henri, 22
Deutsche Luftschiffahrts-Aktien-Gesselschaft
    ("Delag"), 254
Les Deux Midas (etching), **197**
I dialoghi piacevoli (Lucian), **44**
Diamond Dick Jr.: Boys Best Weekly, **269**
"Diamond Dick's Wonder Trail," **269**
Dickens, Charles, 4, 6
Dime novels, 265–269
Dirigibles
    aereon design, 100
    diverse designs, 128
    The Eagle, **280**
    Giffard's design, 110, **239**, 284
    Graf Zeppelin, **340**
    Muzzi's designs, 233
    Santos-Dumont's design, **341**
    whimsical designs, 206
    See also Zeppelins
Disasters and accidents, 204
    airplane crashes, 131, 343
    balloon disasters, 113, 153, 199, 210, **219**, 228, **277**
    Cocking's parachute descent, 230, 231, **232**
    Coxwell balloon ascent, 114, 240
    Le Géant, 18, **19**, **242**, 283
    glider crashes, 116, 158, 339
    Hindenburg explosion, 340
    legend of King Bladud, 10, 48
    Ornen expedition disappearance, 122
    La Patrie disappearance, **290**
*A discourse concerning a new world and another
    planet* (Wilkins), **50**
The Discovery of a World in the Moone
    (Wilkins), 50, 53
Dollfus, Charles, 245
Donaldson, Washington Harrison, 19, 108
Donne, John, 37
Douhet, Giulio, 134
Dover Castle (etching), **200**
Draner (pseud.). *See* Renard, Jules
Draper, Allyn, **266**
*Dresdener Chroniken, und Geschichts, Calender
    1809* (pamphlet), 23, **85**
Dresser, Comfort C., 155
Dresser, Robert W., 150
Dubonnet, Emile, 257
The Duchess (airplane), **5**
Dumas, Alexander, Jr., 283

Dumas, Alexander, Sr., 283
Durant, Charles Ferson, 279
Dürer, Albrecht, 8–9, **40**
Duret, Matthieu, 14
Duruof, Jules, 156
Du Vol des Oiseaux (Esterno), **98**
Dyer, Susan, 199

E

Eagle, as glyptic symbol, **314**, **316**
The Eagle Aloft (Crouch), 200, 271, 278, 279, 295,
    307
The Eagle (dirigible), **280**
Ebert, Johann Heinrich, 182
Educational Demonstration Presenting Mr.
    Claude Grahame-White (program), **294**
E.J. Willis Company, **309**
Embrâsement déplorable de la Machine
    Aérostatique (engraving), **195**
L'Empire de l'Air (Mouillard), **112**
En Ballon! (Tissandier), 21, **104**
Endymion (Keats), 87
Enslen, Karl, 208
Enterprise (balloon), 97
L'Entreprenant (military balloon), 20
Environs of Liège (lithograph), **226**
Erfahrungen beim Bau von Luftschiffen (von
    Zeppelin), **127**
Eroticism, 88
Essai sur les machines aërostatiques (etching),
    184
Esterno, Henri Philippe Ferdinand, Comte d', 98
Etana, 7, 8
*An exact and authentic narrative of M. Blan-
    chard's third aerial voyage* (Blanchard), **79**
An exact Represenation of M. Garnerin's
    Balloons (etching), **211**
Excelsior Standard Screw Fastened Boots &
    Shoes, **262**
Expérience aérostatique faite Versailles le 19
    Sept 1783 (engraving), **176**
Expérience aéerostatique (etching), **217**
Expérience de la Machine Aréostatique
    (engraving), **171**
Expérience du Vaisseau Volant (etching), **187**
Expérience faite à Versailles (etching and
    painting), **173**, 175
Experimenta nova (von Guericke), 11, **11**
Experimentation
    aerodynamic
        with air and gas, 11–14, 55, 81
        during balloon flight, 201
        balloons as research instruments, 111
        with hot air balloons, 330
Experiments in Aerodynamics (Langley), **117**

F

Fabrique de Pellerin, **214**
Facius, George Sigmund, 9, **166**
Facius, Johann Gottlieb, 9, **166**
Fagan, George V., 4
"The Fall of Icarus" (Dürer print), 8–9

Fan, ivory and paper, **311**
Fantasy fiction. *See under* Fiction
Farman, Henri, 256, 304
Fashion
    balloon costume, **185**
    19th century fashions, **213**
The fatal Descent of the Parachute by which
    Mr. Cocking lost his life (lithographs), **232**
Faujas de Saint-Fond, Barthélemy, 15, 16, 74, 147,
    171, 189, 196
Ferber, Ferdinand, 131, **343**
Ferrand, Pierre, 237
Ferris, Dick, 26, 297
Fête donnée par la ville de Paris (etching), **222**
Fête du 14 Juillet an IX (engraving), **220**
Fête du sacre (etching), **221**
A Few Remarks (Stringfellow), **118**
Fiction, aviation, 26–30
    Cyrano's mythical moon voyages, 56
    dime novels, 265–269
    fantasy fiction, 54, 65, 107, 159 (*See also*
        Verne, Jules)
    "Peter Parley" series, 94
    science fiction, 72, 101, 123, 159, 337
    of Sinclair Lewis, 143
    Tom Swift series, 139
    See also Autobiography; Satire; Voyages,
        imaginary
Le Figaro, 286
Fire
    during balloon ascensions, 199, 204
    during Napoleon's coronation, 219, 221
The First Carriage, the "Ariel" (lithograph), **234**
The First Men in the Moon (Wells), **123**
Fischer, Fred (songwriter), 298
Five Weeks in a Balloon (Verne). *See Cinq
    Semaines en Ballon*
Flammarion, Camille, 111
de Flesselles, Jacques, 186
Flight, airplane, 24–25, 118, 135, 137, 275, 286, 343,
    344
    See also Wright, Orville; Wright, Wilbur
Flight, human-powered, 52, 53, 56, 61, 63, 64
Flight, manned, 59, 60, 63
    See also Balloon ascents
Flight, study of. *See* Aviation research
Flight, winged, **36**, 58, 71, 73, 152
A flight to the moon (Fowler), **87**
Flugmaschine. Erfunden von Jacob Degen
    (etching), **216**
Flyer I (airplane), 342
Flyer III (airplane), 163
Flying machines, 55, 135
    aerial steam carriage, 234
    balloons (*See under* Balloons)
    Degen's winged machine, 85
    de Luze airship, 237
    dirigibles, 100, 110, 128, **280**
    early airplanes, 24–25
    early designs of, 57, 58, 59, 60, 66, 68
    emulation of birds, 86, 98, 339
    flying boats, 140–141, 142
    gliders, 158, 339

governmental lack of support of, 157

helicopters, 68

ornithopter, 9–10, 23, **77**, **169**, **216**, 217

parachutes, 47, 149, 167, 211, 212

Passarola, 12–13, **13**, 59, 60

Pétin's locomotive aérostatique, 238

Pilcher's machine, **273**

rigid airships, 160

Roger Bacon on, 42

18th century designs for, 70, 72, 79

19th century designs for, 84, 86, 117, 155

used in advertising, **262**, **264**

wooden dove of Archytas, 51

zeppelins, 22–23, 127, 160, 254, 258, **258**

See also Airplanes; Balloons

Fonvielle, Wilfrid de, 105, 110

Forney, Mathias, 120

14-bis (airplane), 125

Fowler, George, 87

Fox, G., 211

Fraenkel, Knut, 122

La France (zeppelin), 127, 128

Francis, Day, and Hunter (publishers), 296

Franco-Prussian War, 20–21, 156, 243, 338, **338**

Franklin, Benjamin, 15, 164, 171, 177

"Frank Reade, Jr.'s Air Wonder," **267**

Frank Reade Weekly Magazine, **267**

Frank Tousey publishers, 266

Das französische Luftschiff (postcard), **290**

French Revolution, 222

G

Gabriel, Pierre (engraver), 175

Gale, George Burcher, 153

Galien, Joseph, 14, 66, 78

Galluzzo, Leopoldo, 229

Gambetta, Leon, 21

Games, board, **242**

Garis, Howard. *See* Appleton, Victor

Garnerin, André Jacques, 16

   Napoleon's coronation, 221

   parachute descent from a balloon, **149**, 211, 212, 220, 231, **276**, **334**

Garnerin, Elisa, 213

Garnerin, Jeanne-Geneviève (née Labrousse), 18, 149, 213

Garnerin's descent by parachute (gouache), **212**

Gatteaux, N. (medalist), 330

Gatti de Dura (publishers), 229

Gautier, Jean-Baptiste, 221

Le Géant (balloon), 18, **19**, **242**, **283**

Gellius, Aulus, 51

George V, King of England, 291

Germany, 4–5

Gervais, A. de Rouvelle, 128

Gibbs-Smith, Charles, 93, 300

Giffard, Henri, 22, 110, 128, 239, 245, 284

Gimbel, Adam, 2–3

Gimbel, Bernard, 3

Gimbel, Ellis A., 2–3

Gimbel, Fridolyn Kahnweiler, 2

Gimbel, Isaac, 2–3

Gimbel, Jacob, 2–3

Gimbel, Minnie Mastbaum, 2

Gimbel, Richard, **2**, 2–6, **5**

Gimbel's Department Store, 3

Girard, E., 128

Glaisher, James, 114, 240

Gleanings in Bee Culture (Root, ed.), 25, **126**

Gliders, 158, 339

Le globe aërostatique construit à Versailles (etching), **174**

Globo Aerostatico di Diametro (etching), **207**

Godard, August, 245

Godard, Eugène, 111, 245

Godard, Eugénie, 245

Godard, Jules, 105, 245

Godard, Louis, 245

Godard, Pierre, 245

Goddard, Robert Hutchings, **31**, 31–32, 91, 123

Godwin, Francis, 29, 54

Gollin, Alfred, 286

Gomgam (Bordelon), **61**

Goodrich, Samuel Griswold, 26–27, 94

Gordon Bennett, James, 304, **345**

Gordon Bennett Cup, 140–141, 304, 305, **345**

Le Goût du Jour no. 8 (lithograph), **213**

Graf Zeppelin (airship), 340

Graham, George, 18, 223

Graham, Margaret, 18, 223

Graham, Tom (pseud.). *See* Lewis, Sinclair

Grahame-White, Claude, 4, 26, 137, 293, 294, 305

Grand Ballon (balloon), **110**, **284**

Grand Ballon captif à vapeur de la Cour des Tuileries (handbill), **284**

Le Grand Ballon Captif à Vapeur (Tissandier), **110**

Grand-Carteret, John, 237

Grande Semaine Aéronautique de la Champagne (ticket), **304**

Grand New Balloon, to be called Vauxhall Royal Balloon (letterpress), **281**

Grands détails circonstanciés sur l'apparition prochaine (letterpress), **227**

Great astronomical discoveries lately made by Sir John Herschel (Locke), **88**

Great Balloon of Nassau. See Vauxhall Royal Balloon

The Great Nassau Balloon (lithograph), **230**

Great Western (balloon). *See City of New York*

Green, Charles, 17, 281, **335**

   Cocking's parachute descent and, 232

   Nassau ascent, 151

   Vauxhall Royal Balloon, **225**, **226**

Griffin, as glyptic symbol, **318**

Grolier Club, 4, 6

Grösseste Denkwürdigkeiten der Welt (Happel), **57**

Guericke, Otto von, 11

Guidotti, Paolo, 10, 52

Guillé, Louis Charles, 18, 22, 218

Gulliver's Travels (Swift), 62, 152

Gusmão, Bartholomeu Lourenço de, 12–13, 59, 78

Guttemberg le jeune (engraver), 182

H

Haenlein, Paul, 22

Hamilton, Charles Claude, **152**

Hamilton, Charles K., 4

Handbills, 276–286

Happel, Eberhard Werner, 57

Hargrave, Lawrence, 24

Harmon, H.R., 6

Harper, Harry, 137

Hart, Clive, ix, 37–89, 147-163

Harvard-Boston Aero Meet (September 3-13, 1910), **293**, 294

Heinrich Ferdinand Adolf August, Graf von Zeppelin. *See* Zeppelin, Heinrich Ferdinand Graf von

Helicopter designs, 68

Helicopter toys, 10–11

Henson, William Samuel, 24, 118, 234

Herschel, John Frederick, 30, 37, 229

Herschel, William, 30

Hike and the Aeroplane (Lewis), **143**

Hindenburg (airship), 340

de la Hire, Philippe, 67

Hiroshige (printmaker), 248

Histoire aéronautique (Bruel), **133**

Histoire des Ballons (Tissandier), **113**

Histoire des balloons et des ascensions célèbres (Sircos and Pallier), **109**

Historia Alexandri Magni, 7–8, **39**

The History and Practice of Aerostation (Cavallo), 12, **81**, 168

The History of Aeronautics in Great Britain (Hodgson), 302

History of Donaldson's Balloon Ascensions (Amick), 19, **108**

Hoaxes

   balloon hoax, 19

   Degen hoax, 23

   moon hoax, 30, 88, 229

Hodges, E., 203

Hodgson, J.E., 302

Hodson, E., 224

Hokusai (printmaker), 249

Holland, Robert, 151, 226

L'homme aerostatique ou mon pauvre oncle (etching), **193**

Hooke, Robert, 9, 11, 12, 53, 58

Houdon, Jean-Antoine, 189

How We Invented the Airplane (Wright), **144**

Hugo, Victor, 283

A Hundred Years from Now (Caddigan, Brennan and Story), **299**

Hydrogen, 13–15, 82–83

See also Balloons, gas-filled; Experimentation

I

Icare (Desportes and Massé), **300**

Icaromenippus (Lucian), 28, 44

Icarus and Daedalus, 8–9, **40**, 78, **166**, 300, **326**, **328**

Imprimerie de Nicolas, 227

International Aviation Tournament, 1910 (ticket), **305**

J

J. M. Montgolfier, Member de la Légion d'Honneur (engraving), **192**

Les Jacobins allant révolutioner la lune en ballons (intaglio), **209**

James Gordon Bennett International Aviation Cup. *See* Gordon Bennett Cup

Janinet, Jean-François, **195**, 196, 197

Japan, kites in, **248**, **249**

JeanJean, Marcel, 17, **179**

Jeffries, John, 16, **16**, 200, 302, 333

Jeu du ballon. Le Géant (lithograph), **242**

Johnson, Samuel, 71

Jourdan, Jean-Baptiste, 214, 215

Journal of my forty-fifth ascension (Blanchard), 82–83

Journal of Natural Philosophy, Chemistry and the Arts (Nicholson), 24

Jugement définitif en faveur des Srs. Miolan et Janinet (etching), **196**

June Bug (airplane), 140

K

Kant, Immanuel, 29

Kaufman, Phil, 297

Kean, Charles, 153

Keats, John, 87

Keegan, Allen, 204

Keith, B.F., 294

Kelly, Fred C., 144

Kennon, Beverly, **265**

Kepler, Johannes, 28–30, **29**, 49, 50

King, Samuel Archer, 18

Kircher, Athanasius, 9, **51**, 78

Kites, 10
    construction of, 46, 95
    flying by means of, 152
    in Japan, **248**, **249**
    theory of design of, 124

Kites over Sakura District Viewed from the Emperor's Castle (woodcut), **248**

Kitty Hawk. *See* Wright, Orville; Wright, Wilbur

Krebs, Arthur, 22, 128, 244

L

Lachambre, Henri, 122

Lafayette, Marquis de, 278

La Follie, Louis Guillaume de, 30, 72

Lambert, Count de, 257

Lana de Terzi, Francesco, **12**, 57, 69
    aerostat, **168**
    floating globe theory, 12, 55
    influence on aviation, 78, 81
    military aviation, 19–20, 23, 55, **55**

Landauer, Bella, 5

Landells, E., 28, 95

Langley, Samuel Pierpont, 24, 117, 147, 162

Lash's Bitters Tonic Laxative, **264**

de Launay, Nicolas (engraver), 170, 175, **175**, 181, 189

de Launay, Robert, 189

Laurent, François, Marquis d'Arlandes, 16, 76, 177, 179, 194, 195, 199, 331

La Vaulx, Henri, Comte de, 138

Lavoisier, Antoine-Laurent, 13, 15

Leaflets, 276–286

Le Beau, Pierre Adrien, 215

Le Brun, Charles, 166

Le Brun, Victoire, 219

Le Coeur, Louis, 221

Lecornu, Joseph, 10, 124, 218

Legends. *See* Myths and legends

Lehmann, Caroline, 235

Lehmann, Christian, 235

Lehmann's Luftfahrt mit seinem Riesen Ballon (engraving), **235**

Leichter als Luft (Leismann), 165

Leloir, Maurice, 202

Le Mans racetrack, 129

Lennox, Comte de, 280

Le Noir, Rose (engraver), 171, 189

Le Noir (publisher), 189

Lenormand, Sébastien, 211, 334

Leo, Frank, 296

Leonardo da Vinci, 47, 78, 86, 121, 211, **329**, 334

Lesot, Claude (medalist), 341

Letters, **146**, 148–163

Le Vachez, Nicolas-François, 177

Lewis, Sinclair, 91, 143

Liébert, Alphonse J., 245

The Life and Adventures of Peter Wilkens (Paltock), **65**, 229

The life and astonishing adventures of John Daniel, **70**

Lilienthal, Gustave, 131

Lilienthal, Otto, **24**, 91, 116, 158, 159, 273, **339**

Lindbergh, Charles Augustus, 6–7, 253

Lion, as glyptic symbol, **316**

Lisbon, Portugal, 12–13

Literature. *See* Autobiography; Fiction; Satire

Locke, Richard Adams, 88, 229

"Locksley Hall" (Tennyson), 92

Locomotive aérostatique Pétin (lithograph), **238**

London, England, 1–2, **3**

London Illustrated News, **270**

Loos, F., 333

Lorimier, Étienne Chevalier de, 170, 173, 175, **177**, 181

Los Angeles Aero Meet, 297

Loup, Michel, 93

Lowe, Thaddeus Sobieski Constantine, 17, 20, **96**, 96–97, 241, 271, 272, 336

Lucangeli, Carlo, 207

Lucian of Samosata, 28, 29, **44**

Lucretius, 69

Lunardi, Vincent, 17, 84, 201, 202
    decline in popularity of, **205**
    first British balloon ascent, **80**, 203, **303**, **332**
    use of oars in a balloon, 207

de Luze, Carmien, 22, 237

LZ1 (zeppelin), 127

LZ3 (zeppelin), 127

LZ5 (zeppelin), 254

LZ6 (zeppelin), 254

M

MacDonald, James (illustrator), 144

Machinæ novæ (Veranzio), **47**

Machine aérienne par Carmien de Luze (lithograph), **237**

Machine aërostatique, destiné pour la ville de Boulogne (etching), **198**

Machuron, Alexis, 122

Maggs Brothers, 5

Magiae naturalis libri viginti (della Porta), 10, **46**

Magiae universalis naturae et artis (Schott), 12

Magnes (Kircher), **51**

Maitland, Lester J., 253

Man and woman sitting in airship gondola (postcard), **260**, **288**

The Man in the Moone (Godwin), 30, **54**

Maravelas, Paul, ix, 165–259

Marchand, Jacques, 221

Marchand, Roland, 262

Marriott, Frederick, 234

Martello, Pierjacopo, 13, 60

Massé, Victor, 9, 300

Mathematicall magick (Wilkins), **53**

Maxim, Hiram, 24

McCurdy, J.A.D., 140, 143

McFarland, Marvin W., 145

Means, James, 121

Medals
    Alberto Santos-Dumont, **341**
    balloon medal, **21**
    Blanchard, **333**
    City of New York, **336**
    Ferdinand Ferber, **343**
    first flight in England, **332**
    first manned flights, **331**
    "The Flight of Icarus" medal, 9, **326**, **328**
    Garnerin, **334**
    Gordon Bennett Cup, **345**
    Graf Zeppelin, **340**
    Green and Sparrow, **335**
    Jules Verne, **337**
    Leonardo da Vinci, **329**
    Louis Blériot, **344**
    Montgolfier brothers, 17, **330**
    Otto Lilienthal, **339**
    pigeon post, 21–22
    Siege of Paris, **338**
    the Wright Brothers, **342**
    See also Numismatics

Meerwein, Karl Friedrich, 77, 148

Meloni, G. (artist), 228, 233

Merke, H., 211

Mesopotamian seals, **314**, **315**, **316**

A messieurs les souscripteurs (etching), **172**

Michel, Soeur, 148

Miger, Simon Charles (engraver), 183

Military aviation
    airplanes, 134

airships, 22–23, 128, 258
　Chinese use of balloons, 246
　Civil War use of balloons, 153, 154, **241**, **272**, 336
　"dynamite balloon," 244
　Franco-Prussian War, 243, 338
　La Patrie airship, **290**
　potential for, 19–21, 55, 84, 114, 286
　Spanish-American War, 251
　War of the First Coalition, **214**, **215**
Milton, John, 37
La Minerve, vaisseau aërien (Robertson), **84**
Minerve (airship), 84, **206**, 227
Miolan, Abbé, **195**, 196, 197
Mirrour for magistrates, 10, **48**
Moisant, John, 305
Le moment d'hilarité universelle (etching), **182**
Monck Mason, Thomas, 151, 226
Monsieur Pilatre de Rosier (aquatint), **199**
Montgolfier, Étienne, 13–16, **14**, 182, **189**, 196
　first balloon ascent with payload, 173, 174,
　　306, **310**
　first manned balloon ascent, 74, 76, 331
　first public balloon ascent, 170, **171**, 327, **330**
　Montgolfier balloon, **180**
Montgolfier, Joseph, 13–16, **14**, **189**, 192
　first balloon ascent with payload, 174, **310**
　first manned balloon ascent, 74, 331
　first public balloon ascent, 170, **171**, 327, **330**
　invention of the parachute, 211
　Montgolfier balloon, **180**
　only balloon flight of, 186
　satire of, **190**
Montgolfier, Pierre, 202
Montgolfière of November 21, 1783 (painting),
　178
Montgolfier in the Clouds (etching), **190**
Montgolfier vole au Rang des dieux (etching),
　191, 196
Moon travel, 30, **49**, 54, 56, 67, 70, 87, 88, 102, 123,
　229
Moorfields. *See* Lunardi, Vincent
Moreau, Guyton de, **311**
Moret, Chevalier de, 203
Morghen, Filippo, 67
Morris, Ellen, ix, 313–325
"The Motor Boys" series, 27
"The Motor Girls" series, 27
"Motor Matt's Air Ship," **268**
Motor Stories Library, **268**
Mouillard, Louis Pierre, 24, 112
Murrow, Edward R., 2
Music, sheet, 9, 26, 295–301
Muzzi, Luigi, 233
Muzzi, Muzio, 22, 233
My Air-Ships (Santos-Dumont), 22, **125**
My Life and Balloon Experiences (Coxwell), 20,
　114
The Mysteries of Nature and Art (Bate), 10
Mystics, 45
My Three Big Flights (Conneau), **142**
Myths and legends, 78
　Abaris, 61
　effect on aviation development, 37–38

Endymion, 87
Etana, 7, 8, 314
Icarus and Daedalus, 8–9, **40**, 78, 166, 300,
　326, **328**
King Bladud, 10, 48
King Midas, 197
　space travel, 43
　transportation of St. Mary's house, **41**
See also Mystics

N

Nachricht. Unterzeichneter hat die Ehre
　(letterpress), **277**
Nachricht von dem fliegenden Schiffe
　(Gusmão), 12, **59**
Nadar. *See* Tournachon, Gaspard-Félix
Napoleon
　abdication of, 222
　coronation of, **221**
Nassau (balloon). *See* Vauxhall Royal Balloon
Natterer, Johann F., 235
Naudet (artist), 215
Navis aeria et Elegiarum monobiblos
　(Zamagna), 12, **69**
Neptune (balloon), 156
The New Dynamite Balloon (engraving), **244**
New Haven, CN, 5–6
New Hungerford Market (watercolor), **223**
The new mode of picking pockets (etching), 18, **203**
Newspapers, 270–275
"The New Sport of Flying" (magazine article),
　275
New York Times, **272**
Niepce (balloon), 21
Nitrogen, 13–15
　See also Balloons, gas-filled; Experimentation
Nobel, Alfred, 122
North Front of the Heath (lithograph), **224**
North Pole expedition, 122
Le nouveau Dédale (Rousseau), **63**
Nouveau manuel complet d'aérostation
　(Depuis-Delcourt), 218
Numismatics, 9, 327–345
Nye, Russell, 265
Nymphe (balloon), **208**

O

Oars
　used in a balloon, 80, **80**, 207
　used in a dirigible, 233, **280**
Oberth, Hermann, 28
Occasional reflections upon several subjects
　(Boyle), 11
Octavie No. 3 biplane of 1909 (chromolitho-
　graph), **256**
Les oeuvres diverses (de Bergerac), **56**
Olivari, Francis, 228
"On Aerial Navigation" (Cayley), 216
Oresme, Nicole, 55
Orlandi, Francesco, 228
Orlandi, Guido, 228

Orlando Furioso (Ariosto), **43**
Ornament, **310**
Ornen (balloon), 122
Ornithopter, 9–10, 23, 65, **77**, **169**, 187, **216**, 217, 333
Oscar, King of Sweden, 122
Ostoya, Victor E. (cartoonist), 129
Ovid, 8, 37, 40, 64
Oxford University, 50

P

Paine, Thomas, 4, 6
Pallier, Thomas, 109
Paltock, Robert, 65, 88, 229
The Papers of Wilbur and Orville Wright
　(McFarland, ed.), 24–25, **145**
Papin, Denis, 12
Parachutes, 95, 167, 211
　first American descent, 218
　first descent, 149, 212, 220
　Great Nassau descent, 230, **231**
　history of, 334
　night descents, 149
　Veranzio's design of, 47
　women parachutists, 213
Paris, France, 15–17, 257
　Paris Exposition, 245
　Paris Mint, **329**, **330**, **334**, **341**, **343**, **344**
　siege of, 104, 156, **243**, **338**
Parley, Peter (pseud.). *See* Goodrich, Samuel
　Griswold
Parody. *See* Satire
Pass, J., 194
Passarola (airship), 12–13, **13**, 59, 60
Patents, 163, 238
　compendium of, 119
　litigation over, 141, 144
La Patrie (airship), **290**
Paucton, Alexis Jean-Pierre, 68
Paulhan, Louis, 137
Pêche, Dom, 187, **311**
Pellerin, Charles, 214
Periodicals, 270–275
Petin, Ernest, 22, 238
Pewtress, T., 230
Peyrey, François, 130
Phaedrus (Plato), 7
"Phil in the Balloon Corps" (Kennon), **265**
Le philosophe sans prétension (La Follie), 30, **72**,
　152
Philosophical Collections (Hooke), 9–10, 12, **58**
Philostratus, Flavius, **45**
Pickpockets, 18, 203
Pilâtre de Rozier, Jean-François, **15**, 15–16, 196,
　198, 331
　books of, **76**
　death of, 228
　first manned balloon ascent, 177, 178, 179,
　　194, **199**
　Joseph Montgolfier's balloon ascent, 186
Pilcher, Percy S., 273
Pillas-Panis, 246, 247
Pinacotheca imaginum (Rossi), 10, **52**

Pisano, Dominick A., ix, 261–309
Pittman, Holly, ix, 313–325
Placita physica (Vanossi), 12
Plates, decorative, **311**
Plato, 7
Pluck and Luck: Complete Stories of Adventure (Draper), **266**
Poe, Edgar Allen, 4, 6, 19, 229
Poems (Tennyson), **92**
Poetry, 300
Porta, Giovanni Battista della, 10, **46**, 78
Porter, Rufus, 22, 273, 307
Le possibilità dell'aeronavigazione (Douhet), **134**
Post, Augustus, 140–141
Postal service, use of airplanes by, 289, 291
Postal service, use of balloons by, 19–21, 106, 156, 243, 338
   See also Carrier pigeons
Postcards, **260**, 287–292
Prandtl, Ludwig, 136
Première Expérience de la Machine Aérostatique (etching), **206**
Première expérience de la Montgolfière (Pilâtre de Rozier), **76**
Première suite de la description (Faujas de Saint-Fond), 175, 177
Les Premiers Hommes-Oiseaux (Peyrey), **130**
Pressure airships, 125, 128
Priestley, Joseph, 15
The Prince of Abissinia (Johnson), **71**
Printers
   Chez Bassett, 187
   Chez Le Noir, 171, **172**, 182
   Chez Le Vachez, 170, 188
Probst, 176
Probst (printer), 176
Prodromo (Lana de Terzi), 12, 55
Programs, printed, **293–294**
Progress in Flying Machines (Chanute), 10, 24–25, **120**
Projet de ballon planeur (print), **218**
Proust, Joseph-Louis, 76

Q

Quaritch, Bernard, 5

R

Raccolta (Morghen), **67**
Rasselas. See The Prince of Abissinia
Read, Ezra (songwriter), 301
Recherches sur l'art de voler (Bourgeois), **78**
Reims Air Meet, 1909 (stereograph slides), **308**
Religion, 9
   effect on aviation development, 37–38
   heretical writings, 49
   transportation of St. Mary's house, **41**
   view of flying, 45
Renard, Charles, 22, 244
Renard, Jules, **243**
Renard, Paul, 128
Représentation du globe aérostatique (Charles), 75

Research. *See* Aviation research
Restif de la Bretonne, Nicole Edme, 73, 88, 167
Revolving Air Ship Tower, Coney Island, NY (postcard), **292**
Reynolds, Quentin, 265
Riedrer, Friedrich, 40
Rigaud, J.F., 201
Riots, during balloon ascents, 85, 203, 216, 280
Le Rire journal, 274
Robert, Anne-Jean, 15, 75, 171, 184, 194, **311**
Robert, Marie-Noël, 15, 16, 75, 171, 194, **311**, 331
Robertson, Étienne Gaspard, 84, 206, 227
Robertson, Eugene, 278
Robinson, C. (artist), 240
Rochette, Edward, ix, 327–345
Romain, Jules, 228
Roosevelt, Theodore, 251
Root, Amos Ives, 25, 126
Rosenbach, A.S.W., 4
Rossi, Gian Vittorio, 10, 52
Rouen en ballon (lithograph), **236**
Rouillard, Jean Sebastian, 236
Rousseau, Jean-Jacques, 63
La route de l'air (Berget), **132**
"The Rover Boys" series, 27
Rowlandson, Thomas, 200, 205
Royal Aeronautical Society. *See* Aeronautical Society of Great Britain
Royal Air Force, 1–2
Royal Cremorne (balloon), 153
Rozière (hybrid balloon), 198, 228

S

Sage, Mrs., 201, 202
Sails, used on balloon, **311**
Sambucus, Johannes, 37
Samosatensis, Lucianus. *See* Lucian of Samosata
Santos-Dumont, Alberto, 22, **23**, **125**, 162, **341**
Satire
   of aviation technology, 64, 71, 72, 135
   balloon costume, **185**
   in books, 87
   of Janinet and Miolan, **195**, **196**
   of Lunardi, **205**
   of Montgolfier, **190**
   of provincial ignorance, 172
   of travelers' tales, **44**
   of venality of balloon promoters, **203**
Savery, Thomas, 12
Saxby, Charles, 297
Schott, Gaspar, 12
La Science en Ballon (Fonvielle), **105**
Science fiction, 72, 101, 123, 159, 337
Scientific American magazine, 22, 273, 307
Scientific Ascent of Mr. H. Coxwell's Mammoth Balloon (lithograph), **240**
Scorpion, as glyptic symbol, **316**
The Scribleriad (Cambridge), **64**
Seals, cylinder, 7, 313
   fabulous beast and its earthly relative, **322**
   goddess leading a worshipper, **317**
   hero and lions attacking a caprid, **315**

   hero dominating caprids, **314**
   lions, birds, and a scorpion, **316**
   man and Old Syrian creatures, **318**
   man facing a mixed being, **321**
   two winged bulls frolicking, **319**
   winged genius dominating two mixed beings, **312**, **320**
Seals, stamp, 7, 313
   human-headed winged bull, **324–325**
   various animals pictures, **323**
Second voyage aérien (etching), **181**
Selfridge, Thomas E., 140
Sellier, François Noël (engraver), 175
Shafter, William R., 251
Sheldon, John, 204, 302
Sheppard, Joseph (medalist), 9, 326, 328
Siège de Paris (lithograph), **243**
The siege of Paris (journals and manuscripts), **156**
Silvestrini, Phillipe, 228
Siquier, J. (painter), **311**
Sircos, Alfred, 109
Sivel, Theodore, 113
Soapine laundry product, **263**
Society of Medalists, **328**
Solution du Problème da la Locomotion Aérienne (Loup), **93**
Somnium (Kepler), 29–30, **49**, 50
Space travel, 28–32, 43, **43**, 50, 62
   See also Moon travel
Spanish-American War, 251, **251**
Sparrow, Isaac E., **335**
Spiegel der waren Rhetoric (Friedrich), **40**
Spooner, William, 225
Stability in Aviation (Bryan), **136**
Star of the West (balloon), 150
Steeplechase Park, NY, **292**
Steiner, John H., 340
Stereographic slides, **308**
Stock certificate, **307**
Stratemeyer, Edward, 27, 139
Street & Smith (publishers), 265
Strindberg, Nils, 122
Stringfellow, Frederick, 118
Stringfellow, John, 24, 118, 234
Sturmis, Johannes, 168
Swift, Jonathan, 62, 87
A System of Aeronautics (Wise), 19, **89**

T

Talbott, Harold, 6
Tatin, Victor, 138
Tavenard, P.G., 164, **164**, 170, **177**, 249
Taylor, J. (artist), 240
Taylor, Robert B., 68
Tennyson, Alfred Lord, 37, 92
Terameno, Pietro, 9, 37, **41**
Thackeray, William Makepeace, 153
Thayer, Russell, 22, 244
Théorie de las vis d'Archimede (Paucton), **68**
Thirty-six Views Around Fugaku (woodcut), **249**

Through the Air (Wise), 19, **90, 106**
Tickets, for aerial events, 302–305
Tientsin military academy, China, 246
Tinker, Chauncey, 143
Tissandier, Albert, 109, 128, 244
Tissandier, Gaston, 12, 21, **21,** 22, 284
    books of, **104, 110, 113, 115**
    powered dirigibles of, 128, 244
Tom Swift and His Air Glider (Appleton, pseud,), **139**
"Tom Swift" series, 27, **139**
Le Tour du monde en quatre-vingt jours (Verne), **107**
Tournachon, Gaspard-Félix, 18, **18,** 109, 242, 283
Tower jumpers, 10
Toys and games
    board game, **242**
    helicopter toys, 10–11
    kites, 10, 46, 95, 124, 152, **248, 249**
    paper zeppelin model, **258**
Transatlantic flight, 89, 108
Translatio miraculosa ecclesie beate (Terameno), **41**
Travels Through the Air, 240
Traversee de Paris par Em. Dubonnet (collotype), **257**
La traversée par Pilâtre de Rozier et le marquis d'Arlandes (lithograph), **179**
A treatise upon the art of flying (Walker), **86**
Le Triomphe de las Navigation Aérienne (de la Vaulx), **138**
A Trip Around the World in a Flying Machine (Verne), **28**
Trowbridge, John, 135
Tsiolkovskii, Konstantine, 28
Turnor, Christopher Hatton, 99

U

United Kingdom Aerial Post 1911 (postcard), **291**
United States Air Force, 1–5, **5**
United States Air Force Academy, 6–7, 32
United States Army Air Corps, 4
Universal Postal Union, British India postcard, **289**
L'Uom Volante (print), **167,** 211
Up in My Flying Machine (Saxby and Kaufman), **297**

V

Le Vachez, Nicolas-François, 170
Vaisseau volant (flying vessel), **187,** 211

Vanossi, Antonio, 12
Vauxhall Royal Balloon (renamed *Great Balloon of Nassau*), 151, **225, 226, 230, 231,** 232, **273, 281**
Vera Historia (Lucian), 28
Veranzio, Fausto, 10, **47**
Verne, Jules, 283, 327
    books of, **101, 102, 107**
    impact on aviation, 28, 30–31
    medal of, **337**
Versi, e prose (Martello), 13, 60
Ville d'Orleans (balloon), 338
Vincenzo Lunardi Luchese, Anfiteatro Corèa (ticket), **303**
Virgil, 69, 202
De Vita Apollonii (Philostratus), **45**
Der Vogelflug als Grundlage der Fliegekunst (Lilienthal), 24, **116**
Vole, Wright! (Ostoya cartoon), **129**
Volo del Bolognese Muzio Muzzi (lithograph), **233**
Volo dell' aeronauta Francesco Orlandi (lithograph), **228**
Voyages, imaginary, 72, 73, 101, 102, 107
Voyages aériens (Flammarion), **111,** 240
A Voyage to Cacklogallinia (Brunt), **62**
Vuë d'Annonay en Vivarais (etching), **170**
Vuë d'avant du Vaisseau Volant (etching), **169**
Vue de la Terrasse de Mr. Franklin à Passi (etching), **177,** 249

W

Walker, Thomas (painter), 86
Walpole, Horace, 166
Walpole, Robert, 166
Warfare. *See* Military aviation
War of the First Coalition, **214, 215**
War of the Worlds (Wells), 31–32, 91
Washington, George, 83
Watch case, **310**
Waulstaine (artist), 206
Wecker, Johann Jacob, 45
Wells, Herbert George, 26, 31–32, 91, 123, 159
Wenham, Francis Herbert, 103
Whittington, Harlequin, Mayor of London, 276
Wilcox, Philip W., 275
Wilkes, John (publisher), 194
Wilkins, John, 29, **50, 53,** 55
Wind power, 152
Wine taster, **310**
Wise, John, 19, 22, 89, 90, 100, 106, 218
Woelfert, Karl, 22

Wohl, Robert, 274
Woman, man and child sitting in airplane (postcard), **287**
Woman on balcony looking at balloon (dry point), **250**
Women
    as balloonists, 18, 79, 153, 201, 213, 219, 223, 277
    as parachutists, 149, 213, 276
Won't You Come Up and Spoon in Coey's Balloon (Smalley and Adler), **295**
Wooden dove. *See* Archytas of Tarentum
World War I, 134
World War II, 1–5, **3**
Wright, Milton, 147, 161
Wright, Orville, 131, **145, 253, 342**
    Amos Root and, 126
    associates of, 119, 120
    financial issues, 161
    first flight, 327
    Gimbel's collection pertaining to, 24–26, 147
    history of, 130
    lack of official support for, 157
    patent litigation, 144
    photograph of glider, **252**
Wright, Wilbur, 131, **145, 257, 293, 342**
    Amos Root and, 126
    associates of, 119, 120
    financial issues, 161, 163
    first flight, 327
    Gimbel's collection pertaining to, 24–26, 147
    history of, 130
    lack of official support for, 157
    satirical cartoons of, 129, 274
Wright Flyer (airplane), **25**
Wright glider in flight (photograph), **252**
Wyatt, E., 201, 204

Y

Yale University, 3, 5–7

Z

Zamagna, Bernardo, 12, 69
Zambeccari, Francesco, 228
Zénith (balloon), 113
Zeppelin, Heinrich Ferdinand Graf von, 22–23, **23,** 127, 160, 254, **340**
Zeppelins, 22–23, 160, **258**
Zeppelin über dem Bodensee (lithograph), **254–255**

About the companion CD-ROM

What you will find on the disk
The accompanying CD-ROM contains multimedia presentations of the items in *The Genesis of Flight*. Video introductions describe the origins of the Gimbel collection and the collection's home at the United States Air Force Academy. Search engines enable you to select items by keyword. A zoom function permits you to examine the items close up.

System Requirements
The hybrid program on this disk runs on multimedia- equipped Macs (Power PC with OS 7.6 or later) and PCs (Windows™ 95 or later). To enjoy the sound and the color images, you should have at least a 4X CD-ROM drive and a 100 MHz processor with 32 MB of RAM and 16-bit color, though you may be able to run the program with some loss of performance on slower machines. Macs need QuickTime™ 3 or later for the movies.

Starting the program
To start the program, insert the CD-ROM into your CD-ROM drive. After a few seconds, the program will begin running on most computers. If the program does not start automatically on your PC, go to either "My Computer" or "Windows Explorer" and double-click on the "gimbel.exe" file. If the program does not start automatically on your Mac, double-click the "GimbelMac" icon. Then double-click the "GimIntro" icon.

Finding items in the program
In this program, as in the book, holdings are grouped by medium. Clicking a medium on the main menu takes you to the introductory screen for your chosen medium. On the introductory screen click the "List" button to see a list of all the items in that section or click the "Search" button to find the items dealing with a topic of your choice. Clicking any title after clicking the "List" or "Search" buttons takes you immediately to the selected item. To scan the entire program for a topic of your choice, use the "Global Search" button on the main menu.

Using the special buttons
Turn Music Off and **Turn Voice Off:** These toggle buttons on the main menu enable you to view the program silently, or with music and voiced introductions. **Zoom:** When a magnifying glass appears in the upper right corner of the screen you can click it for a movable, close-up view. **Voice:** When a gramaphone appears on the right side of the screen, you can click it for a voiced introduction. **Tell Me More:** A "Tell Me More" button appears at the bottom of the screen when additional scholarship is available. Click this button to read the scholarship.